THE BOOK OF FOOTBALL

BOOKS BY CLIVE LEATHERDALE

Football
THE BOOK OF FOOTBALL (*as editor*)
WIMBLEDON: FROM SOUTHERN LEAGUE TO PREMIERSHIP – A COMPLETE RECORD
ABERDEEN: THE EUROPEAN ERA – A COMPLETE RECORD
ENGLAND: THE QUEST FOR THE WORLD CUP – A COMPLETE RECORD
SCOTLAND: THE QUEST FOR THE WORLD CUP – A COMPLETE RECORD
IRELAND: THE QUEST FOR THE WORLD CUP – A COMPLETE RECORD

Dracula and Vampirism
DRACULA: THE NOVEL & THE LEGEND
A STUDY OF BRAM STOKER'S GOTHIC MASTERPIECE
THE ORIGINS OF DRACULA
THE BACKGROUND TO BRAM STOKER'S GOTHIC MASTERPIECE
THE JEWEL OF SEVEN STARS (*as editor*)
CALMET'S TREATISE ON VAMPIRES AND REVENANTS (*as editor*)

International Relations
BRITAIN AND SAUDI ARABIA 1925-1939: THE IMPERIAL OASIS

Far Eastern Travel
THE VIRGIN WHORE AND OTHER CHINESE CHARACTERS:
TIANANMEN, TRAVELS AND TRAUMAS
TO DREAM OF PIGS: TRAVELS IN SOUTH AND NORTH KOREA

Education
SO YOU WANT TO TEACH ENGLISH TO FOREIGNERS

The BOOK *of* FOOTBALL

Edited by

CLIVE LEATHERDALE

Desert Island Books

First Published
in 1997 by
DESERT ISLAND BOOKS
34 Hamlet Court Road, Westcliff-on-Sea, Essex SS0 7LX
United Kingdom

British Library Cataloguing-in-Publication Data
A catalogue record for this book is available from the British Library

ISBN 1-874287-13-9

Printed in Great Britain
by
Redwood Books, Trowbridge, Wiltshire

CONTENTS

THE PRESIDENT OF THE FOOTBALL ASSOCIATION.

LORD KINNAIRD.

IT is safe to say that few men have done more to advance and encourage the great winter pastime than Lord Kinnaird, President of the Football Association, who, in his early years, whilst at Trinity College, Cambridge, took a prominent part in the movement which ultimately resulted in the establishment of the Association game. In the course of his active football career, Lord Kinnaird played in nearly every position on the field, from goalkeeper to forward, and received a winner's medal no less than five times in the great Cup Final.

Lord Kinnaird was born on February 16th, 1847, and when twenty years of age became captain of the Eton Club at Cambridge. In the same year he played for the celebrated Wanderers Football Club, which had already begun to make its quality felt among the London clubs.

A year later he was elected to the committee of the Football Association, on which he has served loyally and faithfully ever since, being appointed treasurer in 1877, and president in 1890, upon the retirement of Sir Francis Marindin from that post after fifteen years of distinguished service. It is as president of the Football Association that we greet him to-day.

As a player Lord Kinnaird had few equals, no superiors. His versatility was astonishing, and whether as goalkeeper, half-back, or forward, he played with an excellence that may be held up as a shining example to the players of to-day. His first appearance in an important match was for Scotland against England in 1870, a match which was not recognised as an International, because the Scottish team was composed of Scotsmen resident in England. In 1873 he played forward for Scotland v. England at Kennington Oval, when England won by four goals to two.

Great astonishment was aroused on this occasion by the presence of 3,000 spectators at the Oval—an attendance that would bring a pitying smile to the face of a manager of a leading League club to-day, but which was then something like a record

Lafayette.]
THE RIGHT HON. LORD KINNAIRD.

The distinguished President of the Football Association, was one of the finest footballers of his day. He played for both the Old Etonians and the Wanderers, two famous clubs whose names are writ large on the annals of football history. He was the hero of five Cup Finals, playing on three occasions for the Wanderers in the winning team, and twice for Old Etonians. His versatility was astonishing, as, under Association Rules, he filled nearly every position on the field. At the Cup Final in April last Spencer, the Aston Villa captain, had the honour of receiving the Association Cup and medal from his hands. Our photograph on another page hands this historic incident down to posterity.

Lord Kinnaird played in the historic first London v. Sheffield match in 1872, at Sheffield, when, among his opponents was Mr. J. C. Clegg, the esteemed and admirable chairman of the Football Association at the present time. In the same season he captained the first London team to play Nottingham on the Trent Bridge ground.

It was also in the season 1872-3 that he assisted the Wanderers to win the Association Cup, and secured the first of his five Cup medals.

Owing to the Old Etonians claiming his services, he did not assist the Wanderers in the Cup-ties in 1875 and 1876, but in 1877, when the Etonians scratched in the first round, the Wanderers managed to get Kinnaird into their team again, and he kept goal in the Final, which the Wanderers won. The following year he gave further evidence of his striking versatility by playing at half-back in the winning team.

In 1879 the Old Etonians competed for the Cup again, and Lord Kinnaird once more changed his colours, but not his fortune, for the Etonians won, and he secured his fourth Cup medal. From this time onward he played regularly for his favourite club, and with them he won his fifth Cup medal in 1882.

He played regularly down to 1890, and nothing was more remarkable than the ease with which he adapted his play to the ever-changing tactics of the Association game.

He was absolutely devoid of fear, and, however rough a game became, he would be found in the thick of it, revelling in the spirited charges, and invariably escaping scathless from the fray. He was extraordinarily quick upon his legs, and never adopted the precaution of wearing shin-guards.

Since those early years at Eton and Cambridge, Lord Kinnaird has been unceasing in his efforts to promote the love of manly sport amongst the youths of England, and it is with loyal love and respect that we greet him to-day as president of the Football Association.

THE ANTIQUITIES OF FOOTBALL.

By J. E. VINCENT.

The dim beginnings of football—Modern football commenced in 1870—Classic ball games—A quaint description of the game—Football forbidden by statute in the Middle Ages—King James's criticism of football—The game in Elizabethan days—How Roger Ludforde, yeoman, was killed at South Mims—Norfolk "camping"—Modern football the outcome of the public school games.

FIVE thousand nine hundred and five years ago, according to Biblical chronology, Cain and Abel were about beginning to feel their feet. They used them to kick an apple about, and that was the beginning of football. There is no documentary evidence to this effect, not so much as an incised stone to be deciphered by a man of science after taking an impression in squeegee; but there is conclusive evidence of the *a priori*—or, what do you think was most likely?—character. We know that they were boys; we know that apples were abundant—there was, at least, one too many; we know that to kick is even more natural than to throw; and that is enough. We know, also, that Biblical chronology is, for our present purposes, liberally short, making no allowance for Neolithic man, who may be seen looking like a kippered herring *accroupi* in the British Museum, and probably played football, too.

But the Scriptural date for the beginning of the antiquities of football is quite early enough for me, since they ended only in the 'sixties or 'seventies of the last century. Here we get to the bedrock of fact, and I can supply a piece of personal evidence.

In the season of 1879 or 1880—it would be rash to say which—the captain of the Oxford University Association team raised me to the seventh or eighth heaven by asking me to beg, borrow, or steal a 'Varsity shirt, and to play against Cambridge next day. The shirt which I borrowed was historic, being, in fact, the first 'Varsity shirt ever made, and it was not much more than ten years old. The making had marked the period at which football, ceasing to be the game only of schoolboys and the masses, as it had been from time immemorial, became the formalised and important pastime of robust men. So, if we allow Cain and Abel four years in which to devise embryonic football and take the beginning of modern football as 1870, or thereabouts, there remain 5,870 years of history to be condensed into less than half as many words.

When and where did football begin? Probabilities and convenience point to Cain and Abel, since they were boys, and they were the first boys whose names are familiar. But probabilities will not serve the purpose in a scientific age. When does the history of football begin? That depends very much on what is meant by football. Is a game, like the Rugby game of the past, in which the feet are used only occasionally, so far as the ball is concerned, entitled to be called football? I suppose, inveterate admirer of "Soccer" though I am, that the title may be maintained, and that football, in its most primitive form, came into existence when sides were first organised with a view to forcing, without the use of any extraneous instrument, something in the nature of a ball between, over, or past two given marks.

It has been the fashion—set in the Badminton volumes, for example—to lay the classics under contribution. Nausicaa and her maidens play their part in the history of football, but it is long odds that they never played the game. Ulysses, disguised, betrayed his sex by drawing his knees together instead of spreading them apart, so as to utilise his apology for a skirt when he had muffed a catch; but he, Nausicaa, and the maidens, were manifestly playing only handball, or "catch." They fooled about with a ball; no more. They might as legitimately be claimed as the prototypes of cricketers. The *follis*, apparently a large inflated ball, recommended by Martial to old men and young, was not, so far as we know, ever kicked; and its lineal successor may be seen to-day in Southern Europe, where football certainly does not flourish. *Harpastum*, a ball game borrowed by the Romans, with its name, from the Greeks, sounds rather like Rugby Union football, save in one respect.

There was a ball; the players struggled to possess themselves of it, and doubtless to dispossess him who held it. We are told that it involved violent exercise, and in the plural the games are described as *pulverulenta*, "dusty," an epithet which serves to remind us simultaneously of "muddied oafs," and of the fact that there is no new thing and no new idea under the sun. But very little is known of the rules of the game—if there were any—or of its object; and nothing is mentioned in any of the classics as to goals to be passed, or of kicking—not that, to the true Rugbeian, that is very essential.

In fact, the writers, of whom I have been one in my time, have recourse to ancient Greek and Roman literature for professional purposes only, and they all know quite well really that while every football, although not necessarily round, is a ball, there is no excuse for supposing, or pretending to suppose, that every mention of a ball involves the idea of a football. The real truth of the matter is that, in relation to these primeval games, it is impossible to trace origins with precision. Cricket, tennis, hockey, racquets, golf, croquet—all these and many other games of the kinds that involve instruments more or less elaborate can be followed, and their evolution can be traced with scientific accuracy.

But the case is otherwise when Nature has supplied the plaything itself in a rudimentary form from the beginning of time. Cricket and croquet have their histories from the beginning. Football and marbles—for the first of which a blown bladder sufficed, while the second could be played with pebbles or with nuts, as the great Augustus played them—are prehistoric. Old-time students of contemporary manners and customs who descended to such trivialities found them in existence, as they found hop-scotch, and were quite unable to explain their origins. The reason, clearly and obviously I think, is that in their inception and essence such games as football suggested themselves to the first children who played.

Of all such students, Joseph Strutt is the most profound and learned. He flourished in 1801, and my edition of his "Sports and Pastimes of the People of England," edited by the quaintly learned William Hone, was printed for Thomas Tegg and Son, of Cheapside, in 1834. From him we learn nearly all that is to be known, except from casual references in Shakespeare, in statutes, and—save the mark!—on gravestones.

Strutt does not pretend to give the origin of the game, but finds the first mention of it in a statute of Edward III. (A.D. 1349), wherein it was prohibited, mainly because it, like other games, interfered with archery practice. Probably it interferes with rifle practice now. Strutt's description of the game is interesting:

> "When a match at football is made, two parties, each containing an equal number of competitors, take the field, and stand between two goals, placed at a distance of eighty or a hundred yards the one from the other. The goal is usually made with two sticks, driven into the ground about two or three feet apart." [In passing, the nearest modern survival of this microscopic goal is that of the Eton Field Game, in which the goal is as minute in proportion to ordinary goals as the ball.] "The ball, which is commonly made of a blown bladder, and cased with leather, is delivered into the midst of the ground, and the object of each party is to drive it through the goal of their antagonists, which being achieved, the game is won. The abilities of the performers are best displayed in attacking and defending the

FOOTBALL IN THE OLDEN TIMES.

In the early days of the fourteenth century football became so popular in the streets of London that the merchants petitioned the King to put it down. Edward II. therefore issued a proclamation forbidding the game on pain of imprisonment ; but, despite the many attempts that have been made to stamp it out, football has flourished through the centuries, and is recognised to-day as the great national winter game of Great Britain.

goals; and hence the pastime was more frequently called a goal at football than a game at football. When the exercise becomes exceeding violent, the players kick each other's shins without the least ceremony, and some of them are overthrown at the hazard of their limbs."

Strutt quotes Barclay's eclogue:

> "The sturdie plowmen, lustie, strong, and bold,
> Overcometh the winter with driving the footeballe,
> Forgetting labour and many a grievous falle."

He quotes Waller's "Ship of Fools" too:

> "As when a sort of lusty shepherds try
> Their force at football; care of victory
> Makes them salute so rudely breast to breast,
> That their encounter seems too rough for jest."

The prohibitive statute of Edward III., a fighting king, who was zealous for efficiency in a military sense, by no means stands alone. A law of Edward II. in 1314, directed against "rageries de grosses pelotes," may or may not have been directed against football, but there is no question of the reference to football in a statute of 1389 (Richard II.), of 1401 (Henry IV.), in the Scottish statutes of 1457 and 1491. What do they prove? Simply that the lawgivers of the fourteenth and fifteenth centuries found football a flourishing pastime, distracting the people from military exercise, which they were entirely unable to repress. In the seventeenth century, law having done its worst—not that repressive enactments were discontinued—kings and preachers turned their attention to football in vain. King James described it as "Meter for laming than making able the users thereof," and Stubbes, the rancorous author of "The Anatomie of Abuses in the Realme of England" (1583), is unique in the violence of his language.

Football is classed by Stubbes among "develyshe pastimes" practised on the Sabbath Day, and therefore a portent foretelling the end of the world.

> "As concerning football playing, I protest unto you that it may rather be called a frendlie kinde of fyghte than a play or recreation—a bloody and murthering practice than a felowly sport or pastime. For dooth not everyone lye in waight for his adversarie, seeking to overthrow him and picke him on his nose, though it be on hard stones, on ditch or dale, or whatever place soever it be he careth not, so he can have him downe? And he who can serve the most in this fashion, he is counted the only felow, and who but he."

Stubbes, who hated football on Sunday only a degree worse than he loathed it on any other day, on the ground that it withdrew men from godliness and virtue, and "haled" them to wickedness and sin at all times, had probably in his mind, not so much the plowmen's pastimes of which Barclay piped sympathetically, as the annual Shrove Tuesday games, played on the Roodee at Chester—where they were discontinued in 1540—and at other places, from time immemorial; for many of them were played in the streets, and they were practically rough-and-tumble fights, involving more loss of life and broken limbs than even eager Englishmen and sturdy Scots ought to be permitted to court.

Candour compels the admission that there may have been something to be said for both the timid and the moral objection to football, "as she was played." In the Badminton volume Mr. Shearman, K.C. (with whom I had the honour of collaborating exactly twenty years ago in a forgotten volume, now out of print, called "Football: its History for Five Centuries") has collected many gruesome records out of the archives of the law. In the reign of Elizabeth, in the County of Middlesex, were two bad cases, though it is hard to put the second down to the discredit of football. In the first, Arthur Reynolds, husbandman, and five others of Ruyslippe, and Thomas Darcye, yeoman, with seven others of Woxbridge, were indicted for playing "a certain unlawful game called foote-ball, by means of which unlawful game there was amongst them a great affray, likely to result in homicides or serious accidents." In the second an inquest was held at "Sowthemymes" on the body of "Roger Ludforde, yeoman, there lying dead." And it appears that when the ill-fated Roger came with his friend Simon Maltus on to a field where Nicholas Martyn and Richard Turvey were playing football, he was seized by spectator's fury. "Cast him over the hedge!" he cried, in reference to Martyn. And Martyn shouted back: "Come thou and do yt." In ran Roger and tried to kick the ball, but Martyn and Turvey, making common cause, with "the fore-parts of" their right and left arms respectively, "struck Roger Ludforde on the fore-part of the body under the breast, giving him a mortal blow and concussion, of which he died within a quarter of an hour, and that Nicholas and Richard thus feloniously slew the said Roger."

Hard-hearted although it may seem to say so, the tear of sympathy must be denied to Roger Ludforde. He came to the field at South Mims, which was then called "Evanses Field," and found Martyn and Turvey engaged "with others" in a friendly game, or perhaps even in an Elizabethan Cup-tie. As, during a House match at Eton, I have heard a monotonous cry from the sides of "Knock him down!" so Roger adjured Martyn to throw Turvey over the hedge. There was no great harm in that, perhaps; it was merely a rough Elizabethan version of the shouts of encouragement and advice that may be heard from the crowd during a twentieth-century match. Then Roger, without the slightest excuse, tried to interfere with the game, and both sides made common cause against him. He was hit twice.

If anybody tried the same adventure in these days he would certainly be hit more than twice, and probably be kicked into the bargain. Roger, however, was clearly a weakling, else he would hardly have succumbed to a couple of blows on the body.

It is not quite certain that he did not deserve his fate, and, in any case, his death is most unjustly attributed to football.

If I rushed in and disturbed the balls in the middle of an exhibition game of billiards between John Roberts and Stevenson, and the players hit me on the head with the butts of their cues, as I should richly deserve to be hit, that would not illustrate the dangers of billiards but the bad manners of a

Bowden Bros.]

THE GRAND STAND AT ASTON LOWER GROUNDS, BIRMINGHAM.

The Aston Villa ground has been for many years among the finest in the kingdom. It was built upon what was once the kitchen-garden of Aston Hall, and from the stand the magnificent Jacobean pile can be seen rising above the serried ranks of the spectators and the advertisement hoarding that marks the confines of the football enclosure. It is as likely as not that the retainers of Sir Thomas Holte played football of some kind near this very spot in the old days.

spectator; and ancient football was not any more to blame than is its modern successor for the disorderly behaviour of the lookers on.

In his comprehensive book on Norfolk Mr. William A. Dutt tells us how, at the beginning of the present century, a rough and rowdy game called "camping" was very much in vogue in East Anglia. It took the form of a kind of football match between teams representing different villages, districts, or counties.

In these "camping" matches there were practically no rules to prevent rough, and what would now be called "foul," play.

Free fights were a common accompaniment of the game, which was often attended with fatal results. There are men still living who can remember the last of these matches, and they speak of them as having been riotous and terrible encounters.

Similar games were common in Hampshire and what is perhaps the last survival of this form of the game has but in recent years dwindled away beneath the frown of the police of Dorking.

Football, then, throve through many centuries in spite of the opposition of military kings, timid kings, milk-and-water critics, and fire-and-brimstone divines. It grew, perhaps, the more by reason of efforts at repression; but it flourished most of all because, in any of its forms, it was, and is, one of the most strenuous games on earth, the quickest over, and the one that requires least in the way of apparatus. A bladder, such as one may see village boys using now, a strip of green for choice, or of deserted road where no green is available, a couple of coats or sticks at either end for goals—these are all the essentials, and in less elaborate days I have played many a good game with no more sumptuous equipment. Those of old time pinned their faith to the bladder of a pig; but, believe one who has tried both, that of an ox stands more kicking. Then, opposition being relaxed, football seems to have dwindled—that, at least, is the opinion of Mr. Shearman and of Joseph Strutt—but the truth may be that it was merely unnoticed.

Be that as it may, football, in its modern shape, is entirely the product in two forms of the various public school games, especially of those of Rugby on the one side, and of Eton, Harrow, Westminster, and Charterhouse on the other, and for robust young men and boys it is the finest game conceivable, for it is the very creative force of the spirit embalmed in the Harrow song that was sung before King and Queen last summer:

> "God give us bases to guard and beleaguer,
> Games to play out, whether earnest or fun,
> Fights for the fearless, and goals for the eager,
> Twenty and thirty, yes! forty years on."

Russell and Sons.]

FOOTBALL IN 1905—THE KICK-OFF IN THE CUP FINAL.

No greater contrast could be shown to the picture on page 3 than the above photograph, which represents Aston Villa starting the game in the last great Cup Final against Newcastle United. Had first-class football enclosures and playing-fields been permitted by King Edward II. London might have witnessed a Cup Final centuries ago.

THE ROMANCE OF ASTON VILLA.

Winners of the English Cup, 1887, 1895, 1897, 1905. Finalists, 1892. Winners of the Football League Championship, 1894, 1896 1897, 1899, 1900.

By WILLIAM MACGREGOR (Father of the League).

The early days of Aston Villa—The arrival of George Ramsay—His influence on the Villa style of play—Old stagers—A dispute with the Bridge Trust School trustees leads to a change of ground—The arrival of Archie and Andy Hunter—The Villa team of 1897 a great side—The Cup Final, 1905.

Club Colours: Claret and Light Blue. *Ground: Aston, Birmingham.*

IF there is a club in the country which deserves to be dubbed the greatest (and the matter is one of some delicacy), few will deny the right of Aston Villa to share the highest niche of fame with even the most historic of other aspirants. For brilliancy and, at the same time, for consistency of achievement, for activity in philanthropic enterprise, for astuteness of management, and for general alertness, the superiors of Aston Villa cannot be found. They may have rivals of equal worth, but in all the characteristics named they have never been surpassed, and their playing record is probably the best in the country. Blackburn Rovers have excelled their English Cup record, but the Lancastrians are hopelessly behind in respect of League achievement.

A glance at the Villa League record is sufficient to justify all this eulogy. Since the inception of that body the Villa have always held their place in the Senior Division, and have aggregated 622 points to 595 obtained by Everton and 579 by Sunderland. Directly or indirectly they have been the means of raising over £30,000 for the cause of charity, and in the General Hospital is to be seen the Aston Villa F.C. Bed, endowed at a cost of £1,250.

In the old days the social side of the club was one of its most pronounced characteristics. The tours they used to take in Scotland (usually under the management of the writer) were productive of more fun than any journeys I have ever read of. There was a wonderfully strong bond of fellowship in those days among footballers, and I have never come across a happier band of brothers than Aston Villa were. In death, some of the old cronies are not divided, for at Witton Cemetery, Birmingham, there is a Villa corner. There is to be seen the headstone which the club erected to the memory of Archie Hunter, and close by lies the fleet outside-left who helped him to win many a great victory, Eli Davis. A. Allen lies there, too, but Andy Hunter's last resting-place is in far Australia, and the remains of Teddy Lee are under the illimitable veldt.

Like many football organisations which have grown until they have obtained national importance, the Aston Villa Football Club was started by a number of young fellows connected with a place of worship. The famous Birmingham club owes its origin to the energies of a band of young men who were associated with the Aston Villa Wesleyan Chapel, Lozells, on the Aston side of Birmingham. The club was founded in quite a casual way, and for some time the members were content to kick a ball about various pieces of semi-waste ground in the neighbourhood of Heathfield Road. They had one fairly good pitch in the thoroughfare mentioned, which was then just beginning to come into the hands of the builder. Most of their matches were played on Aston Park, even then the football nursery of Birmingham. This was in 1874, and practically Aston Villa was one of the city's pioneer clubs. They had formidable rivals in their early days in the old Birmingham Cricket and Football Club, which utilised the even then famous meadow at Aston Lower Grounds. Aston Lower Grounds was the home of Birmingham sport. The Birmingham Football Club was the strongest organisation in the district.

The Aston Villa Club members were playing in a casual way on Aston Park when something happened which had a great effect upon the destinies of the body. A young fellow, small of stature, but trimly built and firmly knit, walked up and looked—probably almost compassionately if the members only knew it—upon the crude attempts at dribbling and shooting of the novices. The onlooker was George Ramsay, who had played football, and, indeed, excelled at it, in Glasgow. He had come to Birmingham for business purposes, and this was the first time that he had seen his favourite pastime in operation in his new surroundings. He asked if he might be allowed to join in, and the permission being readily granted, he speedily gave those present an object lesson in the art of dribbling.

I have heard some of the old members speak of the fascination which Ramsay's dexterous manipulation of the ball—if the term manipulation may be fairly used in such a connection—had for them. They had never seen anything like it. He had it so completely under control that it seemed impossible for them to tackle him. The members were ready to thrust all sorts of honours upon him, and he was literally compelled to accept the captaincy.

He does not rank, however, as the first captain of the club; W. H. Price was the original choice. But it was George Ramsay who first moulded the style of the club's play, and the Aston Villa team have never lost the reputation they gained for short, quick passing under Ramsay's direction. It is true that Archie and Andy Hunter, two of Ramsay's brother Scots, completed the work which the present secretary began; but the club undoubtedly owed the rapid advance they made among Midland organisations to the valuable and practical example which young Ramsay set them.

Aston Villa were content for some years with a strictly local programme, and for a while they could not hold their own with such strong Black Country clubs as Wednesbury Old Athletic, Wednesbury Strollers, and Stafford Road; indeed, they could scarcely claim to rank as the leading football organisation in Birmingham. But while they were

Russell and Sons.]

ASTON VILLA'S FIRST GOAL IN THE LAST CUP FINAL.

As all the world knows, Aston Villa defeated Newcastle United in the Cup Final at the Crystal Palace in April last by two goals to nil. It was one of the finest games ever witnessed. The striking photograph above shows Hampton, the dashing young Villa centre-forward, scoring the first goal at close range. The ball curled into the right-hand corner of the net, giving Lawrence, the Newcastle United goalkeeper, no chance to save.

advancing most of their rivals were either standing still or receding. Calthorpe and Saltley College, once the two best teams in Birmingham, never advanced beyond a certain stage; and the Villa were of no special account until Archie and Andy Hunter arrived upon the scene. Andy came from Third Lanark, and was one of the best, if not the best, outside-right in Scotland. Archie Hunter came from Ayr Thistle, and the brothers introduced a combination of dribbling, short passing, and long passing which marked an epoch in Midland football.

The first regular home that Aston Villa had was the pitch which was destined to become historic as the Wellington Road field at Perry Barr. It was a capital field, although when the Villa took it there was a hayrick not far from the centre of the ground, a number of trees along the touch-lines, a pool not far away, and a nasty hill near the left-hand corner of the top goal. It was not an ideal enclosure, by any means; but it was quite good enough for those days. The trees were not removed for many years after the Villa started playing there. I well remember the early reporters, who used to have to trudge the touch-lines, finding a rest for their weary backs against these trees, and doubtless they blessed them as the itching Scot is credited with having blessed the Duke of Argyll. The trees were useful to those reporters, for sometimes the spectators got irate with them for obscuring their view of the game. But spectators were often few and far between at Wellington Road in the early days. I can recall more than one match where there were only two spectators, myself and George Ramsay's brother; but the crowd soon began to come.

The first time that a gate was taken the noble sum of 5s. 3d. was raked in, and that was deemed a satisfactory sum by the club treasurer. George Ramsay did the Aston Villa Club many good turns, and not the least of them when he found Perry Barr field. He and a compatriot, named Lindsay, were taking their walks abroad one Sunday, and the thought was in their minds that Aston Villa had had enough of waste grounds and public parks. Ramsay was struck with the eligible look of the field in Wellington Road, and, always good at striking a bargain, he obtained it for the rental of £5 per annum from the tenant farmer. I don't suppose the Bridge Trust School trustees, whose property it was, realised that those tenants were soon destined to pay them hundreds of pounds a year for the use of the same enclosure. The tenant farmer must have looked greedily upon their growing gates, for he raised the rent to £8 in the second year, and finally demanded £10. This was paid, but the Villa found they must have security, so they obtained a three years' lease from the Bridge Trust School trustees, and those gentlemen, whose motto probably was that charity begins at home, condemned them to pay £60 per annum for the privilege. Later they demanded £120, and finally £200 per annum, and even then refused the club certain privileges which the latter deemed legitimate. But the Villa struck at last, and the club's magnificent ground at Aston was the outcome of the demands—exorbitant some of us thought—of the owners of Wellington Road. It was a wrench for some of the old school to be divorced from Wellington Road, but there can be no doubt that the Villa acted wisely when they launched their great Aston scheme, for at the present time the accommodation there is not one whit more than the club requires; indeed, after inspecting the Queen's Park, Crystal Palace, Chelsea, and Fulham enclosures, one is forced to admit that the Villa ground is not the unique coliseum it was when it was originally constructed.

A GLIMPSE INTO THE PAST. ASTON VILLA TEAM AND OFFICIALS—SEASON 1879-80.

This team, which contains the names of many famous exponents of the dribbling code—many of them, alas, now gone for ever!—won the Birmingham District Association Cup in the season 1879-80. It will be noticed that G. B. Ramsay, the present Villa secretary, who was a delightful player to watch, then captained the team, whilst William MacGregor was vice-president.

J. Hughes, Umpire. William MacGregor, Vice-President. W. B. Mason. T. Lee. H. Simmonds. Tom Pank. Eli Davis. F. Johnstone, Vice-President. H. Jefferies, Hon. Sec.

Andy Hunter. G. B. Ramsay, Captain. W. M. Ellis, President. Archie Hunter. C. S. Johnstone.

S. Law. H. Ball.

I shall never forget one Saturday afternoon when a friend and I were watching Aston Villa playing a club called Burton Robin Hood. We arrived on the ground rather late, and the match was in progress when we took up our positions near the touch-line. There was a player unknown to me operating on the wing. I had not the faintest idea who he was. The crowd was restricted to little knots of people dotted here and there.

I made some inquiries, but no one seemed to know who the new man was. Someone did say that he was a Saltley College man, and they gave me the name of a well-known footballer who was in residence there at the time. It did not surprise me to hear he was a Saltley man, because some of the finest footballers in the Midlands were then connected with the college. Never had I seen a forward show such perfect command over the ball. The unknown dribbled, dodged, and centred in a way which took everyone by storm. But he was not a local expert; he was none other than the great Archie Hunter, the man who made Aston Villa, the man who was probably the greatest centre-forward, and unquestionably the greatest captain ever associated with the game.

No one can tell what Archie Hunter did for Aston Villa. After thinking over the matter carefully, I can say, with all honesty and without being inspired by any partisan feeling, that I can recall no individual in football who was quite so much to his club as Archie Hunter was to Aston Villa. And yet Aston Villa were lucky, in a sense, to get him, because when he came to Birmingham he tried to find the Calthorpe Ground. He had played against the Calthorpes at Ayr in a previous season when the club were on tour in Scotland. However, the ground was a long way out, and not finding it he returned to Birmingham, and a business friend introduced him to Aston Villa, telling him, by way of an extra inducement, that there were several Scotsmen connected with the club.

It is usually held by people who do not know the facts that Archie and Andy Hunter came to Birmingham to play football. They did not; they came to Birmingham on business, and in the early days of the club, at any rate, they never had any money for playing. When they started in business as "A. and A. Hunter, drapers," at Birchfield, the club advanced them £200, but bills were given for the amount. The Hunters needed no inducement to play football. Good men came with a rush now, for Arthur Brown, the cleverest centre in the district, Archie Hunter excepted, left Aston Unity and joined the Villa, and the famous Wednesday Strollers' left wing, Eli Davis and Howard Vaughton, both Birmingham men, by the way, also threw in their lot with the club. The Villa's forward play was very fine when Andy Hunter, Crosland, George Ramsay, Archie Hunter, Vaughton, and Davis constituted the vanguard. Lee, Pank, and Law were excellent halves, Law being one of the cleverest tacklers I have ever known. He was the father of a family then, but in some mysterious way football was born in him. Andy Hunter was a delightful fellow to watch. He was at my business place for some years, and to this day in some of the drawers are to be seen diagrams in pencil illustrative of methods which might with advantage be adopted in some particular game. Andy died in Australia, and Archie expired at the Royal Exchange, Six Ways, on the highway from the city to the Villa Ground. To the last the dying man insisted on the bed being placed so that he could see the crowd hurrying to Perry Barr. John Hunter, a third brother, who played for Third Lanark, also passed away, the three brothers being the victims of consumption. Archie Hunter captained Aston Villa for nine years, George Ramsay having occupied the position for the four previous seasons. Arthur Brown and Howard Vaughton obtained their Scottish caps in 1882, and Olly Whateley, the finest shot I can recall, was successful in the following year. Howard Vaughton, the all-round champion of the club, in addition to being a great footballer, was prominent at half a dozen sports. To-day he is one of the most consistent batsmen in Birmingham League cricket.

Aston Villa first won the English Cup in 1887, but long before this they had swept the board in local competitions. The redoubtable Dennis Hodgetts had come into the team by this time, he and Vaughton making a perfect left wing. Albert Brown was fleet and clever at outside-right, but he had not quite the heart that some of the men we have had in that position possessed. A man of indomitable pluck was Joe Simmons. He would tackle anyone and it used to be one of the sights of the season to see him lying in wait for William Gunn, the Notts Forest, and, later, Notts County, giant. Gunn was one of the most courteous men that ever played football, although his physique was abnormal, and the crowd used to roar with laughter at the cheeky way in which Simmons went for the great Nottingham sportsman.

The Villa's fortunes were often at low ebb, but they were never without talented performers. William Groves, Tom Robertson (the famous Scottish referee), and Peter Dowd were three talented Scots who helped to make the Villa an attraction wherever they went. The Villa was naturally one of the clubs invited to form the Football League, and with rare exceptions they have been uniformly successful therein. Indeed, they have, as stated above, scored far more points in the aggregate than any team associated with the League. Under John Devey's captaincy they won the League five times and the English Cup twice in a period of eight years. One can safely say that no team will set aside such a record as that. Their crowning triumph came in 1897, when they emulated Preston North End's example, and won the English Cup and the League Championship in the same season. Expert judges agree that the Villa eleven of 1897 was only excelled by Preston North End's matchless combination of the early eighties. Never since that day has there been a club eleven so crowded with celebrities as the Villa team of '97 was; Whitehouse in goal, Spencer and Evans at back, Reynolds, Cowan, and Crabtree at half, and Athersmith, Devey, John Campbell, Wheldon, and Steve Smith, forwards, constituted the side, the equal of which we have not seen since, and, in my estimation, are not likely to see. There is no half-back line in Great Britain to-day comparable with the line constituted by Reynolds, Cowan, and Crabtree. Crabtree was indeed the most versatile and adaptable footballer of all time. If there was a man, however, who made the side more than another, that man was John Campbell. The Villa had had no centre since Archie Hunter was compelled by failing health to give up the game. Centres are hard to procure, and the Villa could not get one. Then they introduced John Campbell, and he filled the position perfectly. He was the one man in the football world who was suited to Aston Villa's methods, and when he left them to join the Celtic the club went down materially, and it was not until Hampton's appearance on the scene last season that Aston Villa's glories were revived. The club won the League in 1897 by the extraordinary margin of eleven points, their aggregate being forty-seven, Sheffield United being second with thirty-six

Chas. Urban.]

HOWARD SPENCER, THE ASTON VILLA CAPTAIN, RECEIVES THE CUP FROM LORD KINNAIRD.

The scene of enthusiasm which marked the termination of the Cup Final at the Crystal Palace this year will live long in the memory of all those fortunate enough to witness it. In the above unique photograph, which we have reproduced by kind permission of Mr. Charles Urban, of the Urban Trading Company, Spencer, the Villa captain, will be seen holding the precious cup in his hands. His delight is apparent. Lord Kinnaird, in the centre, who gave the cup and medals to the victorious team, looks as pleased as if he had just received a sixth winner's medal himself; and Mr. F. J. Wall, secretary of the Football Association, and other men famous in football, can be easily recognised amongst the group of the select.

ASTON VILLA. THE TEAM THAT WON THE CUP.

Top Row:—G. B. RAMSAY, Secretary. F. MILES. H. TONEY, Director. H SPENCER, Captain. F W. RINDER, Chairman. W GEORGE, Goalkeeper. J. DEVEY, Director. J. GRIERSON, Trainer.

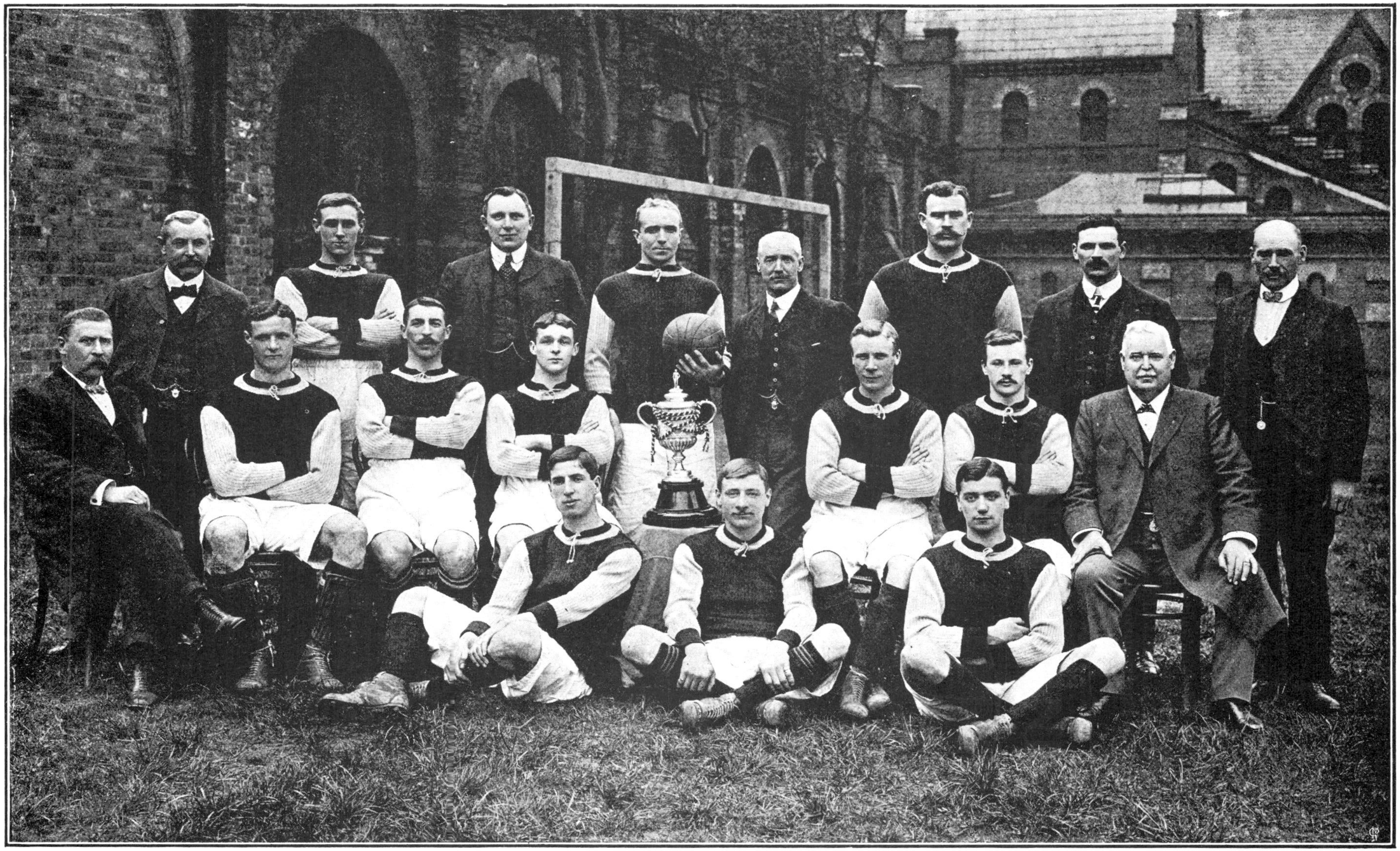

Photo by A. Wilkes, West Bromwich.]

THE ENGLISH CUP.

Middle Row:— D. V. A. JONES, Director. W. BRAWN. W. GARRATY. H. HAMPTON J BACHE. A. HALL. J T. LEES, Director.

Bottom Row:—J. PEARSON. A. LEAKE. J. WINDMILL.

Whitlock and Sons.]

HOWARD SPENCER, THE VILLA CAPTAIN.

The famous full-back was born in Birmingham in 1875. His height is 5ft. 10½in.; weight, 12st. 10lb. The only club he has played for, with the exception of Aston Villa, is Birchfield Trinity. He is a model of what a professional footballer should be, and one of the finest backs that ever played the game. He is scrupulously fair, and one of the brightest ornaments of football. As an International he played for England v. Scotland in 1897, v. Wales in 1897, 1900. Again represented England in 1903; and in his last International match v. Scotland this year, and in the Cup Final, he showed that his judgment and resource were as good as ever. May he long continue to play the game!

Such a margin was unprecedented, and is likely to remain unique. Last season the Villa opened tamely. The secret of their failure was an open one—they wanted a centre. They could do nothing right until young Hampton, who had been acquired from Wellington at the close of the previous year, was drafted into the eleven almost as a last resource. He was an instantaneous success; he revolutionised the Villa's style of play; he gave point to all their attacks; and not only was the English Cup won for the fourth time, but the club secured a highly satisfactory position in the League, finishing fourth. Their display in the Cup Final at the Crystal Palace will never be forgotten. There was a dash and vigour about their football which was irresistible. They did not restrict themselves to the short passing, which, generally speaking, has been the feature of the club's forward work; they swung the ball out to the wings, and did so with an accuracy which has never been excelled. Time after time Hall and Brawn, the outside men, were left in undisputed possession of the ball, and the long passing baffled the Newcastle defenders—no mean set—in a way that they had never been baffled before.

If the Villa's fame as a great team rested on their displays in their last two Cup Finals alone, they would go down to posterity as one of our greatest sides. Their work against Everton in the Cup Final of 1897 was of the most brilliant description, and only slightly inferior was the exhibition of the beaten side. Aston Villa enjoy a great popularity in London, and after these Finals who can wonder at that being the fact? In their games with the Corinthians the Villa have also displayed football of the best type.

There were great rejoicings in Birmingham over the club's Cup triumph last year, and they received an overpowering welcome when they returned home. There would have been an official reception in the fullest sense, but for the melancholy fact that the Lord Mayor of the city died suddenly on the eve of the Cup fight. The Villa wore bands of crape round their arms at Sydenham. A large party of officials and friends of the club were entertained by the management in London, their headquarters being the Hotel Metropole. It is significant as showing the altered conditions which govern football, that, although there was much jubilation at the winning of the Cup, and although the party were staying in London, which to the provincial is the home of revelry, I never saw a single member of the party, which was quite fifty strong, show the slightest sign of undue exhilaration during the four days we were there. I am afraid that could not be said of any of the trips we used to have in the old days.

A. Wilkes, West Bromwich.]

W. GEORGE, THE VILLA GOALKEEPER.

As a goalkeeper the name of W. George ranks with the finest in the land. His height is 6ft. 1½in., his weight well over 16st. He learnt his football, one might say, in the Army. Played for Royal Artillery, Trowbridge, and Trowbridge Town. Aston Villa, after long persuasion, succeeded in inducing him to leave the Army, and he has represented them between the sticks ever since. He invariably plays a high-class game, and was England's best goalkeeper in 1902. He is also a good cricketer, and has played county cricket for Warwickshire, Wilts, and Shropshire.

I was chairman of the club when the Villa won the Cup in 1887, and Mr. Isaac Whitehouse filled that position when the team played in the Final in 1892. Mr. Margoschis was chairman in 1895 and 1897, and Mr. Rinder in 1905. We were all included in the party which went up from Birmingham for the purposes of last year's Cup Final match.

Aston Villa's list of honours is a notable one. Local Cup competitions do not fill the bill as they did in the old days, but when the Birmingham Cups were highly esteemed, Aston Villa almost farmed them. They have won the English Cup four times, the League Championship five times, the Birmingham Senior Cup thirteen times, the Mayor's Charity Cup eighteen times, the Staffordshire Cup six times, while their Reserves have six times been champions of the Birmingham League, and have carried off the Foresters' Cup and the Walsall Cup. The Villa also rank as former winners of the Sheriff of London's Shield.

Russell and Sons.]

VILLA'S SECOND GOAL. THE CUP FINAL, 1905.

No greater testimony could be given to the outstanding excellence of the Villa forward line in this historic match than the above photograph. It will be seen that the forwards have run right through the Newcastle defence, and Lawrence, the United goalkeeper, is left helplessly gazing after the ball, which has been driven with unerring aim by Hampton, the centre-forward, into the net.

THE GROWTH OF MODERN FOOTBALL.

By J. J. BENTLEY.

Establishing the date of modern football—Early Cup games—A rapid advance in interest of recent years—Some Cup Tie figures—The legalisation of professionalism—MacGregor and the League—The importance of the Football Association—The sub-committees—The vitality of the Association game.

MODERN football must be an elastic sort of term to cover the doings of the Football Association, for in 1872 the Cup was first competed for, and in the same year the series of International matches with Scotland was inaugurated. It thus does not require much mathematical skill to show that the Association game has been seriously played for thirty-two years. But one is apt to regard football in the early seventies as rather ancient, and, by comparison, it was, for at that time the game had not a real head like it now possesses, and my youthful recollection of it in '72 was that we heard of London Association rules and Sheffield Association rules, while those which my club—how proud I was to be able to scrape together, by maternal assistance, that half-crown necessary to become a real member!—favoured more the rules which governed the game at Harrow School.

But very soon London rules and Sheffield rules disappeared, and there was one set; although under Football Association régime I have played with sides numbering twelve, and against sides which included three-quarters and half-backs. But time worked changes, and about 1880 the three half-back system was generally adopted, and remains to-day; so that, for a quarter of a century, the men have been disposed of as a goalkeeper, two backs, three half-backs, and five forwards. It is considered almost a crime to alter the position of your forces, if even temporarily, and the one-back game is generally denounced as unsportsmanlike. Why so described I cannot say—it is merely a question of tactics. But, still, for all practical purposes, we play in the same positions on the field as we did twenty-five years ago. It is the only game I know which has changed so little in this respect, although an old-time cricketer, suddenly dropped on one of our county fields after an absence of twenty-five years, would wonder what had happened to his favourite pastime.

But in many other respects, football has altered more than any other game, and mainly in legislature. Up to 1880 or thereabouts, while public interest was yearly increasing, Association experts were chiefly confined to the 'Varsities and Public Schools, although such clubs as Notts Forest, Sheffield Wednesday, Darwen, and Blackburn Rovers had given a pretty broad hint that provincials intended taking the Cup out of London; but it was not until 1882 that Blackburn Rovers appeared in the Final, only to suffer their first defeat of the season at the hands of the Old Etonians, for whom the President of the Association, Lord Kinnaird, played. However, the following year, another Blackburn club, the Olympic, conquered the Old Eton Boys, who played an extra half-hour without the valuable services of the late A. T. B. Dunn; and from then up to 1901 the Cup never saw the metropolis, except for a brief sojourn during the Final Tie, Tottenham Hotspur then taking it back for one year only.

But, comparatively speaking, the interest taken in the competition was not striking up to a dozen years ago, and Preston North End played Wolverhampton Wanderers on one half of Kennington Oval, in 1889, with rope barriers, and only one little stand, which still remains. But the next three years witnessed a wonderfully increased enthusiasm; and, after allowing the Final to be played right across the sacred cricket pitch, the Oval authorities decided to have no more of it. Following two Finals in the provinces, the Crystal Palace people made a football ground out of the old lake, and there the great match of the year has since taken place, 110,000 paying for admission to see Tottenham and Sheffield United in 1901. That is a record attendance for any match, and, as showing the strides made in the Association Cup competition, is worth comparing with the attendance little over a decade previously at Kennington Oval. But not only did the Final "gate" substantially increase, but those of the previous rounds were of a magnitude which, to old stagers, must have smacked of the incomprehensible.

Russell and Sons.] TOTTENHAM HOTSPUR v. SHEFFIELD UNITED.

CUP FINAL, 1901.

How modern football has grown can easily be realised when one compares the attendance of 3,000 spectators at Kennington Oval on the occasion of the England v. Scotland match in 1873, an attendance which then created something like a sensation, with the number of lookers on at the match between Tottenham Hotspur and Sheffield United. To witness the game at the Crystal Palace in 1901 upwards of 110,000 people assembled. The photograph above shows a section of densely packed humanity, and was taken just after Tottenham scored their first goal. The burly Foulke looks very disgusted as he goes to pick the ball out of the net.

I will give last season's figures, and these being taken from official sources, may be accepted as correct. Prior to the Final Tie, 998,568 had paid admission fees amounting to £37,339, and altogether 1,070,000 persons witnessed the various rounds of the competition. It will thus be seen how popular is the yearly struggle for the Cup, and how it has grown far beyond the dream of anyone officially connected with the game in the eighties. And there is a cause, which, probably, many readers will not agree with.

First of all came

the legalisation of professionalism in 1885. But that alone was not responsible for the rapid rise. Indeed, it is open to question whether that of itself did much good, and it certainly decreased the number of prominent amateur clubs. But open professionalism looked like spelling financial ruin to the clubs who had embraced it, and the turning point came when, in 1888, Mr. W. MacGregor, of Birmingham, suggested the League system. It was in a crude form, 'tis true, but it was there, and the early development of it saved professional football, and very soon popularised it. It did more than popularise the little League of twelve clubs—the system permeated the whole of the football world, and not only in England, but in Scotland, Ireland, and Wales was it introduced, and, by causing increased interest in club football, it naturally aroused enthusiasm in Cup-ties and Internationals. It is quite possible something else might have been devised, but certainly nothing of more lasting good, and to-day we have Leagues in almost everything appertaining to sport.

But the League system alone, beneficial as it has proved itself to be, could not have produced the almost unprecedented enthusiasm which now prevails. It is all very well to have a system—that is something to work with—but the most admirable system in the world is rendered futile unless it be properly carried out. The League management has, I think, fairly controlled its competitions, and the same may be said of the committees directing other League competitions; but their duties, to a great extent, were chiefly parochial—as, indeed, they desired them to be. For a considerable period they were allowed to run pretty much as they pleased, but eventually the Football Association realised that it ought to be the governing body, and that Leagues were fast undermining their authority. Then arose a considerable amount of jealousy and friction; but common-sense ultimately prevailed, with the result that, while the Football Association controls the Leagues, the Leagues — or the principal Leagues—are allowed to govern themselves. This seems to be a reasonable state of affairs, and one likely to continue, unless one or the other seeks to obtain powers outside the present jurisdiction, which, under existing conditions, is not at all probable.

J. J. BENTLEY, Esq.,
President of the Football League, and Vice-President of the Football Association.
(A biographical sketch of Mr. Bentley's career will be found on page 14.)

Briefly put, the situation is this. The Football Association governs the sport as a whole, and the leading Leagues—subordinate ones to a great extent as well—are allowed to control their own affairs, subject, of course, to the rules of the parent body being duly observed.

And to what a big, important corporation the parent body has grown! My first recollection of it was in a modest, badly-furnished little room in Paternoster Row, wherein sat a small number of gentlemen, entirely unknown, except by repute, to anything provincial—and I am bound to say that anything provincial was not particularly well received. But the claims of the provincial could not be ignored, and in 1887 a new scheme of representation was drawn up, which first of all divided the country into ten districts, and afterwards provided that each affiliated association consisting of fifty duly qualified clubs should be entitled to a representative. This scheme is still in force, with the addition of a representative each for the Army, the Public Schools, and the 'Varsities, so that it may be said to include everything and everybody entitled to a voice in the government of the game. It has really become a business in the sense that the work involved is of such an important character as to render it compulsory that business-like methods must be absolutely observed. Instead of the unpretentious, back-staircase room in Paternoster Row, offices were secured on Holborn Viaduct. These were found inadequate, and a suite of rooms were taken in Chancery Lane; but in a few years there was overcrowding, and a move made to 104, High Holborn, where the secretary is assisted by a staff of clerks.

Mr. C. W. Alcock performed the secretarial duties for many years in an honorary capacity, but this was too much to expect of any man; and on Mr. Alcock resigning and being elected a vice-president, Mr. F. J. Wall was appointed. He has what may be considered a big salary, but not too large for the duties he is called upon to perform. Then the Council grew too unwieldy to carry out the requirements of the modern growth of football, and it became necessary to appoint sub-committees, all, of course, subservient to the will of the general body, but still sufficiently powerful to command almost universal respect, and we now have, among others, the following:

EMERGENCY COMMITTEE.—Three vice-presidents, who decide cases of emergency which arise between meetings.

INTERNATIONAL SELECTION COMMITTEE.—Nine members, who visit almost the whole of the principal grounds in the country, closely watch budding Internationalists, select trial teams, and afterwards choose the sides to do duty for England against Scotland, Wales, and Ireland. It possesses the fullest powers in everything which relates to matters international.

REINSTATEMENT COMMITTEE.—Seven members, who consider applications from professionals desiring to play as amateurs, and recommend suitable applicants. In their work they are greatly assisted by affiliated associations, who inquire into local cases.

RULES REVISION COMMITTEE.—Each year rules require revision, and five gentlemen revise them for submission to the Council.

AMATEUR CUP COMMITTEE.—A large and important body, practically governing the Amateur Cup competition, now most popular, but it would be rendered more so by the active co-operation of the Old Boys' clubs.

INTERNATIONAL BOARD.—Messrs. C. Crump and R. P. Gregson attend the annual meetings, and carry into effect, if possible, the alterations to laws of the game adopted by the Council.

BENEVOLENT FUND COMMITTEE.—Large and comprehensive. Formed for the purpose of assisting old football players or anyone connected with the game. Possesses ample funds, but is not often troubled with applications.

There are other committees, but these fairly represent the practical ones, and will afford some idea as to what is now required in order to carry on the work of managing Association football. Then there is the Consultative Committee, consisting of the officers and ten others, generally ten old members, and in this committee is vested the absolute powers of the full Council, and it is necessarily a most important section of the sub-committees.

It will thus be observed that the Football Association attempts to carry out its multifarious duties in an eminently business-like fashion, and, although it has many detractors, it may safely be said that it has followed the times, and that the process has been almost inconceivably successful. But to place it on a proper footing has necessitated a vast amount of

Russell and Sons.]

INTERNATIONAL FOOTBALL.—ENGLAND v. SCOTLAND, 1905.

International football has kept pace with the growth of interest shown by the public in League and Cup-tie games. In 1873 3,000 persons witnessed the England v. Scotland match at the Oval. In 1900, twenty-seven years later, 62,000 people assembled to see the struggle between the two countries at Celtic Park, Glasgow, and £4,387 9s. 6d. was taken at the gates—an International match record.

diplomacy, and even now this art is by no means allowed to lie dormant, for there are constantly arising instances which require very delicate handling, and sometimes one is inclined to regard the actions of the Association as bordering on the autocratic, but this it is almost impossible to avoid.

The clubs forming the two important leagues—the Football League and the Southern League—have been fully considered in the arrangement of Cup-tie dates, and nothing better need be desired than the present Conference fixtures, for midway in the League competitions comes a break in the shape of Cup-ties, which cease to possess a personal interest to the majority of clubs in the short space of a month, and they are then at liberty to once more devote themselves to League requirements.

The playing strength of the two Leagues named may be gathered from the fact that, since the inauguration of League football, only clubs representing one or other have appeared in the Final or even in the Semi-final, and since 1889 the Cup has been won by League clubs sixteen times, and once by a Southern League club. This shows the immense popularity of the League; and the one sorrowful note is that it marks the decline of superior amateur football so far as the Cup competition is concerned. But I share the opinion with many others that if the Corinthians would only seriously enter and play for the Cup, they would prove as good as any of our professional organisations, and would do football generally a vast amount of good, while it would enable them to devote an enormous sum of money each year to charity. And, even in these compulsory, business-like days of football, charity is by no means forgotten. I should say that Association football contributes more to it than any other game, and one club alone, Aston Villa, has been the means of handing over the sum of at least £25,000.

The modern growth of the game may be, and is, distasteful to many old and respected players, who—without, in my opinion, just cause—have ceased to take a personal interest in it, but it has developed more than any sport under the sun, and still claims the patronage of prominent gentlemen, who have stuck to and followed it through its peregrinations of the last quarter of a century, and are justifiably proud of the little baby they nursed in the early seventies—now a sound, substantial, and, indeed, superior man. In this connection I will confine myself to three honoured names—Lord Kinnaird, C. W. Alcock, and J. C. Clegg—all three Internationals long before it became necessary to write anything about the growth—modern or otherwise—of our great national game.

Russell and Sons.] FOOTBALL AT THE CRYSTAL PALACE. THE CUP FINAL OF 1901.

An anxious moment after a corner kick.

THE HEAD OF THE FOOTBALL LEAGUE.

MR. J. J. BENTLEY.

Mr. J. J. Bentley was elected president of the Football League in 1894, a position to which he was more than entitled by the sterling worth of his work for many years in what may safely be called the "politics" of football; and as a tribute to the sound judgment of those who elevated him from the post he had honourably filled as chairman of the Football League First Division to that of president of the League, may be cited the fact that he still occupies the premier position, coupling with it the honour of being vice-president of the Football Association.

J. J. Bentley played his first game of football at Turton, Lancashire, the place in which he was born, and he was then a boy of thirteen.

In his youthful days Mr. Bentley was employed in the goods department of the London and North-Western Railway at Bolton. He afterwards began business as an accountant in that town, and to this he subsequently added the duties of secretary of the Bolton Wanderers Football Club. The latter position he relinquished subsequently when he took up the editorship of "The Athletic News."

He became a member of the Lancashire Association in 1886, and of the Football Association Council in 1888, and amongst the long list of honours showered upon him may be mentioned those of president of the Manchester and District Football Association, president of the Bolton and District Charity Cup Association, president of the Lancashire Amateur League, member of the Sheriff of London's Shield Committee, and President of the Manchester, Bury, Bolton and District Referees' Association.

As a player, Mr. Bentley represented Lancashire in inter-county games, and his best work was done for Turton at forward and half-back when that club held a prominent place in Lancashire football in the pre-professional days.

He was also well known as a referee, in which capacity he officiated in the League's best games for some years and in Football Association Cup-ties.

Mr. Bentley has been known as an uncompromising champion of the interests of professionalism and the League systems upon the Council of the Football Association, but he is an absolutely fair-minded, if militant, advocate.

An excellent portrait of Mr. Bentley as he appears to-day will be found on page 12.

THE BIGGEST CROWD EVER SEEN AT A FOOTBALL MATCH.

Russell and Sons.]

THE RECORD CROWD AT THE CRYSTAL PALACE

IN THE CUP FINAL OF 1900-1.

This striking photograph can give but a faint idea of the actual appearance of the crowd of over 110,000 people which gathered at the famous Crystal Palace enclosure in April, 1901, but it is an eloquent testimony to the fascination of modern football. The record created on the occasion of the great match between Tottenham Hotspur and Sheffield United in the year the Cup came South still stands; but that it will be broken, and before many seasons are passed, seems a safe prophecy. At Celtic Park, Glasgow, a sudden wave of enthusiasm may place it in danger; and at the Palace itself, with the game making such rapid strides in popularity in the South, the record should soon be easily passed.

THE HISTORY OF WOOLWICH ARSENAL.

By A. E. KENNEDY (Vice-Chairman of the Woolwich Arsenal F.C.).

The inception of the Woolwich Arsenal Football Club—Some first season results—The "Gunners" v. Millwall—Brilliant play in 1889-90—The adoption of professionalism and its consequences—The struggle for First Division honours—Success—The suspension of the club ground—Prospects of the season 1905-6.

Colours: Red Shirts, White Knickers. *Manor Ground, Plumstead*

OUR greatest concerns have sprung from small beginnings, and in nothing is this more exemplified than in football clubs. The Woolwich Arsenal Club, one of the leading professional organisations in the South, was no exception to the rule, for their first venture was indeed, in a very small way—in fact, the seed from which the present flourishing club has sprung was sown in one of the workshops of the nation's great factory—the Royal Arsenal—as far back as 1886; and I doubt if any of the few enthusiasts who first set the ball rolling on Plumstead Common ever thought the club would reach the dimensions it has to-day, a concern which has been formed into a limited liability company, with a bank business last year which amounted to close on £14,000. No; the club, as many others have done, started in a very humble way. But the men at the head of affairs, keen, hard-headed men of the world—albeit they were mostly skilled mechanics employed in the Government factory—had proclaimed as their motto the one word "Forward!"; and in spite of many disappointments and setbacks that only those thoroughly acquainted with the inner workings of the club are aware of, "Forward!" has been their motto ever since. And it may be taken as an undoubted fact that the same will continue till both the English Cup and the trophy for the championship of the First Division of the League find resting-places on the sideboard of the "Reds'" club-room.

In dealing with the history of the Arsenal Club, I may mention that prior to 1886 Association football was practically unknown in the district, "Rugger" holding the sway; and of the latter there were a number of really first-class teams playing each week. In this year, however, a number of enthusiasts for the "Soccer" code, who had migrated from the North and Midlands, conceived the idea of forming an Association club, with the result that a meeting was held at the Royal Oak, Woolwich, and the present club saw its inception under the title of the Royal Arsenal Football Club. Of the first officers of the club but few are now remaining in the district, but prominent among these few is Mr. John Humble, the present chairman of the company, whose connection with the club has been continuous but for one short break, when, owing to business reasons, he had to retire from active participation in the club's affairs. During their first season the team played on an open space called Plumstead Common, and of the 10 matches played, 7 were won, 1 drawn, and 2 lost, with a goal average of 36 for and 8 against.

This part of a season was more in the nature of an experiment; but so much interest was taken in the games that the committee felt emboldened to hire a private ground for the following season, and the old "Sportsman" Ground, a pitch almost contiguous to the present Manor Ground, was rented; the club made a start in earnest, and from that time to the present has never looked back. This season is important too from the fact that the first meeting between the Arsenal and their subsequent keen rivals, Millwall, took place, with the result that the "Dockers" had to acknowledge defeat at the hands of the "Gunners" by 3 goals to nil. This encounter is memorable in more ways than one, but mostly so because it was the first game played by the Arsenal team on their present playing pitch—the Manor Ground. How it came about is as follows: There had been very heavy rains, and the "Sportsman" Ground, just before the game, was found to be flooded. The committee were in a quandary, and at their wits' ends as to know what to do. Looking up the Manor Road they spied a field under pasturage which appeared playable, whereupon a deputation waited on Mr. Cavey, the tenant of the field in question, requesting permission to play their match on it. The desired permission was readily given, and thus the famous "Reds" first appeared on the present historic enclosure. So well pleased were they with the pitch that they rented it the following season for football, and doubtless many of the Woolwich readers of this article can bring vividly back to mind the old field as it then was, with its roped-in enclosure on the north side, and its grand stand of military waggons borrowed on the occasion of big matches. When one contrasts the ground then and now, we can form an idea of the progress that has taken place in the interval.

The season 1889-90 saw the Woolwichers coming in for a good deal of attention in the South by reason of their brilliant play, and of four cups for which they entered they succeeded in annexing three of them. They came an awful cropper in the English Cup competition, however, when they met the Swifts, for the latter brought down a team composed almost solely of International players, and the gallant "Reds" were humbled, losing by a heavier margin than they would now like to be reminded of. I have always thought that this defeat was one of the best things that could have happened to

Bowden Bros.]
THE WOOLWICH ARSENAL ENCLOSURE AT PLUMSTEAD.
This photograph was taken on the occasion of the first match of the season against Liverpool. The ball is being thrown back by the crowd, after being kicked out by a Woolwich forward in an unavailing effort to score. Though the ground at Plumstead has few claims to beauty, the densely packed crowd invariably presents a most impressive picture.

the Arsenal, for it brought home to them the fact that, however omnipotent they might be in club football in the South, they yet had a lot to learn before they could be classed amongst the higher flight. The lesson was not lost on the management, and the following season saw the team strengthened, and further successes were placed to their credit.

This season (1890-1) also saw the "Reds" leave their old quarters for a spick-and-span new ground replete with all modern improvements in the shape of dressing-rooms, stands, and terraces, known hereafter as the Invicta Ground, and it was here on one frosty day that the Southerners ran Derby County to a goal in the First Round of the English Cup. The "Reds" created quite a sensation by the form they showed in this match, particularly Peter Connolly and Bobbie Buist, names of a bygone past; and I can well remember how Johnnie Goodall, then in his prime, was most anxious to secure their services for the "Rams." It is not generally known that it was owing to the action of certain of the players who participated in this match that in the following season the club embraced professionalism; but it is so, and some day I may be tempted to tell the story. Of course, professionalism was bound to come sooner or later, but the action of the players referred to respecting this match precipitated matters.

It was in 1891-2 that the momentous decision was arrived at, and I have still vivid recollections of that meeting at the Windsor Castle, when Mr. Humble, one of the then committee, and now the present chairman of the club, moved the resolution which was to eventually revolutionise Association football in the South: "That the Arsenal Club do embrace professionalism." This was carried by an overwhelming majority, and, of course, brought down the vials of wrath of the London Football Association on the devoted heads of the Arsenal executive. But the latter proceeded on their way with a dogged determination to overcome all obstacles, and it must be admitted that right well have they succeeded.

This action led to most of the Southern clubs cancelling their fixtures with the Arsenal, with the result that the Woolwichers had to look further afield for opponents, and thus began that association with the Midland and Northern clubs, who this season were met in friendly combat, which has been further strengthened as the seasons went by. It has often been wondered why the Arsenal never joined the later Southern combination of clubs. But this is the reason—a spirit of loyalty towards those who held out a helping hand to them when they were most in need of it. Up to 1892-3, the Arsenal had been very comfortable in their quarters on the Invicta Ground; but at the close of this season the landlord imposed such exorbitant terms on them that they could not be acceded to, and at one time there was a prospect of the club going under.

The opposition they met with, however, only served to knit the club's supporters closer together, and at a meeting called to consider the position of affairs it was decided to form the club into a limited liability company, with a share capital of £1,000. Most of the share capital was at once taken up, and the directors set to work to find a new ground.

As luck would have it, their old home—the Manor Field—was in the market, the freehold was quickly secured, and thus once more the plucky "Gunners" settled down in their old quarters. A small army of men was quickly set to work, and with many of the shareholders assisting in the evenings, the grounds were quickly laid out, and a grand stand and terraces erected.

1893-4 saw everything ready for them, and this season also saw them, for the first time, members of the Second Division of the League, then in its second year. A strange coincidence, also, is the fact that their first opponents in the Second League were Newcastle United, as they were also their first opponents after working their way into the First Division of the League last year.

Thus began the long, weary struggle for First Division honours, which at times appeared so near, but as the end of April came round just as regularly receded, till any club but the Arsenal would have given up the struggle in despair.

The spirit, however, which dominated the early pioneers of the club, and which enabled them to overcome obstacles which to an ordinary club management would have been insurmount-

THE MEN BEHIND "THE GUNNERS"

MR. JOHN HUMBLE
(Chairman).

No reference to the Arsenal Club would be complete without recording the name and services of Mr. Humble. The present chairman hails the North country as his home, but, coming South, he formed one of the early pioneers of the Arsenal Club. First as a player, then a committeeman, next a director of the company, and finally as chairman of the directors, his services have been of the highest value to Woolwich Arsenal, and many and important are the projects that he has set on foot and carried through successfully for the club. He makes a strong chairman at the company's annual meetings, which are not always of the most peaceful character. He has expressed his intention of retiring at the end of this season, but as he can ill be spared from the council of the club, it is hoped that he will reconsider his decision.

MR. PHILIP KELSO
(Secretary-Manager).

Was appointed secretary-manager at the close of the season 1903-4, and by the successful manner in which he has managed the affairs of the club during the first season of his office, has justified the choice of the directors in selecting him for this important post. It need hardly be said that Mr. Kelso is one of the best types of the Scot. Before coming South he was associated with the famous Edinburgh Hibernians for many years, and the success of this powerful organisation was in a great measure due to his efforts. "Phil," as his friends delight to call him, was one of the best known men in Scottish football circles, and has a big reputation for his talent of discovering and bringing to the front young and promising footballers. The Hibernians' loss proved to be the Arsenal's gain, and it is hoped that his connection with the famous "Reds" may continue for many years to come. A thorough enthusiast where football is concerned, he has proved the right man in the right place.

MR. ARTHUR E. KENNEDY
(Vice-Chairman).

A versatile Irishman and the handy-man of the directorate. First joined the board in 1898 as financial secretary, and after successfully filling this important and onerous position for four years became a director. He carries the confidence of the shareholders with him to such an extent that, upon coming up for re-election last June, he was easily returned at the top of the poll. Mr. Kennedy has the reputation of being a keen business man, particularly in football legislation, and his views are always treated by his colleagues with the greatest respect. Is a member of the management committee of the London League, and recently formulated a referee's scheme for that body which is highly thought of.

able, was also strongly imbued in the later officials, and they still lived up to the old motto "Forward!"

As is now well known, the season 1903-4 saw their efforts rewarded, for in that season they managed to secure the second place on the Second League Table after a desperate struggle with Manchester United, and, accompanied by Preston North End, they passed at last into the higher division.

Many interesting incidents and changes in the club's affairs had taken place in the interim. On one occasion the ground was suspended for six weeks for a spectator's assault on a referee—Mr. Brodie, the famous centre-forward of the "Wolves." Then came the sad death of poor Joe Powell, who succumbed to an injury received whilst playing at Kettering. Later, an Archery Tournament was held, the first of the kind in the South, and from the proceeds the club enriched their coffers by about £1,200.

This was in 1902-3, and I always reckon that this was the turning-point in the club's later career; for, with this money, the management were so enabled to strengthen their team for the following season that they won the long-desired promotion to the First League.

In 1897 the Arsenal also made a new departure by engaging a secretary-manager at a high salary. Mr. T. B. Mitchell was the first holder of the post, and he was subsequently followed by Mr. Elcoat, Mr. Harry Bradshaw (the present manager of Fulham), and Mr. Phil Kelso, who occupies this important and onerous position at present.

This practically brings the story of the Arsenal Club down to the present time. Last season was their first in the First League, and it is generally conceded that they did remarkably well for their initial appearance. They finished tenth on the Table, being bracketed with Sheffield Wednesday for points, and but for a series of mishaps should have occupied a much higher position.

However, they have proved to the football public that now they have attained First Division honours they mean to retain them, and there is to be no going back. They have won for themselves by their perseverance and indomitable pluck a warm place in the regard of all football communities, and wherever football is spoken of to-day the name of the Woolwich Arsenal Club is referred to with affection and respect.

And now as to the prospects for the present season. The players are always so well cared for and kindly treated at Woolwich that there are, as a rule, very few desertions from their ranks at the end of a season. The only two players of last season's team that the management were desirous of keeping, and who left them for fresh fields and pastures new, were Jackson and Hunter. The former has been appointed manager of the newly-constituted Leyton team, whilst the latter joined his old friend Buick at Portsmouth. The remainder of last season's team elected to stay, so that Mr. Kelso had not many positions to fill.

JOHN DICK

(Right Half-back), the Woolwich Captain.

The popular skipper of the team, though young as years go, is now the oldest playing member of the club. It was in the season of 1897-8 that he left the Airdrieonians to throw in his lot with the "Reds," and he has not been desirous of a change since. During the whole of this period he has been one of the most whole-hearted and hard-working players that it has ever been the good luck of any club to possess, and it looks as if he has many seasons of good play in front of him yet. As a keen and fearless tackler he has few equals, and many forwards have had good reason to remember the pertinacity with which he has stuck to them and worried them off their play.

The two most important captures were Blair, a forward from Kilmarnock, and Sharp, a full-back, who played last season for Fulham, but originally hailed from Dundee. In addition to these a number of promising young juniors have been engaged, so that there will be no lack of talent for the present season. One of the most important catches, however, is T. T. Fitchie, the young West Norwood amateur. Last season he frequently assisted the "Reds," and invariably did well; but this season he has given a definite promise to assist them whenever his services are required, and this, I fancy, will be always.

With the best of last season's players available, and strengthened as the team will be by the inclusion of the players mentioned above, the prospects of the Arsenal Club, from a playing point of view, are distinctly rosy, and there is every prospect of them finishing higher up on the League Table than last season. This view is also borne out by their form against Liverpool in the opening match of the season, when Tom Watson's team went under to the tune of 3 goals to 1; and though they failed to reproduce this form when playing at Sheffield the following week, their prospects are none the less reassuring.

From a financial aspect, the club also appears to be secure. Last season the gates quite came up to expectation, and there is every likelihood, with the improved accommodation provided for the spectators this season, that the gate receipts will be considerably increased.

This article would not be complete without a list of those gentlemen who are at present responsible for the welfare of the club. They are Messrs. John Humble (chairman), Arthur E. Kennedy (vice-chairman), J. Grant, E. Mercer, R. Clark, C. Hithersay, W. Craib, E. Radford, and W. Lamley (directors), W. T. Weeks (financial secretary), and Phil Kelso (secretary and manager). From what I know of these gentlemen, the future of the club may be safely left in their hands.

Bowden Bros.]

ANOTHER VIEW OF THE ENCLOSURE AT PLUMSTEAD.

The success of League football is plainly shown by the above photograph. A crowd such as this gathers in the sixpenny enclosure at Plumstead every other Saturday throughout the football season, and whatever discomfort the spectators suffer during the hour and a half that play lasts is completely forgotten in the excitement of the game.

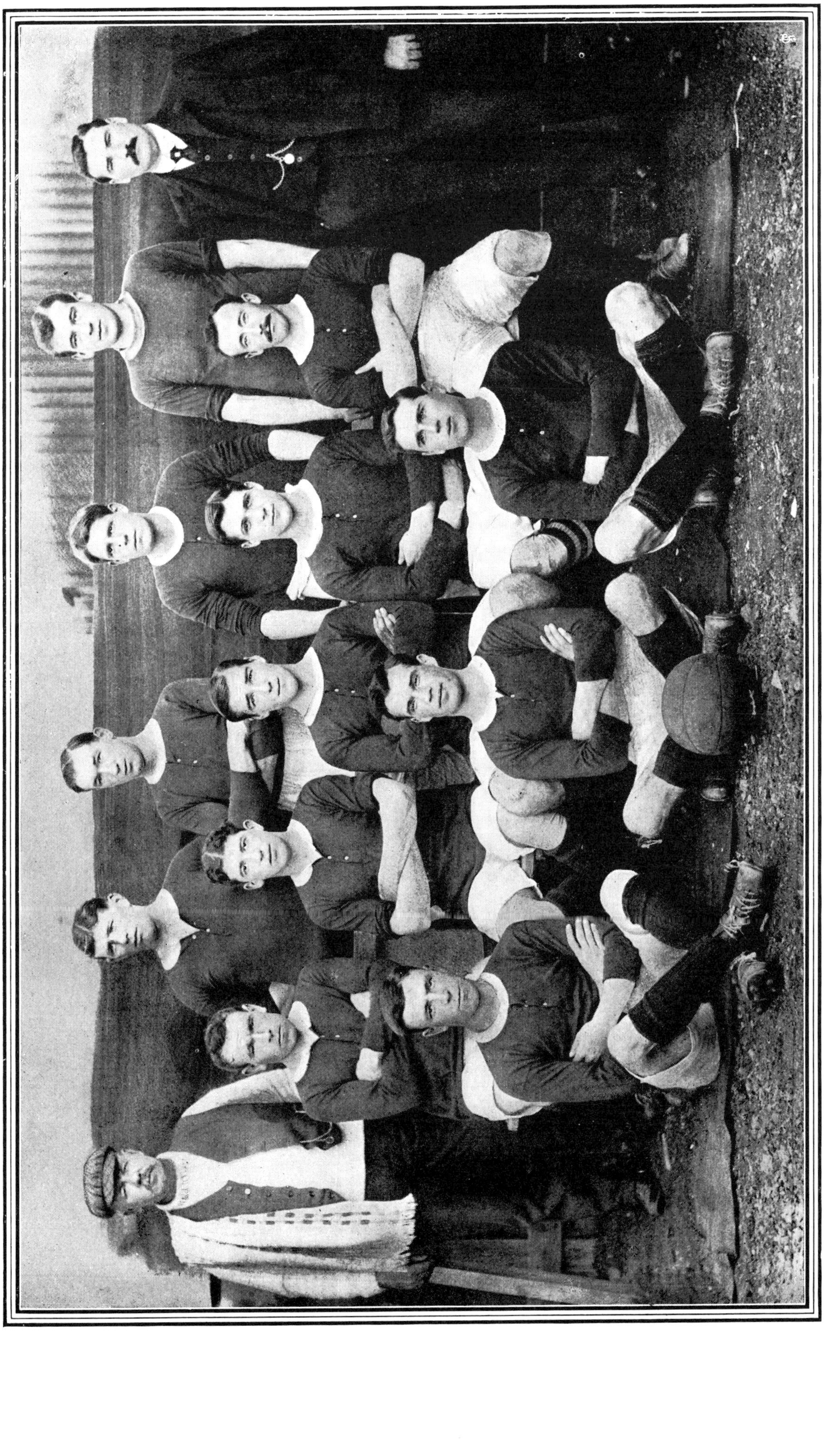

E. G. Elbourne, Plumstead.]

WOOLWICH ARSENAL. THE TEAM FOR 1905-6.

Back Row: P. R. Dunmore, Trainer. J. Sharp. J. Ashcroft, Goalkeeper. P. R. Sands. A. Cross. Phil Kelso, Manager.

Middle Row: A. Gray. R. Templeton. A. Ducat. T. T. Fitchie. P. J. McEachrane.

Front Row: J. T. Bellamy. J. Dick, Captain. J. Blair.

THE MAKING OF A PLAYER.

PART I.—THE FORWARD GAME.

By W. I. BASSETT (the Famous International).

The popularity of a good forward with the spectators—Brains and muscle a useful combination—Nothing new in Villa's up-to-date forward play—The old kick-and-rush style of the Albion explained—Good halves an absolute necessity to good forward play—The qualifications that go to make a fine wing-player—Ground-passing—The pass with the side of the boot—Accuracy in placing the ball the only way to score goals—The value of a hustling game—A last word to the professional.

IN football, as indeed in most pastimes, every member of the side has his own particular function, and a brilliant man in any position is sure to catch the eye of the spectator. But in football there are certain positions which in themselves bring a man into prominence whether that prominence is creditable or otherwise. By this I mean that a man who plays a bad game in certain positions is more likely to attract attention than a player who gives merely an ordinary exhibition in other positions. Take, for instance, the goalkeeper. If he plays badly he is at once an object of derision, or worse, just as he may be referred to as the saviour of his side if, in the face of great odds, he acquits himself creditably. In my opinion, the goalkeeper has more than anyone on the field a chance of catching the eye of the spectator. I should not like it to be thought from that, however, that I regard the position of custodian as the most important on the field, although the responsibility resting upon the man between the posts is undeniable. My opinion has always been that the men upon whom the greatest responsibility devolves are the members of the intermediate division. Their duties are more multifarious than those of any other members of the side. They have to be both attackers and defenders. When the defence is sorely pressed the halves have to lie moderately near goal to be of assistance when they can, and when their side is attacking no one can estimate the service which judicious, fast, and cunning halves can render to the forwards.

But next to that of the goalkeeper the position which lends itself naturally to prominence is that of the forward, and as a side's success is gauged by the number of goals scored, it is easy to imagine that a brilliant forward has a far better time with the crowd than most of the members of the side. I am not one of those who think that forward play has improved in the same ratio as that of other positions. Of course, defenders, particularly the goalkeeper, have a much happier time now than they had years ago, and there has been in recent years a great levelling up in this department of the game. When I first played football good goalkeepers were the exception rather than the rule. In first-class football to-day there are few exceptions to prove the rule. All the leading clubs have excellent custodians. In the days when pluck and daring counted as much and perhaps even more than ability, there were few goalkeepers of outstanding brilliance. I do not want to say too much about goalkeepers, however, for the province of this article is to deal with forward play. I merely wished to make it clear that the forward who possesses real merit has an exceptional opportunity of becoming the idol of the public.

Brains, and the ability to use them, are essential in all positions on the football field, but in no position are they more essential than in the forward rank. One is amazed at the lack of common-sense occasionally displayed. The secret of all success in the playing field is the aptitude which the contestants manifest to take advantage of opportunities. I remember very well that at the time when the Albion were credited, if credited is the proper word to use, with playing "a kick-and-rush game," we had a system of passing which was so styled because many people in those days did not understand it. There was more method in that kick-and-rush style than many people imagined. I notice that the very system of passing which we utilised in those old days is the one which Aston Villa have perfected to-day; and one can trace the recent success of the famous Birmingham team to the adoption of methods which were rather derided by the scientific sides of a decade ago. In those early days the short passing game was believed to be the beginning and end of all success on the football field. Mind, I am not saying anything derogatory to the short passing game. It has its uses to-day as much as ever it had, and when the attacking side are close in goal there is nothing more effective than a short pass, or a series of short passes, always provided, of course, that the defenders are in such a position that such a style is warranted. But the one-style team is not the successful one. The team which is successful to-day is the one which manifests most resource. Certain methods only suit certain conditions, and if forwards cannot adapt themselves to all conditions they are not likely to be permanently successful.

Bowden Bros.]

A FINE DRIBBLE BY THE HOTSPUR CENTRE.

Vivian Woodward in full flight.

The kick-and-rush game for which the Albion were famous was, in reality, a system of passing from the inside-left to the outside-right, and from the inside-right to the outside-left. The Albion forwards knew that style; they were prepared for it. Few teams understood it at all, and consequently it became known as a kick-and-rush style. Because it was little understood it was successful; and it is because it has not been universally adopted that Aston Villa found it successful in their Cup-tie games last season. I am not going to say that Aston Villa copied it from West Bromwich Albion. I do not suppose for one moment that they did. They merely discovered that it is a paying style, and all credit to them for making the most of it. We made the most of it when we discovered it, and many of the triumphs of the Albion are due to it. But it is merely one move in the great game of football. Adopted as a basis for all play, I dare say it would be no more successful than, say, dribbling or short passing, but when combined with other methods it is distinctly useful. It all resolves itself into a question of common-sense. A player without brains, no matter what his natural ability so far as pace and stamina are concerned may be, will never become brilliant.

Speaking of forward play generally, I should assert, without fear of contradiction, that no front line can be wholly successful unless they have a good trio of halves behind them. And in this connection I might mention that not a few good half-backs received their early training in the forward line. W. Groves of Aston Villa, Abbott and Taylor of Everton, and the great James Crabtree might be instanced. I believe generally in the principle of the inside men being left to get the goals—indeed, I have always been an advocate of the advantage of playing to the inside. The three inside men are naturally better placed as a rule than the wing men. It is the duty of the three inside men to draw the opposing halves on to them. When they have succeeded in this, they can pass out to the wings, and the wing men, having a clear course, can make ground unhampered, and, gradually getting close into goal, will find the inside men well up in front of the goalkeeper ready to receive the final pass at the most opportune moment. One thing a forward should always remember, and that is never to lose the ball unless he can do so to advantage. A spasmodic kick never did any good. A colleague may get it accidentally, but the ball is far more likely to be met by an opponent who is waiting than by a comrade who has no idea where it is going. Another thing an inside man should always bear in mind is that when he has beaten the half and drawn the back on himself, it is often more advantageous to pass to another inside man, or, indeed, to try himself to beat the back than to pass out to the wings. By passing out to the corner flag much valuable time is often wasted, and when the outside man gets in his centre practically all the defenders are up. The time when a centre could be turned to advantage by a long rush which would end in the ball and the goalkeeper being bundled into the net together has gone by. Much of Bloomer's success has been due to his skill in beating the back single-handed, and then carrying the ball so near goal that it is an easy matter to trick the goalkeeper with a neat touch which is more like a pass than a shot, although the objective, of course, is that part of the aperture which is unguarded by the custodian. And although Bloomer does so much individual work, he cannot be described as a selfish player. He is one of those men who are quick to see an opening, and, what is more important still, to act quickly. He plays the game with his head as well as his feet, and his style is one which present-day forwards would do well to copy.

Russell.]
A CHARACTERISTIC RUN BY THE RIGHT WING.
This photograph shows Meredith, of Manchester City, sweeping down the field in the Cup-tie Final of 1904 between Manchester City and Bolton Wanderers at the Crystal Palace.

Possibly I know more of the functions of the outside man than of any player on the field. The first essential for an outside wing player is, of course, speed, and the faster a man the better it is for his club. The next essential, I should say, is the ability of a player to gather the ball while on the run. If a wing player would only consider that if he has to lose a second in getting control over the ball, even the slowest opponent can run five or six yards in that brief period, while a really fast half can run nearly twice that distance before the forward is away, he would soon see the advantage of this.

Then the outside man should always be able to centre while on the run. If a man has to slacken his pace before he can get rid of the ball, it almost invariably happens that the back gets up and intercepts the pass. Of course, precision is necessary, and in my playing days I never went a week without devoting some time to practising sharp runs along the wing and quick centres into the goal mouth. Many young players figuring on the wing to-day make the mistake of shooting hard at goal from acute angles. I wonder whether they ever stop to consider how remote is the possibility of scoring? Would it not be far more advantageous if, instead of driving hard at goal, the player gently dropped the ball either to a comrade whom he sees is well placed, or among the ruck of men who are clustering round the goal? If the forwards know their business, they will have taken advantage of the time occupied by the wing man in making his run to place themselves in good positions for shooting, so that by the time the ball comes across to them the only advantage the defenders can possibly have is that special one which the goalkeeper has over all other players on the field. I commend this suggestion to all young wing players. I know a good deal of satisfaction is derived from the scoring of a goal, but the paramount duty of every footballer is to subordinate his own ambition to the best interests of his side. I should like to point out that it is well to remember that wherever the ball is there you will find a crowd of players. Obviously, then, if a side is to be successful, it is the duty of the forwards on the other side of the field to that where the scrimmaging is taking place to lose no time in getting into the best possible position. How often do you see players waiting, sometimes in an off-side position, and sometimes in an equally hopeless position, either near the half-way line or on the extreme wing? If these men would have some confidence in their comrades, and get right into goal, they would at least be in a position to meet the ball should their colleague succeed in beating the man by whom he has been tackled. Another point which should not be lost sight of is that it is far more advantageous for a forward to pass sharply along the ground than to lift the ball. The reason is obvious. Of course, there are times when it is essential that the ball should be lifted well over the heads of the opposing defenders; but, unless it is necessary, a forward should always

Bowden Bros.]
In these days of universally fine goalkeeping it is an absolute necessity for forwards to practise the art of accurate shooting. The photograph shows a well-intentioned shot by the centre-forward going straight to the hands of the goalkeeper. The match was between Tottenham Hotspur and Millwall.

remember that space is saved and speed is gained by passing on the ground. Nine times out of ten the short, sharp pass along the turf is better than lifting the ball into the air, though perhaps the point I am driving at is so patent that there is no need to labour it.

One of the most surprising things to me, as an old footballer, is the poor use forwards make to-day of the pass with the side of the foot. It has become almost a lost art; and yet if players would only stop to consider for a moment, they would see very clearly that it is much easier to make an accurate pass with the broad side of the foot than it is with a narrow toe. When passing with the toe, one is also far more apt to lift the ball than when hitting it with the side of the boot. At first blush it may seem a small matter. Let the forward devote some attention to the practice of this kick; he will not think it is a small matter when he has perfected the touch. In dribbling it is essential; it is a great advantage at all times.

It is not the province of this article to deal with training methods, but a few hints are never out of place. Apart from the practice which I have advocated for the wing men, there are many other little things which the forwards could do, and from which they would derive considerable advantage. The whole line could practise forward movements; forward and back passes between the outside and inside men, with occasional touches to the halves; long swings from the inside men to the extreme wingers on the opposite side of the field, and a hundred and one other movements, all of which would prove useful in actual strife. There cannot be too perfect an understanding between the members of the attack. The whole secret of success on the field is the ability which the players have to divine a comrade's intentions. Players ought to know precisely what each will do under certain conditions, and if they do know that—well, it is unnecessary for me to point to the advantage. But of all the functions of the forward in which either lack of ability or, worse still, lack of common-sense is manifested, I think it will be universally agreed that shooting stands pre-eminent. How many really good shots are there in first-class football to-day? Some of the most brilliant forwards I know often rouse the ire of the crowd simply because they throw all their good work away by indifferent shooting. A forward for whose shooting prowess I always had great admiration was McLuckie, late of Aston Villa. He was an awkward man on his legs—so awkward, in fact, that I have heard it humorously suggested that he used to trip up sometimes over a blade of grass, or fall over his own shadow; yet McLuckie was one of the neatest goal-scorers I ever saw. You rarely heard of McLuckie getting past the backs and then failing to score. What was the secret of his success? Why, McLuckie used his head. He saw at once that being out by himself he had a tremendous advantage, and he made the most of it. He might have shot the moment he saw he had no one to beat but the goalkeeper, but McLuckie always recognised that it would be much easier to score if he ran a few feet nearer to goal, and he always ran those few feet. If the goalkeeper came out to meet him, the Villa centre would gently touch the ball in the direction of the goal a moment before the custodian reached him. A second later he would probably be picking himself up, but that mattered little, for the ball was then in the net. If the goalkeeper did not leave his charge, the result would be precisely the same: for McLuckie, taking in the position at a glance, would see where there was most room, and there he would drop the ball. One seldom saw McLuckie shoot hard. His object was to shoot straight, and although everyone likes to see a good hard drive, is it not far better to gently touch the ball into the corner of the net than to make the upright quiver with the force of the shot, or to send the ball flashing at a great pace a few inches wide of the mark? John Goodall was another man who always placed his shots well; and if Bloomer sometimes puts a good deal of strength behind his shots, it is only because he has confidence in the accuracy of his aim.

Chas. Urban.]

THE POINTS THAT MAKE A GOOD WING FORWARD.

"The first essential for an outside wing player is, of course, speed, and the faster a man the better it is for his club. The next essential is the ability of a player to gather the ball while on the run. If a wing player would only consider that, if he has to lose a second in getting control over the ball, even the slowest opponent can run five or six yards in that brief period, while a really fast half can run nearly twice that distance before the forward is away, he would soon see the advantage of this."

Chas. Urban.]

FORWARD *versus* HALF-BACK.

"The men upon whom the greatest responsibility devolves are the members of the intermediate division. Their duties are more multifarious than those of any other members of the side. They have to be both attackers and defenders. When the defence is sorely pressed the halves have to lie moderately near goal to be of assistance when they can, and when their side is attacking no one can estimate the service which judicious, fast, and cunning halves can render to the forwards."

Forwards should always try to hit the ball forward while on the run; they cannot afford to steady themselves to trap the ball. My advice is, always hit the ball; it keeps the defenders on the move. If the forwards do not keep it more than a fraction of a second, the defender has no one to tackle. He is running aimlessly from one player to another, while the forwards all the time are making ground. Of course, it is not always possible to take the ball right into the mouth of goal, and those are the occasions when a good hard shot, with sufficient strength to reach its mark before the goalkeeper can get to it, is advisable. But there are very few forwards who can drive straight as well as hard. Men can scarcely have too much shooting practice, and when they are being coached in this regard they should be taught to discriminate. I can scarcely recall a game in which opportunities of scoring have not been thrown away through sheer carelessness. The long shots which are necessary will often fail through faulty aim, but a failure of that kind is not nearly so galling to the spectators as one such as we often see where the forward apparently tries to burst the net at the back of the goal when all that is required is a simple touch out of the way of the goalkeeper. How often do we see it recorded that "So-and-so failed ignominiously when the most difficult thing seemed to be for him to miss scoring"? We have seen the position ourselves, and it is very aggravating. Let footballers take to heart some of the points I have raised; but, above all, I should like the young footballer to remember that it is his duty to take as intelligent an interest in his football as he would be expected to do in his work in other spheres. After all, professional footballers have adopted the game as their calling in life, and those who employ them have a right to expect that their servants shall make themselves as proficient as their intelligence and natural endowments in other directions will allow.

Russell and Sons.]

A CORNER KICK. CUP FINAL—MANCHESTER CITY v. BOLTON WANDERERS—AT THE CRYSTAL PALACE IN APRIL, 1904.

One of the most essential qualifications of a wing forward is the ability to middle accurately, and by his fine judgment in kicking from the corner flag he may very often win a match for his side.

ENGLAND'S NEW INTERNATIONALS.

Taken altogether, the International sides selected to represent England during the season 1904-5 were not quite up to the standard of the previous year; yet there was a redeeming feature in the games, inasmuch as form was levelled up until there was little to choose between the sides representing the different countries. England had the decided advantage of playing all three of its International matches at home, and this may perhaps have given the teams the stimulus necessary to win.

The relative positions read as follows. :

		P.	W.	D.	L.	Pts.	Goals. For	Goals. Agst.
1.	England	3	2	1	0	5	5	2
2.	Wales	3	1	1	1	3	6	6
3.	Ireland	3	0	2	1	2	3	7
3.	Scotland	3	1	0	2	2	5	4

That neither England nor Scotland was quite up to the standard of previous years is quite certain. On the other hand, Wales had a very good side, and, with luck, might easily have done better than the table indicates. Irish football shows a distinct improvement, and it seems as if, where International affairs are concerned, Ireland will soon have to be seriously reckoned with.

The new Internationals, some of whose portraits appear on the following page, were F. Booth, Manchester City; J. Carr, Newcastle United; R. Bond, Preston North End; Herbert Smith, Reading; H. Ruddlesdin, Sheffield Wednesday; W. Balmer, Everton; H. P. Hardman, Everton; J. Sharp, Everton; C. Roberts, Manchester United; A. Bridgett, Sunderland; J. V. Bache, Aston Villa; and R. G. Williamson, Middlesbrough.

Arthur Bridgett was born at Stoke-on-Trent, and is twenty-one years of age. He stands 5ft. 8½in., and weighs 12st. 9lb. He first played with Stoke St. Peters, a school team; then played for Burslem Park. Then followed a period with Trentham and with Stoke, from which latter club he was transferred to Sunderland. He is a teetotaller and non-smoker, and played for England against Scotland.

Herbert Smith is the famous amateur captain of the Reading team. He was born at Witney, and is twenty-seven years of age. His height is 5ft. 11in.; weight, 12st. 10lb. Has played for Richmond Association, Oxford City, Stoke, and Reading. Is a total abstainer, and smokes moderately. Played left-back v. Scotland and Wales.

Harry Linacre, the Nottingham Forest goalkeeper, is twenty-four years of age. He stands 6ft. in height, and weighs 11st. 8lb. Has played for Aston-on-Trent, Draycott Mills, Derby County, and Notts Forest. Kept goal last season for England v. Wales and Scotland, and v. Scottish League. Is a moderate drinker, and likes a smoke now and then.

Harold P. Hardman was born at Kirkmanshulme, Manchester, and is twenty-three years of age. He stands 5ft. 6¼in., and weighs 10st. 7lb. Has played for Blackpool and Everton, appeared as outside-left for England v. Wales, and in the Inter-League match against Scotland. Is a total abstainer and non-smoker.

ENGLAND'S NEW INTERNATIONALS

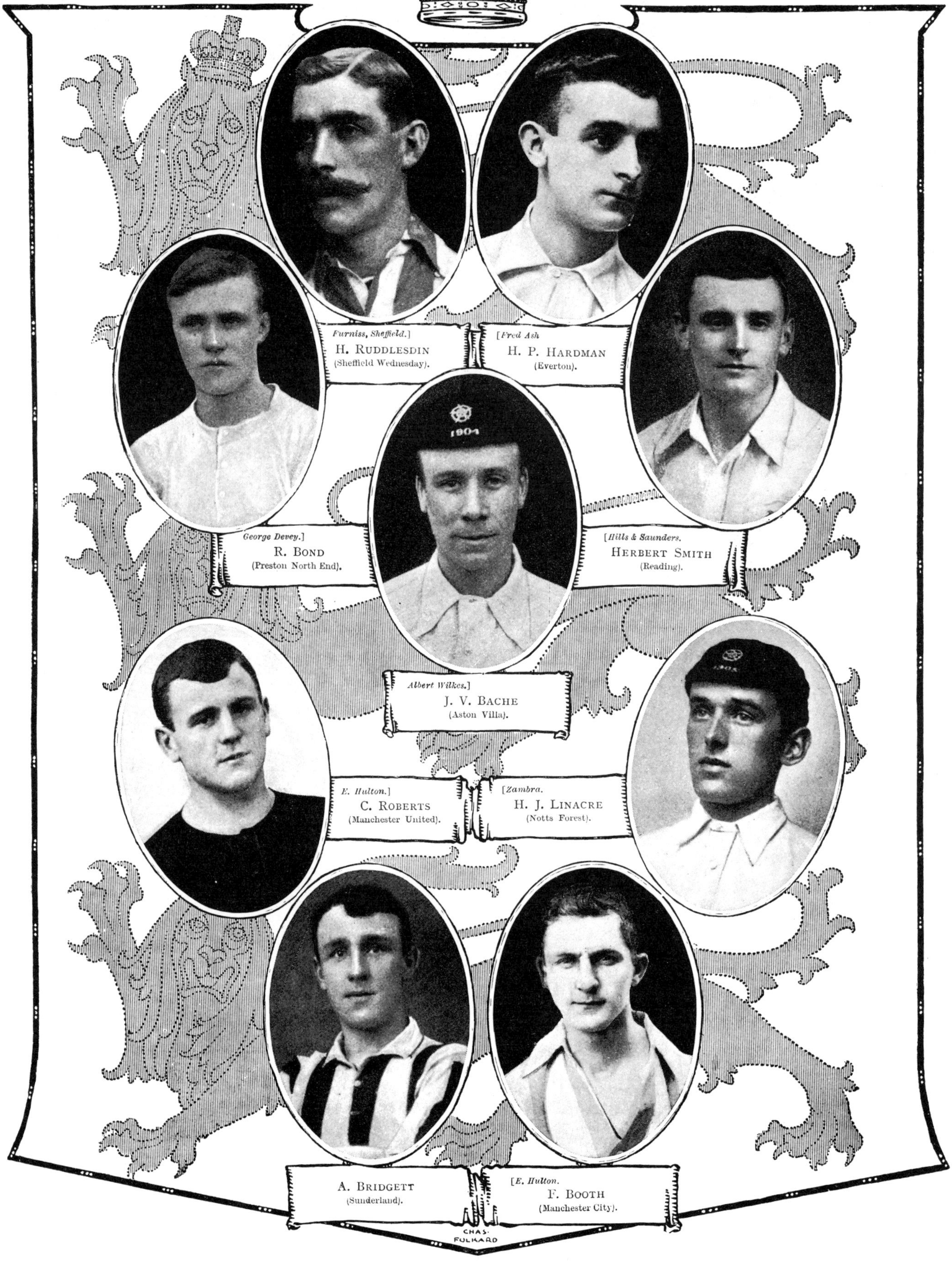

Furniss, Sheffield.] H. RUDDLESDIN (Sheffield Wednesday).

[*Fred Ash* H. P. HARDMAN (Everton).

George Devey.] R. BOND (Preston North End).

[*Hills & Saunders.* HERBERT SMITH (Reading).

Albert Wilkes.] J. V. BACHE (Aston Villa).

E. Hulton.] C. ROBERTS (Manchester United).

[*Zambra.* H. J. LINACRE (Notts Forest).

A. BRIDGETT (Sunderland).

[*E. Hulton.* F. BOOTH (Manchester City).

From a drawing] [*by Ernest Prater*

AN EXCITING MOMENT NEAR GOAL—THE CENTRE-HALF RELIEVES

Russell and Sons.]
The team that won the League Championship. They are seen standing in the goal mouth at the Crystal Palace. The photograph was taken just before the Cup Final match started.

THE RISE OF NEWCASTLE UNITED.

Football League Champions, 1905

By J. H. MORRISON.

The early Newcastle Club and troublous times—Tom Watson to the rescue—The first "gate" at St. James's Park—The rivalry between East and West End—The wages paid in the old days—The amalgamation of the rival clubs—The present club-title adopted—Mr. Watt takes up the position of secretary—The unsatisfactory test matches—Newcastle United elected to the League First Division—From poverty to affluence—Newcastle United's proud position at the present day.

Colours: Black and white vertical stripes, black knickers. *Ground: St. James's Park, Newcastle.*

ALTHOUGH Newcastle United is a club of comparatively modern growth, without the great and glorious past which admirers of the old Preston "Invincibles," Aston "Clarets," or Sunderland's "Team of All the Talents" so often delight to conjure up, it existed in the days when the game was first gaining a grip on the people, when the man paid for playing football was looked upon as a person beneath contempt. In pre-limited liability times it survived vicissitudes which cannot possibly befall the splendidly financed organisations now springing up in most of the large industrial and manufacturing centres, and no longer is it necessary for the heads of the club to meet in solemn conclave to decide whose chronometer should be sacrificed in order to provide funds for the next away engagement.

In the early eighties, when men of the Mr. Alec Peters and Mr. James Phillips type—pioneers who laboured stupendously to give the game root on Tyneside—migrated to the Colonies, there arose one who was destined to play a big part in revolutionising public ideas—Mr. Tom Watson, the cheery and optimistic present-time Liverpool secretary.

Mr. Watson was then located at Rosehill, building up the club now known as Willington Athletic, one of the best League nurseries the country through, and he took up the management of Newcastle West End when it had neither a sou in the bank nor an enclosed ground to play upon.

Backed by the late Wm. Neasham, a fourteen years' lease was obtained on a few acres owned jointly by the corporation and freemen, and under the high falutin title of St. James's Park, with a little cabin for the players' accommodation, a pill-box for the gentlemen of the Press, and a frail rope to keep the people off the playing-pitch, the enclosure was formally opened. The colossal sum of seven shillings and elevenpence was taken at the gates, and Mrs. Watson was the only lady present. At the opposite end of the town another club—East End—was bidding fair to improve considerably in public support, and displaying more enterprise than the Tyne or Rangers, after a brief existence, had ever attempted.

Chas. Urban.]
NEWCASTLE ENTHUSIASM.
The enthusiasm and loyalty of Newcastle United's supporters fairly bubbled over on the occasion of the last great Cup Final. Parti-coloured umbrellas, such as that shown in the photograph, were everywhere in evidence, and victory was the one thing wanting to make the joy of the Novocastrians complete.

The persuasive eloquence of Mr. David Crawford, one of the lights of the present Newcastle United directorate, induced Mr. Watson to go East, and there he remained until 1888, when he took over the Sunderland secretarial reins. Right up to the 1891-2 campaign there was strong, and ofttimes bitter, rivalry between the two Ends, and many fine players were left behind by Scottish clubs after playing friendlies at Newcastle, amongst them being

Ralph Aitken, Bob Kelso, Bob Creilly, Willie Graham, "Surefoot" Watson, Jas. Miller, Joe Wallace, Sorley, and M'Kane.

In those days the remuneration was a situation and 15s. per week for a win, 10s. for a draw or defeat, and a shilling per goal—truly a poor reward compared with the present-day £4 per week maximum. Yet there was no lack of strenuous endeavour. The shilling per goal had a magic influence upon the East Enders, and, in fact, upon the whole destiny of Newcastle football; for after conquering their great rivals seven to one and eight to one, the first cry for amalgamation arose.

It was self-evident that Newcastle could not give adequate support to both clubs, and at length the proposal took definite form when representatives met at the residence of Mr. Joseph Bell, now vice-chairman of Newcastle United. The names of those attending may be fittingly quoted, as at this gathering the foundation-stone was laid for an organisation which ultimately attained national celebrity, and failed by the merest mischance to emulate the striking performances of Aston Villa and Preston North End in winning the English and League Cups in one season. Mr. Wm. Neasham, Mr. Geo. Milne, Mr. Jas. Telford, Mr. Jno. Black, Mr. Geo. M'Connachie, and Mr. Wm. Bramwell represented West End; Mr. Joe Bell, Mr. Alec Turnbull, Mr. Carmichael, Mr. John Graham, Mr. John Cameron, and Mr. Jas. Neylon represented the East End, and it was decided that East End should take over the St. James's Park lease.

Still the struggle for existence in no way abated. East End achieved only moderate success in the Northern League, and even when the open sesame to the League Second Division was secured in 1893, the exchequer was invariably in a most attenuated condition. Fourth place was secured on the League chart to Liverpool, Small Heath, and Notts County, by no means a disappointing return from a playing standpoint. But the descent was so rapid in 1894–5 that nothing short of a public meeting and a spirited revivalist policy saved the situation.

Mr. Frank Watt came from Dundee, ripened in experience as a legislator, referee, and team builder, and courageously accepted the secretaryship. A fresh wave of enthusiasm spread over the town. Ten-shilling shares were liberally taken up, the rechristening from East End to Newcastle United was completed on September 5th, 1895, and all the gentlemen enumerated above consented to sit on the board. Football in Newcastle had at length emerged from the chrysalis stage. Mr. Watt certainly had a very long row to hoe, but efficient management ran hand-in-hand with increased public support, and, whenever the funds permitted, investments were made in ground and team improvements.

In the 1895–6, 1896–7 seasons, Newcastle United were out-distanced by Liverpool, Manchester City, Notts County, and Newton Heath; but men of the Jackson, Aitken, Campbell, Ghee, Peddie, Stott, Wardrope, Ostler, and Roger's stamp landed the club into the test matches a season later. Test, forsooth! Never was the word more misapplied. Stoke and Blackburn Rovers, as First Division tailists, were set to contest a miniature tournament against Burnley and Newcastle United, the Second Division leaders. Everything moved along serenely until the last game of the series, Stoke v. Burnley. A draw would ensure a place "upstairs" for both, defeat for Burnley would secure Newcastle's promotion. The result was a goalless draw, both teams "finding touch" so regularly that the onlookers became incensed, and refused to return the ball into play. Three balls were in use at one period. The disgusting character of the game led to the abolition of the Tests, and the enlargement of each League Division from sixteen to eighteen clubs, Blackburn Rovers and Newcastle United securing election to the upper house when the extension was made.

Thomson and Gee.]
THE NEWCASTLE UNITED CAPTAIN.

A. Aitken, centre-half, was born at Ayr in 1876. His height is 5ft. 8in.; weight 11st. 8lb. He played for Ayr Parkhouse before signing a League form for Newcastle. He represented Scotland against England in the International games of 1901-2-3 and 1905, and played against Wales in 1903. Was right-half for Anglo-Scots in 1903. He is a player of the first class, and one of the very best.

Hence, in September, 1898, Tyneside's debut was made in the highest-class game, the regular performers being Kingsley, now with Queen's Park Rangers; Jackson, Leyton's player-manager; Wm. Lindsay, the Grimsby terror, now at Watford; Peddie, Manchester City's sharpshooter; Wardrope, still footing it at Fulham; Niblo, the Forest stylist; Aitken, the great Scottish International half, who remains a Newcastle fixture; Macfarlane, now with Dundee; and Stevenson, Ostler, Stott, and Higgins, who long since joined the retired list. Occasional service was rendered by erstwhile Sunderland cracks—John Campbell and "Wee" Harvey—and after a tempestuous campaign, United escaped returning from whence they came with very few points in hand.

Improvement marked the 1899–0 doings, when the defence was strengthened by the advent of Dave Gardner from 3rd Lanark, the middle division brightened by the introduction of Alec Gardner from Leith Athletic, and John Carr from Seaton Burn, and the left wing given stability by John Fraser's transfer from Notts County.

Newcastle United accomplished something better than to flash meteorlike across the League firmament. They opened with 30 points, and progressed steadily to 36, and thence to 38 in the 1900–1 tournament. The gate receipts at St. James' Park had jumped from the few shillings under Mr. Tom Watson's regime to a thousand pounds under Mr. Frank Watt's auspices.

Three years of First Division football had raised Newcastle foremost among "gate" attracting clubs, and steadily the funds accumulated, until Mr. Wm. Bramwell became the envy of club treasurers the country over.

Prosperous playing and financial days continued throughout 1901–2, a season notable for the introduction of John

Chas. Urban.] THE GREAT CUP FINAL.
The eagerness of Hampton lands him in the Newcastle goal.

Chas. Urban.] MAGNIFICENT DEFENCE.
Newcastle clear within two yards of the goal.

Rutherford, a winger who attained International honours ere reaching his majority, and has proved the best of Newcastle's local discoveries. Other new-comers were Roberts, from West Bromwich Albion, and now located at the Crystal Palace; Ronald Orr, who afterwards partnered Templeton and Smith on Scotland's left wing against England in 1902 and 1904; Sandy Caie, Colin Veitch, Bob Bennie, and that prince among Scottish pivots, R. S. McColl. With so many famous players banded together, Newcastle naturally entertained championship hopes; but there came a surprising deterioration in 1902–3, when Agnew, now of Middlesbrough, Bennie, Aitken, Watson, Benson, and Davidson were tried in defence, with more or less, particularly less, success. United were weak in backs, strong in forwards, this latter division being increased by Templeton's transfer from Aston Villa, Arthur Turner's migration North, and Andrew Gardner's removal from Grimsby. The defensive lessons did not go unheeded by the management. Thus, a season later, when halves and forwards had attained perfection, there arrived a pair of backs of International repute in quick succession—McCombie and McCracken. No sooner was the full-back famine remedied, than Carr came along, hand over hand, to take English International honours; and it may be fairly stated that no club in the League during the past two seasons has been better equipped in defence than the Novocastrian club.

Chas. Urban.]
LAWRENCE, THE NEWCASTLE GOALKEEPER, SAVES HIS CHARGE AND CONCEDES A CORNER.

As all the world knows, Newcastle United won the League Championship last season with a points total only once excelled in the long history of the competition by Aston Villa in 1899–0, and reached the English Cup Final for the first time. The double event was within their grasp, but the great rush of fixtures in the closing months, caused by playing five games in the two opening Cup rounds, caused a collapse before the rejuvenated Villa hosts.

Newcastle's financial return from the English Cup contest has never been equalled. They shared £2,017, less the usual percentage and expenses, with Plymouth Argyle, £2,396 with Tottenham Hotspur, £1,471 with Bolton Wanderers, and their cheque from the Football Association, as a reward for competing in the Semi-final and Final ties, reached £2,668 10s. The club balance-sheet for the 1904–5 season's working was a wondrous document, showing a profit of £5,487, and a balance credit of £16,379. This balance has been secured by level-headed management under the guidance of three chairmen—Mr. Wm. Neasham, Mr. Jas. Telford, and Mr. John Cameron; and it has been almost wholly expended during the past five months by converting St. James's Park into an enclosure worthy of the League champions and their great and loyal following.

The fourteen years' lease secured in the days of Mr. Watson expired last November, and there were serious thoughts of the club purchasing ground elsewhere. Newcastle, however, has most of its open spaces devoted to public use, and a new home for football was unattainable within the city boundaries.

St. James's Park has its advantages, chief among them being its situation in the heart of the town; and this, more than anything else, led to a new lease of seven years being entered into. Its disadvantages lie in the joint ownership, and permission cannot be obtained for erecting the necessary covered accommodation on one side of the ground. Greater St. James's Park is now a replica of the Queen's Park enclosure at Glasgow, with terracing on three sides, and a pavilion with 5,000 holding capacity on the fourth. Sixty thousand onlookers may be comfortably and safely housed. When Derby County visited the United on September 23rd, the terracing was half empty with an attendance of 34,000; thus the engineer's estimate of the accommodation may be considered accurate.

In the current tournament the whole of last season's players are available, for it is a rarity indeed to find a footballer with migratory tendencies when once he has experienced the Tynesider's hospitality. One of the great secrets of the success attending the team has been the fatherly interest, instead of rigid supervision, taken in the players by the directorate, whose boast it is that they handle the best-conducted body of men in the League. Many a talented player has been refused by the club because his credentials off the field won't bear inspection; whilst from a playing standpoint the chief aim has been to secure warriors who play the game free from undesirable roughness. The consequence is that wherever Newcastle United may operate

Chas. Urban.]
A HOT TIME IN THE GOAL MOUTH.
Lawrence fists away.

NEWCASTLE UNITED—LEAGUE CHAMPIONS, 1905.

Top Row: { JOSEPH BELL, Vice-Chairman. } HIGGINS. GARDNER. McCOMBIE. { J. CAMERON, Chairman. } McWILLIAM. LAWRENCE. TILDESLEY. T. S. ROWLANDSON. { R. MACKENZIE, Director.

Second Row: { J. P. OLIVER, Director. F. WATT, Asst.-Sec. } WILLS. McCRACKEN. AITKEN. RUTHERFORD. FINDLAY. HOWIE. McLEAN. McCLARENCE. CARR. { J. GRAHAM, Director. J. McPHERSON, Trainer.

Stuart and Winfield, Newcastle.]

Third Row: { THOS. GHEE (sitting), Asst. Trainer. } BOLTON. McINTYRE. HARDINGE. APPLEYARD. ORR. GOSNELL. DONNACHIE. { FRANK G. WATT, Secretary.

Bottom Row: CRUMLEY. VEITCH. WHITSON. WATTS.

Bowden Bros.]
NEWCASTLE UNITED'S GOALKEEPER.

James Lawrence stands 5ft. 10in. in height, and weighs 11st. Prior to signing on for Newcastle he played for Glasgow Perthshire. He is considered a very clever goalkeeper, and all those who have had occasion to play against him when at his best will readily admit that there are few custodians so difficult to beat.

their reputation for clean, scientific football has preceded them. The strength includes one Irish International—McCracken; two English Internationals—Rutherford and Carr; and five Scottish Internationals—McCombie, Orr, Howie, McWilliam, and Aitken. Of this batch, McCombie alone had figured in League football prior to joining the United, and only he cost anything substantial in the way of a transfer fee. In fact, seven of the players who figured at the Palace last April were secured at an aggregate cost of £100, therefore it cannot in justice be said that the money bags are at the bottom of the club's success.

Quite a large array of locals figure on the club books, and they, with the assistance of a few importations, form a reserve team which has swept the Northern Alliance and Northern League boards for six or seven years past. The team at present operating in the Northern League would give the majority of the League Second Division clubs a sterling fight, for it includes Charles Watts, the former Ironopolis and Burton Wanderers' keeper; Tildesley, a Halesowen back sought for by Liverpool; Findlay, a Scottish Junior International half-back; McLean, last with Chatham; Hardinge, the Kent county cricketer; Donnachie, of Greenock Morton, who, on current form, will soon secure a permanency in first-class company; and Bolton, of Port Glasgow.

The gentlemen who are so capably controlling Newcastle United's business affairs are Mr. John Cameron, chairman; Mr. Joseph Bell, vice-chairman; Mr. Geo. Milne, Councillor Geo. Archibald, Mr. J. Graham, Mr. J. P. Oliver, Mr. Robt. Oliver, Mr. John Bell, Mr. Jas. Lunn, Mr. D. Crawford, Mr. S. F. Bates, Mr. Robt. Mackenzie, Mr. Frank Watt, secretary and treasurer, and Mr. Jas. McPherson, trainer. With few exceptions they have been associated with the game since its earliest days on Tyneside. All are men of rare ability, and possessed of level-headed business qualifications, and so long as they continue a harmonious whole, no fears need be entertained for the future of the Association code in the great metropolis of the North.

The geographical position of Newcastle necessarily entails upon the United Club more railway travelling than any club in the League, for, with the exception of the Sunderland and Middlesbrough games, they must travel overnight to meet their engagements. This is, of course, a serious handicap in the race for honours, and the occasions are numerous when, after playing a match, the men have less than a quarter of an hour to dress, jump into a hansom, and catch the return train. Blackburn has often proved one of the most difficult towns to leave behind, as Ewood Park is a fair distance from the station, and the hilly streets are paved with something closely approaching boulders. On one occasion the driver of the four-in-hand containing United's players beat all driving records over this stretch, and was incontinently hauled before the magistrates, to be fined forty shillings and costs.

The Newcastle players travel between 9,000 and 10,000 miles each season, and occupy most of the time with the engrossing game of solo whist. Such a thing as horseplay on the journeys is unknown, but they are great practical jokers. The special saloon provided by the North-Eastern Railway Company is divided into two compartments, and these lend themselves to a lively bit of fun when a too officious ticket-collector interrupts the whist and delays the train by counting the party. "How's this, there's twenty-two of you and only tickets for sixteen?" he will inquire, after making a count at each end of the saloon. "Nothing of the kind; there's only sixteen of us all told!" More counting and slamming of doors precedes the arrival of the stationmaster, who finds the number tallies with the tickets and retires bewildered. The ticket-collector little knows that after counting one end of the saloon several players have slipped through the sliding door to be counted a second time.

Billiards is the favourite pastime on the morning of the match, and until this season United possessed a pair of players in Appleyard and Templeton unequalled on the green cloth by any other club couple in the League. The majority of the men are superstitious, and when driving to the ground consider it a sure indication of success if they meet a wedding-party, or failure if they chance across a funeral. Moreover, they are invariably led into the arena at the start and at half-time by "Uncle Joe," the club vice-chairman, who has been justly described as the father of the team. It is a very rare occasion when "Uncle" fails to materialise, and it is even rarer to find a victory recorded in his absence.

Stuart and Winfield.]
A. McCOMBIE,

Newcastle's right-back, was born in Inverness. He stands 5ft. 9½in. in height, and weighs 12st. 6lb. He learnt the art of first-class football with Inverness Thistle, and joined Sunderland in 1899. He is a grand tackler, and a sure kick, and has been an unqualified success ever since he appeared in the ranks of the Newcastle Club.

THE ALL-CONQUERING NEW ZEALANDERS.

By W. S. DOUGLAS.

The Rugby Union XV. handsomely beaten by New Zealand in 1904—Distinguished New Zealanders who have played in the Mother Country—Our cousins from "down under" have modified the Rugby formation—A team of seven forwards and eight backs—Has their innovation come to stay?

Colours: Black. Silver fern-leaf on breast.

THE fame of the New Zealand Rugby players now touring in this country may be said to have preceded them, for New Zealand handsomely beat the Rugby Union XV. which visited Australasia in 1904, after its having practically carried everything before it in the Australian Commonwealth. Moreover, some of the individual talent of this daughter State has been in evidence here at home ere now. There has been a galaxy of brilliant Colonial Rugby men in Great Britain, beginning with G. C. Wade, one of the famous Vassall XV. at Oxford; and one of the most brilliant of all of them was the New Zealander, Dr. A. N. Fell, whose fine three-quarter game for Devon County and for Scotland is fresh in memory still.

Our visitors this winter of 1905-6 are a splendid side, and fully entitled to the fine advertisement they got in their series of sweeping successes at the start. Some of those wins were to a certain extent discounted, to be sure, by the fact that their opponents had not got into form for the season, whereas the winners themselves were trained to the minute. But there is something much more momentous to be taken into account than that slight difference. The New Zealanders have modified the Rugby formation; they have gone a step farther than the Principality of Wales when it forced upon all the other countries, a dozen years ago, the adoption of the four three-quarter system; and the question of the hour, or rather, of the season, is whether the Colonial innovation has come to stay as that did.

Briefly put, the difference is this. Wales drove England and her other neighbours into playing eight forwards and seven backs instead of nine forwards and six backs. Now, New Zealand is virtually putting into the field seven forwards and eight backs; and the chief technical and tactical point of interest about the tour will be to see whether her opponents adopt that new grouping in the Internationals, which begin with Scottish and Irish contests in October, and include a match against England on December 2, and another against Wales on December 16.

Bowden Bros.]

THE NEW ZEALAND CAPTAIN.

D. Gallagher, captain of the all-conquering New Zealanders, is the electric wing-forward whose position on the field has been so freely criticised in the Press. He is a player of exceptional merit, and his judgment, like most of his comrades', is almost faultless.

It should be said that, nominally, the Colonials still adhere to the accustomed arrangement in having more forwards than backs; and there are times when they play eight men in the scrummage, if that suits the run of the game better. But the system by which they have been winning renown in England involves, when all is said and done, the playing of five three-quarters. They have one half-back, and a so-called "wing-forward," who is, to all intents and purposes, a second half-back; they have two "five-eighths," who are nothing more nor less than extra three-quarters. Thus the three three-quarters of their match-cards are in reality one more in number than the four whom the Welsh system introduced; and, with the usual full-back, they play eight men behind the scrum to only seven in it.

The alternate method to which they can resort on occasion is, however, not to be left out of account. For let it be observed—if it be not wearisome to repeat the rather curious fractions which the New Zealanders have introduced among us—that the matter of one five-eighth or of two five-eighths is of no little importance to the future of Rugby football. The fact mentioned above that the Colonials arrange and re-arrange their men according to circumstances, indicates their adaptability, and keeps one from speaking of their system as a hard-and-fast one like the Welsh.

They might spring a surprise of tactics in any one of the International matches which

Bowden Bros.]

NEW ZEALAND SCORE A GOAL.

In this photograph, taken on the occasion of the New Zealand v. Middlesex match at Chelsea on October 4, the ball is seen soaring high above the bar, placed accurately by the unerring foot of Wallace, one of the finest backs that have ever played the Rugby game.

Bowden Bros.]

NEW ZEALAND SCORE A TRY.

The skill with which the men from "down under" dodge and feint after invading their opponents' "in-goal," in order that they may touch-down right behind the posts, has won for them unstinted admiration. In the above photograph it will be noticed that the player scoring the try has broken right away from the opposition, and his touch-down renders the scoring of a goal almost a certainty.

force the solid avoirdupois in the rank before them), the arrangement approaches the ideal.

This compactness would be sacrificed if eight real forwards were played. Therefore one may expect to see the Colonials abide by the grouping described at the outset of this article; and in turn meet Scotland, Ireland, England, and Wales with virtually eight backs behind their seven forwards. (They have yet another choice—of seven forwards, two so-called wing-forwards, and six backs; but that is too unusual, from a British standpoint, to be discussed.) The question whether nine forwards and five backs would have a ghost of a chance against them is highly interesting, because stopping a forward rush is the one part of Rugby in which the New Zealanders are not notably proficient. But all one can say as to that is that Munster would be well advised to try the experiment if it fares ill with Ireland three or four days before

await them. If they should take the field against England or any of the other countries with eight forwards, two half-backs, one five-eighth, three three-quarters, and a full-back, it would be with a view to upsetting the calculations of their opponents.

But to do so would perhaps be to spoil that which very largely helps the New Zealanders in gaining their successes—their scrummage formation, to wit. The tour so far has shown how excellently serviceable a pack the seven men make. The eight forwards of home Rugby form in a front row of three, a middle row of two, and a back row of three. The New Zealanders pack 2—3—2; and as the front couple are picked for their skill in "scraping" the ball to them whenever it is put in, and the trio behind for their shoving power and weight, and the rearmost couple for their quickness in heeling out (as well as ability to rein-

Bowden Bros.]

NEW ZEALAND v. MIDDLESEX, OCTOBER 4, 1905.

The breaking up of a scrum.

Bowden Bros.]

NEW ZEALAND v. MIDDLESEX.

A scrum. The New Zealand method of packing a scrum is 2—3—2, and it seems, judging by results, to be better than the British 3—2—3. The New Zealand team, as seen in the photograph, are getting the better of the tussle.

the Province match, or the Western Scottish XV. if Scotland be beaten at Edinburgh.

The fact, on the other hand, that any ordinary British team cannot hold the visitors by dint of its usual modern Welsh formation may be regarded as established, even though the New Zealanders are only as yet in the preliminary stage of their tour, and have still the greatest representative sides to meet in what are virtually test matches.

There are excellent reasons why Rugby experts should, in weighing up the New Zealanders so far as they have gone, put in the forefront these questions of formation and tactics. For it is quite on the cards that the tour will leave a lasting legacy to British Rugby players—the legacy of a new system and a re-formed fifteen, in which the backs, for the first time in Rugby history in this country, outnumber the forwards. That step in advance of the Welsh system is the question of the day.

NEW ZEALAND FOOTBALL TEAM, 1905.

Back Row: G. Gillett. S. Casey. D. McGregor. A. McDonald. F. Roberts.

Second Row: E. T. Harper. J. O'Sullivan. C. Seeling. R. G. Deans. W. Johnston. G. N. W. Nicholson. J. Corbett. W. Cunningham. F. Newton. J. Duncan, Coach.

Hardie Shaw, Wellington, N.Z.]

Third Row: H. L. Abbott. W. J. Wallace. G. A. Tyler. D. Gallagher, Captain. G. H. Dixon, Manager. J. W. Stead, Vice-Captain. W. Mackrell. F. Glasgow. W. S. Glenn.

Front Row: G. Hunter. H. G. Mynott. G. W. Smith. E. E. Booth. H. D. Thomson.

THE HISTORY OF SHEFFIELD UNITED

League Champions, 1897-8. English Cup Winners, 1898-9, 1901-2. Finalists, 1900-1.

The inception and early history of Sheffield United Football Club—How the club won its way into the First Division of the League—Early disappointment gives way to brilliant success in the League championship competition in 1896-7—The championship won in 1897-8—Splendid performance in the Football Association Cup competition—The International eleven of 1903—Some biographical sketches—A distinguished list of directors—Finance—Players who have helped to make Sheffield United famous.

Colours: Red and white vertical striped shirts, dark knickers. *Ground: Bramall Lane, Sheffield.*

Henderson, Sheffield.]
CHARLES STOKES,
Chairman of the football section of Sheffield United Cricket and Football Club.

FOUNDED in 1889, Sheffield United may not be able to boast of old traditions, such as possessed by Stoke, Notts County, Notts Forest, or Sheffield Wednesday, but the team can lay claim to having done more than many an older club in the making of football history. For instance, only three other clubs—Aston Villa, Preston North End, and Sheffield Wednesday—have won both the League championship and the Football Association Challenge Cup, in addition to which the United have had the honour of appearing before the largest crowd that has ever witnessed a football match.

It would perhaps be as well to start with the inception of the club. It may safely be asserted that to Mr. Charles Stokes belongs the chief credit of the idea of forming a football team in connection with the Sheffield United Cricket Club, and with him must be associated Mr. Joseph Tomlinson, whilst Mr. Allan Hall, the then secretary of the now defunct Heeley Football Club, rendered valuable assistance. Mr. Stokes approached Mr. J. C. Clegg, the chairman of the Football Association, on the subject, and the result was that a meeting was held at the offices of Mr. J. B. Wostinholm, secretary both of the Yorks County Cricket Club and the Sheffield United Cricket Club. It was at once decided to form a football club, the Bramall Lane Ground committee, with Mr. Joseph Tomlinson, Mr. David Haigh, and Mr. W. F. Beardshaw, to act as the executive. Mr. J. B. Wostinholm was the first secretary, with Mr. H. H. Stones as assistant.

The new club possessed a fine ground, and had the promise of support from several of the principal local clubs, so that their prospects seemed of the brightest description, despite strong opposition from a number of gentlemen on the cricket section.

The troubles, however, of the United were only just commencing.

The football section was formed in March, 1889, but the clubs that had promised their support withdrew, with the result that the United possessed a club without players.

However, this was soon remedied, and by August everything was in readiness for the season 1889-90.

A private practice match was held at Sandygate with Sheffield Club as opponents, the United winning by 3 goals to 1. The first public match was against Notts Rangers at Nottingham, the latter team winning by 4 goals to 1. The following are the names of the players who took part for Sheffield in this match: C. H. Howlett, E. Stringer, J. Gordon, S. Mack, W. Hobson, J. Hudson, W. Madin, D. Galbraith, W. Robertson, J. Duncan, and W. Mosforth.

The next match was against Heeley at Sheaf House, Sheffield, which the United won by 2 goals to 1. And thus the club was successfully launched on its career. In their first year they succeeded in working their way through the qualifying competition of the Association Challenge Cup, and actually beat Burnley in the first round of the competition proper, but in the second round they waived their right to play at home for a paltry consideration, and were badly beaten by Bolton Wanderers.

Previous to this, however, Mr. Joseph Smith was induced to join the management. The team was strengthened, and application was made for admission to the Alliance—a competition second only to the League—in 1890, but this was refused, so the club joined the Midland League. In the following season United joined the Northern League, and had a most successful season.

In 1892 the Football League decided to increase the number of clubs, and an application was made for a place in the premier combination, but it was rejected. A Second Division was formed, and this the club joined. Small Heath—now Birmingham—and United ran a desperate race for the championship, but, perhaps fortunately for the United, Small Heath finished at the top. In the test matches United beat Accrington, but Small Heath succumbed to Notts County.

From this point United never looked back. Meanwhile a new secretary, in the person of Mr. Winnill, a schoolmaster, had been appointed. The first League match was against Everton at Goodison Park, and the new-comers made a most auspicious start by gaining a clever and well-deserved victory by 3 goals to 2. They finished tenth in the League the first season, sixth in 1895, and twelfth in 1896. After which they had a brilliant run of success.

In 1896–7 they finished second and in 1897–8 won the League championship; in 1898–9 they won the Association Challenge Cup; in 1899–1900 they again finished second in the League; in 1900–1 they were beaten in the Final for the Association Cup, after playing a drawn game with Tottenham Hotspur; whilst in 1901–2 they again won the Association Cup, after playing a drawn game with Southampton.

Their most successful season was undoubtedly 1897–8, when they were justly regarded as the best football team in Great Britain. They won the League championship, played home and away matches with Glasgow Celtic—who had won the Scottish League without meeting with a reverse—beating them at Sheffield 1—0, and drawing at Glasgow 1—1. They also played two drawn games with Notts Forest, who in that season won the Association Cup.

In 1899 Mr. J. Nicholson took over the secretaryship, and has had a big hand in the welfare of the club.

In 1903 the United possessed what no other club has ever possessed—viz., twelve International players all taking part in the game. These were W. Foulke (goal), H. Thickett and P. Boyle (backs), H. Johnson, B. Wilkinson, T. Morren, J. E. Needham (half-backs), W. Bennett, A. Common, A. Brown, F. Priest, and H. B. Lipsham (forwards). Altogether, the club has turned out sixteen International players, the others being H. Lilley, M. Whitham, R. Howell, and G. A. Hedley.

After this brief history of the inception and progress of the club, it would perhaps not be out of place to give a few particulars concerning those who have had most to do with bringing the United into its present prominence. First and foremost must be placed Mr. Charles Stokes, to whom, as stated, the club practically owes its existence. Mr. Stokes, who is the chairman of the football section, has the distinction of also being one of the founders of the Sheffield Wednesday Football Club, and

SHEFFIELD UNITED—THE TEAM FOR 1905-6.

Top Row: J. Nicholson, Secretary. Mr. Smith, Director. Johnson. Groves. Lensley. Benson. Waller, Trainer. Mr. Tomlinson, Director.

Oswald Parkin, Sheffield.]

Middle Row: Donelly. Brown. E. Needham, Captain. Drake. Priest. Lipsham.

Bottom Row: Lang. Wilkinson. Master Smith.

represented Heeley Football Club on the Sheffield Association executive in 1869.

A Sheffielder, and a prominent and successful athlete in his youth, Mr. Stokes has always been identified with all that is best in sport, and his broad-minded views and tactful management has been of inestimable benefit to the club. For a long time he has been treasurer of the Yorkshire County Cricket Club, and it is only natural that most of his interest should be centred in Bramall Lane.

He has, for close on thirty years, held the position of chairman of the Heeley Cricket Club. He takes little part in public or political business, although pressed on several occasions to do so. He is well known in musical circles, and is honoured and respected by all with whom he comes in contact.

To Mr. J. B. Wostinholm, the first secretary, the club owes a debt of gratitude, though perhaps he did not take a very active part in the management. Mr. H. H. Stones, his assistant, however, was full of zeal and energy, and probably few know how much he has done towards laying the foundation upon which the present success of the club is built.

Mr. Joseph Tomlinson, who is still one of the directors of the club, is a sportsman in the finest sense of the word. As a Sheffielder, he learnt his football with Heeley, and was regarded as one of the fastest forwards of his day.

Mr. Joseph Smith, who joined the club directly after its formation, brought an amount of experience with him that proved of immense value to the club. Like Mr. Tomlinson, he had been cradled in the game, and his judgment as to the capabilities of a player was seldom at fault.

Another gentleman who devoted a tremendous amount of time to the club's interest was the late Mr. Joseph Beardshaw. For years he went away with the team; and railway travelling was a far different affair then to what it is to-day.

These gentlemen in their official capacity had most to do with building up the fortunes of the club successfully, facing all opposition and gradually gaining the confidence and patronage of the public.

THREE SHEFFIELD INTERNATIONALS.

Parkin.]
ERNEST NEEDHAM.
Sheffield United's captain and famous International half-back. One of the most distinguished professionals that have ever played the Association game.

Parkin.]
ARTHUR BROWN,
Sheffield's centre-forward, gained his International cap in 1904. He will not obtain his majority until April, 1906. Stands 5ft. 9in., and weighs 10st. 10lb.

Parkin.]
HARRY JOHNSON,
Right half-back. He stands 5ft. 10in., and weighs just under 12st. Has already secured many International caps for England.

Later Mr. T. Bott joined the board of directors, and during the past eight years—the most successful period experienced by the club—he went with the team to their away matches and invariably took charge of the players when away training. The way the men came up for the important matches showed how well they were looked after when away.

Yates, Sheffield.]
THOMAS BOTT,
Vice-Chairman of the football section of Sheffield United Cricket and Football Club.

In May, 1899, Mr. John Nicholson was invited by the directors to take over the secretaryship of the club, an important post for a young man.

He very quickly proved his worth, and is undoubtedly one of the smartest and most tactful secretaries in the League. He holds a most unique position, being secretary of both the cricket and football sections.

There is no special team's manager at Bramall Lane, so that it will be understood Mr. Nicholson is pretty well occupied.

The company is managed by a board of directors who number twenty. The present directors are the Right Hon. Lord Hawke, Hon. F. S. Jackson, and Messrs. J. C. Clegg, C. Stokes, M. J. Dodworth, J. B. Wostinholm, F. Atkin, E. Barber, A. Bingham, T. Bott, J. Tomlinson, J. Smith, W. Sissons, A. Neal, A. Cattell, C. E. Vickers, W. Chesterman, A. A. Tasker, G. K. Thorpe, and A. J. Gainsford.

J. NICHOLSON,
Secretary.
He took over the important position of secretary to Sheffield United Cricket and Football Club in 1899.

Mr. J. C. Clegg, the chairman of the Football Association, is chairman of the directors, and this in itself is a sufficient guarantee that the club is carried on in a thoroughly legitimate, sportsmanlike, as well as business-like manner.

The financial position of the club is a sound one. The ground, which consists of twelve acres of freehold land, is owned by the club. Since May, 1899, the club has expended over £31,000 in improvements to it. To enable this expenditure to be met, preference shares to the value of £9,130 were issued, and, with the exception of £1,300 owing to the bank as per last year's balance-sheet issued in June last, the balance of these improvements has been paid out of income.

This history would not be complete without a reference to some of the players who have done so much to enhance the reputation of the club.

In 1890-1 R. Howell and M. Witham, two local players, were engaged, and each succeeded in getting International honours whilst with the club. For the season 1891-2 a number of new players were engaged, these including Ernest Needham, Bob Cain, Sammy Dobson, W. Hendry, Jack Drummond—the last three from Preston North End—and Harry Hammond of Everton. The engagement of these players marked the turning-point in the career of the club.

In 1893-4 William Foulke, the giant goalkeeper, was engaged, and perhaps he has as much as any player the club ever possessed helped to place the club in its proud position. Great credit is also due to W. Hendry, who, as captain, and by his skilful play, has practically made the team.

Perhaps the best known and most highly respected player the club has ever had is Ernest Needham. Born at Whittington Moor, near Chesterfield, in 1873, he learnt his football at Staveley, and joined the club when eighteen years of age. He played for Sheffield Association against Glasgow when only sixteen, and has been captain of the club ever since Hendry left.

Many Northern players have been in the United ranks, prominent amongst these being Tommy Morren, Fred. Priest, and G. A. Hedley.

One of the most important persons in a big football organisation is the trainer; and the club have every reason to be more than satisfied with theirs. A first-class football player in his day, George Waller commands both the respect and confidence of his employers and the esteem and admiration of the players. He has made a special study of the muscles, and it has to be a very serious breakdown indeed that Waller is beaten by. He joined the club in 1892. Quiet-spoken, well-mannered, and a gentlemanly fellow, Waller is an ideal trainer. He is a Sheffielder, and played football for Sheffield Wednesday. J. N.

FOOTBALL FIASCOS.

By WILLIAM MACGREGOR.

Pressure of numbers a fruitful cause—The fiasco in the English Cup Final at Manchester, 1893—Aston Villa v. Preston North End—The gates rushed—35,000 people swarm into the enclosure—The game repeatedly stopped—"The military called out" at Perry Barr—The Tottenham Hotspur v. Aston Villa Cup-tie fiasco of two years ago—The match abandoned—Tottenham ordered to pay £350 to London charities—Many fiascos in Scotland—Football in the snow—The terrible disaster at Ibrox Park.

CONSIDERING the dimensions to which football as a national pastime has grown, it would be remarkable indeed if the game had not had its crop of fiascos. Football stirs the pulse as possibly no other pastime does; and, what is more, it stirs the pulses not of a handful of unprejudiced sportsmen, but of tens of thousands of people, many of whom have served no apprenticeship to sport, and are therefore inclined to give their passions free vent.

Many of the fiascos I have seen have been caused by sheer pressure of numbers. Those who are well placed are only anxious to see the game go on, but those who cannot command a good view are apt to push and struggle in the hope that possibly their situation may be improved thereby. Realising that they cannot see where they are, they reason that any change in position cannot be for the worse. That has been the cause of practically all the fiascos I have noted in connection with football. There has always been a keen desire to see, and it was because they could not see that those who were responsible for the trouble got out of hand.

One of the most remarkable fiascos—although possibly it is stretching a point to so label it—was seen in the English Cup Final at Fallowfield, Manchester, in 1893. We were then at the beginning of the really big modern gates, and it is an admitted fact that the Association and the officials who were in immediate charge of the game woefully underestimated the interest that the match was destined to arouse. I do not know that any blame attaches to them; it is so easy to be wise after the event.

But I recollect another fiasco prior to that, in which everyone was amazed by the sudden interest manifested in a particular tie. I refer to the Aston Villa v. Preston North End game in 1888. When a pastime is in a stage of transition anything may happen. We, who make such admirable arrangements now for housing the crowd, are benefiting by our own failures, or by the failures of others, in the past.

R. Banks, Manchester]

A CUP FINAL FIASCO—WOLVERHAMPTON WANDERERS v. EVERTON, MARCH 25, 1893.

An early Cup Final fiasco was witnessed in the game between Wolverhampton Wanderers and Everton in 1893 at Fallowfield, Manchester. The tremendous excitement attaching to the game, owing to the fact that it was being played in the provinces, drew an enormous crowd, for whom no proper provision had been made. The people were perfectly orderly for a time, but as they could not see the game they pushed and fought and threw clinkers and turf at those in front. The barriers were broken down, and a wild scene of confusion occurred.

(*From a photograph in the possession of the Football Association.*)

The Fallowfield Ground is an old one, and it did not possess the banking-up which modern grounds invariably have. There was, theoretically, space for a large number of people, but there was not room for more than 15,000 to watch the match in comfort. Fifteen thousand is quite an excessive number when they practically have to watch the match from the level.

The people were perfectly orderly for a time, but they could not see what was going on, and consequently those at the back grew restive. They saw a nice open space between the people close to the ropes and the players, and they naturally tried to get there. They pushed and fought, and then they threw clinkers and turf at the people in front. Finally the strain became too great for the barriers, which were frail, wooden palisadings; they crashed in at many points, greatly to the danger of the reporters on one side of the ground, and soon there was wild confusion. However, the people wanted to see the play; there can be no doubt on that point; and, although there were interruptions to the game—the crowd were often encroaching over the touch-lines—the match was finished, Wolverhampton Wanderers winning by a goal—scored by their great International captain Harry Allen—to nil.

All sorts of wild rumours were afloat in regard to the proceedings at Fallowfield. It was alleged that there was a plot afoot to seize the gate-money; but football officials are pretty wide awake in those matters. A great many people were injured—few seriously, I believe—and more than one football journalist carried home with him traces of the excessive enthusiasm which the crowd manifested.

There was another fiasco at Fallowfield, but the circumstances were not so sensational as those identified with the proceedings at the Cup Final. The barriers used at the replay of the Semi-final between Sheffield United and Liverpool—the third meeting of the teams in the struggle—in 1899 were altogether insufficient, and again the mistake was made of leaving a big space between the crowd and the touch-lines. There were plenty of police there, but they were powerless to keep back the crowd when once a few of the more daring spirits had jumped the palisading.

By dint of organised charges the police managed to force the crowd back, and the game was renewed. But it did not extend beyond the interval, for when once the teams got into the pavilion it was decided not to allow them to turn out again, and the crowd slowly melted away. An effort was made, I believe, at the match first mentioned, to get the barriers used on the occasion of a recent Royal visit to Manchester, but, from what I can understand, the Watch Committee did not see their way to lend them.

One of the most interesting fiascos I ever remember was that which occurred when Aston Villa and Preston North End met at Perry Barr in 1888 in the English Cup competition. Both teams were in magnificent form at the time. The Aston Villa eleven at that period was a most brilliant one, while, of course, North End had a reputation quite unique. The Villa had a well-appointed ground, as football enclosures then went, and every effort was made to cope with an abnormal rush of spectators. As much as ten shillings was charged for some seats; such a price was unheard of in connection with football of that day.

The Villa really thought that they had made adequate arrangements, but the match stirred the pulse of the Midlands, and, indeed, the football public generally, as no game had ever stirred it before. The prospect of witnessing the two greatest teams of the year, captained by the two greatest football heroes of their time—Nicholas Ross and Archie Hunter—compelled everyone's attendance.

It is computed that 27,000 people were present; but the gates, and, indeed, the barriers, were rushed at a dozen points, and I have always thought there were quite 35,000 people on the ground.

Whatever the number was, not more than half of them saw, so that the precise attendance was not material. But I doubt if more than 20,000 could have seen in comfort. I shall never forget the sights witnessed that afternoon. The stands were soon crowded, and char-a-bancs, brakes, waggons, lorries, and traps were all utilised as temporary stands. Plenty of people paid anything up to half a crown for the privilege of standing on a lorry, and so getting a reasonably good view of the play.

But the pressure from the rear occasioned by those who could not get a glimpse of the players, and who only knew that the game was going on by the occasional skying of the ball, became too great, and the people were soon swarming over the touch-lines. The game was repeatedly stopped, but it was finished, North End winning by 3 goals to 1.

They were most emphatically the cleverer team, but there were circumstances connected with the match which caused grievous dissatisfaction. It was agreed by the respective captains quite early in the game that the match should not rank as a Cup-tie. That was a fair decision, too, because, although the people desired to see the game, and were not anxious to encroach, they were forced over the line by those in the rear, and the players were unquestionably handicapped.

But North End claimed the match, and the Association ruled that the Villa should be disqualified because they had failed to take adequate means to keep the crowd in order. That decision was a mistake, and is now generally admitted to be such. Some of the newspapers, local and otherwise, had some startling bills in connection with that event. "The military called out!" was one. I will tell you how that impression arose. When it was seen that the crowd was becoming unmanageable, mounted police were telephoned for, but they could not be got expeditiously. A couple of soldiers who happened to be on the ground were, however, placed on horses, and they trotted up and down the touch-line near the goal at the Perry Barr end. The horses were not military animals; they were taken from some cabs which were standing on the ground. However, there were mounted soldiers before the gaze of the public, and their presence gave rise to the sensational phrase, "The military called out!"

Then the Tottenham Hotspur and Aston Villa Cup-tie at Tottenham two years ago will not readily be forgotten. I am quite sure that I shall not be accused of partisanship when I say that that fiasco was entirely the fault of those who had

THE FOOTBALL FIASCO AT PERRY BARR IN 1888

Provided a semi-comic incident. The crowd became unmanageable, and, failing the arrival of mounted police, a couple of soldiers, who happened to be on the ground, were mounted on horses dragged from cabs, and they trotted up and down the touch-line near the goal at the Perry Barr end.

charge of the arrangements in connection with the match. Considering the amount of money Tottenham had drawn out of the Cup competition, they might have been reasonably expected to provide barriers of a modern type.

The whole match was bungled. It was right to play on, but it was not right for the referee and players to act in a manner which proved to the crowd that the game was not a Cup-tie. Everything ought to have gone on in a normal way, and then the crowd would have remained quiet to the end.

As it was, they speedily realised that they were being fooled, and they resented it. I am afraid a big crowd of Englishmen will always act as the Tottenham crowd did that afternoon. It may be regrettable, but the fact had better be faced. The teams finally left the field, but I am convinced that had other methods been employed there need have been no disturbance.

The referee reported to the Association the circumstances under which the match had been abandoned, and the chairman and members of committee of the Tottenham Hotspur Club explained the arrangements made for the accommodation of the spectators, and also gave their impressions of the cause of the encroachment on the field of play. The decision of the special commission was that the match should be replayed on the ground of the Aston Villa Club, and that in the event of there being a drawn game that it again be replayed at Stoke.

Tottenham were ordered to pay to the Football Association the sum of £350 out of their share of the gate receipts, the amount to be distributed by the Association amongst the London charities—that was a decision which, generally speaking, was well received.

R. Banks, Manchester.]

THE FALLOWFIELD FIASCO DURING THE MATCH BETWEEN WOLVERHAMPTON WANDERERS AND EVERTON IN 1893.

This photograph was taken soon after the kick-off, and shows the touch-line clear. Later on the crowd swarmed on to the field and interfered with the game. The match was, however, finished.

(From a photograph kindly lent by the Football Association.)

Scotland has had plenty of fiascos, but then the crowds there have always been so huge that this is not surprising. Some of them have been of modern date. There was a narrow escape at the International at Queen's Park Ground in 1890. The crowd were on the touch-lines all the time, but it was agreed to go on with the game, for perfect good humour prevailed.

I remember a Scottish fiasco in the early days. Aston Villa went on a Scottish tour in January, 1887, the year they won the English Cup for the first time. They were a remarkable side then. They beat the Hibernians, then very strong indeed—I recall how brilliantly William Groves played; I believe he made his debut for them that afternoon—by 8 goals to 3, and then travelling on to Glasgow they met Queen's Park at Hampden Park.

There was a tremendous snowstorm, but the Villa, playing against it, scored 5 goals, and looked like routing the powerful Scots. But then the storm increased in severity, and the "Spiders" would not come out again. I am not blaming them; the weather was pretty bad. But the Villa were willing to go on with the game, and I see no reason why the match should not have been finished. But Charlie Campbell, the Queen's Park captain—a good sportsman enough surely!—declared that he would not come out again for ten thousand devils, and the match was abandoned.

The spectators were very angry, but made a great fuss of the Villa men. As they did not get football value for their money, they proceeded to tear down what property they could. Among other excesses they uprooted the goal-posts.

There was also a lively scene at one of the early Cup-ties in the Lancashire competition between Blackburn Rovers and Darwen, those old and historic opponents whose matches were always thrilling, and at which the fur was wont to fly. There was a great deal of contention over that splendid back, Fergus Suter, who, after settling down at Darwen, threw them over and joined the Rovers. This particular bother was inspired by an action of Suter's, and the crowd swarmed over the field, and the enclosure was a perfect pandemonium. How those two clubs did love one another! But their rivalry did great things for the spread of the game in East Lancashire.

But all football fiascos must pale before the terrible disaster at Ibrox Park on the occasion of the International game between England and Scotland in 1902. There was a great crowd that afternoon, and all went well until, as the result of the swaying on the part of the crowd, the great wooden stand at the rear of one of the goals collapsed, and thousands of people were precipitated to the ground. Hundreds were injured; all told over four hundred were affected, and many were killed.

The horrors of that afternoon will never be forgotten by those who witnessed them. It was a ghastly spectacle to see the poor maimed and dying fellows carried in; but some of our football magnates worked like heroes to alleviate their sufferings. Hats, coats, vests, tobacco-pouches, anything and everything were utilised for bandages and pads, and sticks and umbrellas were hastily converted into splints.

Much adverse comment was occasioned by the fact that the match was played to the end, although there was no idea of allowing it to stand. But the criticism showed how completely our critics failed to grasp the real position. 'Twas ever thus! Had not the game gone on, the greatest difficulty would have been experienced in dealing with the wounded. Everyone would have crowded upon the helpers, the approaches would have been blocked, and everything would have been chaos. Everyone concerned wanted to abandon the game, the players more particularly, but it would have been madness to do so.

The accident called forth the generous sympathy and practical support of all good sportsmen, and there was a magnificent response to the Scottish Football Association's appeal for funds. The huge sum collected was most wisely administered; indeed, the committee, although having to deal with so many cases, settled the whole of them without indulging in litigation. This is a result which reflects credit both upon the committee and the members of the public. When one remembers how difficult the average man—and especially the average Scot—is to deal with when he is claiming money for injuries, real or imaginary, it is difficult to overpraise the committee responsible for the administration of the Ibrox Park Fund.

It was feared that the disaster would do irretrievable harm to football, but people had the good sense to realise that such accidents will happen when huge crowds are brought together, no matter whether the occasion be a football match or a religious meeting. The English Association acted promptly in the matter, and their generosity and advice were much appreciated by the Scottish Association.

THE MOST TERRIBLE OF ALL FOOTBALL DISASTERS.

The calamity at Ibrox Park, Glasgow, on the occasion of the International match between England and Scotland in April, 1902, is the unhappiest page in football history. No less than 25 persons died from injuries received by the collapse of the stand, 153 were badly hurt, and 172 slightly injured, as classified by the police. The picture shows Mr. Fulton, of the Caledonian Railway, giving first-aid to a girl whose leg was broken. The corrugated iron screens were quickly pulled down and used as stretchers to carry away the most severely injured for surgical treatment.

BRISTOL ROVERS.

CHAMPIONS OF THE SOUTHERN LEAGUE, 1904-5.

The foundation of the club—The first match—The formation of the Reserve XI.—The starting of the Western League under the title of Bristol and District League—The club formed into a company—The present ground acquired—Professionalism is adopted—The title of Bristol Rovers chosen—The first appearance of the club in the Southern League—Champions of the Western League in 1899-1900—Champions of the Southern League, 1904-5.

Colours: Black and white stripes. *Ground: Stapleton Road, Bristol.*

MR. WILLIAM SOMERTON, CAPTAIN OF EASTVILLE ROVERS, 1884-5, 1885-6, 1889-90, and 1890-91.

Mr. Somerton learnt his football in Oxford. He came to Bristol in June, 1883. Upon the formation of the "Black Arabs" in that year he became vice-captain, and was elected captain the following season. First played as forward, but developed into left full-back, in which position he played for the club when it won the Gloucestershire Association Cup in 1888-9. Finished active participation in the game about 1892 owing to a badly crocked knee, but is still an enthusiastic member of the Bristol Rovers Football Club.

IN September, 1883, a party of five young men laid the foundations of the club now champions of the Southern League. At that time there were only three or four Association clubs in the district. Scarcity of members necessitated practice taking the place of matches for a time. The young enthusiasts played on a hill known as Purdown, and in the vicinity a Rugby team known as the "Arabs" played the other code. Their name suggested to the promoters of the new club the title of "Black Arabs," which was the name the Rovers' club bore at its birth. Many of the original players were engaged in scholastic work.

Of its earliest members, the Rovers still retain Messrs. F. Channing, now a director, and H. J. Horsey, the financial secretary; while Mr. Braund, who was the first secretary, and Mr. W. Somerton, the first vice-captain, are still staunch supporters. The first fixture of the "Black Arabs" was in December, 1883, when they were badly beaten at Wotton-under-Edge by the local team. The following season was more successful, and the popularity of the game was growing rapidly. They arranged about twenty matches in the season 1884-5, and dropped the name of "Black Arabs" in favour of Eastville Rovers. Mr. Somerton took over the captaincy; and that season found the name of Mr. W. Hodgkinson, who afterwards became identified with Bristol City, amongst the committeemen.

MR. FRED CHANNING, CAPTAIN OF EASTVILLE ROVERS, 1886-7, 1887-8, and 1888-9.

Mr. Channing was born in Bristol, but first learned to play the game in Nottingham in 1876. Played right-back for St. Mark's Training College, Chelsea. Joined the "Black Arabs," afterwards known as the Eastville Rovers, in 1883, and was elected captain in 1886. He acted as secretary for the Rovers in 1892-3, was afterwards elected president, and has been a director of the Bristol Rovers Club for the past seven years.

The next few seasons found the Rovers making good headway. Their fixtures were all friendlies, for competitions, as far as Bristol was concerned, were unknown in those days. They changed their playing-ground several times. Mr. Braund, after being secretary for four years, retired in favour of Mr. W. G. Perrin. After one year as honorary secretary, that gentleman relinquished the office to his brother, Mr. W. S. Perrin. Messrs. Channing and Somerton practically shared the captaincy until the close of their playing days.

Prothero, Bristol.]

THE BRISTOL ROVERS' GROUND.

The present ground was at one time used by the Harlequin Rugby team. It will accommodate 30,000 people. The opening match was played here on April 3rd, 1897, when an Aston Villa team defeated the Rovers in their first home match by 5 goals to 0.

It was in the season 1886-7 that an extension was made by the formation of a reserve eleven. This step has never been regretted, and to this day the Rovers run a second team, which last season had the proud record of not having lost a match.

Amongst the local citizens associated with the club was Dr. W. G. Grace, the famous cricketer, who more than once

MR. GEORGE HUMPHREYS,
Chairman of the Bristol Rovers' F. C.
He is a great lover of football, and was for many years an ardent follower of the Rugby game. Is a crack shot with the rifle, and has been a member of the Bristol Rifle Volunteers for over thirty years.

acted as referee. In 1887-8 the Gloucestershire Football Association was formed, and in the following year the Rovers won the cup offered by that body. Mr. Channing was secretary that season, and in the following year Mr. S. S. Rinder, a brother of Mr. Fred Rinder, the chairman of Aston Villa, was a vice-president of the club, and afterwards became more closely connected with the working of the Rovers. The Rovers rarely made good progress in the Gloucestershire Cup in their early days.

In 1892-3 the present Western League was started under the title of "The Bristol and District League"; but it was some seasons before the Rovers attained much distinction in the competition. In 1895-6 they were runners-up.

In the last season of their amateurship the Rovers engaged George Pay as trainer, an office he holds at the present time. He was a Bristol man, but his taste ran in the direction of being a professional athlete. Many of his old admirers and friends would recognise in George the man who, as "C. Lewis," figured in many of the best meetings in the country. He ran in the Sheffield and Manchester Handicaps, and was also the Welsh 150 yards' champion. It is his proud claim that he was never beaten in a match for money. His success as a trainer has been great, and many first-class players have been put on the market who owed their quality in no small measure to the watchful supervision of George Pay.

Mr. H. J. Horsey was secretary of the club when it was formed into a company in 1896. The present ground was acquired by syndicate. It was formerly used by the Harlequin Rugby team—that is when it was not flooded—and the Rovers laid it out to accommodate 20,000 people. The opening match was played there on April 3, 1897, when an Aston Villa team defeated the Rovers by 5—0.

In the following season professionalism was first adopted in Bristol by the Rovers, who obtained the signature of George Kinsey, the old Wolverhampton Wanderers' International. The directors who constituted the company were Messrs. Rinder (chairman), S. Joy, W. H. Brown, F. W. Hunt, A. J. Bevan, H. J. Horsey, and I. Hewys, the last-named acting as secretary. In that season the players' wages accounted for £1,051, whereas last season the amount for the same purpose was £2,652. The gate-money was nearly £2,000, and that of last season nearly three times as much.

After running the team in the name of Eastville Rovers, the company changed it to Bristol Eastville Rovers for the first professional season. That season they were fifth in the Western League, and met with fair success in the Birmingham League. They were knocked out in the second round for the Gloucestershire Cup, and were defeated in the Association Cup by Southampton

A. CARTLIDGE.
Bristol Rovers' Goalkeeper.

A. Cartlidge was born in 1880. He is a splendid specimen of an athlete, standing 6ft. 0½in. in height, and weighs 14st. He first came into prominence whilst playing for Stoke, and his fine goalkeeping of last season raised him to a prominent position among the crack goalkeepers of the Southern League.

by 1—8 at Southampton. At the close of that season the name of the club was changed to Bristol Rovers. Mr. Hewys ceased to be a director, and his place was taken by Mr. G. W. Humphreys. Mr. Hunt was chairman at the time, and Mr. Humphreys was elected vice-chairman, but the following year took the superior position, and has held it ever since. He is a Bristol man, and for many years was a follower of the Rugby game. When the other code became more general, he developed a greater fondness for it.

Mr. Humphreys, however, does not devote himself entirely to football, for he has a great liking for shooting. For over thirty years he has been a member of the Bristol Rifles (Volunteers), and has displayed remarkable skill in the handling of a rifle. On two occasions his marksmanship won him a place in the International matches, while he has also shot in the final for the King's Prize at Bisley. As the result of the shooting matches in which he has taken part, he is now the holder of many badges.

Last season, when a large portion of the banking was covered in on the popular side of the Rovers' ground, and a great deal more covered accommodation provided on the grand stand side, the work was carried out under the supervision of Mr. Humphreys. He gave to his club the great assistance to be derived from his experience as a contractor, and though the work, involving an expenditure of several hundred pounds, was carried out during a few weeks of the season itself, not the slightest inconvenience was caused, and the expeditious manner in which the improvements were effected was a matter for much favourable comment.

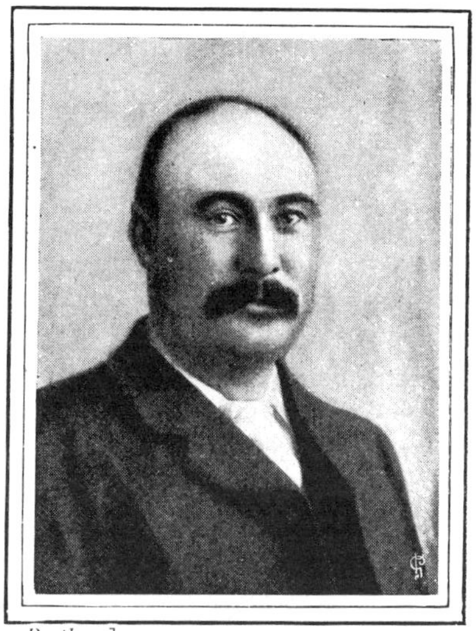

Prothero.]
MR. A. G. HOMER,
Secretary of the Bristol Rovers' Football Club.

The Rovers now have accommodation for about 30,000, of whom a third can be placed under cover.

The other changes in the directorate resulted in the election of Mr. F. Channing and Mr. T. G. Walker, while later Mr. J. H. Machin also found a seat. Mr. Machin has a good deal to do with the working of the Schools' Association League, and deserves every commendation. The League is now a flourishing concern, and it owes its success largely to the efforts of Mr. Machin. Since his election the directorate has been unchanged.

In the season 1898-9 the Birmingham and Western Leagues were competed in. In the former the Rovers did well, but their efforts in the latter did not meet with great success. In the Association Cup they only played one game, being defeated by Reading at Eastville.

The heavy secretarial work prompted the Rovers to consider the desirability of having a paid secretary who could also manage the team. They decided on this course, and in 1899 Mr. A. G. Homer commenced his work with the club. His association with football has extended over many years, penetrating well into his minority. He is a native of Birmingham, having been born at Aston. When in his teens he became honorary secretary

THE CHAMPIONS OF THE SOUTHERN LEAGUE, 1905.

Top Row:—G. Pay, Trainer. H. Dunn. A. Cartlidge, Goalkeeper. B. Appleby. D. Pudan.

Lewis R. Protheroe, Bristol.]

THE CHAMPIONSHIP SHIELD

Middle Row:—D. Clark. T. Tait. G. Jarvie. A. E. Dunkley.

Bottom Row:—J. Lewis. W. Beats. A. Smith.

of the Lozells Football Club. He helped to form, and was the first secretary of, the Birmingham Junior League. He resigned his position with his old club, and was then instrumental in forming the Birmingham Charity Association.

He had for some time been under the notice of Aston Villa, and seeing in him a man of the right sort, the Villa gave him the post of assistant-secretary to Mr. G. B. Ramsay. This necessitated the resignation of the two positions he then held.

During the time he worked for Aston Villa he was instrumental in securing for them Wilkes, the goalkeeper, Steve Smith, the outside-left (now of Portsmouth), Garraty, and Templeton.

At the close of last season the Crystal Palace Club and a Southern League club would have liked to secure his services, but the Rovers' directors were prepared to show their appreciation of him, and he has now signed for them for another five years. It is a matter in which Mr. Homer may take some credit to himself that each year since he has been with the Rovers their profits have increased.

On the appointment of Mr. Homer, Mr. H. Horsey was elected financial secretary, an office which he holds at the present moment. Mr. Horsey is a Bristol man, and, as the article shows, he has long been connected with the club—first as a playing member, then as secretary, director, secretary again, and finally financial secretary.

THE OFF-SIDE RULE EXPLAINED.—I. OFF-SIDE.
CLEAR PASS TO ONE OF SAME SIDE.

A has run the ball up, and having **D** in front passes to **B**. **B** is off-side because there are not three opponents between him and the goal-line when the ball is passed by **A**. If **B** waits for **E** to fall back before he shoots, this will not put him in play, because it does not alter his position with relation to **A** at the moment the ball was passed by **A**.

In the season 1899-1900, the Rovers made their first appearance in the Southern League. In that season they were tenth out of fifteen. In that same year they won the Western League, though only four teams competed. The Association Cup saw the last of them in November, when, after a drawn game at Bristol, Portsmouth won at home by 4—0.

The following season found the Rovers a little higher in the Southern League, their position being seventh. In the Western League, however, they were bottom.

The next season they were seventh in the Southern League, and bottom in the Western. They reached the semi-final for the Gloucestershire Cup, and in the Association Cup were knocked out by Reading. In 1901-2 they were ninth in the Southern League and fifth in the Western, while they held the Gloucestershire Cup jointly with Bristol City.

In the Association Cup they received Stoke, 19,860 people watching the game. This "gate" stands as a record for Bristol. In 1902-3 they were fifth in the Southern League, and runners-up in the Western; they won the Gloucestershire Cup. In 1903-4 they were third in the Southern League, and bottom but one in the Western, the Gloucestershire Cup being taken from them by the City.

The Rovers entered upon their championship season with a defeat at Northampton; but the following week they showed their true form in a splendid victory over Portsmouth at Eastville. Then came a win at Brentford, and the following Saturday Queen's Park Rangers dropped their first point at Bristol. The Rovers then lost a point at Millwall, so that the start hardly suggested a championship season. The "Spurs" were next hopelessly outplayed at Bristol, and the Rovers added to their list two lucky points at Luton.

In their next three matches at home—Swindon, Wellingborough, and Fulham—and a similar number away—New Brompton, Southampton, and West Ham—the Rovers took all the home points, but lost three away.

December gave the Rovers seven points, two each for the matches at home with Plymouth Argyle and Northampton and away at Brighton, while Reading secured a point at Eastville.

Following a win at Fratton Park at the opening of the New Year, the Rovers sustained their heaviest Southern League defeat at the hands of Queen's Park Rangers at Park Royal on the following Saturday, losing by 0—5.

The Rovers, the "Saints," and Reading were now running close together at the top of the table. Victories over Millwall and Luton at home were very acceptable, but a defeat at Swindon came as a great surprise; and then New Brompton drew at Eastville.

In March victories were recorded against Southampton (6—1), Watford at home, and another win at Watford. The only point dropped was at Craven Cottage. April found the "Saints" in a strange plight, and, Reading falling off somewhat, the Rovers were certain of the championship after the defeat of Brentford at Eastville. The anxieties occasioned by a defeat at Plymouth, and a draw at Reading, were dispelled by the collapse of the "Saints." In the same month the Rovers won at Boleyn Castle, and defeated Brighton at home, while the season closed, as it had begun, with a defeat, this time at White Hart Lane. The season's summary in the Southern League was:

	P.	W.	L.	D.	Goals. For	Goals. Agst.	Pts.
Home	17	13	0	4	51	11	30
Away	17	7	6	4	23	25	18
Total	34	20	6	8	74	36	48

In the Association Cup, Brighton and Hove were defeated at Brighton, and then came a splendid draw at Bolton. In the replay, the Rovers could not muster full strength, and lost by 3 goals to nil.

In the Western League, the Rovers finished up last but one.

The Gloucestershire Senior Cup, however, was won by them for the second time in their days of professionalism. After a drawn game, the trophy was wrested from Bristol City.

Last season the Reserves also had a most successful time, winning the Bristol Charity Cup and the Western League (Division II.) Bowl.

The Rovers owed their success largely to the remarkable consistency they displayed. They were fortunate in having very few accidents in the field.

W. Beats, the captain, sustained a rather bad injury at Fulham, but this only kept him out of the team for a few weeks. He played in 29 matches out of the 34. "Billy" is a great favourite in Bristol, where he has lived since 1903-4. He is a true sportsman and an excellent skipper, the influence he has with the players being very far-reaching. The seventeen years he has been playing football for front-rank clubs do not seem to have had the slightest effect upon him. He is still as hard as a nut, and seems fit to lead the Rovers for many seasons to come. He was born at Wolstanton in 1873, and the first big club he played for was Burslem Port Vale. After six years with the Port Vale, he went to Wolverhampton Wanderers.

It was not until 1891-2 that Beats was awarded his International cap. In that season he played against Scotland and Wales. The Rovers had a couple of brilliant backs in Dunn and Pudan, while the halves — Tait, Appleby, and Jarvie—were as clever a trio as could be found in the League. The forwards were generally Clark, Lewis, Beats, Smith, and Dunkley. This championship team has been retained for service this season.

A. C.

THE ASSOCIATION GAME IN SCOTLAND.

By R. M. CONNELL.

The sport that appeals to the masses—Early history of the game—£130,000 spent in Glasgow upon grounds, stands, &c.—The standard of play—The Scottish Cup competition and its early history—No goal lost in seven years—Dawn of the Celtic Club—The "Snow Final" —The legalisation of professionalism—A run of triumphs—The rise of Third Lanark—A sensational victory—The League system introduced into Scotland—A record sixpenny gate.

IF golf is more typical of Scottish life generally, football is the sport that appeals to the masses. One has got to be in Glasgow on International day to realise adequately how tremendous is the hold the game has on the Scottish mind. The enthusiasm of the Scot for the Association game is without parallel in any other race for any particular sport or pastime. Every village can boast of its goal-posts, budding Arnotts, Campbells, and Bobbie Walkers. For nine months the major portion of the male inhabitants of the land of cakes, Bibles, and whisky, discuss little else than the Saturday performances of their favourite clubs and players, and during the other three months of the year they indulge in extravagant speculations in regard to the team that is to wipe out England next April.

The early history of the game is lost in the hoary mists of antiquity, but organised football dates from the birth of Queen's Park F. C. in 1867, years after the game had been cradled in Sheffield. The most remarkable evidence of its growth in recent times has been the enormous outlay in ground extension. In Glasgow alone, the Celtic, Queen's Park, and Rangers clubs have collectively spent £130,000 on ground purchase, stands, and the general equipment of their enclosures. The Celtic lead with £50,000, and the most recent outlay was the acquirement by the club of the palatial iron and glass stand erected by one of the directors at his own expense.

The Rangers come next with £42,000, and operations are not at an end. Since the fateful loss of life at the England-Scotland match in 1902, the club has had in view the abolition of all wooden structures on the terraces, and earth banking on a more extended scale is in progress. Queen's Park, so far, has spent £38,000 on New Hampden Park, a pavilion has yet to be erected at a cost of £5,000, and the pen system of accommodation still further enlarged.

There are those who contend that football is still in its infancy in Scotland, and among those who have expressed this view is Mr. J. H. McLaughlin, ex-president of the Scottish Football Association.

The Celtic chairman has ranged himself on the side of the League reformers, who are endeavouring to combat the hostility of the district cliques in the S. F. A. committee, in affecting the best interests of the game. In recent years, the Scottish League has accomplished more in the direction of improving the standard of refereeing than the S. F. A., and it is matter for regret that

Maclure, MacDonald and Co.]

THIRD LANARK—WINNERS OF THE SCOTTISH CUP, 1904-5.

Top Row: S. M. WYLIE, Secretary. J. COMRIE. T. KELSO. T. SLOAN. J. RAESIDE. J. CAMPBELL. J. NEILSON. J. CAMPBELL, Trainer.

Middle Row: R. BARR. J. KIDD. MR. J. B. LIVINGSTONE, Chairman. MR C. MACDONALD, Director. H. WILSON, Captain. T. MACKENZIE. W. MCINTOSH.

THE SCOTTISH CUP.

Bottom Row: J. JOHNSTON. D. MUNRO.

Maclure, Macdonald and Co.]

CELTIC FOOTBALL CLUB—SCOTTISH LEAGUE CHAMPIONS, 1905.

Back Row:—R. DAVIS, Trainer. R. G. CAMPBELL. D. MCLEOD. H. WATSON. D. HAMILTON. A. MCNAIR. A. WILSON. E. GARRY. J. MCCOURT. D. ADAMS.

Front Row:—J. YOUNG. J. HAY. A. BENNETT. J. MCMENEMY. W. LONEY. J. QUINN. P. SOMERS. W. MCNAIR.

its progressive policy is stultified by its subsidiary position. The shrewder and more independent men in official life are found in the League circle, and, unlike the parent body, there is not the deplorable change in its officers that we see at headquarters from year to year.

In modern football, half-back and goal are the only positions where improvement is visible. The standard of back play and the forward game has deteriorated so very much that only those who have been in touch with the game from the early days can pass judgment on the poverty of its exponents in the more strenuous activity of the present age. One has only to point to the extraordinary prospecting that goes on nowadays by the International Selection Committee on both sides of the Border to illustrate the decline, which is the more inexplicable considering the greater number of clubs that have sprung up.

The standard of play in the national matches in recent years is vastly inferior to what it was twenty years ago. The English teams of 1886, 1888, and 1892, or the Scottish elevens at Blackburn in 1887, at the Oval in 1889, and later still, in 1897 and 1900, are not to be compared with the ill-assorted combinations put into the field within the last few years. The Anglo-Scot turned the scale in Scotland's favour nine or ten years ago, but in the last two Internationals even the Anglo-Scot has failed woefully.

Only so far as Wales and Ireland are concerned has the utilisation of the home-bred player in the service of other countries been productive of improved results in national games. For the first time since Wales and Ireland were included among the national fixtures, Scotland failed to score a win in any of the three games in 1904, the Welsh and Irish matches being drawn, and the English one lost. This year no betterment occurred. Wales beat a strong Scottish team at Wrexham for the first time in thirty years by 3 goals to 1, but a triumph over the representatives of Ireland by 4 goals to 0 at Celtic Park encouraged official hopes in Scotland that in the greater struggle with England consolation would be forthcoming for other disappointments.

The Scottish team contained but four resident players, three of whom—Walker, Wilson, and Thomson—were members of the Heart of Midlothian Club. Glasgow, the "City of Football," had but one representative in the team, which unique circumstance was a decided change from the days when Queen's Park could supply a winning eleven. The public protest when the team was disclosed, and the clamour in the hour of defeat, may lead to a more liberal encouragement for the home player this season.

The game was notable for the super-excellence of the half-backs, a fair standard of back play, and the most hollow forward exhibition ever seen in an England-Scotland match.

Inaugurated in the season of 1873-4, the year following the first International between the representatives of England and Scotland, the Scottish Cup competition is enshrined with the most cherished memories of the game. In later days the League system has proved its utility by providing an attractive series of fixtures with a championship attached to maintain competitive interest, but the Cup still appeals to the masses in a manner no other interest can disturb.

The early history of the Scottish Cup is largely the history of Queen's Park, whose officials cling as tenaciously and loyally to the amateur traditions of the club as in the days of yore, when it revolutionised the forward game by the introduction of combination in passing, a system perfected in later times by Preston North End, the most brilliant team of all time, and the pioneers of professionalism.

In the first seven years of its existence, Queen's Park never lost a goal, and in the season of 1881-2 none of its three elevens lost a match. The club has suffered by the inroads of professionalism, but the magnetic influence of the name still attracts to it the better class of the youth of the West of Scotland.

Regularly four elevens play every Saturday under the old colours, and there are sufficient players at the call of the officials to comprise another two were ground available. Beginning 1873-4, down till 1882-3, when the old Dumbarton, served at the time by such brilliant exponents of the game as James McAulay, Peter Miller, and Joseph Lindsay, triumphed over that powerful local organisation, the Vale of Leven, the Scottish Cup was won alternately by Queen's Park and Vale of Leven. Queen's Park led with three successive victories, then the hardy Vale held it for three more, following which Queen's Park repeated the early sequence by accomplishing the "hat trick" a second time.

It was these performances, coupled with the preponderating element of Queen's Park players in the national teams, that endeared the club to the hearts of the Scottish populace—a sympathy and support intensified when the club made such praiseworthy attempts to capture the English Cup at a time when Blackburn Rovers proved invincible.

The spread of the game and the rise to power of the three great Dumbartonshire clubs—Renton, Dumbarton, and Vale of Leven—followed by the attainment of Cup honours on the part of Hibernian, Renton, and Third Lanark in the later eighties, relegated Queen's Park to a less exalted station, from which it has fitfully emerged to revive the lustre of a glorious past.

The dawn of the Celtic Club in 1888-9 marked a new era in Scottish football. The triumph of the Hibernian Club two years previously in the Cup Final, inspired the Irishmen of Glasgow to emulate the brilliant deeds of their copatriots in Edinburgh by the creation of a similar organisation in the west part of the country.

Adherents flocked to its standard from all parts, and recruited by players of the highest class in James Kelly and Neil McCallum (Renton), P. Gallacher, M. McKeown, James MacLaren, John Coleman, W. Groves, and M. Dunbar from the Hibernian Club, together with the aid of the brothers Tom E. Maley and W. Maley, who had served the Partick Thistle and Third Lanark clubs, the Celtic had a sensational rise. Its first Scottish Cup tie saw the old Cowlairs vanquished by 8 goals to 0, and the defeat of Dumbarton by 4 goals to 1 on the historic and dreaded Dumbarton Ground paved the way for the appearance of the Celtic in the Cup Final of 1888-9 against Third Lanark.

The story of the memorable "Snow Final" that year with its subsequent replay, and triumph of the "Volunteers" by 2 goals to 1, has been often told.

One recalls with pride the achievements of that team so ably served by Andrew and W. Thomson, John R. Auld and James Hannah, later of Sunderland, John Marshall, and last, but not least, James Oswald, the International centre-forward, who afterwards gained fame and renown in the ranks of Notts County.

An early series of Cup struggles in 1877-9 against the Vale of Leven established the Rangers in the affections of the public, and the popularity then gained never deserted the "Light Blues." Founded in 1872, by the brothers Tom and Alexander Vallance, and the brothers McNeil—identified so closely with Queen's Park and Rangers—the old Kinning Park combination found its proper place after the legalisation of professionalism by the Scottish Football Association in 1893.

After the legalisation of professionalism, the Rangers took a new lease of life. The season following its adoption, the club signalised its majority by a maiden Scottish Cup triumph over the Celtic by 3 goals to 1, the feat being achieved by one of the best trained teams ever seen on a football field. The late Nicol Smith and John Drummond for more than a decade were partners at back, and this stalwart couple laid the foundation of the remarkable spell of prosperity that ensued for Ibrox Park.

In the interval, the national trophy was three times won by its representatives, who also enjoyed an unprecedented run of triumphs in the Glasgow and Glasgow Charity Cup competitions. In the season of 1896-7 the Rangers followed the Celtic's notable achievement in 1892 by capturing all three cups.

In 1898-9, the club put up a new record in the Scottish League by winning every match, with a goal aggregate of 79 for and 18 against. The next three years the championship monopoly was continued, and over the four years the Rangers lost but six League matches out of 74, of which number five were drawn, with a goal record of 251 for and 99 against.

Simpson, Falkirk.]
COUNCILLOR ALEXANDER STEVENSON (FALKIRK),
President S. F. A.

An all-round sportsman and a man of many interests. A firm believer in the physical benefits to be derived from open-air exercise. Has hunted with the Linlithgowshire and Stirlingshire Foxhounds for twenty-one years, golfs at Prestwick and Falkirk during the best months of the season, a keen curler and bowler, and patron of many recreative organisations in his native county. The "Bailie," as he is familiarly designated by brither Scot, has held honorary office in the Falkirk F. C. for about a quarter of a century. Came late into official life in Scotland, and is serving a second term as chairman of the S. F. A. In the public life of Falkirk Councillor Stevenson plays a prominent part. For over a dozen years he has been a member of the local Town Council, and for six years was honorary treasurer of the burgh.

Slowly, but none the less surely, the Third Lanark regained its old position, and the first indication of its rise was the overthrow of the Celtic in the Glasgow Charity Cup Final at the Glasgow Exhibition, the improvement in the play of the team synchronising with the advent of the veteran Sunderland half-back Hugh Wilson. Success followed in the Glasgow Cup and Scottish League Tournament, and the end of 1903-4 found the club eulogised as "the team of the year."

This brings our narrative down to the Cup Final of 1904-5, when Third Lanark and Rangers were left to decide the ordeal of the survival of the fittest. Singularly, the clubs had never met in a Scottish Final, and each won its way to the last stage by all-round merit. For four months preceding the match Third Lanark never lost a game.

The game was decided at Hampden Park, and popular anticipation was verified in the result, Third Lanark proving successful, after a drawn match, by 3 goals to 1.

Following England's lead in 1889-90, the League system was introduced in Scotland a year later with the most beneficial results to the game in the bigger centres. Two years previously the Rangers and Celtic met in a Cup-tie, and the "gate" drawings yielded some £80. That same year the record attendance for any match in Scotland was 18,068. Last year, when the same clubs met in the Scottish Cup Final, 64,472 persons passed through the turnstiles, and £1,854 3s. 3d. was drawn, a sum which established the record for a sixpenny "gate." These clubs, and the Heart of Midlothian, are the best exponents of football in Scotland at the present day.

Of the clubs originally forming the League, only Celtic, Third Lanark, Rangers, Heart of Midlothian, and St. Mirren remain in the First Division, which was extended this year to include the Aberdeen and Falkirk clubs with the object of broadening interest in the competition. Unfortunately, the League has always had a pronounced "tail," and the championship has been monopolised by the Celtic (5), Rangers (5), Heart of Midlothian (2), Dumbarton (2), Hibernian (1), and Third Lanark (1). Dumbarton and Rangers held the championship jointly in 1890-1, and last season a tie again occurred, but as goal average is ignored, and a deciding match is necessary, the Rangers and Celtic played a rubber match at Hampden Park, which Celtic won by 2 goals to 1.

THE MAKING OF A PLAYER.

PART II.—HALF-BACK PLAY.

By JAMES W. CRABTREE.

The work of the halves—Their duty to attack and defend—The qualifications of a first-class half—The necessity of physical perfection—Good shooting at goal a requisite—Some famous half-backs and their good points—Keeping the game going—Helping the forward line—Great halves in the old days.

Whitlock, Birmingham.]

JAMES W. CRABTREE,

The famous half-back.

Football has known few better players than he whose portrait appears above these lines. James Crabtree was born at Burnley, stands 5ft. 10in. in height, and weighs 13st. 2lb. He played for Burnley Reserves, Rossendale, and Heywood before signing on for Aston Villa, and also played for Plymouth Argyle. Was given his cap for England four times while with Burnley, and nine times when serving under the Aston Villa claret-and-blue. James Crabtree was equally good at back or half-back, and has shown his amazing versatility by giving satisfaction in the forward line. He has played for England, in all, fourteen times.

WHILE it would not be profitable to institute comparisons between the various sections of a football team so far as relative importance goes, one would be justified in frankly stating that no side can hope to do well which does not possess three capable halves. Personally, I have never seen a club achieve distinction without material assistance being derived from the intermediate trio, and all the great teams of various football eras have boasted half-back sections of exceptional skill.

Of course, it would be useless for a team to rely upon the most brilliant trio of halves the world had known if that team had not also full-backs who could defend sturdily and forwards who could kick goals. But I should feel justified in saying that, given reasonable ability in all departments, the half-back line is the backbone of a football team.

This is so because the work of the half-back is more widely distributed than that of any other player. He is always busy. Backs and forwards often have their periods of rest, or, as we term it, idleness; but the intelligent half-back is always at work. He is there to fill a double purpose. You have all of you seen the goalkeeper on a frosty afternoon wildly waving his arms about to keep his blood from freezing in his veins.

Well, you never see a half-back resorting to such extraneous expedients to keep himself warm. He is always on the alert; the ball may come to him at any moment. The full-back is there to defend, and so long as he is reliable at the pinch he has merely to do a little backing-up when his side are on the aggressive, and then no fault will be found with him. His forte is strong and resolute play in an emergency; defence must ever be his primary consideration.

But the halves are privileged persons. It is as much their duty to attack as defend. While they should always have a slight leaning in favour of defence—the robbing of an opponent is a half's primary duty—they are also there to help their side to attack. "Look after the opposing forwards first, and then see what you can do for your own attacking force" would be an excellent maxim for a half-back to stand by.

Give the ball to the man on your own side who is best placed for receiving it, but make it your first duty to prevent a forward on the other side getting off with it. You need not mind kicking out, although I always like to see the ball kept in play, and the crowd have a similar liking. Do what you will, but clear. That is the first essential. Check the dangerous attack; then let the thought of what you can do to get your own side attacking come to you.

But, all the same, a man will never be accepted as a really great half who can only tackle. That is the elementary stage, so to speak; he must be well grounded in that, but he must not be satisfied to remain in a low standard. The halves have not only to check the opposing forwards, and so relieve the backs of a great deal of work, but if they are to be regarded as worth their salt they must have the skill necessary to aid their own forwards in offensive movements.

The halves are the connecting link between the backs and the forwards; they are the most vital part of a piece of complex machinery. If anything goes wrong with them, then the whole mechanism is thrown out of gear. Reverting to what I said concerning the

Bowden Bros.] A THROW-IN—A CUP-TIE MATCH ON THE VILLA GROUND.

The duty of throwing-in when the ball has gone into touch at the side of the ground generally falls to the lot of the two wing-halves. As the rule is now framed they must stand with both feet on the line and throw-in over their heads with both hands to the player in the best position for receiving the ball.

supreme value of a powerful and intelligent half-back line, an illustration of my contention comes to my mind. I have always had a high regard for the Corinthians; any first-class footballer that played against them was bound to respect their prowess. And yet we do not quite recall their famous elevens as we recall the Preston North End team of the late eighties, the Villa of 1897, and Sunderland in an intermediate epoch. This is mainly due, in my opinion, to a slight deficiency at half. They were not so clever or so methodical and sound as the best professional sides were in that department.

I have no hesitation in saying that I have seen Corinthian sides which, had they possessed a half-back line equal to that of North End in the time of Robertson, Russell, and Graham, or Reynolds, Perry, and Groves of West Bromwich Albion, or Reynolds, Cowan, and Groves of Aston Villa, would have been virtually invincible. Forward they were brilliant in the extreme; they would have been even more brilliant in that department had the forward quintette been fed by three high-class and astute professional halves.

Russell and Sons.]

HALF-BACK PLAY—A TUSSLE NEAR THE TOUCH-LINE.

"Halves are privileged persons. It is as much their duty to attack as defend. While they should always have a slight leaning in favour of defence—the robbing of an opponent is a half's primary duty—they are also there to help their side to attack. 'Look after the opposing forwards first, and then see what you can do for your own attacking force' would be an excellent maxim for a half-back to stand by."

Russell and Sons.]

HALF-BACK PLAY—A FAIR CHARGE.

England v. Scotland at the Crystal Palace, April, 1905.

An excellent method of tackling an opponent is to use one's weight to charge him off the ball. It has the weakness that, having charged one man off the ball, it is often difficult to get it under control again before another forward comes up; but there is also the chance that one of one's own side may get the ball after the one man is temporarily disposed of.

Now, as to the qualifications of a first-class half-back. They are multitudinous. In the first place, he must be a skilful tackler. It is wonderful what a good tackler can do. Forwards learn new tricks, but your astute half seems to tumble to them naturally. He must be acquainted with all the wiles of individual forward play, and he must know what players can do in combination. His judgment must be of the unerring type; he must divine what a forward's intention is before that intention can be translated into action.

He must have the knack of being able to cover a hard-pressed colleague without leaving his own wing—the wing for the checking of which he is primarily responsible—too dangerously open. And when he has robbed his opponent of the ball, and can afford to think of offensive play, he must be able to place the ball to a comrade with never-failing accuracy.

And not only must he place it to a colleague, but he must give it to the colleague best placed for receiving it. He must do this intuitively; there is no time for him to make a critical survey of the position. He must make up his mind, instantly and instinctively, what is the proper thing to do. He must feel what his duty is. It is that instant realisation of the full possibilities of the position which distinguishes the great half from the general crowd of players.

You know that some men will do the right thing; you feel that they will. But this, while it may look an easy matter to those who watch, is, in effect, the most difficult thing in football. Some men never learn how to act intuitively. I can give you no sovereign specific for the acquiring of the habit. It may be to a large degree a gift; I often think it is. Some men enter upon pastimes with a natural ability which others lack. Perseverance will do much, but perseverance will scarcely make a dull player into a sharp-witted and discriminating one. Practice will improve anyone's game, but there are traits in football and other pastimes which are essentially gifts.

A half-back has need to be physically perfect, or he can never expect to last out a hard game. The half-back who is found to be blowing soon after the interval is destined to let his side down badly. During the last season that I played I used to find half-back work very exacting; I could figure at full-back much more comfortably.

It is easy to over-do the practice of following the ball. Ernest Needham used to follow it in a way which some of us would not dare to imitate. I have seen him leave his wing open in a way which I should style highly dangerous. Over and over again I have expected to see some danger accrue as the result of the wing man being neglected. The goal has been invaded, and, just as the ball seemed certain to go into the net, the errant

Needham has dropped, apparently from the clouds, and headed away at the crucial moment.

But one needed Needham's supreme ability to play Needham's game; it would not do for every young half to model his play on Needham's style.

A half-back should be a good shot; a half who is a deadly shot at goal is of incalculable benefit to his team. My theory is that few halves shoot as well as they might. You get some wonderful chances, because the ball often comes to you at comparatively short range, and often it comes when the goalkeeper has men between you and himself, and this places him, in one sense, at a disadvantage.

William Groves was a grand shot at goal; in fact, he was grand at whatever he did at one time. Hugh McIntyre, now dead and gone, was, I hear, a wonderfully good shot; he used to place the ball so that it just went out of reach of the goalkeeper. In the seasons when he was at his best, Albert Wilkes, of Aston Villa, used to get in some awkward shots; and Abbott, of Everton, has no superior in this art.

There can be no doubt that old forwards make exceptionally good halves. I always attributed some of my success to the fact that I was originally brought up as a forward. Abbott was a forward, and Taylor, the Everton centre-half, used to play in the front line. There are many instances, in fact, on record in which a once capable forward has developed into a high-class half.

One of the chief points in a half-back's duty is to keep the game going. It is wonderful how an attack can be sustained if the halves support their forwards cleverly. One of the best shows of this kind ever given was when Wheldon and Spikesley formed the left wing for England in the International at Glasgow in 1898. They had Needham behind them, and the three made all sorts of triangular exchanges which puzzled the Scottish defence completely, and materially helped to keep England on the attack. Needham was a grand fellow at giving his forwards a lift, but then he could play forward himself as well as most men.

Bowden Bros.]

AN INTERCEPTED PASS.

It is part of a half-back's duty to break up the combination of the opposing forwards. By anticipating and intercepting a pass he can not only check the opposing side, but, by cleverly transferring the ball to his forwards, place them in a position to make an immediate onslaught upon the enemy's goal.

The three Preston North End half-backs were almost the first trio to realise the full importance of helping their forward line. No trio of halves ever did their work better than Robertson, Russell, and Graham. It was axiomatic that when North End were attacking they had eight forwards at work. I do not see how any forward line, however powerful it may be, can hope to break down a sturdy defence often if they have to make all their own openings. I wonder how many times Bloomer has benefited by reason of the perfect placing of the ball to him by Archie Goodall at centre-half? Archie Goodall never quite ranked as high as some halves who were his contemporaries, but I seriously question if any half-back of his era ever played fewer poor games.

David Calderhead, of Notts County, was another centre-half whose form was thoroughly reliable. I never heard of Calderhead playing a poor game. He may have done so, but he was notorious for quite another kind of football. Then Tom Crawshaw of Sheffield Wednesday was always a sincere worker, and one of the most judicious centre-halves I ever saw was J. R. Auld when captain of Sunderland. Auld was one of the greatest of players, and left his mark both on English and Scottish football.

It would take me a long time to tell you all I know about famous half-back lines I have either seen or have heard of on such authority that I almost seem to know their form personally. I doubt if Robertson, Russell, and Graham have ever been excelled as a trio, and I have referred to the famous lines of West Bromwich Albion and Aston Villa respectively. Hugh Wilson, Auld, and Gibson, of Sunderland, were a good trio, but were not quite so well balanced as some of the sets I have mentioned, although, prior to the abolition of the one-handed throw-in, Hugh Wilson was the most dangerous individual half in football.

I have often thought what invincible half-back lines Scotland might have had if they had lost their prejudice against English professionals sooner. Hugh Wilson, Cowan, and Groves would have formed a half-back department at least equal to anything ever known. Sheffield United once had a clever half-back line composed of men of small stature. Needham, Morren, and Howell were ultra-skilful footballers, but I am rather prejudiced in favour of men of more substantial build, and I should not think of comparing them with the North End trio.

Everton had a clever set when Wolstenholme, Booth, and Abbott were in their prime, and we have had few better centre-halves than Raisbeck of Liverpool. Andrew Aitken is also a real expert, and when he, Neil Gibson, and Robertson were at their best, Scotland had a trio which caused the English forwards much annoyance. So greatly do I esteem the worth of half-backs that I have always considered that the supremacy of the North over the South has been largely a question of superiority in the intermediate line.

There were some great halves in the old days. I never had the pleasure of seeing such stalwarts as N. C. Bailey and J. F. M. Prinsep, but I recall James Forrest and George Howarth, and I have not seen better tacklers and more judicious players all round than they were. One of the most typical halves I recall was J. Keenan of Burnley. His reputation throughout England was not so great as some of the men I have mentioned, but if he were playing to-day he would be sure of his International cap. His great misfortune was that he was engaged in football at the time that James Forrest was supreme.

I do not think half-back play is so good to-day as it was ten years ago. It may come again, but England has been short of good halves for some seasons. There is no reason for this. There has been a falling off in the quality of forward play, but, generally speaking, the defence is as good as ever it was, and the time may not be far distant when England will again have a trio of exceptional halves. The half-back must bear in mind that he should keep the ball as low as possible in passing to a comrade; he should always keep in touch with his back, and subordinate himself entirely to him, and tackle with spirit, as if defeat or victory depended upon him gaining possession of the ball.

THE RISE OF THE FOOTBALL ASSOCIATION.

By F. J. WALL, the Secretary.

The eventful meeting at Freemasons' Tavern in 1863—The clubs that formed the Football Association—Association rules compiled—Mr. C. W. Alcock occupies the secretaryship for twenty-five years—The Association Cup competition established—Wonderful growth of International games and the Cup competition—Professionalism sanctioned by the Association in 1885—Consummate diplomacy of the Association's council leads to a cordial understanding between amateur and professional in 1905—The future prospects of the game—Income of the Association.

OPEN before me, with ink hardly yet beginning to fade, lie the minutes of the first meeting of The Football Association, held at the old Freemasons' Tavern on October 26, 1863. This meeting was not due to any sudden inspiration, but was the inevitable outcome of the events of the two preceding decades. With the revival of athletics about the middle of the nineteenth century, football of one sort or another again became popular at the great public schools, each of which played its own peculiar game.

When the players proceeded from the schools to the Universities or into the outside world, and, mixing with each other, desired to continue their game, the difficulties arising from the differences in the various school codes soon resulted necessarily in attempts to construct a body of rules acceptable to all. The first of these efforts was made at Cambridge during the late "Forties," and the compromise then arrived at seems to have been maintained or revived at intervals until 1863, when football codification was evidently "in the air" at all athletic centres.

In that year, not only did Cambridge again bring out a set of model rules, but the public school captains met for a similar purpose; and last, but most important, the leading clubs which had recently been formed in or near London came together at the Freemasons' Tavern, as recorded above, intent upon evolving order out of chaos. As was to be expected, the London business-men took a wider view of the situation than did the others; and, while these latter were content to secure merely local uniformity of method, the eleven London club representatives who gathered at the old hostelry in Great Queen Street forthwith claimed for themselves a position which, subject to their being able to maintain it, was bound ultimately to make them the controlling body of the whole sport. They commenced business by passing the following resolution, viz.:

"That the clubs represented at this meeting now form themselves into an association to be called 'The Football Association.'"

They then enrolled their clubs as the first members of the Association, and proceeded to compile the first rules of the Association and the first laws of the game.

Bowden Bros.]

MR. F. J. WALL,
Secretary of the Football Association.

No one works more earnestly and conscientiously for the good of the Association game than Mr. F. J. Wall, who for the past ten years has occupied the onerous and responsible position of secretary of the Football Association. Mr. Wall was born in 1856. He was a playing member and hon. secretary of the Rangers' Football Club from 1875 to 1888, and kept goal on occasion for London. The members of the London Football Association elected him to the committee in the second year of its existence, and in 1892 appointed him to the position of vice-president. Mr. F. J. Wall also did first-class work for the Middlesex Football Association, with which he became associated in 1888. He found it a weakly body, but when he left it he had the satisfaction of knowing that it was one of the largest and healthiest organisations connected with the game. In 1895 he took up the duties of secretary of the Football Association upon the retirement of Mr. C. W. Alcock. Mr. Wall has done a very great deal for the game in the South of England, and manages to discharge his difficult duties to the entire satisfaction of all concerned. The photograph above was specially taken at the Association offices for THE BOOK OF FOOTBALL.

The clubs which took part in this first meeting were:

"N. N." (Kilburn), represented by Mr. Arthur Pember (first president),

Barnes, represented by Mr. E. C. Morley (first hon. secretary),

War Office,

Crusaders,

Forest (Leytonstone),

Perceval House (Blackheath),

Crystal Palace,

Blackheath,

Kensington School,

Surbiton, and

Blackheath School.

These clubs represented practically every variety of football then played, and, but for what was, as it turned out, merely a transient difference of opinion on a minor point, there would probably have been no Rugby Union, and, therefore, only one form of football throughout the country at the present day.

"Hacking"—*i.e.*, "kicking an adversary on the front of the leg, below the knee"—was one of the most cherished features of the game as played at Rugby, and by the clubs whose play was modelled on that of Rugby; and while, in the settlement of the new code, unanimity seemed likely to be secured on all other points, the decision of the majority to abolish hacking caused the revolt of the Rugby clubs, who, led by Blackheath, decided in December, 1863, to withdraw from the Associa-

Slater, Llandudno.]

THE FOOTBALL ASSOCIATION'S TREASURER.

Mr. D. B. Woolfall (Lancashire Association) was formerly connected with Blackburn Rovers. Although he is treasurer of the Football Association, he is little in touch with practical football; but he has rendered immense service to the game by his genius for finance. By profession he is Clerk to the Commissioners of Income Tax for East Lancashire. He succeeded the late Mr. C. E. Hart as treasurer of the Football Association in 1901.

tion, as they were not prepared to give up "their favourite game of hacking." This was the parting of the ways which has ended in the existence, side by side, of two such different games as our present "Soccer" and "Rugger."

Weakened by the Rugby secession, but encouraged by the fact that the rules formulated at Cambridge were closely akin to those which they had decided to adopt, the fathers of the Association code published the rules from which the present laws of the game have directly descended, and invited such clubs as were willing to adopt these rules to become members of the Association. There was, of course, no idea of compulsion, but only an earnest effort to bring as many clubs as possible into line.

Old traditions are hard to kill, however, and progress at first was slow. But the founders of the Association were resolute workers, and knew how to wait. So they played their game and awaited developments, modifying the laws as experience showed this to be necessary. All over the country the game soon began to be taken up, and as it spread the advantages of a unified code became more fully appreciated.

Away from London and the Universities, the chief centre of the game before the Association was formed was Sheffield, whose club, founded in 1854, was the oldest in the country. Although the Sheffielders formed their own Association, adhered to their own early code of laws, and did not bring these into line with those of the central body until 1877, they were from the outset most loyal friends of the Association, and the most notable event of these early years was the receipt of a challenge from Sheffield in February, 1866—the month in which Mr. C. W. Alcock first joined the committee of the Association. This match was thus the first of the Association's representative games.

By the spring of 1868 the membership of the Association had increased to twenty-nine clubs, there being, as at present, many minor clubs in addition who did not seek membership. Mr. Arthur Pember had been succeeded by Mr. E. C. Morley as president of the Association in 1867; and in 1868 the Hon. A. F. Kinnaird (Old Etonians) made his first appearance on the committee. As Lord Kinnaird, he is now president of the Association, and, things being as they now are, it must be interesting to him to recall the fact that, at his first committee meeting, he found no funds in hand and the annual expenditure estimated at only £5!

The records of the previous season showed both that the Association's playing code was

Midwinter, Bristol.]

G. S. SHERRINGTON (SUFFOLK F. A.), Vice-President.

Mr. Sherrington first played football at Ipswich School, and afterwards became captain of Ipswich Town Club. He continued to play "Soccer" at Cambridge, and only missed his "blue" through an unfortunate accident that kept him out of the field for some time. After his 'Varsity days he played for Brentwood, the Crusaders, and represented London F. A. and Suffolk County. He retired from active participation in the game as a player in 1890. As a linesman Mr. Sherrington won quite a reputation, and officiated in many important matches, including International games. He is an indefatigable worker, and is invaluable in connection with Commissions and the general work of the Football Association.

Bennett Clark.]

MR. C. CRUMP (BIRMINGHAM AND DISTRICT COUNTIES F. A.), Vice-President.

Mr. Crump is universally known and respected as a kindly and courteous gentleman. He was born at Kingsland, Leominster, in December, 1840. He was elected to the committee of the Football Association in 1883, and was made a vice-president in 1886. As a player he was a member and first captain of the Stafford Road Works Club (Wolverhampton), which was established in 1872, and became prominent in connection with the Birmingham and District Cup and other Midland competitions. He holds an important position with the Great Western Railway Company at Wolverhampton, and has done much in endeavouring to cultivate an honourable understanding among professional clubs and players. Is an active member of the F. A. Emergency Committee, and is the backbone of football in the Birmingham district.

Russell and Sons.]

MR. C. W. ALCOCK, Vice-President.

No name is better known to cricketers and footballers than that of Mr. C. W. Alcock, secretary of the Surrey Cricket Club, and vice-president and late secretary of the Football Association. He was born at Sunderland in 1842. Played football at Harrow, and later with the Forest F. C., from which sprang the famous Wanderers F. C. in 1864. He became honorary secretary of the Wanderers, and was their captain when the F. A. Cup was won in 1871-2. This was the first of the Wanderers' five Cup victories. He was secretary of the Football Association for 25 years, being appointed to that post in 1870. Mr. Alcock has had a distinguished journalistic career, and his name is inseparably associated with the history of the Football Association.

R. P. Gregson.]

R. P. GREGSON, Association Representative for Lancashire.

Mr. Gregson is a native of Clitheroe, Lancs. He is secretary of the Lancashire Association, to which position he was appointed in 1882, and has done much good work in connection with the great winter pastime.

Bowden Bros.] FOOTBALL ASSOCIATION PORTRAITS.

These pictures hang in the committee-room of the Football Association at the offices in High Holborn. They are, reading from left to right, the late Dr. E. C. Morley, late president; the late Colonel Sir Francis Arthur Marindin, K.C.M.G., late president; and the late Mr. E. C. Hart, late treasurer. The splendid work they did for the Football Association will never be forgotten.

being received with ever-growing favour and that the Association might consider itself to be firmly established, the playing of the first county match, Middlesex v. Surrey and Kent, on November 2, 1867, being an unmistakable indication of sound progress. In fact, in commenting on this match, a leading journal of that time remarked that "football has lately increased to such gigantic dimensions" (!) that county matches had become a necessity.

Several changes had taken place in the honorary secretaryship of the Association before the post was accepted, in February, 1870, by Mr. C. W. Alcock, who held it for the next twenty-five years.

It was the year 1870 that first saw the beginning of the International contests, two games being arranged between English and Scottish players belonging to the clubs included in the Association. The Association Cup competition was established as the result of a committee meeting held at the office of the "Sportsman" on July 20, 1871. These innovations were both the sign of the continued growth of the game and the direct cause of much of its subsequent prodigious development.

Bowden Bros.]

THE COMMITTEE-ROOM.

Specially taken for THE BOOK OF FOOTBALL by kind permission of the Football Association.

In the Cup's first year the Association had so grown as to include about fifty clubs, of which fifteen entered for the Cup competition. Besides these, unaffiliated clubs had sprung up in all directions as the charm of the game was felt, not only in England, but in Scotland also, and, though to a less extent, in Wales and Ireland. Local associations soon came to be formed in the provincial districts as the need for organisation and the disadvantages of over-centralisation at headquarters were realised; and as these local associations became affiliated to the parent body, and worked in complete harmony with it, the unity of the game became more and more assured. Space prevents any detailed reference to the growth of this marvellous network of clubs and affiliated associations; but throughout the Seventies and early Eighties the phenomenal spread of the game, and the spontaneous linking up of clubs into local associations, and of these with the central authority, form one of the most remarkable records in the history of sport.

Over this wonderful growth, and the development of the International games and the Cup competition, Mr. C. W Alcock watched with fatherly care, having as his colleague a gentleman who first took office as a member of the committee in the year of the Cup's birth, who succeeded Mr. E. C. Morley as president of the Association in 1874, who guided the fortunes of the Association through all the storm and stress of the Eighties, and to whom the Association probably owes more than to any other of its many able past officers—the late Colonel Sir Francis Marindin, K.C.M.G. He retained the presidentship until 1890.

In the autumn of 1872 things had so far advanced that it was decided, "in order to further the interests of the Association game in Scotland," to send a team to Glasgow to play a match against Scotland. Hence the first genuine International game, played at Glasgow on November 30, 1872. This was followed by the return match at Kennington Oval, on March 8, 1873. The resulting enthusiasm led immediately to the formation of the Scottish Football Association, over which, from the outset, as over all local associations, The Football Association claimed an overlordship—never fully recognised in Scotland, and, ultimately, not insisted upon. In due course, as the game spread, the Welsh (1876) and Irish (1880) Football Associations were established; the first Welsh International being played in 1876 against Scotland, but England not meeting Wales until 1879; while Ireland played both England and Wales in 1882, and played Scotland for the first time in 1884.

For the next few years the Association was mainly occupied in controlling its Cup competition, in arranging for the International and other representative matches, and in fostering the growth of the game in all directions. So greatly was it developing, so popular had the Cup competition become, and so well attended were the chief Cup-ties, that, in April, 1882, the committee found their financial position so satisfactory that, after the Semi-final between Sheffield Wednesday and Blackburn Rovers, they divided £70 of the gate receipts between the charities of Sheffield and Blackburn, while, later in the same month, they sent a cheque for £50 3s. 0d. to the Lord Mayor for the benefit of London charities, that sum having been realised at a charity match at the Oval. Thus was established that honourable connection between football and charity which has since been so striking a feature of the modern game.

Bowden Bros.]

THE GENERAL INQUIRY OFFICE OF THE FOOTBALL ASSOCIATION.

At the end of 1882, the long "nursing period" having been brought to a close, and the general organisation of the game completed, a conference was held at Manchester, attended by representatives of the Football Association, and of the Scottish, Welsh, and Irish Associations, when a universal code of laws was established, to be observed by all clubs and players throughout the United Kingdom. Thenceforward, no change has been made in the laws of the game except with the consent of the four nations, the International Board being established in 1886 for the purpose of considering and, if approved, sanctioning such changes as may appear to be necessary.

But, with the completion of its long-continued labours in this direction, the Football Association found itself face to face with other more difficult and far less pleasant problems, a settlement of which had become necessary as the "football fever" spread among the working-class population of the Midlands and the North. The over-mastering desire to win their games led certain Northern clubs to look about for the most skilful players anywhere to be found; the big "gates" which resulted from the great popularity of the game enabled them to offer such players monetary inducements to join them; the players were not unwilling to earn better wages by playing football than they could earn at their work; and so the importation of paid players became a regular practice among the Northern clubs.

This professionalism was not openly acknowledged, all the arrangements between clubs and players being kept secret—a state of things which was most unsatisfactory. The founders of the game were resolved to maintain it as an amateur sport, and to eject any club convicted of professionalism. The clubs practising veiled professionalism were resolved to continue to do so, and were determined not to be found out. Stringent measures for the suppression of the evil were adopted, but were skilfully evaded and rendered futile, and at length the long struggle came to an end by the governing body recognising that, as professionalism could not be stamped out, it would be wiser to legalise it under stringent conditions, and to undertake the duty of properly controlling it. So, after some years of anxiety and strife, professionalism was sanctioned at a special general meeting of the Association held in July, 1885.

Yates, Sheffield.]

MR. J. C. CLEGG,

Chairman of the Football Association.

It is impossible to over-estimate the value of the good work accomplished by Mr. J. C. Clegg as chairman of the Football Association. His connection with the council dates from 1886, and within three years of that date he was elected vice-president, and became chairman of the council in 1890. Since then his fine administrative ability has been revealed again and again; and to-day Mr. Clegg is, perhaps, the most valuable member of the council of which he forms a part. He has grown up with Association football, for he played in the first match between England and Scotland, and in the earliest matches between Sheffield and London and Sheffield and Glasgow. Mr. Clegg was a noted athlete in his day, and graced the cinder path from 1867 to 1874, during which time he won no less than 120 prizes. His time for the 100 was 10 secs., although such a record was not accepted by the A. A. A. until many years afterwards. He ran a quarter-mile at Sheffield in 50½ secs., and established a grass record for the same distance of 51½ secs. His time for the half-mile was 2 mins. 3 secs.; and he accomplished a record at 600 yards, which was not beaten for some years. He has been a life total abstainer and non-smoker.

Had professionalism not appeared upon the scene, the constructive work of the Football Association would have been completed with the establishment of the principle of the joint control of the game by the four Associations; and there would have remained for the governing body only the current work of supervision and control. But the decision of July, 1885, threw this consummation forward to a date not yet reached, though, happily, nearly so. The struggle for the recognition of professionalism, and the events that followed upon its recognition, put and kept both amateurs and professionals in a state of impatient unrest for many weary seasons.

The sudden and remarkable development of the great professional clubs, the establishment of the Football League, the acquisition by professional players and clubs of practically all the honours and influence of the game, and the apparently inevitable transfer of authority, gave grounds for serious alarm among those who had spent half their lives in establishing the game. Small wonder, therefore, that the amateurs of the South, the fathers of the game, could not watch this development with philosophic calm, but felt disappointed, irritated, and more and more inclined to withdraw from the Association.

Fortunate, indeed, was that body in having—to guide it and act as mediators amidst all the "excursions and alarms" of those troublous years—men of such courage, steadfastness, devotion and tact as Sir Francis Marindin, Lord Kinnaird (who succeeded Sir Francis Marindin as president in 1890), Mr. J. C. Clegg, and Mr. C. W. Alcock (who, in 1895, exchanged the office of secretary for that of vice-president). These, aided by other old and wise members of the council, succeeded both in keeping within due bounds the robust and aggressive enthusiasm of the great League, and in moderating the disappointment of the amateurs. The tension was gradually relaxed, but it was not until last year (1904) that one could feel that the end of nearly half a century of strenuous, constructive work, and of the even more zealous work of maintaining intact the edifice so carefully reared, was in sight, when a cordial understanding was arrived at between the executive of the Football Association and the representatives of the universities and public schools.

Such, briefly told, is the history of the rise and the present position of the Football Association. Upon much that is interesting it has been impossible to dwell here—upon the evolution of the laws of the game, the control of referees, the development of the rules of the Association, the extension of its influence throughout the world, the history of the Cup competitions and of the International games, the finance of the sport, and all that it has done and is doing in the cause of charity. These things would fill a book—at present, I have only room to draw a few contrasts which may furnish some food for reflection:

MEMBERSHIP OF THE ASSOCIATION.

In 1863 there were eleven clubs. In 1905 the Association—by direct affiliation and through the forty-nine County Districts and Colonial Associations which are directly affiliated, and the minor Associations which have received its sanction—had under its jurisdiction upwards of 10,000 clubs.

INCOME OF THE ASSOCIATION.

In 1863	Under £5
In 1905	£16,986 17s. 9d.

THE ASSOCIATION CUP COMPETITION.

1871-2—15 clubs competed. There is no record of attendances or gates, but both must have been very small.

1904-5—272 clubs competed. The gross attendance was approximately 1,500,000, and the gate receipts upwards of £60,000.

INTERNATIONAL MATCHES.

	Attendance.	Receipts.
1873—England v. Scotland (the only match played) ..	3,000	£109 0s. 0d.
1904—England v. Wales ..	16,100	£610 11s. 6d.
,, England v. Ireland ..	21,700	£1,070 15s. 0d.
,, England v. Scotland ..	27,559	£2,436 1s. 6d.

SCOTLAND'S NEW INTERNATIONALS

Crawford.]
G. WILSON
(*Heart of Midlothian*).

R. Thiele.]
CHAS. THOMSON
(*Heart of Midlothian*).

Maclure MacDonald.]
J. HAY
(*Celtic*).

Maclure MacDonald.]
P. SOMERS
(*Celtic*)

Stuart and Winfield.]
P. MacWILLIAM
(*Newcastle United*).

Elbourne.]
T. T. FITCHIE
(*Woolwich Arsenal*)

Furniss.]
J. LYALL
(*Sheffield Wednesday*).

Starfield.]
A. YOUNG
(*Everton*).

J. H. Thompson.]
J. HOWIE
(*Newcastle United*).

THE RECORD OF THE SOUTHAMPTON FOOTBALL CLUB.

Finalists, English Cup, 1899-1900, 1901-2.
Semi-finalists, 1897-8.

Winners of Southern League Championship, 1896-7, 1897-8, 1898-9, 1900-1, 1902-3, 1903-4.

By A. E. JONES.

The formation of St. Mary's F. C.—The connection with St. Mary's severed and the title Southampton chosen—A rapid rise in the football world is followed by the adoption of professionalism in 1892—Application for admission into the Southern League upon its formation in 1895 refused—Accident, however, led to Southampton taking their place, and they finished third in their first season—A singular coincidence of results in the Southern League and Association Cup the following year—The Southern League Shield won—The club turned into a limited liability company in July, 1897—The Southern championship retained—Southampton as Semi-finalists for the Cup—The famous snow-storm match—The Southern Shield won for the third time—More brilliant Cup performances—"Saints" Southern League champions a fourth time—The champions invincible—A breakdown loses the "Saints" the Southern Shield in 1904-5.

Colours: Red-and-white striped shirts, dark-blue knickers. *Ground: The Dell, Southampton.*

Russell.]
MR. G. H. MUIR,
Secretary of the Southampton F. C., 1886-7-8-9.

IN 1906 the Southampton Club will attain its majority. In 1885 the members of a Young Men's Association connected with St. Mary's, the parish church of Southampton, held a meeting, under the chairmanship of the late Rev. A. B. Sole, at which it was decided to form a football club, to be named St. Mary's F. C., and Canon—now Archdeacon—Wilberforce became its first president.

In such humble circumstances as these was the present world-famous Southampton Club born. The connection with St. Mary's Church was afterwards severed, although the original title was retained, and it became a town club, absorbing the cream of local talent. Continuing its ascent of the ladder of fame, it embraced professionalism, entered the principal leagues in the South, and ultimately made a determined effort to wrest the F. A. Cup from the League.

The "Saints" have always been noted cup-fighters. They commenced "pot-hunting" in 1887-8, in which season they competed for the Hampshire Junior Cup and succeeded in winning it. The very first cup-tie played by the team was at Totton, a village midway between Southampton and the New Forest, and it is interesting to recall the players who did duty for the club on that occasion. They were: R. Ruffell; G. Carter, G. H. Muir; A. Varley, C. Deacon, F. J. Crossley; A. Fry, A. G. Fry, C. E. Bromley (capt.), M. Warn, and A. Gandy. Only Mr. Carter is still connected with the "Saints," and the position he occupies is that of manager of the Reserves. His partner in the match referred to is now a well-known referee.

MR. G. CARTER,
The oldest official connected with the Southampton Club.

The club never yielded possession of the Junior Cup, and in 1890 was able to claim it as its own property.

The next season saw St. Mary's classed as a senior organisation and

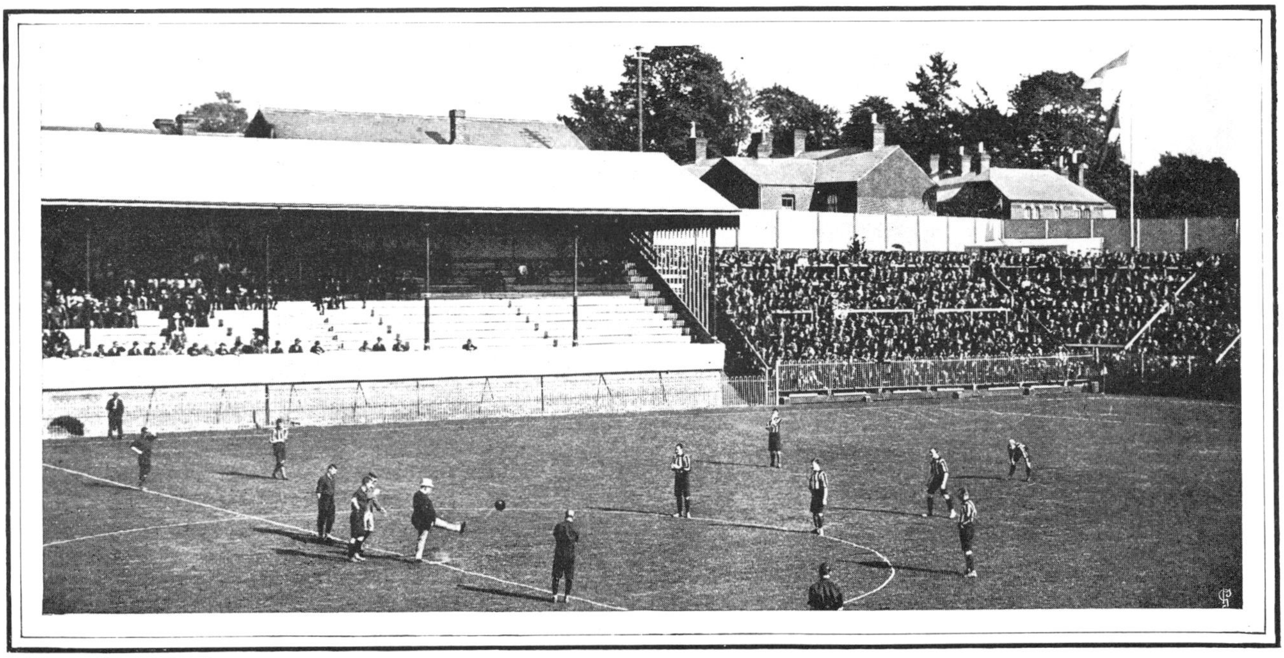

Stuart, Southampton.]
THE DELL, SOUTHAMPTON.
Opening of the ground, September 3, 1898. On this historic occasion G. J. Filling, Esq., Mayor of Southampton, set the ball rolling by kicking-off for Brighton United v. Southampton in the first match on the new ground, perhaps the prettiest in the South.

meeting the strongest combinations in the county; nevertheless, its triumphant career was continued, and it captured the Senior County Cup as well. The team's opponents in the final were the Royal Engineers, holders of the trophy, who had won it twice in succession.

In this season the club also competed for the first time in the Football Association tournament. In the second stage of the qualifying series a great victory was obtained over Reading, the score being seven goals to nil. A technical contravention of the rules, however, nullified this excellent performance.

St. Mary's had drafted into the team for the occasion two soldiers belonging to the 93rd Highlanders, who, it subsequently transpired, were not eligible. Reading lodged a protest and was awarded the match.

About this time the club ceased to be identified with the parish church, and, as a consequence, Canon Wilberforce resigned the presidency. His successor was Dr. Russell Bencraft, J.P. "The Doctor," who held the position for many years, assisted the development of the club most materially, even to the extent of taking a place in the team. Most of the original players, too, had disappeared, and among them G. H. Muir, who also had performed the duties of secretary for several seasons. One of the very few now remaining was G. Carter, and he was, and continued to be until 1894, one of the pillars of the team.

Stuart.]

W. DAWSON,
Trainer.

W. Dawson has a record which few trainers can boast. He has trained six League champion teams, two F. A. Cup Finalists, and a Semi-finalist. Moreover, while under his charge, the following players obtained their International caps: J. Robertson, A. Turner, A. Lee, A. Chadwick, and G. Molyneux, and J. Farrell, T. Barlow, and F. Harrison were picked for the South, and E. Bluff as first reserve against Ireland. In his younger days Dawson was a runner well known in the Midlands, and won many important handicaps.

The season of 1892-3 is memorable in the annals of the club from the fact that the first advance towards professionalism was made. Considerable difficulty had been experienced in obtaining amateurs of ability, while those who joined were not able to spare the time or to incur the pecuniary loss involved by the long journeys which were now being undertaken. It became obvious, therefore, that if St. Mary's was to retain the position it had secured, professional exponents of the game would have to be engaged. The first professional who played for the club was J. Doling, an outside left, and, later, he was joined by J. Dorkin, a Royal Engineer, and J. Angus from Ardwick. A more ambitious programme of matches was arranged; but still the "Saints" pursued their winning career almost without a check.

In the spring of 1893 Stoke paid St. Mary's a visit, and in the Potters' ranks were several men who afterwards became "Saints"—viz., Lachie Thompson, C. Baker, A. Littlehales, and "Chippy" Naughton. Two years later the present trainer, Dawson, was engaged, and with him came J. Turner, Keay, Meston—now completing his eleventh season with Southampton—Farrell, and Naughton, and with the advent of this contingent the team was composed entirely of professionals.

Stuart.]

MR. C. B. FRY.

Mr. C. B. Fry gained most of his football honours during his connection with the "Saints." It was while he was a regular playing member of the team that he received his International cap against Ireland, 1901, and appeared in the F. A. Cup Final. Mr. Fry, whose home is at Westend, a village only a few miles from Southampton, played for the "Saints" in the seasons 1901-2 and 1902-3, and was a conspicuous success. He, Molyneux, and Robinson constituted a wonderfully sound defence; indeed, there was not a superior trio then playing. So well known are Mr. Fry's achievements in other branches of sport that it would be superfluous to recapitulate them here.

At the close of 1894 the club ventured beyond the borders of Hampshire in League warfare. On the formation of the Southern League in 1895, application was made for admission, but was refused. However, as one of the original selections resigned soon after being elected, St. Mary's was asked to fill the vacancy, and consented. The team, which included Barrett (goalkeeper), "Taffy" Hamer (a ponderous punter), Thompson, Dorkin, Offer, Holland, Baker, and Angus—all professionals—did well in the competition, finishing third with twenty points. Millwall was first with twenty-eight, and Luton runners-up with twenty-two points. It was in this season that the "Saints" made their debut in the F. A. competition proper, and in the first round they were fortunate enough to be drawn at home against an English League club. Notts Forest was their opponent, and the Midlanders won easily by 4—1. By a singular coincidence, in the following season, too, the club finished third in the Southern League, and was defeated in the first round proper of the F. A. Cup-ties, Sheffield Wednesday this time administering the knock-out.

Stuart.]

MR. E. ARNFIELD,
Secretary.

No club in the country has a secretary who enjoys more widespread popularity than Mr. Arnfield. He was born at Mellor, Derbyshire, but has been resident at Southampton for fifteen years. He became officially identified with the club in 1894, being elected on the committee, and since that time he has not missed a single meeting in connection with its management. This is a record which is eloquent testimony of his devotion to the club's welfare.

The campaign of 1896-7 was a brilliant one, and St. Mary's inaugurated a record of League successes that no club in the country has equalled. The championship of the Southern League was won without a single reverse being sustained.

This brings us to the most momentous period in the club's history. In July, 1897, the organisation was turned into a limited liability company floated by Dr. E. H. Stancomb (the present chairman of directors), Sir G. A. E. Hussey, Mr. G. Thomas (owner of the Dell, and now a director of Chelsea F. C.), Mr. R. B. Horne, Mr. H. M. Ashton, Mr. W. Newnham, Mr. C. Robson (the well-known Hampshire cricketer), Mr. E. Brown, junr., and Mr. G. S. Payne. The provisional board of directors comprised Dr. Stancomb, Sir George Hussey, and Messrs. G. Thomas, H. M. Ashton, and G. Payne. The late Mr. A. W. McMinn was general secretary, and Mr. Arnfield financial secretary.

The club became the Southampton Football and Athletic Company, Limited, and the headquarters were transferred from the Antelope—which had passed into the possession of builders — to the county cricket ground, whither success followed the team. The Southern League championship was retained, and in the F. A. Cup competition a succession of victories landed the team into the Semi-final.

The draw dictated a meeting with Notts Forest at Sheffield. Each side scored once, and the second contest was played at the Crystal Palace, where, for some inexplicable reason, Southampton players have never been at their best. Mr. John Lewis was referee. It was a bleak, wintry day, and the commencement of play was accompanied by a slight sleet, which grew in density as the game advanced. Eventually the conditions developed into a raging blizzard that forced the teams to suspend "hostilities" in the course of the second half.

However, Mr. Lewis insisted that the players should finish the game, and in the last five minutes the Forest scored twice and won. A protest was lodged by the Southampton Club, but it was not sustained.

Many important developments happened in 1898. The first board of directors elected by the shareholders pursued the progressive policy previously adopted, and engaged a constellation of "stars" in order to maintain the prominent position now held in the football world. The new players included H. Wood (captain for seven seasons), J. W. Robinson, J. T. Robertson (the present manager of Chelsea), A. Hartley, and P. Meehan. And a selection of these, with A. Chadwick, R. Petrie, W. Keay, T. Nicol, and H. Haynes, formed perhaps the most powerful eleven ever possessed by a Southern club up to that time. This team was the first to play on the Dell. The ground. which had just been completed, had been leased from Mr. George Thomas, and it is still the home of the "Saints." For the third time in succession the Southern League shield was won, and, to mark this unprecedented achievement, the executive of the League presented to the club a silk flag, which is "broken" on all important days. It was only after a most exciting struggle that the Southampton team was able to retain the championship.

Southampton's career in the Cup-ties that

Stuart.]
F. HARRISON,
Centre-forward

The most prolific scorer in the South in recent years, F. Harrison, Southampton's centre-forward, is a local production. His great speed and perfect marksmanship enable him to effect some extraordinary feats, and two seasons ago he was the highest scorer in the Southern and Western Leagues. He has improved with experience, and is one of the most dashing individualists now playing.

year was cut short at the third round by Derby County; but a monster attendance softened the effect of the defeat, and the sum taken was £1,255 1s. In 1900, however, Southampton succeeded in getting into the final round of the Cup-ties, only to collapse before Bury, after performing excellently in the preceding stages. The "Saints" were beaten by 4—0.

For five seasons the team alternately won the Southern League championship or figured in the Cup Final. Its second appearance at the Crystal Palace was much more satisfactory, although the irony of Fate willed it that the very side that should have made the first serious attempt to bring the Cup down South should be the one to allow it to be taken North again. In the initial round in 1902 So'ton was opposed to the holders—Tottenham Hotspur—and three games were necessary before a decision was obtained. Then the Hampshire team won at Reading by 2 goals to 1. A magnificent display was given by the "Saints" against Liverpool in the second round, and the Lancastrians were beaten by 4 goals to 1.

The Semi-final, played at Tottenham, saw the blizzard fiasco avenged, and So'ton's opponent in the Final was Sheffield United, which team the "Spurs" had defeated in the ultimate round the previous season. On an oppressively hot day the "Saints" and the "Blades" drew, each scoring once; and on the following Saturday, Southampton failed to accept an easy chance of winning, and was beaten by 2 goals to 1.

It is interesting to note that Mr. Fry was the first amateur to play in the F. A. Cup Final since Topham assisted Wolverhampton Wanderers to win the Cup in 1893. The famous athlete rendered Southampton excellent service for two seasons, and was invariably at his best against Tottenham Hotspur.

Since 1902 Southampton's successes have been almost exclusively confined to the Southern League. But for a complete breakdown last April the club would have secured the championship again, and, had the event taken place, would have won the shield in three consecutive seasons for the second time. As it is, however, the record of the club is a magnificent one, and, it may be safely predicted, will stand for many years.

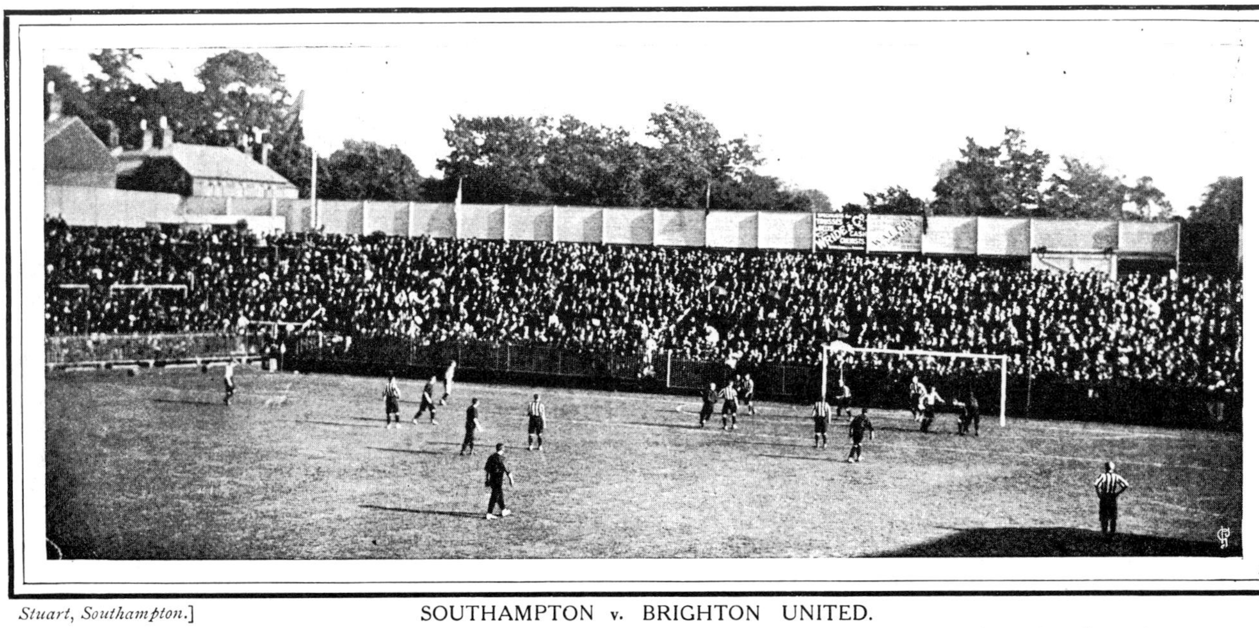

Stuart, Southampton.]
SOUTHAMPTON v. BRIGHTON UNITED.
The first match at the Dell, September 3, 1898. United give Southampton a warm time in front of goal.

SOUTHAMPTON FOOTBALL CLUB—OFFICIALS AND PLAYERS, SEASON 1905-6.

Top Row: J. Warner. W. H. Clark. G. Clawley, Goalkeeper. Burrows. A. Hartshorne.

Second Row: A. Lee. S. Meston. T. Edmonds. G. A. Hedley. A. E Houlker.

F. G. C. Stuart, Southampton.]

Third Row: Dawson, Trainer. Tomlinson. F. Jefferies. J. Soye. H. M. Ashton, Director. Harrison. Sir G. A. E. Hussey, Director. Brown. Harris. F. W. Mouncher.

Bottom Row: E. Arnfield, Secretary. G. Payne, Director. W. Bulpitt, Director. Dr. E. Stancomb, Director. A. A. Wood, Director. C. Robson, Director. W. Jarvis, Director.

THE £ s. d. OF FOOTBALL.

BY WILLIAM McGREGOR.

Powls and May.]
WILLIAM McGREGOR.
"Father" and life member of the Football League.

Football a big business—Men who are lovers of football for its own sake direct the game—The last balance-sheet of the Football Association—Club finance—Gains and losses—Some unique balance-sheets—Travelling expenses and receipts—The abnormally large figures of to-day compared with early gates of famous clubs—The payment of professionals in the old days—Some amusing figures—Room for a model balance-sheet.

FOOTBALL is a big business. The turn-over of some of our clubs is considerably larger than the turn-over of many an important trading concern, and the manifold details incidental to the conduct of a successful club entail a vast amount of labour. Yet the sum spent in salaries is in every case small. This is due, of course, to the fact that directors cannot be remunerated for their services.

The Football Association very rightly insists that the men who run football clubs shall do so as a matter of sentiment. Naturally, it is permissible to pay a secretary, and, if necessary, a clerk, or even a staff of clerks; it would be unreasonable to expect such work to be done voluntarily. But the dictum of the Association that directors shall not be paid is a wise one.

It is wise because it brings into the work the right class of men—that is to say, men who love football for its own sake, and for the pleasing prominence—and this is in no way discreditable to those who like such prominence—which a position on the directorate of a leading club brings in its train. Our football directors are, generally speaking, men who love the game, and they make great sacrifices for the game.

I am not saying that here and there you will not find a man who is a director for the money he indirectly makes out of it; but that cannot always be avoided. I can tell you candidly that the position of football director of a League club carries with it an amount of work which, if a man looked at it through business spectacles, would call for heavy remuneration. But it would be a bad day for football if you divorced the sportsman and substituted for him the guinea-pig, or the man who does not mind doing any work that he is well remunerated for.

Yes, football is a big business. Let us confirm this statement by taking a glance at the last balance-sheet of the Football Association. The sum of £8,018 1s. 1d. was brought forward from the previous season; and the ordinary receipts, such as entrance-fees, subscriptions, sale of professional forms (including a sum of £860 19s. for "complaints, protest fees, and fines"), were £1,553 17s. 1d. The new over-riding percentage on the gate receipts in all Cup-ties produced the handsome sum of £1,633 15s. This is a new but very legitimate source of income. Then the special Cup receipts were: Semi-final at Manchester, £1,467 13s. 6d.; Semi-final at Stoke, £1,798 11s. 5d.; and the replayed Semi-final at Nottingham, £1,443 16s.; making a total yield from the Semi-finals of £4,710 0s. 11d.

The Association's share of the Final Tie at the Crystal Palace was £4,789 19s. 4d., making a gross yield from the later stages of the Cup competition of £9,500 0s. 3d.

The Amateur Cup competition produced £349 9s., and the International matches furnished the following receipts: North v. South at Bristol, £220 4s.; Amateurs v. Professionals of the South, £264 19s. 9d.; England v. Scotland, at the Crystal Palace, £2,436 1s. 6d.; England v. Ireland at Middlesborough, £1,070 15s.; England v. Wales at Liverpool, £610 11s. 6d.; a full total of £4,602 11s. 3d.

The total receipts from all sources were £25,004 18s. 10d.

Now as to the payments. Items paid relating to the previous season absorbed £4,640 16s. 1d. of the balance brought forward. The expenses of meetings were £1,895 2s. 11d.; rents, rates, and taxes ran away with £337 17s. 5d.; salaries accounted for £478 13s.; and a special grant of £676 13s. 2d. was made to the Benevolent Fund, making total ordinary expenses of £4,107 7s. 7d.

The Cup-tie expenses for the Semi-final and Final were £747 9s. 5d., and the expenses of the Amateur Cup competition were £158 3s. 9d.; the expenses of the International games absorbed £1,311 8s. 7d.; and the balance carried forward was £13,915 8s. 7d.

The cash balance of the Football Association in 1905 compared with that of the first year of its existence.

The balance-sheet proper showed assets as follows: By investments, £4,190 9s.; office furniture, £100; cash in bank on deposit account, £3,000; cash in bank on current account, £13,915 8s. 7d. Truly a huge business! And yet that veteran worker, Mr. C. W. Alcock, well remembers the time when, at the end of the first year of the Football Association's existence, the members were proud of the fact that there was a balance in hand of over a sovereign!

The amount divisible among the clubs competing in the Semi-final and Final Ties was £8,024 0s. 7d., and this was apportioned as follows:

THE ENGLISH CUP.			
Aston Villa	£3,362	13s.	5d.
Newcastle United	£2,668	10s.	0d.
Everton	£1,257	14s.	3d.
Sheffield Wednesday	£563	10s.	11d.
THE AMATEUR CUP.			
West Hartlepool	£65	8s.	2d.
Bishop Auckland	£58	2s.	2d.
Clapton	£27	13s.	10d.
Ilford	£20	7s.	10d.

What a difference from the time when West Bromwich Albion performed their stirring English Cup-tie feats! Then the Football Association found it necessary to appropriate practically the whole of the Semi-final and Final gates. One year the Albion had the noble sum of £4 10s. as the reward of their efforts in the penultimate and final stages!

Now let us turn to the question of club finance. In response to a circular I recently issued I was furnished with the balance-sheets of fourteen of the eighteen clubs which were members of the First Division last season, and they offer a very interesting comparison. I must preface my remarks, however, by drawing attention to the fact that to collate the various expenditures has been a task of great difficulty—scarcely two clubs adopt the same way of keeping their accounts.

During the first year of the legalisation of payments to players by the Football Association, seeing that they were interfering with the financial and internal management of football clubs, I suggested that they should exercise a control over the balance-sheets of the organisations, or they could never enforce their own rules. Wherever there is money it is one of the natural laws of our very human system that some of it should leak into channels that cannot be regarded as strictly legitimate ; and football is not free from suspicion any more than any other institution.

TABLE SHOWING PROFIT AND LOSS ACCOUNTS OF LEAGUE CLUBS FOR THE SEASON 1904-5.

Name of Club.	Net Gate.	Season Tickets.	Wages and Transfers.	Training, Travelling, and Hotel Expenses.	Net Profit or Loss.
	£ s. d.	£ s. d.	£ s. d.	£ s. d.	£ s. d.
Aston Villa	14,329 14 2	621 0 6	5,940 5 5	2,499 19 1	1,876 18 3 (p.)
Small Heath	7,209 3 1	559 8 0	4,438 3 6	820 7 9	949 9 6 (p.)
Wolverhampton Wanderers ..	5,450 15 4	380 2 0	3,617 17 1	844 6 5	119 6 8 (p.)
Newcastle United	17,065 0 5	715 10 6	5,118 9 2	*3,265 14 6	5,487 17 4 (p.)
Middlesborough	8,177 14 2	525 10 6	7,730 2 7	1,209 5 8	1,035 2 5 (l.)
Woolwich Arsenal	8,600 14 3	1,000 10 6	5,802 10 0	1,003 19 6	1,674 2 5½(p.)
Everton	14,053 14 4	333 17 0	3,748 9 7	1,780 15 7	5,108 17 7 (p.)
Sheffield United	8,074 13 1	362 9 6	4,039 12 2	570 4 11	†1,473 19 0 (p.)
Sheffield Wednesday	8,893 5 6	203 3 6	4,733 9 0	748 17 3	1,433 8 8 (p.)
Blackburn Rovers	5,743 2 0	380 4 0	5,174 5 0	964 11 9	1,542 13 10 (l.)
Bury	5,181 13 9	330 18 0	4,848 17 6	945 19 1	1,049 18 0 (l.)
Preston North End	6,957 13 11	131 15 0	4,345 17 0	895 9 10	917 5 0 (p.)
Derby County	4,410 17 10	745 1 3	3,998 1 3	930 3 7	1,467 4 7 (l.)
Notts Forest	5,504 0 0	750 0 0	4,645 0 0	455 0 0	545 0 0 (l.)

* Indicates police, gatekeepers, advertising, &c. † Gross profit.

The above table shows at a glance how the various League clubs fared last season in regard to receipts and disbursements, and whether they rejoiced in the possession of a profit or mourned over the grim reality of a loss.

There is food for reflection here. As I previously explained, some of the figures must be treated as approximate amounts, for, owing to the absence of a model balance-sheet, various clubs have included their wages and transfer fees under one head, and in not a few cases training, hotel, and travelling expenses have been lumped together. Naturally such a course goes far to explain differences which at first sight are almost startling.

Aston Villa's first gate at Perry Barr was 5s. 3d.

The astonishing growth of professional football is shown by the above figures, which represent Aston Villa's net gate for the season 1904-5.

Some clubs give only their net profit, and others (such as Aston Villa) publish their gross profit ; and in the latter case I have deducted the amount put down for depreciation to bring the Villa in a line with the other clubs. Though it is impossible to analyse the balance-sheets with perfect accuracy, the above table will be found to afford as careful a comparison as can safely be made.

It will be seen that Middlesborough have made the biggest loss, with Blackburn Rovers and Derby County close behind ; and that Newcastle United and Everton have made the biggest profits, both being well over £5,000. The profits of the two Sheffield clubs are curiously alike, and the losses of Blackburn Rovers and Bury are similar.

Everton, with the second largest gain, have the smallest wage-bill of all the organisations, with the exception of Wolverhampton Wanderers. Derby County have the smallest total gate-money, but the amount put down for season tickets is nearly the highest.

Woolwich Arsenal claim pride of place in this respect, and there is little doubt that if the team had sustained its earlier promise the gate-money would have challenged comparison with the total of any other club. It is not difficult to see how Blackburn Rovers' misfortunes have arisen. Their bill for wages and transfer fees amounts to £700 more than that of the Villa, though they do not retain half the men to be found in the service of the Aston club. The latter, however, do not show their transfer fees on the balance-sheet as the Rovers do.

Newcastle United seem to have made a good thing out of their transfer fees, netting £800 on this account.

Aston Villa paid away £3,415 13s. 1d. to visiting clubs, whereas Everton paid only £936 7s. 6d.; and Newcastle, who shared with the Villa the honour of reaching the Cup Final, paid only £1,620 under this head. The travelling and training expenses of the Villa amounted to £2,000, while those of Small Heath and Wolverhampton Wanderers, who cover much the same distances, were practically only one-third of that sum.

In wages and transfer fees the Villa paid about £1,500 more than Small Heath, and over £2,000 more than Wolverhampton Wanderers. The Aston Villa balance-sheet aroused some criticism in football circles, mainly owing to the large amounts that appear under the heads of "payments to visiting teams" and "travelling and training expenses." The large sum which is set down to the former account is calculated to attract particular attention, but it may be quite capable of explanation. At the same time, I think the Villa would have been better advised if they had entered into more detailed explanation and split up this amount under different heads.

As I see it, if there had been any attempt to make illegal payments they would scarcely be found under this heading, for the very size of the figure was bound to attract criticism. I have just heard of a case in which a club, certainly too poor itself to pay bonuses to its players, was helped by "outside influences." The men did receive certain "considerations," but they did not come out of the club exchequer, though the organisation in question undoubtedly owes its position to these same kindly "outside influences."

One of the stock arguments against the League when it was first instituted was that it would vastly increase travelling expenses, but the fallacy of this notion has been proved. What is the £570 paid by Sheffield United for travelling as compared with the £8,000 they receive as gate-money? In 1888-9, the first season of the League, the gross gate-money of the Villa was £1,999 10s. 8d.; but out of this they paid £368 12s. to other clubs. The amount taken in that season for all their League matches was £1,042 4s. 3d. This amount has been exceeded in the takings of a single League game at Villa Park on several occasions in recent years. Only ten years ago (1894-5) the Villa gate-money amounted to £6,177 4s. 3d., from which had to be deducted the sum of £912 17s. 1d. paid away to other clubs. Players' wages that year were £3,926 10s. 1d.

Wolverhampton Wanderers the year before the League started took only £821 3s. 7d. in gate-money, from which £146 14s. 1d. had to be deducted, being half gates to visiting clubs. "Wages and loss of time" cost £395 19s. 2d. Training, even in those days, cost £122 18s. 9d. For the year 1893-4 the Wanderers' gate-money had increased to £3,356 9s. 3d., and the wages of players to £2,535 14s. Their travelling and hotel expenses then were £392 16s. 3d., and their training account £159 11s. 6d. In the year 1897-8 the Small Heath gate-money amounted to £2,725 8s. 6d., and their wages account was only £1,918 9s. 6d. Training cost £117 8s. 7d., and the travelling and hotel expenses £348 11s. 7d.

The club balance-sheets for the season 1904-5 show that Newcastle United heads the profits' list with a gain of nearly £5,500——

In striking contrast to some of the abnormally large figures mentioned here are the amounts which clubs handled in the early days. Aston Villa's first gate at Wellington Road, Perry Barr, was 5s. 3d. Small Heath's first gate at their original ground in Ladypool Lane in 1876 was 4s. 3d., and their first gate at their present ground at Coventry Road in 1877 was 6s. 8d. When in 1871 the Football Association appealed for funds for a challenge cup, Queen's Park's income was £6 per annum, and yet they cheerfully voted a guinea towards the trophy.

The gate at the first Birmingham Cup Final in 1877 at Bristol Road, Birmingham, the ground of the Calthorpe Club, was £15, 2,000 people being present. Bury's first gate (with Wigan) was £1 16s. 7d., but an exhibition match played prior to this just to give the club a send-off, in which the teams were Accrington and Church, realised £11 9s. 0½d.

Everton's first big match was a local Cup-tie with a neighbouring club—Bootle. This produced £39, Everton's share being £19 11s. 6d. One of Small Heath's first Birmingham Cup-ties at Coventry Road was with a local club—the Calthorpe. The gate-money amounted to £2 18s. 2d., and Small Heath's share of a Cup-tie at Brownhills was 10½d.!

The Albion and Small Heath played an English Cup Semi-final at Aston Lower Grounds in the early eighties, and each club obtained £4 5s., the Association taking the rest. Sheffield Wednesday played an English Cup-tie with the Crusaders at Leyton, when the gate was £15, and after waiting many months Sheffield Wednesday received a cheque for 8s. 4d.; and even then there was some dispute over the signature on the cheque! Wednesday also played Long Eaton Rangers in a Cup-tie. Their share of the gate was £4 15s., and the Long Eaton secretary gravely handed the Wednesday official 1,140 pennies. These the Wednesday officials declined to be burdened with, so finally silver was substituted. Stoke paid their first batch of professionals — Birch, Montford, Tom Clare, G. Shutt, E. Smith, A. Edge, and B. Rhodes—half-a-crown each, and the famous W. Rowley also commenced with the Pottery club at that wage. There was extraordinary excitement at Stoke when Preston North End made their first appearance there in 1885, £114 12s. 3d. being taken at the gate. Stoke's previous gates that season had been: Walsall Swifts, £21 13s.; Third Lanark, £20 6s. 6d.; Derby County, £19 7s.; Bolton Wanderers, £26 7s.; Accrington, £14; Crewe Alexandra (English Cup-tie), £26 14s. 3d.; and Blackburn Rovers, £23 14s. 6d.

West Bromwich Albion's first gate was 30s., and when they won the English Cup for the first time the wage-list was £10 per week. Similar figures to these could be given in connection with most of the leading clubs. Bloomer's first wage with Derby County was 7s. 6d. weekly.

Finally, let me say that the Football Association would do well to draw up a model balance-sheet, and make the clubs adhere to it, or there will be room for all kinds of abuses. Either the Association must ignore all financial relations between club and player, or they must take a firm stand, and see that their rules are carried out. There ought to be no half measures, or any possibility of it being said, as has been said, that "it's your own fault if you are not able to make out your accounts so that the Association can't tell what you've been doing." Some sympathy can be extended to club managers, knowing how difficult it is to keep within the strict letter of the law. To say that the rules of the Football Association are strictly observed would be sufficient to cause many faces to wear a wide smile.

But I do not believe that the rules are so widely broken as some people would have you believe. I know one club, and it is a club which is very wealthy, and it is a club which is currently accused of breaking the rules of the Association in regard to maximum wages and bonuses, yet some years ago that club parted with three of the finest footballers that ever lived, simply because it would not continue to pay them the exorbitant prices they had received. The club did moderately for a season, and it took advantage of the fact that it was not going at full pressure for the League championship to overhaul its finances.

Whilst the Middlesborough Club made a dead loss of over £1,000, the sum they paid for the transfer of Common from Sunderland.

Up to that time it had never troubled about its payment to professionals.

Then it decided to come into line with the bulk of the clubs, and pay no more wages such as £6 10s. per week. Mind you, this was before the day of the maximum wage rule. I have no doubt that isolated players are getting more than the maximum wage, although, candidly, I could not prove that. I have a shrewd suspicion that it is so; but there is every disposition to impute evil in this world, and, personally, I am rather of the opinion that clubs do their best to conform to the rules instead of wilfully seeking to set them at defiance.

BLACKBURN ROVERS F. C.

Winners of the Football Association Cup, 1883-4, 1884-5, 1885-6, 1889-90, 1890-1. Finalists, 1881-2.

The Blackburn Rovers' magnificent football record—Early history—Great fights for the Football Association Cup—J. H. Forrest's fine record—Moderate displays in the League—Some great players who have worn the blue-and-white—MacIntyre and "Jimmy" Brown—International players—Future hopes.

Colours: Blue and white quarters, white knickers.

Ground: Ewood Park, Blackburn.

Hawthorn.]
R. O. EVANS,
Goalkeeper and Captain
The popular Blackburn Rovers' goalkeeper learnt his football in Wales, and did many brilliant things when playing for Wrexham. He stands 5ft. 10½in. in height, and weighs 11st. 10lb. His fine goalkeeping received due recognition by the authorities when he received his International cap for Wales.

THE town of Blackburn holds a unique position in the football world, for it is the only one in the provinces in which the Football Association Challenge Cup has reposed—after being won—on six occasions. It is with the history of Blackburn Rovers that we are dealing, but in referring to the living organisation one cannot omit mention of the dead—in other words, the defunct Olympic Club, which had the great honour of first wresting the trophy from London. This was in the season 1882-3, and the importance of the achievement is increased when it is stated that the metropolis never saw the Cup again until eighteen years had elapsed, when Tottenham Hotspur beat Sheffield United in a re-play at Bolton. A season prior to the Olympic's success, however, the Rovers had been at the Oval, and had failed against the Old Etonians—much to the surprise of Blackburn people, who were cocksure of victory. But once the ice had been broken by the Olympic, the Rovers sailed in and made for themselves a name which will live as long as football exists. They mastered Queen's Park two years in succession, conquered West Bromwich Albion the season after, and thus equalled the feat of the Wanderers in 1876, 1877, and 1878. Then they had a rest, but in 1890 they captured the Cup again, and as they repeated the performance a year later, they now hold the honour of having their name inscribed five times on the most valued prize in the game.

The history of this famous organisation dates back to November 5, 1875, and, according to the small minutes' book which is still in existence, the first resolution was: "That this club be called The Blackburn Rovers."

Hawthorn, Blackburn.]
EWOOD PARK, THE HOME OF THE BLACKBURN ROVERS.
This famous enclosure has the reputation of possessing one of the finest playing pitches in the First Division of the League.

Then follows: "That the Brookhouse Ground be applied for"; "That the rules be those of the Football Association." At a later date are to be found: "That the colours be white jersey, blue-and-white skull cap, trousers optional"; and, later still: "That a Maltese cross be worn on the left breast." The prime movers in the foundation of the club were Mr. John Lewis, who has this season (1905) retired from active service as a First League referee, and Mr. Arthur Constantine, both of whom were fresh from school, and full of enthusiasm. It was a modest beginning, and as the enthusiasts had no idea of the future that was in store, no complete records were kept for the first few seasons. It was in 1879-80 that the "Blue-and-Whites," to give them their present-day popular title, tried their hands as Cup fighters, but after beating Tyne at home by 5 goals to 2, and Darwen by 3 goals to 1, they came a big cropper at Nottingham, the Forest beating them by 6 goals to 0. A year later they were knocked out in the second round by Sheffield Wednesday, and it is interesting to note in this connection that, although the two clubs met several times afterwards in the competition, the Sheffielders never triumphed until 1904-5. In 1881-2 the Rovers reached the Final, and, before they were beaten by the Old Etonians, they thrashed Park Road, a well-known Blackburn club, by 9 to 1, Bolton Wanderers by 6 to 2, Darwen by 5 to 1, Wednesbury Old Athletic by 3 to 1, and Sheffield Wednesday, after a drawn game—0 to 0—by 5 goals to 1. The following season, the one in which Olympic won the Cup, they made merry at the expense of Blackpool by 11 goals to 1, and were then given their congé by Darwen by the only goal of the match. In connection with their defeat in the Final by the Old Etonians, it is no exaggeration to say that Blackburn was thoroughly dumbfounded when the result became known. It is said that the parent of one player lost in wagers a row of houses; but

R. B. MIDDLETON,
The Blackburn Secretary.
A hard-working, tactful, and zealous official who has the welfare of his club at heart.

Hawthorn.]
W. BRADSHAW,
Left half-back.
A fearless tackler and clever exponent of the Association game.

while the accuracy of that statement cannot be vouched for, it shows what the opinion was in the town of the chances of the Rovers.

Sobered by this defeat, the players were not quite so sure in 1884-5 when they were called upon to meet Queen's Park. In fact, the boot was on the other leg. And the Scottish gentlemen had every reason for their optimism, seeing they had no fewer than ten Internationals in their ranks. The Rovers' goals were scored by the two "Jimmys," Brown and Forrest, and Allen obtained that of Queen's Park. Their second success in 1884-5 was obtained at the expense of Queen's Park by 2 goals to 0, and again their goal scorers were Brown and Forrest. This was the last appearance of Queen's Park as finalists, and in 1885-6 the Rovers' progress is shown as follows: Clitheroe by 2 to 0, Oswaldtwistle by 1 to 0, Staveley by 7 to 1, Brentwood by 3 to 1, London Swifts by 2 to 1, and West Bromwich, after a drawn game at the Oval—0 to 0—by 2 to 0 at Derby, the last being the first time a Final was ever fought out of London.

Hawthorn.]
R. CROMPTON,
Right full-back.
The famous Blackburn Rovers' back was born at Blackburn in 1879. He gained his first experience with Blackburn Trinity. Joined the Rovers' Reserves in 1896, and was promoted to a position in the first team soon afterwards. Is a big, fine, resolute back, of whom Blackburn is deservedly proud. Stands 5ft. 10½in. in height, and weighs 13st.

The next Cup-tie triumph of the Rovers was in 1889-90, and their victory was achieved at the expense of Sheffield Wednesday by 6 goals to 1, a score that continued a record until 1903, when Bury swamped Derby County by 6 goals to 0. In their successful combination there were only two players who appeared in the previous Final in 1886, and they were Nat Walton and Forrest. The same couple also figured in the Rovers' Final Tie victory against Notts County in 1890-1, and Forrest, who had thus played in five Finals, shared with Lord Kinnaird and Mr. Wollaston, of the Wanderers, the distinction of holding a quintette of National Cup medals. For this unique feat the Rovers were presented by the Football Association with a silver shield, on which is inscribed: "Presented by the Football Association in commemoration of their winning the Challenge Cup three times in succession." Then follows particulars of the

Hawthorn.]
A. WHITTAKER,
Outside-right.
Arnold Whittaker is a local production, for he was born at Blackburn in 1880. He stands 5ft. 5½in., and weighs 10st. Has played for Blackburn, Queen's Park, and Accrington Stanley. He joined the Rovers in 1899.

J. Frankland, Blackburn.]
BLACKBURN ROVERS—ONE OF THE MOST FAMOUS ELEVENS—1883-4.
EAST LANCASHIRE CHARITY CUP. ENGLISH CUP. LANCASHIRE SENIOR CUP.
Standing: J. M. LOFTHOUSE. H. MACINTYRE. J. BEVERLEY. H. ARTHUR. F. SUTER. J. H. FORREST. R. BIRTWISTLE.
Sitting: J. DOUGLAS. J. E. SOURBUTTS. J. BROWN. G. AVERY. J. HARGREAVES.

victories. This shield was, until his death, the honoured possession of Dr. G. S. Morley (brother of Mr. John Morley, M.P.), who was one of the most enthusiastic supporters of the club for over a quarter of a century, and for many years the president. Twice afterwards the Rovers reached the Semi-final, and on each occasion they were thrown out by the teams which proved the ultimate winners. In latter years they have performed only indifferently, and the furthest stage to which they have advanced was the third round two seasons ago.

As far as the League is concerned, the Rovers have never made much headway; in fact, they were only saved from relegation to the Second Division in 1898-9 by the number of clubs being increased from sixteen to eighteen. They joined the League on its formation, and in the second season were third to Preston North End and Everton. This is the highest position they have ever occupied, and their next best season in point of merit was in 1901-2, when they were fourth. In this season they were running well for the championship up to March, when they were beaten at home by the ultimate leaders — Sunderland. The Lancashire Senior Cup has been won eight times, and the East Lancashire Charity Cup on innumerable occasions, but these are rather barren honours in these days when the two competitions are of minor importance as compared with the National

THE SHIELD PRESENTED TO BLACKBURN ROVERS BY THE FOOTBALL ASSOCIATION.

The inscription on the shield reads as follows: "Blackburn Rovers' Football Club, 1886. Presented by the Football Association in commemoration of their winning the Challenge Cup three years in succession—viz., 1884-5-6. 1884: At Kennington Oval, beat Queen's Park, Glasgow, 2 goals to 1. 1885: At Kennington Oval, beat Queen's Park, Glasgow, 2 goals to 0. 1886: April 3, at Kennington Oval, drew West Bromwich Albion, no goals; April 10, at Derby, beat West Bromwich, 2 to 0."

Cup competition and the League. Of the many great players who have worn the blue-and-white colours opinions, of course, differ as to which was the greatest. Good judges, however, are pretty well agreed in according the place of honour to Hugh MacIntyre, whose death occurred only a few months ago in a London hospital, and "Jimmy" Brown, both of whom were without equals in their respective positions at half-back and centre-forward.

In all, the Rovers have furnished 19 English International players, who have figured in 66 games. Their names are: H. Arthur, J. Beverley, F. Blackburn, J. Brown, R. Crompton, J. Forrest, D. H. Greenwood, J. Hargreaves, A. E. Houlker, J. Lofthouse, J. Southworth, T. Booth, F. Hargreaves, W. J. Townley, S. Wolstenholme, J. Barton, H. Chippendale, Nat Walton, and J. Whitehead. In addition, Tom Brandon and J. Forbes have played for Scotland, and R. O. Evans, the present goalkeeper, for Wales.

Ewood Park, the home of the Rovers' Club, was taken over in 1890, and bought for £2,500 in 1893-4. The playing pitch is one of the finest in the First Division. A fine covered stand was erected last season, and what is now needed is another with better-class seating accommodation. For the sake of the club's glorious record in the past, it is to be hoped that the name of Blackburn Rovers will ever be found in first-class football.

Hawthorn Blackburn.]

BLACKBURN ROVERS—THE TEAM FOR 1905-6.

Top Row: SMITH. MACGILL. CAMERON. EVANS, Captain. MCIVER.

Middle Row: R. B. MIDDLETON, Secretary. WOLSTENHOLME. WILSON. CROMPTON. ROBERTSON. BIRCHALL. PENTLAIND. R. HOLMES, Trainer.

Bottom Row: MOIR. WHITTAKER. W. BRADSHAW. DAVIES. BOWMAN. CHADWICK. MCCLURE.

THE MAKING OF A PLAYER.

PART III.—THE FULL-BACK GAME.

By HOWARD SPENCER (Aston Villa's Captain).

The responsibility of the full-back position—Every man must play the type of game that suits him best—A great change in method during the last twenty years—The old style and the new compared—Combination of forwards the great danger that has to be feared—The huge kick a mistake—The essential qualifications for the full-back position—Some points to study—Accurate passing and pace an absolute necessity in the game—Keep the ball in play as much as possible—And, above all, never allow yourself to get flurried—A last word on the value of straightforward, honest, and honourable football.

Draycott]
HOWARD SPENCER,
the Villa's famous captain and English International. The portrait was taken some years ago.

THE full-back in an Association football team has a responsible office. He is the individual who has to share with the goalkeeper the responsibility of every lost goal. I don't know why it is, but the crowd never seem to blame the half-back, who, by blundering work, gives away his side and is the direct cause of a goal being scored. No; the blame is invariably reserved for the back or the goalkeeper, usually (I was almost about to add "I am glad to say") the custodian being the scapegoat. Of course, there are men round the ropes who can discriminate, and put the blame upon the proper shoulders, but the crowd usually blame the man who was the last to be passed. This is natural; they do not follow the play so closely as the men engaged in the game do; they see that a goal has been scored, and they want to know why the back, or the goalkeeper, or both, did not arrest the course of the ball. And yet the fault may have been committed by a half, or even by a forward. Every back that ever played has lost goals for his side. It is an old saying that a man who never makes a mistake never makes anything, and that saying is profoundly true as applied to football. All that a man can try to do is to let his side down as seldom as he can. He cannot hope to be immaculate.

It is hard to define the duties of each type of footballer one finds in a team. There is no royal road to success. One man does best by the adoption of tactics which another would be inclined to condemn, and would not, at any rate, dream of adopting; and yet the one who favours those tactics and he who objects to their utilisation may both be first-rate players.

Every man must play the kind of game which suits him best, but one can safely say that a full-back should experiment very little. He cannot afford to take the risks which a half is often justified in taking. The half has a kind of roving commission; he is there to assist the forwards as well as the backs; he is there to help both in attack and defence. He is a chartered libertine compared with a full-back, who should be, above all things, orthodox. The latter must not play a speculative kind of game. When he is beaten, the defence of his side has all but given out, for the goalkeeper is at once the strongest and the most vulnerable member of the defence. A goalkeeper may stop anything; anything may beat him. Therefore, there is an immense responsibility upon the full-back. The faults of a half may be covered up, but who is going to repair the errors of the full-back? There is no time in which to repair them, unless, indeed, the goalkeeper comes to the rescue. Therefore, it follows that the full-back is bound to take as few risks as possible. He may, if the coast is absolutely clear, take the ball up the field, and earn the cheers of the crowd, but that is a feat which requires to be executed warily. One slip, and it may be fatal. It is not the first duty of a full-back to excel in offensive tactics. He is there to illustrate the art of defence. If he keeps his goal intact, then he has done his share. Of course, there are refinements of back play which have to be studied, but the man who makes the safety of his goal his first thought will not go far wrong.

There has necessarily been a great change in the methods of back play during the last twenty years. Forwards have changed their methods, and, naturally, defenders have had to shape their play accordingly. I often hear people who desire to be unduly critical say: "You backs have a much easier time than the backs of old used to have. You have not to meet forwards of the class of E. C. Bambridge, W. N. Cobbold, Harry Cursham, Archie Hunter, or W. H. Mosforth; a nice dance you would have been led if you had had to face those men." Far be it from my desire to say anything slighting concerning either the great forwards or the great backs of old. There have been brilliant defenders and brilliant forwards in all ages, and I dare say the balance of ability between the two parties has been well preserved. I do not believe in

Bowden Bros.]
THE "SPURS" v MILLWALL
A rare tussle in front of the Millwall goal. The Millwall defence is hard put to it to repel the "Spurs'" attack.

thinking too highly of one's own generation, but I am also averse to speaking deprecatingly of them. Depend upon it that there are forwards playing to day who would have led the great backs of old a dance, and I also believe that there are backs to-day who would make a good show against the best forwards of by-gone ages. There are compensations in everything. Now I may say that I would not mind being opposed to the most brilliant forward that ever lived, if he were playing the game which, according to my reading and the reminiscences of others, the forwards of old played. The difficulty to-day is the perfection of the combination. If a full-back goes for a forward, and that forward elects to stick to the ball, you may depend upon it that that back thinks that he has a reasonable chance of wrestling that ball from him. I should think that I had a good chance of beating a man, and I am quite sure that I have no desire to over-rate my own powers. At the worst, it is simply a duel between the two men; the back pits his skill against the skill of the forward, and who shall say that the back will not come off victorious as often as the forward? Speaking quite impersonally, I should say that a high-class back operating against a clever but selfish forward would be disposed to think that fortune had delivered his adversary into his hand.

You see, when an old-time back went to tackle an old-time forward the back had a fairly correct idea of what the forward's methods would be. Now that is a great initial advantage. He had a shrewd idea that the ball would remain in possession of the forward as long as his ability enabled him to keep it. The back knew that he had to go for that man, and him only. Therefore, the back must have gone for him with a certain sense of self-confidence. And that feeling of self-confidence is essential if a man is to make a good full-back. It is useless for a man to tackle another in any but a self-confident way. Each man should know his own ability, and act up to that knowledge. There is a wide difference between self-confidence and self-conceit. The self-confident man is the man who regularly does himself justice; the self-conceited man—well, anything adverse may befall him at any time. But the man who is not self-confident is as a rule nervous, and nervous men are of little service on crucial occasions. That is what I mean by self-confidence; a reasonable and rational belief in one's own abilities, and a reasonable belief in the abilities of others.

You have this position then: That a self-confident full-back went to the clever forward knowing that it would merely be a trial of skill and strength between them. There was nothing to complicate the position. But what happens in this, the era of combination, when a full-back goes for a forward? Why, just as he is about to tackle the man with the ball he finds that it has gone elsewhere. There has been a dextrous pass to a waiting colleague; and the full-back realises that he must look for success elsewhere. Now I do contend, in all fairness to present day full-backs, that the backs of old rarely had that to contend with; at any rate, not to the extent that we have to contend with it to-day. The difficulties which the perfecting of the art of combination present more than counterbalance any falling off in the ability of forwards of the present day as compared with the heroes of the past. Nowadays a back is often in a quandary. The man who has the ball is threatening danger, but it does not follow that if you go to tackle him you will at least arrest the attack for a time. You may get to the man, but that does not mean that you will get to the ball. The man is there, and you may put him out of action, so to speak, but that does not mean that you have obtained possession of the ball. The full-back does not fear one man so much as two; a pair of wing men who know each other's movements are far more difficult to fool than the most expert forward that ever set his toe to a ball. Combination will beat the back, while individual trickery fails as often as not.

Russell and Sons.]

ENGLAND v. SCOTLAND.

APRIL 1, 1905, AT THE CRYSTAL PALACE

Herbert Smith, the amateur International and famous Reading captain and left full-back, cleverly secures the ball, and, wheeling, sends it mid-field. He is a clever and brilliant exponent of full-back play.

There were some magnificent backs in the old times, and it would not become me to say anything which would belittle their fame. I have no intention of doing so, but I am naturally anxious to say all I can in favour of the present generation. I have heard old players speak of the Hon. Edward Lyttelton, E. Field, C. J. S. King, and P. J. De Paravacini, and, later still, of Walter Arnott, Nicholas Ross, Dan Doyle, and Tom Brandon. Experts seem to agree that Nicholas Ross and Walter Arnott were the two finest backs that ever lived; and I am not going to question their judgment. Some of the old backs, I understand, kicked a tremendous length, but that, of course, must not be taken as representing the highest capacity of a back. It is not often that you want to kick so heavily. The great point is not to kick beyond the sphere of influence in which your forwards are operating, so that I sometimes get it into my head that possibly some of these old backs may have kicked further than was judicious. I only suggest this as a possibility, and as, in a sense, a plea on behalf of the men of the present day, none of whom, so far as I know, are famed for their prodigious kicking. Of course, the game has changed considerably; and I am one who objects to the institution of comparisons between

Bowden Bros.]

FULHAM v. BRENTFORD AT GRIFFIN PARK.

The Fulham attack led by Wardrope and Fraser, is rudely repelled by Riley, Brentford's right full-back. The match was played on October 7, 1905.

players of different epochs. It is illogical to expect a back to play the same game to-day that a full-back was accustomed to play twenty-five years ago. Each man adapts himself to the requirements of the time; his style is, in a sense, forced upon him. Environment always tells, and what is true in other walks of life is true of football. Running off a little, I never could understand why people should seem to imagine that footballers must be exceptions to all rules. They are only mortal men, and they have their weaknesses and their traditions, and a man is made by his traditions and his environment. When I hear of men being huge kickers, I put it to myself as to how many times in a match a back wants to make a really huge kick. There is nothing like having the capacity to make huge kicks—all backs desire to have that capacity—but judicious kicking is the great thing a full-back has to consider. The man who puts the ball further than his forwards is merely giving a back on the other side a chance of doing something better than he himself has done.

To wind up this phase of the discourse, I think I would rather have played football as a full-back against the famous old forward lines of years gone by than I would play against the present generation. They made a better mark for the full-back than the elusive and slippery gentlemen of the present generation make. Quick exchanges among wing men baffle a back far more than talented individual dribbles, and most puzzling of all is the long-passing game, such as Aston Villa played so perfectly in last year's English Cup Final. I will tell you why that style of game is so dangerous and so little relished by full-backs on the opposing side. When a man comes dribbling through, the ball, if it comes to you at all, comes to you straight, whereas in the long-passing game the ball comes swerving across with a lot of spin on it, and as often as not comes to the full-back's toe either at right-angles or at an extremely awkward angle. As any novice could tell you, that is the most difficult kind of ball to meet, and I feel glad as a defender that we did not have the same class of work to do that afternoon as fell to the lot of Newcastle United. If we had had that work, it is just possible that we might not have done it any better than they did.

Now, what are the essentials of a full-back? A typical full-back should be a well-built fellow, and if he is blessed with substance and weight so much the better. Naturally, a full-back does not require more poundage than his frame and muscular development will carry effectively, but so long as the weight he has is what I may call, to use a phrase of my own, "good weight," so much the better. Little men have had their places in football—little men are shining in football to-day—but there are not many football managers who, given the choice between two backs of equal ability, one weighing 11st. 5lb. and the other 12st. 5lb., would not plump for the heavier man. This is natural enough; however clever a light back may be, he must occasionally be brushed aside, and that may often mean disaster for his side. The crowd dearly love to see a little man shine against big opponents, but good little men have been in the minority, and the position is aptly expressed in the old adage in sport that "a good big one is better than a good little one." The ideal back is a good, solid, 12st. man, with his strength well distributed, but lying for choice in the loins and thighs.

Bowden Bros.]
WOOLWICH ARSENAL v. LIVERPOOL AT PLUMSTEAD, SEPTEMBER 2, 1905.
If a forward is allowed to break through the defence the position is well nigh hopeless. Yet on this occasion Parkinson, of Liverpool, perhaps the fastest forward playing League football, fell at the critical moment as he was about to net the ball. The result was a fractured wrist, which kept the gallant fellow out of the field a number of weeks. The ball went just wide of the post, and Ashcroft is seen watching its course with some concern. Woolwich won the match by 3 goals to 1.

Then a full-back should be a strong kicker, and, above all, he should be a reliable kicker. He must learn to discriminate in his kicking, so that he never sends the ball to the opposing full-back. While a full-back does not have to concern himself with the feeding of his forwards to the same extent that a half-back does, it follows that the man who provides the men in front of him with abundant opportunities of attacking is of far more service than the back whose work ends when he has pulled the other side up. The evil of injudicious kicking is seen when a team are playing against a strong wind. To kick to the opposing full-back then is a criminal offence. Accurate kicking is what is wanted, and that is the first thing for a back to master. When he can use either foot accurately as the ball comes to him simply, then he will gradually begin to improve when he is in a tight corner. The resourceful back who can clear from amid a host of opponents, and get rid of the ball without having his kick charged down, is a great help to his side. It is one thing to kick well when you have plenty of room to move about in and are in no way pressed, but it is a very different matter to get rid of the ball judiciously when the kick may itself become a source of danger to your side.

When all is plain sailing, it is well for the full-back to send the ball out to the wing, as the men there have a greater chance of making ground than those who operate in the centre. The wing men are generally fleeter than those who occupy inside positions, and experience shows that when ground is made rapidly it is usually made on the wing rather than in the centre. But, of course, this advice must not be acted on blindly. It must be accepted with certain reservations. The one plan which will never be adversely criticised is to give the ball to the man who is best placed to receive it, no matter what his position in the team may be. Every back should learn to keep the ball down. There is nothing in high kicking. A ball which goes high does not travel. When your side are under pressure and the wind is against you, there is nothing which gets you into so much trouble as a soaring ball. It must necessarily return to bother you, and sometimes it will return without even a kick on the part of your opponents. Backs should cultivate a hard, low, volleying kick, as nothing is so calculated to get your side out of trouble, and no kind of kick is less calculated to bring back an awkward return.

A back who is well up in the finesse of the game will always look out for a chance of getting the ball well down to his own forwards when his own side are being pressed. I have learned from experience that the best time to catch a side napping is not when the full-back and goalkeeper are expectant and are prepared for any kind of emergency. At that time it usually takes a clever and well-sustained attack to wrest a goal from them. But when their side have been attacking for a time, and the backs have ventured up the field, then is the opportunity for the really skilful defender on the other side to get in a kick which may go far to affect the destiny of the game. You put the ball nicely to your centre-forward, who may be lying well up but just on-side, and in an instant he rushes rather than dribbles through, and the opposing defence is beaten. You often see what I call a "snap" goal scored after a side have been steadily overplayed for a considerable time. Of course, the cry goes up that the side which have been attacking have had "hard lines." But sometimes there is more method in this sudden attack than people imagine. At any rate, that is the time to take the back and goalkeeper at a disadvantage. They have their moments of carelessness, and the knowledge that the other side have, up to this point, had to bear the brunt of the attack, is not infrequently the cause of their undoing.

A full-back has no need to bother his head about dribbling, but he should be a perfect master of the art of giving an accurate pass. He has the option of passing to his halves or to his forwards, and often a neat pass to a half-back only a few yards away is infinitely better than a lungeous kick which may send the ball anywhere, the kicker knows not whither. Indeed, there are times when a well-judged pass is practically the only safe method of a back getting himself and his side out of a difficulty. A thorough understanding between all the various divisions of a football team is essential if the defence is to be of a high order. Let that proper understanding be in existence, and the work of each section is materially lightened. Let it be absent, and certain men may get far more work than they can cope with. The full-back should have a thorough understanding with the half-back on his side of the field, and also with the centre-half, as to the plan of campaign to be adopted in various emergencies. It is a great help to a full-back to know that the half-back in front of him will at least check the advance of the forward line to a certain extent. I can recall no half-back who did this better than the ex-Aston Villa right half, John Reynolds. He was not a fast man, but he had a peculiar knack of always doing something which meant a delay in the attack of the other side. He might or might not get the ball, but he always did something which placed you at a better advantage than you were before he interfered with the aggressive movement. He had a wonderful head; there was no trick in football that he did not thoroughly understand.

IN MEMORIAM.

Albert Wilkes.]
THE VILLA CORNER AT WITTON CEMETERY.
The grave of the famous Villa forward, Archie Hunter.

Pace is an invaluable quality for a full-back to possess—in fact, a man must be abnormally clever if he is to atone for lack of speed. There have been good full-backs who were not fast, but those who recall the play of Nicholas Ross and W. J. Oakley will appreciate what a great factor speed is in the making of an eminent back. The full-back who can sprint well, or who is at least exceptionally fast with the ball, can afford to make mistakes. The slow man cannot afford to be at fault. Therefore, it follows that the fast man can attempt that which the slow back dare not run the risk of attempting. Every full-back should be able to use either foot with equal facility.

There has never in all football been a finer instance of adaptability than was presented by the play of an old colleague of mine, James Crabtree. Crabtree could play in any position on the football field, and it mattered nothing to him whether he played left or right back. There are not many Crabtrees, however, but every full-back should make a point of learning to use both feet. The one-footed back often loses his side a goal. Then, again, a back should always be careful, while covering his goalkeeper thoroughly, to leave sufficient room in which the custodian may operate freely. No goalkeeper can do himself justice who is hampered by a back getting in his way. There should always be a complete understanding between the backs and also between the goalkeeper and the backs. A good club pair would often be more serviceable in an International team than two brilliant performers who knew nothing of each other's methods. It should be the aim of a full-back to keep the ball in play as much as possible. There are times when you are forced to kick out, but when that is so, you need not irritate the crowd by kicking over the stand. It is always better to keep the ball in if you can, but, naturally, it is better to put it out than to get a certain return from a full-back on the other side. I always like to see a back who can kick the ball along the touch-line to the outside wing man without actually putting it out of play.

Then a man who can head well is invaluable. I am told that Crabtree's head saved England repeatedly in that International which was played in a gale of wind at Villa Park. Coolness is a quality which every back should study to obtain. The back who is flurried will make a hash of matters. The man who can head out well is invaluable in saving corner kicks. But you should learn to play with your head in a dual sense. Above all, believe me, there is nothing to be gained by unfair play. I have always believed that it is possible to get the best results by straightforward, honest, and honourable football. Even supposing that once in a way you do, by a little mean trick, gain an advantage, surely the time comes when you attempt something illegal, and so give away a penalty which will probably carry with it a goal.

Wilkes, West Bromwich.]
THE VILLA CORNER AT WITTON CEMETERY.
The grave of Eli Davis, one of the men who helped to make Aston Villa's undying fame.

F. G. O. Stuart, Southampton.]

THE HOME OF THE SOUTHAMPTON FOOTBALL CLUB.

The Dell was opened on September 3, 1898, when Southampton played Brighton United. The beauty of this ideal playing enclosure can be fully realised from the above excellent photograph.

Bowden Bros.]

THE CHELSEA ELEVEN IN THE NORTHERN GOAL AT STAMFORD BRIDGE.

WATSON. MCROBERTS. KEY. WINDRIDGE. MACKIE. FOULKE, Captain. COPELAND. J. T. ROBERTSON. MCEWAN. MORAN. KIRWAN.

THE CHELSEA FOOTBALL CLUB.

By J. T. ROBERTSON (Manager, and Famous Scottish International).

The newest London club and its sudden rise to fame—How the Chelsea football club was launched—Its strong financial position—The fine new grand stand—Chelsea the biggest ground in London—All about the members of the team and their past triumphs—Some amusing applications from would-be professionals—Determined to succeed.

Colours : Light-Blue and White. *Ground : Stamford Bridge, Fulham Road.*

IN the whole long history of football no club has rushed into fame with such sensational suddenness as Chelsea.

In 1904 they did not exist, now everyone interested in the game has heard of their splendid ground, their fine eleven, and the great chance the club has of getting into the League proper at the first time of asking.

Chelsea have come in on a huge tidal wave of popularity. The game is booming as it never boomed before. London is now as enthusiastic as Birmingham, Manchester, Liverpool, or Glasgow, and it is the opinion of all the experts that the greatest of all cities will soon be the headquarters of the greatest of all winter games. I may be biassed, but I believe, and a large number of men who have had a vast experience of the game think with me, that Chelsea is destined to be the leading club of the metropolis.

How this great football enterprise came to be launched is an interesting story. Some eight years ago, Mr. H. A. Mears, who is a son of the late Mr. Joseph Mears, the well-known contractor, conceived the idea of turning the Stamford Bridge Athletic Ground into a football arena. He and his brother, Mr. J. T. Mears, have played football all their lives, and being as fond of sport as they were wealthy, determined to buy the piece of ground that seemed to them so eminently suited for their purpose. It was more centrally situated than any other existing ground, and it was large enough, when treated by a skilled architect, to hold the biggest crowd the most ambitious club-manager ever dreamt of. Difficulties had to be overcome. A Mr. Stunt was the freeholder of the property, and a clause in the lease laid down that the London Athletic Club should be leaseholders until two years after the death of this gentleman. He lived until 1902, which gave the Athletic Club a long run. Directly it was possible, Mr. Mears bought the ground, having some four years previously secured the adjoining property. The Chelsea Club, with its present influential directorate and distinguished patrons, was then formed.

R. Thiele.]

J. T. ROBERTSON,
Manager.

Chelsea's manager was born at Dumbarton in 1877. His height is 5ft. 8in., and he weighs 11st. 6lb. Chelsea secured him from the Glasgow Rangers, and the success of the team under his able management is an eloquent testimony to his ability as an organiser. Mr. Robertson has played for Greenock Morton, Everton, Southampton, and Glasgow Rangers. He is a famous International, having received no less than sixteen caps for Scotland, and has represented the Scottish League on seven occasions. Plays left half-back for Chelsea, and is as keen a footballer as ever, despite the cares of management. He is married.

Last April I was engaged as manager. I was at that time a member of the Glasgow Rangers. We then set to work at once on the engrossing and intensely difficult task of marshalling a strong side.

Meanwhile work had been proceeding apace on the new ground. Mr. Mears said he was willing to spend £100,000 in order that our enclosure might be perfect in every detail; when the whole of the plans are completely carried out, it will fulfil this exacting description. The great grand stand is 120 yards long; the roof is suspended on great iron

Bowden Bros.]
THE HOME OF THE CHELSEA CLUB—STAMFORD BRIDGE GROUND, LOOKING SOUTH.
In the photograph the West Bromwich right back can be seen clearing his lines on the edge of the penalty area.

columns 70 feet from the ground, and it will accommodate 5,000 people.

The ground itself, when complete, will hold close upon 100,000 spectators, each of whom may enjoy an uninterrupted view of the game. When the roof, which is to be erected over the at present unprotected side of the ground, is finished, 50,000 enthusiasts will be enabled to watch Chelsea pulverise their opponents, well sheltered from bad weather. It is hoped that some day the F. A. Cup Final will be played on the Chelsea Ground. Already it is generally regarded as London's leading sports arena.

The London Athletic Club continue to hold their sports on the new cinder-track. And a short time ago 10,000 lovers of the Rugby game gathered to see Middlesex play the New Zealanders. That the League authorities are impressed by the enclosure is proved by the fact that they have arranged for the match between the English and Scottish Leagues to be played at Chelsea in March, 1906.

Top Row: H. A. MEARS. F. W. PARKER. JAMES MILLER. HARRY RANSOM, Trainer. WILLIAM LEWIS, Secretary.

Second Row: J. T. ROBERTSON, Manager. BYRNE. MCROBERTS. FOULKE, Captain. COPELAND. MACKIE. MCEWAN. CRAIGIE. JACK WHITE, Asst. Trainer.

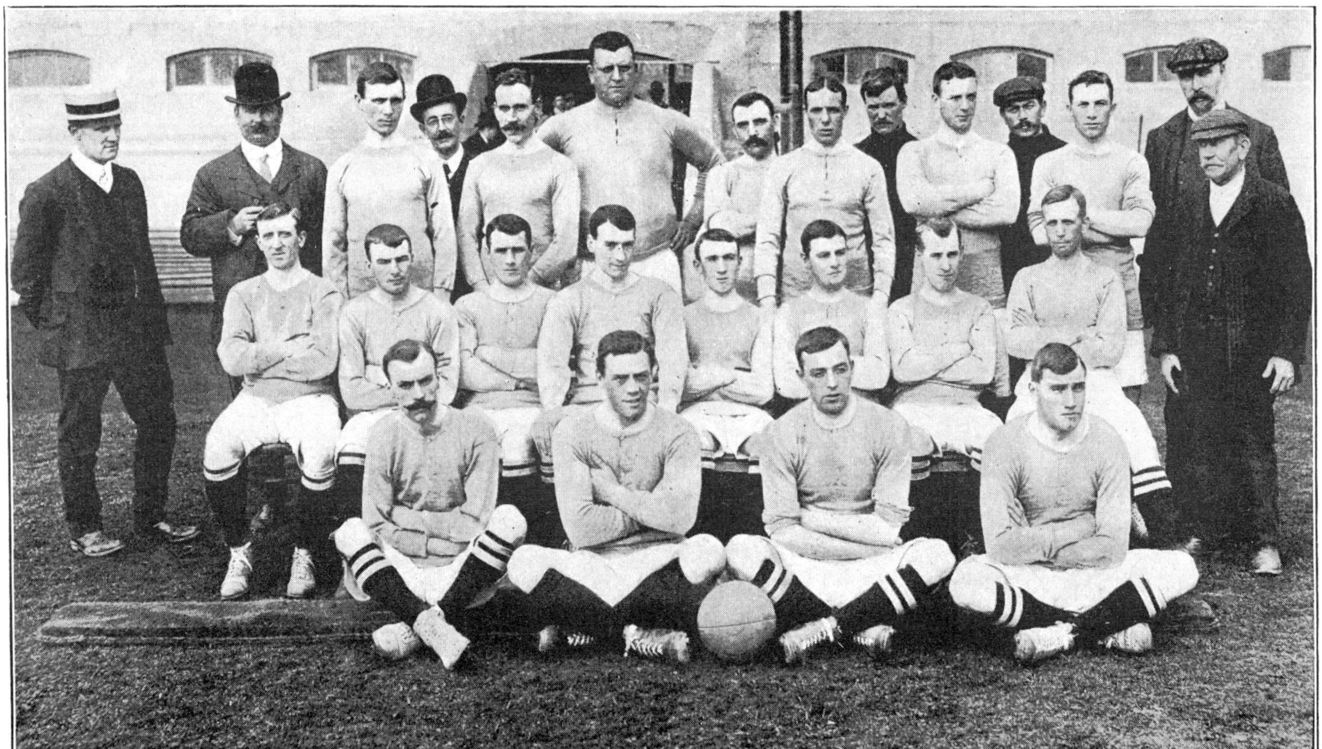

Baker and Dixon.]
THE CHELSEA FOOTBALL TEAM—1905-6.

Third Row (sitting) MORAN. DONAGHY. T. MILLER. J. ROBERTSON. O'HARA. WINDRIDGE. KEY. KIRWAN.

Bottom Row: M. DOWLAND. A. V. SLATER. WOLFE. WATSON.

But in football, as in war, the crux of the matter is the men. The best ground in the world would serve little purpose without an efficient eleven. So far, the players we have engaged have more than fulfilled expectations. The captain is Foulke. He is already one of the most popular players in London. When people first come to Chelsea, they fall to admiring the proportions of the ground, then the proportions of Foulke, and next his unquestionable skill as a goalkeeper. He weighs 22st. 3lb., only 1lb. less than both the backs put together, yet is as agile as a kitten. As a draw alone Foulke is worth his weight in gold, and the way he is playing at the present moment proves him to be one of the best goalkeepers in the League. He stops low "daisy-cutters" and high dropping shots with equal ease, and his punch despatches the ball to a distant point of the horizon. He has accomplished many good performances this season, but perhaps his best so far was his fine fantasia at the close of the match against West Bromwich Albion. The "Throstles" tried strenuously to equalise, and sent in a perfect bombardment of shots, but Foulke was as imperturbably calm as he was adequate. The crowd gave him an ovation after the game.

Bowden Bros.]

WILLIE FOULKE,

Chelsea's captain and goalkeeper, was born at Wellington, Shropshire, twenty-nine and a half years ago. He stands 6ft. 3in. in height, and weighs 22st. 3lb. Foulke is a veritable wonder, and his astonishing activity and goalkeeping ability have aroused almost a fever of interest in his doings beneath the bar for the Chelsea Club. "Little Willie" played for England against Wales in 1897, and has gained two Cup-winners' medals. Sheffield United secured his transfer from a Derbyshire colliery club for £19. He has played cricket for Derbyshire, and his talent for directing a team is very valuable to the Chelsea Club.

The regular backs are Mackie, of the famous Heart of Midlothian team, and McEwan, late of Glasgow Rangers. They are reliable kickers and tenacious tacklers, and play together with a nice understanding. Mackie has a happy facility for getting in his kick, no matter in what attitude he may be, when the ball comes his way.

Key, from the Heart of Midlothian Club, plays half, and last year got his cap for Scotland. Those who have seen him acting as a sixth forward and then assisting the defence, and generally making himself exceedingly inconvenient to opponents, are not surprised he obtained this honour.

Watson, another clever Scotsman, or Craigie, Manchester City, generally play centre-half. Both are good, and I am the third of the line. I gained my experience playing for Southampton, Everton, and Glasgow Rangers, and was capped for Scotland sixteen times.

The forwards are an accomplished set of players. They can play the three-inside game, or indulge in those long, swinging passes out to the wings that are more effective against some teams. R. McRoberts, of Small Heath, is in the centre. He was the first player signed on by the club. He is a splendid shot, and when he does not score a goal a match one hears rumours that he is not well. But that is only because of his sad expression. Nothing is more cheering to "Mac" than scoring a good goal.

Moran is outside-right. He made a big reputation while with the Heart of Midlothian Club, but has never played so well in his life as he has since donning the light-blue jersey of the Chelsea Club. His sensational centres are quite one of the striking features of the game.

Copeland, of Tottenham Hotspur, generally acts at inside-right. It was the Copeland and Kirwan left wing that played such an important part in gaining the Cup for Tottenham. Now Copeland means to do as much towards gaining promotion for Chelsea into the First League. James Robertson is a clever player and a fine shot at goal, and can also play in the latter position. Kirwan, the other member of the famous wing, still retains his old place for Chelsea. His partner is Windridge, of Small Heath. Both combine well together, yet do not fail to keep in close touch with the rest of the line. We have secured a number of other well-known players. Among them is McDermott, of Everton. He is regarded as one of the cleverest inside forward players in the country, and several League clubs were anxious to secure his services.

He first made a reputation when wearing the colours of the Celtic Club, but while playing before the critical crowd at Everton he won fresh laurels. He is essentially a polished player, with a mastery of those deft touches one expects of an Everton man. He is 11st. 7lb. in weight, and twenty-five years of age.

Another new man, who has a brilliant past, but should have a still more brilliant future, is Pearson, of Manchester City. He plays effectively at centre-forward, and has the happy facility of being able to combine well with his wings, and yet never misses an opportunity of threading a way through his opponents by himself.

One hears club managers on every side bemoaning the lack of forwards who possess initiative. The player who can get rid of the ball tamely whenever he is tackled, and who always does the same thing every time, is easy enough to find. He will never help win a Cup-tie or a League match. It is the player who can do things his rivals do not anticipate, and who is above all not afraid to shoot when he draws near goal, that we are all hunting for, and these we think we have found.

Our idea is to have a strong body of reserves, so as to ensure Chelsea always having a first-class side in the field.

The Chelsea football programme, with its topical notes on the game in general and the club in particular, has proved very popular. The two lads in light-blue jerseys who throw up the ball when it goes behind have also provoked a good deal of comment and amusement. They form a striking contrast to Foulke. My work has also not been without its humorous side. Amongst the many applications for positions I received, was one from a man who said he was a splendid centre-forward, but if that position was not vacant he could manipulate a turnstile. Another wrote: "You will be astonished to see me skip down the touch-line like a deer." A third was willing to "be linesman, goal-keep, or mind the coats."

Lastly, it may be said that nothing is certain in football, and therefore no one can be sure of success; but, at any rate, Chelsea are determined to deserve it.

A RUGBY MATCH—THE BREAKING UP OF A SCRUM.

The intense exhilaration of the Rugby game cannot be understood by those who have not played the code. Half its delight is occasioned by the scrummage, and a man who has once placed his head and shoulders down to help pack a scrum never loses his delight in the Rugby phase of our great national winter pastime.

Bowden Bros.]

'VARSITY FOOTBALL—RUGBY. OXFORD *v.* CAMBRIDGE AT QUEEN'S CLUB.
Following up a punt.

THE RUGBY UNION.

By C. J. B. MARRIOTT.

Hacking—A divergence of opinion leads to the secession of the Blackheath Club from the proposed amalgamation of the running and dribbling codes—The historic meeting at the old Pall Mall Restaurant on January 26, 1871—The Rugby Union formed—The first committee—Hacking abolished—The Calcutta Cup presented to the Union—Rowland Hill is appointed to the dual office of secretary and treasurer in 1881—An International dispute leads to a uniform code of laws—The evolution of the game as regards running—The formation of the professional Union—The first visit of the New Zealanders—Canada visits the mother country—Rowland Hill retires, and Mr. Percy Coles becomes secretary of the Union—Rowland Hill, president—Some passing references.

BEFORE giving a detailed account of the formation of the Rugby Union, a glance at the condition of the game and circumstances which led to the Union's inception will not be out of place.

At the commencement of the sixties, or a little before, it had occurred to many of the old Public Schoolmen resident in London that the game to which they had been devotees when at school was worth following in after years. The first regular club of which we can find trace round London was formed by the old pupils of the Blackheath Proprietary School in 1858. Their antagonists were chiefly drawn from the numerous cramming establishments in that neighbourhood. Later, in 1860, the name was changed from Blackheath Old Boys to the Blackheath Club, which has been retained ever since. In a photograph before us of the Blackheath team of 1862—we believe the oldest photo extant of a Rugby club team—the rig-out of the players is hardly in accordance with present-day notions. Two wear long white cricket flannels, the rest simply their ordinary trousers with the ends tucked into their socks. All are in jerseys, and look a very formidable side.

A few years subsequently, in 1863, Mr. Edwin H. Ash founded the famous Richmond Club. During the first year of its formation the Harrow rules were followed, but in the ensuing season a change was made to those of Rugby, as exponents of which the club have been from that day to this among the most famous.

Bowden Bros.]

FAMOUS RUGBY MEN.

Mr. F. M. Stout, England's famous International captain, and Mr. Rowland Hill, the honoured president of the Rugby Union.

The drawback to the enjoyment of inter-club matches in those early days was the divergence existing in the rules. Most schools had peculiarities and restrictions of their own, which were afterwards adhered to by their old boys, and the complications thus occasioned can easily be imagined.

Recognising the desirability of one governing code, the representatives of the chief public schools resident at Cambridge met at the beginning of the season of 1863, and drew up a set of rules, which embodied a mixture of the running and dribbling games. Later in the same season a similar meeting for a similar purpose was held in London. One of the moving spirits for the adoption of a uniform code was Mr. C. W. Alcock, the now popular secretary of the Surrey Cricket Club and lifelong football enthusiast.

After the necessary preliminaries, a meeting was held, at which the crux of the whole position turned on the question of the retention or elimination of hacking. In the old days, when the majority of the followers of the game had been trained at schools where the number of players in the scrummage would amount to thirty or more, the necessity for hacking to loosen the ball from the forest of legs was absolutely necessary. This feature of the Rugby game was dearly cherished by the alumni of the big

Bowden Bros.]
W. LLEWELLYN (NEWPORT).
He is a magnificent three-quarter, and as captain of the Welsh International fifteen has earned undying fame.

schools who took to playing the game around London. Certain concessions the followers of the dribbling game were willing to make to their Rugby brethren, but on the question of the elimination of hacking they stood firm.

The treasurer of the proposed amalgamated body, Mr. G. Campbell, secretary of the Blackheath Club, was the stoutest advocate for the retention of hacking, and in a vigorous speech which he made to the assembled delegates he asserted that if hacking were abolished from the game he would undertake to bring over a team of Frenchmen who would beat the exponents of the proposed new code after a week's practice. Little chance did there appear when this sturdy devotee of the old-style football made the above statement that the time would come that France would play England under Rugby rules.

On the motion for no hacking being carried by nine to four, Blackheath seceded from the proposed amalgamation, a course which was followed by several others.

For some years longer the Rugby-playing clubs still continued without any governing body or official code of laws. Many new clubs were springing up around London at this time, notably the Gipsies, founded by F. Luscombe and W. J. Parker in 1868, the Ravenscourt Park, founded in 1865, the still extant Wasps Club, which dates from 1868, and the famous Queen's House Club, started by the late Colonel Cleary Hill, elder brother of the present respected president of the Rugby Union, the club taking its name from the family domicile of the Hills; and other teams too numerous to mention.

In 1870 it occurred to Mr. Edwin H. Ash, the secretary of the Richmond Club, that the time had arrived when the exponents of the running game should have a properly constituted governing body and an official code of rules. This gentleman, to whom the inception of the Rugby Union is largely due, in conjunction with the secretary of the Blackheath Club, convened a meeting for the purpose of forming a Rugby Union. This historic meeting was held at the old Pall Mall Restaurant on January 26, 1871. It was then unanimously decided that the Rugby Union should be formed, and an official code of rules drawn up. The entrance-fee and subscription was first fixed at 5s., but was later increased to £1 1s. The entrance-fee, by the way, has at the time of writing been suspended, to induce more of the smaller clubs to join the Union.

The following clubs were enrolled as original members, a certain number of whom are still in existence: Blackheath, Richmond, Marlborough Nomads, West Kent, Wimbledon Hornets, Gipsies, Clapham Rovers, Law, Wellington College, Guy's Hospital, Harlequins, Queen's House, King's College, St. Paul's School, Lausanne, Civil Service, Addison, Mohicans, Flamingoes, and Belsize Park.

MR. J. E. RAPHAEL,
The famous Oxford University three-quarter.

While the first committee was formed as follows: President, Algernon Rutter (Richmond); hon. secretary and treasurer, Edwin H. Ash (Richmond); R. H. Birkett (Clapham Rovers), F. T. Currey (Marlborough Nomads), W. F. Eaton (Ravenscourt Park), A. J. English (Wellington College), J. H. Ewart (Guy's Hospital), A. G. Guillemard (West Kent), F. Hartley (Flamingoes), E. C. Holmes (Richmond), R. Leigh (Law), F. Luscombe (Gipsies), L. J. Maton (Wimbledon Hornets), E. Rutter (Richmond), and F. Stokes (Blackheath). Of the above six hailed from Rugby, and one each from Haileybury, Wellington, Tonbridge, and Marlborough.

It is needless to say that the rules drawn up were almost entirely based on those in use at Rugby, the only important exception being the elimination of hacking. This feature of the running game, which had led to the secession of the Rugby clubs from the Association in 1863, was now forbidden

Baker and Dixon.]
RUGBY COUNTY CHAMPIONSHIP—DURHAM v. MIDDLESEX, APRIL 20, 1905.
The championship game was played at West Hartlepool on April 20, 1905, when Durham won by the narrow margin of three tries (nine points) to one goal and one try (eight points). The above admirable photograph shows Durham intercepting a pass.

by Rule 57, which read : " No hacking or hacking-over or tripping-up shall be allowed under any circumstances."

Early in 1871 circumstances occurred which led to the institution of International matches. An Association team, comprised of Scotsmen resident in London, and called the Scotch International team, had been beaten by an English International team.

Scotsmen resident in their own country were not unnaturally dissatisfied, both by the title and result of the match, and a challenge speedily appeared in " Bell's Life " that a team of Scotsmen resident beyond the Border were willing to play any team of Englishmen under Rugby Union Rules. With both sides willing, arrangements were duly made, and the first English and Scotch match was played at Edinburgh on March 27, 1871. Twenty aside constituted the teams, and the position of the players in the field was as follows : Three backs, one three-quarter back, three half-backs, and the rest forwards.

F. Stokes, an old Rugbeian and captain of Blackheath, led the English team, ten of whom hailed from the famous Warwickshire foundation. The game was very warmly contested, and resulted in a victory for Scotland by one goal and a try to a try. In the heat of the match, which was umpired by the late Mr. H. Almond, headmaster of Loretto, a desire was expressed to revert to the old hacking rules.

A. G. GUILLEMARD, Esq.

As he was in 1871, and as he is to-day.

This famous Rugby player and authority was one of the twenty Englishmen who played in the first International match against Scotland, March 27, 1871, at Edinburgh. The field in that famous game measured 120 yards in length by 55 yards in width. The Englishmen were somewhat handicapped by the narrow dimensions of the playing field, and were defeated, after a splendid fight, by a goal and a try to a try. In the following year, on February 5, at Kennington Oval, England won by two goals and two tries to a goal. Mr. Guillemard was president of the Rugby Football Union from 1878 to 1882.

Happily this was averted by the firm action of Mr. Almond, who refused to remain umpire if such a course was adopted.

In the following year the Scotch team made their first appearance in London, the match being played at the Oval, when England had the satisfaction of reversing the result of the match by scoring two goals and two tries to one goal.

In the following year, 1873, the spread of the game in the North of England led to the necessity of the merits of the Northern players being more systematically recognised by the authorities, and for this purpose the annual North and South match was instituted. The first game between the two sections was fittingly played at Rugby, and resulted in a draw, the South scoring three tries to one. The rules, be it remembered, at that time required a goal to be scored before a match could be lost or won.

The same year the Scotch Rugby Union was formed. Up to this time several of the leading Scottish clubs—notably the West of Scotland, Edinburgh University, and the Glasgow Academicals—had been members of the English Rugby Union.

In 1875 the popularity of the game in the North led to Messrs. E. Kewley of Liverpool and the late James Maclaren of Manchester being appointed as Northern representatives of the Rugby Union executive. The latter, father of the well-known cricketer, was one of the most active pioneers of the game in the North, and his work on the committee only terminated with his death a few years ago.

Another important event of this year was the challenge received from Ireland to play an International match. This was willingly accepted by the Rugby Union, and the match duly came off at the Oval, when England won by two goals and one try to nil.

The Irish representatives, as was natural, showed any amount of vigour, but their knowledge of the finer points of the game, and especially of back play, was by no means commensurate with their zeal.

In 1877 it was thought desirable, in International matches, to follow the example introduced by the Oxford and Cambridge representatives of playing fifteen a side, which has been the recognised number of the Rubgy team ever since. The almost interminable scrummaging of those days was thereby somewhat curtailed. An alteration in the rules the following year, whereby a player, when tackled and the ball held, was obliged to immediately put it down, had an important bearing on the game. The development of the present game dates from the introduction of this word " immediately." The old plan had been to wait to put the ball down until the forwards had formed up in compact phalanges. The breather thus gained enabled players of Homeric girth, whose sole qualification was their avoirdupois, for pushing purposes, to take part in the game. These now disappeared, and the lighter, speedier, and more youthful forwards appeared in their place.

The arrangement of players in the field now was two full-backs, one three-quarter, two halves, and ten forwards. As the passing of the halves to their outsides developed, the number of three-quarters has been successively increased to two, three, and four, and the full-backs reduced to one.

The same year the handsome cup, known as the Calcutta Cup, was presented to the Rugby Union, to be annually held by the winning side in the Scotch and English match, under the following circumstances: The famous Calcutta Rugby Club, which was composed of old Public Schoolmen, and had never suffered defeat, disbanded through many of the members adopting polo. Being embarrassed with funds at their bankers to the amount of £60, the members, who had all learnt

RUGBY—DURHAM, THE CHAMPION COUNTY TEAM, 1904-5.

After a keen struggle Durham defeated Middlesex at West Hartlepool on April 29, 1905, for the Rugby Union County championship. The team was composed as follows: H. C. Nielson, Sunderland, back; B. Wellock, West Hartlepool, J. T. Taylor, West Hartlepool, C. Adamson, Durham City, and H. Imrie, Durham City, three-quarter backs; J. Harrison, Hartlepool Old Boys, H. Wallace, West Hartlepool, half-backs; G. Summerscales, Durham City, J. Elliott, Durham City, R. Caseborn, T. Hogarth, F. Boylen, Hartlepool Rovers, G. Havelock, Hartlepool Old Boys, C. J. H. Stock, Sunderland, and J. M. Hall, Westoe, forwards.

the game at home, and were loyal members of the Rugby Union, voted that this sum should be expended in a cup of Indian workmanship and presented to the Rugby Union on the conditions mentioned.

In 1881 Wales, largely through the instrumentality of Mr. Richard Mullock of Newport, made their first appearance in an International contest. Somewhat unfortunately for them they had to meet an exceptionally powerful English side, the last, by the way, in which Lennard Stokes was a participator, and as was natural, at such an early stage of their existence, the Welsh representatives met with a heavy reverse.

The same year is also memorable for the appointment of Rowland Hill to the dual office of secretary and treasurer. From that time to the present Mr. Hill has been a dominating personality in the Rugby world. His unselfish labours have gone far to spread the good fellowship of the game both on and off the field of play. A born politician and diplomatist, he has always been ready to waive unimportant points; but on matters of principle, or where the welfare of the game would appear in the least degree jeopardised, he has been immovable.

Baker and Dixon.]

RUGBY—THE WELSH INTERNATIONAL FIFTEEN AGAINST ENGLAND, 1905.

W. M. DOUGLAS (Touch Judge). G. TRAVERS, Pill Harriers. D. JONES, Aberdare. W. JOSEPH, Swansea. H. WATKINS, Llanelly. C. M. PRITCHARD, Newport. C. LEFEVRE, Belfast (Referee).

W. NEILL, Cardiff. J. J. HODGES, Newport. D. REES, Swansea. WILLIE LLEWELLYN, London Welsh (Captain). R. T. GABE, Cardiff. E. MORGAN, Lond. Welsh. A. F. HARDING, Lond. Welsh.

R. M. OWEN, Swansea. GEORGE DAVIES, Swansea. R. JONES, Swansea.

The match was played at Cardiff on January 14, when Wales won by the overwhelming majority of twenty-five points—two goals, five tries—to nil.

In 1882 Ireland achieved the best result so far with England, drawing the match of that year, two tries being gained by either side. Five years subsequently they were rewarded for their long uphill fight by defeating England by a try. Since then the victims of Ireland in the football field have been many and great.

The first discordant note to interrupt the harmony of the Rugby Union occurred in 1884. In that year an unfortunate disagreement as to the legality of a try gained by England in the Scotch International match led to a prolonged discussion, and as a result the Scotch and English match was not played the following season.

In 1886 wiser counsels prevailed, and the Scotch allowed the legality of the try, which the referee had given against them, on the understanding that in future International questions or disputes should be referred to an International Board, and the annual match was resumed.

Unfortunately, however, a question cropped up as to the Rugby Union's right to frame the laws for International contests. As a result, no International matches were played in the two following seasons. This regrettable deadlock was finally overcome by submitting the points in dispute to the arbitrament of the late Major Marindin, the President of the Football Association, and Lord Kingsburgh, Chief - Justice Clerk of Scotland.

The result of the deliberations of these two gentlemen were as follows:

1. International matches shall be played under one code of laws.

2. The laws presently existing of the Rugby Football Union, except such parts of Laws 25 and 30 as impose a penalty of a free kick if the ball be knocked on when thrown in from touch, shall be the first code of laws for International matches.

3. The International Rugby Football Board shall consist of twelve members, six of whom shall be elected to represent England, two to represent Scotland, two to represent Ireland, and two to represent Wales.

4. The International Board shall have power to settle all disputes arising at or in connection with International matches by a majority of their number.

5. The International Board shall have power, by a majority of not less than three-quarters of their number, to amend, alter, or cancel any law in, and add new laws to, the International code.

Since that date the Rugby Union have happily not been involved in dispute with the Unions of the other countries, and the rulings of the International Board have always been loyally followed.

In 1891 a welcome change was made in the scoring laws. In the old days no match could be won unless a goal had been scored, and one goal would thus outweigh in value any number of tries. The first step was to make three tries equal to a goal. This, after a trial, was thought not to be an adequate arrangement, and the following rule was passed:

A match shall be decided by a majority of points. A try shall equal two points; a penalty goal three points; a goal from a try (the try not to count) five points; any other goal four points.

This system of scoring remained in force for some years with slight alterations, but in the present year it has been thought advisable to get the sanction of the International Board to the following revision:

A try equals three points; a goal from a try (in which case the try shall not count) five points; a dropped goal four points; a mark goal, and a penalty goal, three points; the field goal being abolished.

In 1892 it was found desirable to re-codify the laws. These had been altered and patched about from time to time, and it was felt that a re-draft was desirable. The work was duly taken in hand by Mr. W. Cail, the Union's treasurer, and the result gave entire satisfaction.

The last vestige of prohibiting the ball being run with was done away with—namely, that it could now be picked up and run with when dead. It is interesting to note the evolution of the game as regards running. We learn from that interesting work entitled, "The Origin of Rugby Football," published by the Old Rugbeian Society in 1897, that there was a time at Rugby when running with the ball was not known, the habit being when a fair catch was made to allow a kick at goal, the opposite side lining up at the spot where the catch occurred.

In 1823 one, Ellis, disregarded this rule, and, on catching the ball, rushed forward with it towards the opposite goal. This innovation gradually led to the introduction of running with the ball from a fair catch; and then, as running became popular, a player picking the ball up on the first bound was allowed to run. Later, running was allowed if the ball was moving when picked up, and finally, in 1894, the rule was passed permitting a player to pick the ball up when dead and run.

Equally interesting is it to note the gradual elimination of so many of the complicated formalities which existed in the old days. At one time there were almost as many ceremonies connected with a place-kick from a try as at a coronation. Any infringement or omission invalidated the kick. Gone, too, are the complicated punt-outs and punt-ons, as also that relic of barbarism a maul-in-goal.

PERCIVAL COLES, Esq.,
Secretary of the Rugby Union.

Mr. Coles, the old Oxford captain, was appointed secretary of the Rugby Union upon the retirement of Mr. Rowland Hill, who now ably fills the presidential chair. He is a splendid worker, played with great distinction for his 'Varsity, and is an admirable referee.

Though the game in the 'Eighties had made great strides in the North, especially in Yorkshire and Lancashire, both of which counties produced many fine teams, a dark cloud of professionalism was enveloping what was intended by its founders to be an amateur sport.

Emoluments to attract players from smaller clubs were known to exist, and in many ways indirect payment was obtained for play.

The Rugby Union authorities, viewing the position of the amateur element in the sister game of Association since the legalisation of professionalism, determined to take action before the professional section became too strong. Nor had they long to wait.

In 1894 two Yorkshire members of the Rugby Union committee brought forward at a special general meeting the following motion :

"That players be allowed compensation for bona-fide loss of time."

This was felt to be the thin edge of the wedge, and, after very warm arguments for and against at the largest meeting the Rugby Union has ever had, the motion for compensation was thrown out by a majority of 146.

Shortly after this the professional element, seeing the firm front displayed by the Rugby Union governing body, started a Union of their own, and have existed as a separate body ever since. In the season 1888-9 the Mother Country received the first visit of a Rugby team from the Colonies, when a team from New Zealand came home and played a series of matches. The visitors showed good form, and their physique and powers of endurance were certainly of a high order. They played no less than seventy-four matches, of which only twenty resulted in their defeat, and at this time it must be remembered, whatever may be the comparative state of Rugby football in the South, in the North at all events the teams were far and away stronger than those of the present day.

The excellent form which the New Zealanders then showed gave promise, which has now been so fully realised, that, with a due appreciation and cultivation of the finer points of the game, that colony would be able to produce a team the equal of any other country.

We likewise more recently welcomed a team from Canada who showed fair form. It must, however, always be remembered that the exigencies of the Canadian climate precludes the duration of the football season lasting more than about three months. The Canadians, therefore, have a very short season in which to perfect themselves in the intricacies of the game.

At the time of writing the team from New Zealand are carrying all before them, and grave doubts are expressed whether any team will be able to defeat them. Their visit will, no doubt, do good to English football, for, as with our cricket before the advent of the Australian teams, our Rugby game has tended for some years to get into a groove. That the present tour of the New Zealanders may stimulate all sections of the football world to endeavour to bring the game to a higher state of proficiency is devoutly to be hoped for.

For next season arrangements have already been made for a visit of football players from South Africa. This part of the Empire has thrice been visited by football teams from England, and on the last occasion the South Africans did so well, and showed such improved style, that they, if not so powerful as the New Zealanders, will certainly render a good account of themselves in the matches in which they engage.

Last year, owing to having received an important appointment in his Majesty's Court of Probate, Mr. Rowland Hill, after twenty-three years' devoted service, felt compelled to resign the position of secretary.

As the necessary work devolving on the secretary has now so vastly increased from the early days, it was found impossible to select a candidate with sufficient leisure to carry on the work as an honorary official of the Union. It was, therefore, decided to appoint a paid secretary, and from the large field of candidates Mr. Percy Coles, the old Oxford captain, was selected. The loss of the old pilot could not but be greatly felt, but his kind interest in initiating his successor in the secretarial duties, coupled with the latter gentleman's energy for his work, has a good deal to do with the fair sailing of the good ship Rugby Union. As a small expression of their appreciation of Mr. Hill's many years of unselfish and zealous work, the general meeting of club delegates elected him with acclamation to the presidential chair, a position he has consented to occupy for another year.

RUGBY—THE ENGLISH INTERNATIONAL FIFTEEN AGAINST WALES, 1905.

Top Row: C. J. Newbold. J. L. Matthias. E. W. Dillon. W. L. G. Rogers. F. H. Palmer. W. T. Carr.

Centre Row: S. F. Coopper. S. H. Irvin. V. H. Cartwright. F. M. Stout, Captain. B. A. Hill. J. E. Raphael.

Bottom Row: F. C. Hulme. T. A. Gibson. W. V. Butcher.

The match was played on January 14 at Cardiff, when England were handsomely beaten by twenty-five points to nil

Bowden Bros.]

THE "SPURS'" GROUND—TOTTENHAM HOTSPUR v. MILLWALL.

The "Spurs" pressing. A tussle on the fringe of the penalty area.

THE TOTTENHAM HOTSPUR F. C.

ITS STORY AND PROGRESS.

Winners of the Southern League, 1899-1900; Winners of the English Cup, 1900-1; Winners of the Dewar Shield, 1901-2; Winners of the Southern Charity Cup, 1901-2.

By JOHN CAMERON.

How the Tottenham Hotspur Club was started—Big oaks from little acorns grow—Rapid progress of the club—A change of ground in 1887-8—Professionalism adopted—The first of the great Cup-tie victories—A second change of ground—Champions of the Southern League—The English Cup won—A glorious victory—The club's splendid record.

Colours: White shirts, black knickers. *Ground: High Road, Tottenham.*

MAY one not say, without the slightest suspicion of egotism, that no club has left such a mark upon football in the South of England as the Tottenham Hotspur? The club is about twenty-three years old, and it began its career in the most modest way. In the year 1882-3, some young men of the name of Robert Buckle, John Thompson, and Sam Casey might have been observed hard at work in the region of Northumberland Park with saw, plane, and paint-pot.

It had been decided to start a football club, and with an enthusiasm identified with schoolboys the idea had been forthwith put into practical effect by the making of a set of goal-posts.

Then came a day destined to be historic, when, the goal-posts finished, a start was made on the Marshes, with Robert Buckle as captain, and Jack Thompson as secretary. Matters went along very smoothly. The excitement and joy of that successful day is often talked about by many players, most of whom, happily, survive, and have lived to see their small venture grow into an organisation, the fame of which has reached to the utmost limits of the "Soccer" world.

At that time there were two centre-forwards and only two half-backs, the former position being occupied by Buckle and Thompson, while Sam Casey played back.

That first season was a very successful presage of glorious victories to come, and after a number of

J. Pettingall.]

THE OFFICIALS OF THE TOTTENHAM HOTSPUR F. C.

J. HAWLEY. T. A. DEACOCK. M. F. CADMAN. R. BULLOCK.

JOHN CAMERON, Secretary and Manager. THE ENGLISH CUP. C. D. ROBERTS, Chairman.

Of these Mr. Bullock is now in America, his place being filled by Mr. George Cox, this being the only change that has been made in the directorate since the "Spurs" won the Cup.

TOTTENHAM HOTSPUR FOOTBALL CLUB—TEAM AND OFFICIALS, SEASON 1905-6.

Top Row: J. OVER, Groundsman. T. DEACOCK. W. HICKLING. J. WHITBOURN. J. EGGETT, Goalkeeper. J. SHACKLETON. W. BULL. T. A. DEACOCK, Esq., Director. M. F. CADMAN, Esq., Director.

Second Row: T. SINTON, Steward. J. CAMERON, Esq., Sec. and Manager. J. WATSON. J. WALTON. E. HUGHES. T. MORRIS. O. BURTON. J. GEORGE. J. FREEBORO'. C. D. ROBERTS, Esq., Chairman. J. HAWLEY, Esq., Director

W. Clement Pardie. Chingford.]

Third Row: F. McMULLAN. H. CHAPMAN. A. GLEN. H. STANSFIELD. A. TAIT, Captain. C. O'HAGAN. W. MURRAY. P. KYLE. J. McNAUGHT. J. BREARLY. G. COX, Esq., Director.

Bottom Row: S. MOUNTFORD, Trainer. J. CHAPLIN. W. BERRY. C. CARRICK. J. DARNELL. J. NIE, Asst.-Trainer.

meetings—held usually under a street lamp, for funds were low, and members all poor—it was decided to risk another season. In 1883-4 the club entered upon its second season. At this time the club had the good fortune to secure the services of J. Jull, than whom no more sterling player ever put on boots for the "Spurs." He proved a tower of strength, and the young Tottonians began to be talked about. The next season Jull was elected captain, and retained the post right up to 1896, when a long and honourable career was brought to a close.

In 1887-8, so keen had the interest in the club become, it was decided to migrate to the Northumberland Park Ground, and charge for admission. The opening match was against the Old Etonians in the English Cup, and the visitors included in their team such celebrated players as A. T. B. Dunn, R. C. Gosling, A. H. Studd, &c., &c.

Of course, this galaxy of talent settled the "Spurs'" aspirations, the score being 8 goals to 2; but for a long time the Old Boys had a hard job to shake off the tough little "Spurs." The possession of a private ground brought increased support and new players, and slowly, but surely, the club forged ahead.

It was in December, 1895, that the executive—including their popular president, Mr. John Oliver—found it impossible to continue under amateur rules, and at a memorable meeting held shortly afterwards the club took the plunge into professionalism.

At this period the "Spurs" were greatly indebted to such sterling players as Stanley Briggs, Charlie McGahey, Ly Burrows (a magnificent back), and Ernie Payne (a fine forward). The last-named player cost the club dearly, as in providing him with a pair of boots they came under the ban of the Football Association, who suspended them for a fortnight.

The beginning of the year 1899 marked an epoch in the club's career. After working through the preliminary rounds of the Cup, they were drawn against Newton Heath (now Manchester United) at home. The result was a draw, but on the replay a glorious win was recorded, and since then the "Spurs" have done exceedingly well in Cup-ties.

The following season it must be admitted they were knocked—rather unluckily—out in the first round by Preston North End; but that year they became Southern League champions, which was then the highest ambition that was entertained in the minds of those in command at the time.

W. H. Prestwich.]

THE ENGLISH AND SCOTTISH CUPS.

This unique photograph was obtained in the following manner: The Heart of Midlothian Club, winners of the Scottish Cup in the previous season, paid a visit to Tottenham on September 1, 1901, to play a friendly match with Tottenham Hotspur, holders of the English Cup. They brought the Scottish Cup with them, and under these circumstances the two cups were photographed side by side.

During that season the executive removed their quarters from Northumberland Park to their present ground in the High Road. More commodious stands were erected, and increased accommodation provided all round; in fact, the ground was then second to none in the South. The F. A. were soon alive to this fact, and conferred upon the ground such honours as two of their International trial matches, one of their Semi-final ties, and also the final of the Amateur Cup. All that is wanted now to give complete satisfaction is a "real live International" to be played at Tottenham.

Their second season on the present enclosure proved the brightest in the club's history, and the story of how the Cup was brought back to the South after twenty years weary waiting is inscribed on the scroll of fame.

However, it may not be out of place to give the names of the players who were instrumental in this big achievement, and they were as follows: Goal, G. Clawley; backs, H. Erentz, A. Tait; half-backs, T. Morris, E. Hughes, J. L. Jones; forwards, T. Smith, J. Cameron, A. Brown, D. Copeland, and J. Kirwan.

Dissecting the various nationalities of the team, we find England had three representatives; Scotland, five; Wales, two; and the "poor distressful country," but one. To find all four countries represented in the winning team of the "Final" is unique in the records of the game. How the Southern football world was stirred to the innermost core is now a matter of history, and, if only for the great fillip that was given to the game through their fine victory, the "Spurs" have made a landmark in Southern football which will never be effaced.

The team were not content with winning all the premier honours, but in quick succession laid their eager grasp on the Dewar Shield, the Southern Charity Cup, Western League, London League, and South-Eastern League championships. No other club in the South can boast of such a record, and, consequently, can it be wondered why the "Spurs" hold such a warm place in Londoners' hearts?

Perhaps no other club of late years provided the various Associations with so many International players. In one year alone it is on record that they provided England, Scotland, Wales, and Ireland with some of their best International players, which is surely another record in the annals of the game.

How much Ireland is indebted to Kirwan and O'Hagan, Wales to E. Hughes and J. L. Jones, England to V. J. Woodward, and Scotland to A. Brown, cannot be expressed.

The social side of the players' lives has been well looked after, and the club-room at White Hart Lane has witnessed many a pleasant evening. Here directors, players, and their friends often meet in the evening for a friendly game of billiards, an hour at cards, or a quiet chat. It is a high compliment to hear that other clubs are following in their footsteps; and I am looking forward to the time when home-and-home friendly matches at billiards, whist, draughts, &c., between London clubs will be quite a common occurrence.

I have left till near the close another great reason for the phenomenal success of the club, and that is the excellent management that it has always enjoyed.

The board consists of only five directors—to wit:

Mr. C. D. Roberts, M.C.C. chairman, Mr. J. Hawley, Mr. T. A. Deacock, Mr. M. F. Cadman, and Mr. George Cox.

Perhaps the highest testimony that can be paid to their worth is the fact that at each annual general meeting they are invariably unanimously re-elected. Since the Cup was won in 1901 only one change has taken place, Mr. George Cox taking the place of Mr. Ralph Bullock, who, in consequence of crossing the herring-pond on a permanent engagement, had reluctantly to resign his position.

When things were at their blackest, they steered, both by their courage and by their great financial support, the club to the position it at present enjoys.

The balance-sheets of the club for the last few years provide interesting reading.

In their first season as a professional organisation (1895-6) the sum total of their income only amounted to £1,166. It has increased gradually year by year, until at the end of last season it reached the record sum of nearly £12,000.

The directors have a great scheme on hand at present, and negotiations will be completed within a few weeks for the purchase of the freehold of the ground and also for a large piece of adjoining land.

When all is completed, the ground will hold at least 60,000 people, and the "Spurs" will not only have secured a permanent home in High Road, Tottenham, but an enclosure which will meet all likely requirements for many years to come.

SOME FAMOUS FORWARDS

Elbourne.]
R. TEMPLETON
(*Woolwich Arsenal*).

Moyse.]
T. A. SOAR
(*Fulham*).

Parkin.]
LIPSHAM
(*Sheffield United*).

VIVIAN WOODWARD
(*Tottenham Hotspur*).

Wilkes.]
HAMPTON
(*Aston Villa*).

B. B. and B.]
JACK SHARP
(*Everton*).

Reeves.]
F. BLACKBURN
(*West Ham*).

Dee.]
I. LONG
(*Reading*).

Stuart & Winfield.]
APPLEYARD
(*Newcastle United*).

THE BALL AND THE BOOT—HOW THEY ARE MADE.

SOME INTERESTING FACTS ABOUT A GREAT INDUSTRY.

By WILLIAM SHILLCOCK.

The commercial side of football—My connection with the business side of the game—How I lost the English Cup—The importance of being well shod—The football of to-day—A tip about inflation—Old players don't like a lively ball—Footballs are made by hand—Army lieutenant's criticism of a football—A trade secret—The football-boot—Where the modern boot differs from the old—How the boots are made—One of the most wonderful machines in the world—Where hand labour beats the machine at boot-making—The life of a football-boot—What J. W. Robinson says—A word of warning to those who rail against the game.

THE ball and the boot are the two most essential adjuncts to football. Without the ball, indeed, there would be no game. Possibly, therefore, we might put the ball and the player as the two essentials, leaving the boot as the primary adjunct. Now, I have always been interested in the ball and the boot—interested in a practical way. I need not say that football has its commercial side. Everyone can appreciate that fact; but few can be aware of the magnitude of the business which has sprung up as the result of the expansion, the great and almost stupendous expansion, of the game which some of us recall as the pastime of a handful of enthusiasts to whom the ball was everything, and who scarcely gave a thought to the question of general equipment.

I have had a long and, I hope, not unimportant connection with football. There is one incident which has indissolubly identified me with the game. It was an incident which seemed to me at the time a great and unprecedented calamity. I pictured myself a ruined man. I seemed to see myself a hated individual—to see my business boycotted. What was this heinous offence of which I was guilty? Why, I was the man who lost the English Cup. It was on view at my establishment when the Villa won it in 1895, and apparently it was looked at with envious eyes by a festive Birmingham burglar. He and his colleague—for there must have been at least two—adopted time-honoured methods. They removed a portion of the shop roof, and the Cup disappeared, and has not since been heard of. I am not joking when I say that I believed that incident was destined to ruin my connection with football, but happily such has not been the case. But you see that I shall ever be a man with a record unique in the annals of football.

But let us talk more definitely of the ball and the boot. Time was when any boot was deemed sufficient for a footballer, and when anything in the nature of a ball was kicked at with perfect satisfaction on the part of the kicker. Many a grand exhibition of football has been given in an ordinary pair of old-fashioned elastic-side boots; indeed, some of the more famous of the old players never troubled to use any other. But we live in a fastidious age, and the boot is now chosen with scrupulous care. So it should be. Given two elevens of equal calibre, victory would probably go to the better shod team. Any great player will tell you that a perfect-fitting pair of football boots are a luxury. Rarely is a player guilty of serious neglect in this important matter to-day. Yet as late as October this season I heard that one of the Woolwich Arsenal forwards at Small Heath was greatly prejudiced by the fact that his boots were new, and had lamed him before the match had run its course.

IN A FOOTBALL-BOOT FACTORY—A RIVETING MACHINE.

The machine shown in the above photograph, which was specially taken for THE BOOK OF FOOTBALL, turns out as many as 500 pairs of football-boots per day, and it is kept busily working throughout the football season.

The football of to-day is as perfect as a football need be. Its method of manufacture may change, but it is difficult to imagine the invention of a better process than that which now obtains. You have players grumbling about footballs. I heard a man grumble at my "McGregor" once, and if he will grumble at that, he will grumble at anything. "What was the matter with it?" I inquired. "Well, it was too light. It bounced over the horizon every time it dropped." But really you must not blame the maker for that. The ball was blown up too tightly. It is quite easy to blow a football up too much. Many people are not aware of that. Well, THE BOOK OF FOOTBALL has given them some valuable information.

Some clubs wet the ball before playing with it. That is not at all a bad method of obviating the excessive volatility of the ball. But a good football should bounce. The maker would laugh if you asked him to produce a ball which only bounced moderately; and here, in a whisper, let me tell you that it is the old player who generally complains of the volatility of the ball. It makes the game too fast for him.

Everything in connection with the making of a football is done by hand. Now, nothing beats hand labour. You know that fact, of course. The leather is carefully cut out by hand, the stitching is done with scrupulous care, and the lacing is now so artistically done that there is practically no possibility of accident. In the old days, when the lace was not so carefully inserted and hidden away, accidents to the eyes of the players were by no means scarce. The leather in general use is what is known as cowhide leather. It is hard, and yet pliant. It is most durable, and is practically waterproof. The bladders are made so perfectly that one rarely has trouble with them. Years ago one never knew when they were likely to go wrong. My own speciality is an improved chrome leather called "tufisto."

THE STUD-MAKING MACHINE.

This machine is an English patent. It drives five rivets through three plates of leather, and leaves the stud ready for fixing in one operation. A boy can work it, and it turns out thirty gross of studs per day.—From a photograph specially taken for THE BOOK OF FOOTBALL.

The difficulty is to wear a good football out. Last June I received a letter from Lieut. R. A. T. Alton, of the 21st. Battery of the R. F. A. It is interesting as showing what kind of usage a well-made modern football will stand. It reads: "About a month ago you very kindly sent a football for the use of the men of this Battery to kick about in the barrack-square. I am now writing to report that the ball has been kicked about every day, and has really had a severe trial as regards wear and tear. The ball has not been kicked about on grass, but on gravel, and the men often used clogs to kick it. The football has been used very roughly, and has lasted much longer than any I have purchased before for the Battery." I have that football at my establishment now. There is scarcely a scratch to be seen on it.

A football of the type used twenty years ago would not have endured such usage. But there is a good deal about the manufacture of a football which cannot be told. The great point is to get your leather properly stretched. Unless it is thoroughly stretched, the ball will not keep its shape. This stretching of leather to its fullest capacity is a trade secret—a valuable secret too. Not until the whole of the stretch has been eliminated can the leather be utilised for football purposes. The balls which go out of shape are, for the most part, made of leather in which some of the stretching property has been allowed to remain. Naturally there is infinite variety in footballs. We make upwards of thirty different patterns, ranging from the old-fashioned "Button End" ball to the "McGregor," which, by the way, was used in the England v. Scotland matches for 1899, 1901, 1902, 1903, 1904, and 1905, and in the English Cup Finals for 1899, 1900, 1901, 1902, and 1903.

So much for the ball. Now for the boot. There are few secrets, I take it, concerning the football-boot. Some firms make better boots than others. They have more up-to-date machinery and better workpeople to finish the article off. There are patents, too, but there are no secret processes, so far as I am aware. All that is wanted is good leather—and some is naturally better finished than others—and good workmanship. The modern football-boot differs from the old-fashioned football-boot in that it is lighter, stronger, and more durable. The aim is to get it light, yet strong, and it can safely be said that no boot used to-day is constructed on more scientific principles than the football-boot.

Come with me to my factory, and see it made. You will not regret it. Every process is interesting, and I can venture to say you have seen nothing more ingenious and striking in the whole realm of mechanical invention than some of the American boot-making machinery.

You see that huge press? That is English, by the way—Messrs. Whitfield and Hodgson's. It cuts the sole out of thick chrome leather as hard as iron and tough as oak at the rate of 250 or 300 pairs a day. It can be worked by anyone, but we have it handled by a good man, because a bad hand would cut leather to waste, and that no manufacturer can afford to do in these days of stern competition. How neatly it cuts the leather to the shape required!

There you see a smaller press cutting out the stiff cap which is inserted in the toe of the football-boot. You want something solid there. An ordinary boot would give at every kick, and then the kicker's toe as well as the boot would suffer, and the flight of the ball too. Then mark how that skiving machine bevels the edge of the cap, enabling it to be sewn in at the edges, while the middle retains the full strength and thickness of the leather. There is an ingenious stud-building machine, which drives five rivets through three plates of leather, and leaves the stud ready for fixing. That is an English machine—Messrs. Gimson's, of Leicester—and it builds up thirty gross of studs a day. A boy can work it. You see how neatly and expeditiously that trimming machine does its work?

THE WONDERFUL AMERICAN LASTING MACHINE.

It is practically a steel pair of hands. It grips, clutches, and pulls the uppers where it will, and rivets where it likes. It lasts or rivets the uppers to the soles at the rate of 1,500 pairs of boots per week.—From a photograph specially taken for THE BOOK OF FOOTBALL.

What is that human-looking machine?

That is an American lasting machine; in my estimation, one of the most wonderful machines the world has known. It is practically a steel pair of hands. It grips, clutches, and pulls the uppers where it will, and rivets where it likes. Mark the double race-way for the tacks. You simply throw a handful of tacks into that reservoir, they automatically fill the race-ways, and are conveyed to the machine, which uses them itself with human —nay, I would almost say superhuman—ingenuity. That machine lasts or rivets the uppers to the soles at the rate of 1,500 pairs per week.

Yonder is a riveting machine with one race-way for the rivets. It rivets 500 pairs of boots a day.

That is a sole-levelling machine, which levels both outside and inside of the sole. That hammering machine has done much to give a nice finish to the soles.

There you see the tops being cut out by hand. Why by hand? Well, because it is a process where the judgment of the workman is valuable.

The man cuts out the leather where the leather is uniformly good, whereas a machine has no power of discrimination and would furnish us with tops good, bad, and indifferent, whereas we require them all to be good—that is, of sound leather of uniform thickness.

That is the eye-letting machine. It can be worked by a young girl. It places the eyelets at even distances, and gives each the same blow. So fast does it work that we never really keep pace with it. That is a neat little German skiving machine with a band knife. It is a pretty little worker.

There you see the perfectly finished boot, after inspecting all the processes incidental to its building-up. That is my special boot, the "McGregor," bearing a photo of the founder of the League thereon.

That boot is, I believe, the model of what a football-boot ought to be. There have been all sorts of fanciful boots, but a fanciful boot will not do for heavy football grounds. The strain on a football-boot is tremendous. That boot will not be sold for at least four months. No boot should be sent out as soon as it is made. I keep £2,000 worth of football-boots in my stock-room regularly. It never gets below that.

Of course, there is always a demand for footballs. You can have no conception of the magnitude of the football outfitting trade to-day. It is a great industry. If football were to cease, England would lose a great and a profitable industry. England leads here, believe me.

I am only one manufacturer. There are plenty of others, yet I have taken a single order for 6,000 footballs! How many footballs do I sell a year? Well, between 40,000 and 50,000 a year, and I have customers all over the world; so has every leading maker.

What is the life of a football-boot? Well, that depends upon the quality of the boot, and also in a sense upon the wearer. Here is a letter which came quite spontaneously from J. W. Robinson, the great goalkeeper. He says there that he had a pair of my boots in constant use, both for match play and practice, for eight full seasons.

"I have played in over 400 matches and innumerable practice games in these boots, and they look like lasting for many years to come."

But, mind you, I doubt if I should like all my boots to wear as Mr. Robinson's have done, because that would mean one pair one customer one lifetime, and that might not be all I could wish financially. But, whether you buy my boots or someone else's, don't buy cheap ones. Good boots are not only a luxury, but they are infinitely the cheapest in the long run. But don't let people talk of abolishing football, or this country will suffer industrially as well as physically.

Football is a valuable health agent; there can be no doubt on that point. Some silly people talk about professionalism ruining the game, and shout about so few playing and so many looking on. It is nonsense—arrant nonsense. The players now are as legion compared with their number at the time that I started in this business. Any manufacturer of football outfits and apparatus will bear out this statement. If we had to rely upon professional clubs for our business we should have a poor time. I am glad to get an order from a professional club—very glad indeed; the fact that they patronise me undoubtedly influences other orders, and they buy of the best, too. But they are not the backbone of my trade, or of the trade of anyone situated as I am. The thousands of enthusiastic junior players—players to whom their Saturday game is everything, and who would not dream of sacrificing their match even to watch an International engagement—are the class which keep athletic outfitters going. There are ten players to-day to every one you found at the time that professionalism was instituted. Football is a grand game—a game which needs little outlay and brings in its train a maximum of healthy enjoyment and good exercise.

William Shillcock.

WHERE THE FOOTBALLS ARE MADE.

THE INTERIOR OF A FOOTBALL FACTORY—A SIDE-LIGHT ON A GREAT INDUSTRY.

Everything in connection with the making of a football is done by hand. Cowhide leather is used, and it is practically waterproof. The stretching of the leather is a valuable trade secret, and it is all important, for a ball made of badly stretched leather will quickly lose its shape. The above photograph shows only one section of a great football factory, and was specially taken for The Book of Football.

ANNALS OF STOKE FOOTBALL CLUB.

By W. W. COCKBILL.

The antiquity of Stoke F. C.—Early records—The Staffordshire Cup won in 1878-9—Ground changes—Professionalism introduced—How "pros." were paid in the old days—A club crisis—Stoke take their place among the clubs forming the League—The cultivation of local talent—Amateurs introduced to League football—Hard times in 1904-5—The present season's fine record.

Colours : Claret shirts, white knickers ; or white shirts, black knickers. *Ground : Victoria Ground, Stoke-on-Trent.*

H. J. Gover.]

H. D. AUSTERBERRY

Was appointed secretary of Stoke F. C. in 1897. He has for fifteen years been a member of the council of the Staffordshire Football Association.

FOOTBALL, we are assured, was introduced into this country somewhere about the time of the Roman invasion, but it was in 1863 that the game, previously a brutal sport, first obtained a foothold as a pastime and healthy recreation. Modern football history can truthfully be said to have commenced in that year, and one of the clubs which sprang into existence at that time was Stoke. Founded by some Old Carthusians --Armand, Bell, Matthews, and Phillpott, young men who were at the time pupils at the North Stafford Railway Works—the club has had a continued, if chequered, existence. It has the honour of being, with one exception, the oldest club in the League, a combination in which, with the solitary exception of one season, it has kept its place through good report and evil.

The four enthusiasts who formed the club were not long in obtaining support. Sons of business men, manufacturers, and county gentlemen, joined the club, and Mr. J. W. Thomas, then connected with the Stoke Victoria Athletic Club, became its first secretary. In those days every club, or, perhaps, it would be more correct to say, every district, had its own rules, and played the game in its own way. Stoke favoured a modified form of Rugby, and amongst the early recruits were W. H. Hallam, Harry Allen, Percy Trubshaw, Walter Ansdell, "Chad" May, and others, but the man to whom the credit of setting the club on a firm footing is due is the late Mr. Tom C. Slaney. He was by profession a schoolmaster, and as a boy showed great promise on the football field, his prowess being developed during the time he was training for his certificate at Saltley College, Birmingham. He was the leading light and mainstay of the club, for, from the time he joined it until 1883, he was hon. secretary, and was captain from 1875 to 1882. It was he who formed the Staffordshire Football Association in 1877.

Brandebourg.]

LEN. HALES,

One of the most brilliant forwards Stoke ever had. He was badly injured in a Cup-tie at Bristol in 1901, and retired from the game.

In those days football as a spectacle was practically unknown in the Potteries, but when such clubs as Derby Town, Burton Town, Walsall, Notts County, Notts Forest, Shropshire Wanderers, Ashbourne, and Tutbury were the visitors, Sweetings Field was thrown open to the public at the moderate charge of 2d., and as many as 200 people have been known to congregate on those important occasions.

In 1878 and 1879 Stoke secured the Staffordshire Cup, which is interesting, inasmuch that they have never since won the trophy, though they were joint holders with Wolverhampton in 1904.

When Mr. Slaney's long and honourable association with the club as secretary came to a close, he was succeeded by Mr. Walter Cox, who shortly afterwards handed the reins over to Mr. Harry Lockett. Mr. Lockett for some time held the dual office of secretary of the Stoke Club and secretary of the Football League, but when the League assumed such importance that it was considered advisable to have a secretary not officially connected with any of its clubs, Mr. Lockett resigned the Stoke secretaryship.

Stoke had removed from Sweetings Field, the scene of many stern encounters, to the old Athletic Ground, and from thence to their present ground in 1883. During his term of office, Mr. Lockett, who was not slow to appreciate the change which was coming over the game, introduced professionalism. This was in 1883, and one of the first professional players was Tom Clare, who did great work at back, and is now the manager and secretary of Burslem

THE TEAM THAT REPRESENTED STOKE IN SEASON 1877-8.

Top Row: T. KINGSLAND. G. LOCKHART. R. SLEIGH. G. LAKE.

Second Row: T. C. SLANEY, Captain. W. BODDINGTON. J. MALLETT. H. ALLEN.

Bottom Row: R. McMILLAN. H. R. BROWN. E. JOHNSON.

Port Vale. His wage was like that of the six other professionals, 2s. 6d. per match. What would the present-day "pro." think of that princely remuneration? And yet there are few better backs playing to-day than Tom Clare was in those days, not to mention W. Rowley, Stoke's International goalkeeper, who was in receipt of the same wage.

There was a crisis in the history of the club about this time. Rowley and Clare discovered that another well-known player was in receipt of the munificent salary of 5s. a week. There was a strike of the professional players, and the club had to concede the demands of Rowley, Clare, and the others, and raise their wages to the same standard as the man who was receiving 5s. a week. It may be interesting to here give a few of the largest "gates" during this first season of professionalism, if it can be called by such a name: Crewe (English Cup), £26 14s. 3d.; Bolton Wanderers, £26 7s. 0d.; Blackburn Rovers, £23 14s. 3d.; Walsall Swifts, £21 13s. 0d.; Third Lanark, £20 6s. 6d.; and Derby County, £19 7s. 0d.

Gover.] TOM HOLFORD, Captain.

He stands 5ft. 6in., and weighs 10st. 2lb. Is one of the finest half-backs playing. Played for Wales in 1903. Is a home-bred player, and works hard at his trade, playing football in his spare time. Is a life-long abstainer and non-smoker.

It was in this season that Stoke met the all-conquering Preston North End for the first time, and a "gate" which produced £114 12s. 3d., a gigantic sum for those days, saw the home team go under by a goal. Many will remember the stonewall defence of Rowley between the sticks and Clare and Underwood at back. After retiring from the playing-field, Rowley became secretary in 1895.

As everybody knows, Stoke was one of the original twelve clubs which composed the League when it came into existence in 1888-9, and they got together a team which, following the lead set by other clubs, contained several Scotsmen. The club's choice of players was not a happy one, however, for they finished at the bottom of the table in company with Notts County, each club having secured twelve points. They were re-elected, but the following season saw them again in the humiliating position of being at the bottom of the table, and for a season Stoke had to turn their attention to the Alliance. Championship honours fell to their share, however, and this performance enforced their claim to re-admission to the charmed circle, a claim which was duly recognised, and in 1891-2 they were again members of the League. Again, at the end of this season, Stoke had to seek re-admission. The application met with success, and since those troublesome days they have always managed to keep their place in the tournament, though in 1895 they figured in the test matches. Newton Heath were their opponents, but the "Heathens" were well beaten.

After the resignation of Mr. Lockett, Stoke were served by Mr. J. Bradshaw and Mr. A. E. Reeves as secretaries; but in 1895 a financial crisis in the affairs of the club led to a series of meetings being held in the town. The result was that between £800 and £900 was taken up in shares in Stoke and the adjoining towns, and W. Rowley, the late goalkeeper, was appointed the first secretary of the company. In 1897 Mr. Rowley resigned and Mr. H. D. Austerberry, who had some few months previously taken an important part in the re-organisation of the Burslem Port Vale Club, and had acted as the first secretary of the limited liability company, was appointed secretary and manager of Stoke. Under his regime, and after the appointment of Mr. W. A. Cowlishaw as chairman in 1899, the directors gradually dropped the policy of relying upon imported players, and the club began to assiduously cultivate the local talent with which North Staffordshire abounds.

It was in the season 1901-2 that Stoke tried the daring experiment of including three amateurs in their team—L. R. Roose, S. B. Ashworth, and Len Hales. This season was in every way a phenomenal one, and one of the most remarkable of many strange occurrences was the fact that 31 points proved only just enough to keep the club out of the Second Division.

In 1902-3 Stoke had their most successful season, finishing sixth on the table of merit with 37 points, their record aggregate in any one season. They also reached the third round of the Football Association Cup, being knocked out by Derby County at Derby. The following season saw Stoke again escape the bottom two by a single point, Liverpool reaching the total of 26, and Stoke being just one step above with 27. Last season, after a moderate commencement, the club finished in the twelfth position with a total of 30 points. However, the club was in such a serious financial position that during the past summer the question was seriously considered as to whether the club should not dispose of some of its best players. Thanks, however, to the patriotism of the directors, all difficulties were overcome, and the month of September was entered upon with a debt of something like £2,500.

It is an open secret that the future of the club depended almost entirely upon the results of the early part of the season, and, although the directors were confident that they had a sound team, they hardly anticipated that the splendid results of September and October would be achieved. The present side is certainly one of the most serviceable that the old club has ever had.

Gover.] MR. W. A. COWLISHAW.

He has been a director of the club since 1896, and was appointed chairman in 1899. He is one of the keenest and most successful business men in North Staffordshire.

Taylor.] MR. JOHN DAVIS.

He has been a director of the club since 1896, and his advice has been invaluable to his colleagues.

LEIGH RICHMOND ROOSE,

Stoke's famous Amateur Goalkeeper.

He first played for Stoke against the Blackburn Rovers on October 19, 1901, when he gave a magnificent display of goalkeeping.

MR. SAM LAKE.

He forms the connecting link between the old club and the new. He was with his brother George a playing member in the early 'Seventies, and was appointed a director of the club in 1899.

Gover.] W. ROWLEY.

He kept goal for Stoke, and was appointed first secretary of the company. He resigned this post in 1897.

STOKE FOOTBALL CLUB—TEAM AND OFFICIALS FOR THE SEASON 1905-6.

Top Row: Mr. W. Atkins. Mr. Davies. Mr. Lake. L. E. Holdcroft. H. N. Benson. L. R. Roose. C. Burgess. A. Sturgess. H. D. Austerberry, Secretary.

Scott and Co., Manchester.]

Bottom Row: J. Eccles, Trainer. R. Fielding. G. Baddeley. F. W. Rouse. T. Holford, Captain. J. H. Hall. J. Miller. W. A. Cowlishaw, Chairman. C. Osborne.

Rischgitz Collection.]

FOOTBALL! (From a photograph of the picture by T. Webster, R.A., 1800-1886.)

THE EVOLUTION OF THE PLAYING PITCH.

By H. J. W. OFFORD.

In the olden days, before football was the highly organised game that it now is, all that the players cared about was a ball, an open space to play upon, and two more or less rudely constructed goals. Wherever the ball chanced to go, there pell-mell followed the players; but though the variety of scene doubtless had its charms, the necessity for a limitation of area gradually became apparent.

When the Football Association was formed in the 'Sixties its first care was, of course, to draw up a code of rules for the government of the game; and, as a ground to play on was a prime necessity, it followed naturally that Rule I. dealt with the dimensions of the playing area.

There was more than a suspicion of "go as you please" about it; for though the maximum length and breadth were definitely stated as 200 yards and 100 yards respectively, there was no minimum, and players often disported themselves upon curiously shaped pitches.

There were no lines. The length and breadth had to be denoted by flags, and some of the more enterprising clubs supplemented those at the corners by others along the length of the field. Another curious fact was that the law provided for a "tape" across the goal-posts.

There were many interesting discussions in those days as to whether the ball went just over or just under the tape, especially when the game was played with a breeze blowing.

And, of course, the absence of touch-lines provided the extreme wing players with much more latitude than they now possess, though the "crowds" that then assembled had a decided partiality for wandering on to the pitch.

In 1875, when the F. A. Challenge Cup competition was in its fourth season, the desirability of minimum measurements as well as maximum had forced itself upon those entrusted with the making of the laws. A minimum was therefore inserted, and it was further provided that across the goal-posts a bar

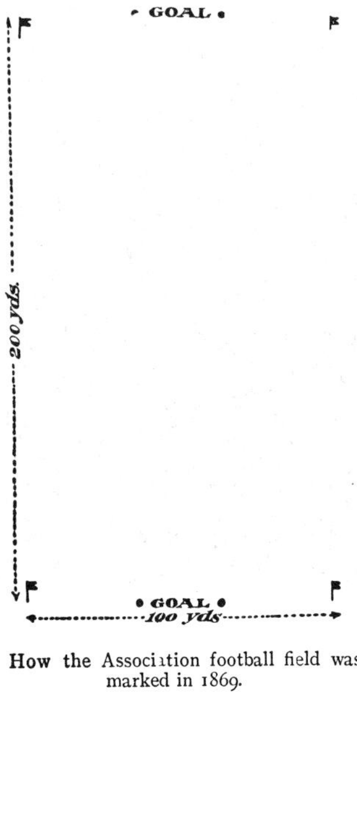

How the Association football field was marked in 1869.

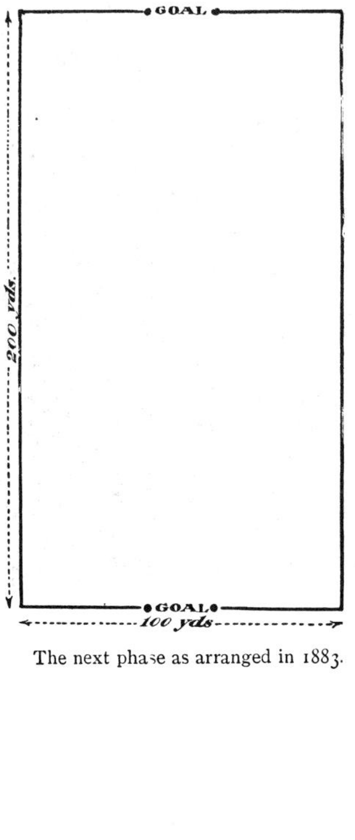

The next phase as arranged in 1883.

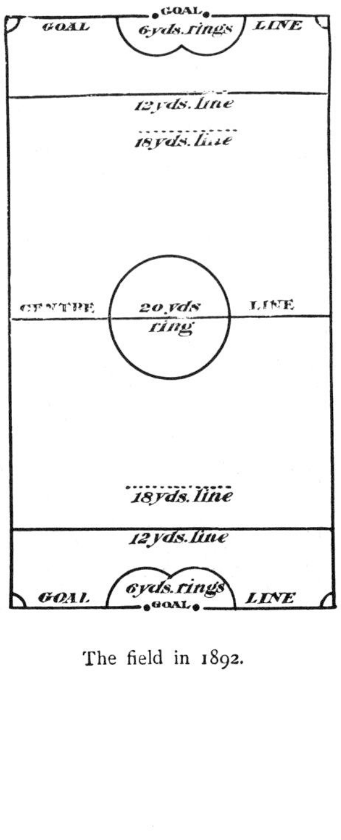

The field in 1892.

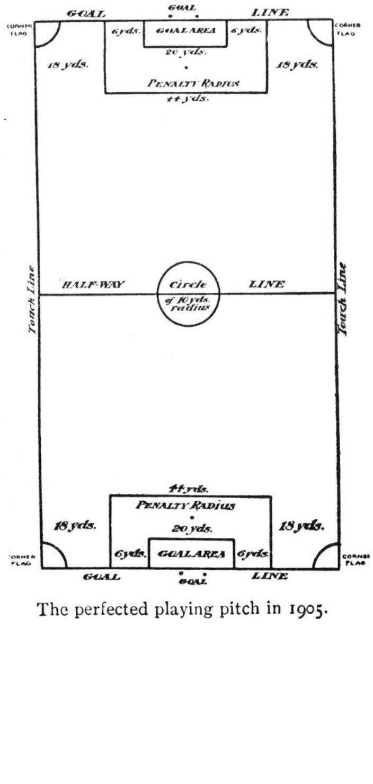

The perfected playing pitch in 1905.

THE OFF-SIDE RULE EXPLAINED—(*continued*).

CLEAR PASS TO ONE OF SAME SIDE.

2.—NOT OFF-SIDE.

A has run ball up, and having **D** in front passes across the field. **B** runs from position 1 to position 2. **B** is not off-side, because at the moment the ball was passed by **A** he had three men between him and the goal-line.

3.—OFF-SIDE.

A and **B** make a passing run up the wing. **A** passes the ball to **B** who cannot shoot because he has **D** in front. **A** then runs from position 1 to position 2, where he receives the ball from **B**. **A** is off-side because he has not three opponents between him and the goal-line when the ball is played forward by **B**.

might be used instead of a tape. Eight years later, in 1883, the first lines made their appearance, and the date is also memorable from the fact that tapes were no longer officially recognised.

But the lines that were then required were merely those denoting the length and breadth of the field, hitherto indicated by the positions of the flags. The interior of the playing pitch remained unmarked, and when the ball was placed in the centre the spot was not precisely indicated.

For seven seasons the simple outline of the ground sufficed, but in 1892 there were striking developments, the following words being added to the law: ". . . and lines defining six yards from the goal-posts and twelve yards from the goal-lines shall also be marked out. The centre of the ground shall be indicated by a suitable mark, and a circle with a ten-yards' radius shall be made round it."

The circle in the centre was to denote to the side that was not kicking off where they were forbidden to approach while the kick-off was being made. The lines showing six yards from the goal-posts marked the positions from which the kick-off from goal was to be made, and the twelve-yards' lines enclosed the area in which the commission of certain offences entailed a penalty kick.

These alterations brought the markings into something approaching those of the present day. But though the penalty kick was introduced at the same time into the laws, no eighteen-yards' line was mentioned, although all players had to stand six yards behind the one taking the kick. Most of the important clubs, however, marked a line eighteen yards from the goal-line; but it was not until nine years later, in 1901, that "a short dotted line eighteen yards from each goal-line" was prescribed.

Though it was in 1897 that the "lines defining six yards from the goal-posts" were first definitely stated to be semi-circles, yet that was naturally the interpretation that was put upon the requirement, and in most cases those particular lines had been made semi-circular.

In 1902 the semi-circles, the dotted eighteen-yards' line and the twelve-yards' lines, disappeared, and the markings assumed the form that is so familiar to the players and spectators of to-day. It is unnecessary to enter into any detailed explanation of the modern markings.

The goal area serves practically the same purpose as the semi-circles; the penalty radius combines the purposes of the twelve and eighteen yards' lines; and the penalty-kick mark rigidly defines the spot from which the kick shall be taken.

How long these markings will remain is problematical. They appear at the moment to satisfy all requirements; but should the need arise in the future, any necessary additional lines will assuredly be ordered by the "powers that be."

CLEAR PASS TO ONE OF SAME SIDE (*continued*).

4.—NOT OFF-SIDE.

A and **B** make a passing run up the centre, and **A** being confronted by **D** passes back to **B**. **B** is not off-side because, although he has not three opponents between him and the goal-line, he is not nearer the goal-line than **A** at the moment **A** passes the ball to him.

5.—OFF-SIDE. RUNNING BACK FOR BALL.

A centres the ball. **B** runs back from position 1 to position 2, and then dribbles between **D** and **E**, and scores. **B** is off-side because he has not three opponents between him and the goal-line at the moment the ball was played by **A**.

THE MAKING OF A PLAYER.

PART IV.—GOALKEEPING.

By L. RICHMOND ROOSE.

A goalkeeper is born, not made—The most responsible position on the field, and the most fascinating—Pluck, physical agility, and mental alertness the qualities which go to make a good goalkeeper—The severe mental tension attached to a strenuous match—The value of originality in goalkeeping—The best goalkeeper is he who makes the fewest mistakes—The advantage of height—Hesitation a fatal error—When a goalkeeper should leave his goal—Combination in defence—A hint to referees—Some last words of advice to the aspirant for goalkeeping honours.

A GOOD goalkeeper, like a poet, is born, not made. Nature has all to do with the art in its perfection, yet very much can be done by early training, tuition, and practice. A "natural" goalkeeper seems to keep his form without much effort. All the training possible will not make a man a goalkeeper. You must coach him, explain the finer points of the game to him, and show him the easiest and best way to take the ball to the greatest advantage, and how to meet this or that movement of the attacking forwards, and then he will be something more than a mere physical entity or specimen. Granted that the aspirant has the inherent and essential qualities in him to become successful, it is the early work and coaching that are the determining causes of after success, without which he can never hope to attain to the ideal.

In the other positions in the field success is dependent upon combined effort and upon the dovetailing of one player's work with another. With the goalkeeper it is a different matter entirely. He has to fill a position in which the principle is forced upon him that "it is good for man to be alone"—a position which is distinctly personal and decidedly individualistic in character. His is a most onerous post, and one which is equally responsible. Any other player's mistakes may be readily excused, but a single slip on the part of the last line of defence may be classed among the list of the unpardonable sins—especially when the International Selection Committee is on business bent. His one mistake or lapse may prove more costly than a score of errors committed by all his fellow-clubmates put together.

Bowden Bros.]

L. RICHMOND ROOSE,

Stoke's famous amateur goalkeeper, and Welsh International.

He is, in the opinion of many eminent critics, the most brilliant goalkeeper who ever played the game.

Nevertheless, a goalkeeper's position is a most fascinating one to take up, and the intense application which an aspirant willingly gives to it is the best proof of the powerful attraction of the duties incumbent on one filling that post. The attraction of "paddling one's own canoe," as it were, in this pastime is equally pronounced as in the orthodox river pastime itself.

To prove a successful goalkeeper, a man must be one of those destined by Nature to be "on his own," as the resources for reliably filling the post are entirely in himself; and, unless he wishes to be purely imitative, the goalkeeper, like the silkworm, must produce his materials from himself. He must not even have a nodding acquaintance with "nerves," the *bete noire* of many a man who otherwise would have been successful. The responsibility which it involves and entails should not have a tendency to make him feel timid, otherwise he must give up the idea of ever excelling. He should be full of pluck, as in a very short time experience will teach him that an ounce of that genuine and useful attribute is worth a ton of the elusive element known as luck. Individually he should be extremely keen, and his physical agility should be commensurate with his mental alertness.

Goalkeeping is looked upon as the easiest position to take upon one's self in the field. The belief is as erroneous as it is common, and those people who suggest such betray gross ignorance. Certainly there are occasions when the goalkeeper has nothing more strenuous to do than to support his own frame and weight, yet

Russell and Sons.]

INTERNATIONAL FOOTBALL—ENGLAND v. SCOTLAND, APRIL 1, 1905, AT THE CRYSTAL PALACE.

H. J. Linacre, the Notts Forest goalkeeper, kept a fine goal in this match, and his previous magnificent display at Craven Cottage in the Cup-tie between Fulham (winners) and Notts Forest stamped him as a custodian of the highest class. In the picture he is seen leaping cleverly to a long shot dropping from the Scottish forwards.

even then the routine and monotony are positively irksome to those whose preference is for something more than the "simple life" from the keeper's point of view, and on such occasions they scarcely put credence in the sentiments contained in the phrase that "they also serve who only stand and wait."

It is this long waiting for shots that tries a goalkeeper—this watching and waiting when you see your forwards and backs being slowly but surely driven in on you that will make a man unsteady at the critical moment. Only those who have followed an important Cup-tie from start to finish can appreciate the strain on the nerves of the spectators. What must it be, then, to the players engaged, particularly the goalkeeper. No doubt a good deal depends on temperament, but even the most light-hearted and careless acknowledge that the mental tension is severe, and when there is not much to occupy a goalkeeper's attention, what John Stuart Mill called "the disastrous feeling that nothing matters" is apt to creep over the best of custodians when the spur is removed and the keenness taken away or only present after long intervals.

Only those who are active votaries rather than passive critics can appreciate the merit or the charm of goalkeeping, and such expect to find a little originality concurrent with that which we see brought to bear upon other games of skill. Everything that the aspirant to first-class rank attempts to accomplish should be marked by a steady, quiet confidence. There should be nothing to denote the novice about his play, albeit a champion in embryo. As a rule, men are clever at a game because they are fond of it, and when a man is fond of anything in which he takes part, he does not usually or as a rule scamp such work as he participates in.

Players with intelligence to devise a new move or system, and application to carry it out, will go far. And for that reason the possession of personal conception and execution is desirable, although a "player with an opinion" nowadays which is not in consonance with the stereotyped methods of finessing and working for openings is shunned to no small degree, as though he carried about with him the germs of an infectious disease.

A goalkeeper, however, can be a law unto himself in the matter of his defence. He need not set out to keep goal on the usual stereotyped lines. He is at liberty to cultivate originality, and, more often than not, if he has a variety of methods in his clearances and means of getting rid of the ball, he will confound and puzzle the attacking forwards.

Trickiness and ability to dodge an opponent are as absolutely necessary to a goalkeeper's art as that a boxer should feint with his right and deliver a blow with his left. A custodian should confound his opponents when hard pressed by clearing exactly similar shots in totally different ways, and should not allow them to decide or guess by mere theory how he will act in getting rid of the ball or in clearing. He should "bounce" the forwards, but keep it within proper limits.

A goalkeeper should be one possessed of acute observation and independent thought. He should be aggressive, and have the fighting instinct or spirit in him, and if in combination with a modicum of "temper"—so-called—he will be none the worse for that. Temper is only a form of energy, and, so long as it is controlled, the more we have of it in a custodian the better. He should know every move of the game as well as he knows the alphabet, and study the mysteries of attack and the intricacies of defence, at the same time carrying his individual attitude with perfect balance. If he can give to his work the spice of a little originality, it will prove to his advantage. Stale minds rather than stale bodies and muscles are responsible for many of the indifferent displays we read of. When a person's mannerisms (*sic*) seem part of the man, unconscious and necessary to the full self-expression of his work or play, it is folly to attempt to cramp one's methods for the sake of conformity to a general type. When, however, they are foreign to his role, they become a just source of irritation, and the reason for their adoption is possibly found in the fact that the person who has aped somebody's methods, which were in turn sub-aped by others, was suffering at both extremities of his person in that he was the possessor of a swollen head and had grown too big for his boots.

Russell and Sons.]

CUP-TIE FOOTBALL—THE FINAL AT THE CRYSTAL PALACE BETWEEN ASTON VILLA AND NEWCASTLE UNITED, APRIL 15, 1905.

Although twice beaten by the ubiquitous Villa forwards, Lawrence was in no way to blame for Newcastle's defeat. The photograph shows how cleverly he anticipated a splendid cross-shot from the flying right wing, W. Brawn. Hampton, who had broken through, gave him little time to clear.

The fairest judgment of a man is by the standard of his work, and the best goalkeeper is the one who makes the fewest mistakes. Perfect custodians are not in evidence in this mundane sphere. There certainly are degrees of comparison in the best of goalkeepers, albeit of a limited kind, as the tactics indulged in by keepers are merely matters of personal equation.

"Some men are born great, others achieve greatness, others have greatness thrust upon them." A goalkeeper may be of all these, but the best keepers are principally the first.

They are expected to be perfection personified in their form—never to lapse or even make a mistake, and to possess all the virtues of the man who was sorry he had only the Ten Commandments to keep and no more. Granted perfection is desirable, but it is usually presentable only to the imagination in this imperfect world.

Let a goalkeeper be successful in his clearances, and great will be his triumph. Let him fail, and oblivion will be his portion. Orthodox views to the contrary notwithstanding, a goalkeeper and his methods of defence are the result of the physical make-up of the individual. This relative truth no one need gainsay. He should stand about six feet and no nonsense. Size gives one the impression of strength and safety and enables a goalkeeper to deal with high and wide shots with comparative ease where a smaller and shorter man would be handicapped. On the other hand, a tall and ponderous goalkeeper is at a disadvantage with the smaller and more agile rival when required to get down to swift ground or low shots. To the agility of youth should be coupled the sagacity of veterancy. His first duty, and, indeed, the primary responsibility incumbent upon him, is to ensure his team against defeat, and he should always play the game that is calculated to be most effectual in obviating defeat for his side. He should not be one of those incapable of anything out of the ordinary, but should be able to rise to the occasion when such is demanded of him ; otherwise, even if his critical friends are unable to locate any particular weakness, there will be feelings of unreliability somewhere in connection with his work. The plans which he has in his head should be carried out unhesitatingly, and he should try to make himself fit naturally into the team's fabric. To be on the tip-toe of expectancy is a quality necessary in a top-grade custodian. Like the figure of Aunt Sally on a fair green, he is there for any of the opposition to take a cheap shy at him when, how, and from what position they please. The manner in which some forwards score from unexpected positions and are successful at long range shows not only how often it is possible for a goalkeeper to be unsighted in the line of fire, but, on the other hand, it is a striking illustration of the forward's well-developed, natural abilities for taking in a position at a glance, and the defence is not found to be of the calibre supposed against such incisive attacks.

A keeper should be thoroughly in union with his backs, and thereby not only make his own work easier but help them to play better. If he is what is called a natural custodian, he will soon fit in with the defence's fabric, and there will be a blend of style which does not suggest to the spectator the idea of being put together "at twice" and where the establishment of a clearing house for adjusting differences should be requisitioned. There should be combination in defence just as well as in attack, and a complete understanding.

A class back will not merely rush an opponent and spoil his progress. He will time his tackle so as to yield the best opportunity to enable him or his goalkeeper to capture the ball and place it to the best advantage. Neither should get rid of the ball in haphazard fashion, unless in exceptional instances. They should "sweep the horizon" for the best spot to place the ball, probably to an unmarked forward who stands an excellent chance, or has the opportunity to make good headway, and, in course of time, such a defence will make the best attack appear not quite the deadly article they imagined, presuming the defenders have the ability to accept the opportunity consequent on the opposing forward's mistakes or finnicking methods. The tendency of the present-day with forwards is to over-elaboration and excessive finessing for positions in the vicinity of goal, with the inevitable result that their combined movements, carried out almost on draught-board lines, have proved ineffective against the timely virile and robust opposition to be encountered. There is too much mere trifling, unprofitable fiddling about for nothing in the forward's game. Players are not allowed a certain time, as in chess, to decide upon a move, and immediate action should be taken by a forward in front of goal, and then would goal-scoring be much more frequent than at present.

Bowden Bros.]
WOOLWICH ARSENAL *v.* EVERTON AT PLUMSTEAD, SEASON 1904-5.
How severe was the attack of the Everton forward-line at one period of this match is clearly shown by the photograph above. Ashcroft is seen making a fine save at close quarters.

Bowden Bros.]
THE INTERNATIONAL GAME BETWEEN ENGLAND AND SCOTLAND AT BRAMALL LANE GROUND, 1903.
Doig, who is now playing for Liverpool, is seen saving a hot shot from the English forwards. He kept a good goal for Scotland on this occasion. Scotland won the match by 2 goals to 1.

There is a speculative element in every goalkeeper's venture from under his posts. Leaving one's goal is looked upon as a cardinal sin by those armchair critics who tell a goalkeeper what he should do and what he should not do, and administer advice from the philosophic atmosphere of the grand stand. They wobble mentally, in proportion with the custodian's success or want of success in rushing out to meet an opponent even when the result is as inevitable as when a man's logic is pitted against a woman's tears. A goalkeeper should take in the position at once and at a glance, and, if deemed necessary, come out of his goal immediately, even if things were not what they at first seemed. Never more than in this case is it true that he who hesitates is lost. He must be regardless of personal consequences, and, if necessary, go head first into a pack into which many men would hesitate to insert a foot, and take the consequent gruelling like a Spartan. I am convinced that the reason why goalkeepers don't come out of their goal more often is their regard for personal consequences. If a forward has to be met and charged down, do not hesitate to charge with all your might. If you rush out with the intention of kicking, don't draw back, but *Kick* (with a capital K !) at once.

If a thing is worth doing at all, it is worth doing properly and with all one's energy, and he who gives hard knocks must be prepared to accept hard knocks in return. A goalkeeper should believe in himself. If you don't have confidence in yourself, it is a moral certainty your backs cannot, and their play will show it by lying close to goal, and doing most of your work. As a consequence of this, the half-backs have too much defence thrown upon them, and are thus hampered, and cannot feed their forwards, so that there is a weak display all round, which takes its origin from the defects of one man, and a want of confidence in the last defensive unit on the side.

Consistency should be aimed at. A goalkeeper on whom you cannot rely or depend is like a man to whom you ask an inconvenient question, and who prevaricates in his answer. He should not be one of those who " keep " one day with extreme brilliance, and another day make repeated and egregious mistakes. His works hould be notable for its uniformity and in distinct contrast to the curate's egg, which was found to be good only—in parts.

Real power in a goalkeeper is indicated by a combination of mental and physical skill. Separately the qualities are of great personal worth, but combined they undoubtedly characterise genius, and if a genius for guarding a goal shows itself in a young player, he is bound to come to the front. Goalkeeping is not only a physical exercise, but a moral discipline when looked upon in its true light and from a right and proper standpoint. It develops courage, perseverance, endurance, and other qualities which fit one for fighting the battle of life. It is an education both of body and mind. For the position a " mens sana in corpore sano " is requisite. Nothing is impossible, and inability to accept an opportunity consequent upon some hesitancy has often been the cause of a goalkeeper failing by a few inches, or the proverbial coat of varnish, to reach what would at one time have been a chance.

The goalkeeper's position tends to keep one's energies on the stretch, and it comes in the list of those pastimes, participation in which makes a man far younger when he arrives in the suburbs of the fifties than if he had in his youth dawdled over roses or dozed over parish magazines. Goalkeeping will take it out of a man if his heart is not in the game, and will soon kill his enthusiasm. On the other hand, if he is attached to his position until it becomes part and parcel of his nature, he will guard his lines until he is ready to drop or collapse like a concertina.

Every clearance should be designed to do something, and every return quick. The custodian should never make capital out of any doubtful point, for though he be eager to win, he should be still more determined to win like a sportsman. He will be kicked here, there, and everywhere, but should be content with appeals to the referee, and not take the law into his own hands. He should never appeal for anything he considers to be unfair. Appeals by the goalkeeper have had value, but he is scarcely the best man for the same. When granting a free kick to the opposition within scoring distance from goal, the referee should hint to the goalkeeper the nature of the free kick given, as it may be granted for one of those offences in respect of which the ball must be played by a second party before the shot would be allowed to count. It would be a great benefit if referees generally would adopt a " double " whistle for a free kick from which a goal could *not* be scored direct, and it would tend to simplify matters, especially for goalkeepers, as some referees, with extensive knowledge, give equally peculiar decisions; and it would need a desperate surgical operation of the sort suggested by Sydney Smith to introduce the why and the wherefore of these decisions very often, even to the most receptive intelligence. If a player has the ability to keep goal, he should set about trying to improve his style. He may possibly be a little unfinished at first, but he is bound to improve if he combines with the agility of youth a matured observation of the game which time alone can give. A sure eye, a perfect sense of time, and a heart—even as big as a hyacinth farm—are necessary to a goalkeeper's art, for it is an art of the rarest type. He should be as light on his feet as a dancing master, yet nothing is more reprehensible in a goalkeeper than taking wild, flying kicks, or using his feet in any way, when he can use his hands, as there is safety in numbers, and two hands are better than one foot. When he does kick, his kicking should be accuracy itself, so as to land the ball exactly where he intends. There must be boot behind the ball, muscle behind the boot, and intelligence behind both. He should be as cool as the proverbial cucumber, and good temper is an essential. Excitability and an uncontrollable disposition or temper are antagonistic to good judgment, and the goalkeeper who is devoid of judgment is useless for all practical purposes. If a player is mapping out a goalkeeper's career for himself, his course should be one of moderation, regularity, and simplicity. Nothing is ever achieved without effort or even sacrifice in one's pastimes, as in the higher walks of life, and only a study of its points and experience will educate him up to the standard expected of him. Let a player take that for granted, and he will succeed.

L. Richmond Roose.

Russell and Sons.]

AN EXCITING MOMENT NEAR GOAL IN THE GREAT FOOTBALL ASSOCIATION CUP FINAL, ASTON VILLA v. NEWCASTLE UNITED, APRIL 15, 1905.

Lawrence has just brilliantly saved his goal, after taking the ball from off the very toe of the Villa forward. The photograph is a splendid testimony to his ability as a goalkeeper.

RECORDS OF BURNLEY FOOTBALL CLUB.

By J. SUMMERSGILL.

Burnley Rovers—An Amalgamation—The Association code adopted in 1881—A Charity Cup competition instituted—Importation of Scottish players—Preston North End beaten—Banned by the English F. A.—A Royal match at Turf Moor—Burnley's League record—Official and financial records—Some memorable games—Complete list of Burnley's performances in the F. A. Cup competition.

Colours : Green jerseys, white knickers. *Ground : Turf Moor, Burnley.*

THE game of football was played at Burnley under Rugby rules about thirty years ago by a club known as the Burnley Rovers, a team composed of gentlemen of the district, the ground being situated at Calder Vale. In the late 'Seventies, the Rovers breaking up, a meeting was called by a number of gentlemen connected with the Young Men's Christian Association, the Rev. M. W. Hall, curate at the parish church, presiding. It was decided to form a club, but the title was soon changed to the Rovers. Some of the members of the original Rovers assisted to forward the movement. A warm discussion ensued on the subject of the code to play, but it was decided to adopt Rugby rules. However, in 1881, another club sprang into existence, the two amalgamating ; and at the end of that year it was decided to adopt the dribbling code, and the club became known as "Burnley." In 1882 the club migrated to Turf Moor, where its headquarters have been ever since.

A. Greenwood.]
COUNCILLOR S. McFARLANE,
Member of the Burnley F. C. committee and chairman of club, 1886-7.

B. and C.]
COUNCILLOR EDWIN WHITEHEAD,
Chairman of Burnley directors since 1898-9.

King.]
MR. R. H. WADGE,
Vice-chairman of Burnley directors since 1899-1900.

Once the Burnley Club was launched, other teams sprang into existence, such as Burnley Wanderers and Burnley Trinity ; and to foster the game, Dr. Dean, medical officer of health for Burnley, offered a cup for competition amongst local clubs for the benefit of charities, and this trophy was won and subsequently presented to the secretary, G. C. Waddington, who took part in the contest, his companions being R. Chase (who subsequently officiated in the capacity of referee), S. Hargreaves (now a member of the Burnley Town Council), J. Marsland, H. Culpan, T. Cross, J. Eastwood, H. Birley, W. Brown, T. Midgley, and R. Horsfield.

Before the season of 1883-4 was commenced, the services of Dannie Friel (a Scottish International hailing from the Vale of Leven), who was then a playing member of the Accrington Club, were enlisted, and in the course of practice games he put the budding Burnley dribblers through their paces.

In October, 1883, Friel accepted a tempting offer to become permanently attached to the Turf Moor organisation, which was further strengthened by W. Ronaldson, of the Hearts, and one of the brothers Gair, and the club made rapid strides, coming off the conquerors in eight consecutive games.

In 1884-5 Burnley were, indeed, a team to be reckoned with, for they could not only hold their own against Lancashire teams, but organisations further afield, as is shown by the fact that in November, 1884, they gained a victory over Preston North End. This was an achievement to be proud of. They also defeated Blackburn Rovers by 5—0.

In consequence of the importation of Scottish players, Burnley,

A. Greenwood, Burnley.]
A ROYAL ENCLOSURE. THE HOME OF THE BURNLEY FOOTBALL CLUB—TURF MOOR GROUND.
From the time the club joined the League the Burnley directorate have devoted constant attention to the improvement of their ground at Turf Moor, and it is now one of the best equipped enclosures in Lancashire. It was here that Burnley played Bolton Wanderers in the memorable match in October, 1886, at which the late Prince Albert Victor was present. Bolton won the game by 4 goals to 3.

along with two or three other clubs, came under the ban of the Football Association, and these clubs played each other until professionalism was legalised.

In 1887-8 Burnley played the Corinthians twice, beating the crack amateur club by 4—1 at Turf Moor, and drawing (2—2) in London. In that season they played 59 matches, 29 of which were won, 20 lost, and 10 drawn. Mr. S. McFarlane, who was a generous supporter of the club, that season presented the team with white jerseys with blue sashes bearing a badge of the Royal arms, in commemoration of the visit of Prince Albert Victor, who came to Burnley on October 13, 1886, to open the Victoria Hospital. A match took place at Turf Moor, Burnley being opposed by Bolton Wanderers, and the new rig-out was first worn, appropriately, on the next meeting of the two Royal teams. The Royal match, which attracted a large crowd—the receipts (£250) being handed over to the funds of the hospital—was won by Bolton by 4—3; but Burnley turned the tables when they wore their new costume, winning by 3—2.

This brings us to the League days, and a summary of doings in the First Division may not be out of place. It is as follows:

					Goals.			
Year.	P.	W.	L.	D.	For	Ag.	Pts.	Posn.
1888-9	22	7	12	3	42	62	17	9
1889-90	22	4	13	5	36	65	13	11
1890-1	22	9	10	3	52	63	21	8
1891-2	26	11	11	4	49	45	26	7
1892-3	30	13	13	4	51	44	30	6
1893-4	30	15	11	4	61	51	34	5
1894-5	30	11	15	4	44	56	26	9
1895-6	30	10	13	7	48	44	27	10
1896-7	30	6	17	7	43	61	19	16
1898-9	34	15	10	9	45	47	39	3
1899-1900	34	11	18	5	35	54	27	17

MR. W. R. THORNTON,
Burnley F. C.

In the second season of the League they came dangerously near losing their place among the select, for up to the beginning of March, 1890, they had not won a single match; but in January of that year they infused a lot of fresh Scottish blood, and extricated themselves from their difficulties at the expense of Stoke, who were voted out.

The re-organised team defeated Preston North End at Turf Moor by 1—0, and from that time theirs was something of the nature of a triumphal procession, for out of the next twenty-four matches they only lost four matches—two League games and two ordinary club fixtures—and wound up by winning the Lancashire Cup, defeating Blackburn Rovers, the winners of the English Cup that year, at Accrington, in the presence of 12,000 people, by 2—0. The victory caused a scene of the wildest enthusiasm. This set the club on its feet.

In 1890-1 the chairmanship of the committee fell to Mr. A. F. Sutcliffe, and the constitution of the governing body underwent a change, though the treasurer and secretary were the same.

About this time a scheme for floating the club was proposed by Mr. T. Heaton and some colleagues, the intention being to raise capital by £5 shares. Though there was every reason to believe that the scheme would succeed, it was strenuously opposed by some of the officials and the main body of the members, and the opposition succeeded; though in the light of subsequent events the step was not in the best interests of the club, for it could assuredly have been floated with a larger capital than was raised when eventually a £1 per share scheme was adopted in 1897-8.

In 1891-2 Mr. H. Bradshaw became hon. secretary, and Mr. J. Walmsley treasurer, and Mr. S. Thomas, an ardent supporter of the Burnley Union Stars F. C., which had ceased to exist, joined the committee and later became hon. treasurer.

In 1893-4 Mr. Bradshaw was chairman and Messrs. S. Thomas, D. Tillotson, and A. F. Sutcliffe the treasurer, hon. secretary, and secretary respectively. Mr. J. Walmsley became chairman in the succeeding season, with Mr. Bradshaw the hon. secretary. Amongst the committee was Mr. C. E. Sutcliffe, whose first official connection with the club this was, and in 1896-7 he was appointed chairman, a position he subsequently held on the provisional directorate during the process of floating the club, and when that was an accomplished fact Mr. Edwin Whitehead, who had been a staunch supporter of the Union Stars, joined the committee in 1896-7, and was vice-chairman in 1898-9, succeeding Mr. Sutcliffe in the chair in 1899-1900, since which time the directors have been the same, with Mr. Whitehead as president, though for two seasons they have been assisted by a committee of members of the club. Mr. H. Bradshaw, from being secretary pro tem. to the club during the provisional period, became secretary for two or three seasons—until, in fact, he accepted the position of manager for Woolwich Arsenal. He is now employed in a similar capacity at Fulham.

Between Mr. Bradshaw's departure and the appointment of Mr. J. E. Mangnall, who after four years' service accepted the post of secretary and team manager to Manchester United F. C., Mr. W. R. Thornton, one of the directors, performed the secretarial duties, and on Mr. Mangnall leaving, Mr. Spen Whittaker, who had had a long connection with football in the Accrington district, and whose brother is Mr. N. Whittaker, of London, became his successor, and he still occupies the position.

The high-water mark of financial success was reached in 1890, but gradually, owing in great measure to the largely augmented wages bill necessary to maintain a team capable of holding its own against all comers, including, of course, competent reserves, a change came over the scene. When the club descended to the Second Division at the end of 1896-7, the adverse balance was a substantial one, and it was computed that the regaining of lost prestige cost nearly £1,000. However, in 1898-9, despite the fact that the club was at one time in serious running for the championship of the First Division and finished up third—higher than ever before—there was a further loss of nearly £1,000. At the end of the season 1895-6 the club was indebted to the bank to the extent of only £242. This was increased to £989, although the share capital called up amounted to £570 by the end of 1897-8. The adverse balance was next year reduced to £412, mainly through the transfer of players, the income from this source reaching £608. At the end of the season 1899-1900 the amount owing at the bank was £1,051, and by the end of the succeeding season the adverse bank balance had gone up to £1,826, despite the fees for the transfer of players realising £244.

F. Hopwood.]
MR. SPEN WHITTAKER,
Secretary of the Burnley F. C.

In 1901-2 there was a reduction to £1,782, largely owing to the transfer of players bringing in £785. During the subsequent years to 1904-5 the amount owing at the bank had been reduced to £1,350, at which figure it stood at the commencement of 1905-6. Thus, reckoning from the year 1895-6, the expenditure had exceeded the gate receipts to the extent of £4,098—£2,475 5s. from the transfer of players; £1,046 share capital; and £576 15s., profit on the bazaar held in 1898, and opened on September 22 by the Lord Mayor of Liverpool. During the last two years the club managed, by the exercise of strict economy, to pay its way for the first time for a number of years.

In addition to the matches referred to above, the more memorable games played by Burnley are: The defeat of Sunderland by 3—2 on September 13, 1890—this being the Wearsiders' first defeat on joining the League—which was accomplished by the same combination which won the Lancashire Cup; the defeat of Preston North End at Turf Moor on March 7, 1891, by 6—2, Tom Nicol making a sensational debut for the club by scoring 4 goals; the defeat of West Bromwich Albion at Turf Moor on December 6, 1890, by 5—4, after being 1—4 at half-time; the victory over Everton by 3—2 on March 14, 1891, the winning goal being got in the last minute; the defeat of Darwen by 9—0 in a League match at Burnley, this being Burnley's largest score in connection with the First Division; the defeat of Everton in an English Cup-tie at Everton on January 23, 1892, by 3—1; the Test match at Turf Moor against Notts County, when Burnley were defeated on April 26, 1897, by 1—0, through bad luck and a blunder by the referee, which relegated Burnley to the Second Division; the defeat by 3—1 by Everton in an English Cup-tie at Turf Moor on February 26, 1898, before the largest gate on record at Burnley (£794); the defeat of Blackburn Rovers in both Test matches—by 3—1 at Ewood and 2—0 at Turf Moor—and the draw (0—0) at Stoke in the Test games (all at the back end of 1897-8), which, following on the championship of the Second Division, caused Burnley to re-appear in the First Division; the winning of the East Lancashire Charity Cup by beating Blackburn Rovers at Ewood on April 20, 1892, and again winning the trophy against Accrington on April 28, 1893, having previously beaten the Rovers; the defeat of the Blackburn Rovers by 1—0 on October 7, 1899; and the reverse sustained in the English Cup-tie at Stoke on February 20, 1896, by 7—1, after a draw of 2—2 at Burnley.

Though Burnley have at times achieved noteworthy feats in cup competitions, they have not generally done well in the English Cup-ties. They have only once been in the third round, and that was when they fell to Everton before the record crowd at Turf Moor. Besides winning the Lancashire Cup, they have figured three times in the final—three years in succession—a feat which was recognised by the County Committee giving the players medals. They last season won the East Lancashire Charity Cup, beating Blackburn Rovers in the final by 3—0. Burnley have held the trophy almost all the time since they first won it in 1892.

As most followers of the club will be interested in Burnley's record in the premier Cup competition, a complete summary of their games will be found in the subjoined table :—

1885-6—Burnley, 0; *Darwen Old Wanderers, 11. (Burnley played their second team, the first not being eligible.)

1886-7—Burnley, 3; *Astley Bridge, 3. *Burnley, 2; Astley Bridge, 2. (Burnley scratched.)

1887-8—*Burnley, 4; Darwen Old Wanderers, 0. Burnley, 2; *Accrington, 3.

1888-9—*Burnley, 4; Old Westminsters, 3. Burnley, 1; *West Bromwich Albion, 5.

1889-90—Burnley, 1; *Sheffield United, 2.

1890-1—*Burnley, 4; Crewe Alexandra, 2. (Extra time played, before which score was 2—2.) Burnley, 1; *Notts County, 2.

1891-2—Burnley, 3; *Everton, 1. Burnley, 1; Stoke, 3. (The game with Everton was a re-played tie, Burnley winning the first match.)

1892-3—*Burnley, 2; Small Heath, 0. Burnley, 0; *Sheffield Wednesday, 1.

1893-4—Burnley, 0; *Notts County, 2.

1894-5—Burnley, 1; *Newcastle United, 2.

1895-6—*Burnley, 6; Woolwich Arsenal, 1. *Burnley, 1; Stoke, 1. Burnley, 1; *Stoke, 7 (re-played).

1896-7—*Burnley, 0; Sunderland, 1.

1897-8—*Burnley, 3; Woolwich Arsenal, 1. *Burnley, 3; Burslem Port Vale, 1. *Burnley, 1; Everton, 3.

1898-9—*Burnley, 2; Sheffield United, 2. Burnley, 1; *Sheffield United, 2 (re-played).

1899-1900—*Burnley, 0; Bury, 1.

1900-1—Burnley, 0; *Newton Heath, 0. *Burnley, 7; Newton Heath, 1. Burnley, 0; *Small Heath, 1.

1901-2—Burnley, 3; *Bishop Auckland, 2. Burnley, 0; *Walsall, 1.

1902-3—Burnley, 0; *Reading, 1.

1903-4—*Burnley, 8; Keswick, 0. Burnley, 0; *Darwen, 3.

1904-5—*Burnley, 1; Lincoln City, 1. Burnley, 2; *Lincoln City, 3 (re-played).

* Indicates ground on which game was played.

BURNLEY FOOTBALL CLUB—THE TEAM FOR 1905-6.

Top Row: Mr. S. WHITTAKER, Secretary. O. PICKLES, Groundsman. DIXON. GREEN. MOFFAT. TAYLOR. MCFARLANE.

A. *Greenwood. Burnley*]

Second Row: BARRON. D. WALDERS. PARKER. CRETNEY.

Bottom Row: J. WALDERS. DAVIDSON. R. SMITH. WOOD. MURPHY.

Bowden Bros.] THE ARMY v. THE NAVY AT QUEEN'S CLUB GROUNDS, WEST KENSINGTON.

Played on Saturday, February 25, 1905. This match, in which the Army proved victorious by two goals to nil, was graced by the presence of His Most Gracious Majesty King Edward VII. and His Royal Highness the Prince of Wales. In the photograph the Navy are seen making a hot onslaught on the Army goal.

FOOTBALL IN THE ARMY.

ITS HISTORY AND RECORDS.

By Captain E. G. CURTIS, Hon. Sec. Army Football Association.

How the Army Challenge Cup competition was instituted—H.R.H. the Duke of Cambridge becomes President of the Association—Rapid growth of the Association—The Army Cup Final at Aldershot—First season's entries—The Association's secretaries—The first representative Army team—The Army F. A. becomes affiliated to the Football Association—Well-known Army players—The Army Cup winners defeated in India—Formation of the Cavalry Football Association and institution of the Cavalry Cup—Ireland establishes an Army F. A.—The Cup lost, and found—The Association's indebtedness to the Press—Some points on finance—A few words of thanks.

April 10th, 1888.

Dear Sir,—A proposal having been made to start an Army Association Football Challenge Cup, to be competed for by Regiments, Battalions, &c., quartered in the United Kingdom, a meeting to discuss the matter will take place at No. 1, Whitehall, on Friday next at 3.30 p.m. Major Marindin, K.C.M.G., President of the Football Association of England, has kindly consented to take the chair, and has lent his offices for the meeting. It is requested that all officers who take an interest in football will attend and aid in forming a committee to draw up rules, &c., for the competition.

We are, dear sir, yours truly,
H. McCALMONT, Scots Guards,
F. E. LAWRENCE, Rifle Brigade,
Acting Honorary Secretaries.

Such was the first intimation of the intention to create football as a competition in the Army. Previous to the issue of the above notice, inter-regimental football matches were practically non-existent; it is true that there had been military football teams; none more famous than the Royal Engineers' team of the Seventies, which figured in the Final Tie of the Football Association Cup four times in seven years. It is even recorded that more than twenty years before this history opens, a match had been played at Aldershot between the Army and the Wanderers Football Club. There does not appear to have been any record kept of the result of this game, and this can hardly be wondered at when one recalls the primitive arrangements of the friendly, but none the less spirited, contests of those days.

THE LATE SIR F. A. MARINDIN, K.C.M.G.

To return to that Friday in April, 1888—how incongruous it now seems to mention Friday in connection with the game—the meeting was held, Major Marindin presided, and some fourteen military officers attended to "discuss the matter." One alone of those fifteen now remains on the committee of the Army F. A.—Lieutenant (now Lieut.-Colonel) J. Winn, of the Royal Engineers, who subsequently for one season held office as the honorary secretary.

As the outcome of the meeting, it was decided to start the Army Cup competition; rules were drafted to the number of fifteen, all of which remain in force at the present time. An honorary secretary was appointed and also a working committee.

To anyone who has ever followed Army football, it would be superfluous to recall the name of the first honorary secretary; his association with the soldiers' winter game is known to all; the prime mover in its inauguration, the mainspring in its early days, and the keenest of its supporters up to the time of his painfully sudden death in December, 1902.

Referring to the first handbook of the Association—a leaflet one might term it—one finds that two pages were devoted to what are now known as the "rules," but which were described in those days as "primary conditions." The remaining six pages testify to the sound basis on which the Association was founded.

Within six weeks of the first meeting, H.R.H. The Duke of Cambridge consented to be president of the Association, an office which he held until the time of his death in 1904. For the first few years of the competition H.R.H. made a point of attending the Final Tie and presenting the Cup to the winning team; doubtless his personal interest in those days went far towards fostering the sporting spirit of the competition. His Royal Highness the Duke of Connaught is now president of the Association, whilst His Majesty, King Edward the Seventh, has graciously consented to be the patron.

THE LATE COLONEL H. L. B. McCALMONT, C.B.
First secretary of the Army F. A., 1888 and 1889.

On August 21, 1888, the first circular of the Army F. A. was issued (it is a coincidence that this circular bears the same date as the present honorary secretary's first commission); but a few weeks elapsed before the Army Cup was purchased; it is described as follows:

"The Cup is a reproduction in smaller size of the celebrated Warwick Vase found in the River Tiber, and now in the possession of the Earl of Warwick. It is of solid silver, and very massive; the workmanship is a fine specimen of the silversmith's art, being skilfully executed in every detail. The Cup stands upon a square silver pedestal, and the height is twenty inches."

The silver pedestal is now full up with the records of the Cup competition, and an ebony plinth with silver faces has been added, and is shown in the accompanying photograph.

What rapid strides the Association has made in the few years of its existence is well known. Not so many months ago, the writer, who has not the pleasure (?) of residing at Aldershot, inquired of a well-known supporter of the game there if the interest in Army football was general in the Aldershot command. His reply was characteristic. It was to this effect: "The men talk nothing else, they know it all; they know more about the Army rules than you yourself could tell them." What a change in a few years! Football has emptied the barrack-rooms (shall it be said the canteens also?); the present-day soldier spends his leisure in the open air, and is doubtless all the better for that. Go to any one of the large garrisons and this statement can be easily verified; but the biggest proof of the popularity of the game with the soldier is to be seen at Aldershot on any Easter Monday—the day which is now recognised as being set apart for the Army Final. There, on a ground which could not be surpassed by any in England, will be found thousands of spectators—certainly anything up to twenty thousand—a fair sprinkling of civilians, but in the main the soldier—the soldier of every rank, the soldier's wife and the soldier's child; uniforms and badges of every regiment in the Army; rows and rows of "parked waggons" which serve to seat the masses stand at the side and at the end of the ground, a full band playing, and the pipers taking their share; the Army Cup carried round the ground before the match so that all may see it, and then deposited in the enclosure reserved for the committee.

THE ARMY FOOTBALL ASSOCIATION CHALLENGE CUP.

Ninety minutes—perhaps more—of breathless excitement, the final whistle, and the stupendous rush of cheering soldiery all making for the same point—the roped enclosure of the committee.

A few words of congratulation to the teams from some valiant officer of high rank, the Cup handed to the captain of the winning team, the medals presented, the usual cheers—and one cheer more!—and away go the thousands—to wait for the next season to come round.

Gregory and Co.]

HOW TOMMY ATKINS LEARNS HIS FOOTBALL—THE ART OF KICKING.

A scene on the parade ground with the Queen's Royal West Surrey Regiment.

The arrangements are admirably made by the Army Athletic Club, who give the Army F. A. a guarantee for the match ; this amount, together with the profits of the Semi-finals, and the residue of the entries, go to make up the fund from which is voted annually to the teams which have journeyed farthest the grants in aid of travelling expenses. The football spectator who seeks his full of enthusiasm should go and see the Army Final!

COLONEL W. P. PULTENEY, C.B., D.S.O. (Scots Guards), Secretary of the Army F. A., 1891, '92, '93, and '94.

To return to the first season's competition, entries for the Cup competition were called for in August, 1888, and forty-four teams responded ; of that number of original entrants, nine of the teams have since figured in the Final rounds of the competition ; the majority of the entries came from the Infantry battalions, but it is noticeable that all branches of the service were represented. By the time the Semi-final was reached there only remained the 2nd Battalion South Staffordshire Regiment, 1st Scots Guards, 1st Battalion Cameron Highlanders, and the 2nd Battalion Argyll and Sutherland Highlanders ; the last named eventually won the Cup by defeating the 2nd Battalion South Staffordshire Regiment at Kennington Oval by 2 goals to 0 on March 27, 1889, and on which occasion Major Marindin acted as referee. At the end of the first season there was a balance credit of £28, after paying all expenses, including the purchase of the Cup. A very satisfactory commencement.

It would be tedious to enter into details of each subsequent year's competition ; let it suffice to reproduce from this year's handbook the record of the results of the Final ties, together with the number of entries in each year.

WINNERS OF THE ARMY CUP.

	Number of Entries.
1888-9—2nd Bn. Argyll and Sutherland Highlanders beat 2nd Bn. South Staffordshire Regiment [2—0].	44
1889-90—2nd Bn. Black Watch beat 2nd Bn. Scots Guards [3—1].	45
1890-1—2nd Bn. Scots Guards beat 2nd. Bn. Argyll and Sutherland Highlanders [2—0].	46
1891-2—2nd Bn. Scots Guards beat 1st Bn. Scots Guards [2—1].	45
1892-3—2nd Bn. The Queen's Own (Royal West Kent Regiment) beat 1st Bn. Sherwood Foresters [1—0] (after a drawn match, 0—0).	47
1893-4—2nd Bn. Black Watch beat Royal Artillery (Gosport) [7—2].	54
1894-5—Royal Artillery (Portsmouth) beat 2nd Bn. Black Watch [2—0].	64
1895-6—1st Bn. Royal Scots beat 2nd Bn. The Queen's Own (Royal West Kent Regiment) [3—1].	58
1896-7—Royal Artillery (Portsmouth) beat 1st Bn. Lancashire Fusiliers [1—0].	54
1897-8—2nd Bn. Gordon Highlanders beat Royal Artillery (Portsmouth) [2—0].	52
1898-9—1st Bn. South Lancashire Regiment beat Army Service Corps (Aldershot) [3—0].	54
1899-1900—No Competition.	
1900-1—2nd Bn. Highland Light Infantry beat 3rd Bn. Coldstream Guards [1—0].	44
1901-2—Details Black Watch beat 4th Bn. Lancashire Fusiliers [1—0] (after a drawn match, 0—0).	37
1902-3—Service Bn. R. E. beat 2nd. Bn. North Staffordshire Regiment [2—0] (after a drawn match, 1—1).	43
1903-4—Royal Marine Artillery beat Service Bn. R. E. [1—0].	72
1904-5—2nd Bn. Grenadier Guards beat Service Bn. R. E. [2—1].	77

It will be seen that the number of entries has steadily increased ; an average of fifty-two per season shows that the competition is as popular as it is widespread. One knows of teams in the Football Association Cup competition travelling from Plymouth to Newcastle, and vice-versa ; but regimental clubs have gone further than that to play in the Army Final. A further reproduction from the Army handbook shows the list of officers who have acted as honorary secretaries to the Association ; out of eighteen seasons it will be seen that Major Lowther and Captain Curtis have each served for four seasons, whilst Colonel Pulteney is close up with three.

List of Officers who have held Office as Hon. Secretary and Hon. Treasurer since the formation of the Association in 1888.

April, 1888—	Secretary ..	H. McCalmont, Scots Guards.
	Treasurer ..	F. E. Lawrence, Rifle Brigade.
Jan., 1890—	Secretary & Treasurer	J. Winn, R. E.
Nov., 1890—	,,	F. E. Hanbury, Scots Guards.
Sept., 1891—	,,	W. P. Pulteney, Scots Guards.
Jan., 1895—	,,	H. C. Lowther, Scots Guards.
Sept., 1898—	,,	R. Ford, Army Service Corps.
Oct., 1899—	,,	W. Simpson, Royal Fusiliers.
Sept., 1900—	,,	H. E. B. Newenham, Royal Fusiliers.
Feb., 1901—	,,	E. G. Curtis, Bedfordshire Regiment.
Sept., 1901—	,,	R. Ford, Army Service Corps.
April, 1902—	,,	E. G. Curtis, Bedfordshire Regiment.

In December, 1891, the Football Association Council decided to recommend affiliated Associations to admit to their matches, free of charge, soldiers in uniform ; the majority of the County and District Associations were pleased to grant this privilege, and it is only right now to say that their kindness in doing so is much appreciated, not only by those who benefit directly, but by those who realise what such a concession entails.

It was in the winter of 1892 that the Army F. A. first put a representative Army team in the field. On Christmas Eve of that year the Army and the Corinthians teams met at the Oval. The soldiers' team included: Wood and Hyslop, both of the 2nd Scots Guards (holders of the Army Cup), the last-named was afterwards a Scottish International ; Reed, of the Cameronians, and Powell, of the South Staffordshire Regiment, who, on leaving the Army, joined the Woolwich Arsenal team, and subsequently died from injuries received at football. The Corinthians included : W. N. Winckworth, A. G. Topham, with G. Brann, A. G. Henfrey, G. H. Cotterill, J. G. Veitch, and R. R. Sandilands. What a front line! At half-time the Army led by 3 goals to 1, but later the game underwent a startling change ; Veitch and Cotterill each added a goal, and then on the stroke of time Sandilands fairly snatched the match out of the fire, and the Army "went down" to the tune of 4—3.

MAJOR H. C. LOWTHER, D.S.O. (Scots Guards), Secretary of the Army F. A., 1895, '96, '97, and '98.

In January, 1894, the Army F. A. was affiliated to the Football Association, and in due course was permitted to be represented on the Council of that body. Of late years the Army representative has been a constant attendant at the Council meetings ; at the present time, when leagues and competitions are springing up in every direction, it is not surprising to find that the Army F. A. is directly concerned in many matters that come before the F. A. Council.

In January, 1895, Captain W. P. Pulteney resigned the post of honorary secretary on proceeding abroad for special service. He was succeeded by Lieutenant H. C. Lowther, of the Scots Guards. During the time that each of these officers was honorary secretary, by their indefatigable efforts the welfare of the Association progressed very considerably. Entries for the Cup competition increased by leaps and bounds, the existence of the Association was brought into prominence, and the Army teams, although not always fully representative, rendered very good accounts of themselves.

CAPTAIN E. G. CURTIS (Bedfordshire Regiment), Secretary Army F. A., 1901, 1903, 1904, and 1905. Secretary of the Punjaub-Bengal A. F. A., 1895 to 1899.

To Colonel Pulteney—as we know him now—must be attributed to a great extent the credit of having brought the Association to maturity. Since his return to England from East Africa, where he gained the Distinguished Service Order, he has taken a prominent part in the management of the Association; in fact, since his return from the South African campaign, he has acted as the president of the committees. Well-known players of the Army, between 1892 and 1896, were: Lieutenant W. S. Gosling, of the Scots Guards; Private Hyslop, of the same corps; Reilly, of the Royal Artillery, Portsmouth (since an International); Hanna, of the Portsmouth Gunners; Menham, of the 3rd Battalion Grenadier Guards; Lambie, of the Highland Light Infantry; and Sergeants Sharp and McGregor, both of the Royal West Kent Regiment. George, the famous Aston Villa "keeper" of the present time, was also serving in the Royal Artillery at that time, but his light passed undiscovered!

CAPTAIN W. SIMPSON (late Royal Fusiliers) has refereed ten Army Cup Final Ties.

In September, 1895, the Punjaub-Bengal Army Football Association was affiliated and inaugurated in Northern India. Colonel P. J. Hughes, of the Cameronians, and the writer, were responsible for its inception. The rules of the competition adhere firmly to those of the Army F. A., and the competition itself is regarded in India as the blue riband of Army football there. So far as can be traced, no regiment or corps has won both these Army Cup competitions.

It is noticeable that the Army Cup winners of 1897-8 went out to India in October, 1898, and were defeated in the first round of the P. B. A. F. A. Cup in the following December, although nine of their Cup winners figured in the team. It was interesting to watch this team endeavouring to accustom themselves to the very different style of play; for in India the ball is always in the air and seldom on the ground. Many of the poor fellows in that team lost their lives in South Africa within twelve months of the match, and their much-beloved secretary, Lieutenant "Jackie" Outhwaite, died of enteric fever before he had been six months in India and whilst he was the honorary secretary of the P. B. A. F. Association. His enthusiasm for his regimental team is spoken of still in Aldershot. He *was* keen, and considered nothing an extravagance when his team was to benefit thereby. The system of completing the competition differs to the English methods, for when eight teams only remain, they are collected at a military centre—generally Umballa—and the matches are played off there. Drawn games are not infrequent, and these are re-played on the following morning at 6 a.m., before the sun is up. And isn't it cold, cheerless work looking on!

In 1896 the Cavalry Football Association was formed and affiliated to the A. F. A., and a Cavalry Cup competition instituted.

A record of the results of this competition is attached hereto.

CAVALRY CUP.

RESULTS OF THE COMPETITION.

1896—8th Hussars	beat	9th Lancers.
1897—2nd Life Guards	,,	15th Hussars.
1898—Royal Horse Guards	,,	12th Lancers.
1899—10th Hussars	,,	8th Hussars.
1900—No Competition.		
1901—No Competition.		
1903—6th Inniskilling Dragoons	,,	1st Royal Dragoons.
1904—17th Lancers	,,	14th Hussars.
1905—3rd Dragoon Guards	,,	14th Hussars.

HON. SECS., CAVALRY FOOTBALL ASSOCIATION.

1896-1897—Capt. Burns Lindow, 8th Hussars.
1897-1905—Capt. Viscount Crichton, D.S.O., R.H.G.
1905—Surg.-Capt. B. Pares, 1st Life Guards.

The institution of a separate competition for the cavalry was a very sound idea. Although no cavalry regiment has as yet gone far in the Army Cup competition, it is not suggested that the mounted man is not a good exponent of the game; anyone who witnessed the Cavalry Cup Final Tie on the Fulham Ground this year would agree that the football was of no mean type. The work and duties of the foot-soldier are more suitable for the game, and the cavalry man has not quite so much time to himself as his comrade in the infantry. For five seasons, not including the two years when the competition was in abeyance, Viscount Crichton has been the honorary secretary; his close association with the work of the Emergency Committee of the A. F. A. has enabled him to keep the Cavalry competition thoroughly up-to-date, and it is due to his individual efforts that the work of the C. F. A. committee is not very arduous.

In 1897 the Irish Army Football Association came into existence, and was affiliated to the Army Association. There is an Irish Army Cup competition conducted on exactly the same lines as the home competition. The rules of the Irish A. F. A. conform in every detail to those of the parent Association, and teams feel, when in Ireland, that they are as well cared for as if they were in Aldershot.

MAJOR R. FORD, D.S.O. (Army Service Corps), Secretary of the Army F. A., 1899 and 1902.

At the commencement of the 1898-9 season, Captain Reginald Ford, of the Army Service Corps, took over the Army secretaryship. Towards the end of this season arose the sensational disqualification of the Portsmouth Royal Artillery from the Amateur Cup competition. The lesson was most beneficial; the old rule of seven days' training limit was abolished, and regiments have since found themselves on a more equal footing. The Army Cup has since then wandered about considerably. Long may it wander!

CAPTAIN VISCOUNT CRICHTON, D.S.O. (Royal Horse Guards), Secretary Cavalry F. A., 1897 to 1905.

In October, 1899, the entries numbered forty-five, but the unforeseen occurred; amongst the many thousands who were destined for South Africa, Captain Ford was one of the first to go. His term in office had been brief but eventful. The Army F. A. is much indebted to him for certain improvements which he brought about. Captain W. Simpson took over the post. His name had for some years been prominent in the football world. As a referee his experience must be unique. It is not given

2nd BATTALION GRENADIER GUARDS' FOOTBALL CLUB.

WINNERS ARMY CUP, HOUSEHOLD BRIGADE CUP, AND GREAT WESTERN SUBURBAN LEAGUE, 1904-5.

Top Row: Pte. R. Griffiths. Cpl. T. Drabble. Pte. J. Smith.

Second Row: Drill-Sergt. J. M. Myles. Col.-Sergt. W. Napier. Pte. P. Joyce. Sergt. F. Godfrey, Captain. Sergt. I. V. O. Hill. O.R. Col.-Sergt. F. Martin, Secretary.

Gale and Polden, Ltd.]

Third Row: Lieut. and Adjt. B. N. Brooke. Lieut.-Col. R. G. Gordon Gilmour, C.B., M.V.O., D.S.O. Sergt.-Major W. E. Acraman.

Bottom Row: Pte. S. C. Harris. Pte. H. King. Pte. J. Shepley. Sergt.-Mstr.-Tailor J. Kelly. Pte. D. Chapman.

to many to take ten successive Army Finals in addition to one F. A. Cup Final, but this is his record. His tenure of office was brief. The war in South Africa caused the competition to fall through, and before the following season had come round, Captain Newenham, of the Royal Fusiliers, had taken up the secretaryship, but only for a few months, for he, in turn, followed in the never-ceasing stream for South Africa. On his departure the writer took up the work. The Cup competition was kept going somehow. In the meantime the Army Cup had disappeared! It was eventually traced to a very safe resting-place in a bank in Lancashire, whence it was recovered. The "holders" at the time were on the veldt, and communication with them was difficult. However, all's well that ends well.

In September, 1901, Captain Ford returned to take up the reins of office which he had temporarily vacated. The movements of troops were uncertain, so that it was a matter for congratulation to get even thirty-seven entries. About that time Captain A. H. Marindin was elected to the committee to perpetuate the memory of his uncle, the late Sir Francis Marindin. Colonel Sir Edward Ward also became a vice-president then. At the end of the 1900-1 season the Cup had for a change returned to Aldershot, throughthe agency of the 2nd Highland Light Infantry, but twelve months later found its way North again, in charge of the Details of the Black Watch. A few months in office sufficed to impress upon Captain Ford that his leisure was too much taken up to enable him to devote to the work the time necessary to cope with the ever-increasing correspondence which the post entails. At the end of the season he resigned, and the writer returned to the post, which he had previously held for a few months.

It is hard to write of one's own work, so the record for the past few seasons must be omitted. What has been done during that time has been done with the best of motives. Progress is always open to criticism, but criticism is sometimes encouraging. The entries have risen to as many as seventy-nine. The Army teams have won a few matches (not forgetting a victory over the Corinthians) and lost quite as many. The first representative match against the Royal Navy has been played—and won; and the unique event of the Sovereign and the Prince of Wales attending the match has to be recorded. All of these events are fresh in every footballer's memory. It only remains to be added that the correspondence of the Association has assumed alarming proportions, and that the work of the committee is by no means a sinecure.

Leagues and competitions spring up in every direction. The "stars" of the Army teams are tempted away to fresh fields, but few of them seem to live up to the reputation which caused them to give up their soldiering. Oh, if these would-be Internationals would but listen to the words of advice which are so often showered upon them! Words from their own comrades or their superiors all seem of no avail. To those soldier-players, who think that life outside the Army is bristling with attractions, would I say: "Look before you leap." From the front rank of Army football to the reserves of a League team is not a very big jump, and from there to the ranks of the unemployed footballer is not so very far.

The Army Association has always been indebted to the Press for giving early intimation of their doings, and for their fair accounts of matches played. No doubt the gentlemen of the press-box appreciate the many difficulties which the selectors of the teams have to contend with, and make allowance accordingly. Certain it is that when the Army team is playing every member does his best, and "sticks it" to the bitter end—and this is as it should be.

Much of the financial success of the Association is attributable to the "gates" of the Semi-finals. These matches are invariably played on the grounds of the best-known professional clubs. The Association pays for the use of the ground, and all expenses of advertising, posting, &c.; but the club secretaries by their own personal interest are the men who make the matches draw, and to those gentlemen, as well as the club proprietors, are thanks due. Before closing this history, which I do not for one instant claim to be complete, I would take this opportunity of thanking all those who, during my term of office, have given me their support—not only those whose names are prominent in the control of the Army's winter game, but those in the non-commissioned ranks of the Service who have frequently and willingly given me their opinions and assistance, both of which we of the governing committee are proud to have received.

E. G. CURTIS.

Gregory and Co.]

EASTER MONDAY—A GREAT FOOTBALL DAY AT ALDERSHOT. THE FINAL FOR THE ARMY FOOTBALL ASSOCIATION CHALLENGE CUP.

This annual contest is looked forward to with the greatest interest by the men who serve their King, and no more stirring sight can be seen than that presented at Aldershot on the occasion of the great Army Cup Final. The Challenge Cup is carried round the ground before the match so that all may see it, and the twenty-two stalwarts are cheered on in the game by the rank and file who muster some 20,000 strong to do honour to the occasion. Last year victory rested with the 2nd Grenadier Guards, who defeated the Service Battalion Royal Engineers by 2 goals to 1.

A HOT TIME IN THE GOAL MOUTH.

The goalkeeper saves his charge.

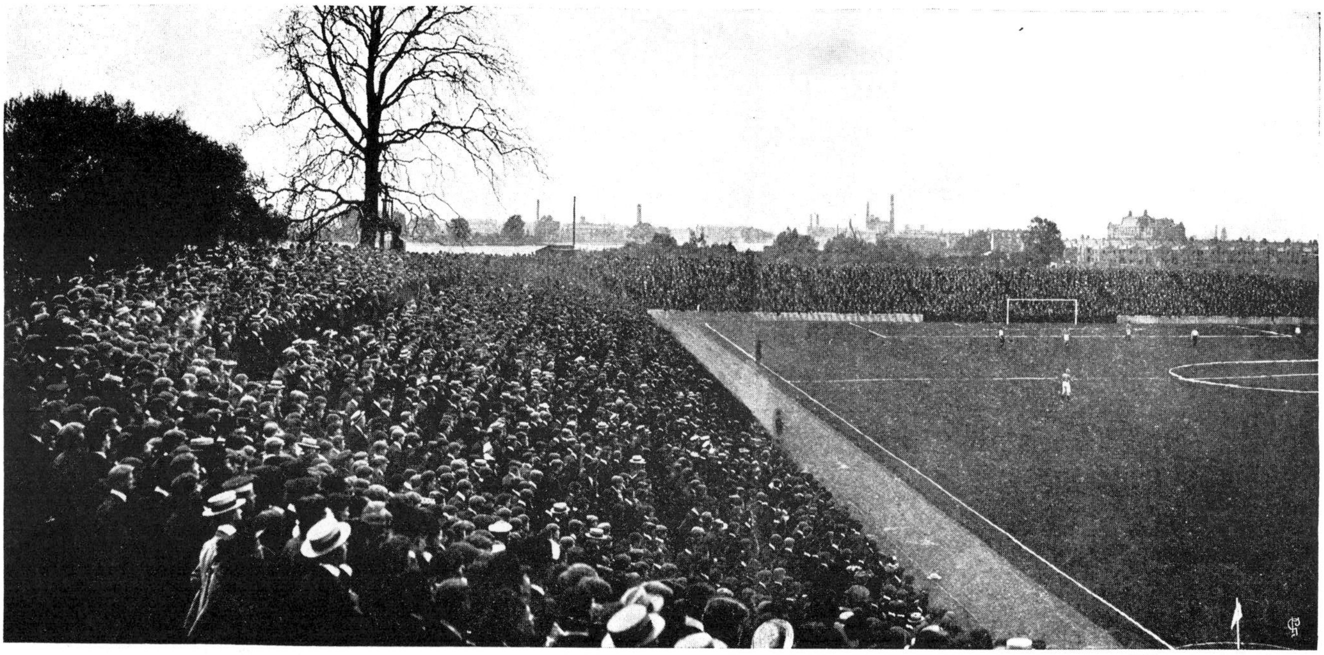

[Photograph by Moyse.

CRAVEN COTTAGE—FULHAM'S MAGNIFICENT

No Southern League club of recent years has made such rapid strides as Fulham. Even those who knew the playing field at Craven Cottage a year ago perfect, and that at the eastern end, not fully shown in the photograph, rises over eighty tiers in height, and when packed with spectators

FULHAM'S FORWARD MOVEMENT.

By H. E. JACKSON.

The origin of Fulham Football Club—Jack Howland, the goalkeeper—Old memories—Fulham and the Wasps at the Half Moon Ground—Craven Cottage Ground—A historic spot—How a workman discovered an old well—The surface of the ground raised above water-level—How Fulham's "pros." were engaged in the old days—Fulham's fight for elevation from the Second Division of the Southern League—A test match with Brentford—A limited liability company formed—Jack Fryer signed on—How Fulham were elected to the First Division of the Southern League—Splendid performances in 1904-5—The watchword of the club, "Enterprise."

Colours: White shirts, black knickers. *Ground: Craven Cottage, Fulham.*

WHILST I was a boy at school football was just beginning to take "hold" in the South of England, and though Fulham originated as Fulham St. Andrew's as far back as 1880, few, if any, of its originators even dreamt that from that small "acorn" would grow the gigantic "oak" of the Fulham Football Club of to-day.

It will be a surprise to many to know that the club was not founded in Fulham at all, but had its origin in the Sunday-school of St. Andrew's Church, West Kensington. Amongst the early 1880 players I remember Jack Howland, a big, vigorous man who, in the course of his career, came to grief in almost every imaginable manner, and finally retired from the game with a compound fracture of the right leg. He was a natural player, with great physical advantages, for his height exceeded six feet by two inches, and his big frame carried, then, nearly thirteen stones of weight.

To-day—I saw him recently—the genial Jack is a fat and comfortable boniface, and he actually blushed when I asked how many pounds he would have to reduce to reach playing weight again.

Other founders have passed to the "great majority," and one remembers with regret that Jack May and Arthur Thomas are no longer with us. Looking back over the years when Fulham were "small fry," Jack May seems to have been the only goal-keeper the club ever had, for his years of duty numbered so many. Others came, had trials, and departed, and Jack took up his place between the sticks again; but though he "retired" so many times, he usually came back again to fill the gap and get another limb broken. Poor chap, he died suddenly, not twelve months ago, and the inquest revealed the fact that nearly every bone in his body had been broken at various times.

I remember seeing him strip in his last playing season—about 1897—and what with bandaged ribs, rubber ankle-pieces, and knee supports, he looked more like an Egyptian mummy than one of the best goalkeepers London ever produced. His only club was Fulham, although he occasionally took trips with the City Ramblers in the days of Charley McGahey and Frank Whithington.

Poor Arthur Thomas was more than a father to the club, and to him, more than any other soul, Fulham owes its very existence to-day. His playing days were short, for ill-health caused his retirement from active participation in the game, but as a member of the committee he rendered excellent service, and for years he acted as treasurer when the club's coffers were mostly empty, and the "necessary" was provided by the holder (?) of the funds.

Enough of sad memories. As a local team, Fulham St. Andrew's prospered, and when the building fiend drove them from their home in Lillie Road, Fulham Cross, to Barn Elms, Barnes, the little crowd of supporters that had gathered round the Fulhamites did not desert them. Other grounds that Fulham claimed as "home" in the early days were Ranelagh House, a ground adjoining the present Hurlingham Club, and Stansfeld's Field, adjoining the famous Swan Brewery in Fulham Road. At neither of these were the Fulham "Saints" allowed a lengthy stay, for the advance of the brick-and-mortar merchant claimed the space on each occasion.

Again Fulham—for by this time "St. Andrew's" had been dropped—had to find a ground on the other side of the River

Putney.]

ENCLOSURE ON THE BANKS OF THE THAMES.

are astounded at the wonderful transformation that has been made at the Fulham Ground. The grand stand is 120 yards in length, the terracing quite presents a spectacle imposing to a degree. The ground has the additional advantage of placing the spectators close to the field of play.

Thames, and for some years they shared the famous Half-Moon Cricket Ground at Putney with the Wasps' Rugby fifteen. Even in those days the Association game took precedence over the carrying code, for when half of the ground had to be given over to the builder, Fulham were able to outbid their Rugby rivals for the remaining strip.

What memories that old Half-Moon Ground brings back! With a threepenny "gate" the black-and-whites gathered round them one of the most one-sided crowds I have ever seen, and about this time Fulham began to be almost able to pay their way.

"Old followers of Fulham will remember Jack May knocking Smith, the Paddington centre-forward, senseless. It was in a West London Cup-tie, and Smith got his head to the ball just as Jack was punching it out of goal. The result was disastrous for the Paddington man, in spite of his hard head, and I know it *was* hard, for earlier in the game our craniums collided when we both jumped up to head a kick out from goal.

Moyse.]

MR. H. BRADSHAW,
Fulham's Manager.

He was for twenty years connected with Burnley F. C. as player, secretary, and manager. He was with Woolwich Arsenal as manager when the Plumstead team won their way into the First Division of the League.

That May was not always so fortunate was borne out by his mishap during the same season, for keeping goal at Newbury he was knocked unconscious into his own goal in endeavouring to save from a corner kick.

Ten years ago this season the Half-Moon Ground was taken over by the speculating builder, and Fulham had to seek another new home, and, after much searching, the present Craven Cottage Ground was discovered.

To-day it is a football pitch replete with the latest and most up-to-date conveniences, with banks and stands that any club in the country may well envy, and a playing pitch second to none in the kingdom.

But ten years ago Craven Cottage—historical place that it is—could boast nothing level but Craven Steps, which still form a River Thames land-mark, and for one whole season the Fulhamites had to play all matches on opponents' grounds whilst their own place was being put in order.

Hills and valleys, trees and shrubs, mud and lakes, were the great features of the pitch when Fulham acquired it on the "half-gate" principle. Lest some of my readers should not understand the latter term, let me explain that half of the money taken at the "gate" was the landlord's rent.

I mentioned earlier in this article that Craven Cottage was of historical interest, and during the course of laying out the ground, a subterranean passage, which led from the old Cottage under the river to the Barnes side, and which in the olden days was doubtless an acceptable way of giving foes the slip, had to be filled up, and another relic, discovered in a peculiar way, was a well, some twelve feet deep, now also filled in. Perhaps to this day that well would never have been discovered had not a man fallen through the rotten lid which covered the top of it. When Fulham took possession of Craven Cottage, the land lay some feet below the level of the river at high tide, and to remedy this it was decided to raise the surface six feet all over.

Moyse.]

H. E. JACKSON,
Secretary.

He has been connected with Fulham F. C. for many years, as player, committeeman, and secretary. He publicly advocated for a first-class side in 1899 without success. An untiring worker and a real enthusiast.

Ten years ago who would have dared to forecast such a future for Fulham as the club has achieved? Horace Wilkins was secretary then, but Jack Aylott succeeded him soon afterwards, and it was in his time that Fulham took their first step in the right direction by adopting the paid player in a humble way.

"Ten bob a week and a job" was the usual term of engagement with Fulham's "pros." in those days, and what awful duffers we were induced to sign on at that "exorbitant" price!

It was in 1899 that Fulham first embraced professionalism in this small way, and the strength of the team may be judged from the fact that at the end of the season only Uxbridge and Maidenhead stood below us in the Second Division of the Southern League, and we were only saved from one of the bottom positions by having a slightly better goal average than Uxbridge, with whom we tied for points.

A big advance was made in the following season, for "the boys" gained second place in the table; but though Watford, the leaders, won their way into the First Division of the Southern

League by beating Sheppey United in the test matches, Thames Ironworks proved too good for our boys at Tottenham, and we failed to qualify for the "upper circle."

The 1900-1 season was a disappointing one, for Fulham had to be content with fifth place on the list; but after a most exciting struggle Fulham's name figured at the top of the Second Division table in the next season, but again the test match failed to gain admission for us into the First Division, Swindon beating us somewhat luckily at Reading.

Moyse.]

ATTACK.

FREDERICK THRELFALL, Fulham's brilliant outside-left, was born at Preston in 1880. Is 5ft. 10in. in height, and weighs 11st. He came to Fulham from Manchester City.

Again, in 1902-3, our team proved to be the best in the Second Division of the Southern League, for we lost only one game and had only seven goals scored against us in all the competition games, and when we had to meet Brentford in the test match at Shepherd's Bush we felt quite sure of gaining promotion at last.

Alack and alas! Brentford had won but two of their thirty games that season, and we had only had seven goals scored against us, yet, though we scored first, the test match was lost to us by 7 goals to 2. Poor Jack Head—our goalkeeper—his feelings may be imagined!

However, during the close season in 1903 the "Cottagers" determined to take the bull by the horns. A general meeting of the members was called, and at this it was decided to turn the club into a limited liability company, gather together a first-class team, and apply for admission to the First Division of the Southern League.

It cannot be said that funds were too abundant, and consequently operations were somewhat retarded.

Here I may pay a well-merited tribute to Mr. H. G. Norris, for it was through him that Jack Fryer first signed for Fulham.

Bowden.]

JACK FRYER,

Fulham's famous Goalkeeper and Captain.

He was born at Cromford in 1877, stands 6ft. 2½in., and weighs over 13½st. He is thought by his admirers to be well worthy of International honours, and is a great goalkeeper.

This was on May 14, 1903, and as the old Derby County goalie's was the first signature that we obtained that season it will easily be understood that Fulham's choice of players was somewhat limited.

However, of the team gathered together between May 14, 1903, and the annual general meeting of the Southern League, Fryer, Soar, and Robotham are still with us, which goes to prove that some good men are left even after every club in the country has had its pick of the market.

Personally, I have always been lucky—must have been born under a lucky star—for I have taken on "forlorn hopes" and come out on top; but my luck was never so much in as when the Southern League held a preliminary meeting of the First Division clubs on the Friday night preceding their annual general meeting on the Saturday, to decide between themselves whose claims they should support.

There were two vacancies in the "upper circle"—Kettering disbanding and Watford having to apply for re-admission through being one of the two bottom clubs—and three applicants: Watford, Fulham, and Plymouth Argyle.

Watford had been members of the League for seven years, and Fulham for five seasons; but the meeting of First Division delegates decided to support the applications of Plymouth Argyle—an unknown club—and Watford, leaving us out in the cold.

However, the final and deciding meeting was not until the following afternoon, and I never wish to undergo such a trying time again as I had between the close of the Friday's meeting and the opening of the "general" on Saturday.

Anyway, we of Fulham were able to impress our claims upon certain wavering delegates, and, to our great joy, but Watford's sorrow, Fulham and Plymouth Argyle were elected to the First Division of the Southern League.

This was the one really great step to fame that Fulham made, and with becoming modesty we ask the world if we have been like "Lot's wife" since.

We can soon conclude this history now, for by this time we had "arrived." We secured eleventh position in the Southern League in our first year, with a team gathered together after the 14th of May. Mr. Harry Bradshaw, who had just been successful in piloting the Woolwich Arsenal Club into the First Division of the Football League, was secured as manager, and the team he got together finished sixth in the Southern League competition, and ran into the fourth round of the English Cup competition, being beaten by the team which ultimately secured the Cup—viz., Aston Villa.

To-day we have a ground second to none in the kingdom, for Craven Cottage can accommodate 60,000 on the popular sides, where everyone can obtain an uninterrupted view from its terraced banks; 5,000 in one of the most palatial stands ever built; and 3,000 more in the terraced enclosure, which is protected from the weather by the same roof which covers the stand.

At the moment of writing Fulham are making a bold bid for the championship of the Southern League, therefore I feel justified in asking, "Did the Southern League delegates make a mistake when they voted the 'Cottagers' into the 'upper circle'?"

We paid the maximum dividend to our shareholders in our first year as a first-class side; we paid it again last year; and, considering we draw "gates" equal to any club in the South, we hope to pay it again this season.

Moyse.]

DEFENCE.

W. MORRISON, Fulham's fine centre-half, was born at West Benhar, Lanark, in 1879. Is 5ft. 9½in. in height, and weighs 12st. 10lb. Has a great future before him.

"Enterprise" is the watchword of the "Cottagers'" management, and I cannot do better than conclude this all too curtailed article by handing down to posterity the names of the directors who control the fortunes of one of Fortune's favourite clubs. Messrs. Dean (chairman), Allen, Norris, and Foulds were on the first board, and to these gentlemen in particular Fulham's go-ahead policy is due. Such names as Messrs. Hitchcock, Hymers, and Apps, stalwarts in the old days, have given place to Messrs. Hall, J. Watts, and Dudley-Evans; but good work as they have accomplished, no "history" of Fulham would be complete without mention of Tom Walker—our trainer in the days when I wore Fulham's colours, now the father of the playing pitch at Craven Cottage—who has put in over twenty years' service, and seen Fulham grow from a very small concern to a powerful club.

HERBERT E. JACKSON.

FULHAM FOOTBALL CLUB—PLAYERS AND OFFICIALS, SEASON 1905-6.

Top Row (from left to right): J. STUTTARD, Trainer. MR. W. HALL. MR. W. GALLEN. MR. J. DEAN. MR. H. G. NORRIS. ROSS. FITCHETT. SHELLEY. THOMPSON. FIDLER. WATERSON. MR. J. WATTS. MR. D. EVANS. MR. C. BARKER. MR. H. E. JACKSON, Secretary. HAMILTON, Asst.-Trainer.

Moyse, High Street, Putney.]

Middle Row: HAWORTH. THORPE. MORRISON. EDGLEY. WOOD. FRYER, Captain. ROWBOTHAM. COLLINS. WARDROPE. THRELFALL. MR. H. BRADSHAW, Manager.

Bottom Row: SOAR. HOGAN. GOLDIE. A. HARWOOD. FRASER. BELL. KIRBY. THOMAS. CATTERALL.

[Wilkes, West Bromwich.]

WEST BROMWICH ALBION OUT FOR A TRAINING-WALK.

Back Row: F. Shinton. E. Bradley. J. Stringer. J. Pennington. C. Simmons. G. Young.
Front Row: W. Barber (Trainer). J. Manners. A. Haywood.

THE DAY'S WORK.

HOW THE PROFESSIONAL FOOTBALLER IS TRAINED.

By W. I. BASSETT.

Is special training a mistake?—The up-to-date professional has too much leisure—A typical day's work—The value of skipping as an exercise—Ball-punching—Running—Ball-practice once a week—Stereotyped methods are of more service to the defence than the attack—Why should not sides be formed?—Hot, cold, and plunge baths—The old style and the new—Doctor's morning—Special training for Cup-ties—Modern training too artificial—Mr. McGregor's suggestion—Some good advice to young players.

THE average man has but a dim and imperfect idea of the way in which a professional footballer fits himself for his work. He has a suspicion that he fills in his time at the ground, but he has little knowledge of the routine through which the expert footballer goes. Training has reached lengths of which we old footballers never dreamed. I want the reader of this article to carefully note that I am not writing this as a director of the West Bromwich Albion Football Club. I do not want that club to think that I am referring to them or their methods. I am not. I am dealing with the whole question of football training from my own point of view.

Personally, I do not mind admitting that I am no believer in this organised system of training. I believe the man plays football best who works for his living in the ordinary way. Take the case of that great centre-half of years ago, Charles Perry. He always worked, but was there a fitter man in the kingdom? No. But conditions have changed. Men are receiving £4 per week for their football now, and there is no necessity for them to work. You cannot blame a man who is in receipt of such an income for refraining from tying himself down in any way. He is a free agent, and with few exceptions he elects not to work. So be it. I am not finding fault with him. But allow me to say that all this special training is solely for the benefit of the man who does not work; the other man merely wants a little special exercise—say three nights per week—to keep him fit. Time hangs heavily on the paid footballer's hands, and club directors know to their cost that a programme of exercise has to be mapped out for him, otherwise he would soon become fat and sleek and well-disposed towards everyone, but scarcely a deadly opponent. There you have the sum and substance of the why and wherefore of this special training which has become such a big business. But you must not tell me that the man who practically lives on a football ground is going to enjoy his football, or look forward to it with such keenness as the men of old did. I say it is a practical impossibility for these men to be as enthusiastic as we were; and this constant attendance at the ground is, in my opinion, the cause of all the stereotyped, listless, and automatic play we get. But I am not here to moralise; my mission is to give you a typical day's work at a football ground.

MR. W. I. BASSETT.

He was born at West Bromwich in 1869, stands 5ft. 6in., and weighs 11st. He played outside-right for the Albion for sixteen seasons, and was capped sixteen times for England. He is at present helping his old club to revive its ancient glory.

The bulk of the trainers vary in their methods, but I will endeavour as far as possible to let the reader know what a normal day's work is. Monday is often a *dies non*. Many clubs allow the men to do as they like on that day, providing that there is no mid-week engagement. They do not report themselves for special training on Monday. On the Tuesday morning they get to the ground at ten o'clock, and the trainer takes them for a good walk into the country. They probably cover five or six miles, and do it at a fair pace

There is no racing, but also there is no sauntering about. This is a form of training I cordially approve of. Not only do the men get what I regard as the best exercise in the world, but they also get plenty of good fresh air. There was a time when walking was overdone. There was an individual connected with Wolverhampton Wanderers in the old days who used to walk the men off their feet. He would take them ten or twelve miles at a fast pace day after day. The result was that the leg muscles got too hard; the men were jaded; and a trifling accident was likely to result in a complete breakdown. Plenty of good, sound walking is highly beneficial, but it is possible to overdo even the most legitimate form of exercise.

Should the morning not be conducive to pleasant walking, then the trainer orders alternative exercise. But here there is an attempt made to treat the individual according to his special requirements. One will be set to skip vigorously for half an hour, and even longer. Skipping is a grand exercise. One of the greatest full-backs of the day is in the habit of skipping every morning; practically he does little else, and he is always in the pink of condition. The exercise affects every muscle of the body. It makes for increased agility, it improves the wind, and it renders the muscles pliable and elastic. It would make the ordinary man smile—and I am not sure that he might not sneer—to see these grown men skipping for an hour. Oftentimes, the great back I have mentioned will do a thousand revolutions at a time; but it is good training, and half an hour of it every day would do good to the man who is not a footballer. Most of our leading clubs have a well-equipped gymnasium on the ground for the use of the players on days when exercise cannot legitimately be taken in the open air. Another player will have a long turn with the Indian clubs, and others will punch the ball for an hour. Now, ball-punching is one of the finest, and also one of the most interesting, exercises ever devised. There is something very attractive to the individual in ball-punching, and there is also a measure of skill to be acquired in the art. If you have never seen a clever American ball puncher, see one at the first opportunity. A man like Tucker is well worth watching. Some of our leading pugilists are very fine ball-punchers. There is no exercise like it for a goalkeeper; but it gives stamina to everyone. It teaches a man to be quick on his feet, and it is particularly good for improving the wind.

Albert Wilkes.]
THE PLUNGE BATH AT ASTON LOWER GROUNDS. GARRATY ENJOYS A DIP.
Elaborate and costly plunge baths are fitted at many of the best-equipped football enclosures, and are greatly appreciated by the players. It is luxuries such as these that swell the list of expenses of a big football club. From a photograph taken expressly for THE BOOK OF FOOTBALL.

Then there is running exercise. Most of the players will run round the ground a few times or many, according to the amount of exercise each is deemed to require. This was the only real training that I ever did. I used to have a brisk walk several times a week, and a few spells of running; this is to improve the wind, and also to give lasting power to the player. Then there is sprinting exercise; this is to improve the pace. The men indulge in short bursts at top speed, and most of them are all the better for this class of work. Very few players possess the speed they might have if they trained properly; but there is always a danger of overdoing this kind of training. Men who indulge in it much are liable to sudden breakdowns. Men of Templeton's type and build are much given to indulging in sprinting practice, and they are somewhat prone to get the muscles too rigid, and then a breakdown is liable to follow. Personally, I never used to do sprinting practice. I was fast enough for all requirements, and, therefore, I deemed it best to husband all my strength. My favourite practice was running with the ball and centring when going at top speed.

But, I fancy I hear the reader ask, what about learning to play football? This may be all very well, but when do the men learn new tricks with the ball? When do they practise dribbling and shooting? Well, remember that I am not telling you what I should do with men; I am not a trainer. I am simply telling you what they do. Once a week, and once a week only, the men have ball practice. So far as I have been able to see, the men simply kick in. The goalkeeper gets in position, two men play back, and eight or nine others kick in. You can see them dribbling deliberately, passing deliberately; they stop the ball dead, and then shoot. That is to say, they do precisely what they never would have time to do in the course of actual football. Now, I cannot see that this is beneficial. The backs and goalkeeper may get good practice, but I don't see where it is going to improve the other men's play. Personally, I would much rather see sides formed. Then the men could please themselves whether they dribbled excessively; but I really do not see why they should not practise dribbling and practise racing off at top speed and centring on the run. It would be infinitely more interesting and infinitely better practice than the stereotyped methods now in vogue. My own opinion is, that men get nothing like as much actual work with the ball as they need. When I was playing, I always made a practice of doing plenty of work with the ball, and I never went to our

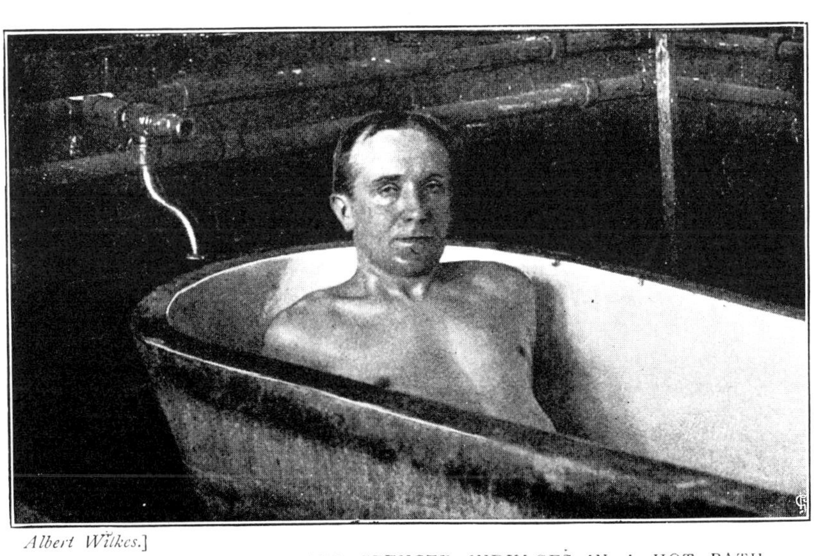

Albert Wilkes.]
AFTER EXERCISE—HOWARD SPENCER INDULGES IN A HOT BATH.
Hot baths are a great luxury. In the old days at the Pike's Lane Ground at Bolton the players were content to wash themselves down in the mud round a great waterbutt.

ground to practise football without devoting special attention to taking the corner kick.

When the hard work is over you get the baths. Most important clubs have hot and cold baths available, while many of our leading organisations have all the latest steam and douche baths that human ingenuity has contrived. In some of the excellent illustrations by that practical footballer, Albert Wilkes of Aston Villa, you will see well-known footballers in the act of taking baths. I may tell you privately that poor Garraty, who has been induced to go into the big plunge bath that Aston Villa have, for the purpose of the photograph, is saying pitifully: "For goodness' sake, Albert, be quick! It's jolly cold in here!" But all this is strictly in confidence. A hot bath is a great luxury, but as I am writing with the pictures of these well-favoured footballers before me, my mind reverts back to the early League matches at the old Pike's Lane Ground, Bolton, where you could see a crowd of practically naked Albion and Bolton footballers splashing themselves after a match in the mud round a great waterbutt. There were no such elaborate baths in those days as the reader can see so excellently depicted in these photographs. The large plunge baths are not to be found everywhere, but they are very handy; and a tour round the dressing-room quarters of a famous football club would lead the ordinary man to have some slight idea where the money goes.

When the baths have been used, then the player submits himself to the attentions of the trainer. He is rubbed down vigorously, and you feel a fine glow of health after a vigorous rubbing down following a good bath. I do not think there is anything in the world to equal it. Special massage is given, of course, in the case of any weak muscle or seat of injury, and this is also beneficial.

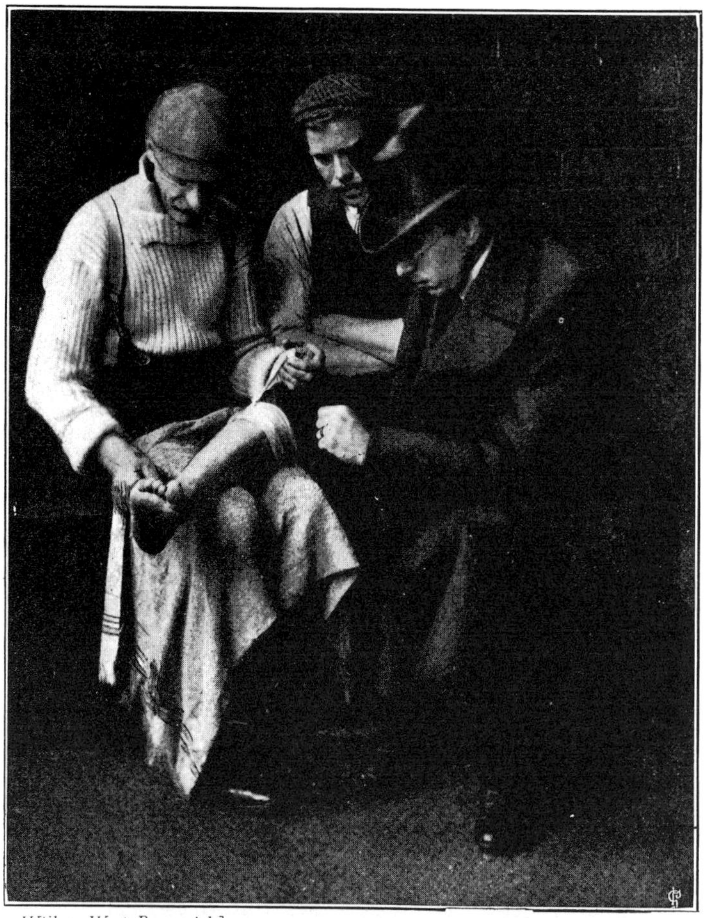

Wilkes, West Bromwich.]

DOCTOR'S MORNING—INSPECTING A DAMAGED LEG.

The members of a big football team are periodically examined by the doctor, who exercises a kind of general supervision over them, apart from any urgent call that might be made upon him. This is necessary, as prevention is better than cure. In the photograph above, which was specially taken for THE BOOK OF FOOTBALL, the doctor is seen examining a damaged leg in the presence of the trainer.

The doctor is in constant demand by those responsible for the keeping of a football team in first-class condition. In the old days it was only deemed necessary to call in a doctor in the case of serious injury; but a different policy is pursued now. Footballers have not yet adopted the Japanese policy of paying a doctor when they are well, and of depriving him of his fee when they are ill; but there is just a suggestion of that principle about their methods. The men are periodically overhauled by the doctor, who gives special advice for special cases. Of course, in the case of serious injury, unremitting attention is given by the medical man; but he also exercises a kind of general supervision quite apart from any urgent call made upon him. This is necessary, as prevention is better than cure in regard to these matters. One of the illustrations is a capital picture showing the doctor examining a damaged leg in the presence of the trainer.

I have merely given you here a typical day; of course when a team are in training for an important Cup-tie different methods obtain. Possibly they go away to some seaside hydro. and there, up to a point much benefit is likely to accrue. Change of air is naturally beneficial; but I have often found that the tendency is for the players to get out of their usual routine, and, probably, find the fare too good for them. Then, even if the team do not go away, they make special visits to health resorts, such as Droitwich, for the purposes of having brine baths. These are excellent tonics, and are highly favoured by footballers. But you want a great deal of discretion in regard to these matters. Granting that all this training is necessary, mainly because of the fact that men have so much time hanging heavily on their hands, which, if it were not artificially taken up, would probably be devoted to purposes which would not be conducive to good football later in the week, I cannot see that sufficient is done to improve the quality of football. But, there again, one would scarcely think it necessary for anyone but the individual footballer to trouble about that. It should be a matter for the personal ambition of each player. One would think that for his own sake he would make himself as expert in every department of the game as possible. But I do not see that he does, and I am quite sure that directors would be wise if they encouraged the men to indulge in more actual game practice. There is something altogether too artificial about football training, to my mind. I may be heterodox in my ideas, but they are my ideas, and there the matter ends. I admit that we get teams who can last their game out well; there is no doubt on that point, and to that extent the training justifies itself. But I think it should be more educational and less artificial.

My old friend, Mr. McGregor, has made a valuable suggestion in regard to football training. He advises the men to go in for golf, and cites the views of Dr. Charles Robertson, an expert Rugby footballer, and one of the greatest golfers in the Midlands, in support of his contention. On the general principle I agree with Mr. McGregor cordially, but I am afraid there are difficulties in the way. To begin with, golf clubs are generally somewhat exclusive. One might almost say that this is natural; it is a game the upkeep of which is expensive. It is played by the wealthy class, and, naturally, they like to keep their links pretty much to themselves. That is to say, they like to restrict the membership to persons of their own social circle. At any rate, if all the professional footballers in a team were to make application to a club for admission, I do not think they would get in. The only way out of the difficulty would be to provide municipal golf links everywhere, and I am afraid this is still only a dream. Still, municipal golf links are coming, and when they are universal, perhaps the professional will include the game in his regular day's routine. Anything which can be done intelligently, if I may put it so, is far more valuable than anything which is more or less mechanical and stereotyped. But whatever is done, I am quite sure that the men ought to be induced to take more personal interest in perfecting themselves in the art and science of the game than they do. They seem to

Albert Wilkes.]

J. STRINGER

(West Bromwich Albion) takes sprinting exercise.

Sprinting is indulged in to improve the pace, and when not overdone is very beneficial to the player.

me to go from week to week without trying to add to their accomplishments. Now, I do not see how a man is to be a great player if from the time he gets into a professional football team he never troubles about the pastime excepting when engaged in an actual match. Match practice is the best practice, I admit, but then a man does not get sufficient match practice in the course of a season to turn him from a moderate player into a high-class one. This is quite apart from training, and it ought to be sufficient to draw attention to the matter, and leave each footballer to work out his own improvement. I am afraid some of them think they have nothing to learn, in which case they will learn nothing. But they are not all like that, and the rest would do well to lose no single opportunity they may obtain of perfecting themselves in all the methods which go to make up the sound footballer.

Football is a very exact science; there is far more in it than the average player is disposed to think. There are many good players to-day—there will always be many good players—but there is a great deal of slovenly football. Many men play moderately, who, if they gave the game the attention which, in my opinion, it deserves, might improve their football markedly. It is a game worth studying; in fact, men who adopt it as a profession ought to study it. No man should try to skip through a profession. There is a great demand for good players, and even if there is no chance of earning fancy wages which men used to earn years ago, £4 per week all the year round is not a bad wage for the average man who plays football.

Besides, if a man gets out of the ruck and proves himself to be a really good player, his name is remembered, and that recognition may be of use to him in after life.

There is one thing which is going to tell more in football than it has ever told before, although the tendency has all along been in the direction of good. Character is going to tell. Let young players note that, and note it carefully. There used to be a lot of wild doings in the old days, and they make very interesting reminiscences. No one delights to hear them chatted about more than I do. I don't suppose that the footballers of the future will ever have quite such riotous fun as their predecessors had. But they may not be much the worse off for that. After all, it is easy to overdo the wild Bohemianism which characterised some of the footballers of the old school; and it must not be forgotten that there are often sore heads after a night out. There is every encouragement given to-day for the formation of character. There is a daily increasing tendency for clubs to look askance at men who have not a clean record. Clubs have begun to learn—nay, they have learned!—that it does not take many black sheep to lead the whole flock astray.

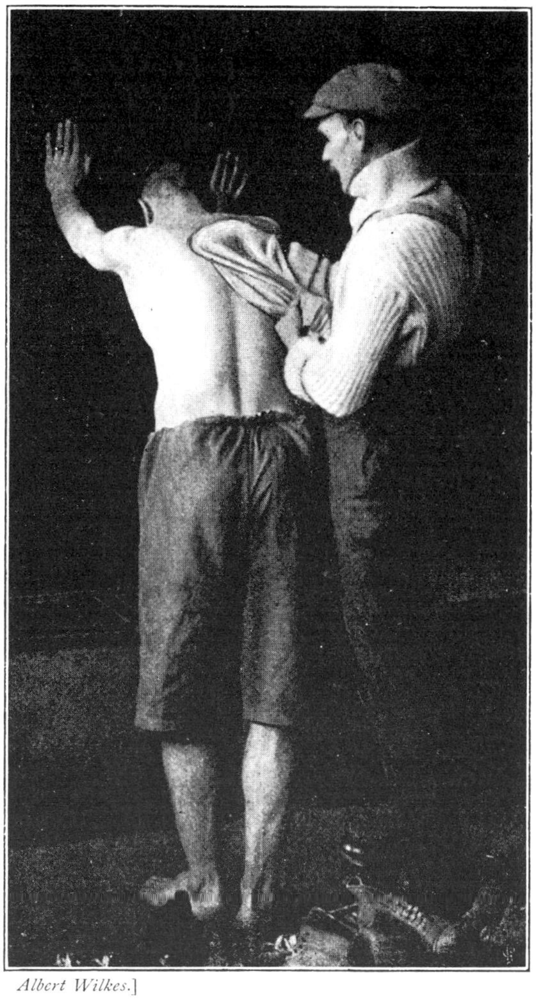

Albert Wilkes.]

A RUB DOWN BY THE TRAINER.

After the day's exercise and the bath the player is taken in hand by the trainer and vigorously rubbed down, any weak muscle or seat of injury receiving special attention and massage. This most important part of football training keeps the men in perfect health. From a photograph specially taken for THE BOOK OF FOOTBALL.

So long as I am connected with football I shall never sanction the admission into a team of any man who has not a clean record. It is all very well to be a fine footballer; but the man who can play good football, and is occasionally unfit to do so, is of doubtful value to a side.

I have even gone to the length of seriously advising players to pay some regard to their personal appearance. This may appear to some as a rather small matter, but personally I regard it as a somewhat important one.

I do not like to see footballers getting £4 per week—or even £3, if you like—slouching about in mufflers and dispensing with collars. It brings the game into contempt with the very class we want to draw to our matches.

There is no reason why footballers should not always look neat and trim; they will be doing good to the pastime generally if they are reasonably careful as to their personal appearance.

Albert Wilkes.]

J. PENNINGTON

(West Bromwich Albion) at skipping exercise.

Skipping is magnificent exercise. It affects every muscle in the body, renders them pliable and elastic, and improves the wind. Professional footballers often skip for an hour at a time.

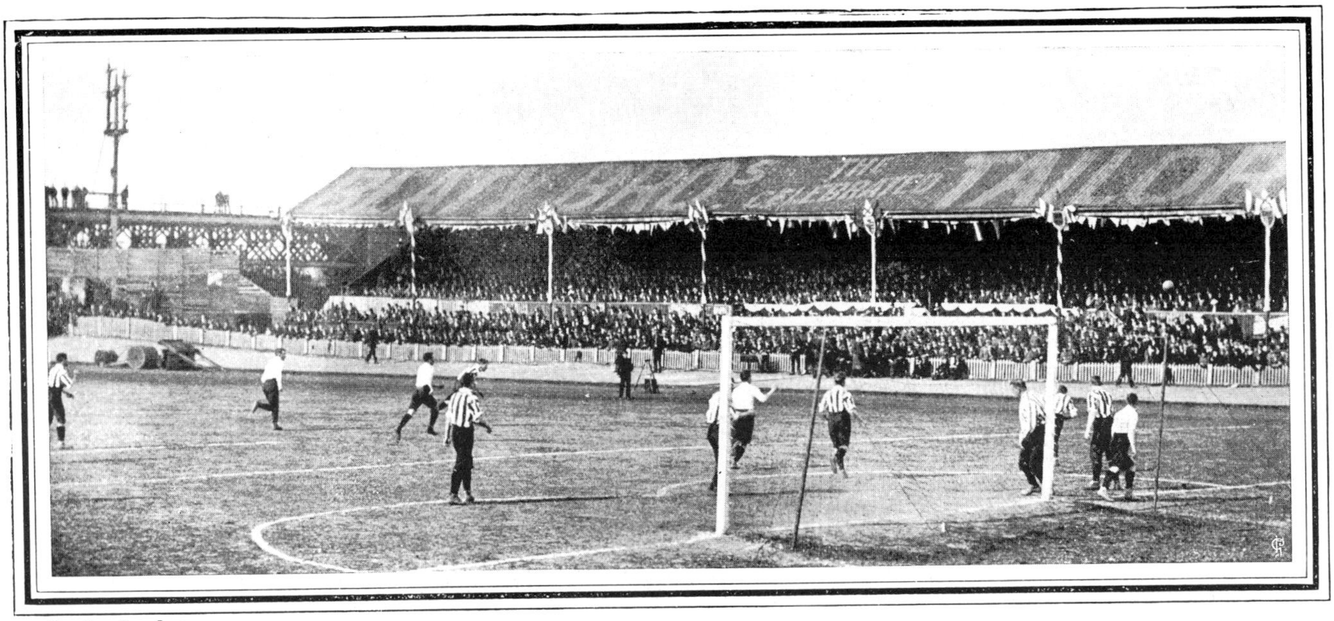

Bowden Bros.]

BOLTON WANDERERS' GROUND—THE RE-PLAYED CUP FINAL OF 1901.

Tottenham Hotspur met Sheffield United at Burnden Park in the year the Cup came South after a drawn game at the Crystal Palace. The "Spurs" won by 3 goals to 1. Sheffield United repel the "Spurs'" attack.

THE FOOTBALL HISTORY OF BOLTON WANDERERS.

By J. K. FLETCHER.

How the club was started—The vicar disagrees with the members of the Christ Church Club—A memorable meeting and a change of name—Mr. Parkinson joins the club—A Scottish invasion—Early Cup games—The arrival of Mr. J. J. Bentley—A split in the camp—Bad times—The Bolton lottery—Bolton's League experiences—The Cup Final of 1903-4—Pike's Lane and Burnden Park—How the present ground was secured.

Colours: White shirts, blue knickers. *Ground: Burnden Park, Bolton.*

THOUGH there may be clubs with more brilliant histories, few can point to such a career of usefulness as can Bolton Wanderers, who claim to be one of the oldest clubs in the League.

Like many other first-class football clubs, Bolton Wanderers owes its inception to the desire of the scholars and teachers of the Christ Church Sunday-school to indulge in outdoor recreation. The first president was the Rev. J. F. Wright, the vicar, whose son, Dr. J. F. Wright, himself an old Rugbeian, is now a large shareholder in the club.

The schoolmaster, Mr. Ogden, was chosen as captain, and the members of the club were called upon to pay a subscription of 1d. per week—a magnificent sum which, when we remember what a tremendous business the management of a League club is nowadays, seems ridiculously small.

The match list was at first confined to local clubs, but a rift in the lute came when there arose a split with the vicar, who objected to the club holding meetings in the schools unless he was present. The members did not approve of this idea, and at a meeting held on August 28, 1877, the following resolution was passed: "That we alter the name of the club from Christ Church to Bolton Wanderers." The name was suggested by the fact that they had to wander to a neighbouring hostelry, the Gladstone Hotel, near Pike's Lane. Subsequently the headquarters were removed to the Britannia Hotel, where they remained until the meetings were transferred to registered offices.

It was in 1878 that Mr. Peter Parkinson was admitted a member of the club, and for several years he was the prime mover in the management of the Wanderers. His object was to bring the club to the front, and he obtained its recognition throughout England and Scotland. He was the means of the introduction of Scotsmen into Bolton, W. Struthers, one of the finest of centre-forwards, and J. Devlin, an Arbroath full-back, being the first of the importations. Others came down in 1881, and it was no secret that, though professionalism was not then legalised, players were being paid sub rosa.

On one occasion a Commission of the Football Association was appointed to inspect the books of the Wanderers, but they were above suspicion. Of course, the Commission were ignorant of the fact that an official had sat up all night preparing a fresh set of books for their inspection. Some of the older school of players can divulge interesting stories of how an extra half-crown was included in the weekly salary when a match was won, and how half-a-crown was stopped off them when they lost. But this was in the good old days, and such practices would never be tolerated now by either players or the powers that be.

It was in 1881–2 that the Wanderers' president, Mr. J. W. Makant, J.P., himself a rare type of the gentleman-sportsman, was elected, and he still manifests an active and healthy interest in the welfare of the club. Having been successfully launched on the tide of prosperity, further laurels were gained in 1883–4, when the club ran into the fourth round of the English Cup, there to be beaten at Bolton by Notts County, after a drawn game at Trent Bridge, where £360 was taken in gate-money.

The professional question came to the front in 1884, and the Wanderers and Preston North End headed the movement, which resulted in the formation of the British Football Association, consisting of a federation of forty clubs. The following season saw Mr. J. J. Bentley appointed—in February, 1885, to be precise—as secretary; and what good fortune he brought with him! Out of 69 matches, 56 were won and eight lost, whilst

BOLTON WANDERERS' FOOTBALL CLUB—REPRESENTATIVE FIRST ELEVEN, SEASON 1905-6.

[Howard Barrett, Southwell.]

BOYD. STOKES. MARSH. BAVERSTOCK. GREENHALGH. DAVIES (Goalkeeper). SHEPHERD. STRUTHERS. TAYLOR. WHITE. MCEWAN.

there was a balance of £102. However, internal dissension led in 1885-6 to the resignation of Mr. Parkinson as president, Mr. W. Barnes as treasurer, and Mr. E. Parkinson as a member of the committee; but from a playing point of view the Wanderers were again successful, and their extraordinary feat in winning the Lancashire, Bolton Charity, and Derby Charity Cups led to remarkable scenes of enthusiasm in the town. No fewer than seven of the players were Boltonians when the Lancashire Cup was won from Blackburn Rovers, who had held it the four previous seasons. But despite this success, there was a feeling of unrest in the camp, and the next annual meeting was of a stormy character. When the voting took place for the secretaryship, about fifteen second team players, who were not members, were brought into the room, and Struthers, receiving 112 votes against Mr. Bentley's 101, took up the reins of office, rather against his will; but he did not take kindly to the duties, and resigned before the end of the season. Mr. Fitzroy Norris succeeded him in February, and Messrs. A. H. Downs, F. E. Brettell, and now Mr. J. Somerville have also wielded the secretarial pen.

When the last match of this troublous season had been played at West Bromwich, the players were dismissed, most of them going over to the neighbouring Halliwell Club, though, with about two exceptions, they returned before the commencement of the next season. One of the stalwarts, however—Jimmy Trainer to wit—was lost for ever, and the club was fast falling from its high estate when, in October, 1887, Mr. Bentley was prevailed upon to again throw in his lot with the club. A work of restoration followed, and the debts of the concern were paid off as the result of a lottery, which the police sought to prevent; but it took place at the shop of one of the committeemen whilst some of the officials occupied the office for the purpose of deceiving the guardians of the law. The first prize of £100 went to a Manchester man. Then came the adoption of the League system, the competition being formed in the season 1888-9, when the Wanderers were one of the first twelve clubs to join.

On the whole, the Wanderers may claim, without ever having won the championship, to have had a fairly successful League career, though they have experienced their share of ups and downs; and when they dropped into the Second Division at the end of the season 1898-9, there were many pessimists who predicted that this was the beginning of the downward grade, and that the club had fallen permanently from its once high estate.

But what are the facts? They romped back along with Sheffield Wednesday into the higher sphere a season later, winning no fewer than twenty-two matches against four defeats. The policy of securing promising juniors and training them was a costly one. The authorities had given big prices for men with reputations, and were dissatisfied with the results, and so likely youngsters were encouraged and introduced into League football. As was only to be expected, the club sacrificed much at the shrine of experience, and at the end of the season 1902-3 they were again compelled to retire from the First Division.

There was no extension movement to save them from the humiliation, and yet a team that had to muddle through another season of Second Division football proved capable of fighting its way to the Final of the English Cup. They were unfortunate enough to be beaten by Manchester City by a goal which will ever remain one of the most unsatisfactory that has decided the destination of the national trophy. This was the second time that the Wanderers had advanced so far as the Final Tie, for in 1894 they were thought to have a gift of the Cup when, at Everton, they had to meet Notts County, then a Second Division club; but, owing to injuries, the team was not decided upon until the last minute, and even then the players, in a fit of jealousy, would not allow a sound and anxious player to turn out. Four goals were registered against the famous triumvirate, Sutcliffe, Somerville, and Jones, who formed one of the finest defences in the annals of football.

Turning to dwell for a moment on the old Pike's Lane Ground, many players and club officials will have vivid recollections of this historic enclosure, now more or less built upon. It was often a veritable mud-heap, but it was associated with many of the Wanderers' most memorable achievements. In 1889 it was leased to the club at a yearly rental of £35, a sum which five years later had increased to £175. It became more and more apparent, however, that the ground would fall under the inexorable sway of the builder, and the inevitable was accepted in the early Nineties. Land was then rented from the Bolton Corporation in the Burnden district, and in 1895-6 the Burnden Park Ground, which was formerly a disused tip, was opened, the club being turned into a company. This ground is now one of the most commodious and well-equipped in England.

Bowden Bros.]

A MEMORABLE MATCH—THE LAST CUP FINAL PLAYED IN LANCASHIRE—TOTTENHAM HOTSPUR v. SHEFFIELD UNITED, 1901.

After a draw of 2 goals all at the Crystal Palace the "Spurs" met Sheffield United at Burnden Park Ground, Bolton, and here, after a splendid game, they were victorious over the Yorkshire team by 3 goals to 1. T. Morris, the right half, has just thrown the ball in from the touch line, and John Cameron and Erentz, the Tottenham right back, can be seen eagerly watching the flight of the ball

SOME FAMOUS HALF-BACKS

Scott and Co.]
M. PARRY
(*Liverpool*).

Wakefield.]
PARSONAGE
(*Brentford*)

Wilkes.]
A. LEAKE
(*Aston Villa*).

Prestwich.]
BULL
(*Tottenham Hotspur*).

Adams.]
COMRIE
(*Millwall*).

Howie.]
G. T. HENDERSON
(*Middlesboro'*).

Wilkes.]
PHEASANT
(*West Bromwich*).

Moyse.]
GOLDIE
(*Fulham*).

Stuart and Winfield.]
A. GARDNER
(*Newcastle United*).

BIRMINGHAM (late SMALL HEATH) FOOTBALL CLUB.

FORWARD

Holders of the Birmingham Senior Cup, Birmingham Charity Cup (joint holders with Aston Villa), and the Staffordshire Cup.

By WILLIAM McGREGOR.

The evolution of Small Heath Alliance—Formation of the club at Bordesley—The first team that played for the club—A removal of headquarters to Sparkbrook—Notable players in the early days—The Birmingham Cup, a tempting offer, and Small Heath's base ingratitude—Fine Cup performances in 1883-4—The Semi-final at Aston Lower Grounds—Professionalism adopted—A limited liability company formed—Small Heath enter the Alliance—How Sheffield Wednesday beat Small Heath in the Cup competition in 1891-2—Small Heath win the Second League championship, but fail in the test game—They enter the League proper—Fluctuating fortunes—Prominent officials and financial records.

Colours: Blue shirts, white knickers. *Ground: Muntz Street, Small Heath.*

THE club we now know as Birmingham has had three titles since it commenced its eventful career in 1875. Originally it was called Small Heath Alliance, and then, when its history was well advanced, it became a limited liability company, and dropped the word "Alliance," and this season it is having its trial trip under the title of "Birmingham." It will be more convenient for the purposes of this article to use the term "Small Heath" on all occasions, because practically the whole of their history has to be dealt with under that title.

Small Heath have not obtained the same amount of publicity that Aston Villa have had extended to them, and they have not won such high fame as their neighbours. With the exception of one or two unsuccessful seasons, Aston Villa have always been at the top of the tree. Small Heath have had few fat seasons and many lean ones. Their history is not so fully, or so consecutively, recorded in minute-books as is the history of Aston Villa. Still, it is possible to follow the career of the club, and it has not been devoid of incident.

A few young fellows connected with Trinity Church, Bordesley, were ardent members of a cricket club which bore the title of the religious organisation which gave it birth. Cricket was their great hobby, and during the summer months nothing else was required to keep the members loyal to the club. But it was feared that during the dark days of winter the members might get scattered, and so it was decided in the autumn of 1875 to form a football club. It was possibly deemed expedient to give it a wider title than their cricket club possessed, and so they christened it Small Heath Alliance. The three brothers Edden—Will, Tom, and George—the brothers Tom and Fred James, and W. H. Edmunds were the actual pioneers of the club. It was not difficult to procure a playing pitch in those days, and it was lucky that it was so, for a rental would have been out of the question. There was then a wide tract of waste land in Arthur Street, the turf of which was thoroughly good, and there the club commenced its career.

There were not many Association clubs in the district, and as a consequence engagements were not easy to procure, but it is recorded that the first game was played against Holte Wanderers, then a well-known team in the Aston district. It is interesting to recall Small Heath Alliance's eleven on that occasion. It consisted of W. Edden, Arthur Wright, Fred James, Tom James, G. H. Edden, W. H. Edmunds (captain), T. Edden, D. Keys, C. Barmore, C. Barr, and J. Sparrow.

Two years were spent in this unconventional way, and then a move was made to Ladypool Road, Sparkbrook, where a properly enclosed ground was available. The club soon began to boast a following, and many of those who either played or watched in those early days are still enthusiastic in their support of the club. A lengthy programme was fulfilled each winter, and by 1877 it was felt that a better ground ought to be secured, so a move was made to the present enclosure in Muntz Street.

Some of their leading players began to obtain more than a local reputation, and prominent among these was Arthur James, the finest outside-right the club ever boasted. From 1878 to 1885 he was the captain of the team, and he possessed a popularity on the Small Heath side similar to that possessed by Archie Hunter at the other end of the city.

A notable match was that played at Small Heath on September 27, 1879, for it marked the first meeting of Small Heath Alliance with Aston Villa. The Villa had not as strong a team as they sometimes played, and they were beaten by a goal, and one disputed—you often heard of disputed goals then—to nil.

Small Heath's ground was not a favourite one with visiting teams. Its furrows were as pronounced as any you would see in the district. And so we read that in the same year, when Wednesbury Old Athletic were drawn against them in the Birmingham Cup, they offered the Small Heath men £5 to change the venue of the match. Five pounds was a tempting bait, and Small Heath accepted it. They were guilty, however, of an act of base ingratitude, for they beat the Old Athletic before their own supporters. As the Old Athletic were the holders of the cup, this match naturally added materially to Small Heath's reputation. The "Heathens," as they were popularly called, were afterwards able to get a much better class of fixtures than they had previously enjoyed, for they met Aston Villa, Aston Unity, Walsall Swifts, Wednesbury Old Athletic, Saltley College, Wednesbury Strollers, and various teams of lesser ability.

In 1882-3 the club won their first cup, for in the final of the Walsall competition they beat Wednesbury Old Athletic at The Chuckery, Walsall, by 4 goals to 1. Charlie Knowles, who had all too short a career with the club, played a fine game that day at outside-left. But the club quarrelled with the Walsall Association during the following season, and the committee passed a resolution that the cup should be returned.

The season of 1883-4 was a busy one, although Excelsior knocked them out of the English Cup after a drawn game. Those were remarkable games indeed! Walter Hart had acted as hon. sec. to the club in succession to S. Gessey; but in 1884-5 the present secretary, Alfred Jones, took office. That was an eventful year, the club reaching the Semi-final of the English Cup. They had a somewhat easy journey, Derby County being the only powerful side they met, and the whole of the five ties prior to the Semi-final were decided at Coventry Road—a big slice of luck. In succession they defeated Burton Wanderers by 9—2; Darwen, 3—1; Derby County, 4—2; Davenham, 2—1; Redcar, 2—0; and they met West Bromwich Albion in the Semi-final at the Lower Grounds, Aston.

In the game at Aston the ground was four inches deep with snow, and the "Heathens" played tamely, being beaten by 4 goals to 0. The crowd pelted Bob Roberts, the Albion goalkeeper, with snowballs, and altogether the match was not a particularly enjoyable one.

The club adopted professionalism in 1885. Harry Stansbie,

BIRMINGHAM FOOTBALL CLUB TEAM AND OFFICIALS, SEASON 1905-6.

Back Row: { SIMMS, Asst.-Trainer. } NORMAN, Trainer. } GLOVER. ROBINSON. { W. ADAMS, President. } STOKES. HOWARD. DOUGHERTY. DR. STANLEY. { ALFRED JONES, Secretary. }

Percy Wynne, Small Heath.]

Front Row: BEER. GREEN. MOUNTENEY. WIGMORE. W. H. JONES. WILCOX. FIELD.

BIRMINGHAM SENIOR CUP. BIRMINGHAM CHARITY CUP. STAFFORDSHIRE CUP.

the celebrated St. George's goalkeeper, was engaged, but he was re-transferred to St. George's when the season proper opened. Mr. Hart carried a resolution that the men should be remunerated according to the takings at the gate. This is a principle which has much to recommend it.

In 1888 Small Heath became a limited liability company; they were the first to adopt the principle. They dropped the title "Alliance," and were known as Small Heath Football Club, Limited. The step was not generally approved locally, but history has made it clear that they acted sensibly. Mr. Hart was the first chairman, and Messrs. Greatorex and Starling were the secretaries. They went into the fifth round of the English Cup, and were only beaten by an odd goal by West Bromwich Albion.

At the close of the season 1888-9 Small Heath were elected members of the Alliance, the body which subsequently became the Second League. They did not earn distinction in the new competition; in fact, they had some poor sides in certain seasons about this time. Fred Wheldon and W. Walton joined the team in 1890, and for six seasons the former was their greatest forward, and was indeed one of the greatest inside-lefts the country has seen.

In the season 1891-2 money was not plentiful, and when, after beating Woolwich Arsenal in the first round proper of the English Cup, they were drawn with Sheffield Wednesday at Small Heath, the "Blades" offered them £200 to take the match to Sheffield. Greatly to the annoyance of some of their supporters, the directors accepted the offer, and they lost by 2 goals to 0 after a rough and stormy game.

1892-3 witnessed the formation of the Second League, and Small Heath proved to be the first winners of the championship shield, but they failed in the test games, Newton Heath beating them after a draw. In the following season Small Heath ran up to Liverpool in the Second League, and in the test match at Stoke they beat Darwen by 3 goals to 1. Chris. Charsley emerged from his retirement to keep goal in this match, and very proud was he when his team were returned victorious. The funnel of the engine was decorated with the club colours when the team returned to Birmingham, for were they not now a First League organisation? Here is the eleven which gained for the club the distinction they had so long coveted: Charsley, F. Short, and Purves; Ollis, Jenkyns, and E. Devey; Hallam, Walton, Mobley, Wheldon, and Hands. The players were entertained to dinner at The Colonnade Hotel, and rejoicings were general. They occupied twelfth position in the First League table in the following season. In the season 1895-6 the team went all to pieces; indeed, some of the performances were little less than discreditable. Fourth position was secured in the Second League in the season 1896-7; but it was not until the season of 1900-1 that the club regained their position in the First League; then they finished second to Grimsby Town. But they did badly in the season of 1901-2, for they had to be content with seventeenth position, and once more they had to spend twelve months in the lower ranks. 1903-4, however, saw them again installed in the senior Division. They made a wretched opening, but their form of the latter half of the season was positively thrilling. They were one of the cleverest and most consistent sides in the country. The directors had shown commendable enterprise. They strengthened the team at every point. Stokes, Green, Wilcox, Glover, and other players were secured at substantial transfer fees, but never was money better spent. Charles Athersmith left Aston Villa on a point of principle, and although past his best he proved a very useful man to the "Heathens." After leading in the League table for a considerable portion of the season 1904-5, they met with accidents to their players, and, being short of capable reserves, they could finish no higher than seventh, but they had the best side the club had ever possessed, and they were first-class in every department.

For the present season Aaron Jones and Cornan, inside-forwards, were secured from Barnsley; and Mounteney, of Leicester Fosse, was also signed on. The last-named has apparently made his position in the team secure, Tickle, who succeeded Athersmith, having dropped out.

Just a word as to the workers. In addition to the names already mentioned, J. Tatton, J. Bodenham, and Councillor John Wilkinson have been firm friends of the club. Then the president, Councillor William Adams, has been most generous, and few men have been less content than he to be regarded as an ornamental official. Chris. Charsley, the famous goalkeeper, was always an amateur. He was made the recipient of a valuable piano and a purse on the occasion of his wedding, and he was a genuine amateur in the strictest sense of the term. He is now Chief Constable of Coventry.

Then as to finance. The club made a profit last season, and the figures they had to deal with are in strong contrast to those which the early officials dealt with. The first gate at Ladypool Road in 1876 was 4s. 3d., and the first gate at their present ground was 6s. 8d. That was in 1877. One of their early Birmingham cup-ties produced as their share the sum of 10½d. Out of this they had to pay the fares of the team and officials to Brownhills. Even when they got into the Semi-final of the English Cup they only drew £4 5s. as their share of the gate; the Football Association took all the rest. The expenses were, of course, correspondingly small. In the year that professionalism was introduced, Small Heath spent only £70 14s. 9d. in wages.

Albert Wilkes, West Bromwich]

THE HOME OF BIRMINGHAM FOOTBALL CLUB AT SMALL HEATH.

The energy and enterprise of the officials controlling the Birmingham F. C. have improved the playing enclosure at Small Heath until it now leaves little to be desired. The playing field is well cared for, and the splendid team representing the club in this season—1905-6—should assure the recently re-christened Small Heath Club a future of unqualified prosperity.

PUBLIC SCHOOL FOOTBALL.

PART I.—ASSOCIATION.

By W. D. NIXON.

Where the game is played for its own sake—The wall game at Eton—Winchester and the Association game—The objection to peculiar school games—The Association game at Charterhouse and its famous players—Westminster—Malvern College—Repton—Shrewsbury—The smaller schools—"Old Boy" clubs—The Arthur Dunn Memorial Cup—A glance backward and some records—The value of football at the schools.

ATHLETICS under Public School auspices strike a very pleasant note in the ear of the true sportsman, and football is probably one of its chief branches.

The reason is, that nowhere can one find athletics in such a pure atmosphere. The schoolboy plays his games in the most perfect surroundings, under the eye and guidance of those who have his moral welfare to guard. The game is played for the game's own sake, and every boy is keen to shine in his sports and to get on to the goal that lies before him—the highest distinctions and honours that his school can give him.

In our biggest and best-known public schools, where the game is played at all under recognised codes, enthusiasm is about equally divided between Rugby and Association.

It is a curious fact that our greatest public school—Eton—should not play a recognised game. Etonians have their own particular style, known as the "wall game," but there is a leaning towards Association, especially among the past members of the school; and the Old Etonians have won a great name in the football world, especially in former years, when the competition of professional teams was not so great. In fact, we find the Old Etonians figuring in six Finals of the English Cup, which they managed to secure in 1879 and 1882, beating the Blackburn Rovers in the latter year. In the first two Finals in which they took part, it is rather curious to note that a re-play took place in each case, no definite decision being arrived at at the first attempt.

Harrow also have played a game peculiar to themselves, but it runs very much on the lines of the ordinary Association game. It is rather curious, therefore, that a school of such a size and reputation should not have turned out more Association players who have made a name in after years. Old Harrovian football is very weak, and this may be the cause of the authorities deciding to start a new era in the school football. However, whatever be the reason, Harrow are going to take up Rugby, and, being situated so near to London, should be able to turn out a fifteen who should prove above the average, and there ought to be no difficulty in getting a full and regular fixture list with all the chief clubs playing in and around London.

Winchester, one of our very oldest schools, and, consequently, one with many a cherished association and tradition, has also its own particular game. This has been played by Wykehamists for many and many a generation. However, with the advance of years and the growth in the popularity of the recognised codes, these schools have had to give up their own particular game, and bring themselves in line with more popular methods. Thus it has come about that Winchester has drifted towards Association; and it is now played by them for one of the two winter terms, whilst their own game holds sway during the rest of the season. Winchester has turned out many good "Soccer" players.

Probably it is only a matter of time before all these schools play entirely under one of the two recognised codes, for as matters stand at present any school playing its own game suffers two serious disadvantages. Firstly, there is bound to be difficulty in getting matches, and this must detract somewhat from the enthusiasm the game infuses into the school life. The aim of a public schoolboy is to get into his school team, and that team's status must depend upon its success, which, without matches with opponents capable of giving it a good game, must be a difficult matter to gauge.

There is another strong objection to any school playing a game peculiar to itself, that objection being that when schooldays are over a young fellow has got no credentials with which to join any club, and keep up his exercise; and this every man should endeavour to do as long as he is able. It is distasteful, and even difficult, for a player of eighteen or nineteen years of age to start to learn a new game. In Association, all clubs who draw their recruits from the public schools play the game up to a very fair standard, and would be unable to find an opening for a complete novice. Consequently, many a young athlete on leaving one of these schools has to abandon football, whereas he might have made a fine player under a recognised code of rules.

I will now turn my attention to those schools which do play the Association game pure and simple, and endeavour to

Bowden Bros.]

ST. ANDREW'S DAY AT ETON—THE FIELD GAME—MASTERS v. OLD ETONIANS. "ROUGE HIM!"

The field game is closely allied to the Association code, and is played by eleven a side. The field is 100 to 120 yards long by 80 to 100 yards wide. The ball is about half the size of the Association ball. Play is characterised by combined forward rushes down the field. There are eight forwards, a short behind, long behind, and goal. The main object is for the forwards to drive the ball over the enemy's base-line or through the goal.

give a brief outline of their position and strength one by one.

It is among our more old-established schools that we find the best teams. It is a matter of some difficulty to absolutely decide the best school at Association football, but if the matter were put to public vote, pride of place would probably go to Charterhouse.

For a long time Carthusians have held a high place in the amateur world, and since the Charterhouse was moved from London to Godalming, in 1872, the school has year after year turned out players of a very high order.

The names of those players who have made great reputations for themselves after learning their first steps at Charterhouse make a long list, but there are probably few followers of the game who are not familiar with the names of G. O Smith, W. N. Cobbold, the Stanboroughs, the brothers Walters, G. C. Vassall, and the Wreford-Browns.

These men are all so famous that it seems imperative to give a brief outline of their records. G. O. Smith, the great "G. O.," was probably the greatest centre-forward we have ever seen. He played centre-forward for his school, and subsequently filled the same position for Oxford for four years. He gained his first International cap against Ireland at the age of twenty-one, and has altogether played in twenty International matches.

W. N. Cobbold also holds an unique record, for he took up Association after playing Rugby at Cranbrook. He played for Cambridge for four years, and during that time Cambridge won every match.

The brothers Walters won great renown as full-backs. They played together for England from 1885 to 1890. They went to separate Universities, A. M., the younger brother, playing for Cambridge, and P. M. getting his "Blue" at Oxford. It is worthy of note that P. M. Walters failed to get into the Charterhouse team when at school.

G. C. Vassall is a forward of a more recent date. He went from his school team into the Oxford eleven, which he captained in 1899. He also has done great service for the Corinthians, and got his International cap in 1899 against Ireland. Their chief school match is with Westminster, whom they severely defeated last season, and they have lately secured a fixture with Winchester.

Westminster must come second, if only by reason of its honoured name. The school has not had a team of recent years at Vincent Square quite capable of keeping up the name it once had. Their chief match is with Charterhouse, and in recent years the "Pinks" have done none too well. However, everyone will wish them better times, and these are bound to come with a few new players of the calibre of the Moons and R. N. R. Blaker. The chief school fixture is with Charterhouse, as already stated, and it takes place at Westminster and Godalming in alternate years. Before leaving Westminster football, one word of appreciation must be given to S. S. Harris, Westminster's "star" production of late years, and one of the most brilliant amateur forwards now playing Association. He came into great prominence at Cambridge, and since then has done some sterling work for the Corinthians, notably in the final of the Dewar Shield in 1904, when he scored 5 goals off his own foot against Bury. He got his International cap against Scotland in 1904, and again in 1905 he was twice "capped." He has played this season for Portsmouth.

Malvern College, in Worcestershire, must certainly claim next place. This school is of much more recent date, and was only opened forty years ago, therefore its sudden and complete success in the football world is the more remarkable. Probably no school has turned out a larger percentage of "star" performers. C. J. Burnup, J. Balfour-Melville, G. L. Mellin, W. H. B. Evans, and the famous Foster family all learned their football here. All these players are Corinthians.

Another school of "stars" is Repton. It has certainly been established for over 300 years, but only containing some 300 boys it has always done remarkably well. They generally have a very good team, and annually play two very keen matches with Malvern and Shrewsbury, both of which they managed to win

Bowden Bros.]
ST. ANDREW'S DAY AT ETON—THE FIELD GAME—MASTERS v. OLD ETONIANS. TRYING TO CONVERT A "ROUGE."
A "rouge" is a minor point scored by forcing the enemy to play the ball over their base-line. The attacking side then endeavour to convert the "rouge" into a goal. A "bully" is formed a yard in front of the posts (the goal is 12ft. wide by 6ft. high), and by sheer weight the attacking forwards try to "worry" the ball through the goal. A goal score is equivalent to that of three "rouges."

Bowden Bros.]
ST. ANDREW'S DAY AT ETON—THE WALL GAME—COLLEGERS v. OPPIDANS. A "BULLY" BEING BROKEN UP.
The wall game is played by eleven a side, and is started by a "bully" in the centre of the field against the wall. A "bully" consists on each side of five players, who are sub-divided into "walls" (three in number) and "seconds" (two in number). The rest of the players are "outsides" and "behinds." The first principle of the game is to score "fair shies" in the enemy's "calx."

last season. Of their "stars," Charles B. Fry is certainly the chief. And it was Repton which produced that most artistic batsman, L. C. H. Palairet, and his brother, R. C. N.; and, still more recently, R. A. Young, the brilliant young Cantab. The name of F. G. J. Ford, popularly known as "Alphabet" Ford, must be added to this list. All these names will be familiar to cricketers, but these men have also figured largely in the football world; and if the Rev. W. Blackburn and G. S. Harris are added to the list, we have a fair sample of the class of players Repton has given us. Charles Burgess Fry is probably the greatest athlete England ever produced. He played Association for the West Kent Club at the age of twelve, and subsequently for Repton for three years. On going up to Oxford, he played for the "'Varsity" from 1892 to 1895, captaining the team in 1894. He played regularly for the Corinthians from 1895 to 1900, and then turned his mind to professional football. Fry assisted the Southampton team from 1900 to 1902. During this period he did much to bring professional and amateur players together, and established a closer feeling of friendship between the two classes.

Shrewsbury also play the Association game, and though it is a small school numerically, and plays a less prominent part in the public eye, nevertheless there have been Salopians of more than average merit. W. J. Oakley and M. M. Morgan Owen are two of Shrewsbury's most famous players, Oakley making a great name as a full-back in partnership with C. B. Fry. Oakley played for England every year from 1895 to 1901, except in 1899, and he assisted G. O. Smith to write the Badminton Library volume on the game.

There are many smaller public schools playing under the dribbling code, and of these Brighton, Bradfield, Lancing, Radley, Rossall, and Sherborne are the chief.

Brighton is about sixty years old, and with 150 boys generally have a pretty sound team, and can boast of L. H. Gay and G. H. Cotterill amongst its past members. L. H. Gay played for Cambridge and England.

Bradfield and Lancing have teams of about the same standard of strength. The former school plays an annual match with Radley, in which the results are about equal; and Lancing's chief rival is Brighton.

Radley has a small number of boys, and the team would be stronger if there was not a counter-attraction in rowing. The Radleians play their two chief matches with Bradfield and Malvern, but the Worcester school is generally too strong for them.

At Rossall the boys play under rather novel and pleasant surroundings. The school stands on the Lancashire sea coast, and the playing fields extend right down to the sands, and every Rossallian can speak of the keen games played in the bracing air of the "Hoi."

Most public schools endeavour to keep together their Old Boys in athletic clubs; and this branch of football has received great assistance owing to the competition for the Dunn Memorial Cup. This trophy was first competed for in the 1902-3 season, and was instituted in memory of one of the most famous and popular Etonian footballers—the late A. T. B. Dunn.

Judged by the Dunn Cup competition, Charterhouse bears off the palm, for it has been "there or thereabouts" every year. In the first year of the competition no definite result could be arrived at, and the Old Carthusians and Old Salopians became joint holders. In the following two seasons, however, the Carthusians were undisputed winners, beating the Old Rossallians 2—0 in the season 1903-4, and the Repton representatives by the same margin last year. Looking through the results of the other principal cup competitions open to amateur clubs, the Carthusians figure very prominently, and still further strengthen their claim to be considered the best Old Boys' side. They secured the English Cup in the year 1881, and have won the Amateur Cup twice, and the London Senior Cup four times. The Old Westminsters come next with five victories, all secured in the London Senior Cup, which has also been twice secured by the Old Foresters. The Old Malvernians secured the London Cup in 1902, and the Amateur Cup in the previous season. To the Old Etonians belongs the record of having been the only schoolboy team to win the English Cup twice, in the years 1879 and 1882, but they have never won any other important cup contest.

Finally, the discipline and regularity of school life helps to keep a boy in good condition, so that little real training is necessary. The right spirit is infused into his life and games, and everything tends to bring out those manly qualities which go to make up the true Briton and sportsman.

Bowden Bros.]

THE WALL GAME AT ETON—COLLEGERS v. OPPIDANS. OPPIDANS TRYING TO KICK INTO CALX.

The field of play in the wall game is 120 yards long by 6 yards wide. The goals are: In "good calx," a door in the wall; in "bad calx," a section marked on a large elm to correspond with the door. Calx is a term given to an area thirty feet distant from the end of the wall, and is clearly defined by a chalk line running down the wall from the top to the bottom. It is within calx that the "shies" are scored. A "shy" is scored by a player getting the ball between his outside foot and the wall, thus raising it off the ground. He then has the privilege of "shying at the goal." If a goal is scored (a very rare occurrence) it takes precedence of any number of "shies."

READING FOOTBALL CLUB RECORDS.

1871 to 1905.

BOROUGH OF READING

Reading's proud record—The Berks and Bucks Cup—A famous Cup-tie with Old Etonians—The tragic death of Reading's captain on the field—The "Spurs" defeated in 1880—A move to Coley Park—An amalgamation with Earley—Formation of the Southern League—Professionalism adopted—Elm Park enclosure secured—A limited liability company formed—Prominent Reading players—Southern League records—The fatality of the fifth position—Astonishing success with a new team in the season 1904-5.

Colours : Dark blue and white stripes (vertical). *Ground : Elm Park, Reading.*

THE Reading Club is very proud of being one of the very oldest football organisations in the country, its existence dating back to the year 1871. Mr. J. E. Sydenham (afterwards the first hon. secretary of the club) called a meeting at the old Bridge Street Rooms—curiously enough within a short distance of the present offices and headquarters—and from that first meeting the present important and strong organisation has developed.

The first matches were played on the Reading Recreation Ground, and the colours of the club were then, as now, the well-known dark blue and white stripes. Of the original team, which did not lose a single match during the first season, two or three are occupying important positions in the town—notably Mr. J. W. Martin, J.P., and ex-Mayor of the borough ; Messrs. Edward Margrett ; C. Holbrook, J.P., now at Gloucester ; W. J. Martin, now in Chili ; E. B. Haygarth, a leading solicitor in Cirencester, and then a grand full-back ; J. Ewart ; and A. Hart. The latter player was nearly fifty years of age when he took up the position of goalkeeper.

Others, who have since passed away, were Harry Miller, the first captain ; H. F. Rogers, who died on the football field at Coley Park ; and Tom Cook. The late Mr. James Simonds, J.P., was the first president, and until the club embraced professionalism he retained that honoured position and did yeoman service.

The matches played were confined to the best clubs in Berks, Bucks, and Oxon—viz., Henley, Marlow, Wycombe, and the famous Swifts.

During 1872-3-4 the club seldom lost a match, and prominent players in those years included Alderman C. G. Field, another ex-Mayor of the town, F. W. Albury, and J. Henderson. In 1877 the club included in its ranks the members of another local association called the "Hornets," and the amalgamation considerably strengthened the town club, several good players amongst them—Messrs. A. J. Richardson, G. J. Gibson, and G. Sillence—doing splendid service. W. H. Barnett, Stanley Hayward, J. R. Morgan, and T. H. Turner were included in the team during 1878-9, and all these gentlemen left their mark in local football history. W. H. Barnett was for many years the club's hon. treasurer and secretary, retiring in 1890. Stanley Hayward first played half-back in 1875, but afterwards appeared regularly in goal. For sixteen years Hayward kept goal splendidly, and during twelve of these seasons he played in all the Berks and Bucks games with conspicuous ability. Mr. Hayward afterwards was the official club scribe until his retirement in 1890.

J. R. Morgan, afterwards of Cambridge University, and an International, together with Edgar Field, also an International, were magnificent backs at this period—1877-8.

The Berks and Bucks Cup was first offered for competition in the season 1877-8, and the Reading Club, after disposing of Wallingford and Maidenhead, met Marlow in the final tie. After playing the usual ninety minutes no goals had been scored, and it was not until the last minute of an extra half-hour that Reading scored the winning goal, and thus secured the Berks and Bucks Cup—a great local trophy.

The victorious team was—S. Hayward, goal ; E. Field and J. R. Morgan, backs ; A. J. Richardson, H. F. Rogers, half-backs ; W. Holbrook, T. Lewis, G. Sillence, T. H. Turner, C. G. Field, A. C. Bartholomew, forwards. It was customary to play six forwards and two halves in those days.

During the season 1877-8 the club did remarkably well, and only lost to the Old Etonians, then in their palmy days, by a hotly disputed goal to nil in the second round of the Football Association Cup. The Etonians won the English Cup that year.

W. Henry Dee, Reading.]

ELM PARK, THE HOME OF THE READING FOOTBALL CLUB—SHOWING A VIEW OF THE GRAND STAND

The following season was as disastrous and as melancholy as the preceding one had been successful, for during the third match of the year, against the "Pilgrims," the captain—H. F. Rogers—died on the field from an epileptic fit, and the ensuing matches up to Christmas were cancelled.

In 1882 the club sought fresh playing quarters, and moved from the old Reading Cricket Ground to Coley Park, where for many subsequent seasons their matches were decided.

Up to the season 1885–6 there is little of importance to note.

The famous Old Carthusians—then in their greatest days of the Brothers Walters—were met in the English Cup-ties in 1887 at the Oval, and only after a close and splendid game did Reading go under by 2 goals to 1 (scored by C. E. Murdoch).

The season 1889–90 saw the amalgamation of the Reading and Earley clubs, also the change of playing quarters to the Caversham Cricket Ground, and, in addition, the succession of Horace Walker to the combined offices of hon. secretary and treasurer, Mr. W. H. Barnett, after many seasons of loyal work, seeking retirement.

The following year Frank Deane, one of the cleverest half-backs that ever represented Reading, made his entry into the team, and in 1890–1 S. Justins, W. Knight (Reading Albions), J. Warburton, H. Read, and J. Vinard all came into the team, E. Harrowell being captain.

The winning of the Berks and Bucks Cup in 1892 aroused all the dormant local football enthusiasm, and the interest which this success created has steadily increased as the years rolled onward.

Hills and Saunders.]

HERBERT SMITH,
Reading's famous Amateur Captain.

He has been associated with the club for six seasons. He learnt his football at the Oxford County Schools and Beccles College. He stands 6ft., and is splendidly built. Is a sportsman and an amateur of the highest type, and is idolised by the players of his club. He played last year for England against Scotland at the Crystal Palace, and also against Wales.

The success of League football in the North was at this time interesting the southern clubs, and a series of meetings in London ultimately led to the formation of the present Southern League in 1894, Reading forming one of the clubs therein. By many of the old brigade this step was considered a preliminary one to the embracing of professionalism and such finally proved to be the case.

Mr. A. W. A. Webb was appointed hon. secretary in succession to Horace Walker. The season was not a particularly brilliant one, as only six League matches were won and the fifth position secured.

The management began now to seriously consider the advisability of seeking the assistance of paid players.

Naturally there was strong opposition to the introduction of the professional element by many old supporters of the game, including the president, Mr. James Simonds, who had for so many years ably occupied this honoured position. The inevitable step was, however, taken, and the first professional organisation was established in 1895. Councillor F. A. Cox was the first chairman, Councillor W. Frame became hon. treasurer, and Mr. J. Warburton proved an ideal hon. secretary for the reorganised club.

After a very moderate start the team went splendidly, and finished up fourth in the League with twenty-three points.

The following year Reading only secured the sixth place in the table.

Dann and Co.]

READING FOOTBALL CLUB—FIRST PROFESSIONAL TEAM, SEASON 1895-6.

Top Row: A. Babes. S. D. Justins. M. Cannon. (Goal). E. Watts.

Middle Row: D. Spiers. Phil Bach (Captain). C. Wheeler.

Bottom Row: A. Hadley. G. Reid. J. Reid. W. Cunningham.

Dee.]
J. B. MESSER, Esq.,
Chairman of the Reading Football Club.

The difficulty of securing a new and more convenient playing ground, with greater accommodation for the increased numbers of spectators, was this season surmounted, and a lease of the present commodious and capitally equipped ground at Elm Park was secured. Mr. C. T. Murdoch, the late lamented borough member, performed the opening ceremony on Saturday, September 5, 1896, when a match with Holloway College was played. This game is memorable from the fact that it was mainly instrumental in making the Football Association more clearly define the standing of scratch teams.

During the season 1897-8 it became expedient to change the constitution of the club, and it became hereafter a limited company, Mr. J. B. Messer being appointed chairman, and Messrs. F. A. Cox, G. R. Jackson, E. Bird, A. H. Bull, J. C. Fidler, H. Lewis, W. Frame, J. Warburton, E. Knowland, J. Higgs, and A. Ridout forming the first board of directors. Mr. T. Sefton was chosen as secretary. The club's team was fairly successful, and the fifth position in the Southern League was secured.

The next season saw the inclusion of some splendid players in the team. Notably, Walter Whittaker, now with the "Bees"; J. Holt; J. Plant, who secured his Scottish cap the following year; and Harry Miller, one of the cleverest centres the club has possessed. This team did splendidly until the later stages, and again the fifth position in the League was reached.

Dick Evans, J. Barlow, and W. Ross were the principal additions to the team of 1899-1900. The fourth position was reached in the Southern League with thirty-two points.

The present social and athletic club was opened in 1899, and boasts a membership of over four hundred, who use the commodious premises in Bridge Street and at Elm Park.

Harry Mainman, the present Notts County captain, was in the team of 1900-1, when Cotton kept goal, and the terrier-like Bull played right-half and Clinch full-back.

Onward to season 1901-2, we have the advent of that brilliant back Frank Stokes, now with Birmingham City, and also the addition of Allison, Alec Davidson, Griffiths, and Blackwood. The favourite fifth position was once more reached with thirty-nine points.

Brilliant Craggs and the present captain, Herbert Smith, came into the powerful team of 1902-3, which probably was the strongest eleven that have represented the Reading Club. After a splendid tussle for League honours, Southampton just securing the premier position by three points, Reading finished an easy second. There was quite an exodus of players at the end of the season, and a new team had to be fixed up for 1903-4. The players included Willis and Naisby (now with Sunderland), Henderson (Leeds City), and Fred Bevan, undoubtedly the star centre-forward of the South. A rattling good playing season was enjoyed, and the favourite fifth place attained with forty-one points. Bolton Wanderers, who reached the F. A. Cup Final this year, were decidedly lucky to defeat the "Biscuit" team in the re-played Cup-tie at Burnden Park by 3 goals to 2.

The management were again faced with the necessity of fixing up a new eleven for 1904-5, and, excepting Herbert Smith and Tom Naisby, a brand-new team was signed. W. Henderson, an old favourite, was secured, and also Higginson, Bainbridge, Long, Bannister, Riley, and Brown.

The success of the team was surprising, and but for a series of injuries to players and the lack of good-class reserve men, the Southern League championship would have at last been won. The club, however, had to be content with the second position to the Bristol Rovers.

Five memorable Cup-ties were played with Brentford and Fulham, and the latter club ultimately triumphed at Tottenham. Honours were shared with the "Spurs" as joint-holders of the Southern Charity Cup. Financially the season was a record one, and enabled the club to re-engage practically all the old players they desired, the new-comers for the present season being: Newbigging (Notts Forest), goal; Lindsay (Renton), back; Gettins (Middlesborough) and Allman (Burslem), forwards.

Dee.]
H. MATTHEWS,
Secretary and Manager, Reading Football Club.
He has done splendid work for his club during the last fifteen years.

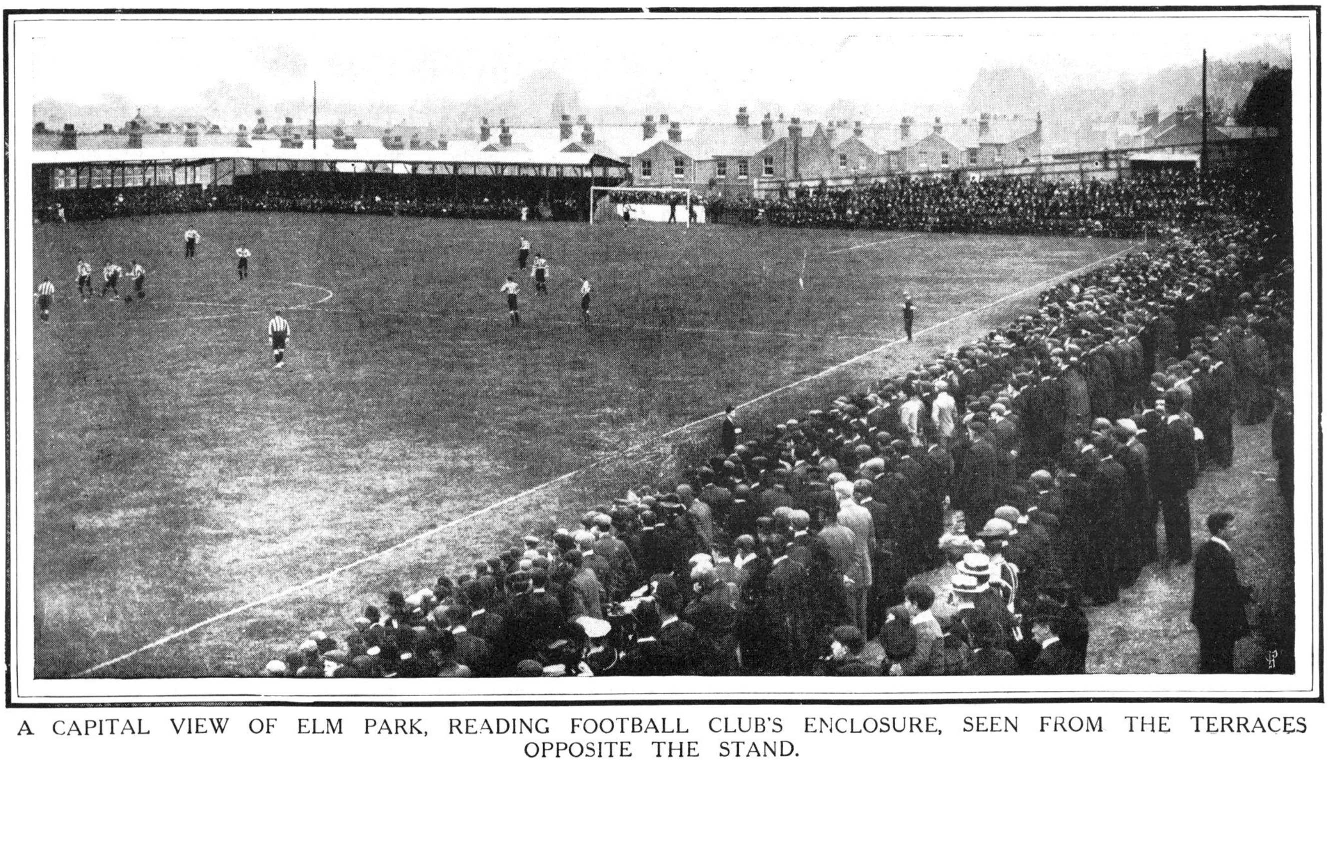

A CAPITAL VIEW OF ELM PARK, READING FOOTBALL CLUB'S ENCLOSURE, SEEN FROM THE TERRACES OPPOSITE THE STAND.

READING FOOTBALL CLUB, LTD.—THE TEAM AND OFFICIALS, SEASON 1905-6.

Top Row: T. J. Stacey, Esq. Henderson. W. Brown Newbigging (Goalkeeper). Riley. Bannister. C. Brown H. J. Matthews (Secretary).

W. Henry Dee, Reading.]

Middle Row: F. Paley (Trainer). Lindsay. Bainbridge. Higginson. Long. Gettins. Allman.

Garbutt. Devlin.

Baker and Dixon.]

SCHOOL FOOTBALL (RUGBY).—LONDON v. THE REST.
A forward rush. London getting away.

PUBLIC SCHOOL FOOTBALL.

PART II.—RUGBY.

By W. D. NIXON.

Rugby essentially a public school game—The lack of playing-fields in the old days—Rugby School, and the game that bears its name—Blackheath, Richmond, Harlequins, and the Rugby Union—William Webb Ellis and his connection with the handling code—Rugby School conforms to the laws of the Union in 1881—Cheltenham—Marlborough—Merchant Taylors—Leys School, Cambridge—The superior class of Scottish public school "Rugger"—The value of their Public Schools championship—Big schools and their principal fixtures—The necessity of cohesion in public school Rugby, and the necessity for an English School championship.

TO the amateur mind this heading gives promise of a subject of great interest. No branch of sport is more purely amateur than Rugby Union football, and it must, therefore, appeal to those who have at heart the love of sport for its own sake. The game, too, has come so much to the front during the present season that this brief discourse should have additional interest ; and the New Zealand invasion has shown us an example that the Rugby world is anxious to emulate and, if possible, eclipse.

The game of Rugby is essentially a public school game—its very name tells us so ; and it is from the celebrated old school where the great Dr. Arnold spent so many of the best years of his life that the game had its origin and name.

Turning to the historical side of the game, there are many facts of interest that come to light.

The early days of football are rather buried in oblivion and obscurity. In its earlier stages football does not seem to have flourished in our schools—the mode of life and the clothing of the time were not compatible with the rough treatment that might be received on the football field.

Neither were the great schools of a century ago endowed with that wealth of open space and playground which has been obtained by some of our more modern institutions.

This undoubtedly had an effect on the development of their various games, and it was from confinement of space that we find such a game as the "wall game" growing up at Eton.

Rugby was more blessed than any other school in the matter of space, and in 1749 there was a playground of over two acres in size ; and this was luxury in those days.

History tells of the various forms of football at the different schools, hybrid forms of Association and Rugby, but at the Midland School alone do the laws appear to have allowed a player to run with the ball.

Running with the ball led to tackling, and it is not too much to say that the running game came entirely into its present form from Rugby School, although, doubtless, before it was taken up by the public at large, other schools, such as Cheltenham and Marlborough, had adopted a game of the type so lucidly depicted in "Tom Brown's Schooldays."

In the year 1850 football had greatly increased in popularity, and in 1858 the famous Blackheath Club sprang into being, mainly through the agency and energy of old Rugbeians; and the next year the Richmond side followed, and there was no other regular constituted team for the next five years except the Harlequins.

Through the exertions of these three clubs the Rugby Union was founded in 1871. This was the means of bringing the game into line a bit, and a uniform code of rules was drawn up in this season, when the first English and Scottish International game was also played.

Turning to further details of the game at Rugby School, as being the spark from which the fire of the Union game was kindled, we find that the game in its present form really took shape in 1823.

One William Webb Ellis was the culprit who in that year picked up the ball and ran with it, which was then contrary to the rules.

The game developed at the school from that day onwards

more or less on its own lines, and it was not until the year 1881 that the school conformed to the laws of the Rugby Union. Other schools took the game up, but it will be found that this did not occur until a good many years after the example had been set at Rugby.

Thus Cheltenham, which has always been in the front rank of the public schools, probably took the game up in the late Forties. At this school the "Classical and Modern" match dates from the year 1852, and is supposed to be one of the first fixtures in England that has been played continuously ever since.

Cheltenham commenced their list of "foreign" matches in the year 1875, and it is worthy of note that since their fixture with Rugby was commenced they have won 60 per cent. of the games.

Marlborough followed the lead in the Sixties, and the game has gone on from strength to strength ever since. The year 1878 saw the number of men in the team fixed at the regulation number of fifteen, instead of the twenty who had composed the side up to that date. There are still mementoes of those early days to be seen in some of the caps awarded.

At the Merchant Taylors School, which has probably turned out more sound players than any other in England, the exact history of the game is also rather lost with the lapse of years.

The first fixture recorded was in the early Sixties, and in 1859 the school record contains a paragraph saying "that the bad fortunes of previous

Baker and Dixon.]

THE RUGBY GAME—FETTESIAN LORETTONIANS v. RICHMOND.

Richmond getting away from a scrum.

Baker and Dixon.]

RICHMOND v. FETTESIAN LORETTONIANS AT THE OLD DEER PARK, RICHMOND.

Fettesian Lorettonians make a clever pass over the back.

seasons have been reversed" by the defeat of St. Paul's School. From that point there is a lapse until the year 1878, when the steady improvement of the team began to be recorded year by year.

From the year 1879 onwards, in fact, the history of the Taylors' football is pretty clear and up-to-date.

Moreover, the boys turned out by this school have always played a prominent part in English Rugby, and the style of football taught has never been of the bread-and-butter order.

This strenuous game probably owes its origin to the fact that in the earliest days of the school there was a rough-and-tumble game played on a small asphalt pitch, which was very hard indeed to fall upon. This game is less popular now, but will die hard on account of its antiquity and the large part it plays in school tradition. It doubtless owed its origin to a lack of proper accommodation, that old bugbear, insufficient space, being much in evidence in all the great public schools.

Leys School, Cambridge, has made great strides at the game during the thirty years that Rugby has been the code adopted; and Uppingham has also proved its ability, though one of the most recent schools to take to the handling code, the game having been adopted in 1890. Previous to that, this school, like so many others, had a game peculiar to itself.

There are several other schools of premier importance in public school Rugby, but the above instances will serve to show the approximate period at which the game became popular at our various public schools, and it will be seen that it was left for Rugby School to be the pioneer and show the way in the matter.

Unlike the case of the Association game, it is a matter of much greater difficulty to pick the premier school at the Rugby game. The Dunn Cup serves to show us in Association the relative merits of the various schools through their old boys, but the lack of a similar competition for the Rugby playing schools is much felt, and would be heartily welcomed by all who wish to see the national standard of the game improved.

However, I will return to this point later; and in picking the premier schools in England it would take a great deal of discrimination to find much to choose between Cheltenham, St. Paul's, Bedford, Marlborough, Rugby, and Merchant Taylors.

There is no very elaborate programme of inter-school matches, but more often than not the above six schools would be found to have the best public school fifteen of the year amongst them.

However, Englishmen would probably be the first to admit that in Scotland they have some public school Rugby that is a class above anything we have got in England.

The three Scottish schools, Fettes, Loretto, Merchiston, and, in a lesser degree, Glenalmond, play a wonderful game for boys, a game brimful of vigour and pluck, and played with any amount of robust dash.

The proof of the pudding is in the eating, and the quality of the play at these schools can be judged from the ease with which the boys on leaving these establishments, secure higher honours at the Universities, and from the frequency with which they gain their International caps.

Merchiston, whose history dates back to the year 1833, appears to be the oldest of the Scottish public schools, but even this makes it of much more recent development than similar English institutions, and, therefore, all the more credit is due to them for the rapidity with which they have risen to the top of the tree at football.

In Scotland they have a Public School championship, and to this is due much of the stimulus the game has received, and seems to show that the game would derive great benefit in England from a similar institution. It certainly has done a great deal for Scottish Rugby, and though Scottish temperament and physique do seem peculiarly adapted to "Rugger," the success that has attended the game in the North can hardly be attributed to this alone.

Probably any of the five leading schools in Scotland could turn out a team in most seasons which could put "paid" to the account of the best production of their sister schools in England.

Coming nearer to home, Rugby School has probably quite as much right to premier place as any other college, if only on the score of tradition.

The school has a good list of fixtures, its chief opponents being Uppingham and Cheltenham, and this latter school is very proud of their record against its great opponent. In 1900 they had a team at Rugby which will probably be handed down as one of the strongest ever put into the field by any school. Old Rugbeians have ever been to the fore in the Rugby game. In 1904 there were five past members of the school in the Oxford fifteen; and last year four of the English Internationals—Cartwright, Rogers, Stoop, and Dillon — were all old Rugby boys.

The strength of the game at the Midland school owes a great deal to the untiring energy and coaching of Mr. H. C. Bradby, one of the masters, and himself an old Rugbeian.

Marlborough's chief opponents are Clifton and Wellington, and it is curious to note, in the case of the Wellington match that, though the Berkshire school has won two-thirds of the fixtures, nevertheless Marlborough has managed to secure the bigger aggregate of points, and the Wiltshire school has also a good lead over Clifton.

Cheltenham always indulges in an ambitious programme, playing other public schools—Rugby, Haileybury, Wellington, Sherborne—against all of whom the school has performed consistently well.

Being so near to Wales, Cheltenham has always had the benefit of Welsh training, and tumbled to the four three-quarter game sooner than most other clubs. Old Cheltonians have been prominent in the wider field of subsequent football, twenty-five Internationals having learnt their early game at this school, and such names as G. T. Unwin, F. Jacomb, and F. H. B. Champain are familiar.

Merchant Taylors has fixtures with St. Paul's, Mill Hill, Epsom, and Christ's Hospital, of whom the first is their chief and most dreaded rival.

The great players produced by the school are easily headed by J. E. Raphael, a three-quarter brimming over with individuality and dash, while the school cherishes the names of N. C. Fletcher, C. B. Buck, and the brothers Taylor.

Leys, Cambridge, plays Bedford Grammar, St. Paul's, Merchant Taylors, Mill Hill, Oundle, and Dover, and the players from this school are yearly improving, prominent Old Leysians being G. L. Lloyd, J. H. P. Strong, J. T. Tullock, and A. B. Flett.

Clifton's opponents have nearly all been mentioned already, and Clifton Rugby is famous, if for no other reason, from the fact that J. Daniell, one of the greatest forwards we have ever had, learnt his football there.

Uppingham is a comparatively new convert to the game, playing only one school fixture, viz., with Rugby, but yet such cracks as H. Alexander, C. J. Newbold, and H. F. P. Hearson have all come from that school.

Christ's Hospital, having recently moved to Horsham, is able to offer magnificent playing fields, and will probably come much more to the fore in the near future.

Dulwich, Eastbourne, Haileybury, Sherborne, Tonbridge, and St. Peter's (York) must be added to the list of names already given, and then I think I have taken into consideration all the schools in the front rank.

Finally, may I give one word more in urging the necessity of cohesion and a thorough working together in all public school Rugby. A Public School championship, on the lines of the one that has done so much for Scottish football, between eight schools, selected by means of a qualifying competition each year, would work wonders.

This might lead to a levelling up of public school form, and possibly to a trophy for competition between Old Boy teams on the lines of the Arthur Dunn Cup.

W. D. NIXON.

Baker and Dixon.]

THE RUGBY GAME—FETTESIAN LORETTONIANS v. RICHMOND AT THE OLD DEER PARK.

The breaking up of a scrum. Richmond neatly pick up the ball on the fringe of their opponents' twenty-five.

Baker and Dixon.]

RUGBY—THE FIGHT FOR THE COUNTY CHAMPIONSHIP AT WEST HARTLEPOOL, APRIL 29, 1905.

In this championship match Durham defeated Middlesex by three tries (nine points) to one goal and one try (eight points). The game was played in torrents of rain. In the above splendid photograph the winners are seen reaching for the ball.

THE RISE TO FAME OF LIVERPOOL FOOTBALL CLUB.

League Champions, 1900-1; Second League Champions, 1893-4, 1895-6, 1904-5.

How Liverpool F. C. became established—Keen rivalry with "Papa" Everton—A brilliant first season—Liverpool join the Second Division of the League—Magnificent record in 1893-4 secures the club admission to the Premier Division—Fluctuating fortunes—A fall from grace and a second rise to favour—A League record, 106 goals to 32—The coveted League championship won—Officials and players—Prospects for the present season.

Colours: Red shirts, white knickers. *Ground: Anfield Road, Liverpool.*

LIVERPOOL is a young club which has experienced the troubles peculiar to youth. It is now approaching its vigorous manhood, and seems destined for a green old age—being neither "green" nor aged at present.

The club was first troubled about its birth. That interesting little event might never have been if Papa Everton had behaved himself. Everton were then playing at the Anfield Road ground, and might have been playing there still; but owing to differences with their landlord and president, Alderman J. Houlding, J.P., as to the amount of rent to be paid, they removed their headquarters to Goodison Park, leaving behind them a minority, who constituted and called themselves "Liverpool F. C.," and have made the name their own. At first their title was disputed by a local Rugby club of the same name. Whoever hears of that Rugby club now? Such were the birth-throes of Liverpool.

The split is not at all to be regretted in the interests of football. It created two clubs instead of one, and for years local enthusiasts have seen at least one League match a week at home, while most other centres have to be content with one League match a fortnight.

The split also stimulated local rivalry, and local rivalry keeps the game alive. It is never so much alive as when Liverpool and Everton meet. Then the wonder is that instead of everybody being alive, everybody is not killed dead, as an Irishman would say. It is "Derby Day" in Liverpool; there is a record "gate" and a record struggle.

Liverpool Football Club was launched on March 15, 1892, with Alderman Houlding as president, and Mr. W. E. Barclay as secretary.

Scott and Co.]

MR. TOM WATSON,
Secretary of Liverpool Football Club.

There is no more popular man in all football than genial Tom Watson, the Liverpool secretary. He helped to establish Newcastle United, to build up the fame of Sunderland, the "Team of All the Talents," and is continuing his career of usefulness with the Anfield Road club, with whom he has now seen nine years' service.

The club had a brilliant first season, during which they won the Lancashire League championship with a score of 66 goals to 19, and the Liverpool Cup, in which not a goal was scored against them.

These proved rather expensive triumphs, for both the Lancashire League and the Liverpool Cups were stolen mysteriously, and the club had to replace them at a cost of £127. They had started with only £500 in the treasury, practically a gift from the president, who did not press for repayment. He was a generous, lifelong friend. They had not too many of that sort; the "gates" were poor; the receipts did not repay the guarantee given to Rotherham, the first club Liverpool ever played, who won by a margin of 6 goals. How did the treasurer manage to pay the team? The bank balance was scarcely more than a first-class professional's salary, and yet Mr. James McKenna, the present vice-chairman, had got together a combination that simply scintillated with celebrities—T. Wyllie, of the Glasgow Rangers; Andrew Hannah, J. McBride, Duncan McLean, J. Kelso, and J. Cameron, of Renton; J. Miller, of Dumbarton; and Malcolm McVean, of 3rd Lanark; in all thirteen professionals and sixteen reserves.

The team had not long to wait for League honours. These came first on admission to the Second Division of the League at the end of their first season, and at the end of their second season in admission to First League honours. And well these were deserved, for from September 1, 1893, to April 30, 1894, they lost only five out of all their matches played, defeated nearly every First League club that came to Anfield Road, as well as Preston North End, the then "Invincibles," by 3—2 in the English Cup competition, and went right through the Second League tourney undefeated, winning outright all but two of their 28 matches, with a goal score of 77 to 18. A victory over Newton Heath in the test matches by 2—0 found them at last in the First Division.

The history of Liverpool, so far as high-class football goes, is a history of alternations between the First and Second Divisions of the League. They are a brilliant, but erratic, and rather unfortunate team. They have been champions of the First Division once, and runners-up once. On the other hand, they have been twice relegated to the Second Division, both times through sheer bad luck. Their first "put back" occurred the very season they were admitted to the First League —1894-5—when they finished last, winning only six League games at home, and one away, and, defeated by Bury in the test matches, they had to return to the Second Division. It was a remarkable anti-climax to the achievements of the previous season, and no doubt the prophets of woe alone enjoyed themselves, while sanguine supporters went into mourning. There were reasons for the fall; accidents to players were so numerous that the same team could not be played two matches running; combination was, therefore, out of the question, and it is combination rather than individual excellence that wins League matches. One "star" among ten "sticks" is no use, except for stage purposes. Liverpool fell, to regain First Division honours by a record in goal-getting which has never been equalled in either division of the League. In 1895-6 they won the championship of the Second Division once more with a goal score of 106 to 32 in thirty fixtures. What stout hearts they must have had! League clubs that have never been deposed from their high position—Fortune's darlings!—will not be able to appreciate this statement. Those best able to judge are other former First League clubs relegated to the Second Division and still there. The descent is easy enough; getting out again is a task beyond most of them. For, make no mistake, competition is far fiercer in the Second than in the First Division of the League. It always is, at the bottom, for the individual as well as for the club, which is merely a collection of individuals. If Liverpool had been a craven-hearted lot, they would have sunk never to rise again after 1894; but

LIVERPOOL FOOTBALL CLUB.—THE PLAYERS; SEASON, 1905-6.

Back Row: W. Connell (Trainer) J. Hewitt. C. Wilson. S. Hardy (Goalkeeper). M. Parry. E. Doig (Goalkeeper). W. Dunlop. J. Hardy.

R. Scott and Co., Manchester.]

Middle Row: R. Robinson J. Gorman. D. Murray. J. Hughes. A. Raisbeck. J. Cox. G. Fleming. S. Raybould. A. West.

Front Row: A. Goddard. G. Latham. J. Carlin.

their unwritten motto is: "It's dogged that does it"; and so, by sheer pluck, they forced their way back next season. While they were down, as is the way of the world, their enemies jumped on them, and their friends stood afar off—there were not enough spectators to go round the field, and the smallness of the attendance was emphasised by the emptiness of a fine grand stand that had been erected at a cost of £1,000 to hold 3,000 people. The club's enemies kindly utilised the occasion to try to steal its best players—their skill was unquestioned, it was their misfortune that had brought the club low—but Mr. W. Houlding, who had succeeded his father in the presidency, persuaded the committee not to part with a single player.

We have seen how quickly Liverpool in 1895-6 recovered from their fall; we have now to see how, after triumphs still more brilliant than at the outset of their career, they came a cropper from causes similar to those of 1894-5—sheer misfortune —and found themselves in the Second Division again, and once more asserted their right to the place in the First which they now hold. In 1898-9 they were runners-up to Aston Villa for League championship honours with 43 points to 45. The match, played at Birmingham, drew the largest crowd that has ever witnessed a League match—the proceeds were £1,500. In the season of 1900-1 Liverpool at last won the League championship with 45 points to the 43 of Sunderland. On both these occasions the League championship was decided in the last match of the tourney. The club that was rejected when it applied for admission to the First Division at the outset of its career, and that had twice been in the Second Division—once promoted there, once relegated there—was now League champions. No other League club can point to such a strange reversal of fortune. Liverpool are not the only League champions; but they are the only League champions who have been twice in the Second Division. One other temporary eclipse was still in store for them, and owing to troubles with players, some of whom left for the South and were afterwards suspended, the season of 1903-4 saw them at the bottom of the League ladder once more. But, like water, they are bound to rise to their level, and their level is the First Division. The club that threw them out in the test matches was West Bromwich. The "Throstles" are now themselves in the Second Division, while Liverpool have climbed back, after the hardest fight ever seen in the Second Division, during which they had for opponents Manchester United and Bolton, First Leaguers before Liverpool were ever dreamt of. There was no doubt about the right of Liverpool to their forfeited honours in the First Division; they won the Second Division championship with 58 points, a record, nearest to which came West Bromwich in 1901-2 with 55 points.

So here are Liverpool for the second time among their equals in the First Division; to remain there, at least over the present season, if fulfilment does not belie their early promise.

As English Cup-fighters their history is scarcely inferior to their League strenuousness, for though they have not yet won the Cup, they have been twice in the Semi-finals; first, in the season of 1896-7, when Aston Villa beat them at Bramall Lane and afterwards won the Cup; and again in 1898-9, when they played their memorable three games with Sheffield United—first at Bolton, secondly at Fallowfield—what time Liverpool were leading by a goal when the crowd broke in—thirdly at Derby, when Sheffield United won by a goal to also win the Cup. Hard lines that Liverpool should lose within sight of the Crystal Palace! But they have proved better Cup-fighters than some League champions, not to speak of Second Division teams. So much for national honours; now for local. They hold the Liverpool Cup, for which they defeated Everton last New Year's Day by 4 goals to 1, and they have more than once shown their lusty youth by soundly thrashing their parent club at Goodison.

These successes have not been achieved without clever officials as well as clever players. The late Alderman Houlding had a knack of gathering men about him. Mr. Edwin Berry, solicitor, now chairman of the club, was an old Everton player in amateur days. Mr. James McKenna, vice-chairman, was one of the original founders of the club, and has stood by it, come weal come woe; he is a member of the management committee of the League, represents No. 3 Division on the council of the Football Association, is President of the Lancashire combination, one of the executive of the Lancashire F. A., and devotes all his spare time to the game; altogether a notable figure in the football world. He was recruiting-sergeant for Liverpool in its infancy, when he had many exciting experiences and some dangerous adventures in the hunt after players. And what shall be said of Secretary Tom Watson, with over twenty years' experience of first-class football, beginning as secretary to Newcastle West End, then from 1887 to 1896 secretary to Sunderland F. C., whom he found a struggling team, organised them into a "team of all the talents," popularised the game in Sunderland, and was the "brains" of the team that won the League championship three times. He came to Liverpool in August, 1896, and has there repeated his Sunderland successes and his popularity. There is no more experienced and popular football secretary to-day. Trainer William Connell has been with the club three seasons; he came from Stockport County.

Bowden Bros.]

J. E. DOIG,

Liverpool's famous goalkeeper, was born at Arbroath in 1868. He stands 5ft. 9¾in., and weighs 12st. 9lb. He is a fine custodian, and has played many times for Scotland. Before joining Liverpool he played for Blackburn and Sunderland. He may now be regarded as a veteran, but is still a goalkeeper of the very first class.

Liverpool players have gained many distinctions. Doig, Raisbeck, Parry, Raybould, Cox, and Parkinson are all Internationals. J. E. Doig, a Scotch International, of Arbroath, played for Sunderland first, but has now followed his old chief to Liverpool. He first kept goal for Scotland against Ireland in 1887; nine years later he was goalkeeper for Scotland against England; he is still as good as ever.

A. Raisbeck, centre half-back, is one of Scotland's best, and has represented her several times against England; he is Liverpool's captain for the fourth time. M. Parry, right half, has played for Wales. J. Cox, outside-left, is one of the speediest forwards of the day. He has played in various International matches. S. Raybould, three seasons ago, was top scorer in the League.

J. Parkinson, centre-forward, a local lad, played in the North v. South match at Bristol, and was considered one of the finest forwards on the field.

The Liverpool players for the present season are as follows: Goal, J. E. Doig and S. Hardy; backs, A. West, W. Dunlop, C. Wilson, and D. Murray; halves, M. Parry, A. Raisbeck, G. Fleming, J. Bradley, G. Latham, John Hughes, and T. Chorlton; forwards, A. Copper, R. Robinson, J. Parkinson, S. Raybould, J. Cox, J. Garside, J. Hewitt, and J. Carlin.

Liverpool started the season with the brightest of hopes. They had fought their way through the Premier Division of the League before, and secured the highest honour the competition has to give. Facing Woolwich Arsenal at home they were defeated in the opening match of the season, after Parkinson had left the field with a broken wrist. Disaster followed disaster until it seemed as though the fight would not be for the leadership but one of strenuous endeavour to escape the bottom rung of the League ladder. However, recovery came as suddenly, match after match was won, and the "Reds" have now a fine chance of winning the championship, and already seriously challenge the leaders for pride of place. To once more win the championship of the League is the great ambition of the club.

THE FAMOUS WEST BROMWICH ALBION FOOTBALL CLUB.

THE "THROSTLES."

Winners of the Football Association Cup 1887-8, 1891-2; Finalists 1885-6 1886-7, 1894-5.

By WILLIAM McGREGOR.

The fame and fascination of the Albion—A team with a history—How the Albion humbled proud Preston—The club founded in 1879—The club's pioneers—Early matches—The spirit that made the Albion—Clever footballers—A creditable defeat—West Bromwich beat the Villa—Their first cup won—Famous games—Stoney Lane Ground secured—Albion v. Blackburn in the Cup Final of 1885—The Final again reached—The Cup won in 1888—Preston's assurance sadly disturbed—The Cup won again in 1892—The sensational game in the Final of 1895—Moderate League record—Great players of the past, and brighter prospects for the future.

Colours: Blue and white stripes, white knickers. *Ground: The Hawthorns.*

ALTHOUGH West Bromwich Albion are not the force to-day they were in football in the days when everyone looked for them to qualify for the Final of the English Cup, they have a possession which clubs of a more mushroom type cannot rob them of. They are almost alone among the clubs in the Second League in possessing a history. When West Bromwich Albion go to London to fulfil Second League engagements they draw a big gate. There was a large muster at Chelsea when the Albion appeared there recently, and yet it would not be accurate to say that these people went there expecting to see a display of football such as Newcastle, Aston Villa, or Everton would give. No; the crowd was mainly drawn by the halo of romance which surrounds West Bromwich Albion. The name is a powerful attraction still wherever football is played. I have no doubt that some thousands of people went to Chelsea that afternoon solely because of the kindly recollections they had of the Albion in the brave days of old, when James Bayliss was their leader, and William Bassett was the bright particular star of the forward line. A club's reputation dies hard. Sportsmen are notoriously conservative; and you have only to mention the name of the Albion in football circles to fire the imagination of veteran followers of the game who recall them when they were at their best, and whose fund of reminiscences concerning them is ample.

West Bromwich Albion in the late 'Eighties and early 'Nineties had an almost unique reputation. They proved themselves quite competent to beard the Preston North End lion when his might inspired awe wherever he roamed. Matter unlimited has been written concerning that wonderful match at Nottingham when they threw the proud Prestonians out of the English Cup competition in the Semi-final stage. Even more eventful was their triumph in the competition a year later still, when they and North End reached the Final, and the Albion won one of the hardest games football has known.

The history of West Bromwich Albion is almost unrivalled so far as interest goes. The club was not formed in an hour by those who had wealth at their disposal and the willingness to equip a model enclosure and engage a formidable team.

It was founded in 1879 by a band of youths who had played cricket together, and that band of youths remained practically undivided until they had taken the club from its humble environment and made it one of the foremost football organisations in the country.

They were desirous of having an incentive to keep together during the winter months, so they subscribed

WEST BROMWICH ALBION.

The team that defeated Preston North End in the F. A. Cup Final at Kennington Oval, March 24, 1888, by 2 goals to 1.

Back Row: Mr. J. Buil. Mr. J. Raybould. Mr. G. Salter. Mr. T. Smith (Hon. Sec.). Mr. H. Jackson. Mr. L. Ford.
Middle Row: A. Aldridge (Right-back). C. Perry (Centre-half). E. Horton (Right-half). R. Roberts (Goal). G. Timmins (Left-half). H. Green (Left-back).
Bottom Row: G. Woodhall (Outside-right). W. I. Bassett (Inside-right). J. M. Bayliss (Centre). T. Pearson (Inside-left). J. Wilson (Outside-left).

sixpence each, and a select committee went to Wednesbury to buy a ball, for such an article was not to be found in every street at that period.

The select committee consisted of Stanton, George Bell, Harry Bell, Stokes, Eld, Timmins, and Bisseker. It is only right that the names of these pioneers should go down to posterity as those who made a pilgrimage which will always be remembered so long as people are interested in football lore.

The lads christened themselves the West Bromwich Strollers, and their first ground was a piece of unenclosed ground known as Cooper's Hill, but they played their matches on the excellent stretch of turf in Dartmouth Park. A weekly subscription of twopence for a time sufficed to meet all their requirements. For one thing, they had no rent to pay, and that is an advantage which most men crave, whether they be associated with football or not. They were not disposed, however, to let anyone share their privileges, for the substantial sum of sixpence was exacted from each aspirant who desired to share the comradeship of the Strollers.

DR. ISAAC PITT.

This photograph has a special interest for all lovers and followers of the famous "Throstles." Dr. Isaac Pitt was a director of the club for over twenty years. To him a great debt of gratitude is due, for with unwavering devotion he tended and doctored the players year after year, and had not a little to do with the great success of the famous club. He is still officially connected with the Albion.

From the first their form was promising; and soon a few enthusiasts began to gather to watch their games. This, and the rapidly improving form of the team, seemed to justify a little enterprise, and so, in 1881, we find them leasing a field off Walsall Street. The field had its good points, and it also had its defects. Their means did not enable them to invite tenders for the proper equipment of the enclosure, so they wisely decided to utilise their own labour in getting their new home ship-shape. They gave of their leisure to the work, and every morning saw them do something towards getting the ground fit for football purposes. Whenever a man had an hour to spare he went and put in that hour at the ground. That is a spirit, by the way, which is dying out, even if it be not dead. It was that spirit which made the Albion Club, and, therefore, it calls for eulogy. They levelled and rolled the ground, and put the fences in good order, to the end that they might charge a gate. The Albion were strong on arboreal nomenclature even then, for we get almost a suggestion of the Hawthorns in the title which they gave to their ground, which was the Birches. The veteran Stanton told me that the people who wished to remain dryshod in wet weather used to find their own planks, and the only approach to a grand stand was a manure-heap.

The Strollers were not the leading team in West Bromwich at that time. They were preceded by the old West Bromwich Club, of which George Salter was captain, and also by the Dartmouth, and the Sandwell; but they rapidly left their rivals behind.

The members of West Bromwich Albion—they took their name from the Albion district in West Bromwich, the title seeming to them more distinctive than West Bromwich Strollers—were a very close corporation. They met at a coffee-house in the town, and so jealous were they of the welfare of the club, that they decided that it would be prejudicial to the best interests of the organisation for any of the players to begin courting. They looked with grave suspicion upon any man who absented himself for any reason whatever from the almost nightly meetings they held at the coffee-house.

The chief members of the Albion team at this time were S. Biddlestone, who was the goalkeeper; H. Bell and R. Roberts, backs; T. Smith, J. Wilson, and J. Stanton, half-backs; with the forward line constructed from W. Bisseker, E. T. Smith, G. Timmins, J. T. Stokes, G. Bell, H. Aston, W. Round, H. Evans, and J. Armstrong. Bisseker was the captain, and Stokes the vice-captain.

In 1881-2 the club took a step forward by entering for the Birmingham Cup, and their early performances in the competition left no doubt as to their latent ability. In the first round they were drawn against the Calthorpe, who then had a good reputation in the Birmingham district. It was, in fact, the pioneer Association club of the Midlands. The game took place upon the ground of the Birmingham club in Bristol Road, and although the Calthorpe were then falling away from the high position they had occupied, they looked upon the engagement as a very soft thing; in fact, most of the members had never heard of West Bromwich Albion. Several old members of the Calthorpe have told me that, although some of their leading players were injured, they took the field with unlimited confidence. But the Albion played sound and clever football; they lasted better than their opponents, and won by 3 goals to 2. From that time forward their yellow and white quartered jerseys, with the Staffordshire knot embroidered on the front, became familiar on local grounds.

The late secretary of the Birmingham Football Association, Mr. J. H. Cofield, who refereed in the match, was so pleased with the display that, by the same evening's post, he despatched a long letter of congratulation to them, advising them to keep together, and prophesying

WEST BROMWICH ALBION.

The team that beat Aston Villa in the English Cup Final at the Oval by 3 goals to nil, April 2, 1892.

Nicholson. J. Reader. C. Perry.
W. I. Bassett. J. Reynolds. R. McLeod. S. Nicholls. T. Pearson. W. Groves. T. McCulloch. J. Geddes.

THE ENGLISH CUP.

that there was a great future before the club. Elwells were beaten in the second round, and Notts Rangers in the third. They found their way into the semi-final stage, but were then removed by Wednesbury Old Athletic. As the Old Athletic were the most powerful side in the Midlands, the fact that the Albion, who prior to that season were an unknown team, were only beaten by 3 goals to 2 suggests that their football must have been of a very high order indeed. By sheer pertinacity and loyalty to their organisation they had become a power in Midland football.

MR. W. H. KEYS,
Chairman of the West Bromwich Albion F. C.

A hard-working and enthusiastic follower of the Association game, Mr. Keys makes an ideal chairman, and the club are to be congratulated on having so able a director.

The season of 1882-3 found them competing for the Birmingham and Staffordshire Cups; and Mr. George Salter made an enthusiastic president. In the first round of the Birmingham Cup they defeated Coseley by 26 goals to 1; in the second round they met Wednesbury Old Athletic again, and once more only a goal divided the teams. They ran into the final of the Wednesbury Charity Cup, and therein met Notts Forest. They were beaten by 5 goals to 3 on the Aston Villa ground at Perry Barr, and it is worthy of notice that Tinsley Lindley, then a school-boy, played one of his first games with the Forest. He scored four of the five goals obtained, but considering the calibre of the Forest, this was one of the Albion's most notable performances. The defeat was more creditable than some victories would have been, but the joy of the Albion at making so good a fight was somewhat chastened by the fact that an injury in the match robbed them for ever of the services of their captain, John While.

The Staffordshire Cup competition provided them, however, with ample compensation for all disappointments. In the second round they were drawn against Aston Villa, the greatest side in the Midlands. The Villa did not regard their engagements as seriously as they might have done; in fact, they omitted to cancel their ordinary first team engagement for the day. They split up their forces, but even then they thought the team they put in against the Albion would suffice; but a fierce game ended in a draw, although the Villa had choice of ground. The Villa had a different team in at West Bromwich in the following week; but the Albion won by a goal to nil, and the victory caused quite a sensation throughout the Black Country. The Albion beat Stoke in the final by 3 goals to 2, and thus won their first cup. It was indeed remarkable that the same band of youths who started a few years before in such a humble way should have worked right to the top of the tree so far as Midland football was concerned. They were now located at Four Acres, the ground of the Dartmouth Club, who had abandoned football to devote their undivided energies to cricket.

In 1883-4 we find them competing for the first time in the English Cup competition. They were removed from the first round by Wednesbury Old Athletic, but the Albion had their revenge, for they knocked the Wednesbury cracks out of the Birmingham Cup competition, and thus placed all the Black Country at their backs. They reached the semi-final of the cup, only to be beaten by a powerful team, Walsall Swifts, by 1 goal to nil. They were also in the final of the Staffordshire competition, but lost the cup to Birmingham St. George's, who won by 2 goals to 1. It is illustrative of the progress that the Albion had made that Preston North End gave them fixtures, and they beat the Prestonians at West Bromwich by 2 goals to 1.

There was a notable match between the Albion and the Villa in the third round of the English Cup in 1884-5. They played a goalless draw at Perry Barr, and when the match was re-played at Four Acres rain fell in torrents. The Albion's victory of 3 goals to nil paralysed Midland football opinion for a time. The Albion travelled on successfully until, in the sixth round, they were beaten by the ultimate winners, Blackburn Rovers, by 2 goals to nil. They had the worst of the luck that day, and the referee, Mr. W. F. Beardshaw, of Sheffield, had a bad time with the crowd.

The Albion's fame now rested on a national basis. They bade farewell to the Four Acres, equipping the Stoney Lane enclosure at a cost of £370, and paying £25 per annum for rent. Professionalism was adopted, the remuneration being ten shillings per week to all the first team members.

The opening match at Stoney Lane was on September 5, 1885, when the Albion beat Third Lanark by 4 goals to 1. Their great centre-forward, James Bayliss, migrated to them from Wednesbury Old Athletic, which was on the down grade at this time. He and T. Green, formerly of Birmingham St. George's, were deadly inside players, Bayliss being in particular the embodiment of dash. Greatly to the joy of all Midland footballers, the Albion reached the Final of the English Cup, being the first Midland side to

WEST BROMWICH ALBION F. C., SEASON 1894-5.
English Cup Finalists, defeated by Aston Villa, 1 goal to 0. Winners of the Birmingham Cup, defeating Aston Villa by 1 goal to 0.

Draycott.]

T. HIGGINS. J. TAGGART. J. READER. J. HORTON. W. WILLIAMS.
T. PERRY. W. I. BASSETT (Captain). R. McLEOD. W. RICHARDS. T. HUTCHINSON. J. BANKS.

qualify for this great distinction. They drew with Blackburn Rovers at the Oval, and some say they won the game, but that is as it may be. The late Major Marindin, who refereed, was of opinion that they had scored on one occasion, but no appeal was made—things were ruled differently in those days. In the re-played Final at Derby—the first time that the Final Tie had been removed from London—the Rovers, who were the cleverer team, won by 2 goals to nil. But the Albion were full of honours that season, for, in addition to ranking as Finalists of the English Cup, they carried off both the Birmingham and Staffordshire trophies.

In 1887 they were again in the Final. Their most historic performance was the defeat of the then almost invincible Preston North End team at Nottingham in the Semi-final. What a fever of anxiety the Albion men were in when it was time for them to go on the field and their great custodian, Bob Roberts, had not arrived. He had missed his train, but just as the game was about to begin the crowd at the back of the goal parted, and Roberts, ready dressed, but covered with a long ulster, vaulted over the ropes, and was ready for the fray. Sheer pluck and dash won the game for the Albion by 3 goals to 1, Bob Roberts excelling himself. They were not destined to win the Final, for they fell before Aston Villa, then a great side indeed, by 2 goals to nil.

Nothing daunted, they again appeared at the Oval in the next season, and then they beat proud Preston North End by 2 goals to 1. William Bassett's play on that afternoon created quite a furore, and he gained his International cap the same evening.

MR. F. EVERISS,
The able and popular secretary of West Bromwich Albion Football Club, 1905.

It is related of Preston North End that so confident were they that Nick Ross asked Major Marindin if they could not be photographed with the Cup prior to the match. "Had you not better win it first?" was the laconic reply of the military referee.

The Black Country was aflame with enthusiasm for weeks, for never before had there been such football heroes.

Then came the institution of the League, and that phase of football was not so agreeable to the Albion. However, in 1892, we again find them in the Final of the Cup, and they beat Aston Villa in hollow style by 3 goals to nil.

Next we come to 1895, when the Villa and the Albion again met in the great battle of the year. This was the fifth Final in which the Albion had been engaged in a period of eleven years. The Villa scored in the first half-minute, and won a sensational game by a goal to nil. Bassett and Higgins played wonderful football for the Albion that day; and the late Colonel North, always a large hearted sportsman, was so much taken up by the pluck of Higgins, who played with his head swathed in bandages, that he went to the dressing-room after the match and presented him with a five-pound note. But there the Albion's distinction in football practically came to an end. They have never been prominent in the English Cup since, and in the League they have been, with few exceptions, uniformly unsuccessful. Once they fell into the Second League, but very gallantly they fought their way back, winning the Second League competition in the season of 1901-2 with a record total of 55 points. They won 25 matches, lost 4, and scored 82 goals to 29. They also did well in the First League in the next season, but in 1903-4 they were at the bottom of the list, and have since been members of the Second League. Their prospects are brighter than they have been for a considerable time, for, thanks to the unceasing efforts of Mr. Harry Keys and Mr. W. I. Bassett, the faults of previous mismanagement have been atoned for, and the club have a chance of gradually building up a first-class side again.

Looking back into the past some great names occur to one as belonging to players who proudly sported the Albion's colours. Two of the greatest were William Bassett, unrivalled as an outside-right, and Bob Roberts, unquestionably the finest goalkeeper of his time. Then W. Williams was one of the most dreaded backs that ever played for England, and James Bayliss was a centre who knew no fear. No man ever led West Bromwich Albion to victory so often as did James Bayliss. Harry Green, Harry Bell, Nicholson, and George Cave occur to one as excellent backs, while at one period Timmins, Charles Perry, and Ezra Horton constituted a magnificent intermediate line. Finer still, however, because they were more scientific, were Groves, Charles Perry, and Reynolds. Higgins was another half-back of signal ability. Then forward one easily recalls Spry Woodhall, Tom Green, J. J. Wilson, George Bell, A. Loach, R. McLeod—who made an inimitable partner for Bassett—and T. Pearson; and later day players include G. Dorsett and H. Hadley. A very capable half of years ago was Tom Perry, a brother of Charles; and in Joseph Reader the Albion possessed a goalkeeper who served them almost as long as any professional has ever served a football team.

Wilkes, West Bromwich.]
THE HOME OF WEST BROMWICH ALBION FOOTBALL CLUB—THE HAWTHORNS GROUND.

WEST BROMWICH ALBION FOOTBALL CLUB.—THE TEAM, SEASON 1905-6.

Top Row: W. I. Bassett (Director). W. Barber (Trainer). J. Pennington. G. Young. J. Stringer. A. Adams. A. Randle. Mr. Fred. Everiss (Secretary).

R. Scott and Co., Manchester.]

Middle Row: F. Haycock. C. Simmons. E. Pheasant. F. Shinton. A. Haywood. G. Perkins.

E. Bradley W. Law.

THE ASSOCIATION GAME.

HOW THE BALL SHOULD BE PLAYED.

By WILLIAM I. BASSETT.

The perfection of football—Some great ball-players—Fine football an instinct—Dribbling a question of toe work—How to centre the ball—Taking the ball on the run—Trapping the ball—Where Scottish forwards excel—Centring the ball on the run—The corner-kick—First-class dribbling a lost art—How to tackle—The punt-kick—When to use the inside of the foot—Passing the ball—The value of a forward pass in attack.

WITH many men football is a rough-and-ready art. The player kicks the ball about as a lad, and he kicks it about aimlessly. There is no method, no science, no studied idea in what he does. There is a ball, and it was obviously made to be kicked. Providence, or Nature, as you will, has given the lad a toe, and obviously that toe was mainly designed for the purpose of kicking something. At least, that is how the position presents itself to the lad's brain, although he is not cognisant of the fact that the brain directs the toe to kick. Some men continue to kick aimlessly for the remainder of their football lives. The pastime is in no sense an intellectual exercise to them. They acquire a somewhat more pronounced measure of efficiency each year, and they may become fairly useful members of a minor team, but the game is a mere form of exercise; they bring no brain power to bear upon their methods, and as a consequence the science of the game is a sealed book to them, even when they have attained their maximum efficiency.

But there is a higher grade of football—a form of the game in which brain power tells. I was going to say that we see its highest exemplification in the play of the New Zealanders, but as we are treating on the Association game, perhaps I had better say that we saw it at its highest power in the play of Preston North End, Sunderland, and Aston Villa, and, I am bound to add, Tottenham Hotspur in the year that they won the English Cup.

In the play of those teams we saw the perfection of football. More especially in the forward work Preston North End and Sunderland obtained a perfect ensemble, and their foot work was also perfect. No men ever played the ball better than Gordon, James Ross, John Goodall, and Geordie Drummond; and James Hannah was a delightful footballer. Then, again, David Russell was one of the greatest artists with his feet we have had, and so were Johnny Auld and Donald Gow. Fred Wheldon, of Aston Villa, has probably never been excelled in this particular. Steve Smith was another expert; that hook of his past the half-back I have never seen equalled. In the photos which accompany this article you see a man who has no superior to-day in point of clever foot work. Simmons, of West Bromwich Albion, is not a strong, robust, sturdy fellow; he is a man whose strength wants nursing, but he is the embodiment of scientific method. To him belongs the credit of developing the latent talent of a line of young forwards who at the opening of the present season had no claim to be regarded as they are regarded to-day.

How the ball should be played; that is the text. Some men succeed by methods that others would regard as heterodox. There is no royal road to success in football. I gave the game considerable study, and I believe that my views on this matter will be received with some degree of respect, but I am sensible enough to admit that I see men succeeding who adopt what are to my mind heterodox methods. But heterodoxy has always had its heroes. After all, success is the standard by which men should be judged, and if some thrive on heterodoxy, good luck to them; let them go on thriving, and say: "This man Bassett is all right in his way, but I have my way, and it comes off." The golfer who gets distance with all his shots—when distance is the one thing desired—need not quibble at his own style; and assuredly the opponent he beats need not quibble at it either.

But to the thousands who would be ruined by the adoption of unorthodox tactics sound methods are an essential study. It is only given to the man of exceptional gifts to triumph by reason of unorthodox methods Therefore, a man is on the safe side if he seeks to avoid them. There is a right way and there is a wrong way in everything, and the average man will not succeed by the way of wrong methods.

Albert Wilkes.]

DRIBBLING.

Both the toe and the inside of the foot need to be used expertly in dribbling, and the ball must be kept absolutely under control. With one or two exceptions modern footballers are deficient in this valuable football art, and the forwards who can dribble successfully stand out in a class by themselves, and are a constant danger to the opposing defence.

After all, everything depends upon the man. A really good football player knows by instinct what to do. He scarcely has to think. I have no doubt that James Crabtree was a born footballer; I am sure that Johnny Holt was, and I am sure that Cobbold and E. C. Bambridge were. Such men always have a trump card up their sleeve. Other men play for years without mastering the art of dribbling, passing, and shooting. This is best exemplified in billiards. Ninety-nine men out of a hundred never get beyond a certain stage, and they never would get beyond a certain stage whatever practice they had. To be quite explicit, they soon reach the limit of their capacity.

One of the first things a forward has to learn is to run with the ball properly. Some men do this instinctively in the proper way, others never seem to have the ball really under control. There is a great art in getting along with the ball at your maximum speed and yet always have it under control. I have been told that I did this reasonably well. Charles Athersmith also did it excellently. Athersmith was not a dribbler; he did not dodge an opponent at all artistically, but he could fly along the touch-line, and he always had the ball in his possession. There is no flying forward to-day to compare with him. You cannot teach a man to do this; you cannot say that the ball must never be more than such a distance from your toe; all you can do is to watch a man, and say that he does it well, moderately, or badly. Hodgetts, of Aston Villa, did it well, although he was not what you would call a flying forward. Spry Woodhall could do it, too, and so could William Groves in his forward days. In fact, no one ever did it much better than Groves, for he had great pace.

That is all a question of toe work; you cannot turn your feet out to use the side of the foot when you are sprinting. You touch it on, never losing control, and, above all, never getting out of your stride. Some men do everything with their toe, and are guilty of many inaccuracies as a consequence; but in this one matter the toe alone must be used.

There is no relation between this and dribbling; they are separate and distinct arts. Indeed, the fleet outside man is rarely a dribbler. He should have the power to dribble, but his speciality is the ability to scuttle off with the ball at top speed. At the same time, dribbling power should never be sacrificed for mere speed, or control of the ball will become difficult. While the winger is not called upon to dribble as the inside man is, he will be a poor player if he has not a reasonable amount of dribbling power. I can always tell whether a man has the right forward instinct when I see him use his toe cleverly in getting off and changing to the use of the side of the foot when he comes to make a pass.

Then as to centring. You want to use both toe and side of the foot to get the ball in accurately. If you used the toe only you could not expect accuracy; if you used the side of the foot solely you would not get power. You will see what I mean if you look carefully into the illustration of Simmons taking a corner kick.

Then the wing man must know two important points in the art of playing the ball. He must learn to do two things thoroughly which are quite diverse in character. He must learn to take the ball on the run, and he must learn to trap it dead. He will be under first-class unless he can do both thoroughly.

Albert Wilkes.]

TAKING A CORNER KICK.

In taking a corner kick it is best to come round to the ball. By so doing a "screw" or "bias" is set up which lands the ball accurately in front of the net. The above excellent photograph clearly shows the "screw" there is on the ball. It almost appears as if it were going out of play, but it will come round again, and drop in front of the posts. It is a mistake to centre low, and it is usually best to drop the ball between the centre-forward and the inside-left.

Wilkes, West Bromwich.]

PASSING THE BALL ON THE RUN.

In taking the ball on the run it has to be gathered with the inside of the foot and shot forward straight ahead. It is always better to give a man a pass well in front of him than to send the ball to his toe. He can then take it on the run, and much more danger is likely to accrue than if he had to stop to safely gather it. The above excellent photograph was especially taken for THE BOOK OF FOOTBALL and clearly shows the correct pass forward.

Times without number the man who can take the ball on the run is away with it before the half has a chance of getting near him. If he has to stop to trap the ball there is a perceptible delay, the defenders fall back again, and, what is quite as important, your own forwards as often as not get into off-side positions.

In taking the ball on the run it has to be gathered with the inside of the foot and shot forward straight ahead. It is not easy to explain, but if the ball is coming to you at an angle—as it usually will in this case—and you take it on the inside of the foot—also placed at an angle—the tendency of the ball is to glance off straight ahead of the player. Then he uses his speed for all he is worth.

In trapping the ball you bring the foot down, with the knee bent inwards and slightly extended. The leg should be at an angle of about thirty degrees, so that you catch the ball between the ground and the side of the foot. This is the only sure way of stopping the ball dead, and it requires a large amount of practice to render the footballer at all expert.

Scottish forwards excel at this kind of trick, but, in passing, let me say that the tendency among Scottish forwards is to trap the ball too much. This means that the onward movement which may be in progress is checked. I do not care to see it overdone. It is invaluable near goal, for the expert forward can trap the ball and shoot with rapidity. Scottish forwards are more leisurely, as a rule, than those associated with English clubs. But they are infinitely cleverer in their foot work, though they have not the same dash. I used to notice in our International games how much faster we got along with the ball than the Scottish forwards did. They are deliberate, they do things very prettily, but they do not take the ball on the run and shoot as the best of our forwards do. Bloomer can trap the ball infallibly, but he loses only an imperceptible fraction of a second in doing so and then getting into his stride again.

There is nothing more serviceable in football than the dexterous use of the inside of the foot, and in trapping the ball you can see in a moment whether a man is an expert at the game or not.

There is a great lack of ability in this respect among present-day footballers. There are few Bloomers—men who can stop the ball dead, unless it chances to come to them in a very awkward manner, and then move on without the slightest loss of time. But, then, Bloomer is in a class by himself in respect to many tricks of forward work.

Comparatively few men centre really well. I have heard many glowing accounts of the gifts of Eli Davis, one of the old-time Villa wing players, Andy Hunter, George Holden, and J. L. Kaye, of Queen's Park, but I never saw these men at their best. Athersmith used to centre uncommonly well, so did Gordon; but really, when one comes to think the matter out, the names of men who excelled in the useful art do not come crowding upon one. You want to learn to centre on the run; that was a speciality of mine, I believe. I used to practise it assiduously enough, goodness knows, and few men become really clever who do not try to perfect themselves in their art. There is something in the sudden twist of the foot, in the perfect poise, and in the precise point of contact between toe and ball, which is either not understood by many of our footballers, or, if understood, is indifferently done. You want a considerable amount of leverage for a good centre, more particularly if the ball happens to be a wet and heavy one.

It is the same with taking the corner kick. There is an excellent picture of this. If you look into it you will notice the screw there is on the ball. I invariably took corner kicks in this way. I used to come round to the ball instead of running at it straight—often, by the way, there is no room in which to take a straight run at the ball even if you had the inclination to take the kick in that way. The touch-line is far too close to the spectators at some of our grounds. I can assure you that it is a real pleasure to an outside wing man to play at the Crystal Palace.

But to return to the corner kick. By coming round to the ball you get a bias on it. The ball in the picture appears to be going out, but it will come round and drop well in front of the posts. My practice in taking the corner kick was to drop the ball between the centre-forward and the inside-left. Both in centring and taking a corner kick you want to avoid the near back. The mistake most young players make is that they centre too low. In centring they merely put the ball in with the same action they would use in shooting, and as a consequence it never rises, and five times out of seven either strikes the near back or another defender and is easily cleared.

It always annoys me to see a clever young player bring the ball down the wing nicely and then kick it to the near back. That is childish play; all the good work previously done is thrown away. You want to get under the ball well in centring; you want to centre, not to shoot. The outside man who tries to shoot from near the corner flag is robbing his colleagues in the centre and inside positions of chances of scoring to which they are entitled, and he is not therefore playing the game. Nothing is easier for the goalkeeper to clear than a shot from the wing; nothing is likely to embarrass him more than a centre well taken in hand by the inside men.

Then as to dribbling. One can say little that can be of practical value. You cannot teach men how to dribble. They must teach themselves. There is a knack about dribbling which some men possess naturally, others have to acquire it. But, depend upon it, practice will do much for the footballer who has his heart in his work. There is no jeering crowd to discourage you when you are at practice. And the best way to practice is to take part in an impromptu game with half a dozen on each side.

You want to use both the toe and the inside of the foot expertly in dribbling. Candidly, my opinion is that, with the exception of a few great players, dribbling is a lost art. Men can dodge, but they cannot dribble; they can trick an opponent, but they cannot fool half a dozen. This is because they do not keep the ball close enough. The modern forward can have no conception of the marvellous control some of the old players I remember when I was a youth had over the ball. Men now put the ball to the side of an opponent and get to it first. That is all right in its way, but it is not dribbling. What a revelation it was to watch Cobbold dribble! He used to run through a team at top speed, and yet the ball was always absolutely under control; it never seemed many inches from his toe. But dribbling of that kind is a lost art now.

Albert Wilkes.]

TACKLING.

It is almost impossible to tell a player how to tackle. Each man adopts or fits his own special style to the exigencies of the occasion. Even a great half-back cannot tell you how he gets the ball. He gets it, that is all. His business is to stop a forward rush, and, once in possession, to pass the ball to his forwards. This is best done by a clean pass along the ground to his man, given with the side of the foot, and always two or three yards in front of the player. (From a photograph specially taken for THE BOOK OF FOOTBALL.)

Neither can you teach a man how to tackle. It is impossible to say how tackling should be done. Each man must be a law unto himself. You see your opponent coming, and what you do you do instinctively. I never met a half who could tell you much about tackling. He can tell you how the ball should be placed when it is obtained, but he cannot tell you how to obtain it. Cowan, Holt, Crabtree, Chas. Perry, Forrest, George Howarth, Davie Russell, Graham, and Robertson were all successful, but it would be folly to try to tell you how to tackle. But the neat low pass, along the sward for choice, with the side of the foot to the centre-forward, and the long low drive which places the ball two or three yards in front—not behind, or even at the foot of the player, but well in front—those can be explained. The Scottish halves, Aitken and Robertson, were very fine exponents of the art of helping their forwards. Crabtree and Needham were equally fine, but I doubt if any man ever excelled William Groves in this phase of half-back work. You will see a photo of a player taking a punt kick, or volley. To execute this kick you allow the ball to drop upon the full face of the top of the boot, and with practice the kicker can obtain remarkable accuracy. In the old days Wolverhampton Wanderers and West Bromwich Albion used to be particularly deadly when the ball was punted into goal, and men of the stamp of Jem Bayliss, John Brodie, Tom Green, and Pearson came for the goalkeeper long before he had obtained a fair sight of the ball. Oh, those were merry days—for the forwards! The goalkeeper was then a being apt to wear a rueful countenance.

When the forward is well placed in front of goal he should shoot with the inside of the foot; much more accuracy is obtained in that way. Shooting with the toe is responsible for five-sixths of the shots which go somewhere between the post and the corner flag, and also for the bulk of the shots which soar heavenwards, leaving the cross-bar far beneath.

Albert Wilkes.]
PASSING: SHOWING SIDE-FOOT PASS.
Simmons, the young West Bromwich Albion player, shows how to pass the ball with the side of the foot. He is a clever and scientific exponent of the Association game. (From a photograph specially taken for THE BOOK OF FOOTBALL.)

You rarely raise the ball much if you shoot with the inside of the foot, and you get a great deal of power if you lever the leg properly. Yet how often you see the man with a golden opportunity dig his toe into the ball with clenched teeth and a vicious air! It is a mistake; both in shooting from close quarters and in passing the use of the inside of the foot is most desirable. In the illustration you will see a pass with the side of the foot executed by one of the most accomplished forwards of the day.

When a player is standing in front of the posts a hard shot with the toe is most undesirable. It may beat the goalkeeper—anything may beat him, for he has a big space to guard—but more often it crashes against his chest and bounces back into play. "Hard lines," the crowd say; "how luckily he saved that!" No, bad play, my friends; bad play on the part of the forward. He ought never to have given the goalkeeper a chance of saving. A quiet touch with the inside of the foot would have sent the ball into the net with mathematical accuracy, far out of the reach of the goalkeeper. But old habits die hard; the men lose their heads and probably don't know what they are doing. A touch does it where the reckless shot fails, either from lack of accuracy or from the fact that the ball is banged right into the centre of the goal, and therefore naturally strikes the goalkeeper.

A valuable rule for players to remember is that it is always better to give a man a pass well in front of him than to send the ball to his toe. He can then take it on the run, and much more danger is likely to accrue than if he had to stop to safely gather it. Of course, if an opponent is nigh, then care has to be shown, as the pass may be intercepted; but if there is a margin in favour of your man, let the pass go well ahead of him. It may make all the difference between a virile and a weak attack.

There are hundreds of little touches in Association football, the ability to use which marks the high-class footballer. No one should be destitute of ambition; it is conceit a man wants to avoid, not ambition. The young fellow who enters upon a career of Association football should not be content to come in with the crowd. He should try to make himself one of the giants of the game, because that is sure to benefit him in the long days that will come when he can no longer kick a ball effectively. The man who masters the art of finesse in football will be able to go on some years longer than he who is content with a rough-and-ready, if reasonably effective, style.

A man loses his pace long before he feels that he is not fit to dignify a football field. The inside-man who is a perfect master of all the tricks of the inside-game can continue to give a club reasonably good service long after the International Selection Committee have him in their minds, and long after a percentage of his pace and agility has deserted him.

I need only mention the names of John Goodall and Edgar Chadwick to show what I mean. Edgar Chadwick is still a useful footballer; but then, what he did not know about the inside-game no one need desire to know.

Brains tell in football, and although the club which seeks to win the English Cup or the League championship with a team of veterans will not succeed, yet there is always room in a side for one or two experienced men; men who, although not fleet of foot, can last the game out, can artfully husband their strength, and finish a hard match as fresh as their juvenile comrades.

Constant practice, and the living of a strictly temperate life, go to make not only the skilful but the enduring footballer.

Albert Wilkes.]
VOLLEYING: SHOOTING AT GOAL.
When the forward is well placed in front of goal he should shoot with the inside of the foot; much more accuracy is obtained in that way. Shooting with the toe is responsible for five-sixths of the shots which go somewhere between the posts and the corner flag, and also for the bulk of the shots which soar heavenwards, leaving the cross-bar far beneath.

Bowden Bros.]

PARK ROYAL.

A splendid view of the Queen's Park Rangers' fine football enclosure as seen from behind the Western goal.

QUEEN'S PARK RANGERS' FOOTBALL CLUB.

By H. J. WOOD.

Queen's Park Rangers make a humble start as St. Jude's Institute Football Club in 1885—The men behind the club in the early days—Abundant patronage leads to a change of ground—The failure of the Brondesbury playing-pitch—The club's name changed to Queen's Park Rangers—Migratory seasons—The Rangers make a stir in Metropolitan football—An unfortunate incident—Professionalism adopted and a limited liability company formed—The first professional side—A successful season ends in a big financial loss—A dispute about the Kensal Rise Ground leads to a change of venue—Park Royal's famous enclosure secured—Grand future prospects.

Colours: Green and white striped shirts, white knickers. *Ground: Park Royal.*

WHEN Jack McDonald and Fred Weller in 1885 organised a football team, principally from boys of the Droop Street Board School, Queen's Park, W., they little imagined that out of that lowly beginning would rise the present prominent club in Southern football. Of Scottish birth, McDonald came when but a lad to reside in West London. The schoolboy fever for football, in the metropolis, at least, was not as rampant then as it has become since; but his enthusiasm for the game soon became contagious in the playground, and, with the hearty co-operation of the Rev. Gordon Young, a club was formed. The reverend gentleman started an institute in connection with his church (St. Jude's), which became the headquarters, and they took the name of St. Jude's Institute Football Club.

A gymnasium was fitted up, as, even in those days, it was considered the proper thing to do some sort of physical training, and members were enrolled at a subscription for the season of 7s. 6d. Subsequent events have abundantly proved that they were extremely fortunate to enlist the good offices of Mr. Walter Cross, to whose unflagging zeal, and no inconsiderable monetary support, the club was steered through many vicissitudes, and to-day Mr. Cross is one of the most respected and capable members of the present board of directors of the Queen's Park Rangers. Much useful assistance was also rendered to the club by the brothers Harry and Joe Spurr, Harry Creber, and Tom Handford.

Mr. C. Lynch was the first secretary, and the fixture list was confined to "friendlies" with Stanley, Tottenham, Brentford, Fulham, Old St. Stephen's, Clapton, &c. The colours adopted were Oxford and Cambridge blue halved, and a piece of ground known as Welford's Fields, to the south of the then Kensal Rise Station, was secured at a rental of £8 per season. The club's plant consisted of four upright posts, and two lengths of tape to form the cross-bars. These had to be carted to and fro when a match was to be played. Many of the players who formed the first team are still keenly interested in the fortunes of the present club, though Jack McDonald has long since joined the great majority.

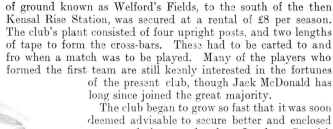

MR. H. J. WOOD,
Secretary of the Queen's Park Rangers' Football Club.

The club began to grow so fast that it was soon deemed advisable to secure better and enclosed accommodation, and the London Scottish Ground at Brondesbury was secured at a rental of £20 per season, the anticipated "gate" being counted upon to meet the additional expenses. But in the matter of the gate, things did not pan out as expected, the takings on many occasions not reaching 1s. 6d.!

With the change of quarters a change was made in the title of the club to Queen's Park Rangers, though the colours were still the two University blues.

In the middle of the second season (1889-90), at Brondesbury, the ground became absolutely unfit for football, and the remainder of the season's matches had to be played on opponents' grounds.

The ravages of the builder prevented any fixity of tenure being obtained, and the next three or four seasons saw the club first at the Home Farm, Kensal Green, the Gun Club Wormwood Scrubbs, and then Harvist Road, West Kilburn. While at the Gun Club the colours were changed to green and white—at that time the colours of the Celtic, Glasgow. Coincident with the change of colours the Rangers won their first trophy, namely, the "West London Observer" Cup. Competed for by clubs in West London, it had generally rested with Stanley

QUEEN'S PARK RANGERS' FOOTBALL CLUB—THE TEAM, SEASON 1905-6.

W. DRAPER (Trainer). W. YENSON. P. McLARNEY. A. HITCH. MATT. KINGSLEY (Goalkeeper). S. DOWNING. G. NEWLANDS.

Bowden Bros.]

NEIL MURPHY. S. H. SUGDEN. F. BEVAN. G. RYDER. A. GARDNER. McLELLAND (Asst.-Trainer).

and Fulham; but after defeating Stanley, Fulham were met in the final at Kensal Rise Athletic Ground, and defeated, after extra time had been played, by 3 goals to 2. The Rangers held the cup for three years, when it was handed over to the London League, and is now competed for annually by the members of that body.

The change to the Kilburn Cricket Club Ground in Harvist Road, West Kilburn, proved the turning-point in the Club's history. With an improved team (among whom West Londoners will remember W. Ward, Jimmy McKenzie, Ted Wallington, Tom Harvey, and Sam Gillam, the Welsh International goal-keeper) a more ambitious programme was entered upon. In addition to the best of the usual friendlies, entry was made for the English Cup, Amateur Cup, London Charity Cup, and the London and Middlesex Senior Cups.

The club now began to make a big stir in Metropolitan football. The visits to London of the great League clubs at that time were confined to the Cup finals, and it was considered a rare stroke of business enterprise to get the famous "Throstles" to play at West Kilburn. The terms were £50 or half gate, and, as £140 was taken, the venture was, financially, very successful. Included in the West Bromwich Albion team that day were Bassett, Flewitt, McLeod, Reynolds, Williams, and Reader, and they won by 4—1.

The gates assumed "alarming" proportions, and the accommodation became totally inadequate. A bold jump was now made to the famous Kensal Rise Athletic Ground, and a ten years' lease was taken at a commencing rental of £100 per annum, increasing to £150. The services of Jock Campbell, who had previously trained the Third Lanark, Woolwich, and Tottenham teams, were secured, and under his supervision great things were expected of the team. This did not, however, materialise. Owing to an unfortunate disturbance at Richmond in a Cup-tie with the town club, occasioned by Sammy Brookes being ordered off the field, the club were fined £4 by the London Football Association, and their ground closed for a fortnight. This sentence was very much resented, the fine was paid, and the club withdrew from all the cup competitions under the ægis of the L. F. A. This robbed the club of their principal fixtures, and, coupled with the great difficulty experienced in keeping some of the best footballers in the team from accepting the inducements of other clubs and the fact that the demand for first-class football had become so apparent in London, the idea of professionalism was mooted. After many wordy discussions in committee, it was decided at a meeting held at St. Jude's Institute to become a professional organisation. A committee was formed, and in due course the Queen's Park Rangers' Football and Athletic Club, Limited, became an accomplished fact, with a nominal capital of £5,000 in shares of 10s. each.

The company was registered on December 28, 1898, the directors appointed being Messrs. A. Lythaby, Leo Hawes, A. Devenish, W. Cross, A. Teagle, Jess Saxby, H. E. Cleverly, W. Hiscox, J. Taylor, and W. L. Wood, with G. H. Mousell as secretary.

It was fortunate for the club that in Jock Campbell they had a man who knew all the ropes of professionalism, and under his guidance the following team were got together:

Goal: H. Clutterbuck (Small Heath); backs: Joe Knowles (Sunderland), and H. McConnell (Woolwich Arsenal); half-backs: Keech (Leicester Fosse), A. Hitch (Grays), and Gavan Crawford (Woolwich Arsenal); forwards: Tom Smith (Southampton), Adam Heywood (Woolwich Arsenal), Frank Bedingfield (Aston Villa), Peter Turnbull (Millwall), and J. Hannah (Sunderland).

Successful applications were made to the Southern League, as also the Southern District combination and the English Cup. The reserves were also admitted to the London League. However, the form shown by the team was very in and out. The club finished midway in the Southern League table with 26 points out of a possible 56, scoring 49 goals to 57. In the Southern District combination the team finished in the ruck, and the reserves wound up third in the London League.

Notwithstanding that the—to the Rangers—huge sum of £1,067 was taken in two rounds of the English Cup, the season ended in a heavy financial loss, and, but for the monetary assistance of the directors, the club would have gone to the wall.

Bowden Bros.]

A MATCH AT PARK ROYAL—QUEEN'S PARK RANGERS v. PLYMOUTH ARGYLE.

After a temporary cessation of play the referee throws down the ball.

At the end of the second season the landlord took advantage of a new point decided in the Appeal Court, and determined the club's lease. In sore financial straits, the directors could not retain their players, only Newlands and Leather remaining.

Thanks to the good offices of one of the directors—Mr. T. R. Eagle—a ground was obtained at the rear of St. Quintin's Avenue, Latimer Road, Notting Hill. Trouble for the club soon rose again, the inhabitants of St. Quintin's Avenue petitioning the owner of the estate to put an end to the tenancy on the score of detriment (?) to the neighbourhood. They so far succeeded in this that the club had notice to leave at the end of the season, and negotiations were successfully concluded for a return to Kensal Rise at a much increased rent, but only for a fixed period of two seasons.

The return to Kensal Rise marked a wonderful increase in the success of the club financially, the gate receipts totalling £4,542, against £3,320 the previous season, the profit on the year's working being over £600, instead of as before a heavy loss, notwithstanding that the team were beaten in the preliminary round of the English Cup, and finished halfway down in the Southern League table.

With practically the same set of players, the club rose (1903-4) to fifth place in the League table, two points only separating them from Tottenham, who were second, and the receipts leapt up to £6,000. This had its effect on the landlord, and when negotiations were opened for a renewal of the tenancy (notwithstanding that he had received in rent for the season £270) nothing but a purchase of his lease, at what the directors considered an exorbitant price, seeing that there was at the most but six seasons to run, could be entertained, and after many efforts were made to obtain a more central ground, a lease was secured of the palatial ground at Park Royal, Willesden, a ground which for its possibilities is second to none in the kingdom; and with the best possible relations existing with the Great Western Railway Company the future of the club seems assured.

Starfield and Co.]
THE HOME OF EVERTON FOOTBALL CLUB—THE GOODISON PARK ENCLOSURE, LOOKING NORTH-WEST.

EVERTON FOOTBALL CLUB.

League Champions, 1890-1 ; English Cup Finalists, 1893 and 1897.

By LOUIS T. KELLY.

A characteristic start of the Everton Football Club—The club's first title—A speedy change of name—Everton's first railway journey—Liverpool and District Football Association Cup won—Alderman John Houlding offers the club tenure of the Anfield Road enclosure—Everton one of the first of the clubs to embrace professionalism—Strenuous Cup fights with Bolton Wanderers—The Liverpool Cup returned—Everton join the League upon its formation—The championship won in 1890-1—League record—Everton's performances in the Football Association Cup competition—A Final fiasco—Everton leave the Anfield Road enclosure and take up their abode at Goodison Park—Remarkable success—Some of Everton's most famous players—Prominent officials—Fine prospects for the future.

Colours: Blue shirts, white knickers. *Ground: Goodison Park, Liverpool.*

IN tracing the history of England's most famous Association clubs right back to their source, it would possibly constitute a rare eye-opener for the game's detractors if one could get them to note the large percentage claiming the precincts of some church or Sunday school as their birthplace. One such organisation is the Everton Football Club, than which there is no name more genuinely honoured where King "Soccer" reigns.

In the year 1878 certain youthful members of the St. Domingo Congregational Church, Everton, thought the time was ripe to introduce a big, healthy baby boy—football. There had been a sister game—cricket—in vogue for some time. The thought quickly took the shape of action, and the club was dubbed the St. Domingo Football Club.

It is interesting to note that the present courteous secretary of the Everton Club, Mr. W. C. Cuff, and Mr. A. R. Wade, a current member of the directorate, were both members of the church when the present club was established. Their "home" games were taken for decision at Stanley Park. Purely local elevens were met, and of "gate money" there was none. The players operated under the wing of "St. Domingo" for but a brief period, and in the November of that same year—1879—as the result of much deliberation at a general meeting held at the club's headquarters, the Queen's Head Hotel, Village Street—within a stone's throw of Ye Anciente Everton Toffee House—the title was changed to "Everton." A month later, December 23, the first match under the new name was played, resulting in a victory over the long defunct St. Peter's eleven. And right on to the present moment Everton's career may broadly be put down as one long string of successes.

MR. W. C. CUFF,

The popular Everton secretary, was born at Liverpool on August 19, 1868. He was educated at Liverpool College, articled to the legal profession in 1888, and admitted 1893. Has been in practice in Liverpool since 1895. He was elected a director of Everton F. C. in 1894, and afterwards appointed secretary upon the resignation of Mr. R. Molyneux in 1901.

Everton were admitted members of the Lancashire Football Association in the season 1880-1, and it is worthy of note that the club's first railway jaunt was rendered necessary through being drawn away against Great Lever—a Bolton team—in this competition. Everton, after a drawn game, were badly routed by 8—1.

About the autumn of 1882 a field in Priory Road was rented from Mr. Cruitt, of Coney Green, and Everton's first "gate" realised the lavish sum of 13s.! Contrast this with the £1,300 gate subsequently taken by Everton in a local "Derby" with Liverpool!

The club's first great personal triumph materialised in the following season—1883-4—when Earlstown were defeated by 1—0 in the Liverpool and District Football Association Cup final, and Everton lifted their inaugural cup. The patronage given to the club at this juncture unmistakably proved that the game had "caught on," and one of the earliest to discover this fact was that keen sportsman and astute business man the late Alderman John Houlding, once Lord Mayor of Liverpool.

That gentleman's love of sport prompted him to offer the club a field in Anfield Road fully equipped for football, and the offer, needless to add, was promptly accepted. This field is now the headquarters of the Liverpool Football Club. Everton's tenancy thereof covered a period of nine years, and over the whole the word "progress" must be writ large. The new enclosure—called the Anfield Road Ground—was opened with a match against Earlstown, and the latter received a 5—0 defeat. In this same season Everton again lifted the local trophy, defeating Bootle in the final round. The rivalry between these clubs had by this time almost lashed itself into fury, beside which that of the present-day Everton v. Liverpool partisanship is calmly dignified.

MR. W. R. CLAYTON.

He is one of the most popular of the Everton F. C. directorate. He took a prominent part in the reconstruction of the club's affairs, and has done much towards making it one of the most successful football organisations in Great Britain.

When, in 1885, professionalism was legalised in England in consequence of an agitation by the Lancashire clubs, Everton were amongst the first to embrace it. George Dobson and the late George Farmer—a captivating inside-left in his day—were the two first professionals on the club's books, and in the following season that daring full-back, Alec Dick, of Kilmarnock, ranked as the "Toffee's" first importation.

It was in the season of 1887-8 that Everton were drawn against Bolton Wanderers at Pike's Lane in the first round of the Football Association Cup competition. Everton were beaten by 1—0, but were successful in a protest against Struthers, the Wanderers' centre-forward.

Ultimately, the teams met no fewer than four times ere the tie was decided, Everton at last gaining a 2—1 victory. But it cost them dearly. Those were the days when protests in Cup-ties were almost as plentiful as blackberries in autumn. The Wanderers lodged a protest on the ground that Everton had infringed the professional rule by offering players situations as an inducement to join them. In the sequel Everton were deemed guilty, suspended for a month, and seven of their players declared professionals.

The Liverpool Association decided to uphold the decision of the Football Association, and the Liverpool Cup—then held by Everton—which occupied a place in a sort of three-cornered cupboard in the Sandon Hotel entrance, was taken from them. One evening Mr. R. E. Lythgoe drove up in a cab, and, amidst the groans of the assembled people, carried off the trophy. A monumental mason who lived in the neighbourhood, and possessed a keen sense of wit, arranged to fill the vacant cupboard, and made a gravestone to take the place of the cup. The original stone is now in the possession of Mr. J. Ramsay, of the Liverpool Football Club, and the inscription reads as follows: "Sacred to the memory of the Liverpool Cup [here follows a facsimile of the cup] which was won by the Everton Football Club 1884, 1886, 1887, and taken from them by the Liverpool and District Football Association April, 1888. 'Gone, but not forgotten.'"

The cloud, however, was not of long duration, and Everton were soon destined to burst out once more into glorious sunshine, thanks in chief to Mr. W. McGregor coming along so opportunely with his scheme of League football and League points. When this scheme took definite shape in the summer of 1888, Everton had forged ahead so pronouncedly that they were amongst the first clubs invited to join the select circle of the "original twelve" League clubs.

In the season 1889-90 Everton's improvement became so marked that they secured second position in the League to Preston North End, who only had a two points' lead. Everton practically lost the championship that season through falling at home by 5—1 before Preston, the former's only home defeat.

However, in the season 1890-1, Everton's cup of joy was well filled, seeing that they secured the League championship for the first and only time. Curiously enough, the second position on the table was held by Preston North End, so that the 1889-90 placings of the pair were exactly reversed.

During "the" League's existence the membership has been spread among twenty-seven clubs, but only two—Everton and Wolverhampton Wanderers—have steered clear of the last four positions. Albeit, the other three—Aston Villa, Derby County, and Blackburn Rovers—have qualified as "life members." It is interesting to set out the points gained by this quintette since "the" League's institution out of a possible 1,020: Aston Villa, 622; Everton, 595; Wolverhampton Wanderers, 505; Derby County, 499; and Blackburn Rovers, 495. These figures undoubtedly testify to the club's claim for consistency.

Glancing at the club's record in the Association Cup competition, it must at once be said that they have never had the good fortune to annex the coveted trophy, which thus far has played the part of a real will-o'-the-wisp. They have, however, twice figured as finalists. The first occasion was in 1893. Everton were a great team that season, particularly in attack, whereas their Final opponents, Wolverhampton Wanderers, had experienced a very moderate season apart from the Cup-ties. To emphasise the brightness of Everton's prospects, the two clubs were due to meet under League auspices the week preceding the Final on the Wanderers' ground. To keep their Cup team fresh and keen the Everton management sent a reserve eleven to the Black Country for the League match—there being no League rule at that time compelling clubs to play their full strength—and the reservists actually defeated the "Wolves'" Cup combination by 4 goals to 2. How much more easily, then, would the Cup be Everton's a week afterwards!

Starfield and Co.]

THE BOARD-ROOM IN THE SPLENDIDLY APPOINTED EVERTON FOOTBALL CLUB'S OFFICES AT GOODISON PARK.

The game was decided at Fallowfield, Manchester, when, as Mr. W. McGregor has already told our readers, the arrangements were totally inadequate to meet the demands of the assembled crowd. But the greatest "fiasco," in the eyes of the thousands of Everton supporters assembled, lay in the fact that their pets were defeated by 1 goal to 0. That match was additionally noteworthy in that it was the first Football Association Cup Final decided on a ground originally chosen out of London.

Everton's second

EVERTON FOOTBALL CLUB—FIRST LEAGUE TEAM, SEASON 1905-6.

Back Row: T. McDermott. T. Booth. R. Balmer. W. Abbott. T. Taylor. A. Young. J. Crelley.

Starfield and Co., Liverpool.]

Front Row: J. Elliott (Trainer) J. Sharp. H. Makepeace. J. Settle. W. Scott. W. Balmer. H. P. Hardman.

appearance as finalists was in the Diamond Jubilee year—1897—when they were successfully opposed at the Crystal Palace by Aston Villa. The "Clarets" won by 3 goals to 2, but they had to struggle desperately for the honour, Everton fighting every inch of the way In fact, this game is being handed down as the finest exhibition of football ever given in the history of the Association Cup competition.

In the year 1892 differences which had arisen between Mr. John Houlding and his committee culminated in the latter terminating the tenancy of the Anfield Road enclosure. Several of the committee had sought diligently for a suitable piece of land on which to erect a first-class football ground. Eventually a likely looking plot of ground, situated the north side of Stanley Park, favourably impressed the search party. This land had degenerated from a nursery into a howling desert, but the committee—prominent among whom were Messrs. George Mahon, W. R. Clayton, and Dr. J. C. Baxter—saw possibilities writ large thereon. With the vast majority of the members to support them, the committee formed themselves into a limited liability company, and at once entered into an agreement for the acquisition of the present magnificent ground at the price of £8,090, the area being 29,470 square yards. The capital of the company is £2,500, in £1 shares.

From the date of settling at Goodison Park the history of the Everton Club must be set down as one of great and rapid progress. The directors, under the chairmanship of Dr. J. C. Baxter—to-day a valued member of the League's management committee—Mr. W. R. Clayton, and Mr. G. Mahon successively, have done all that is possible to make the ground fit to uphold the best traditions of the club, and can now look with pardonable pride upon the result of their labours in that direction, namely, the finest equipped football ground in the United Kingdom. They have, as a fitting climax to their previous efforts, recently erected a magnificent board-room, suite of offices, &c., on the ground at a cost of £3,000.

The holding capacity of the ground is estimated at 55,000 people, for all of whom—best of all—an uninterrupted view of the field of play can be guaranteed. It is estimated that no less a sum than £27,000 has been spent on the ground! The record gate receipts amount to £1,980, taken on the occasion of the Semi-final tie between Manchester City and Sheffield Wednesday two years ago.

The Everton Club is one of the most wealthy in the British Isles. Thirteen years ago they purchased their present ground for just under £9,000. Since then they have erected stands, &c., to the value of £10,000, and to-day stand in the extraordinary position of owning a piece of land—which for building purposes has increased in value from £8,090 to £15,000—free from encumbrances of any kind whatever, the mortgage on the ground being finally wiped off during the season 1904-5. It goes without saying that such a wealthy club has, during the League's history, boasted many of the most brilliant stars of the football firmament. In the season 1893-4 Everton had no fewer than twelve Internationals in their ranks, whilst last season their "capped" players reached double figures—truly a perfect "galaxy of talent"!

Looking back at their list of goalkeepers, the season 1904-5 will not readily be forgotten by reason of the daring and brilliant exploits of Leigh Richmond Roose. It wasn't his fault Everton missed both the F. A. Cup and the League trophy by a single stride. Their present season custodian, Scott, is little if any thing inferior, and possibly the finest keeper Ireland has produced; whilst a far-famed "tenter" seen in Everton's well-known blue jersey was Hillman—now of Manchester City.

Of backs, Everton has enjoyed a profusion. "Nick" Ross was perhaps the most lustrous.

Everton's half-back division has almost invariably been one of great strength. John Holt was essentially a unique centre-half, but what a sweet wing-half was "Dicky" Boyle, the Dumbarton light-weight! "Bob" Kelso was, at his best, a wonderful half-back of the Crabtree type. Then there were D. Kirkwood—now a director—and J. Robertson, the present Chelsea manager.

Coming to more modern days, Tom Booth has had very few superiors in League football. In Makepeace, Everton have a half-back who bids fair to prove the finest locally developed middle man in the club's history.

"The finest vanguard Everton ever placed on the field," did you ask? A ticklish question. But, as a line, Alec Latta, Brady, Geary, Chadwick, and Milward would compare with the best.

The secretarial duties of so vast a concern were for many years fulfilled by Mr. R. Molyneux—now with Brentford. On his leaving the club in 1901, Mr. W. C. Cuff—then in his sixth year as a director of the club—was appointed secretary and manager.

Needless to add, the club has been singularly blessed in the calibre of directors at the helm. To those three long-service gentlemen, Mr. George Mahon, Dr. J. C. Baxter, and Mr. W. R. Clayton, especial encomiums are due.

The remaining members of Everton's board of directors are Messrs. John Davies (vice-chairman), E. A. Bainbridge, B. Kelly, D. Kirkwood, A. R. Wade, Dr. Whitford, and Horace Wright.

The history of "Everton's Rise and Progress" would not be complete without some reference to the League team trainer, Jack Elliott. First as a player, and later as a trainer, Elliott has rendered the club valiant service, of which latter he is now in his sixteenth season.

Starfield and Co.]

THE EVERTON FOOTBALL CLUB'S ENCLOSURE, GOODISON PARK, LOOKING NORTH-EAST.

This fine football arena was completed at a cost of £27,000. The record "gate" receipts for a single match amount to £1,980, and it has a holding capacity of over 55,000 persons.

SCHOOLBOY FOOTBALL.

By H. J. W. OFFORD.

The excellence of modern schoolboy football—The South London Schools F. A.—A challenge shield presented to the London Schools F. A. by the Corinthians—The growth of kindred associations—The Sir Thomas Dewar Shield—Superiority of London schoolboys—Defeat of the Londoners at Glasgow—A 10,000 gate—Rapid growth of the schoolboy game—A national competition instituted—London become champions of England—A splendid gift to charity.

Tutt.]
C. B. DIBB
(Earlsmead School, Tottenham).
A schoolboy footballer, cricketer, and athlete. Played centre-forward for London. Holder of seventy-six prizes.

"THE boy's the father of the man." It is, therefore, a matter for congratulation that the lads of the elementary schools of Great Britain are being trained to play thoroughly good football. From the youngsters of to-day we shall obtain our great players of the future. That the supply will not be deficient is patent to those who have watched the skilful schoolboy teams at work. Young, and overflowing with energy, they enter into the sport with a zest that is refreshing. But they not only bring this delicious spirit of enthusiasm into the game; they play with marked intelligence, and their combination and general tactics would put to shame many a senior club. As a phrase of derision, the saying "They played like a lot of schoolboys" has lost its significance.

MR. T. THOMAS,
Hon. Sec. of the English Schools Football Association.

School football is now highly organised. But it is not the new thing that the uninitiated might imagine. This season the famous South London Schools F. A. celebrates its majority, so that for more than two decades the young South Londoners have had their football welfare cared for. Which was actually the pioneer school organisation is doubtful. South London claims the honour; but there are rumours of another association that, in those early days, operated in the district of the Tower Hamlets. The East End district must have been one of the first wherein an association was formed, for what was probably the earliest of all inter-association matches was played in 1888 between South London and Tower Hamlets, the former winning by 4 goals to 1. The success of these two associations naturally brought about the organisation of others; but the first great impetus was given to the schoolboy game when, in 1893, a thirty guinea challenge shield was presented to the London Schools Football Association by the world-renowned amateurs, the Corinthians. "Pa" Jackson was then the guiding spirit of the club, and his idea of fostering a love of the game by offering this shield for competition was a happy one. For many years the ambition of every London schoolboy footballer has been to help his district to win the Corinthian Shield. Since the inauguration of the competition the London Schools F. A. has grown enormously. There are school associations in all parts of the kingdom; but London, with its sixteen district combinations, ranging from Acton to Ilford, and from Willesden to Greenwich, far eclipses any other. The area under its control must be immense. And it is steadily growing, for Staines and Brentford have expressed a desire to be included.

Ridout.]
TOM REYNOLDS.
This schoolboy footballer is thirteen years of age, and is considered for his years the finest back in England. He holds eight championship medals and the London Badge. He weighs 9st.

GLASGOW v. LONDON.
Played on the Queen's Park F. C. Ground, Hampden Park, Glasgow, April 26, 1905.
Glasgow: Black-and-white. London: White.
After being undefeated for five seasons, London were beaten by Glasgow by 4 goals to 2

Each of the sixteen associations in membership has its local competition, and each carefully selects eleven of its best players to battle with rival districts for the L. S. F. A. trophies. During the twelve seasons that the Corinthian Shield has been in existence it has been won six times by South London, three times by West London, twice by Tottenham, and once by West Ham.

Another stroke of luck befell the London schools when, in 1898, Sir Thomas R. Dewar, ex-Sheriff of London, presented a fifty guinea shield to the Association. This has been devoted to a competition between those schools which secure the various local championships. They meet in the closing weeks of the season, and as the winning team is hailed as the champion school of London, the ties arouse the keenest interest.

Every season since 1899 a team representative of the whole of London has been selected. For a long time it was a hard task to find opponents for this team. Leeds were the first to tackle them, but it was soon manifest that the Yorkshire lads were no match for the Londoners, and, when in 1901 they were beaten on the "Spurs'" ground by 13 goals to 1, it was realised that interest in the match could not be sustained. Then Edinburgh were met, but the laddies of the Scottish capital were also vanquished with comparative ease. For six seasons the London boys were unbeaten.

Recently the Queen's Park F. C., of Glasgow, have sedulously fostered the game amongst the secondary schools of that city. They hope to train players who will in a season or so assist to maintain the high traditions of the celebrated "Spiders." It was in this direction that London next turned their eyes. The move was fatal, for on April 26, 1905, at Hampden Park, before over 10,000 spectators, Glasgow beat London by 4 goals to 2. The Scots played admirable football, and quite deserved to win; but in fairness to the defeated Londoners, it must be mentioned that their average age was fourteen and a half years to the fifteen and a half of their conquerors.

T. E. PLUMB,
Of Munster Road and Upper Latymer School. Aged fifteen years on December 24, 1905. Winner of ninety prizes, eighteen medals, and five certificates. Captained the London Schools' team that won the English championship.

THE ENGLISH SCHOOLS' CHAMPIONSHIP SHIELD.

THE CORINTHIAN SHIELD.

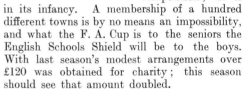

THE DEWAR SHIELD.
London Schools' Championship Competition.

Two days later, with just the same advantage, Edinburgh enjoyed the felicity of at last beating the Southron by 2 goals to 1.

While Metropolitan football was growing, so was the sport in other parts of the country. Sheffield for many seasons has produced formidable school teams. They first met South London in 1890, and the two associations have met regularly since, their opposition arousing considerable interest both in Yorkshire and London. The Lancashire towns, too, played each other whenever a convenient ground could be obtained. Seeing the hold that the game had established in the schools of towns in all parts of the country, Mr. Tom Thomas, meditating in the beautiful village of Llanrwst, North Wales, conceived the idea of a national competition. When submitted to the Associations, it was acclaimed a capital notion, and on November 5, 1904, at Birmingham, the English Schools Football Association was formed. A shield was presented by R. A. Naylor, Esq., and it was decided that the profits arising from the competition should be devoted to the benevolent and orphan fund of the National Union of Teachers.

Twenty-one associations took part. The important clubs of the various towns, both professional and amateur, were extremely sympathetic, and by the loan of their grounds they materially assisted the remarkable success of the competition. The matches were keen, and for the most part even. Eventually London and Sheffield qualified for the final tie, which was played on Easter Monday at Llandudno. The game was most exciting, and it was only after a strenuous contest that London, the heavier side, won by 3 goals to 2, and thus became champions of England and the first holders of the shield.

The English Schools Association has now forty-one districts in membership. One is East Northumberland, and another Plymouth, so that its influence is felt from one end of the land to the other. And this is only the second season of the competition; it is in its infancy. A membership of a hundred different towns is by no means an impossibility, and what the F. A. Cup is to the seniors the English Schools Shield will be to the boys. With last season's modest arrangements over £120 was obtained for charity; this season should see that amount doubled.

The London boys so easily defeated all the teams opposed to them that it was felt that their continued participation in the competition would imperil its success. Little interest is aroused when the result is practically a foregone conclusion. The immense area of selection provided by the Metropolis is undoubtedly a distinct advantage, though it must not be forgotten that it also prevents the chosen boys from practising together with a view to perfecting their combination. However, London will not compete again as a whole. Several of the districts included in the L. S. F. A. have entered, and they may be trusted to uphold the reputation of Metropolitan football, and to put forth strenuous efforts to retain the shield for its present resting-place—the hall of the London County Council.

In conclusion, it might perhaps be well to state that this highly organised school football has not the manufacture of professionals for its aim. Incidentally, no doubt, it provides them. But the sole objects of those who devote so much of their leisure to the boys' games are to provide the youthful Britons with a healthy exercise in the open air, and to instil self-command into them.

THE LONDON SCHOOLS' TEAM, 1905—FIRST CHAMPIONS OF ENGLAND.

BURTON UNITED FOOTBALL CLUB.

ITS GALLANT FIGHT FOR FAME AND FORTUNE.

By C. GREWCOCK.

Early Association days in Burton—The progressive enterprise of Burton Swifts—Peel Croft Ground purchased—The Swifts elected to the Alliance in 1891—The Staffordshire Cup won in 1892—Indifferent performances in the League—The club seeks re-election in 1901—The two premier Burton clubs amalgamate, and the title Burton United is adopted—Poor gates and a first season's loss of over £700—A hard fight with adversity—The mayor comes gallantly to the rescue—Disastrous 1904-5 season—Mr. Mundy, Secretary Grewcock, and an enthusiastic committee gallantly set to work to better matters for 1905-6—An improved team—Poor Cup record—Brighter future prospects.

Colours: Green-and-red shirts, white knickers. *Ground: Peel Croft, Burton-on-Trent.*

WHILE the beginnings of Association football in the Brewing Metropolis are not exactly lost in the mists of antiquity, yet, on the other hand, the dribbling code is not a plant of mushroom growth in Burton, for as far back as the early 'Seventies the town had several clubs of excellent calibre, notably the Wanderers, the Strollers, the Rangers, and Outwood Star, who were able, not only to give a good game, but not infrequently a good thrashing as well to some of the best combinations in the Midland counties. Many of the men connected with these clubs were first-class exponents of the game, and for many seasons such names as David Rutherford, Jack Faulkner, Sam Lawrence, Billy Fellows, Pat Murfin, Tom and Jack Bancroft, Sam Black, Alf Sheffield, Fred Price, Tommy Soar, Fred Roberts, "Jerry" Chandler, Fred Waring, and "Bag'em" West were familiar in the mouths of lovers of the game as household words, and enjoyed quite a Midland reputation. Then came the days of George Kinsey, "Troll" Robinson, Adrian and Arthur Capes, Sam Emery, Teddy Birch, George Hubbard, Jack Thornley, and others, and, with the demise of the Strollers and Rangers clubs, the contest for premier honours was left to the Swifts and Wanderers. Many and keen were the battles fought on the Derby Turn and Shobnall Road grounds, to say nothing of an occasional tussle on Kidger's Field—on which plot of land Gordon Street now stands—and, taking the campaign as a whole, it must be admitted that the honours of war rested with the Derby Turn combination.

A. V. SHAW, Esq.,
Director of the Burton United Football Club.

It is just twenty years—for it was in the autumn of 1885—since professional football first secured a footing in Burton, and the credit for its introduction belongs to Mr. John Parker, who at that time was honorary secretary of the Burton Wanderers F. C. The first local player who received pay for his football was Measham Tunnicliffe, who was known to his many admirers by the sobriquet of "Navvy," one of the best centre half-backs in the Midlands.

In the following season, Burton Swifts (formerly known as Outwood Star) resolved to emulate the example of their local rivals, a course which naturally did much to enhance the keenness of the struggle for supremacy. Better-class football was the immediate result, and, from the point of view of finance, the Swifts had a distinct advantage, thanks to the generous help they received from Messrs. James and J. T. C. Eadie, who not only liberally subsidised the club, but purchased for its use the present playing pitch at Peel Croft, with stands and fencing, at a cost of something like £6,000.

At that time the Swifts were members of the Combination, while the Wanderers were connected with the Midland League, but in 1891 the Swifts secured a well-deserved lift in the football world, being elected members of the Football Alliance, which then included such clubs as Notts Forest, Small Heath, West Bromwich Albion, Sheffield United, Sheffield Wednesday, Grimsby Town, Stoke, the Arsenal, Sunderland Albion, &c.

The following year (1892) saw the two principal combinations —the Football League and the Football Alliance—amalgamate, constituting the finest combination in the world, and thus the Swifts gained a footing upon the League ladder which they retained so long as they continued to exist as a separate organisation.

Their team in 1892 was a very smart one, including, as it did, such experts at the game as Donald Sutherland (ex-captain of Grimsby Town), Arthur Worrall (Wolverhampton), and the brothers W. and E. May (Notts Forest), who were so alike in build and features that it was difficult to say which was which when they were apart. The season was not at all a bad one from a League point of view, as they finished sixth, but it was especially memorable for the fact that they captured the Staffordshire Cup. The match was played on the Mullineaux Grounds, Wolverhampton, their opponents being Aston Villa (the holders of the trophy), who felt so cocksure of retaining it that they had not taken the trouble to bring it with them!

The season of 1893—with the most expensive combination the club ever had, including Sam Jones (the Welsh International goalkeeper), Walter Perry (West Bromwich), Alec Boggie, and the late Jimmy Munro — again saw the Swifts sixth on the list with 31 points; and then in 1894-5 the Wanderers—who, under the capable supervision of Mr. W. D. Clark (with the genial and generous "Father" Cogley as treasurer), had been making very small fry of Midland League clubs—secured admission to the charmed circle. They secured 35 points out of a possible 60, while the Swifts only totalled 24; but in the following season the Derby Turn brigade quite eclipsed all previous performances, and only missed taking part in the test matches by goal average, tying with Grimsby in the matter of points with 42 for third place. The Wanderers' record was a really brilliant one, the men being seen at their best against their most powerful opponents, and no one who followed their fortunes in those halcyon days will easily forget how they defeated Newcastle United by 9 goals to 0, and Manchester United by 8 to 0. The ensuing season, however, proved just as disastrous for the Wanderers as that of 1894-5 had been successful, for they finished last but one on the table, and failed to secure re-election, while the Swifts, who occupied but one rung higher, were given another chance.

From 1897 to 1901 there is very little to record that would be pleasant reading from a Burton point of view, 28 being the highest number of points the Peel Croft club secured during this period, and in 1901 they had once more to seek re-election.

MR. F. B. PEACH,
Chairman of the Burton United F. C.

In the meantime, the parlous state of Association football in the town, and the difficulty of getting an adequate measure of support for two senior clubs, had caused the representatives of the rival organisations to carry on informal negotiations with a view to amalgamation, and, after one or two well-meant but fruitless attempts, a town's meeting, which was largely attended and was presided over by the Mayor, unanimously approved of the fusion of forces. Some discussion naturally took place as to the name of the new club, but eventually, with but one dissentient, it was dubbed "Burton United." The management for the first season was vested in a committee composed of an equal number of representatives of each of the defunct organisations, and the following were chosen to man the new ship on its first voyage: Messrs. George Rae (chairman), W. Matthews, A. J. Woolrych, S. H. Morris, J. Bancroft, H. Meakin, C. Grewcock, with W. D. Clark as secretary-manager. Though late in the day, the committee managed to get together a capital set of men, including Peers (Notts Forest), R. Gray, Archie Livingstone, T. Arkesden, Billy Joyce (ex-Bolton Wanderers and Tottenham Hotspur player), and Chris. Mann (Aston Villa). This team, in transfers, summer wages, &c., cost the new club something like £500, but there is no doubt the money was well spent, as the representatives of the club were, as a result, able to present such a case to the League that their re-election was once more secured, the United tieing with Bristol City for top place in the voting. From a playing point of view, the first season of the new combination was a distinct improvement on its predecessor, 30 points being secured, but the gates were far from realising expectations, and, as a consequence, the committee found themselves faced by a heavy deficit of between £700 and £800 at the end of April.

MR. C. GREWCOCK,
Secretary of the Burton United F. C.
He is an enthusiastic and hard-working official, and has done much to forward the cause of the club for which he works.

It was only with difficulty that they were able to find the wherewithal to pay summer wages to the class men they wished to retain, but they managed to do so, and the players available for 1902-3 included Mann, Livingstone, Harry Ashby (now with Leicester Fosse), Jacky Lewis (of Bristol Rovers), and Arkesden. The financial affairs of the club were entrusted to the management of Mr. George Rae, who had for many years been a hard-working and enthusiastic supporter of the Swifts F. C., while Mr. W. D. Clark was re-elected secretary-manager. Although avoiding the indignity of having to sue for re-election, the performances of the team were anything but satisfactory, the total number of points showing a decrease of 1 on those obtained during the previous season, while the state of the finances was such as to cause the management extreme anxiety.

The team for 1903-4 included Harry Bromage (Derby), Clough (Nelson), J. Reynolds (now of Sheffield Wednesday), Hargreaves (who, with Bromage, is playing for Leeds City), and Orlando Evans (Aston Villa), and, for the second season in succession, the Crofters finished sixth from the bottom with 29 points. Strenuous efforts were made in the close season in various ways to raise the wind so that a better class of men could be secured, but the debt incurred by floating the combined club clung to the shoulders of the committee like an Old Man of the Sea, and so, having to part with several of their best men, including Harry Ashby, Reynolds, and Archie Livingstone, it was not with very sanguine feelings that the season 1904-5 was entered upon; indeed, when Mr. C. Grewcock took over the position of secretary-manager in succession to Mr. Clark, things were, perhaps, as bad as they ever had been, and the general opinion was that we had arrived at "the beginning of the end."

The play of the team only served to strengthen this view, for victories were, like angels' visits, "few and far between," and, with the takings growing "smaller by degrees and beautifully less," and creditors pressing for immediate remittances, some of the more pessimistic patrons predicted that the club would not see the season out. In the meantime, thanks to the public spirit of the Mayor, a town's meeting was called, at which a "Penny Fund" was launched, and the proceeds from this and other sources sufficed to keep the wolf on the right side of the door.

The season, from a playing point of view, proved the most disastrous in the brief and chequered history of the United, for they finished last but one with 20 points. Very little hope was entertained that the League would favourably consider another application for re-election, but the movement for the extension of the League saved them, and great was the delight of the club's supporters when it became known that Burton was not, after all, to lose its place in Second League circles.

With Mr. C. Mundy as treasurer, and a loyal and enthusiastic committee at his back, Mr. Grewcock at once set to work to get a team together for 1905-6, a task which, taking all the circumstances into consideration, would have daunted any but the pluckiest secretary-manager. Only two of the old team could be prevailed upon to remain—Bromage, Mann, Ashby, Evans, C. L. Aston, Gould, and the Brothers Hargreaves all departing for "fresh fields and pastures new." Summer money was, of course, out of the question, but, for all that, a team has been secured whose performances up to date have amply justified the wisdom of the committee in engaging them.

Seven of them, viz., Starbuck (goal), Shreeve, Culland (backs), Davis (half-back), Gutteridge, Burton, King (forwards), are practically local lads, the four who have come from a distance being Battles (Stockport), Robinson (Fosse), Hunt and Bradshaw (Fulham). The eleven does not make any pretensions to brilliancy, but it has proved itself a decidedly hard-working and useful one, and the fact that at the time of writing (November 10) the club had secured 12 points, as against 20 all last season, warrants the habitués of Peel Croft in anticipating that April, 1906, will find the club in a much-improved position as compared with the one they occupied twelve months previously.

So far as the National Cup is concerned, the United have not, up to date, cut a very distinguished figure in the competition, but that has by no means been for the lack of ambitions in the particular direction. "The stars in their courses" have, however, seemed to fight against the Crofters, and the only performance deserving of special mention was the drawn game played with Manchester United at Clayton, in 1903-4—at least, that was the official verdict, although the Burton people who saw the game aver to this day that the Lancastrians' equalising goal was a rank off-sider.

In the pre-amalgamation days, however, both the Swifts and Wanderers created a surprise now and then in the pot-hunting expedition, and perhaps in the not very far distant future the United may rise upon a wave of Cup-tie successes, and inaugurate a period of prosperity for the gallant Second League club, whose prospects seem to grow steadily brighter and brighter.

MR. T. DOTMAN,
Director of the Burton United F. C.

BURTON UNITED FOOTBALL CLUB—THE PLAYERS, SEASON 1905-6.

Top Row: ALLSOPP (Trainer). C. GREWCOCK (Secretary). BURTON. SHRUVE. STARBUCK. KIRKLAND. DAVIS. C. MUNDY (Financial Secretary).

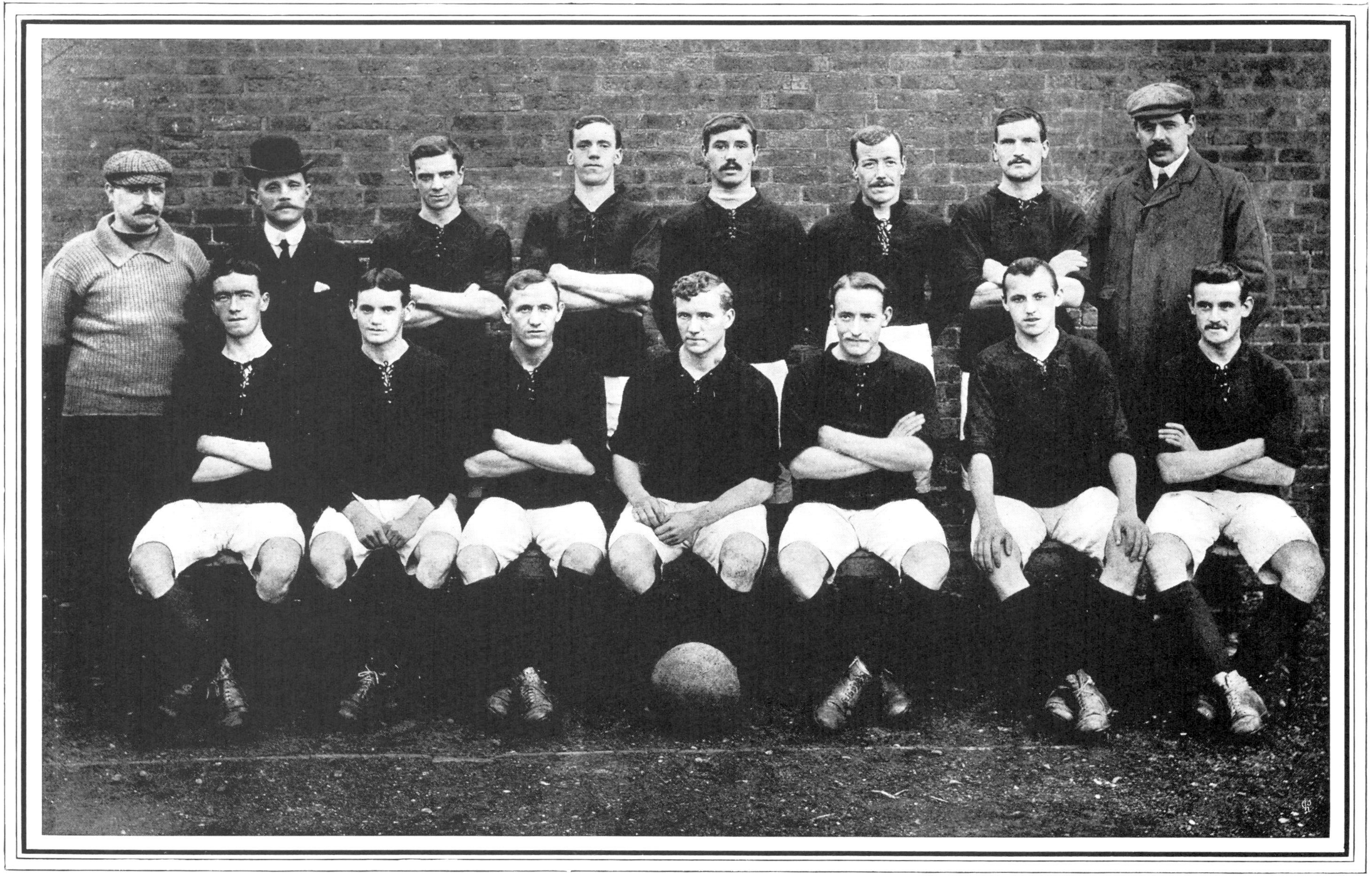

R. Scott and Co., Manchester.]

BATTLES. BRADSHAW. HUNT. ROBINSON. ASTON. GUTTERIDGE. KING.

QUEEN'S PARK.

A HISTORY AND RECORD OF THE MOST BRILLIANT ASSOCIATION FOOTBALL CLUB IN SCOTLAND.

Winners of the Scottish Cup, 1874-5-6, 1880-1-2, 1884, 1886, 1890, 1893; finalists, 1892, 1900. Finalists in the English Cup, 1883-4, 1884-5.

By WILLIAM McGREGOR.

Queen's Park introduce Association football into Glasgow, establish the Scottish Football Association, and play the first International game against England—Financial figures in the early days—How the game was played in 1867—Queen's Park generously subscribe to the English Cup fund—The first International—Queen's Park play the Wanderers at the Oval in 1872—Founding of the Scottish Association—Queen's Park win the first of their brilliant successes in the Scottish Cup—Queen's Park's magnificent record—The establishment of the League—The club falls into line after ten years—Poor League record, and the reason—Famous Queen's Park players—New Hampden Park.

Colours: Black and white hoops, black knickers. *Ground: Hampden Park, Glasgow.*

IF I were asked to specify which club in Association football had done most to inculcate and foster a love of the Association game, I should answer most unhesitatingly, Queen's Park. They were the club which introduced the Association game to Glasgow, their origin dating from 1867. They founded the Scottish Football Association; from their own ranks they found the opposition to England in the first International game between the two countries, and their missionary visits to the Midlands and Lancashire did much to create a true love for Association football in those districts, and also to give a tone and polish to local football effort.

They were the first club to introduce really scientific methods into the game. Their football was as perfect and polished as football has ever been played at a time when most clubs were content with merely scrambling after the ball. What they did is in danger of being forgotten, because many modern footballers seem to be quite convinced that the exponents of the game who preceded them were not of much account. Therein they are mistaken. There were giants in the Queen's Park eleven of early times such as are rarely to be found—at any rate, they are few and far between—in modern football. It is quite safe to say that Weir and McKinnon were dribblers the like of whom do not exist to-day, and they were playing with Queen's Park in 1873-4! The Queen's Park eleven which I remember in 1880 comprised, I think, more really brilliant footballers than any eleven I have seen, except the great Preston North End combination

The Queen's Park Club was formed in 1867, and they took their name from the enclosure on which their early revels were held. Like many other great clubs, Queen's Park originated from a Young Men's Christian Association, and the first annual meeting was held in April, 1868. It is worthy of note that Mr. Klinger, the first secretary of Queen's Park, wrote to the "Sporting Life" and "Cassell's Paper" for advice as to rules to be observed. The letter, by a somewhat roundabout route, reached John Lillywhite, the publisher of the well-known cricket annual. He procured for Queen's Park a copy of the rules of the Football Association, and with the help of these Queen's Park, who had up to this point played in somewhat haphazard style with teams ranging from eleven to twenty-two a side, commenced to work on scientific lines.

THE HOME OF THE GREAT SCOTTISH AMATEUR CLUB, QUEEN'S PARK.

This magnificent enclosure at New Hampden Park, Glasgow, will hold as many as 100,000 people when it is finally completed. It is here that the great International match between Scotland and England will be played in 1906.

How small the beginnings of Queen's Park were, the financial history of the club tells. The yearly subscription of the club when Mr. Alexander Rhind was connected with the finance department was 6d., and the income of that year —1869—was £3 9s. 8d. But the expenditure was £4 2s. 4d., so that a deficit of 12s. 8d. had to be made up. Therefore, a levy was imposed. In the following year, however, Queen's Park made their first profit, for whereas the expenditure was £5 19s. 11d., the income was £6 3s. 11d., so that they had 4s. to the good.

Many of the members desired to christen the club the Glasgow Young Men's Christian Association, but the title Queen's Park seemed more euphonious and less cumbrous, and the latter was decided upon. Their early games would be counted amusing now. There were goalposts for opponents to aim at, and there was a goalkeeper, but there was no bar and no nets. If the ball went between the posts a mile high it was a goal, and as good a goal in the eyes of the players as that produced by the lightning shot which passed within a few inches of the goalkeeper. It was competent to catch the ball on the bound, but it could not be either lifted or carried. Touch-downs had a tangible value, and ends were changed each time a goal was scored.

The original colours were blue; the now world-famous black and white hoops were not adopted until the cup-tie era began. Naturally, the club had to form its own combats, for there were no other teams to play, and such sides as Captain v. Secretary and Light-weights v. Heavy-weights were popular. There was a club at Ayr shortly after this, and an attempt was made to arrange a match, but it had to be abandoned as impracticable. The distance to be travelled was too great; it was thirty miles! The first match—it will surely never be forgotten by Scottish footballers—took place on May Day, 1868, on the public park at Cross Hill. Their opponents were the Thistle, and Queen's Park won by 2 goals to nil. Matches with Hamilton, Eastern, and the Drummond, who played on Glasgow Green, followed.

A SCOTTISH CUP FINAL AT HAMPDEN PARK—THIRD LANARK v. RANGERS, 1905.
This match, which was won by Third Lanark by 3 goals to 1, was witnessed by 65,000 people.

Some of the Queen's Park records about this time are appalling. In the season 1873-4, for instance, their record ran: Matches played, 10; won, 10; goals for, 47; against, 0. Then, in the Black Year, 1876, the year they first encountered defeat, their figures were such as most clubs would yearn to possess. Played, 13; won, 11; drawn, 1; lost, 1; goals for, 33; against, 4.

The first captain of Queen's Park—or, at any rate, the captain at the time when they leased their first private ground and became a responsible organisation—was William Ker He was a brother of the redoubtable Geordie Ker, possibly the deadliest centre-forward Scottish football ever knew. Like most Queen's Park men, William Ker was a most gentlemanly young fellow, and was loved and respected by all who associated with him.

It is on record that, although the income of Queen's Park was small at this time, they were one of the clubs to subscribe a guinea to the fund raised for the purchase of the English Cup. This was in 1871. The subscription to the Football Association was then only 5s. per annum, so that it was impossible to buy a cup out of the funds. Returning to William Ker; he played in the first International at Hamilton Crescent, Partick, when Queen's Park met England single-handed. The game ended in a draw, and was the outcome of a challenge issued by Mr. Alcock, on behalf of the London Wanderers, to the effect that they would meet any eleven that cared to face them. Queen's Park, ever keen sportsmen, replied that they would be glad to meet them on neutral ground in the North of England, and give battle either for a cup of the value of eleven guineas, or eleven medals worth a guinea each.

Queen's Park suggested that the nationalities of the players should be restricted, for two of the greatest members of the Wanderers team, the Hon. A. F. Kinnaird and Colonel Renny-Tailyour, were Scotsmen. The match was played on the delightful enclosure of the West of Scotland Cricket Club at Hamilton Crescent, and not a goal was scored. The gate, 4,000, including a large number of ladies, was the largest that had been seen at a football match in Scotland.

The Scottish team, exclusively Queen's Park, was as follows: R. Gardner (captain), goal; W. Ker and J. J. Taylor, backs; J. J. Thomson and J. Smith, half-backs; R. Smith, A. Rhind, W. McKinnon, D. Wotherspoon, J. B. Weir, and R. Leckie, forwards. Three hearty cheers were given by each team for their opponents. The Englishmen were entertained to dinner, and it was decided to play a return match at Kennington Oval in the following spring—and so Queen's Park established International football.

March 4, 1872, marked an important era in the history of Queen's Park. They entered for the English Cup competition in this the first year of its existence, and received byes until the Semi-final stage, when they were drawn against the Wanderers. A public subscription was started in Glasgow to send the team to London, for this was the first match of its type that Queen's Park had been concerned in.

On the day in March given, the Glasgow men turned out at the Oval, and a stiff game ended in a draw. As, according to the rules as they then existed, it was necessary for Queen's Park to again go to London for the re-play, they decided to retire from the competition. Their team that day was: R. Gardner; W. Ker and J. J. Taylor; J. J. Thomson and J. Smith; R. Smith, J. E. A. Walker, J. B. Weir, D. Wotherspoon, J. Hepburn, and D. Edmiston.

On March 13, 1873, Mr. Archibald Rae called a meeting, at which the Scottish Football Association was founded. The enthusiasm with which Queen's Park played the game was naturally contagious, and clubs were springing up on every hand.

Queen's Park obtained the co-operation of Clydesdale, Dumbreck, Vale of Leven, Rovers, Eastern, Third Lanark R. V., and Granville, and Mr. Archibald Campbell (Clydesdale) was the first president, Mr. William Ker (Queen's Park) the first treasurer, and Mr. Archibald Rae (Queen's Park) the first secretary. A challenge cup was purchased, and great interest was manifested in the final tie.

It took place at Hampden Park, not the New Hampden, and not even the second Hampden that most of us remember so well, but the original Hampden Park, which has now been cut up to form a railway embankment. There was no pavilion; there was a small shanty near the entrance to the field, and that was the only building the ground boasted. The grass was practically uncut, and at the corners was quite luxuriant in its growth.

But in March, 1874, that ground was the scene of the first concluding tie for the Scottish Cup, and 2,000 people watched the match, which I daresay is vividly stamped on their memories. Thirty-three years ago it is, and many of the twenty-two who took part in that game are dead. Queen's Park and Clydesdale were the opponents, and Queen's Park triumphed. Charles Campbell, Thomas Lawrie, Harry McNeill, R. W. Neil, John Dickson, and Angus McKinnon played in that match, in addition to Taylor, Weir, Leckie, J. J. Thomson and W. McKinnon. The redoubtable J. J. Lang, who afterwards played for Sheffield Wednesday, was one of the Clydesdale team, and R. Gardner—who had left Queen's Park as the result of a slight dispute with some of his colleagues—kept goal for them.

And so I have told you of the first International, and of Queen's Park's first cup final. Everything else must be in the nature of a resumé. In their first seven years, Queen's Park had an unbroken run of success; indeed, they did not lose a single goal. From July 9, 1867, to January 15, 1875, their custodian was never beaten. Then, on January 16, the Vale of Leven created a record by scoring against the "Spiders." Notts County were the first English club to score against them, this being on March 12. It was not until March, 1876, that Queen's Park sustained their first defeat, the Wanderers beating them at Kennington Oval. This is, without doubt, the most wonderful record possessed by any Association team. In all they have won the Scottish Cup ten times, the last occasion being in 1893, when they defeated the Celtic. They reached the final in 1900, only to be beaten by the same club. They have won the Glasgow Charity Cup eight times and the Glasgow Cup three times. They have also held the Dewar Shield conjointly with Aston Villa. Up to the beginning of the present year, 122 Queen's Park men had participated in International matches with England, 68 had played against Wales, and 36 against Ireland. No other club can boast such an array of Internationals.

Mention must be made of the two gallant attempts which Queen's Park made to lift the English Cup. On March 29, 1884, they worked their way into the Cup Final, and met Blackburn Rovers at Kennington Oval. They had a magnificent team, practically an International side. Despite the sturdy football of Arnott and Campbell, J. Brown and Forrest notched goals for the Rovers, and Christie scored for Queen's Park, who were beaten by 2 goals to 1. They did not relish some of the decisions of Major Marindin, the referee; but as one who saw the match, I must say that the Rovers played slightly better football, and few begrudged them their victory.

In the following year, Queen's Park again qualified for the Final, and the same men—Brown and Forrest—scored for the Rovers. Despite the brilliancy of their players, it seemed to me that the Scotsmen were clearly beaten in each match; but then they were beaten by the greatest set of Cup-fighters ever known.

From that time onwards Queen's Park made no attempt to win the English Cup. It is the one disappointing point in their record that they failed to get their name inscribed on the English Cup. Yet they were represented in these matches with the Blackburn Rovers by superlatively clever elevens.

As most of my readers know, Queen's Park have kept the amateur flag flying since the club came into being. They have resisted all suggestions as to the advisability of embracing professionalism, and they stand to-day in a unique position. Leaving out the Corinthians, which one can scarcely designate a club in the full and complete sense of the word, Queen's Park may be said to be the only first-class amateur club. No other amateur team plays its part in representative league and cup-tie games.

The establishment of the Scottish League played havoc with Queen's Park. It was prophesied that unless the amateurs joined that organisation they would become extinct. For ten years they held aloof; but the day of friendly matches has gone by, probably never to return. Each year witnessed a waning of interest in their games; indeed, one might say that the only attractive element in their programme was their New Year's Day match with the Corinthians at Hampden Park. That has always been, and probably always will be—at any rate, so long as present conditions obtain—a game of supreme interest and importance. It is the official meeting of the recognised amateur leaders of football in the two countries.

At last it came to this—that Queen's Park must join the Scottish League, or lose their place in first-class football. Very wisely they chose the former alternative.

They have not gained distinction in the competition; I never thought they would. In 1900 we find them taking part in the League tournament; they only aggregated 17 points. Fourteen was all they could obtain in 1901. In 1902 they made but 15, and in 1903 they reached 21. Last year there were only two clubs—Greenock Morton and Motherwell—below them, and they were credited with 20 points as against an aggregate of 41 each for the leaders—the Rangers and the Celtic.

The plain fact is, that Queen's Park found it impossible to avoid the attention of the poacher, and as most of their players are young fellows in business offices they cannot get away at all times, and so they are at a disadvantage when it comes to

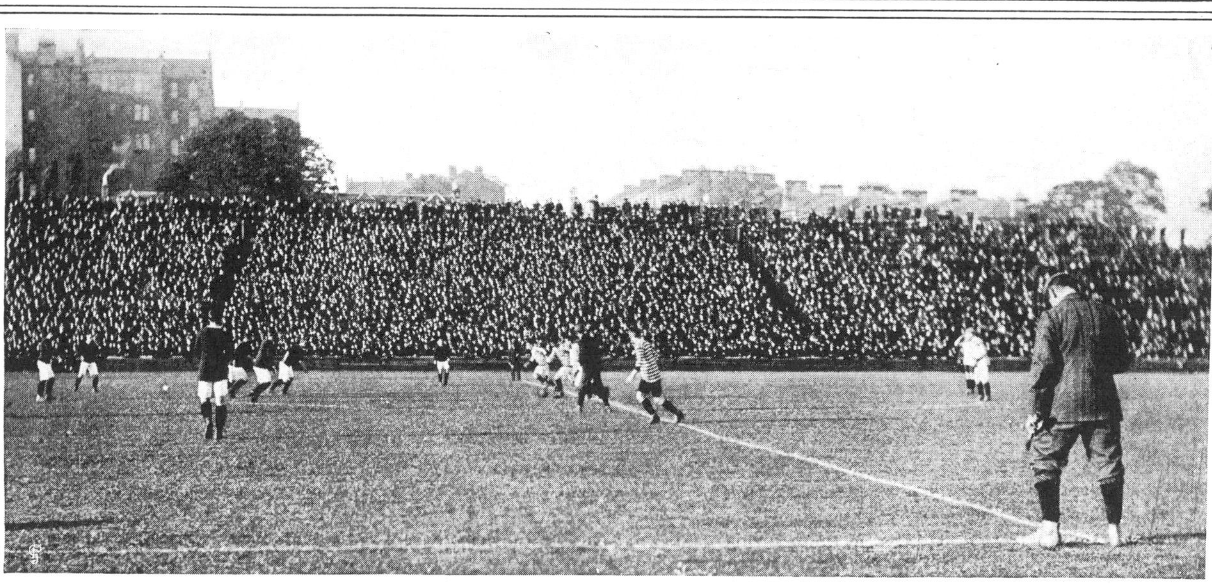

A LEAGUE MATCH AT HAMPDEN PARK—QUEEN'S v. CELTIC (WINNERS OF THE SCOTTISH LEAGUE CHAMPIONSHIP, 1905).

Queen's Park kick off and open the game.

meeting opponents on remote grounds. Could Queen's Park have kept their players, they might have been nearer the head, rather than the foot, of the table.

They have had some bitter blows since the early days when Quentin Neill went to Lincoln City. As the result of professionalism, they lost such great players as R. C. Hamilton, R. McColl, John Cameron, W. Lennie, McWattie, McNaught, Henderson, Fullarton, Graham, McCullam, and Logan, and since McColl left they have, for the first time in their history, been without a first-class centre-forward. McColl was the legitimate successor of Weir, McKinnon, Ker, W. Berry, Dr. Smith, Hamilton, and W. Sellar, and, strangely, he has never been quite the footballer he was since he left the amateur fold.

A GLASGOW CUP FINAL—CELTIC v. RANGERS AT HAMPDEN PARK.

The attendance at this match reached the imposing figures of 55,000 persons, an eloquent tribute to the popularity of the "Soccer" code over the Border.

No club can claim such a wealth of talent as Queen's Park have possessed. The form of their men in the early days was, considering that the pastime then had no history, abnormally skilful. J. J. Taylor was a magnificent back; although light, he was a perfect tackler, he had remarkable speed, and he was a born leader of men. He died at Govanhill about eighteen years ago.

Robert Gardner, their first great goalkeeper and the captain of the original International side, was a most versatile player. He, too, is dead, passing away at South Queen's Ferry about sixteen years since.

J. B. Weir has also gone over to the great majority. For ten years he was an indispensable member of the team, and he, Angus McKinnon, William McKinnon, Harry McNeill, T. Lawrie, and T. C. Highet passed superbly.

Second only to Weir was William McKinnon, who played in eight Internationals against England, including the first. He, too, was a close dribbler, and it is said that he was the finest man at taking a corner-kick ever known.

J. J. Thomson, William Ker, and Alexander Rhind were also great members of the old brigade.

After them came Charles Campbell, possibly the most consistent half-back and the finest header ever associated with football. He played in ten successive games against England. He was a great captain, and he has since proved an able legislator.

Harry McNeill was the idol of the Queen's Park crowd. He had a quick action, and literally seemed to glide along the touch-line. R. W. Neil was one of the best backs I have ever seen.

Then we come to the time of Andy Watson, one of the soundest of all backs; E. Fraser, a cultured young fellow, whom I shall always regard as the prettiest outside-right of all time; William Anderson, who did the rough work for him so unselfishly; John Kaye, unrivalled in the art of centring; J. T. Richmond, W. Harrower, A. H. Holm, and J. J. Gow.

Later came Wattie Arnott, declared by many to be the finest back ever seen and by others bracketed equal with Nick Ross. Alexander Hamilton and William Sellar were two of the most gentlemanly and polished inside-forwards Scotland has produced. Then there were R. M. Christie, J. A. Lambie, W. Lambie, J. Allan, and his brother D. S. Allan, Dr. Smith, and W. Berry, while I fear I have neglected to notice in his proper place the greatest of all centres, George Ker. R. Smellie, D. Sillars, whose melancholy death was noted recently, Tom Robertson, and George Gillespie. Then, later still, came A. J. Christie, Kenneth Anderson, and W. Gulleland.

Queen's Park have always been richly endowed with officials of the highest type. Mr. Archibald Rae, Mr. C. Campbell, Mr. R. M. Christie, Mr. Richard Browne, and Mr. Arthur Geake (*the* worker for the club), have, with others, been responsible for a policy of sound enterprise.

The equipment of the magnificent newest Hampden, which has cost over £35,000, and is by far the finest ground in Scotland, is proof positive that this eulogy is warranted.

THE SCOTTISH CUP FINAL OF 1905—THIRD LANARK v. RANGERS AT HAMPDEN PARK.

The game was witnessed by 65,000 persons.

BIG TRANSFERS AND THE TRANSFER SYSTEM.

By WILLIAM I. BASSETT.

Wild talk about the transfer system—The position of players of to-day—Transfer of players an invention of the Football League—Transfer fees sometimes the means of saving clubs from extinction—The system and its good points—Where the Football Association steps in and prevents the migration of players, offered a full salary, to the South—Early transfer fees, and what the men were worth—Vox populi—Transfer fees and transferred players—A record price for Common, and what he did for Middlesborough—The rules of the Football Association with relation to the transfer of players—The transfer form.

NO system prevalent in modern football has aroused so much discussion than that designated the transfer system. There never was a controversial matter in regard to which the evidence was of such a conflicting character. Some men hate and abominate the transfer system; others declare that it has been the salvation of the weaker section of first-class football clubs. We can dismiss from our minds at once all the silly talk of silly people, who say in a profoundly silly way that it is monstrous, it is a sin against morality, &c., that players should be bought and sold like so many cattle. That is nonsense.

There are plenty of deserving objects of pity in this world. If a man craves for victims for his sympathetic tendencies he has not to look far to find deserving objects. But let us clear our minds of cant before we begin to examine the transfer system. A footballer at £4 per week all the year round can stand a great deal of sympathy before he is tempted to turn and rend those who would fain sympathise with him.

Professional football players are a handsomely remunerated set of men, and call for the commiseration of no one. They are not bought and sold as chattels—there is no law of the Football Association to compel any man to go where he does not desire to go. Nay, I might add that if a footballer makes up his mind to go to a certain club, he has the power to get there sooner or later. The Football Association simply provides for the reasonable protection of the club, just as, in other matters, it provides for the adequate protection of the player.

THIS IS *NOT* THE WAY THE TRANSFER OF A PLAYER IS ARRANGED.

Some people are under the impression that professional football players are bought and sold like cattle. Mr. W. I. Bassett in his excellent article explodes once and for all this erroneous idea. There is no law of the Football Association to compel any man to go where he does not desire to go. The transfer system only provides for the reasonable protection of the club.

The transfer system is the invention of the Football League, and it applies only to the workings of that body. A player may go to the South or elsewhere from a League club, and that club have nothing to pay for his migration. But he cannot go to another League club without the sanction of the club which last engaged him. He is their player for League purposes for ever, unless an arrangement is made for his transfer. It is simply and solely a principle which operates among League clubs; so long as a club holds the signature of a player for League purposes he can go the round of the world outside the League, but he cannot join another League club. Until quite recently it had never had the official recognition of the Football Association. Now, however, the Association have decided that from January 1, 1908, no transfer shall exceed £350. There can be no quibbling at this. There must be an end to the almost insane competition which has been going on for the possession of good men; besides, under unrestricted competition, clubs of moderate strength have been debarred from getting good men. The market has been virtually closed to them.

Generally speaking, the tendency of the transfer system has been in the direction of good. I have no hesitation in saying that it has saved clubs like West Bromwich Albion, Barnsley, and Bury from extinction. Under the conditions which once obtained, when Aston Villa were paying Wheldon and Athersmith £6 10s. per week all the year round, the tendency was for all the best men to go to a few clubs. When a player connected with a club of moderate strength became famous, he naturally wanted to go to one of the leading clubs. Sometimes he went; sometimes his sense of local patriotism impelled him to be loyal to the club which had introduced him to football. Now, without the operations of the transfer, his club would have been powerless to keep him. His services were sought after, but a prohibitive transfer fee was asked. This generally choked the poachers off, but if the worst came to the worst the club which reared him or finished off his football education at least had a financial salve with which to anoint the sore caused by his loss. Sometimes you know that you are bound to lose a great player. He sees that the future is not with you, and he wisely elects to transfer his football services and abilities to where he deems he will work under more auspicious conditions. If you are bound to lose him, then the best thing you can do is to get the highest price you can for him. You will concede this much—that if a player is bent on leaving a poor club for a richer one, you cannot keep him back. Therefore, you make the best of a bad job, and compel the club which acquires him to pay according to their means for him.

I will take the case of the club with which I was connected as a player, and with which I am now associated as a director. I feel confident that West Bromwich Albion would not have been in existence to-day had there been no transfer fee. If one of the wealthier clubs coveted one of our men we naturally asked for a big transfer fee—not more than the man was worth, but still a substantial one. Now, what would have happened, or what could have happened, if we had not been privileged to ask such a fee? The club in want of the player would have been in a position, had they cared to break the law (and such offences are, I have heard, not unknown), to offer the player a good sum down as an inducement for him to come to them at the first convenient opportunity.

THIS ADMIRABLE "LOCKETT" WAS SECURED BY ASTON VILLA FROM STOKE FOR SOME £400.

The transfer fee is the invention of the Football League, and, generally speaking, its tendency has been in the direction of good. It was introduced to prevent the powerful clubs from poaching the best players from their less famous and more unfortunate neighbours in the League.

This has been done, and been done in spite of the existence of the transfer fee; in fact, it is common knowledge that certain clubs who are exempt from the transfer fee have been in the habit of giving players signed by them what they would under normal conditions have had to pay for their transfer. This explains the otherwise unaccountable way in which men have migrated to clubs outside the League. And such migrations would have been far more numerous than they actually have had it not been for the commendable vigilance manifested by the Football Association. Whenever a man has been offered the maximum wage by his club, and has elected to go elsewhere, and the Football Association have been informed of the facts of the case so far as they affect the club he is leaving, they have inquired into the matter, and in several instances, notably the migration of Raybould, Goldie, and Glover from Liverpool to Portsmouth, Cox from Liverpool to Fulham, and Bradley from Stoke to Plymouth Argyle, the registration of the player or players has been cancelled.

There is really nothing very heinous about the transfer system. If one League club takes a famous player from the ranks of another League club, thereby strengthening its playing resources, it is only fair that it should pay for the privilege. It is generally supposed that Everton paid Bury £400 for the services of Settle, their famous forward.

I heard of one case in which a club outside the League paid the man who came to them a handsome sum in consideration of the fact that under other conditions a transfer fee would have had to be paid; and when the Association cancelled the man's registration the club were not in a position to demand the money back, because, had they done so, they would have been self-convicted of a very serious offence, an offence which might have brought in its train a punishment such as a prominent club could only shudder at.

It is difficult to over-estimate the value of any system which gives a club the full benefit of the services of its home-grown players. I think it will be at once admitted that it is not for the good of football that the cream of the players shall be in half a dozen teams. No matter how strong a club may be, it cannot play matches with itself. It must have opponents, and it is well that it should have plenty of able opponents. There have been instances in which a club has been of infinitely less value to itself than to other institutions. I could name several clubs which have, at various times, helped to fill the coffers of other clubs, and have themselves done only moderately well financially. Without the restriction which the transfer system imposed no poor club could have held its players long.

Equally absurd as the clamour against the transfer fee in principle was the outcry which used to go up whenever it was announced that a certain man had been secured by one club from another for what was at the time regarded as a prohibitive fee. It is rather remarkable how the fee has varied. What was prohibitive ten or twelve years ago is regarded as quite an insignificant sum to-day. I recall the time when Groves was transferred from West Bromwich Albion to Aston Villa for £100, and the same club picked up John Reynolds for £40. Even then there were people who demurred, and said that it was foolish to pay prices for players. When you think of what John Reynolds did for Aston Villa, how he played in practically every match during those wonderful seasons when they won the League five times and the English Cup twice in eight years, you begin to realise that this famous half-back came very cheaply to Aston Villa, in that he cost them less than £5 per annum so far as the transfer fee went. I wonder what West Bromwich Albion or any other club would get for two players of the merit of Groves and Reynolds to-day? To begin with, there are not two such players in existence. Half-backs of the present day are not quite up to the standard of those men.

And then what a shout there was when the same enterprising club gave £250—I believe that was the figure; at any rate, it was not more—for Crabtree. If ever any man who played football was worth a thousand pounds, Crabtree was worth that sum; but transfer fees were not then what they are now, and the price the Villa paid Burnley for this great player ranked for some considerable time as a record. I have heard it said that Aston Villa got back the price of Crabtree's transfer in the course of a few matches, because a great many people thronged to Perry Barr to see a man whose fame was unique at that time. I have personally heard of some who went down to Perry Barr out of sheer curiosity to see Crabtree, and who have been season-ticket holders of Aston Villa ever since. It would be impossible to assess the monetary value of Crabtree to Aston Villa. Who knows but that his prowess made all the difference between success and failure in an early Cup-tie — the difference between winning and losing, which might be represented by three or four thousand pounds? I hold that you cannot estimate the value of a good

The big transfer fee of £700 was paid by Newcastle United to Sunderland for the services of McCombie. Probably he has been worth that sum, and more, to the club he now represents. Last year Newcastle United won the League championship, and only just missed the Cup. It would be idle to scoff at the policy of the Newcastle United directorate after such a showing.

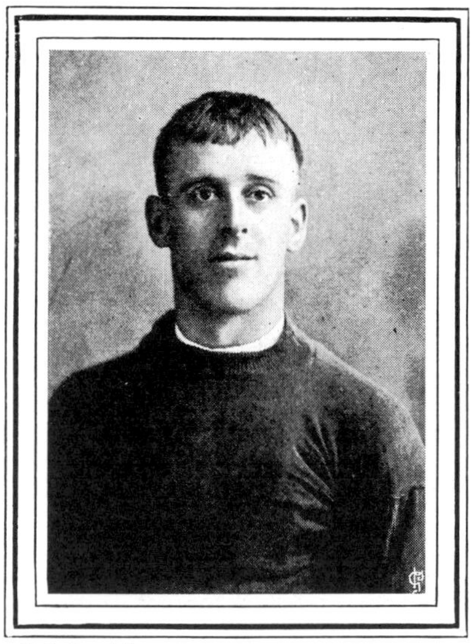

Fairclough.]
ALFRED COMMON,
The hero of the record £1,000 transfer fee.
Common, who was transferred from Sunderland to Middlesborough in the spring of 1905, was born at Sunderland in 1880. He stands 5ft. 8in., and weighs 13st. He has played for South Hilton, Jarrow, Sheffield United, and Sunderland.

man to a club, and if there is one sillier principle than another it is that of selling your best player or players. Small Heath came near to selling McRoberts to Aston Villa for £300. If they had done so, I verily believe the club would never have reared its head again. I say that seriously, knowing the peculiar plight which Small Heath were then in.

There have been many bigger transfer fees than £250 since Crabtree left Burnley. Fred Wheldon was acquired by Aston Villa from Small Heath—the Villa have ever been ready to pay for good men, and a very sound principle it is for a club with their resources—for £350; Settle went to Everton from Bury, the fee, I have always understood, being £400; Aston Villa gave Bury £400 for McLuckie; Dorsett went from West Bromwich Albion to Manchester City at £450; and I understand that Aston Villa paid Stoke £400 for Lockett. It is generally understood that Newcastle paid Sunderland £700 for McCombie, the Scottish International back; and the same price, I believe, was given to Glossop by Manchester City for Thornley and Norgrove. Blackburn Rovers are credited with giving a high price for Cameron, the International back; but the record price is £1,000, paid by Middlesborough for Common. Of course, the old cry went up that no footballer could be worth £1,000, but I am rather inclined to believe that Aston Villa would have given £1,000 for a high-class centre in the early part of last season, and who can say whether Common was a cheap or a dear man? I should say that, under the circumstances, he was a cheap man. It is generally thought that he saved Middlesborough from sinking into the Second League. Now, I take it that the difference between the takings of Middlesborough as a Second League club and Middlesborough as a First League club would be fully £4,000. Let us presume that, at any rate, for the sake of argument; no harm will be done if the figures are not accurate. If Common was largely instrumental in saving them from relegation to the Second League, then it follows that his purchase was one of the best investments any club ever made. Manchester City put a huge sum down—or rather a well-known newspaper proprietor put it down for them—when they secured at one stroke Hynds, Drummond, and McOustra from the Celtic. Few people will deny a statement to the effect that that expenditure was the turning point of Manchester City's history. But for that expenditure the club might have gone the wrong way altogether. Let us be careful, therefore, before we denounce in unmeasured terms the principle of paying heavy transfer fees. If you knew the sums which clubs waste either on inferior men, or in experimenting with juniors, you would understand the avidity with which they seize hold of any chance of getting a ready-made first-class footballer. One man is worth £300 to one club, but he may be worth double that sum to another. If a wealthy club merely wants to strengthen one particular position, then it is idle for anyone to say that they are paying an excessive sum for one bright star. The sum is not excessive if they get what they want, and when you speak relatively you must remember that certain clubs are taking as much in a League game to-day as they took in the whole of their League matches in the season that that organisation first sprang into existence. Therefore, even relatively high-priced men may be cheap.

The Football Association provides for the transfer of players from one club to another in rules 29 and 32. Rule 29 says: "Players may be transferred from one club to another" (see form H.), and "after the 1st of January, 1908, no club shall be entitled to pay or receive any transfer fee or other payment exceeding £350 upon or in respect of the transfer of any player." Rule 32 furthermore says: "The Council shall, subject to these rules, have power to cancel the registration of a professional at any time upon application of the player, or of his club, or may transfer him from one club to another. A professional transferred must be re-registered by the club to which he is transferred." The council will require to be satisfied that the transfer of players is bona fide, and applications for the purpose of obtaining players for special matches will not be acceded to.

The following is a reproduction of the Association's transfer form:

THE FOOTBALL ASSOCIATION, LIMITED.
FORM H. (RULES 29 AND 32.)

FORM FOR TRANSFER OF A PROFESSIONAL FROM ONE CLUB TO ANOTHER.

THE SECRETARY OF THE FOOTBALL ASSOCIATION, LIMITED,—
I am at present a Professional of the..... ....Club and Registered with The Football Association, Limited, and desire the Special Permission of the Council of The Football Association, Limited, to be transferred to the................................Club.

.... *Signature of Player.*

....
.... } *Postal Address.*

Date.................................
I desire the transfer of ....
from..Club
to..Club.
....................................Secretary.
....................................Address.

I assent to .... being transferred from....................................Club
to...Club.
....................................Secretary.
....................................Address.

The bitter opponents of the transfer system were shocked last season when Middlesborough gave Sunderland £1,000 for the transfer of Common. The Tee-side club was then in great danger of sinking into the Second Division. After Common's arrival Middlesborough managed to steer clear of the last two positions on the League table, and if, as many suppose, Common saved them from the Second Division, as Mr. Bassett justly remarks, he was worth the price paid. It is interesting to note that The Football Association has fixed the maximum limit of the transfer fee after January 1, 1908, at £350.

HOME PARK, PLYMOUTH ARGYLE'S PLAYING GROUND—THE ARGYLE v. SOUTHAMPTON.
A throw in from the line.

PLYMOUTH ARGYLE

Western League Champions, 1904-5.

By T. McLEOD.

The inception of the club—Entry into the Southern and Western Leagues—A strong team of players—First season's success—Great Cup-tie fight with Sheffield Wednesday—Old and new managers—Plymouth Argyle's fine showing in the Southern League in the season 1904-5—Historic draws with Newcastle United—Prospects of the season 1905-6.

Colours: Green shirts, black collars, white knickers. *Ground: Home Park, Plymouth.*

THOUGH, comparatively speaking, new to Southern and Western League football, the Plymouth Argyle Club has fully justified its existence. A little more than three years since, Association football in Devon—that is, Association football in so far as first-class teams are concerned—was practically unknown; in fact, the county has for more than a decade been looked upon as a veritable hotbed of the sister code. Five years ago such teams as Aston Villa, Sheffield Wednesday, Notts County, Southampton, Stoke, and Woolwich Arsenal paid visits to Plymouth for the purpose of playing exhibition games, and on each occasion a first-class professional club appeared in the western port the financial support accorded was particularly gratifying. Recognising, some three and a half years since, that it was time Devon took her proper place in the Association football world, a few sporting gentlemen, chief amongst whom were Lieutenant Windrum (who did so much for the Portsmouth Club in its early days), Messrs. Clarence Spooner, John Spooner, Guy Spooner, Stanley Spooner, A. V. Adlard, and, last but not least, Frank Davis, took the initial step in the formation of a professional club. A private meeting was called, and the advice of experts in the launching of a professional club obtained; in fact, the whole matter was thoroughly gone into, with the result that it was decided to run a club upon professional lines. A limited liability company was floated with a subscribed capital of £3,000. This did not include the beautiful ground at Home Park, which is the property of the Argyle Athletic Club. The ultimate financial success of the venture was questioned by many, who were of opinion that a professional side, run as it must be on first-class lines, would not receive in the Three Towns the amount of financial support necessary for its upkeep; in fact, the expression went forth that it would only be a "flash in the pan." But the gentlemen at the head of affairs held a diametrically opposite view, they were prepared to launch out their hundreds for the sake of sport, they had their backs to the wall, and did not intend to forsake their ground without a struggle. They have never looked back. The launching of the club was well received from the first by the local press, to whom the Argyle directors owe a deep debt of gratitude.

THE WESTERN LEAGUE CHALLENGE CUP.

The next thing was the obtaining of a manager. In this respect the choice was, indeed, a happy one. Mr. Frank Brettell, whose name is a household word in Association football circles, was given the helm of the Argyle ship to pilot her through her first voyage. He had a reputation second to none for initial successes. His efforts for Tottenham and Portsmouth are too well known to be tabulated in this resumé; suffice it to say Frank Brettell was the man to make the Argyle Club a success if the task were possible of accomplishment. "Frank," as he is familiarly known in the Three Towns, came to Plymouth, saw, and conquered; of that there cannot be a shadow of doubt.

The next move was to secure admittance to the Southern League. Upon this the future of the infant club absolutely depended. Therefore it was a great relief to learn that Argyle had been received with open arms by the Southern League clubs at that time competing, and the Plymouth directors are not unmindful of the helping hand extended to them at a time when help was sorely needed. Then came the announcement of the players who would do duty for Argyle in the opening season. They were: Robinson (English International and South-

Haddon.]
ANDREW CLARK,
The Argyle Captain.

This full-back, recognised as one of the most daring and fearless defenders in the Southern League, has been with Argyle since the club's inception. He hails from Fifeshire, and before joining his present club figured in the Hearts of Midlothian team and Stoke. He has no superior in the South as a left-back. He stands 5ft. 7in., and weighs 13st.

ampton goalkeeper), Andrew Clark (Stoke), Fitchett (Southampton), Archie Goodall (the Irish International), Banks (West Bromwich Albion captain), Leech (Stoke), Digweed (Portsmouth), Jack (Bolton Wanderers), Peddie (Manchester United), Picken (Bolton Wanderers), Dalrymple (Hearts of Midlothian), Wattie Anderson (Woolwich Arsenal), Winterhalder (Sheffield United), and C. Clark (Everton). Though with only fourteen players signed on, the critics throughout the South considered that Argyle had the making of a fine side, and that their opinion was justified was proved by the accomplishments of the club during the initial season.

The first season, both from a playing and financial point of view, was a success. Without going fully into the record of the club for the opening season, attention should be called to the fact that Argyle defeated all the best teams in the Southern League — Southampton, Tottenham Hotspur, Reading, Portsmouth, and Bristol Rovers. But these achievements were dwarfed by the great games with Sheffield Wednesday. After fighting through the qualifying and intermediate rounds of the great Cup competition, Argyle came into the first round proper. As luck would have it, the Plymouth club were drawn out of the hat with Sheffield Wednesday, but the Devonians had choice of ground. After a desperately hard game, the Argyle effected an eleventh hour draw, and in the re-play at Owlerton were defeated, but not disgraced.

The second season was even more successful than the first, Argyle coming out at the head of the Western League, thereby securing the valuable cup, and fourth in the Southern League, following home Bristol Rovers, Reading, and Southampton in the latter competition. But the outstanding achievement in the history of the Argyle Club is the splendid performances against Newcastle United in the English Cup competition. Curiously enough, last season Argyle were drawn, in the first round of the competition, with the winners of the First Division League, Newcastle United, as was the case with Sheffield Wednesday in the previous season. Argyle went to Newcastle, and, to the astonishment of the whole of the football world, ran the famous Novocastrians to a draw. At Plymouth in the re-played tie another draw resulted, and it was only at the third time of asking that Argyle were disposed of at Plumstead. The outcome of these brilliant performances was to secure for Argyle exemption this season from the qualifying rounds of the competition.

Haddon.]
PLYMOUTH ARGYLE'S MANAGER.

ROBERT JACK, the player-manager of the club, who stands 5ft. 10in. and weighs 11st. 7lb., is in his third season with the club. A Scotsman born and bred, he has played for Alloa Athletic, Bolton Wanderers (six years), Preston North End, and Glossop. He is the fastest man in the Argyle ranks, clever at beating an opponent, and never failing to centre with accuracy.

Haddon.]
J. W. SUTCLIFFE.

A Yorkshireman with the distinction of having played for England under both the Rugby and Association codes. Standing 6ft., and weighing 13½st., he has to be reckoned with as a defending force. Has played in the ranks of the Bolton Wanderers, Millwall, and Manchester United. Joined Argyle at the end of last season. His judgment and resource are as good as ever. Obtained his Rugby cap for England against the Maoris in 1888-9.

The club commenced the season 1905-6 with a considerably altered side. McLuckie, Picken, Dalrymple, Ashby, the Hodgkinsons, and Robinson did not again sign on, but capable substitutes were found in Sutcliffe (the ex-English International goalkeeper), McNeil (Hearts of Midlothian), Bauchop (Alloa, Scotland), T. Briercliffe (Woolwich Arsenal), T. Corrin (Reading), H. Wilcox, Buchanan (Middlesborough and Brentford), and Godley (Stoke). Another notable change in the personnel of the club this year has been the substitution of Mr. Robert Jack for Mr. Frank Brettell as manager. Mr. Brettell holds no official position in the organisation now, but he still retains a warm place in his heart for the Argyle Club. "The Plymouth Argyle F. C. was my last protégé, and will ever remain so," he says, "and I hope one day to see it taking the foremost honour of the English Cup." And who knows but what that honest and sincere wish of the ex-Argyle manager may be gratified before many more football seasons are past.

THE PLYMOUTH ARGYLE GROUND.

The ground at Home Park, situated about a mile and a half from Plymouth, is recognised as one of the best and prettiest in the South. It will accommodate 25,000 people, and is capable of unlimited extension.

PLYMOUTH ARGYLE FOOTBALL CLUB—THE PLAYERS. SEASON 1905-6

Back Row: J. Hughes (Asst Trainer). R. McNeil. P. Saul. H. M. Wilcox. W. Horne. R. Jack (Manager). J. W. Sutcliffe (Goalkeeper). A. Clark (Captain). T. Cleghorn (Trainer).

Hawke, Plymouth.]

Middle Row: F. W. Bauchop. T. Briercliffe. F. Buck. I. Owens. F. Crouch (Secretary). C. Clark. D. Buchanan. J. Wright (Sub-Captain). T. Corrin.

Bottom Row: W. Leech. J. Banks. W. Godley.

SUNDERLAND FOOTBALL CLUB.

"THE TEAM OF ALL THE TALENTS."

League Champions, 1891-2, 1892-3, 1894-5, 1901-2.

The rise and development of Sunderland F. C.—The ubiquitous Scotsmen—Arrival of Tom Watson, secretary—Sunderland admitted to the League in 1890—Early defeats end in a change of goalkeeper—The coming of Doig—The club win the League championship—Remarkable League record—Players' wages—A limited liability company formed—The disastrous season of 1896-7—A change of headquarters—Roker Park Ground secured—Fine struggle for League honours in 1900-1—The League championship won for the fourth time in 1901-2—The ground suspended—Troublous times—The present season and future outlook.

Colours: Red and white striped shirts, dark knickers. *Ground: Roker Park, Sunderland*

THE Sunderland Association Football Club originated from a team of school teachers, chief among whom was Mr. James Allan, at present a schoolmaster in the town, and who still takes a great interest in local football, particularly competitions having for their object the benefit of charitable institutions. Football was rather a novelty at this time (1880–1), and was played more for amusement than anything else. There were only a very few clubs in Durham County, which was federated with the neighbouring County of Northumberland. The game gained in popularity, and new clubs sprang up in different parts of the county, until it was eventually decided to establish the Durham Football Association.

The teachers' team meantime developed into the Sunderland Football Club, which with Darlington formed the chief support of the newly formed County Association. In 1887 Mr. Robert Thompson, J.P., a leading shipbuilder in the town, began to take an active interest in the club, and was elected president. Mr. Thompson was assisted in the management by a most capable committee, at the head of which was Mr. James Marr, who was elected chairman, and Mr. Samuel Tyzack, the club treasurer. The latter gentleman worked very hard and most successfully for the club, and it was mainly due to his efforts that the playing strength was increased by the importation of several prominent players from over the Border.

Culshaw.]
COUNCILLOR F. W. TAYLOR,
Chairman of the Board of Directors,
Sunderland F. C.

A difference in committee, however, led to a split in the club, and as a result a rival football combination was formed by the disaffected and retiring members, who had Mr. James Allan at their head. The new organisation, Sunderland Albion, however, only had a short reign, and after a very few seasons the promoters, owing to a lack of support, found it impossible to continue, and thus the opposition to the club soon collapsed.

In the season of 1887–8 the team was mainly composed of Scotsmen, and now began to make a name in the football world, it having by this time become the most important football combination in the County of Durham. In fact, the only serious rivals Sunderland had in the district were Middlesborough and Newcastle West End.

Towards the end of the season just named, Mr. Tom Watson—now of Liverpool—was elected secretary of the club, having previously acted in a similar capacity for the Newcastle West End.

The matches played by the team during the season 1888–9 were principally with Scottish teams, there being a difficulty in arranging with English clubs, owing to Sunderland not being members of the League. In the following season, 1890–1, the club was successful in obtaining admission to the League, but owing to Sunderland being situated so far away from the headquarters of the other clubs forming the League, the local management had to agree to pay the travelling expenses of the visiting teams.

The team commenced their first League season badly, for they were defeated by Burnley in the opening match by 3—2, and again two days afterwards by Wolverhampton Wanderers by 4—3, after leading by 3—0 at the interval. Both these were, by the way, home matches.

It is here worth mentioning that during five seasons the club only suffered three home defeats, two being those mentioned above, while the other victorious team was Blackburn Rovers. To return to the two defeats named above, several of the players blamed the goalkeeper for these, but whether there were any good grounds for the charges it is not for me to say. However a new goalkeeper was sought, and another visit was paid to the "land of oatmeal," with the result that John E. Doig, of Arbroath, a Scottish International, was engaged, and certainly from this time the club never looked behind.

On the Saturday following the disastrous opening matches, Sunderland went to West Bromwich and defeated the team of that name by no fewer than 4 goals to 0. The two points thus gained were, however, deducted, and the club was fined £50 by the League committee for breach of rule in having played Doig, who was then ineligible owing to insufficient registration.

At the end of this season the club managed to finish seventh, which, for the first season in the League, was considered most satisfactory. The club also reached the Semi-final of the English Cup competition, when they were defeated by Notts County, after playing a drawn game of 3 goals each.

Doig's record with the club was a brilliant one, and is worthy of special mention here. In six seasons he only missed three League games, and his ability was frequently recognised by his being selected to represent his country in International matches.

In the following season, 1891–2, the club won the League championship, and were again successful in reaching the Semi-final of the English Cup, when they were defeated by Aston Villa.

The season of 1892–3 again found the team showing up well, when they established what was at that time a record by winning the League championship with 48 points and scoring 100 goals in the series of matches, a thing never before equalled.

In 1893-4 the team finished second to Aston Villa, who also defeated the Wearsiders in the second round of the English Cup, after a drawn game at Sunderland.

The following season, 1894–5, saw Sunderland League champions for the third time, thus establishing another record. In this season the Semi-final of the English Cup competition was again reached, but the hopes of the club were once more

SUNDERLAND ASSOCIATION FOOTBALL CLUB—TEAM AND OFFICIALS, SEASON 1905-6.

Back Row: J. J. WILSON (Director). Councillor F. W. TAYLOR (Chairman). W. WILLIAMS (Trainer). W. FARQUHAR (Captain). E. RHODES. T. H. NAISBY. J. WATSON. A. BARRIE. ROBERT H. KYLE (Secretary). SAMUEL WILSON (Vice-chairman).

W. A. *Culshaw, Sunderland.*]

Front Row: W. HOGG. D. O'DONNELL. J. GEMMELL. R. MCKENZIE. A. BRIDGETT. H. BUCKLE. E. MCCONNELL. THE MAYOR, Councillor F. FOSTER, J.P. (Director). C. E. THOMPSON (Director).

Culshaw.]
A. BRIDGETT.

He is one of Sunderland's most popular forwards, and his sterling merit was not overlooked by the International selection committee, who gave him his cap for England v. Scotland, April, 1905.

shattered by Aston Villa. In 1895-6 the team did not do nearly so well, only finishing fifth in the League.

The success of the club from the time of being admitted to the League up to this date had been truly remarkable, and it was all the more so when it was remembered that the club never had a large number of players at command, from sixteen to twenty League professionals only being kept at these times. The wages were also very small compared with those of the present day, the average terms being something like £10 bonus on signing, and 30s. a week; of course, with one or two exceptions, these latter receiving £3 a week. When the success of the club was assured, £3 a week became the recognised wage of its first-team players. Among the men who served the club so well at this time were John E. Doig, Donald Gow—one of the finest backs ever seen—John R. Auld, Hughie Wilson, Johnnie Campbell, and Jimmy Miller. The forward division was made up as follows: J. Gillespie, J. Miller, J. Campbell, D. Hannah, and J. Scott, and a finer quintette could not be wished for. The team now became universally known as "The Team of All the Talents."

Culshaw.]
MR. R. H. KYLE,

The popular Sunderland secretary, hails from Belfast. He succeeded Mr. A. Mackie to the secretaryship at the opening of the season 1905-6.

In August, 1896, a change was made in the constitution of the club, it being then converted into a limited liability company with a capital of £5,000, divided into 5,000 shares of £1 each. Mr. Tom Watson severed his connection with the Sunderland Club on his appointment to the position of secretary to the Liverpool Club, and Mr. Robert Campbell was appointed to the vacancy.

From all points of view the season of 1896-7 was a most disastrous one, the team doing very badly, and consequently there was a decided falling off in support. The end of the season found the club last but one in the League table, and, in accordance with the rules then in force, the test matches had to be fought. Fortunately, after a very hard struggle, these were safely got through. In the last test match it may be mentioned that Sandy McAllister played a splendid game, and made his mark as a great player.

Among the matters of note which occurred during the next few years may be mentioned the severance from active work in connection with the club of Messrs. Robert Thompson, C. E. Thompson, S. Wilson, and J. T. Calvert, and the taking of their places by Messrs. John P. and James Henderson, Sinclair Todd, and one or two others. To these gentlemen the club is indebted in a great measure for the prominent position it now occupies.

When the club received notice to leave the Newcastle Road ground, a new home had, of course, to be sought, and it was entirely due to the chairman, Mr. J. P. Henderson, and his brother that the present home of the Sunderland Football Club was obtained. There was quite a distinguished company present at the opening of the ground, which was called Roker Park, and which is regarded as one of the finest in the country.

Another change in the management now took place. Mr. Campbell, the secretary, accepted a similar position with Bristol City A. F. C., and in filling the vacancy the directors considered it advisable to divide the work, and Mr. Alec. Mackie was appointed team manager and match secretary, and Mr. Alec Watson financial secretary. These two continued to look after the affairs of the club until, as is now well known, they were suspended along with the directors a year ago.

In the season of 1900-1 the team finished second in the League, after a most interesting struggle for premier position, the winners not being known until the last day but one of the season, when Liverpool, by defeating West Bromwich Albion, became the holders of the League Cup. The financial result of the season was, however, most satisfactory, a gain on the year's working of nearly a thousand pounds being shown against a loss during the previous season.

1901-2 was one of the most successful seasons in the history of the club, both from a playing and a financial point of view. The team succeeded in carrying off the League championship for the fourth time with the following good figures: Played, 34 matches—won 19, lost 9, drawn 6; goals for, 50; against, 35.

The following season, 1902-3, was not so successful from a playing point of view as its predecessor had been. There was again a keen struggle for the League championship, Sunderland finishing in the third position in the League table with the following record: Played, 34—won 16, lost 9, drawn 9; goals for, 51; against, 36.

Unfortunately, during the season just referred to, owing to the unruly conduct of a number of the spectators after the League match v. Sheffield Wednesday, the ground was suspended for a fortnight, and the League fixture v. Middlesborough, which should have been played at home, had to be played on St. James's Park, Newcastle, kindly lent by the directors of the Newcastle United A. F. C. The season of 1903-4 was one of the most unsuccessful seasons the club had ever experienced. The team only did very moderately in the League, and in the English Cup-ties was again beaten in the first round, this time by Manchester City. It was in this season that the trouble over the McCombie benefit match arose. The circumstances which led in the following season to the suspension of the directors and secretaries are well known and need not be again referred to in this article.

Owing to the circumstances referred to above, it was necessary that a new board of directors should be appointed to take the place of those who had come under the ban of the Football Association, and in October, 1904, Mr. F. W. Taylor was appointed chairman of the board, the other directors being Mr. S. Wilson (vice-chairman), Mr. S. Storey, Mr. C. E. Thompson, Mr. J. W. Taylor, jun., and Mr. F. Foster.

The team did fairly well in the League competition, but again were defeated in the first round of the English Cup.

In June of this year (1905) Mr. A. Mackie was appointed secretary and manager of the Middlesborough Club, and therefore resigned his position with Sunderland, after a very successful term of office. It may be mentioned here that during the last season the club received the record transfer fee for a player, Alf. Common, who was transferred to the Middlesborough Club for £1,000. At the annual meeting the retiring directors were unanimously re-elected, with the exception of Mr. J. W. Taylor, jun., who did not offer himself for re-election.

The board had now to look for a successor to Mr. Mackie, and in August they appointed Mr. R. H. Kyle, of Belfast, to the vacant position. Mr. Kyle had a splendid reputation as a football manager before coming to Sunderland, and there is no doubt but that he will justify the confidence of the directors, and prove the right man in the right place.

Culshaw.]
WILLIAM FARQUHAR,

Sunderland's captain, was born at Elgin in 1879. He stands 5ft. 7½in., and weighs 11st. 5lbs. He is a splendid half-back.

SOME FAMOUS FULL-BACKS

Parkin.]
JOHNSON
(*Sheffield United*).

Culshaw.]
WATSON
(*Sunderland*)

Stuart and Winfield.]
W. McCRACKEN
(*Newcastle United*).

Scott and Co.]
W. DUNLOP
(*Liverpool*).

Wilkes.]
STOKES
(*Birmingham*).

Elbourne.]
J. SHARP
(*Woolwich Arsenal*).

Arthur and Co.]
JONES
(*Wolverhampton Wanderers*).

George Newnes.]
A. TAIT
(*Tottenham Hotspur*).

Moyse.]
ROSS
(*Fulham*).

Howard Barrett.]

BRAMALL LANE, SHEFFIELD—THE HOME OF SHEFFIELD UNITED

One of the most famous League grounds in the kingdom.

THE LEAGUE AND THE LEAGUE SYSTEM

By WILLIAM McGREGOR (the Founder).

The invention of the League system—Its rapid growth and expansion—The rise of professionalism—My first circular to the clubs—The historic meeting at Anderton's Hotel—The title "The League" adopted—The second meeting at the Royal Hotel, Manchester—How the League system revived football in the Midlands—The power of the Press—High standard of play at once commands public attendance—The Cup and the League—The value of the League system to junior football—A popular fallacy exposed—Why the Football Association should always be the governing body.

FOOTBALL has seen many changes. Beginning as quite a desultory pastime, club matches were for long deemed the highest form of football fixture, because no other kind of fixture was known. Then, with increase of interest, came International matches; then district associations took shape, and we had interesting games between picked forces of those associations, and very attractive the games were. Then there came the professional era, and with it came the Football League. As the founder of the Football League, I suppose I am naturally looked to as its apologist. Well, there is not much to apologise for; there is much to explain. I suppose no institution ever founded in connection with a national pastime has been girded at so freely as the Football League. To some the very term "league" seems to act as a red rag is currently supposed to act to a bull. I have heard people say they hated, detested, and loathed the word "league." I have usually put these people down—I was going to say as brainless asses, but perhaps that would be too strong a term, so I will say as foolish people.

I do not see that the title of an organisation matters much; its scope and objects matter vitally. I wonder what would happen if you could blot out the league system from sport from this day onward? I wonder who would be the better for it? Ninety-nine players out of every hundred, and ninety-nine clubs out of every hundred, would be infinitely worse off, because no principle ever formulated in connection with sport has caused so much really genuine, bona-fide competition as the league system.

WILLIAM McGREGOR.

Mr. William McGregor was born at the little village of Braco, in Perthshire, in 1847, and first saw a football at the age of seven. When Mr. McGregor went to Birmingham thirty-five years ago he associated himself with Aston Villa, and has held every honorary office in connection with the club. Mr. McGregor founded the Football League in 1888, and was its first president. When he retired from the office he was elected a life member. He is vice-president and life member of Aston Villa, he represents the Birmingham Association on the council of the Football Association, being a member of the finance committee of that body, and he is a vice-president of the Staffordshire Football Association. He is president of the Birmingham Youths and Old Boys' Association, president of the Birmingham Wednesday Association, and president of the Birmingham Junior Charity Association. He is on the appeals committee of the Staffordshire Association, and also on that of the Birmingham League.

No sooner was the League formed than it was copied throughout the country, and now it is the accepted form of football strife. The colleges at Oxford and Cambridge play their matches on the league system, and they gain greatly in interest by reason of that. The man who says he loathes the word "league" is foolish, and there is an end to the argument.

There can be nothing objectionable in the term "league"; it is a simple principle; the principle is that each club identified with a certain body shall play every club connected with that body. What could be simpler, and what could be fairer and more complete, I cannot imagine.

If you put it to me that the first league ever originated in connection with football made itself somewhat unpopular by its selfish methods during its early history, then I will grant there was much to deplore. But we all make mistakes; every juvenile makes mistakes; possibly the Football League made mistakes during its infancy. It did, and the boycott that it established was calculated to do the organisation infinite harm. But the League legislators recognised that, and withdrew the boycott. To-day there are hundreds and hundreds of leagues in different parts of the country, well organised, and carrying on their competitions in a way creditable to themselves and convenient to the affiliated clubs. I regard the league as a great and imperishable system. It has spread from football to practically every phase of organised sport under the sun. We have our polo leagues, our air-gun leagues, our cricket leagues; and I say the man who declares that the principle is not a good one has the whole sporting world against him. It would scarcely have caught on as it did if it had not possessed good points, and many of them.

The League was originally established in the interests of a handful of senior clubs, the sole object the promoters had in view being to provide a regular and fixed programme for those Saturdays which were not given over to Association and other cup-ties. Prior to the inception of the League, fixtures had been kept or cancelled pretty much at the caprice of the clubs interested, and I recall one period in Aston Villa's history in which, owing to matches being written off at the last moment, and the operations of frost and bad weather, not a single game was played for five Saturdays.

People who rail at the League forget the state football was in at the time that the League was founded. It is a very easy matter to rail at the League, but if some of these wiseacres had been responsible for football government at the time that I introduced the system, they would have known that something of the kind was essential.

Football was rapidly going to the bad, and if something had not been done, I really believe that the game would have received a very severe check, and its popularity would have been paralysed once and for all. I am not saying that football would have died, because football will never die. Even if the time should come when it ceases to be the highly organised sport it is to-day, it will still be the pastime of the juveniles, because it is not easy to conceive the introduction of a game which will prove its superior.

It is all very well for people to talk about the iniquities of the League now that some of our clubs can make £5,000 a year, but they must put themselves into the position of the men who were face to face with a difficult problem at the time the League was brought into being. I was one of those men; I was connected with the management of Aston Villa—officially connected therewith. I may say that the late George Kynoch and I were responsible for the lease of the Aston Villa ground. Someone had to be responsible for these things, because Aston Villa was not then a limited liability company. In fact, people howled when I proposed it should be formed into one; but then people will howl at anything which is novel. It is all very well to howl, but when you are responsible for a lease, and when you get a handful of bills which have to be met, and no gate-money is coming in, then you want something more practical than howling.

The position was this. Professionalism had been introduced, and with the professional came the weekly wage list. Players had had money before, but if there was no money they did not have it; which was a very simple plan, an easily worked system for both club and players. I saw that the only way to meet these weekly wage lists was to obtain good gates. Good gates had become imperative. It seemed to me that if we could get twelve of the leading clubs to pledge themselves to play each other a regular course of matches, such matches to be regarded as inviolate, we should get the crowd regularly.

In the old days clubs were continually crying off engagements at the last moment owing to cup-ties, and poor worried secretaries used to have to rush about, wire, and write all over the country in order to get a match. Very often a match would be written off on the Friday. I have known a fixture wired off on the Saturday morning. Owing to the multiplicity of local cup competitions, clubs ceased to issue fixture cards, and most of our clubs were in a really parlous condition. How dreary

R. P. Gregson, F.R.P.S.]

THE LEAGUE MANAGEMENT COMMITTEE, 1903-4.

W. W. Hart. J. McKenna. H. S. Radford.

William McGregor. T. H. Sidney. J. J. Bentley. John Lewis. T. Charnley (Secretary).

some of the games were! No one enjoyed the really rousing games of old more than I did, but clubs were not then exempt from the preliminary rounds of local and national cup competitions, and it was not edifying to see a strong club beat a minor team by 26 goals to nil. You could not expect people to take interest in such fixtures, but the professionals' wage-bill was there, and it had to be met.

Accordingly, on March 2, 1888, I sent the following circular to Aston Villa, Bolton Wanderers, Blackburn Rovers, Preston North End, and West Bromwich Albion:

"Every year it is becoming more and more difficult for football clubs of any standing to meet their friendly engagements, and even arrange friendly matches. The consequence is that at the last moment, through cup-tie interferences, clubs are compelled to take on teams who will not attract the public. I beg to tender the following suggestion as a means of getting over the difficulty. That ten or twelve of the most prominent clubs in England combine to arrange home-and-home fixtures each season, the said fixtures to be arranged at a friendly conference about the same time as the International conference. This combination might be known as the Association Football Union, and could be managed by a representative from each club. Of course, this is in no way to interfere with the National Association; even the suggested matches might be played under cup-tie rules. However, this is a detail. My object in writing you at present is merely to draw your attention to the subject, and to suggest a friendly conference to discuss the matter more fully. I would take it as a favour if you would kindly think the matter over, and make whatever suggestion you may deem necessary. I am only writing to the following: Blackburn Rovers, Bolton Wanderers, Preston North End, West Bromwich Albion, and Aston Villa, and should like to hear what other clubs you would suggest.

"I am, yours very truly,

"William McGregor.

"P.S.—How would Friday, March 23, 1888, suit for the friendly conference at Anderton's Hotel, London?"

The replies from all the clubs were favourable. Mr. J. J. Bentley wrote to me as secretary of Bolton Wanderers, and gave it as his opinion that the first clubs chosen should be West Bromwich Albion, Preston North End, Aston Villa, Blackburn Rovers, Bolton Wanderers, Wolverhampton Wanderers, Accrington, Burnley, Old Carthusians, Halliwell, Notts County, Mitchell St. George's, and Stoke. In the second circular sent out by me, Accrington, Burnley, Wolverhampton Wanderers, Stoke, Notts, Preston North End, Bolton Wanderers, Blackburn Rovers, West Bromwich Albion, and Aston Villa were invited to meet at Anderton's Hotel, Fleet Street, London, on the night previous to West Bromwich Albion and Preston North End meeting in the English Cup Final at the Oval. The meeting unanimously approved of my suggestion. Later we had to find a name. I proposed that it should be called the Association Football Union, but many thought that this would be likely to cause confusion with the Rugby Union.

Then someone suggested "The League"; but that did not please me, for two reasons, I fancy. One was that, as a lad, I had heard far too much for my comfort of the solemn League and Covenant, and in the second place the Irish National League and the Irish Land League were so unpopular then that I jibbed at the word "league." However, I was soon brought to see

THE ENGLISH LEAGUE TEAM v. SCOTTISH LEAGUE.

First match in Scotland at Celtic Park, 1893.

W. McGregor. T. Clare. J. J. Bentley. J. Southworth. C. Perry. R. Molyneux. W. Rowley. H. Lockett.
W. I. Bassett. F. Geary. R. Howarth. H. Wood. J. Schofield.
T. Reynolds. Ernest Needham.

England won by 4 goals to 3.

that it was a good one, and so it became the Football League, with Mr. Harry Lockett, of Stoke, as hon. secretary, and myself as the first president.

This meeting was at the Royal Hotel, Manchester, on April 17, 1888, when the twelve clubs were selected and rules drawn up. The decision was that the League should consist of Preston North End, Aston Villa, West Bromwich Albion, Wolverhampton Wanderers, Bolton Wanderers, Everton, Notts County, Derby County, Stoke, Burnley, Accrington, and Blackburn Rovers. There were thus six Midland teams and six Lancashire teams. Many other clubs wanted to come in, but we could only see our way to having twenty-two vacant dates during the season, and so it was decided to keep to the twelve. They were all professional clubs, and each club was bound to play its strongest eleven in every match, under a penalty of forfeiting its position. The original idea was to pool the gates, and that was the reason why Everton were admitted, because they were not so powerful as the other clubs at that time, but were growing in power every day.

The rules were short and simple; they were five in number, with two additional ones with respect to referees.

The first contentious item we had to deal with was in regard to regulating the positions of the clubs according to merit. In the paper I read at the first meeting convened in connection with the League, I pointed out—and I really think I am entitled to some little credit for foreshadowing so accurately what happened—the help we were sure to get from the Press in regard to the publication of a weekly table of results. I do not mean to claim that I foresaw that the League table of the future would be of such supreme importance. Still, I did foresee that it would be one of the primary factors in maintaining interest in our doings. I consider that the publicity that the table has received has been one of the main factors in the success of the League competition, and I trust clubs will never forget the debt they owe to newspapers in this connection. If there had been no League table, there would assuredly not have been such widespread interest in the League as there is to-day.

What was the result of the starting of the League programme? Football immediately had a new lease of life. People knew that if a match was announced between Preston North End and Blackburn Rovers, they would see Preston and Blackburn at their best. They would see their strongest elevens, and they would see them fight with grim determination.

Now it may be that this highly competitive form of football has a few drawbacks, but there can be no doubt as to its many excellencies. Its chief excellency is that people like it, and will go to see it. People knew that they could rely upon watching an interesting game each week, and soon the attendance at League games became treble what they had been when the same matches were played as friendlies.

Of course, the League was started at an opportune time; just when Preston North End were at the zenith of their power. But under any conditions it would have been a success. It was a success from the start, and the League, as an organisation has gone on extending its power ever since. It has never had anything in the way of a set-back. The increase in League gates continued, and clubs found that the new order of things had given them what was so absolutely essential, viz., a certain income—an income which enabled them to concentrate their attention on the League, save for the four or five Saturdays when the English Cup competition claimed their attention; and that attention they were only too proud to give.

The remarkably high standard of play maintained in League games compelled the attendance of the public. Prior to the establishment of the League, players had been a law unto themselves. They had shown in-and-out form, varying their play according to the strength of their opponents. No one knew how to estimate the strength of the respective first-class clubs. After a team had been knocked out of the English Cup competition—possibly in the first round—all interest in their doings ceased for the season.

But in the League was discovered a system by which the true form of a club could be determined. The championship of the League does not fall to the team which happens to be in form during one portion of the winter only; it can only be secured by the eleven which has played consistently for the whole term of the competition. The League speedily showed its capacity for raising the standard of professional football throughout the country. The professional was producing big gates; and the labourer is worthy of his hire. His wages rose in relation to the amount of ability he displayed, such ability being represented, more or less, by the magnitude of the crowd which that ability drew.

The league system is as much the property of the amateur as of the professional. Most of the junior clubs are wholly amateur, but I do not know that they find their competitions any the less successful on that account. The league is not a bogey; it is a principle. The mere fact that the League happened to be initiated in the interests of a particular organisation, composed exclusively of professional teams, is no condemnation of the principle, which now obtains almost as much in cricket as in football.

At present, so far as strong teams are concerned, the League competition and the English Cup fit in nicely. Just as some teams may be feeling disappointed at the poor show they have made in the League, the English Cup competition comes along, full of thrilling uncertainty, and it comes along at an opportune time. Nothing will ever interfere with the popularity of the English Cup; it is sure to go on in its present form. But in various parts of the country we have cup competitions conducted on the league principle, and conducted with great success. At first there was a disposition to regard this as a dangerous innovation, but so long as the authority of the district association is paramount, I fail to see that it matters whether the competition under its auspices is upon the league or the knock-out principle. In a small association, whose competition does not embrace more than a dozen clubs, the running of that competition on

Howard Barrett.]

A SECTION OF A GREAT CROWD AT THE ASTON VILLA GROUND, ASTON, BIRMINGHAM.

One of the most famous football enclosures in the League.

league lines is a boon to the association. It rests with the association to turn the league system to their own purposes, and not to inveigh against it, as there was a tendency to do years ago.

In regard to junior football, the inauguration of the league system has been of profound value. It has given the youngsters competitions in which they can take an intelligent and consecutive interest right through the season. And I can assure you that the enthusiasm which the youngsters, as a whole, manifest in their various league tournaments is intense. Leagues, it is true, have crippled the local associations, and they have destroyed interest in the cup competitions, and have quite knocked on the head the old inter-association matches. This is to be deplored, but we live in a world of change, and governing bodies must adapt themselves to varying circumstances.

But the big League game has not killed the junior match. I remember the time when in any district if there was a big match one half the smaller clubs in the neighbourhood would cancel their games to go and watch the seniors play. But now the juniors have their own leagues. They play their games—which to them, at least, are of vital importance—and only take an academic interest in the doings of the senior clubs.

Now, surely, this must be approved by those who declaim against people watching football and say that they should all be playing. Never in the history of the game, I venture to say, has there been less interest in big games on the part of the juniors than there is to-day. Boys do go to see the big clubs play, but wherever you go you come across hundreds of small matches, and I can assure you that these small matches are more rigidly observed to-day than they were prior to the establishment of the league system. This is a great point in favour of the League.

The one evil of the league system is that in the very nature of things it is apt to visit lack of success with punishment out of all proportion to the offence. We know that the League was the cause of some old teams in Lancashire practically dying out. Some of them have revived since by becoming identified with sectional leagues. The tendency of the League is, in a sense, to concentrate interest in the doings of a few clubs. The few do exceptionally well at the expense of the many.

But, as I say, things are righting themselves somewhat, and to-day football of medium strength is flourishing in Lancashire.

There is one point which I must not forget. A league should never aspire to be a governing body. There was a time when I was disposed to think—and I believe I advocated the principle openly, so I must be candid about it—that the League should govern professional football; but, after all, I have come to see that it is best for the whole government of football to be in the hands of the Football Association. And, so far as I know, the leagues do not desire it to be in other hands. The League have their work to do; they have to look after their own interests, but they should not seek to govern. A body whose aims are necessarily selfish, as those of the League are, ought not to desire to be a governing body. When the League meet, they are actuated by the interests of the League clubs. The genera good of football is not then their chief concern.

The Football Association meets to control the game as a whole. It has no interest in professionalism; it has no interest in amateurism. It has to hold the scales fairly as between the two great sections of the football world. The League, in asking whether a certain thing is good for them, does not stop to think what its effect will be upon, say, the next thirty-six clubs outside. All this is natural, but still it unfits the League for being a governing body. All that it should aim at is to make its own competition successful, and leave the government of football to the body which naturally assumes such functions. This, I believe, the League are quite ready to do.

AN ECHO FROM THE PAST—THE BOLTON WANDERERS' TEAM OF THE EARLY EIGHTIES.

Back Row: KENNEDY. DOBSON. BROMILEY. MCKERNAN. STEEL. MR. J. PARKINSON (Umpire).
Front Row: HOWARTH. FALLON. STRUTHERS. GLEAVE. DAVENPORT. SCHOLES.

THE BOLTON CHARITY CUP.

Bolton Wanderers were frequent winners of the Charity Cup here depicted. Of the players, McKernan and Howarth have gone hence.

BLACKPOOL FOOTBALL CLUB.

FROM LANCASHIRE LEAGUE TO SECOND DIVISION.

By J. RAWCLIFFE.

The Blackpool Club established—First officials—Changes of ground—The Lancashire Junior Cup—The club joins the Lancashire League—Blackpool lose the championship through an inferior goal average—The championship won—The club enters the Second Division of the League—A limited liability company formed—A successful season—Back to the Lancashire League—Blackpool enters the Second Division again—Famous Blackpool players who have been transferred—Future prospects.

Colours: Red or claret shirts and light-blue knickers.

Ground: Bloomfield Road, South Shore, Blackpool.

THE Blackpool Football Club has had a long and varied career. Little did the promoters of the present club, when it was first formed in the early Seventies, think that it would occupy the position it does in the football world to-day. After being in existence for a few years, the first Blackpool Club, with practically no expenses, became defunct, and then Blackpool St. John's sprang up. This club played in Masheter's Field, off Caunce Street, and was principally composed of old scholars from St. John's School.

In consequence of a split amongst the players, a public meeting was called in 1887, and it was then decided to resuscitate the old club, and ever since there has been a Blackpool F. C.

Bamber, Blackpool.]
MR. C. RAMSDEN,
Chairman of the Blackpool Football Club.

The first officials were Alderman John Bickerstaffe, president; Mr. John Anderton, secretary; Mr. Joe Hill, treasurer; Councillor Sam Bancroft, Mr. Charles Whalley, Mr. Richard Swarbrick, Mr. Tom Todd, Mr. George McVittie, Mr. George Whittaker, and Mr. Sam Whittaker.

Notwithstanding the fact that the Blackpool Club has been in existence for close upon twenty years, yet only four grounds have been occupied. After playing for a time on a field off Bloomfield Road, a move was made to Raikes Hall, and many memorable encounters took place on this playing pitch. The next venue of play was the Athletic Grounds; but as this was considered to be rather too far from the centre of the town, the officials of the club decided to go back to the old Raikes Hall pitch. Subsequently the Raikes Hall estate was offered for sale by public auction, and, upon it being opened out for building purposes, the club had no option but to seek a new ground, and they again removed to Bloomfield Road, where they have remained ever since.

Few clubs have done so well as Blackpool in the Lancashire Junior Cup competition. The very first time the trophy was put up for competition they ran into the semi-final, being beaten at Southport by 3 goals to 1 by Darwen Rovers. In the season of 1887–8 they achieved the height of their ambition by carrying off the cup, their opponents in the final being Preston St. Joseph's. The following year they ran into the final, and after a drawn game they were beaten by Oswaldtwistle Rovers.

In 1889–90 the "Seasiders" had again an excellent chance of annexing the cup, and probably they would have done so had it not been for an unfortunate accident which occurred in the semi-final. Two old opponents in Blackpool and Fleetwood Rangers met at Preston, and "Billy" Corry, a capital forward at that time, had the misfortune to break his leg. Notwithstanding this Blackpool proved victorious, only to be beaten in the final round, which was played at Blackburn, by Bury.

The following year—1890–1—Blackpool again returned with the cup, defeating Ardwick at Preston in the final round by 3 goals to 0. This was the very last time they ever won the Junior Cup.

When the Lancashire League was formed in 1888, Blackpool were one of the first clubs to join, and their record in this league is exceedingly creditable. In 1890–1 they finished second to Bury, the latter obtaining 33 points out of 20 games, whilst Blackpool came three points short. In the following season the Lancashire League was increased to twelve clubs, and, strange to say, Bury again carried off the championship with 40 points, Blackpool being second with five points less.

The next season saw a remarkable incident in connection with the championship of the Lancashire League. Liverpool had a very strong team that year, but Blackpool defeated them both at home and away. When the last league match was played in April, the two teams had obtained exactly the same number of points, viz., 36; but the Mersey-side team secured the championship in consequence of having a superior goal average. The full record of the clubs was as under:

	Played	Won	Lost	Drn.	For	Agst.	Pts.
Liverpool	22	17	3	2	66	19	36
Blackpool	22	17	3	2	82	31	36

In 1893–4 Blackpool again made their presence felt in the Lancashire League, and after a desperate struggle they carried off the championship, their old antagonists—Bury—being three points behind them. Blackpool secured 33 points out of 22 games, and Bury 30 out of a similar number of matches. In the following season the league was further extended to fourteen clubs, and after a most exciting fight Fairfield proved the champions with 37 points, and Blackpool were the runners-up with 34 points.

It was then decided to apply for admission into the Second Division of the League, and in the circular which was sent out to the different clubs it was stated that "during the past seven years Blackpool have been every year in the first twelve clubs in the averages for the United Kingdom, and at the end of last season won the third position. At present we occupy about the fifth. If elected to the Second Division, we shall do our best to maintain a team that will hold an advanced position, and do credit to the Blackpool Club and the Second Division." However, the application proved unsuccessful, and the team was destined to remain for another season in the Lancashire League. Nelson won the championship that year with 48 points, sixteen clubs then being in the league. Blackpool finished thirteenth in the list with 28 points, and they had to be re-elected to the league.

However, notwithstanding their poor position in the Lancashire League, they again applied for admission to the Second Division, and this time they proved successful. It was then decided to form the club into a limited liability company, with £1,000 share capital, and the first directors were Mr. Whittaker Bond (chairman), Mr. Edward Little, Mr. Richard Swarbrick, Mr. John Walmsley, Mr. Leonard Seed, and Mr. Thomas Sefton (secretary).

A match committee was also formed, consisting of Mr. Albert Bond, Mr. George Gettins, Mr. George Whittaker, and Mr. J Holden.

The first season the club was in the Second Division was the most successful, so far as attendances were concerned, that has ever been experienced. Many competent judges also aver—and with some justification, too—that the team that season was the best which has ever been got together since the formation of the company. At all events, during the first season in the Second Division, Blackpool finished sixth with 31 points, and only once since, viz., in 1900-1, have they obtained a similar number. In the latter year there were more clubs in the League, and Blackpool finished twelfth in the list. The team included: Douglas, goal; Bowman and Parr, backs; Norris, Stirzaker, Stewart, Thompson, and Colville, half-backs; Clarkin, Donnelly, Clarke, Bradshaw, Parkinson, Winstanley, and Martin, forwards.

In the following season the club finished eleventh on the list with 25 points, and in 1898-9 they were in the dreaded last three, and failed to obtain re-election to the Second Division. They accordingly returned to the Lancashire League; but after being there for one season, they were again admitted into League football, and here they have remained ever since.

Owing to the meagre support which the club receives, considering the class of clubs which they oppose, it is impossible for the officials to pay the limit wage, and during recent years very few players have received summer pay. The majority of the team work hard during the week, and they cannot possibly be expected to be in the same condition as players who are always in strict training. This, no doubt, accounts for their position during the last few seasons in the League, for they have generally been found hovering about the bottom of the list.

Bamber, Blackpool.]
MR. T. A. BARCROFT,
Secretary of the Blackpool Football Club.

In 1900-1 they were twelfth with 31 points; in 1901-2 they were in the same position with 29 points; in 1902-3 they were thirteenth with 28 points; in 1903-4 they finished fifteenth with 27 points; and last season they again secured 28 points. The form of the team last year proved so unsatisfactory that the directors decided to make a sweeping change, and a totally new forward rank was secured. Up to the present, however, the new players cannot be said to have done themselves credit. The truth is they lack experience.

The club, however, have accomplished one performance this season which they have never done before. They ran into the semi-final round of the Lancashire Senior Cup, being finally beaten at Preston in a re-played tie with Accrington Stanley by 1 goal to 0. The Blackpool Club also won the Fylde Cup in 1887-8, 1889-90, and 1890-1.

There are probably few Second Division clubs that have transferred more players than the Blackpool F. C. Many noted players have made their mark with the seaside club, but when a substantial offer has been made by a wealthy club, the directors, owing to the impoverished state of the exchequer, have perforce had to part with the men. This, to a large extent, accounts for the poor performances of the club in the Second Division. If Blackpool had parted with none of their players, they would at the present time have a very fine team.

Perhaps the most noted players who have been transferred from Blackpool are J. Cox (Liverpool), J. Birchall (Blackburn Rovers), F. Pentland (Blackburn Rovers), H. P. Hardman (Everton), J. J. Morris (Notts County), R. Norris (Notts Forest), T. Bowman (Aston Villa), F. Griffiths (Preston North End), McEwen (Bolton Wanderers), T. Wolstenholme (Bolton Wanderers), Clarkin (Burnley), G. Colville (Glossop), Edgar Chadwick (Glossop), J. Martin (Walsall), J. Clarke (Luton), R. Hogg (Luton), R. Parkinson (Notts Forest), and T. Bradshaw (Sunderland).

It is not generally known that negotiations had been completed with Sunderland for the transfer of Wilson, a promising half-back, at a very substantial figure, but, before arrangements were finally completed and the transfer money paid, Wilson was seized with an illness which unfortunately proved fatal. It is also worthy of note that Blackpool were the first club to approach Peter McBride, the Scottish International and present goalkeeper for Preston North End, but at that time he refused to cross the Border.

Whilst playing with Blackpool, Griffiths was chosen to play for Wales, and, since they were transferred, both J. Cox and H. P. Hardman have been honoured with International caps.

Considering the size of the seaside town, the Blackpool Club is not supported as it ought to be; and in order to make both ends meet, as the saying goes, the officials have no option but to transfer their best players when they get a big sum offered, and —as was the case last season with Bristol City—they have had to change the venue of their Cup-ties when offered a substantial guarantee.

However, it speaks well for the judgment of the officials that they are able to "spot" promising young players and bring them out, and the policy adopted last season of watching minor clubs, with the object of picking out a player who is likely to turn out a star artiste—a la the theatrical bill—is one to be commended. Some supporters think it would be better if the club joined the Lancashire Combination, and were run at less expense; but so long as the present management control the club there is little doubt that an effort will always be made to maintain a Second Division club in Blackpool.

J. P. Bamber, Blackpool.]
THE BLACKPOOL FOOTBALL CLUB ENCLOSURE AT BLOOMFIELD ROAD, SOUTH SHORE, BLACKPOOL.

BLACKPOOL FOOTBALL CLUB—THE PLAYERS, SEASON 1905-6.

Back Row: MILLER (Asst.-Trainer). H. E. LEIVERS (Asst.-Sec.). JOHNSON. HULL. RILEY. BIRKET. DORRINGTON. PARKINSON. LOWE. THRELFALL. ROTHWELL (Trainer).

R. Scott and Co., Manchester.]

Middle Row: RAISBECK. REILLY. DUCKWORTH. BATE. JONES. T. A. BARCROFT (Hon. Sec.). HANCOCK. BENNETT. LAVERY. CONNOR. SCOTT.

Front Row: ANDERTON DARLINGTON. CREWDSON FRANCIS. GOW.

Stephen Cribb, Southsea.]

PORTSMOUTH'S MAGNIFICENT FOOTBALL ENCLOSURE AT FRATTON PARK.

The Fratton goal, looking west.

THE PROGRESS OF PORTSMOUTH FOOTBALL CLUB.

By P. G. WHITMEY.

The educational influence of Army football in Portsmouth—The historic meeting in April, 1898, and formation of the Portsmouth F. C. upon a limited liability basis—The splendid equipment of Fratton Park—First season's record—Unsatisfactory financial position of the club after two seasons' work—A grand revival and a period of prosperity—Present season's players.

Colours : Pink shirts, white knickers. *Ground : Fratton Park, Portsmouth.*

THE inhabitants of the great naval port were educated up to Association football very gradually, and it is entirely due to the Royal Artillery Football Club that a professional team exists. The Royal Artillery, under the guidance of Sergeant-Major (now Lieutenant) F. Windrum and Sergeant R. Bonney (now the manager of the Portsmouth Club), created a public liking for the game, and the attendances at the matches during the time the team figured in the First Division of the Southern League gave promise of great things if a professional team could be started. The idea developed rapidly, and on April 5, 1898, a meeting of several influential gentlemen was held, at which it was resolved to form a syndicate with a limited liability to acquire a piece of land in Goldsmith's Avenue, Fratton—now known as Fratton Park—at £1,100 an acre, the purchase being completed for £4,950. Thus was founded a club which, from its inception, created a name for itself. The company was formed with a capital of £8,000, in £1 shares, and one very successful condition made was that any purchaser of twenty-five shares would be entitled to a seat on the grand stand in perpetuity for all matches except English Cup-ties.

This proved a great inducement, and at the present time the company finds itself in the happy and proud position of having the whole of its capital subscribed, and a ground second to none in the South. During last summer a very fine clubhouse was erected over the main entrance in Frogmore Road, with board-room, manager's office, reading and card room, and billiard-room for the players, with spacious lavatories and bar.

The embankments round the playing pitch have year by year been built up, and now provide accommodation for a big crowd, and during this summer have been terraced, thereby enabling everyone of the 30,000 which the ground is capable of holding to have a good view. The dressing-rooms both for the visiting and home teams have been entirely renovated, and contain hot and cold water baths and shower baths. The referee, too, has not been forgotten ; his comfort has been made a first study. A bath is provided for him with hot and cold water and every convenience.

The board of directors comprises Sir John Brickwood, chairman, head of the firm of Brickwood & Co., Ltd., the largest brewery firm in the district, John Wyatt Peters, Esq., Alfred H. Bone, Esq., G. L. Oliver, Esq., chairman of the finance committee, W. Wigginton, Esq., John E. Pink, Esq., ex-mayor of the borough, who succeeded Lieutenant F. Windrum on his departure for Plymouth, and B. Murtough, Esq.

The secretaryship of the company has been in the hands of Mr. P. G. Whitmey from the start.

After the formation of the club was completed, the directors engaged Mr. Frank Brettell, from Tottenham, as manager, and delegated to him the responsibility of getting a team which would be capable of more than holding its own in the Southern League. How well Brettell—than whom no better judge of a player exists—fulfilled his mission is demonstrated by the results of the first season's work, from a playing point of view,

PORTSMOUTH FOOTBALL CLUB—PLAYERS AND OFFICIALS, SEASON 1905-6.

Back Row (from left to right): P. G. WHITMEY (Secretary). COWPER (Asst.-Trainer). STEWART. WALKER. BOWMAN. HARRIS (Goal). G. L. OLIVER (Director). SIR JOHN BRICKWOOD. A. H. BONE. B. M'RTOUGH. COOK (Goal). McDONALD. DIGWEED. HALLIDAY. H. WOOD (Trainer).

Cribb, Southsea.]

Middle Row: WARRINGTON. ARCHIBALD. HUNTER. HUGHES. S. SMITH. BUICK (Captain). LEE. MOLYNEUX. JACKSON. R. BONNEY (Manager).

Front Row: BRITTAN. W. SMITH. KIRBY. HOLDEN. CUNLIFFE. DIDYMUS. SALTER. HICKLETON.

Cribb, Southsea.]
THE SPLENDID NEW PAVILION AT FRATTON PARK.
It contains the board-room, manager's office, reading and card-room, and billiard-room for the players, and stands at the Frogmore Road entrance to the ground.

which reads as follows: 1st team—Played, 63; won, 42; lost, 15; drawn, 6. Goals for, 140; against, 70. 2nd team—Played, 31; won, 18; lost, 9; drawn, 4. Goals for, 103; against, 40.

The team obtained second position in the Southern League and third in the Southern District Combination—truly a wonderful record for a new club.

The financial results, however, both in the first and second seasons were far from satisfactory, for at the end of the second the audit of the accounts showed a deficit of £1,530 to date. However, better times were in store, and the close of the following season saw a profit of £1,939 declared, which wiped out the loss previously made, and gave encouragement to the directors to persevere in their go-ahead policy, which next season produced an even better result, no less a sum than £2,045 being declared as profit on the year's work, enabling them to write off £413 for preliminary expenses and pay a dividend of 5 per cent. on the capital.

The season 1903–4 also showed a profit, although somewhat smaller, amounting to £593, but a sum of £100 was written off the accounts for depreciation of stands and buildings, thus reducing the amount of the net profit to date; but following the precept of the season before another 5 per cent. dividend was declared, which materially helped the club to dispose of the bulk of its unallotted capital.

The season 1904–5 was a very successful one, a profit of £1,032 being made on the year's work, thus enabling the directors, for the third year in succession, to declare a dividend of 5 per cent., the utmost limit allowed by the Football Association. A further sum of £125 was also written off for depreciation. It was universally admitted that the value of the ground having increased tremendously since it was bought it would suffice to write off depreciation from stands and buildings only, and take no account of the appreciation.

From the foregoing facts it will be seen that the club is in a prosperous state, and on a sound financial footing. It will now be interesting to see what players were engaged by Mr. Brettell for the first season. In goal was Mat. Reilly, the well-known Royal Artillery custodian, who had made a name for himself by his peculiar trick of bouncing the ball, and to whom a great deal of the success of the "Gunners" was due. At back was also another Royal Artillery player, H. Turner, and Tom Wilkie from Liverpool; while during the season Bob Struthers was transferred from Gravesend. At half the club was ably served by Bob Blyth from Preston, Harry Stringfellow, and T. Cleghorn; while Marshall and Cunliffe formed the right wing, Sandy Brown was at centre, and W. Smith and Clark were the left-wing pair. Of these players, the only ones now remaining are Danny Cunliffe and W. Smith. The last-named was awarded a benefit on November 8, when Reading were met in the Western League.

The trainer for the first two seasons was W. Brierley, He was succeeded by Joe Clayton, from Newton Heath, who remained with the club until April 30 last, when he was succeeded by Harry Wood, Southampton's popular skipper. This year the directors have engaged a second trainer in the person of T. Cowper, from Wellingborough, it being thought that, with twenty-six professionals, besides many local amateurs signed on, there would be more than one man could attend to.

The players signed on for the present season are: Harris and Cook, goal; Molyneux, Walker, Stewart, Archibald, and Brittan, backs; Bowman, Buick (captain), McDonald, Jackson, Digweed, Halliday, and Hickleton, half-backs; Warrington, Kirby, D. Cunliffe, Hunter, Lee, W. Smith, Steve Smith, Hughes, Holden, Salter, Didymus, and Corbin, forwards; while the club has also the invaluable assistance at times of Messrs. S. S. Harris and E. G. D. Wright, the noted Corinthian left wing.

Cribb, Southsea.]
A FINE VIEW OF THE FRATTON PARK ENCLOSURE, LOOKING EAST.
Portsmouth playing arena will accommodate 30,000 persons, each of whom can witness the game in comfort, and the club is to be congratulated upon the success which has attended its energy and enterprise.

Bowden Bros.]

UNIVERSITY FOOTBALL—OXFORD v. CAMBRIDGE AT QUEEN'S CLUB, 1905.
An exciting moment in front of the Cambridge goal.

UNIVERSITY FOOTBALL (ASSOCIATION).

By STANLEY S. HARRIS.

How a 'Varsity team is chosen—The first match of the year—The Freshmen's matches—How the 'Varsity ground is shared—Indifferent form of 'Varsity "Soccer" teams—Special training not necessary—The Captain's trials—The Cambridge fixture-card—The 'Varsity style—The League system in 'Varsity football—Arranging the fixtures—College games—Cup-ties at Oxford—The Corinthians—Famous 'Varsity Blues.

UNIVERSITY football under the Association code is run on much the same lines at both Universities. Up till quite recently, however, there was a certain difference, inasmuch as, while Cambridge had a league competition for the respective colleges, Oxford always held a cup competition on the "knock-out" system. The latter, a year or two back, while still keeping up the cup-ties, also started a league on the same lines as Cambridge. These competitions are intended to stimulate the keenness in the internal football of the 'Varsity, and thus work towards one common end, namely, to give every possible chance to the authorities to turn out the best representative team to play for the 'Varsity as a whole. More as to this later on.

The 'Varsity team is usually chosen by a committee, in which the captain is, or should be, the predominating voice. Whether committees are desirable things or not is a matter of opinion. Personally, my experience of them during my first three years was so unsatisfactory that I resolved to do without one during my year of captaincy and manage the matter alone in conjunction with S. G. Luker, who was then hon. sec. Most fortunately matters went well throughout the season, but I am told that, had things been a failure, there would have been a great deal of criticism levelled at our action. Well, it is, as I have said, the business of this committee to choose the 'Varsity team, and the captain chooses the committee; their task is no easy one, and the fact that, very frequently, each member of the committee has a different opinion, makes it no lighter. If the captain is a decisive person, however, he will take his own way, and merely have a nominal committee to bear some of the responsibility if things turn out badly.

The first match of the 'Varsity year is the Seniors' match; in this game are included all the best players in the 'Varsity—Freshmen excepted—who have failed to get their "Blue."

On the next day follows the Freshmen's match, in which each side is captained by a "Blue." It is usually a fairly easy matter to make up the sides for this match, as the players' reputations precede them to the 'Varsity; and also the college captains, in sending up the names of the Freshmen whom they consider worthy of trial, are invited to comment on the form they have shown. It happens occasionally that a man who has come from a private school is overlooked for a time; and there is certainly no doubt that it is a great advantage to come from a well-known "Soccer" school—such as Charterhouse, Malvern, Westminster, &c.—as it is generally expected at the 'Varsity that anyone turned out by such places must have a certain amount of football in them: it frequently happens, indeed, that a man with a big reputation at school will receive a prolonged trial, even if his form at the 'Varsity is very ordinary; this is often a great mistake, for it may easily happen that a man may show fine form in the class of football played at the best schools, and yet be quite incapable of taking a prominent part in first-class football.

The Seniors' and Freshmen's games give the captain some idea as to whom to play in his first match, the result of which is usually unsatisfactory, for the reason that the players have had no opportunity of getting together. It is curious to notice, however, the different results of this first match. During my time at Cambridge we always played the London Caledonians; the first two years we administered crushing defeats on each occasion, and yet the subsequent career of those two 'Varsity teams was by no means great. In the third year, when we had a season of unparalleled success, we all performed like novices in the first match, and the London Caledonians beat us by 2 goals to 1, being, as it turned out, the only amateur team in England to defeat us. There are usually extensive alterations in the team after the first game; as, of course, it is of the utmost importance to get the eleven settled as soon as possible. And there should be no need, bar accidents, to make any changes after the fourth match, by which time one has had ample opportunity to judge of the material at hand and get together the strongest possible team.

Of late years, at Cambridge, far more matches have been played away than at home; the reason has been that the Rugby authorities always arranged their card first, and usually left very few possible dates for the sister game. An effort was made three years back to remedy this, and since the Rugby captain at that time was quite willing to help in every way, matters were placed on a much more equal and satisfactory basis. A glance at this year's card tells me that the 'Varsity ground is still shared fairly evenly, and I sincerely hope that matters will never return to the old state; for people cannot expect the 'Varsity, as a whole, to take a keen interest in the doings of a team which they scarcely ever see play.

'VARSITY (ASSOCIATION) FOOTBALL—OXFORD v. CAMBRIDGE, 1905.
Cambridge make a dash. The left-winger centres the ball.

It is, from our point of view, a lamentable fact that, whereas the Association game, in England generally, arouses far more wide-spread interest than the Rugby, at the Universities it is the reverse. Probably the reason is that, of late years, while the 'Varsity Rugby teams have usually been among the best in the kingdom, the "Soccer" teams, with the exception of the Cambridge eleven of 1903-4, have not been able to adequately hold their own with the better professional sides. There is promise this season of a good team at Cambridge, a promise which all lovers of amateur football sincerely hope to see fulfilled.

It would be a thousand pities for 'Varsity play to fall below the standard of first-class football; one's love of the 'Varsity is such that it is galling to see her defeated by teams who should not be her superior.

No extensive training is done at the 'Varsity; it is not really necessary. In addition to the representative matches, one has all the college league and cup contests, and players soon attain a state of fitness not to be surpassed.

The inter-University match is always played at Queen's Club, usually in the month of February. The new players are awarded their "Blues" about a week before the event; it is a very rare occurrence for a player, however good, to be given his "Blue" early in the season. I wonder if any cap or colours exist which are more keenly coveted than a "Blue"! I greatly doubt it.

To captain a 'Varsity side with success is no easy matter. It is, of course, impossible to give satisfaction to everyone, for one will always find that nearly every college have their "spot" man or men who, in their opinion, are without equal in the place. How often one hears the remark: "Why on earth can't they give So-and-so a shot? He's far the best centre-half in Cambridge"—and so on. But it may be said that the 'Varsity captain, if he does his duty in the way of watching college matches, may be relied on to get together the best team possible, in spite of what the grumblers say.

Just a glance at the Cambridge fixture-card. We find that there is very little variation from year to year. The Casuals are met twice every season; this match is usually a good one, as the Casuals are able, of course, to put in a pretty warm side. The 'Varsity, however, of late years at any rate, have usually been successful. Then both 'Varsities have a match against Ludgrove Masters, captained by G. O. Smith; while a match of a similar sort is played by Cambridge at Queen's Club against a team got up by C. Wreford-Brown. Three or four matches against professional teams are played by Cambridge; while Oxford, evidently believers in practice against professionals, play rather more. A few Old Boy teams are met, but these do not, as a general rule, provide such a good test for the 'Varsity. Still, it would be a great pity to abandon such fixtures, as they provide, what is all too rare in these days, games in which one finds the good, vigorous football of the old days, when one did not hear the whistle every minute for a hard charge or a robust piece of play.

'VARSITY (ASSOCIATION) FOOTBALL—OXFORD v. CAMBRIDGE, 1904.
Smart dribbling by Oxford. The halves beaten

Let us now turn from the 'Varsity eleven to football as it is played in the 'Varsity itself. There are at Cambridge three divisions of the league, conducted on the same system as the Football League—that is, two points for a win, and one each for a draw. At the beginning of each season a league secretary is appointed, whose duty it is to arrange all the matches before the commencement of term. The secretary's task is by no means an enviable one; there are, if I remember right, about 140 or 150 matches to be arranged, and it is necessary to avoid all days on which there is a 'Varsity match, all days on which there are cup-ties, and also, if possible, Saturdays, as so many people go up to town to play on that day. I know, from personal experience, what a business it is to fix up these matches; for, three years ago, when A. F. Leach Lewis was secretary, he and I spent seven hours in an hotel at Prague, and then another seven or eight hours in the train from Prague to Flushing, I think it was, in our endeavours to get the matter satisfactorily settled.

Every college plays home-and-home matches with every other college. No match may be scratched without the permission of the league secretary or 'Varsity captain, and then only in the event of a University examination, or if the ground is unfit for play. Up to the present, Pembroke have been top of the league table more than any other college. They have had some remarkable sides; on one occasion there were six "Blues" in the team, including S. S. Taylor, L. J. Moon, A. R. Haig-Brown, and H. S. Snell.

OXFORD v. CAMBRIDGE, 1903.

Booker makes a fine run.

At Oxford, in addition to the league, they have the cup-ties which, as I have mentioned before, are played on the "knock-out" system. Oriel has, with a few exceptions, proved itself the strongest team; occasionally, Christ Church and Magdalen have a look in, but it is not often that any other college can overcome Oriel, whose team is, as a rule, largely composed of Old Carthusians. As regards the college friendly matches, a meeting for all the college captains and secretaries is held at the beginning of the season, at which they arrange all the matches for the ensuing year.

Cambridge and Oxford are mainly responsible for the existence of the Corinthians; year after year the best players at each 'Varsity are tried, and then, after they have finished their residence, the elect are chosen regular members of the Corinthian F. C., and thus the two 'Varsities combine to support the greatest of our amateur clubs. After the Corinthians, it is to the 'Varsities that one looks for the most perfect example of amateur play; there the game is played for the love of sport; a deliberate foul is a thing unknown; plenty of hard charging there is, if you like—charging which might be given a foul in our modern-day professional football—but at the 'Varsities they do not mind vigorous play, because they know it will always be fair.

It may be interesting to note some of the men famous in football who belong to the 'Varsities. In the Cambridge team of 1884 we find, for the first time, such names as R. T. Squire, A. M. Walters, A. T. B. Dunn, and W. N. Cobbold, all four Internationals of the first rank; needless to say, Cambridge won the 'Varsity match that year. In the following year P. M. Walters made his appearance at back in the Oxford team. In 1888 C. Wreford-Brown is found playing for Oxford, while J. G. Veitch, Lindley, and Cotterill are representing the sister University. In 1892 we have C. B. Fry at back for the Dark Blues, with M. H. Stanborough on the side of his opponents. In the following year our greatest centre-forward, G. O. Smith, comes in for Oxford, while that famous player, W. J. Oakley, partners Fry at back; on the other side, L. V. Lodge is the best-known player.

From 1894, up to the present time, the most notable players turned out by Oxford have been C. D. Hewitt, B. O. Corbett, G. C. Vassal, W. U. Timmis, M. Morgan-Owen, R. E. Foster, W. Blackburn, G. E. Wilkinson, and O. T. Norris; while for Cambridge we read of C. O. S. Hatton, G. S. Wilson, T. T. N. Perkins, G. P. Dewhurst, C. J. Burnup, E. H. Bray, S. S. Taylor, C. L. Alexander, H. Vickers, H. O. C. Beasley, L. J. Moon, W. Campbell, R. N. R. Blaker, P. P. Braithwaite, R. G. Wright, T. S. Rowlandson, C. C. Page, and E. G. D. Wright. It would take a great deal too long to mention all the great players who have come from the 'Varsities, and therefore I have chosen a few from the many, in an endeavour to show what a great and important part the Cambridge and Oxford teams play in the world of football.

Bowden Bros.]

UNIVERSITY (ASSOCIATION) FOOTBALL—OXFORD v. CAMBRIDGE AT QUEEN'S CLUB, 1905.

Clever passing by Cambridge.

THE FAMOUS SHEFFIELD WEDNESDAY FOOTBALL CLUB.

Winners of the Football Association Cup, 1895-6; Finalists, 1889-90. Winners of the League Championship, 1902-3, 1903-4.

The home of Association football—Early games at Sheffield—Wednesday's first cup—J. C. and W. E. Clegg—Sheffield play London—The Sheffield Association Challenge Cup—A sensational Final Tie—The two first Scottish professionals from o'er the Border—Sheffield Wednesday as Cup-fighters—The Cup won in 1896—The Olive Grove Ground opened—Wednesday enter the League—Dark days—The club moves to the Owlerton enclosure—Wednesday receive influential support—Back to the First Division of the League—The championship twice won—Famous players who have worn the blue-and-white.

Colours: Blue and white striped shirts, navy-blue knickers. *Ground: Owlerton, Sheffield.*

FEW clubs in the country can boast a longer or more honourable record, than Sheffield Wednesday; indeed, of the leading organisations, Nottingham Forest and Stoke alone can claim prior existence. Sheffield may be described almost as the home of Association football, and in the early Sixties, when the game was being played in a haphazard sort of way up and down the country, the town could boast a dozen good clubs whose keen rivalry led to many exciting contests. To present-day footballers in the cutlery capital, such names as Broomhall, Garrick, Wellington, Pitsmon, and Mechanics are unknown, yet these clubs, along with Heeley and Hallam and Sheffield Club—the two latter the only ones now left—were playing football when Wednesday was simply a cricket club. It was in September, 1866, or nine years after Hallam and Sheffield Club had been playing matches, that the members of the Wednesday Cricket Club, which dated back to 1820, decided to start a football section so that they might keep together during the winter. Most of those who took part in the historic meeting at the Adelphi Hotel, at which this decision was come to, have joined the great majority, but Mr. Charles Stokes, the present treasurer of the Sheffield United Club, and Mr. W. F. Pilch, a son of the famous Fuller Pilch, still take a keen interest in both the summer and winter pastimes.

ALDERMAN GEORGE SENIOR, J.P.,
Chairman of the Directors of the Sheffield Wednesday F. C.
He is an ex-Lord Mayor of Sheffield, and has done much to ensure the success of the famous Owlerton Brigade.

The young footballers proved very enthusiastic, and practised assiduously for nearly three months on a ground they had rented at Highfield, now covered with bricks and mortar. The first regular match was against Droufield, on the latter's ground, and the Wednesday boys made an auspicious start by winning by 1 goal to 4 rouges. In the following season Mr. Oliver Cromwell, a local theatrical manager, offered a silver cup for competition, and Garrick and Wednesday met in the final tie at Bramall Lane, when, after a tremendously exciting struggle, Wednesday became the possessors of the first of the many trophies destined to fall to their lot.

In 1870 the brothers J. C. and W. E. Clegg joined the club, and commenced their long and brilliant career in the world of athletics. The same season also saw the club migrate to Myrtle Road, where they played on a hilly field overlooking their future home of Olive Grove. The season of 1871-2 was memorable for the inauguration of the series of inter-association matches between Sheffield and London, and for the first, played on the Bramall Lane Ground on December 4, 1871, Wednesday supplied no less than seven members of the victorious team, while Mr. C. W. Alcock captained the visitors.

Following the lead of the Football Association, the Sheffield Association instituted a challenge cup competition in 1876-7, and Wednesday became the first holders, winning a sensational final tie against their old rivals—Heeley. At half-time the Heeleyites led by 3 goals to nil, but afterwards their opponents levelled matters up, and, extra time being played, Wednesday won by 4 goals to 3. On opposite sides in this match appeared the first two Scottish players imported from over the Border. These were J. J. Lang, a Third Lanark and Scottish International forward, for whom Wednesday found a lucrative situation in Sheffield; and Peter Andrews, another International, who was brought from Glasgow by Heeley under similar conditions. Such famous players as the brothers Clegg, the brothers Stacey, and the brothers Butler, were also in the Wednesday team. The Wednesdayites won the cup again the following year, and altogether they have held it on ten occasions.

In 1878 the Earl of Wharncliffe gave a valuable cup to be competed for annually, the profits to go to the medical charities of Sheffield. Wednesday were the first winners, and have been successful nine times since.

Sheffield Wednesday have always been noted cup-fighters, and although they have only once won the English Cup, they have been in the Final twice, and in the Semi-final seven times.

They first entered for the great F. A. Cup competition in 1878, but it was not until 1895-6 that Wednesday gained the height of their ambition by beating the "Wolves" in the Final by 2 goals to 1, after a splendid game, at the Crystal Palace. What a reception Jack Earp and his colleagues had when they returned to Sheffield on the following Monday with the Cup in their possession! It was the culmination of years of hope and gallant struggling, and such scenes of enthusiasm had never before been witnessed in Sheffield.

To return to the general history of the club's progress, it may be noted that when the Myrtle Road Ground was discarded a move was made to Sheaf House in 1877, followed later by the renting of a field at Endcliffe, now part of the city's most beautiful public park. All this time, the chief matches had been played at Bramall Lane, but when at the close of 1886 it was decided to go in for professionalism, it was recognised that the club must have a first-class ground of its own. After a good deal of consideration, a piece of land close to the Midland Railway line between Sheffield and Heeley was leased from the Duke of Norfolk. It was only three and a half acres in extent, and little better than a swamp, but by utilising every portion to the best advantage, and draining it on scientific principles, it was made to serve the purpose desired.

On September 12, 1887, the Olive Grove Ground was opened, Blackburn Rovers being the visitors, and the result, a draw of 4 goals each, was considered very satisfactory by the Sheffielders. Almost from the start the new venture caught on with the public, and here it may be said that probably no club in the country has had a more whole-hearted body of supporters. Having been refused admission to the newly constituted Football League, Wednesday helped to form the Football Alliance in 1889, other prominent clubs concerned including Nottingham Forest, Walsall, Mitchell St. George's (Birmingham), and Newton Heath. The Sheffielders were the first champions, but in the

SHEFFIELD WEDNESDAY FOOTBALL CLUB—THE PLAYERS, SEASON 1905-6.

Back Row: T. Marrison. J. Reynolds. A. Stewart. T. L. Jarvis. J. T. Brittleton. C. Crapper.

Furniss Sheffield.]

Middle Row: J. Davis (Hon. Trainer). J. B. Jameson. W. Layton. H. Ruddlesdin. T. H. Crawshaw (Captain). J. Lyall. H. A. Burton. W. Bartlett. J. N. Malloch. P. Frith (Trainer).

Front Row: H. Davis. H. Chapman. A. Wilson. J. Stewart. G. Simpson.

T. H. CRAWSHAW
(Centre-half).

Sheffield Wednesday's captain was born at Sheffield in 1872. He stands 5ft. 11in. in height, and weighs 12st. Played for Park Grange, Attercliffe, and Heywood Central, joining the Wednesday in 1894. Has been "capped" ten times for England, and is a wonderful player.

FRED SPIKESLEY
(Outside-left).

He was born at Gainsborough in 1871. Height, 5ft. 7in.; weight, 10st. He joined Wednesday in 1892, after playing for Gainsborough Trinity. Represented the English League in 1894 and 1903, and was seven times "capped" for England.

next season they sank to the very bottom of the table.

When the League was enlarged in 1892, Wednesday was received with open arms, every one of the clubs voting for their admission.

The darkest period in the club's history came in April, 1899, when the end of the season found Wednesday relegated to the Second Division of the League, and ousted from its ground. There was, however, one ray of comfort. In its hour of trial the public had stuck loyally by the old club, and the treasury contained over £2,000 in hard cash. Mr. John Holmes (president), the late Mr. Alfred Holmes, the late Mr. Arthur Nixon, and Mr. A. J. Dickinson, who had acted as hon. sec. since 1891, had been chiefly responsible for the active management of the club, and they were not the men to be daunted by difficulties. Aided by other members of the directorate, they set to work with a will, and every piece of ground, likely or unlikely, within a reasonable distance of the city was surveyed. All sorts of obstacles had to be surmounted, and at times the directors were almost in despair; but eventually, in June, an agreement was come to for the purchase for £5,000 of ten acres of freehold land at Owlerton, just outside the city boundary, on the Primitive Road.

Of course, the conversion of this meadow land into a thoroughly up-to-date athletic ground could not be carried out by a club with a membership of less than fifty and a capital of £250, so the club was turned into a limited liability company. Mr. George Senior, one of the City's leading steel magnates, accepted the chairmanship, and threw himself heart and soul into the work of his new position. Many of the most influential men in the civic, commercial, and professional life of Sheffield became directors, and the capital of £7,000 was quickly subscribed. The new ground was opened on the first Saturday in September, 1899, less than three months after the land had been acquired, the playing-pitch being in excellent condition. One season was sufficient to get the club out of the Second Division of the League, and change of ground evidently brought change of luck in the League competition, for since being at Owlerton the Wednesdayites have been as consistent as any other club in the table. It is unnecessary to go at length into their recent history, but it may be pointed out that Wednesday carried off the League championship in 1902-3 and 1903-4, and in the early stages of last season looked like repeating the feat until a series of accidents disorganised the team. The Wednesday Club has always been managed on sound business lines, with a result that can be seen by a perusal of any of its recent balance - sheets. Last year the total revenue was £9,293 9s. 3d., and expenditure £7,130 8s. 3d., players' wages accounting for £4,334 10s. 6d. of the latter amount. The net profit for the year amounted to £1,433 8s. 8d. According to the last balance-sheet, the club's assets were £3,424 19s. 10d. in excess of liabilities. A good deal has been written of late as to the relations of civic dignitaries to sport, and the personnel of the Wednesday directorate supplies a very striking illustration of what has been noted as an interesting phase of modern civic life. Ald. George Senior, J.P., the chairman, is an ex-Lord Mayor of Sheffield; the present Lord Mayor, Col. Hughes, C.M.S., is a director, and so are three other ex-Lord Mayors—Ald. W. E. Clegg, J.P., Ald. G. Franklin, J.P., and Ald. J. R. Wheatley, J.P. Also on the list are the names of another alderman, three city councillors, and the Official Receiver, Mr. J. C. Clegg, the Chairman of the Council of the Football Association.

This sketch would not be complete without some mention of the many famous players who have worn the blue-and-white. Of the old times, perhaps the most noted were the brothers J. C. and W. E. Clegg, and "Billy" Mosforth. Others of the old brigade who gained International honours were W. H. Carr, W. Betts, E. Brayshaw, and J. Hudson; while, in recent years, T. Crawshaw, F. Spikesley, H. Ruddlesdin, H. Davis, and F. Thompson have all been "capped."

Furniss, Sheffield.]

THE OWLERTON GROUND, SHEFFIELD WEDNESDAY'S FAMOUS FOOTBALL ENCLOSURE.

This playing field was opened on the first Saturday in September, 1899. The record attendance here was that of 36,413 persons, who witnessed the Cup-tie match between Sheffield Wednesday and Portsmouth on February 18, 1905. The ground will hold about 50,000 persons.

THE FOOTBALL HISTORY OF WEST HAM UNITED.

By E. S. KING.

Thames Ironworks are seized with football fever—West Ham an old football centre—A peep into the past—The first match played September 7, 1895—A move to Browning Road, East Ham—The Memorial Grounds, Canning Town—Thames Ironworks enter the Second Division of the Southern League—The club embraces professionalism—The Southern League proper—A bad first season—A limited liability company formed and the title "West Ham United" adopted—Southern League records—Troublous times—The Boleyn Castle Ground secured—A bright future outlook.

Colours: Claret with light-blue sleeves, white knickers. *Ground: Boleyn Castle, Upton Park.*

IN the summer of 1895, when the clanging of "hammers" was heard on the banks of Father Thames and great warships were rearing their heads above the Victoria Dock Road, a few enthusiasts, with the love of football within them, were talking about the grand old game and the formation of a club for the workers of the Thames Ironworks, Limited. There were platers and riveters in the Limited who had chased the big ball in the North country. There were men among them who had learned to give the subtle pass and to urge the leather goalwards. And so when the idea was first suggested that an amateur club should be formed, it met with a ready response from the employés of the Thames Ironworks. These early organisers, of what, in a later age, is known as West Ham United, also found a generous patron in Mr. A. F. Hills.

Before passing along to the first appearance of the club in the field, I ought to point out that West Ham is one of the oldest football centres in the country. The fact is not generally known that Blackburn Rovers have met Upton Park—not the present club of that name—in a late round of the Association Cup competition in West Ham Park. "The oldest inhabitant" tells me that Blackburn Rovers won. I mention these things to show that when the Thames Ironworks F. C. came before the local public a great deal was known about the game; and, indeed, the way had been prepared for the Ironworks by clubs like St. Luke's, Old St. Luke's, and Old Castle Swifts. Canning Town and West Ham, generally in those days even, was a hotbed of football. Old Castle Swifts had the distinction of being the first professional club in Essex, and they played on a field hard by the Hermit Road. Their existence was brief. The Hermit Road "cinder heap"—it was nothing better—lay untenanted after their demise, and it was this barren waste that the Thames Ironworks decided to occupy. A few meetings were called, and the project talked over. Foremen and overseers in the Limited were persuaded to give their support, a committee was elected, and secretaries appointed. Roughly speaking, the membership did not exceed fifty. No thought of professionalism, I may say, was ever contemplated by the founders. They meant to run their club on amateur lines, and their first principle was to choose their team from men in the works.

J. E. Reeves.]
J. GRISDALE,
Chairman of the West Ham United Football Club.

On September 7, 1895, eleven men from the works turned out at Hermit Road to play the reserve team of the Royal Ordnance F. C. The pages of history record that the result was a draw, 1—1, and everybody went home satisfied.

"Bob" Stevenson, who captained Woolwich Arsenal at one period of their existence, was the first captain of the T. I. W., and in those early days the training was done on week nights at a school-room in the Barking Road. The players used also occasionally to go out for a moonlight spin on the turnpike road. Their trainer was "Tommy" Robinson, and he is still trainer to West Ham United. There is a break of several seasons in his service, however, during which we saw him smoking his cigar on match days and thinking hard when the game was going against the side in which he has always taken a deep interest.

The Ironworks' first season came to a close, with happy results.

They had to move from Hermit Road, though, the next year, and they subsequently appeared at Browning Road, East Ham. For some reason, not altogether explained, the local public at this place did not take kindly to them, and the records show that Browning Road was a wilderness both in the matter of luck and support. Still there was a bright time coming, it was thought, and people were beginning to talk about the Memorial Grounds at Canning Town. This vast athletic enclosure was built by Mr. Hills, and, if my memory is not at fault, I think it was opened on Jubilee Day, 1897. History has been made at the Memorial Grounds. Troubles and triumphs are associated with the enclosure, but, somehow, West Ham never succeeded there as it was once thought they would. Thames Ironworks, however, won the London League championship in 1898.

The next season they entered the Second Division of the Southern League and won the championship at the first time of asking. The season 1898–9 will also be remembered as the year in which they embraced professionalism. One of the arguments advanced at the time was that none but a tip-top team of good players could draw the multitude to the Memorial Grounds. Following its adoption there were more trials and troubles. Those supporters who remained loyal will remember the year as one in which certain officials came under the ban of the F. A. It was distinctly unfortunate, and for a time dark clouds threatened the club.

Thames Ironworks were next invited to knock at the door of the First Division of the Southern League. And knock they did. They were admitted, only to discover that the higher you go the more difficulties you may expect to encounter. In September, 1899, then, they made their entry into the First Division. Ill-luck dogged them all the way. They won only eight matches, and finished in the table just above Sheppey United. All this while the man in the street was talking about the club.

The time was ripe for a limited liability company, and the public were shortly afterwards invited to take up shares. Next year the name was changed from Thames Ironworks to West Ham United, and henceforward the doors of the club were open to the rank and file.

The record of 1899–1900, however, would not be complete without some reference to the players who were associated with the club at that time. There was poor Harry Bradshaw, who came from the "Spurs" with Joyce. How well I remember that match with Queen's Park Rangers during the Christmas holidays, when Joyce brought over the sad message to the Memorial

Grounds that our comrade had passed away. Poor Harry was one of the cleverest wing-forwards I have ever known, and he was immensely popular with everybody. He joined the club with me, and with us in the team were McEachrane (now with the Arsenal), Craig (Notts Forest), my partner at full-back, Carnelly, and Joyce. We had some rare talent in our reserve team too, for, if my memory is not at fault, there were J. Bigden (now of the Arsenal), R. Pudan (Bristol Rovers), and Yenson (Queen's Park Rangers).

Retaining several of their old players, in the following season, 1900–1, West Ham finished up sixth on the Southern League table. This, indeed, was progress. It was the first year of the intermediate rounds of the English Cup competition, and it was our fortune to meet Liverpool at the Memorial Grounds. They beat us by only 1 goal, and we were rather unlucky to lose. Goldie (Fulham) played against us, and Satterthwaite, who afterwards became identified with West Ham, was Liverpool's twelfth man. Grassam joined us that year, and Hugh Monteith kept goal for the "Hammers," as we were then styled.

Next season, 1901–2, is the brightest in the history of the club. It was roses all the way, but there was one ugly thorn, and that a beating from Grays United in the National Cup competition. We reached fourth position in the League table, finishing behind Portsmouth, "Spurs," and "Saints."

In that year I was appointed assistant-secretary, and at a later period, as is generally known, I became secretary-manager.

We lost the services of several of our best men the following season, 1902–3. That was the penalty, I suppose, we had to pay for success. All the same, we had a useful team, among whom was Fred Griffiths, the Welsh International goalkeeper; J. Blythe, who afterwards went to Millwall; and Linward, who was transferred to the Arsenal. And the club certainly deserved a higher position than tenth on the table, where we subsequently finished. The Cup competition saw us beaten at Lincoln, and the match will be remembered if only for the accident to Kelly, who, although he broke his ankle, went on playing till within a few minutes of the finish.

Now we come to the season 1903–4. This was one of the most eventful in the history of the club. The West Ham United Football Club Company dates from 1900–1. The open door, so to speak, had been productive of good results. The charge that the club was out of sympathy with the local public was not repeated in 1903. A lot of prejudice had been lived down and forgotten, and I don't suppose any club has had to fight harder for its existence than West Ham United. Even as we stood on the threshold of 1903–4 a great and overwhelming difficulty beset us. It was the last year of our agreement concerning the occupancy of the Memorial Grounds.

But before I pass along to the stirring events which marked the close of that season, let me say something about the team. We were reinforced by a strong contingent from Reading, including Allison, Cotton, Watts, and Lyon. With regard to the performances of the team that year, I regret to say that we did not succeed as we should have liked. Fulham beat us by a goal in the Cup competition, and in the League we were the reverse of comfortable—a fact which did not help to encourage us when we knew that we must leave the Memorial Grounds and that a new home had to be found. The immediate and pressing difficulty of West Ham at the close of the 1904 season was the question of ground. The directors endeavoured to negotiate with Mr. A. F. Hills for a further lease of seven, fourteen, or twenty-one years of the Memorial Grounds at a good rental, the club to have sole control.

Unfortunately as we thought then, but luckily as it afterwards turned out, no agreement could be arrived at. And we had to go. But where to? A piece of waste ground was offered us by the corporation, but this would not do. I well remember the facts concerning our lifting up and being placed on dry land, as it were. It was during our last few days at the Memorial Grounds. A match was being played between boys of the Home Office Schools. One of the Brothers from the Boleyn Castle School was present. We told him of our difficulty, and showed him the letter from Mr. Hills. An arrangement was made with the Brother there and then to go and see the Boleyn Castle Ground. We agreed to take it. A week later we were thrown back into the lap of despair again by being told that the Home Office would not approve of the action of the Brothers. A deputation of directors waited upon Mr. Ernest Gray, M.P., and through his good offices and certain conditions on our part we were finally allowed to take possession of Boleyn Castle.

It is a place with a history. There the unfortunate lady whose name is linked with that of Henry VIII. has resided. There are legends and stories about this fine old mansion—now a school.

At their new ground the West Ham Club hope to make football history, and I may say that 1904–5—our first season at the Castle—was also the first year we have ever made a profit on the season's working.

Before closing I should like to give the names of the present board: Mr. J. Grisdale, chairman; Mr. J. Moss, vice-chairman; Mr. G. C. Fundell, treasurer; Messrs. A. C. Davis, H. Iggulden, W. White, L. Johnson, H. G. Sutton, J. Reeves, and H. Mattocks.

Reeves.]

BOLEYN CASTLE GROUND, THE HISTORIC HOME OF WEST HAM UNITED FOOTBALL CLUB.

It was in the fine old mansion near by, which gave the ground its name, that Anne Boleyn, the unfortunate wife of King Henry VIII., once resided. West Ham United are rapidly making history of another sort here, and it seems that at last the club has embarked upon a flood-tide of prosperity.

WEST HAM UNITED FOOTBALL CLUB—THE PLAYERS, SEASON 1905-6.

Back Row: S. HAMMOND. A. McCARTNEY. G. KITCHEN (Goalkeeper). C. COTTON. D. GARDNER.

J. E. Reeves, Canning Town.]

Middle Row: W. WHITE. E. S. KING (Secretary). T. ALLISON. H. HINDLE. F. PIERCY. L. JARVIS. T. ROBINSON. C. PAYNTER.

Front Row: W. FORD. H. WINTERHALDER. S. McALLISTER. C. MACKIE. G. HILSDON. W. BRIDGEMAN. H. WILKINSON. L. WATSON. F. BLACKBURN. A. WINTERHALDER.

Bowden Bros.]

INTERNATIONAL RUGBY FOOTBALL—ENGLAND *v.* SCOTLAND, 1903, AT RICHMOND.

Scotland (winners) picking up in the loose.

THE RUGBY GAME.

PART I.—FORWARD PLAY.

By J. H. ROGERS

(Hon. Treasurer of the Midland Counties Rugby Union; International, 1890-1; ex-Captain of the Moseley F. C.).

The forwards the backbone of a Rugby fifteen—The New Zealanders and forward play—Keep your eyes on the ball—The ideal forward—The advent of the four three-quarter game and its influence on forward play—The Newport pack of the Nineties—New Zealanders' seven forwards—What is to be done with the spare man?—Scrummaging—Dribbling—Tackling—Mark your man—Combination run wild.

THE success of a Rugby football team is almost entirely to be measured by the strength of its forwards. A side with an excellent line of three-quarter backs with a poor pack in front of them will invariably be beaten by a side with good forwards and only moderate backs. I need scarcely tell any practical judge of Rugby football how helpless is the position of the talented half and three-quarter back who is operating behind a pack of beaten forwards. The probability is that they will be starved for the whole of the game. The play is dominated by the doings of the forwards. What can talented back players do when the opposition pack time after time carry the scrum and come sweeping along with irresistible rushes? All that the three-quarters can then do is to defend. The three-quarters depend for their openings, as a rule, upon the alert-feeding halves, but halves who are over-run by the opposing pack scarcely get a chance of handling the ball, or if they do handle it they are downed immediately, and another scrum takes place, this time nearer their line.

The brilliant play of the New Zealand team this season in the open has been the subject of much favourable comment, both oral and literary. All who have seen them at work will appreciate to the full their speed and cleverness; but they, like other teams, are mainly dependent upon their fine sturdy and intelligent scrummagers.

The New Zealand forwards are players of the highest and best type. While possessing every possible physical advantage in common with the three-quarters and other sections of the team, they utilise their brains in everything they do.

Mr. F. Glasgow, one of the ablest members of their pack this year, states that the cardinal principle of the New Zealanders' forward play is that they shall keep their eyes on the ball. Every forward, when he gets down in the scrum, watches the ball from the moment it is put in until it is out again, and then he instantly knows, from instinct and experience, what to do. There is no blind pushing; the scrummage is cleverly manipulated, and the break-up is timed to give the fleet men a chance of going on with the ball.

More intelligent forward play than the New Zealanders show has rarely been seen; and I give prominence to this because I regard it as axiomatic that the forwards are the back-bone of any Rugby fifteen. You want agile and clever halves, you want fleet and diplomatic three-quarters, if you are to become a heavy scoring team, but you will never have a really dangerous side until your forwards are right.

The Welshmen were brilliant behind the scrum for some years before they began to hold their own in International strife, but they had not a sound pack. Then they paid special attention to forward work, and the moment that they had their forwards right they became, generally speaking, superior to other nations. But I remember a time when the Welsh backs were superlatively clever; but it was generally possible then to beat them forward, and as defence was never the chief characteristic of their back play, they were often seen at a disadvantage, but the failure of the forwards furnished the key to the position.

It follows, therefore, that the position of forward is of paramount importance—a fact not always appreciated by onlookers, as, naturally, a great deal of the best of his work is unseen.

The ideal forward should be strong, of good physique, fleet of foot, able to scrummage, tackle, dribble, and pass accurately. Of modern forwards, V. H. Cartwright, the present captain of the English fifteen, and J. Daniell, of Cambridge University, have been the best examples.

One of the finest packs which existed under the three three-quarter game were the Oxford University forwards of 1882-

1884, so ably led by their captain, H. Vassall. They rushed the scrums, broke up quickly, and handled the ball with a dexterity equal to the best of three-quarters.

With the advent of the four three-quarter system, the forward of the Gurdon brothers type—who were skilful scrummagers and dribblers—and the forward of the Yorkshire type—adept at rushing a scrum—gave place to a heavy and slow class of player with less energy and vigour, the packs of many of the successful present-day teams being composed of mere automatons, whose sole ideas seem to be obtaining possession and heeling out.

After C. Hancock, the famous Cardiff centre, had perfected the modern four three-quarter game, the late Arthur Budd, who was, perhaps, as fine a judge of a player as ever lived, although ultimately he strongly supported the new formation, always deprecated the fact that heeling out destroyed the honest scrummager. "Is it possible," he asks, "for a man to be kicking backwards and pushing forward simultaneously?" This is sound logic, but, nevertheless, it has been demonstrated beyond all doubt that a team playing the heeling and passing game to perfection can still have a pack of forwards who can do something more than automatically heel out to their backs.

I refer to the famous Newport pack of the early Nineties. They not only heeled as occasion demanded, but could rush the scrums, break up quickly, dribble perfectly, form into line, and pass from hand to hand with speed and precision. Any team with a like set of forwards would to-day carry everything before them.

INTERNATIONAL RUGBY—ENGLAND v. SCOTLAND AT RICHMOND, 1905.
Forward play. Wheeling the scrum. The match was won by Scotland by 8 points (1 goal, 1 try) to nil.

NEW ZEALAND v. SOMERSET AT TAUNTON, OCTOBER 21, 1905.
The breaking up of a scrum. Somerset pass the ball while collared. This match was won by New Zealand by 23 points (3 goals—1 penalty, 1 dropped—and 3 tries) to nil.

The triumphant New Zealand team would have been still more triumphant had their forwards been able to indulge in those close dribbling rushes which are now so rarely seen. But the New Zealanders have demonstrated that seven pushers with the two—three—two formation are equal, if not superior, to eight. Does this account for the winger, for in nearly every side there is at least one forward who aspires to be an Evershed—whose equal at his particular style of play has yet to be found. If seven be the requisite number of forwards to pack properly, then the eighth has been wasted—he has become what is known as a winger or "sugarer." He hangs outside, sometimes hooks the ball from the scrum, and dribbles away on his own, leaving the remainder of the pack to share his work amongst them, but more often hampers his own half-backs, and generally does considerably more harm than good; but he obtains the plaudits of the crowd, who vote him to be easily the best forward on the side, because he is the most conspicuous. Further, it may account for the non-success of some of the English packs, owing to the fact that the claims of a particular forward have been advanced by the representative of his particular county committee; and as it generally happens that at least half of the forwards suggested for International honours are players of this description, one or two have almost invariably been included in the English teams.

If seven forwards, all sterling scrummagers, are to constitute the packs of the future, the question will have to be solved as to what position in the field is to be allocated to the extra man—whether as an extra forward with a roving commission—if he be a Frank Evershed, yes—or a five-eighth, or as an extra three-quarter.

In scrummaging, the two in front should endeavour to pack under their opponents as a lift and push combined, which should commence immediately the ball is put in—and a little before, if possible—and which often upsets their balance, and possession of the ball is more easily obtained. Control of the ball is control of the game, and the pack which more often obtains possession should, other things being equal, win the game.

Immediately possession is obtained, if the scrum be in your opponents' half, heel out smartly to your half, who will set the backs in motion; if in your own half, the ball should be retained in front of the last two forwards, and the scrum should be screwed or wheeled towards the more open side of the ground, then a combined rush and dribble or a bout of passing should be indulged in, according to the state of the ground. In case your opponents gain possession, endeavour to rush their scrum. As soon as the ball has left the scrum on either side the forwards should break up immediately.

In dribbling it is most essential to keep the ball close and to guard against kicking too hard and over-running the ball, for all the ground gained by a long dribble may be lost by a forward kicking so far in front as to enable one of the opposing backs to pick up and kick. When a player over-runs the ball he should immediately turn back and get behind again, and not stand about off-side doing nothing. Dribble, with the head well forward, and pass a man by playing the ball on one side of him and running by him on the other. Do not pick up in a dribble unless near the line. How often one sees what promises to be a fine combined effort spoiled by a forward seizing the ball and grovelling with it on the ground.

All these points are a matter of head, and I have come to the conclusion that the football player, like the poet, is *nascitur non fit*, and unless the football instinct is born in him, however well he may be educated, he never seems to turn out quite the genuine article. It is astonishing that a player voted highly intelligent may show absolutely no "brains" whatever on the football field. In the Association game, if a forward makes a mistake it is seen at once by the crowd; but a Rugby forward may commit a dozen blunders, not one of which would be noticed by the onlookers.

RUGBY FOOTBALL—A LINE OUT—NEW ZEALAND v. MIDDLESEX, AT STAMFORD BRIDGE. OCTOBER 4, 1905.

New Zealand beat Middlesex by 34 points (5 goals and 3 tries) to nil.

In tackling one should always go for the man with the ball and endeavour to down him, and although the axiom is "tackle low," I think a grip just above the knee to be the most effective.

In passing, do not pass for the sake of passing, but retain the ball until you can hand to a player more advantageously situated than yourself, and then pass low and in front of the man, to enable him to take it in his stride, for if the ball be passed straight to the player it will check his pace momentarily and the effort may be spoiled.

"Mark every man a man" is such an elementary principle of the game that one would think it unnecessary to repeat it, yet how frequently in a throw-out from touch one observes two or three men unmarked? If each forward accounts for an opposing forward it should be difficult for a man to break away.

This brings to my mind an incident which once occurred in a Yorkshire cup-tie. On a throw-out from touch, every forward was on the ground almost before the ball had left the hand of the thrower-out, so keen were they "marking every man a man."

It seems absurd to say that a Rugby ball cannot be caught in one hand, yet the frequency with which players go for the ball with one hand on a throw-in from touch and invariably knock-on must be my apology.

Where the ball is there should be, not one, but the majority of the forwards, both in attack and defence, if possible.

It is apparent, then, that a forward should always be in the pink of condition, otherwise he cannot play the game with credit to his side or with any enjoyment to himself. It must be remembered that Rugby football is a game, not a pastime, and should be played both with vigour and determination, and if it be not played in this spirit it is not worth playing at all.

While I should be sorry to seem to depreciate present-day players, I am bound to remark that a lack of resource is often to be noted among to-day's exponents of the game. When I was in the English team, every man in the pack could not only do his work in the scrum, but he was deadly outside it. If the chance arose, there was not a man on the side who could not dash over the line himself. He did not seek to pass needlessly; really, some players give one the impression that it is a relief to them to get rid of the ball. They appear not to have sufficient confidence in their own ability to make a dash for the line. They pass, and too often pass, with a total lack of judgment. Let unselfishness be as pronounced as it can be made, but do not let unselfishness give place to mere timidity; or, to put it more mildly, complete lack of resource.

Yet it is not an altogether uncommon spectacle to-day for men to be seen hesitating and looking round for someone to whom they may pass when they have practically a clear run for the line. That is a grievous defect of present-day play. I believe it to be due, in a measure, to combination run wild.

INTERNATIONAL RUGBY—ENGLAND v. WALES, AT CARDIFF ARMS PARK, JANUARY 14, 1905.

A line out. The match was won by Wales by 25 points (2 goals and 5 tries) to nil.

THE STORY OF WOLVERHAMPTON WANDERERS.

Winners of the Football Association Cup, 1892 3; Finalists, 1888-9, 1895-6.

By B. W. MOLTON.

The rise of the club—The fight for local supremacy—The "Wolves" among the foremost of the League clubs—Some anxious times—The Wanderers' Internationals—The "Wolves" as Cup-fighters—The Wanderers win the English Cup—Economy the club's watchword—The "Wolves'" officials.

Colours: Old gold and black striped shirts, black knickers. *Ground: Molineux, Wolverhampton.*

THERE are two themes upon which the admirers of Wolverhampton Wanderers are wont to wax eloquent, and in dilating upon which they frequently display pardonable pride. The first of these is—that throughout the long and trying ordeals of seventeen League tournaments their favourite organisation has never once failed to retain its place in that select circle. The Wanderers and Everton, Black Country enthusiasts truthfully declare, are the only two clubs of the original twelve which constituted the Football League in 1888 that have not either been re-elected by vote, or played in test matches, or else regained their place in the premier section of the League through the medium of the Second Division. The other ground upon which their partisans are given to congratulating themselves is that Wolverhampton Wanderers are among the select few who have qualified to have emblazoned in letters of gold upon their stationery the magic words, "Winners of the English Cup." For it is well that this fact should not be overlooked, that although the first of the series of Football Association Challenge Cup Competitions dates back to 1871-2, in those thirty-four seasons only twenty clubs have laid hands upon the coveted trophy.

Like many another club which has risen to an important place in the football world, Wolverhampton Wanderers owe their inception to the enthusiasm of a band of scholars and choristers. Three young fellows, who afterwards became well-known in the football world, had a big hand in helping to lay the foundation of a club which was subsequently to be recognised as one of the twelve foremost in the country (for the Wanderers were of the select dozen when the Football League was established). In 1877 John Baynton and John Brodie were pupil teachers at St. Luke's School (which is situate in a district called Blakenhall, Wolverhampton), and John Addenbrooke was just then going through the preliminary stages of the scholastic profession. The last-named was a member of St. Luke's Juniors, and amongst the colleagues of the youth who was subsequently to become the secretary of the club were Arthur Lowder, Richard Baugh (each of whom subsequently became an International), and Ike Griffiths. There was also existent in the same neighbourhood a cricket club which boasted the name of Wanderers, in connection with which there was a football section. Several of St. Luke's footballers played cricket in the Wanderers' team, and the two organisations became so closely connected and intermixed that in 1879-80 St. Luke's Football Club amalgamated with the Wanderers Cricket and Football Club, and so the name of Wolverhampton Wanderers Football Club was brought into existence. When the first season's play was entered upon, St. Luke's (that were) became the Wanderers' first team, and the Wanderers (that had been) were relegated to secondary position.

The Wanderers quickly established a name for themselves amongst the best teams in the Black Country, but they were required to prove by playing achievements that they were fittest to survive as the leading Wolverhampton club. For there was another "Richmond in the field" fighting hard for supremacy. Stafford Road Football Club (connected with the Great Western locomotive works situate in that locality) had gained much local fame under the spirited leadership of Mr. Charles Crump, a fine old-fashioned sportsman now so well known as one of the vice-presidents of the Football Association. Besides taking leading parts with Aston Villa, Aston Unity, Wednesbury Old Athletic, and all leading clubs of the Birmingham district, the "Roaders" had earned much notoriety by running the Old Etonians to a goal in an English Cup-tie in the round immediately preceding the Semi-final stage. When the elevens were brought together 5 goals to 1 represented the difference in the scoring (and the larger number stood to the credit of the juniors), and in the return game the Wanderers emphasised their supremacy by winning with 2 goals to spare. Still holding the whip-hand over their eager rivals, the Wanderers removed them from further participation in one of the local cups, and so set the seal to their own greatness, whilst they sealed the doom of the Stafford Road Club, which, after languishing for a time amongst the second-raters, eventually accepted the inevitable, and disbanded.

LIEUT.-COLONEL GEORGE WALTON WALKER,

Chairman of Directors of the Wolverhampton Wanderers' Football Club.

The Wanderers have never reached the summit of the League table, but they have played an important part in many a season's tournament, and the aggregate number of points standing to their credit in League games places them high in the list of merit. Aston Villa lead the field in the grand totals, the famous Birmingham club having earned since the Football League's inauguration until April last 622 points; Everton are second with 595 to their name; Sunderland third with 578; and Wolverhampton Wanderers fill the fourth position with 505 League points. The Black Country team occupies the central position amongst the five clubs who have had an unbroken connection with the whole of the seventeen League tournaments (for Sunderland were not given place till the third year), Derby County having 499 points to their credit, and Blackburn Rovers having won 495 points since the autumn of 1888. A red-letter day in the Wanderers' history, too, was when they swooped down upon the "Invincibles" at Deepdale and defeated the North-Enders for the first time in a League match before the Lancashire club's supporters, and that after Mr. Sudell's famous combination had gone through a League season without losing a single match and had also won the English Cup without having a goal scored against them.

During such an extended association with these exacting contests the Wanderers—as is only reasonable to expect—have sometimes drifted into perilous positions, and their supporters have tasted of those worries and anxieties which are inseparable from fear of losing place in the premier section of the Football League. The first time they stood in real danger of relegation was in the spring of 1896, and, as illustrating the glorious uncertainty of the game, they had that same season reached the Final of the English Cup! Again, in 1902, the "Wolves" made themselves none too secure, being but two points in advance of Small Heath when the last-named club sank into second-class company. In the spring of the current year, too, the patrons of the Wanderers were again placed on tenter-hooks, for their favourites possessed but two points advantage over Bury, who only qualified to continue to rank as top-sawyers by the favour of the votes of their colleagues in annual meeting assembled.

As the Wanderers' teams have always been made up mostly of Englishmen, it follows somewhat in natural sequence that International talent has been found therein in goodly quantities. Some thirty caps have been won by representatives of the club, the following having, whilst associated with the "Wolves," had the honour and personal gratification of being chosen to appear for their country in representative games: Rose and Baddeley, goalkeepers; Baugh and Mason, backs; Fletcher, Allen, Lowder, and Kinsey, half-backs; J. B. Brodie, R. Topham, Wood, and Beats, forwards. Of these Baddeley, Allen, Kinsey, Brodie, Wood, and Beats have had the high distinction of appearing against Scotland, and W. C. Rose had filled the breach in one of these great contests ere he settled in the Midlands, and at the time he was associated with the London Swifts. Tom Baddeley in 1904 received his "triple crown," being selected by the Football Association to hold the fort against the representatives of Scotland, Wales, and Ireland, in addition to fulfilling a similar duty against the chosen of the Scottish League in the same season.

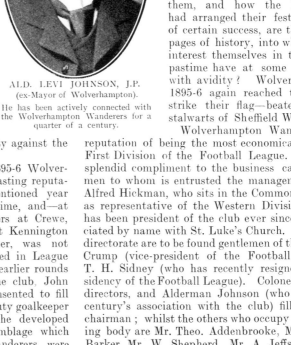

ALD. LEVI JOHNSON, J.P.
(ex-Mayor of Wolverhampton).
He has been actively connected with the Wolverhampton Wanderers for a quarter of a century.

In the seven seasons between 1888-9 and 1895-6 Wolverhampton Wanderers built up for themselves a lasting reputation as dogged Cup-fighters. In the first-mentioned year they reached the Semi-final stage for the first time, and—at the second attempt—defeated Blackburn Rovers at Crewe, and so qualified to meet Preston North End at Kennington Oval. W. C. Rose, the Wanderers' goalkeeper, was not eligible to take the place he so efficiently filled in League games, because he had turned out in one of the earlier rounds for Warwick County; and an ex-captain of the club, John Baynton, in his day a fine centre half-back, consented to fill the position to the best of his ability. The deputy goalkeeper was not a success on Lady Day, 1889, for he developed "nerves" when confronted with the huge assemblage which congregated at London town, and the Wanderers were defeated by 3 goals to 0.

In the following season, 1889-90, the Wanderers reached the penultimate round again, but Blackburn Rovers then turned the tables upon their previous conquerors. Three years elapsed ere the "Wolves" were amongst the last four to survive in the "knock-out" series, and, strange to say, they were for the third time pitted against the redoubtable Rovers in the Semi-final. The Midlanders won the rubber over the Lancastrians and qualified to meet Everton at Fallowfield. About this time a sentimental feeling was gaining ground that English football should be played by English footballers. The Wanderers' eleven contained eight Staffordshire-reared men, and three who first saw light in the neighbouring county of Salop. As the Shropshire border is well within half a dozen miles of Wolverhampton, the players who turned out to oppose the Lancashire club's representatives could not only boast of being all Englishmen, but every one of them could lay claim to local associations. How they won, when high odds were laid against them, and how the Evertonians' followers had arranged their festivities in anticipation of certain success, are they not written in the pages of history, into which most of those who interest themselves in the grand old English pastime have at some time or other dipped with avidity? Wolverhampton Wanderers in 1895-6 again reached the Final, but had to strike their flag—beaten by 1 goal—to the stalwarts of Sheffield Wednesday.

Wolverhampton Wanderers have earned the reputation of being the most economically managed club in the First Division of the Football League. This reputation is a splendid compliment to the business capability of the gentlemen to whom is entrusted the management of the club. Sir Alfred Hickman, who sits in the Commons House of Parliament as representative of the Western Division of Wolverhampton, has been president of the club ever since the days it was associated by name with St. Luke's Church. Upon the Wanderers' directorate are to be found gentlemen of the calibre of Mr. Charles Crump (vice-president of the Football Association) and Mr. T. H. Sidney (who has recently resigned the senior vice-presidency of the Football League). Colonel Walker is chairman of directors, and Alderman Johnson (who claims a quarter of a century's association with the club) fills the position of vice-chairman; whilst the others who occupy places upon the governing body are Mr. Theo. Addenbrooke, Mr. A. J. Evans, Mr. E. Barker, Mr. W. Shepherd, Mr. A. Jeffs, Mr. W. Fleming, and Mr. J. H. Addenbrooke, secretary.

Arthur and Co.]

THE MOLINEUX GROUND, WOLVERHAMPTON.
The classic playing field of the Wolverhampton Wanderers' Football Club.

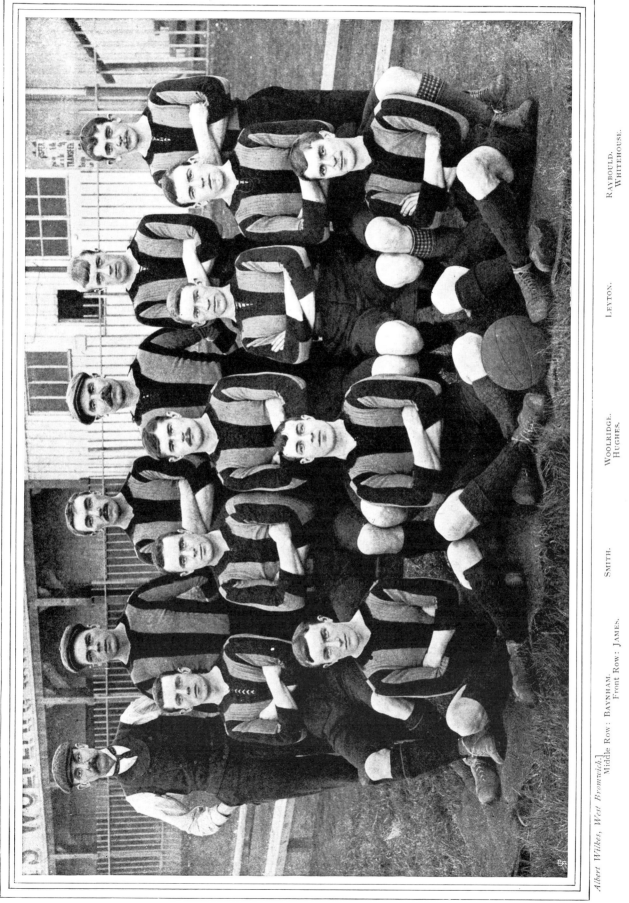

WOLVERHAMPTON WANDERERS—FIRST LEAGUE TEAM, SEASON 1905-6.

Back Row: The trainer. LUNN. JUGGINS. BADDELEY (Goalkeeper). STANLEY. BETTERLEY.

Albert Wilkes, West Bromwich.]

Middle Row: BAYNHAM. SMITH. WOOLRIDGE. LEYTON. RAYBOULD.

Front Row: JAMES. HUGHES. WHITEHOUSE.

THE ASSOCIATION GAME IN IRELAND.

By J. W. GORDON (Secretary of the Irish League).

The introduction of Association football into Ireland—Queen's Park v. Caledonians, October 24, 1878—The game takes root—Formation of the Irish Football Association—The Irish Cup competition—The County Antrim Association—The Irish Football League founded in 1890—Its great influence on the game—"Nick" Ross helps Linfield to win the League championship—Linfield's distinguished English club victims—The first Irish and Scottish League match—The Belfast City Cup competition—International games instituted—Magnificent future prospects of the Association game in Ireland.

THE Association game in Ireland is only in its infancy as compared with the sister countries, England and Scotland. It was not until the year 1877 that a serious attempt was made by Mr. W. Dick, the then secretary of the Scottish Football Association, to introduce the Association code into Ireland, and it was so far successful that an exhibition match was arranged, but, owing to some unexplained reason, the match fell through, and the idea was abandoned. In the following year, however, Mr. J. A. Allen, honorary secretary of the Caledonian Football Club, of Glasgow, having been in correspondence with Mr. J. M. McAlery, of Belfast, a gentleman who afterwards made a name for himself that will live while the game is played in Ireland, and who had chanced to see the dribbling game played in all its beauty while on a trip to Scotland, and being encouraged to hope for success, these two gentlemen determined to renew the attempt, and, putting their heads together, brought about an exhibition match on the Ulster Cricket Ground, Belfast, on October, 24, 1878. The players in the match were selected from two of the leading Scottish clubs, viz., the famous Queen's Park and Caledonian Football Clubs of Glasgow, and several players of International fame took part in the match. The match was under the auspices of the Ulster and Windsor Football Clubs, two organisations at that time identified with the Rugby code. The sides, however, did not exclusively represent these two prominent Scottish clubs, as the idea in coming to Belfast was not to play a club match so much as to introduce the scientific game into Ireland. The match was a great success, and attracted a satisfactory number of spectators, the majority of whom were devotees of the Rugby code. The teams on that occasion were constituted as follows: Queen's Park—Goal, W. C. Mitchell; backs, S. E. Thompson and W. V. O'Brien; half-backs, C. Campbell (captain) and R. M. Sloan; forwards, W. H. Lamberton, T. J. Richmond, J. Smith, J. Goldie, J. Somerville, and J. C. Baird. Caledonians—Goal, G. Cherry; backs, C. Duff and A. Lawson; half-backs, W. Robb and D. Davidson; forwards, H. McNeill, R. M. Liddell, J. Allen (captain), J. Torrance, C. Spence, and H. J. McCreedie. After a splendid struggle the game ended in a victory for the Queen's Park team by 3 goals to 2. The majority of those present at the match were delighted with the display, the game being free from accidents, and anything resembling a scrummage, which is so common under the Rugby rules, was not seen. Altogether the match passed off most pleasantly and successfully.

This was the first Association game played in Ireland, and, the seed being sown, though on Rugby ground, it flourished, and there was soon a bit of dribbling to be seen occasionally on the local football grounds. The Lenzie Football Club now offered to come over and give the novices a match, and the Ulster Football Club organised an eleven to meet the invaders. The game excited great interest amongst footballers and also great amusement, as the amateurish attempts of the home players were often ludicrous in the extreme. However, everything has, or is supposed to have, a beginning, and such was the beginning of Irish Association football. This was the turning point in the history of the game, for up till this match there was no club, properly speaking, playing Association rules, for while there were plenty practising the new code, no club seemed to care to throw themselves wholly into the new game. The visit of the Lenzie team roused the supporters of Association into action, and several attempts at a start were made, but a difficulty presented itself, for there was no ground on which

THE MOST POPULAR TEAM IN IRELAND—LINFIELD FOOTBALL CLUB, SEASON 1905-6.

Back Row: R. Torrans (Trainer). Harper. Jones. Shepherd. Mehaffy. A. Adams (Committee). Stewart. Wilers. Rae. W. MacBride (Committee). J. Peder (Committee).

Front Row: Anderson. Darling Milne Soye. Young.

Webster, Belfast.]

DISTILLERY FOOTBALL CLUB—THE WINNERS OF THE IRISH CUP, SEASON 1904-5.

At Back: SLOAN.
Standing: GRIEVE. WATSON. HARCOURT. M'MILLAN. JOHNSTON.
Sitting: HUNTER. DOWNIE. SOYE. MURRAY. M'DOUGALL.

to play. All the grounds were engaged by Rugby teams, who, though they had no antipathy to the new rules—in fact, rather treated them with contempt—would not allow the Association game to be played. However, help came where least expected in the shape of a resuscitation of the old Cliftonville Cricket Club, and the committee willingly granted the use of their ground for the Cliftonville Association Club, which soon entered into possession, and thus the supporters of the "dribbling" code had at last found a place for their "soles" to delight in.

The committee of the Cliftonville Football Club at once began to extend the game, and a club being formed at the Knock, they were ably assisted by the newly-formed organisation, which spared no exertion in the cause, and their reward came at the end of the season in the shape of four organised clubs playing Association rules only, while others were to be found occasionally practising them. The four clubs now to the fore were: Cliftonville, Knock, Banbridge Academy, and Moyola Park. The following year a few of the moving spirits, headed by Mr. J. M. McAlery, the "father" of the Association game in Ireland, determined to start an Association, and, following the example of the Sister Countries, instituted a challenge cup for annual competition amongst the clubs connected with the Association, it being found from experience across the Channel that there was no better means of developing and spreading the game in the country districts. A meeting was held on November 18, 1880, for the purpose of organising an Association. The meeting was highly successful, and the clubs readily consented to assist the scheme. Lord Spencer Chichester accepted the Presidency, and under His Lordship's auspices everything went well. The Association having been formed, the challenge cup was now to be made a reality; hitherto it had existed only in the imagination of the sanguine supporters of the Association. However, energy and enthusiasm accomplished their purpose, and it was not long before the Irish Football Association were in possession of a trophy which has been competed for every year since. And now came the great period of the game. Hitherto spectators at football matches were practically an unknown quantity, but once the Cup-ties were started, the people turned out, and the Association game rose at once into public favour. Only seven clubs entered for the first competition, but so successful were the matches that, at the end of the season, the Association was firmly established, and the game already popular. The following clubs entered for the Irish Cup competition in the first year of its inception—viz.: Cliftonville, Knock, Moyola Park, Distillery, Avoniel, Old Park, and Alexandra. The final tie was won by Moyola Park, who succeeded in defeating the "premiers" of that day—Cliftonville—by 1 goal to nil.

For a period extending close upon ten years the progress of the Association was one long, uninterrupted success. Clubs multiplied with a rapidity truly astonishing. In a few years such well-known clubs as Queen's Island, Glentoran, Limavady, Ulster, and Wellington Park were formed, only to be followed at intervals of short duration by Clarence, North End, Y.M.C.A., Mountcollyer, Hertford, Linfield, Belfast Celtic, Bohemians, Shelbourne, and Derry Celtic. Several of these clubs have since gone to the wall, it is true, but the more important are still to the fore and more prosperous than they ever were before. Whereas a few years ago the matches were only attended by a few hundred spectators, now thousands are an almost daily occurrence, and the Rugby game that held the field before the introduction of Association has had to take a back seat with the public.

The number of clubs entering for the Irish Cup competition kept on increasing each year till, at the present time, it is very satisfactory indeed, and highly creditable to those who have had the management of affairs for the past number of years. In the year 1887 Mr. J. M. McAlery resigned the position of Honorary Secretary to the Irish Association, and the choice of a successor fell upon Mr. Jack Reid, Honorary Secretary of the Ulster Club. Mr. Reid has held the position ever since, and under his management the Association has prospered in a truly surprising manner.

In the year 1888 the County Antrim Association was launched. This was the first branch of the parent body, and to-day it is often familiarly called the Premier County Association. At the outset it was composed of only eighteen clubs, all, of course, playing the game in the County. To-day its membership is almost one hundred clubs, which speaks eloquently for the rapid rise and steady progress of the game in Ireland. A few years ago it only returned one delegate to the Council of the Irish Association; to-day it sends, on affiliation, ten representatives, and the number is yearly increasing. Nowhere amongst the members of the Council are there to be found more capable legislators than those appointed by the Premier County Association to look after its affairs or fight its battles at the Council of the Governing Body. After its inception, Mr. Robert Ervine, an old player, had control of the affairs of the Association for several years, and when he had to give way to the call of duty he was succeeded in the secretarial department by Mr. James M. Small, an International player of several years standing, who still controls the destinies of the Association. The County Antrim Association is now known by the name of the County Antrim and District Association, the name being altered to enable a Belfast club named Glentoran, one of the oldest clubs in the country, to become connected with the Association, which they could not do, owing to their being situated on the County Down side of the River Lagan, until the change had been made. Although there are to-day five District Associations affiliated to the Irish Football Association, viz., County Antrim, Leinster, North-West of Ireland, Munster, and Mid-Ulster, the first-named still holds the foremost position at the parental board.

But the greatest incentive was given to the game in this country when, in the year 1890, the Irish Football League was formed. At first it was composed of only eight clubs, viz., Linfield, Ulster, Distillery, Cliftonville, Glentoran, Old Park, Clarence, and Milford; but the second season saw the number increased to ten, only to find, before the end of the season, that this number was unwieldy. Consequently, it was reduced to the original figure, and has practically remained at this number ever since. With the advent of the Irish League football improved one hundred per cent. Competition was so keen between the clubs that one of them—Linfield—induced the celebrated "Nick" Ross, of Preston North End fame, to come across and act as coach during the summer months. His training was so thorough that this team carried off the League championship for the first three years it was in existence. Never before or since was such football seen as when Ross was training the Linfield team. Within a couple of seasons the most famous teams in both England and Scotland fell before Linfield, as will readily be seen by a glance at the following list: Corinthians, Preston North End, Blackburn Rovers, Bolton Wanderers, Wolverhampton Wanderers, West Bromwich Albion, Partick Thistle, Notts Forest, and Queen of the South Wanderers.

Webster, Belfast.]

GLENTORAN FOOTBALL CLUB—WINNERS OF THE IRISH LEAGUE CHAMPIONSHIP, SEASON 1904-5.

At Back: M'CLELLAND. LEWIS.
Standing: TORRANS. REID (Secretary). M'MASTER. REA. CONNOR. M'CONNELL. M'COURT. M'KEOWN. KEENAN. CASEMENT.
Sitting: LEONARD. MAXWELL. WARD. KIRKWOOD. DOHERTY.

In 1893 the first match between the Irish and Scottish Leagues was played in Belfast, and, to the surprise of everyone on this side, resulted in a victory for Ireland by 3 goals to 2. Twice since has victory favoured the Irishmen in these International encounters. Last season no match took place owing to a suitable date not being forthcoming. A year afterwards, intercourse between the English and Irish Leagues began, and has continued ever since, notwithstanding the fact that Ireland has not yet won one of the twelve matches played between the two countries. Some idea of the progress the game has made in Ireland may be gleaned from the fact that there are no less than thirty Leagues, Alliances, and Combinations in Belfast alone. In 1894 the Belfast City Cup competition was organised, and although it has up to now been confined to City clubs only, it has proved equally as successful as the League, with which it is, to a certain extent, identified. This year an innovation has been introduced, a Dublin club being admitted into the competition, and, so far, with phenomenal success. The club is the Shelbourne, and it already has had the effect of drawing the two Cities more closely together, and dispelling the bad opinion the one had about the other.

International intercourse proper between Ireland and the three Sister Countries began, in the case of England and Wales, in 1882, and in the case of Scotland, two years after, 1884. We have played twenty-four matches with England, and have yet to achieve a victory, having drawn two and lost the other twenty-two matches. Our record with Wales is not nearly so unsatisfactory, as out of the twenty-four matches played we have won nine, drawn four, and lost eleven. With Scotland we have only won one out of twenty-two matches and drawn two, while we have been on the wrong side of the account no less than nineteen times. Next to International matches, the Irish Cup final tie holds pride of place in the affection of the people. Out of the twenty-five years the competition has been in existence, the Distillery and Linfield Clubs have each won the Cup eight times — admittedly a splendid record, and one that will be hard to beat.

The game is spreading rapidly all over the country. Derry has had a club connected with the Irish League for the past four years—the Derry Celtic; while Dublin has two clubs identified with that popular organisation, viz., Bohemians and Shelbourne, so that the Irish League is now Irish in every sense of the word. In no part of the country has the game made such gigantic strides as in Dublin, where the clubs can now be numbered by the hundred, whereas a few years ago they could have been counted on the fingers of one hand. The enormous number of 250 clubs (senior and junior) turn out weekly in Belfast, and 3,000 players are weekly found playing the game in the City or its suburbs alone. Last year two Belfast clubs carried off the two most important trophies in the country, Distillery again winning the Irish Cup, and Glentoran for the second time annexing the League championship.

Connected with the game we have now an intermediate competition and a junior competition, the clubs comprised in the latter amounting to almost 200, and coming from every part of the country — from Giant's Causeway to Cape Clear.

All other sports and pastimes have had to take a back seat since the advent of Association football in Ireland; and when an International match with England will draw £940, an inter-League match with the same country £400, and an ordinary League match between two local teams £200, it will be admitted that we are progressing rapidly towards that happy consummation so earnestly desired by every devoted adherent of the game in Ireland—when the "gates" will be such as will enable the very best talent to be procured. And that time, I hope, is not far distant.

MR. J. W. GORDON,
Secretary of the Irish Football League.

The present secretary of the Irish Football League is also its founder. The formation of the Football League by Mr. W. McGregor was attended with so much success that Mr. Gordon saw the League system had come to stay, and immediately launched the Irish League. That was in the year 1890, and he has been first Honorary Secretary and then Secretary of the organisation—in fact, he is the only official connected with either of the three national Leagues who was at the inception of one of these bodies. His aim has always been to elevate the game, and no writer in Ireland has done more towards the realisation of that object.

[*Webster, Belfast.*]

SHELBOURNE FOOTBALL CLUB—RUNNERS-UP FOR THE IRISH CUP, SEASON 1904-5.

Standing: PIDGEON. PENSTON. DOHERTY. RONAN (Treasurer). ABBEY. KELLY. MONKS (Trainer). CUNNINGHAM (Secretary).

Sitting: WIMBLE. JACK OWENS. HESLIN. JAMES OWENS. LEDWIDGE.

LAWLESS. CLEARY.

W. H. Cox, Luton.]

A CAPITAL VIEW OF THE NEW IVY ROAD ENCLOSURE, THE HOME OF LUTON TOWN FOOTBALL CLUB.

Match, Luton v. Portsmouth, Southern League competition, season 1905-6.

THE STORY OF LUTON TOWN.

By CHARLES GREEN.

The Wanderers and Excelsiors—The union of the two clubs in 1885 and the title Luton Town adopted—The club's first committee—Luton Town meets the best of the Southern clubs—The paid player—The club's colours changed in 1889-90—The first Southern professional—Luton Town establish a record by being the first club to adopt professionalism—Players' wages—The team—Luton Town beat the Old Westminsters in the F. A. Cup—A fight for the Southern League championship—A duke kicks off at the opening of the Dunstable Road Ground—A limited liability company formed—Luton joins the English League—Disastrous times—The Southern League rejoined—Luton Town takes over a new ground—Capital results, and bright future prospects.

Colours: Light-blue jerseys, white knickers. *Ground: Ivy Road, Dunstable Road, Luton.*

ALTHOUGH the Luton Town Club was not formed until May, 1885, its history would not be complete if it did not start a year or so earlier; for the club came into existence through the amalgamation of the two senior clubs then in the town. It was, in fact as in form, a true union of the Wanderers and Excelsiors, for after the union the proportion was actually six to five, sometimes in favour of one club and sometimes the other, in the composition of the teams. Possibly the Wanderers had made the greater strides as a senior club prior to the amalgamation, for they had entered the Football Association Cup Competition, and had already played a tie against the famous Old Etonians.

The Wanderers were really a combination of working lads and the best players of a local college, chief of whom were three brothers named E. H., J. C., and D. Lomax.

The meeting of both clubs, held at the Town Hall on April 11, 1885, resulted in a resolution being passed that "The Luton Town Club be formed," the proposer and seconder being Mr. G. H. Small (Excelsior) and Mr. E. H. Lomax (Wanderers) respectively. Mr. F. Pitken was elected as the club's first secretary, with Mr. P. A. Findlay as assistant. The committee were as follows: Messrs. G. Furlong, J. Long, G. H. Small, S. Pakes, T. Brookes, C. Abbott, T. C. Brown, H. G. Spratley, and G. Deacon. The colours first adopted were Navy blue and pink halves for both shirts and caps, the resolution reading that both cap and shirt be worn by each player on the field.

At the first committee meeting the secretary was instructed to challenge such clubs as Old Etonians, Old Foresters, Old Wykehamists, Old Westminsters, Grove House, Wellingborough Grammar School, Prairie Rangers, Hotspur, and Berks and Bucks; all well-known clubs at that period, and really representative of the best Southern football of the day.

The first ground used by the Town Club proper was the Excelsior's pitch, and they continued to use this until compelled to move twelve years later.

At the general meeting the following year Mr. F. Pitken retired from the office of secretary, although he continued on the committee for several years after, and Mr. I. Smith and W. G. Wheeler were elected as secretary and assistant; and they continued to work together in these offices until 1896, thus completing ten years' service. Mr. Smith is even now a director, thus being, by many years, the oldest official attached to the club.

I find during the second season the club decided to give three of their players the proceeds of a match, and I think it can be claimed they were the first Southern players who were openly paid for playing football, although they were not registered at this time.

During the season of 1889-90 the club's colours were changed to cochineal, and they were known throughout the Southern world as the "Reds" for several years.

On December 13, 1890, a minute sets out that the sum of 5s. per week was offered to F. and H. Whitby and Read. At least one of these (H. Whitby) accepted this offer, and was certainly paid this amount for the rest of the season. He was probably the first professional who signed a professional form in the South, for it was not until the following season that Woolwich Arsenal went over to the professional ranks.

On February 9, 1891, there was an application from F. Whitby, who at this time was working out of the town, for a further sum to meet his travelling expenses and lost time. But the committee evidently thought they had launched out far enough, for a resolution was passed that "The club could not see its way to spend any more money on professionalism as finances stood at present." It being also recorded in the minutes of that date that an increase in this direction would undoubtedly prove disastrous to the club.

It is patent from the above that Luton were actually the first club to go over to the professional ranks in the South, although Woolwich Arsenal have usually been given the credit, or discredit,

LUTON TOWN FOOTBALL CLUB—THE PLAYERS, SEASON 1905-6.

Back Row: E. Gibbs (Director). J. Bygrave (Groundsman). Bert Else. Fred Hawkes. J. Blackett. A. E. Lewis. W. McCurdy (Vice-Captain). H. Watkins. A. Wales. C. Green (Secretary). W. Lawson (Trainer).

W. H. Cox, Luton.]

Middle Row: P. Gallacher. A. Warner J. M. Dow. J. Pickering. A. McDonald. W. Barnes.

Bottom Row: F. White. Alex. Brown. "Bob" Hawkes (Captain).

of that plunge. Luton's income that season was £203 9s. 5d., and the expenses were £164 10s. 9d., leaving a balance of £38 18s. 8d. So, it will be seen, the players did not exactly get a living wage after all expenses were met by the club.

Still, at the general meeting during the ensuing close season, the question of paying the whole of the team was decided upon. It was left to the new committee to settle terms, and a joint meeting of committee and players was held on August 10, 1891. The ultimate resolution proposed by a committee-man, and seconded by a player, makes curious reading nowadays. It was resolved that players be allowed 2s. 6d. per week, with an extra 6d. for away matches. Also they should be paid for time lost previous to 12 a.m. As this was the first complete professional team in the South, I will give their names:

Burley, Sanders, Hoy, Taylor, Paul, Wright, F. and H. Whitby, Deacon, Chesher, and Oclee.

It is true by September, when the season commenced, Woolwich Arsenal also turned out as a professional side; but I think Luton can justly claim to be really first, although admittedly on a small scale. Taylor, Paul, and Oclee did not reside in Luton; but the other eight were Lutonians. The first captain was Taylor, and he continued to hold that position the whole of the season 1891–2

The following season the players' wages were doubled so far as the local players were concerned; while the committee launched out to the extent of securing Julian, of Woolwich Arsenal, at a much higher figure than 5s. He captained the team, and was a great favourite with the crowd.

In May, 1893, Mr. H. Arnold, the present Chairman of Directors, became officially connected with the club, and Luton rose to fame by beating the Old Westminsters at Wembley Park in the Football Association Cup. As the Old Westminsters had no fewer than half-a-dozen International players in their ranks, the performance was one of real merit. Luton were beaten in the next round by Middlesborough, at "Ironopolis," by 2 goals to 1.

The next season is notable on account of the formation of the Southern League, and naturally Luton were one of its leading clubs; indeed, both this and the following season they ran second to Millwall on the table.

After two seasons with the Southern League, Luton decided to make a change, and application was made to the Second Division of the English League during the summer of 1896. They were unsuccessful in this, but still they left the Southern League, and were content to figure in a new league, known as the United League, which was certainly a more powerful combination. But as it numbered only nine clubs, it did not provide sufficient matches, and the season resulted in a loss.

Owing to an enforced change of ground during this season, a new pitch was prepared on the Dunstable Road, and this was formally opened by the Duke of Bedford on April 3, 1897, when Loughborough played their United League fixture.

Not many clubs can claim to have a duke kick off, but Luton can; for His Grace started the game in question. By this time Luton had got together one of the most powerful sides in the country, among them being Williams (Everton), McCartney (Newton Heath), Stewart (Newton Heath), Coupar (Newton Heath), Docherty (Derby County), and Ekins (Burton Swifts). For two seasons they held the goal record, having scored over 200 goals!

A further advance was made on June 11, 1897, when the annual meeting decided to turn the club into a limited liability company. This became an accomplished fact on October 27, 1897.

At the annual meeting of that body Luton were admitted as members of the English League. This naturally meant stronger opposition, but still the club secured a respectable position, totalling 30 points out of a possible 60.

It was found impossible to retain the same players for the following season, and a side of youngsters was tried, with not too good a result, for although, through the increase of clubs, 68 points were obtainable only 23 were secured.

A still more disastrous season followed, for Luton dropped to the last position but one on the table, only totalling 18 points, and did not put up for re-election.

In February, 1900, Mr. T. Smith was compelled to resign the secretaryship once more on account of pressure of business, and Mr. H. Smart was called upon to wield the pen, which he did until October, 1901, when the present writer took up the position.

During Mr. Smart's reign the Southern League made overtures for the return of Luton to the competition, and at the annual meeting of that body in May, 1900, Luton were unanimously re-elected, and since that time have remained loyal to the Southern League. It is scarcely necessary to relate the progress of the club in detail since their return to their former love, as Luton's recent history is within the recollection of the majority of present-day footballers.

It should be mentioned, however, that at the close of the season 1904-5 Luton were compelled to once again shift their quarters. This would have been a knock-down blow to many clubs, but the present directors faced the situation boldly, and a thoroughly up-to-date ground has been fitted up. During the Christmas holidays of 1905 more spectators have witnessed the matches than have ever assembled on a Luton ground in the history of the club, and both on Christmas Day and Boxing Day a crowd of 10,000 gladdened the hearts of the officials, from which showing it should be safe to predict a period of increased prosperity for the club. In conclusion, it should be mentioned that the club adopted its present colours—the blue and white—upon their return to the Southern League.

Cox, Luton.]

THE NEW LUTON TOWN ENCLOSURE AND GRAND STAND.

Luton v. Millwall, Southern League competition, 1905-6.

THE RISE OF THE MIDDLESBOROUGH FOOTBALL CLUB.

By GEORGE F. ALLISON.

The club formed in 1876—A change of ground—Middlesborough adopt professionalism in 1889—The first professional team—The amateur status re-adopted—Brilliant achievements—The English Amateur Cup won—Forced into professionalism again—The club enters the League Second Division — The club enters the First Division with a grand record — Fine financial progress — The other side of the picture—An enforced change of headquarters—The magnificent Ayresome Park enclosure equipped—The club in debt—Common transferred from Sunderland for £1,000—Relegation to the Second Division narrowly escaped—Middlesborough directors punished by the Football Association—The club directorate reconstructed—Bright future prospects.

Colours : Red shirts, white knickers. *Ground : Ayresome Park, Middlesborough.*

FEW of the clubs participating to-day in representative English football have experienced so many of the vicissitudes of the game as Middlesborough, the subject of this pen sketch. In the days when amateurism flourished on the North-east coast, Middlesborough tasted pretty liberally of the sweets of success, but since the adoption of professionalism, the subsequent reversion to the amateur fold, and, later, the re-adoption of the "ruling passion," their ups and downs have been of a very pronounced character.

Success on the playing field has not always brought its full financial reward, and probably the palmiest days in the club's history were those when they figured amongst the Second Division clubs in the seasons 1899-1900, 1900-1, and 1901-2. Both from the playing and financial point of view, this eventful period in their history may be termed successful, and, financially, they continued to prosper in the two subsequent seasons when playing in the higher flights. But with that I will deal later.

The idea of forming a club was first mooted at a "tripe" supper—a popular sort of convivial gathering—held in the Corporation Hotel about the year 1876, at which several gentlemen, now holding responsible positions in Ironopolis, as the town is frequently called owing to its important association with the iron and steel industry, were present. The idea was hailed with enthusiasm, and in the latter part of 1876 the first meeting of the club was held in the Albert Park Hotel. But it was not until March 3, 1877, that the players took part in their first real match. They played on the old archery ground in the Albert Park before a little knot of admiring spectators.

MR. ALEC MACKIE.

Appointed manager of the Middlesborough F. C. at the end of the season 1904-5. A highly capable and efficient official, who managed the Sunderland Club for seven seasons with great success. He has proved himself to be endowed with all the diplomatic ability, shrewdness, thoroughness, and keen business instinct which are essential in his particular class of work.

After a few seasons' playing in the park the club transferred its home to the Grove Hill Ground, then to the Middlesborough Cricket Field, and in 1892 they settled down on the old Linthorpe Road enclosure.

Middlesborough practically monopolised the Cleveland Cup after its inauguration in 1881-2. They won the trophy five years in succession, and then withdrew from the competition for a season in order to give other teams a chance. The following year they again won the cup, and in the seasons 1889-90, 1893-4, 1895-6, and 1896-7 they defeated all comers.

Under the present professional régime the reserve team in its first year again credited the club with the cup, and during the past three seasons it has graced the Borough chairman's sideboard.

When, in 1889, a wave of professionalism swept with irresistible force over the North, Middlesborough, after an ineffectual attempt to stem the tide which threatened to swamp amateurism altogether, closely followed by Middlesborough Ironopolis, Stockton, South Bank, and neighbouring clubs, embarked upon what proved to be a disastrous undertaking.

Their first game as a professional club was against Sunderland on December 7, and they were represented by the following team : Goal, Barbour ; backs, Walsh and Wynn ; half-backs, Copeland, Stevenson, and T. Bach ; forwards, Tomkins, Sampson, Mason, Wilson, and Dennis. Mr. Fred Dennis is now a First League referee, a vocation in which Mr. Jack Walsh at present figures locally with some prominence.

About this time, too, the Northern League was formed, and it included such teams as Sheffield United, Sunderland Albion, Newcastle East End, and Newcastle West End, and, with rivalry of the keenest character prevailing, some very fine contests were witnessed. With two professional organisations in the town the spectators were well catered for, but the Borough were always more or less overshadowed by their rivals—Ironopolis—during this stage of their career, and, though they ran the "Nops" a close race, the latter carried off the League championship thrice in succession. Three years of professionalism more than sufficed the directors, and at the end of that time they re-adopted the amateur status. Debts innumerable hung like a lodestone around the neck of the club, and for some considerable time subsequently its progress was handicapped by a heavy financial burden. Thanks, however, to the pertinacity and unfaltering enthusiasm of the management, this adverse balance was eventually wiped off the ledger. They got together a team consisting entirely of local talent, which proved itself one of the best in England. In 1894, 1895, and again in 1897 they won the championship of the Northern League. They also twice carried off the English Amateur Cup, defeating all competitors in 1895 and again in 1897.

As time went on, however, and the professional element gradually made great advancement in public favour, the officials of the club, in spite of its glorious record, became tired of amateurism. So, not without misgivings, the club once more decided to adopt professionalism in 1899. Many thought it a daring venture, and others predicted another inglorious failure. But the prophesies of the pessimists did not materialise, for during at least five of the past six seasons Middlesborough has been one of the best supported clubs in the country.

At the first time of asking they were admitted to the Second Division, thanks to the influence of the Northern delegates, and to a brilliant oration by Mr. Harry Walker, of the Football Association, who advocated the claims of Middlesborough for inclusion in the English League. In the season 1899 they relied chiefly upon local talent, aided by a few Scottish juniors, and they narrowly escaped relegation, the transference from Newcastle of Wardrope (now of Fulham) and Niblo (now of Notts Forest) just saving the situation. The year's working, however, showed a clear profit of £176, but they only obtained 23 points for 34 matches. There was a very marked improvement in the team in the following year, and during the whole season they were only twice beaten at home—by Blackpool and Walsall. They won 15 and drew 7 of the 34 matches played, and finished with a total of 37 points to their credit, which placed them sixth on the League table.

During this season the gate receipts amounted to £8,347—nearly double of that of the previous year—and the profits were £447. There is an old saying that the third time pays for all, and its accuracy was for once exemplified in the case of the Middlesborough Club, who at the third time of asking won their way into the higher realms. This was in the season 1901–2.

At the end of the season they were credited with the following splendid record: Played 34, won 23, lost 6, drawn 5; goals for, 95; against, 25; and points, 51. The excellence of this record was enhanced by the fact that they had not only scored more goals than any other team in the First or Second League, but their defence had been penetrated on fewer occasions. It was a record which excites admiration.

Notwithstanding the fact that the gate receipts in this season fell to £7,501, the profit was much larger than in the preceding year. It totalled £922.

I will just say a word or two now in regard to the financial affairs during their First League career.

In the season 1902–3 the receipts amounted to £8,389, and the profits were £1,182, but in the following year that was far surpassed, for a sum of £10,444 found its way into the exchequer, and of that amount £3,314 ranked as profit. But there the story of financial progress must end. A different story must be told—a story bordering upon financial ruin, or thereabouts. The demands of the ubiquitous builder made it imperative that the club should find a new home, and a capital site was selected in a residential part of the town on the Ayresome estate, and to which an excellent service of tramcars run incessantly throughout the day. This ground was opened on September 12, 1903. It is a splendid enclosure, judiciously apportioned, and contains all the adjuncts to an up-to-date club and ground. It is capable of accommodating between 35,000 and 40,000 people, and cost between £10,000 and £11,000. To clear off this sum the whole of the profits made in the first year of its opening—1903-4—were absorbed, and at the end of that season nearly the whole amount had been cleared off. But the strain on the club's financial resources had been tremendous, and with the team performing none too well last season the receipts fell to £8,703, and when the balance-sheet was issued this year it showed a dead loss of £1,635.

LIEUT.-COLONEL T. G POOLE.

A director of the club, and fulfils the duties of honorary financial secretary, a position which he undertook at the end of the season 1904-5.

Reverting to the playing achievements of the club in their first year in the First Division—1902–3—they won 14, lost 16, and drew 4 of the 34 matches played, and finished sixth from the bottom of the League. In 1903–4 they only won 9 of the 34 matches, but 12 were drawn, and 13 lost, and with 30 points to their credit they were tenth from the top of the League chart.

Last season the struggle to escape relegation was even more acute, and as a last extremity, to escape from the inglorious distinction of being one of the two bottom clubs in the League, they paid the fabulous price of £1,000 to the Sunderland Club for the transfer of Alf Common, the erstwhile International and Sheffield United player.

Misfortunes do not come singly, and as if Middlesborough had not already suffered enough, following certain allegations made at the annual meeting some months ago, a Commission appointed by the Football Association sat in solemn conclave at York to sift to the bottom the truths, or otherwise, of the ugly statements made. After months of long-drawn suspense, the decision of the Football Association was made known, and the dread sword of the Football Damocles fell upon the club and old directorate.

Only one director—Lieut.-Colonel T. G. Poole—escaped punishment; and the following eleven gentlemen were suspended for two and a half years: Messrs. R. W. Williams (chairman), W. Allen, A. Barritt, J. Crombie, C. Dobinson, T. Fletcher, A. Mattison, A. McCallum, D. Mullen, G. Pickard, and Dr. Steel. The club itself was fined £250—the most unkind cut of all—and an ex-Middlesborough player, "Teddy" Gettins, now of Reading, was fined £10 for being loyal to his old directors and disloyal to his conscience—so said the Association's indictment.

At the shareholders' meeting on December 14, convened for the purpose of electing a new Board, the following gentlemen were unanimously appointed to act in conjunction with Col. Poole in guiding the destinies of the club: Messrs. G. W. Armitage, T. Burdon, John Davison, T. Dixon, A. E. Forbes, C. G. Hunt, W. Jones, and J. R. Smiles. As a final word I cannot help feeling sorry for the old directors, and I know that the full sympathies of the club's supporters are with them in their period of exile. What they did was purely in the hope of saving the club from relegation to the Second Division.

R. E. Fairclough, Middlesborough.]

THE SPLENDID AYRESOME PARK ENCLOSURE—THE HOME OF THE MIDDLESBOROUGH FOOTBALL CLUB.

This fine football ground will comfortably hold from 35,000 to 40,000 people, and was fitted and equipped at a cost of between £10,000 and £11,000.

MIDDLESBOROUGH FOOTBALL CLUB—THE PLAYERS AND OFFICIALS, SEASON 1905-6.

Back Row: A. McCallum. G. Pickard. D. Mullen. A. Barrett (Directors).

Second Row: Tinsley. Lieut.-Col. Poole. T. Murray. C. Hewitt. W. Agnew. J. Frail. J. Hogg. T. Hedley. S. Aitken. Dr. Bryan. Mr. Allen, Senior.

Third Row: A Visitor. R. Atherton. D. McCallum. J. Cassidy. G. Henderson. R. W. Williams (ex-Chairman). A. Jones. A. Davidson. D. Smith. A. Mackie (Manager). W. Allen.

Front Row: J. Binghley (Trainer). T. Coxon. J. Bell. J. Thackeray. A. Common (Captain). T. Green. G. Reid. W. Barker. T. Coulson (Asst.-Trainer).

AMATEURS v. PROFESSIONALS AT THE ASSOCIATION GAME—THE CORINTHIANS v. SOUTHAMPTON AT QUEEN'S CLUB.

THE FAMOUS CORINTHIAN FOOTBALL CLUB, 1883 to 1906.

By STANLEY S. HARRIS.

England's greatest amateur team—The relation of the Corinthians to the 'Varsities—The Dewar Shield competition—The Corinthians and the Football Association Cup competition—The club founded by Mr. N. L. Jackson—Corinthian Internationals—Some famous players—The great G. O. Smith—The Dewar Shield match of 1898—The Corinthians' annual Christmas tour—Corinthians v. Queen's Park—The Easter tour—A visit to South Africa—The Corinthian style.

Colours: White shirts, dark knickers.

WHETHER a history of the Corinthians has been written on many occasions, I am not, I fear, in a position to state. I only know that it has been written as recently as December, 1904, when, as readers of Mr. C. B. Fry's magazine will tell you, a most capable and interesting article by that gentleman himself appeared in the December number. Consequently, it would be an extremely difficult task to write on the above title, were it not for the fact that Mr. Fry, while dealing very minutely with the doings of the club up to the time of the retirement of G. O. Smith, only gave a very small amount of space to the present generation; for this I am duly grateful, as it will enable me to tell you a good deal about the Corinthians without having to repeat that which has been written before. I will endeavour, therefore while briefly sketching the history of the club from its start, to enter somewhat particularly into its position at the present time.

A NOTABLE QUARTETTE—CORINTHIANS v. TOTTENHAM HOTSPUR, 1902.
L. J. MOON. H. A. LOWE. CAPTAIN SIMPSON (Referee). J. D. CRAIG.

The Corinthians are, as every follower of football knows, England's greatest amateur team; the club is composed exclusively of 'Varsity and public school men, and not more than ten new members can be elected, I believe, in any one year. It is a point of some interest that in the Corinthian side which beat Bury by 10—3 in the Dewar Shield match in 1904 there were five Oxford Blues, five Cambridge Blues, and G. S. Harris, the old Reptonian. To belong, therefore, to a club which is able to confine itself to the 'Varsities and public schools, and yet be, year after year, the first amateur club in the land, is an honour of which one may feel justly proud. It is no wonder that footballers who have met in rivalry on the field at Queen's in the 'Varsity match join together after and strain every nerve to keep the Corinthians in the position they have always held.

When one is at school, there is the feeling that the sense of pride in one's school can never be surpassed; when the schoolboy goes to the 'Varsity, he finds that love of his school is swallowed up in an altogether stronger feeling—a sentiment almost of reverence—towards his University; it is a feeling which nerves him to do all things for the honour of alma mater. Then the 'Varsity man goes down, and the feeling is carried on with regard to the Corinthian F. C. They know that they have the honour to be members of a club without rival, and their one desire is to help it to retain that position. Another point which causes the Corinthians to stand out by themselves is that they never enter into any competition, save once a year, and then in the cause of charity.

The Dewar Shield match, to which I refer, is one of the most interesting events of the football year; the idea is that the make no allowances for circumstances. Still, the stronger reason for abstaining from competition is because, as I have said before, it is against tradition and principle. No, let them go forward, failing occasionally perhaps against a second-rate professional side, but at other times over-running and outclassing the best professional teams in the kingdom.

Let us turn, for a time, to the more intimate history of the club. Founded, as everyone knows, by Mr. N. L. Jackson, it lost very little time in taking a high position, and in nine years from the date of its start, viz., 1883, there had been forty-four Corinthians in the English teams. Among the older generation, perhaps the most interesting figure is the great W. N. Cobbold; he captained the Cambridge team for two years in succession, having the satisfaction, in 1886, of seeing his side beat Oxford by 5 goals to love. He was known as the "prince of dribblers," and though he did not have such a long International career as G. O. Smith and one or two others, yet on his day he was probably the finest forward the world has seen. He still

Russell and Sons.]

A FAMOUS CORINTHIAN ELEVEN.

From left to right: G. C. Vassall. S. H. Day. (H. W. Hewitt.) G. S. Harris. J. D. Craig. (Capt. Simpson.) O. T. Norris. T. S. Rowlandson. M. Morgan Owen. W. U. Timmis. H. Vickers. S. S. Harris. E. G. D. Wright.

match should be between the best amateur and the best professional team of the year. Save on one occasion, the Corinthians have always been chosen for the former. That one exception was when the lot fell to Queen's Park, the great Scottish amateur combination; what is more, they were successful in the match. Apart from that one annual game, the Corinthians have never played in competitive football. Pressure has been, and still is being, brought to bear on them to persuade them to enter for the English Cup. Though such a course might have its advantages, it would be against the principles and traditions of the club. Apart from that point of view, it must be remembered, also, that the men on whom the club has to rely are, for the most part, unable to give themselves up to football; the majority can only get away about once in a week. It is only natural, therefore, that their form is subject to inconsistency; one day brilliant, another moderate; this is not the style of play for Cup-ties. Again, it is extremely doubtful if it would always be possible to get the best team out even for Cup matches, and it would do the club's prestige no good to be defeated in competition games, since the average follower of football would plays—and plays well, too—for West Wratting against the Cambridge colleges. No more ardent supporter of Cambridge is alive, and I believe I am right in saying that he has not missed an inter-University match since the time he was captain—twenty years ago. Other great footballers of that time were E. C. Bambridge, who played outside-left with Cobbold, and Dr. Tinsley Lindley, one of the best of centre-forwards; he and G. O. Smith stand out pre-eminent as the two great Corinthian centres. At outside-right we find George Brann, who still scores centuries with great regularity for Sussex, but, as far as football is concerned in these days, confines himself to kindly criticism and encouragement. Among the defence was that most famous of Old Westminsters, N. C. Bailey, who gained his International cap on no less than nineteen occasions. As a half-back he has never been surpassed, while his old schoolfellow, R. T. Squire, would also take some beating. The latter is also very well known as a full-back. Lastly, where has a finer defence ever been found than P. M. and A. M. Walters at back, and W. R. Moon in goal? It is my great misfortune that I have never seen either of the former two play, but I well

THE CORINTHIANS v. SUNDERLAND, 1902, AT QUEEN'S CLUB.
Ryder dribbling.

remember, during my first term at Westminster, hearing how the brothers Walters came down against the school, and left a very strong impression both on the minds and bodies of the school forwards. Those of us who know them, however, can very easily understand how unpleasant it would be to meet the hard, sinewy frame of P. M., or the rather bigger, but equally hard one of A. M., in open charge. They are both of them excellent cricketers, and all who know them bear them the sincerest liking and respect. W. R. Moon, who frequently turns out for the well-known Hampstead Cricket Club, is probably the greatest goalkeeper of all time. I well remember, even a year or two ago, when he had not appeared in public for over two years, that he was persuaded to keep goal for the Old Westminsters in a Cup-tie against Shepherd's Bush. His form on that occasion was still brilliant; there was one particularly fine save, when an opposing forward had got clean away, but W. R. fell full length just at the right moment, and took the ball off the astonished forward's toe. Lastly, we have G. H. Cotterill, and C. Wreford-Brown of the old generation, though the latter indeed has lasted through all three generations, and still plays fine games at centre-half. An untiring worker and ubiquitous tackler, he never knows when he is beaten; he, Cotterill and Veitch finish our first batch. The two latter were magnificent forwards on the heavy side, and woe betide the back who tried to bustle them.

In the middle generation, the outstanding figure is, of course, G. O. Smith; he is admittedly the greatest centre-forward of all time. Possibly his success lies chiefly in his wonderful knack of adapting himself to all sorts of players; his own method is most unobtrusive. His forte was in making openings for the players on either side of him, though he was never slow to seize a chance himself should such be present. Slight of build and stature, such was his quickness and resource that the heavy charger rarely got near him. There was no dallying or dodging about where G. O. was concerned; just a deft touch to the left or right, and he passed by in his stride, leaving the half-back wondering why it was he thought G. O. was going in the opposite direction.

I well remember seeing the match for the Dewar Shield in 1898, when Aston Villa were beaten by 2—1 by the Corinthians. G. O. Smith, R. E. Foster, and G. P. Wilson were the insides, and, in spite of the fact that the ground was practically under water, we witnessed that day a most perfect exhibition of the inside forward game. G. O., I think, got both goals; the first, at any rate, was his with a lovely left-foot cross-shot into the corner of the net.

R. E. Foster and G. P. Wilson, on their best form, were both about as good as anyone you could wish to see; both were splendid dribblers and fine shots; it is a thousand pities we do not still see them. R. R. Sandilands, a forward who could play in almost any position, had a brilliant career up to the time when he hurt his knee; like Foster, he was several times an International. W. J. Oakley and L. V. Lodge belong to this period; they were both splendid backs and both Internationals; the former, indeed, was one of the best backs ever seen—in the opinion of some, quite the best.

G. C. Vassall and H. Vickers overlap into the present generation; the former, who plays at outside-right, is possessed of tremendous speed, and is a fine shot; the latter is one of the best amateur half-backs we have had for a considerable time.

At the present moment the Corinthians have a side capable of upholding the best traditions of the club. For the past two seasons, indeed, the results have been eminently satisfactory, and there seems to be no reason why they should not be so during the year that is now with us. Certainly towards the end of last year they were rather disappointing, and seemed to get stale; but that, I feel sure, is merely temporary.

T. S. Rowlandson, in goal, has few, if any, superiors in England. Big, strong, and very quick, he is an ideal build for such a place; he is particularly adept at saving penalties. At full-back we have W. U. Timmis, C. C. Page, and O. T. Norris to choose from; they are all bustlers and very clean kicks. Timmis, the old Oxford Blue, has rendered yeoman service to the club for years, and both the last two ought to turn into players of the very first order.

At centre-half we have, in my opinion, the best man in that position in the kingdom, viz., M. Morgan Owen. He has played nine or ten times for Wales. Though not over-heavy, he is very strong and "stocky," and makes the best use of every pound of his weight. A very quick and sure tackler, and a splendid pass to his forwards, he always opens up the game beautifully. Vickers we have already mentioned. J. D. Craig, right-half, is now one of the most dangerous halves it is possible to run up against; very fast, very strong, and with plenty of weight to

THE CORINTHIANS v. QUEEN'S PARK (GLASGOW), 1902.
C. B. Fry saves the situation.

A TRIO OF FAMOUS CORINTHIANS.
M. MORGAN OWEN. G. E. WILKINSON. C. B. FRY.

it is a matter of no small wonder that we generally have one day off form, or that we have all had enough of it at the finish.

However, it is a most delightful arrangement, that eight days' tour. Year after year, a large proportion of the same people meet together, and thus things go with a swing from first to last. There are usually about eighteen people on tour, so that everyone is able to have a rest occasionally.

At Easter it is unusual for the club to get together such a strong side for the tour, and the opposing sides are considerably weaker than those met at Christmas; therefore, the whole affair is taken less seriously, and looked on more as a holiday. In addition to the above-mentioned tours, the club often takes trips abroad. For instance, in 1903, Mr. C. Wreford - Brown took a team out to South Africa. The players whom he had under him were not, perhaps, altogether the best at the club's command; but it was, nevertheless, an excellent team, and, owing to their captain's good judgment in getting them thoroughly well together, they enjoyed a most successful tour; it also had the effect of making a vast improvement in the football of more than one member of the side. Again, in 1904, a strong side of Corinthians toured with great success in Hungary.

One word as to style. The Corinthian style has, I think, always been unique, and never entirely absent, even in the club's worst years. The chief thing about it is the "straight-ahead" theory. The forwards play a good open game, without any crowding, taking the ball on the run and making straight for goal without dallying. The passing is crisp, quick, and along the ground; the shooting is done from all angles. There is plenty of hard charging, but never a suspicion of foul play. There is any amount of life and go, and no one ever slacks. In fact, the impression one gleans from watching the Corinthians is that they play to win the game and to enjoy themselves while doing so.

back him up, he is possibly the best amateur right-half at the present time. H. A. Lowe, at left-half, is possessed of plenty of speed, and passes beautifully to his forwards—and none but a forward can know how much difference that makes.

In the forward line there is a plethora of talent to choose from. Vassall I spoke of above; his place at outside-right is frequently taken by R. G. Wright, who gained renown, in company with S. H. Day, as a right wing at Cambridge. He is a great worker, clever and tricky, and centres from any position. Sam Day, in his best form, has no superior as an inside-right; he is fast, and a very deadly shot. He shows excellent judgment, and if only he had a little more weight nothing would keep him from his International cap; that, however, may yet come. G. S. Harris, at centre, is a player to whom all things are possible. A very fine shot and good dribbler, he goes very straight and requires a lot of stopping. At outside-left we have E. G. D. Wright and E. S. Ward. Both are very fast, and have a good control of the ball. Wright ought to have a great future before him, as far as football is concerned; he can centre from almost any angle when travelling at top speed, and he knows the game to a nicety.

So much for individuals; now to return for a short time to the doings of the club. The Corinthians have, as most people know, two tours in each year — the first one, at Christmas-time, is the serious one; the second, at Easter, the holiday tour. By this I mean that, at Christmas, we go up North and play all the best clubs possible, and put our very best team into the field. In this tour, also, we play what is, in some respects, our most important match of the year, viz., against Queen's Park. As we usually play seven matches in eight days,

THE CORINTHIAN ELEVEN OF 1901.
Back Row: C. WREFORD-BROWN. B. MIDDLEDITCH. A. T. B. DUNN. C. B. FRY. W. J. OAKLEY. C. F. RYDER. B. O. CORBETT. H. VICKERS.
In Centre: R. E. FOSTER. G. O. SMITH. M. H. STANBROUGH.
At Bottom: G. E. WILKINSON.

Bowden Bros.]

THE NEW ZEALAND RUGBY TEAM IN TRAINING, 1905.

Practising a run by the three-quarters. The Colonial flyer, G. W. Smith, is holding the ball. W. Wallace on the left.

THE RUGBY GAME.

PART II.—THREE-QUARTER PLAY.

By ARTHUR J. GOULD, the most brilliant of all Welsh Internationals.

The three-quarter ignored in the early days of the Rugby game—The essential features of three-quarter play—The centre three-quarter—Cleverness and pace—Feeding the wing the first consideration of the centre—The futility of wild play—The drop at goal—Giants of the four three-quarter game—Elliott and Fitzgerald—The wing three-quarter—Don't bungle your pass—Kicking into touch—The three-quarter and defence.

RUGBY football is a very different game to-day to the game which was played on our public school-fields thirty years ago. Then twenty a side was the invariable rule, and the bulk of the forty were to be found in the scrum. What a sight it must have been to see thirty men pushing for all they were worth! They had to push; that was the game. Mr. Arthur Budd, whose knowledge of the code was so ample, has told us that when he played at Clifton School it was not unusual for th sides to be boxed in a scrummage for three or four minutes together, only to discover by that time that the half-back had absconded with the ball to the other side of the ground! There were fifteen a side forward, and they used their strength and avoirdupois. The stronger and heavier side carried the scrum, and the side which carried the scrum usually won. Naturally, in such an era, the three-quarter had a poor time—a poor time, that is, relatively speaking. I have little doubt that to the player the thrill of enjoyment was there. There are many points in the Rugby game which do not appeal to the onlooker which the Rugby player would not willingly see sacrificed.

But the elements of passing were soon introduced. To-day for our passing bouts we depend mainly upon the three-quarters. Passing is their prerogative. It should be essayed by all sections of the team, but it is to our three-quarters that we look for the making of ground in this manner. We cheer them; but other times other manners. Spectators years ago used to cheer the efforts of the tightly packed scrummagers. It was a stern contest of thew and muscle, and it had its good points. It is out of date now, but I am not gratified when I hear modern spectators speak as though the scrum had no right to remain a feature of the Rugby game.

In the first England and Scotland match there was only one three-quarter in the English twenty. Later there were two, then three, and then four. There seems to be a tendency to-day to make the number five, but I doubt if the combination of four skilful, fleet, and agile men can be excelled. Still, the whole drift of football has been in the direction of fostering three-quarter back work, and as we live in an experimental age it is difficult to say what the future has in store for us. As one who helped to make the four three-quarter game

Bowden Bros.]

THE NEW ZEALAND RUGBY TEAM IN TRAINING, 1905.

Duncan collaring Booth. Newton on the left.

what it is to-day, I may say that I am reasonably proud of what little I may have done in that direction, believing, as I do, that the three-quarter game, as played in Wales, is the most enjoyable phase of Rugby football we have had, no matter whether regarded from the point of view of the player or the spectator. Surely there is nothing prettier in football than to watch a three-quarter line in full flight? The ball passes from hand to hand with wonderful celerity; so much happens in the space of a few seconds. Surely, from every point of view, this is better than the stodgy, phlegmatic football seen in the days of the twenty a side, when thirty forwards held the ball tight, when the individual was lost in the crowd?

Bowden Bros.]

THE NEW ZEALANDERS IN TRAINING, 1905.

Duncan collaring Newton. The moment of the fall.

What are the essential features of three-quarter play? There are two kinds of three-quarters — there is the wing three-quarter and the centre three-quarter. There was a time when there was homogeneity in the work done by all the three-quarter line; now there is a marked difference of methods. The centre three-quarter should be strong, active, clever, and, above all, judicious. Of course, every Rugby player should be able to field and pass well; these are elementary essentials; but, alas! we sometimes find proficiency even in these particulars lightly regarded. The centre man should be able to feed the wing men under all sorts of disadvantageous circumstances. Every footballer should cultivate speed, but mere pace is not so essential in a centre as in a wing man; that is to say, that whereas a wing man must be fleet, even if he is not superlatively clever, the centre man would be better equipped with mere cleverness than with mere pace. If he can combine both, so much the better. Rawson Robertshaw, of Bradford, was, in my opinion, the first Englishman to grasp the real possibility of centre three-quarter play. He had wonderfully fleet men alongside him, notably J. J. Hawcridge, Percy Robertshaw, and F. T. Ritchie, and he fed them as no wing three-quarters had ever been fed before. R. L. Aston, in the South of England, also did much to give character to centre three-quarter back work. In Wales good centre three-quarters have always been abundant. A good supply of that type of player has been essential to our game.

LONDON WELSH v. NEWPORT.

Brought down by the leg. The above snapshot shows a magnificent collar by the London Welshman.

But while the feeding of the fleet outside man must ever be his first consideration, the centre three-quarter who is not himself a fairly regular try-getter will always be under suspicion of having been a failure, and mere automatic passing is of little value. The centre three-quarter will often do well to give the impression that he means to go through himself. If he makes straight for the opposing three-quarter, he will draw the defenders towards himself. Then just when he is likely to be tackled he passes to the wing man, who is backing up well on the outside and slightly in the rear, and often the latter will have a comparatively simple task in getting over. But the three-quarter who chucks the ball about before he has drawn the opposing defenders towards him is doing his side little service. It is the potential try which the centre three-quarter has up his sleeve, so to speak, which finally opens out the way for his fleeter comrade on the wing.

Then, again, the centre three-quarter must be able to pass to either side of the field with equal facility. This is a point which some teams overlook. Time after time you see the ball go right across the field, always from right to left. Now, that is playing into the hands of the defenders. Such tactics are, it goes without saying, easy to cope with. The great art of passing is not to let the opposition have the slightest inkling as to whom the next pass will visit. Among youthful three-quarters the inability to pass quickly and effectively from left to right is proverbial. A passing bout among them invariably ends in the wing man who last receives the ball being either tackled or pushed into touch.

Then the centre must always be on the look-out for a chance to drop a goal. He may often find himself favourably placed for dropping, and although the average points per match obtained from dropped goals may be small, yet such a goal has won many a game, and the records of men like Albert Goldthorpe, of Hunslet, prove how great a feature of the Rugby game a dropped goal might be made. The mere fact that few goals are dropped is not a proof that goals cannot be dropped. Never jeopardise the getting of a try by dropping at goal; but instinct should tell a man when to abstain from so doing. There is no royal road to success in football. No team can be really great without able centres. The four three-quarter game has never been quite so finely played as it was by Elliott, Fitzgerald, T. W. Pearson, and Norman Biggs, of the old Cardiff fifteen. Elliott and Fitzgerald were almost perfect centres. The ideal centre must have individual ability and judgment. He must be able to get past opposing centres, he must be capable of scoring by an individual effort, he must inspire opponents with the sense that he can go through if he tries; but his chief game should be to draw the opposing wing on to him, thus leaving an opening for his own wing. While he must be endowed with confidence in his own powers, so that he may himself take a chance without hesitation, he must be absolutely unselfish, and gifted with that judgment which teaches him to transfer the ball to his colleague at the right moment. When the perfect opening is made, the centre's work is done, and he should pass, leaving the wing to score. Never were a pair of centres more gifted with the power to draw the defence upon them, and the judgment to give their wings the ball, than were Elliott and Fitzgerald. Neither was fast, but both were extremely dodgy, and at the time of which I speak their unselfishness and judgment were worthy of all praise, while the accuracy of their passing could not have been improved upon.

NEW ZEALAND v. SOMERSET AT TAUNTON, OCTOBER 21, 1905.
Booth gets away for New Zealand and scores.

Then as to the wing three-quarter. He must be fast, and he should be tricky. He should cultivate the art of dodging adroitly, and if he can get that dangerous swerve which some men are able to command, then he is blessed indeed. There is nothing which a defender dreads so much as the man with a swerve. A. L. Brooke, the Huddersfield crack, had it as pronouncedly as any man that ever played. You get a man with a fast swerve and you have a man who scores tries freely. Pace is one of the first essentials on the wing. Many men have been dangerous scorers who were scarcely high-class footballers in the strict sense of the term. F. T. Ritchie, the champion sprinter, is a case in point. He was not an artistic performer, but the man who can do level time is always to be dreaded, providing that he has a reasonably good idea of the rudiments of the game.

Then the wing man should take his passes perfectly. It is very irritating to the centre men to see perfectly-made passes bungled, and more particularly is this so when the line lies white and tempting before you. Few men take the trouble to practise indoors in the gymnasium as the old Newport fifteen did. The wing man should also be able to find touch infallibly. It should not be difficult for a wing man to find touch, but one of the refinements of the game is the art of finding it at the most remote point possible. After all, possibly a reference to individuals will enable me to tell my tale better than I can tell it by rigidly adhering to abstract theories. I question whether any club ever possessed a finer pair of wing three-quarters than Norman Biggs and T. W. Pearson. Both were exceptionally fast and adepts at taking passes. Often Pearson took the ball with one hand when running at full pace, and he was a magnificent kick. His use of the touch-line was a lesson to three-quarters. As a scorer he had few equals, and in the season of 1892–3 he obtained forty-one tries for Cardiff. Often, of course, combination had done most of the work; but Pearson, though from his height and symmetry he appeared rather slight, was very strong, and he used his left arm with wonderful effect in handing off tacklers. He was also the great exponent of the short punt kick, from which he scored many tries. In Wales we hold that Pearson was the finest wing three-quarter that ever played, and it was a pity that business led to his giving up the game while he was still at the height of his powers. Norman Biggs was tremendously fast, and his dashes for the corner were things to be remembered. In addition, he was great at stopping rushes and a demon tackler. I have devoted some space to these great players because they were perfect exponents of their art, and what I have said of them can be applied generally. But just a word as to defence. The three-quarter must always mark his particular opponent, and the outside one must never allow his man to stand wide. When in his own "25" he should stand just outside, ready to go for his man the instant there is a necessity for doing so. And when he has followed up so as to put his forwards onside, he should always fall back immediately, unless he has a thoroughly good chance of again securing the ball himself.

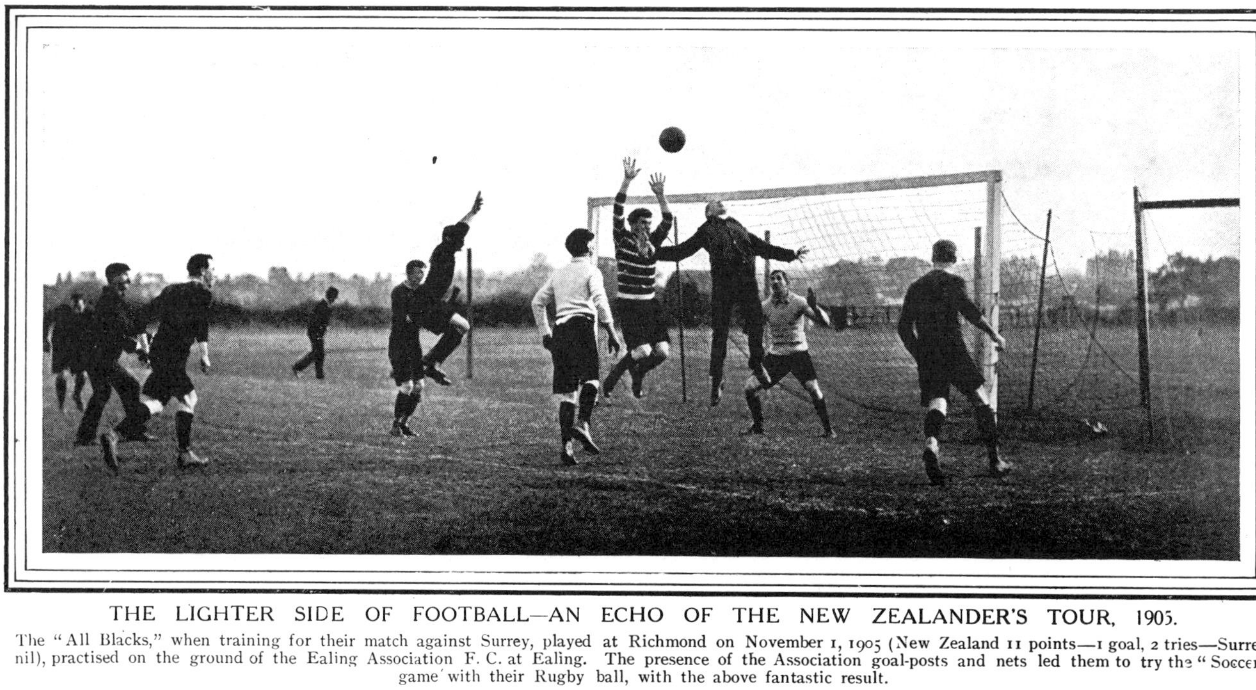

THE LIGHTER SIDE OF FOOTBALL—AN ECHO OF THE NEW ZEALANDER'S TOUR, 1905.
The "All Blacks," when training for their match against Surrey, played at Richmond on November 1, 1905 (New Zealand 11 points—1 goal, 2 tries—Surrey nil), practised on the ground of the Ealing Association F. C. at Ealing. The presence of the Association goal-posts and nets led them to try the "Soccer" game with their Rugby ball, with the above fantastic result.

ANNALS OF THE NOTTS COUNTY FOOTBALL CLUB

Winners of the Football Association Cup, 1893-4 ; Finalists, 1890-1.

Notts County introduce Association football into Nottingham—Mr. Blake Bailon leads the club on the Park Meadows in 1863-4—Great cricketers and the game in Notts—Greenhalgh of the County plays in the first International match—The club plays Queen's Park at Glasgow—A draw with the famous club at Nottingham—An increase of playing strength owing to the demise of the Nottingham Law Club—William Gunn transfers his services from the Forest to the County—The club's grand record in 1883-4—Preston North End defeated at Trent Bridge—The club embraces professionalism—Poor League performances—A limited liability company formed—Relegated to the Second Division—The County win the English Cup.

Colours : Black and white stripes. *Ground : Trent Bridge, Nottingham.*

TO Notts County belongs the honour of initiating the Nottingham public into the mysteries of Association football. Originally the members of the club had themselves to be initiated into its mysteries, but they proved ready pupils, and by their enthusiasm and skill soon contrived to get the sporting public of the lace town interested in their doings. Throughout the whole amateur era Notts County were a magnificent side. No provincial club turned out more redoubtable players ; no provincial club held their own in the front rank more persistently. It was when the days of the paid player came in that Notts lost caste ; just as the Forest did, for the matter of that.

Nottingham, as a centre, did not take at all kindly to the paid player. They were used to watching a higher class of men, and they did not like the altered conditions.

It was in the year 1862 that a number of well-known young fellows, mostly men of good social position, used to practise football in the Park. They included Major Hack, a notable sportsman, who was one of the best rifle shots in the town, F. C. Smith, Bernard Bradley, W. Patterson, A. Blake Bailon, W. A. Hodges, J. C. Hodges, and the well-known Richard Daft. The game came to Nottingham from Sheffield. For a time the doings of the band of enthusiasts did not command much public attention, but the club was rooted firmly, and in the season 1863–4 we find them migrating from the Park to the Meadows. There, clad in shirts of black and amber, the Notts County team gained fame under the leadership of their original captain Mr. Blake Bailon.

Notts sportsmen have always been famous for their all-round ability. You generally found a Notts cricketer a capable footballer, and a Notts footballer a capable cricketer. Practically every member of the Notts County team about this time, and, indeed, for at least ten years later, was first-class, or approaching thereto, at cricket. George Parr, the greatest batsman of his time, was one of the full-backs, and the most deadly shot at goal in Nottingham was Richard Daft. F. C. Smith, later well known as a banker, and the brothers Steegman were also among the prominent devotees of the game.

Notts obtained a notable recruit in the year 1867, when E. H. Greenhalgh was elected a playing member. He was one of the greatest footballers ever produced by Nottingham.

The fame of the County must have spread rapidly, because, prior to 1870, the London Wanderers did not think it *infra dig* to cross swords with them. In the first International Association match between England and Scotland, which took place at Partick, Glasgow, on November 30, 1872, E. H. Greenhalgh was included in the English team. He acted as one of the full-backs. To be more precise, he really played at three-quarter back, or cover goal, the position in which Sam Widdowson frequently used to appear in the early games of Notts Forest.

We find the Notts club showing commendable enterprise, for in 1875 they took a big journey. They visited Glasgow, and there met the then invincible Queen's Park eleven. They were beaten by 6 goals to 0, but they had more than ample compensation for their previous disappointment when, on March 8, 1875, Queen's Park returned the visit. The result was a draw of 1 goal each, but this showed what strides Nottingham had made. When one considers that the men had to pay their own expenses, this journey to Glasgow must be regarded as a great piece of enterprise.

Just as Notts Forest gained a valuable accession of playing strength when the Notts Castle Club collapsed, so the Notts County team profited materially when the strong Nottingham Law Club broke up. They were a very successful team.

It was with the Nottingham Law Club that that magnificent forward, Arthur Cursham, was originally associated. He was received with open arms by the County, and glad were they when his brother Harry, who had been associated with a Sheffield club, the Thursday Wanderers, threw in his lot with them in the year 1876. These accessions

Howard Barrett, Southwell.]

AFTER THE MATCH—A FOOTBALL CROWD CROSSING TRENT BRIDGE.

Those who decry the practice of spectators who gather in their thousands to witness a first-class football match might take a lesson from this picture. All sorts and conditions of men are here shown, even some ladies, and the general expression on their faces is one of happiness and content.

prompted them to enter for the English Cup in 1877, but there is always an ebb and flow of playing strength and public popularity, and about 1881, just when the Forest were at their best, the Notts club was in a rather sorry way. Indeed, there were thoughts of disbanding the organisation, and, as a last resource, a meeting was called at the Lion Hotel, but it was only attended by nine individuals. Mr. Arthur Ashwell, who was in the chair, however, would not hear of the club being disbanded. He moved that it be continued, and made a vigorous speech in support of his views. Mr. Arthur Cursham was equally dogmatic on the point, and it was there and then resolved that there should be no collapse of the famous old organisation.

This meeting was the turning-point in the club's history. That fine full-back, H. T. Moore, joined the club ; Stuart Macrae, one of the sternest half-backs that football has known, also came on the scene ; and, greatly to the joy of the County—and to the sorrow of the "Reds"—the mighty William Gunn, who had been playing brilliantly for the Forest, decided to transfer his affections ; and soon Notts probably had the finest eleven which had up to that time been seen in Nottingham. Instead of being troubled by fears of impending dissolution they marched triumphantly in 1883 into the Semi-final of the English Cup. In that stage they were drawn with the Old Etonians. They opened the score, and their hopes of reaching the Final stage appeared likely to be realised ; but the Eton men eventually triumphed by 2 goals to 1.

We have now come to the brightest days of Notts County football. They were now firmly established at Trent Bridge, and they had won the affections of the Nottingham public. In the season of 1883–4 they were never beaten at home, and they again reached the Semi-final of the English Cup.

A memorable match in the next season was when Preston North End, then the greatest side in the country, visited Trent Bridge, but, amidst intense excitement, Notts beat them by 2 goals to 1, that well-known all-round sportsman, Herbert Emmett, whose death was recorded recently, scoring the winning goal almost on the call of time.

The professional element was now beginning to intrude itself into football. As the purely professional teams came to the fore, Notts, who had always adhered to amateurism, gradually lost caste, as other teams situated as they were had done. At last they saw that they must face the inevitable, and for the season 1885–6 five professionals were retained, viz., Sherwin, Gunn, Emmett, Moore, and A. Peters. The club met with only moderate success, for they did not treat football with quite the business-like precision that some successful teams were adopting. But when in 1888–9 the League was formed, Notts were one of the original twelve selected. They owed much to Mr. Edwin Browne, their secretary. He was a man of considerable influence in the football world, and his tact stood the County in good stead. They finished eleventh, only having Stoke below them with the same number of points—12—but the County had a better goal average. They were re-elected, and the next season they finished tenth. They then became a limited liability company, and in 1890–1 they had an excellent season, finishing third on the League table to Everton and Preston North End, and reaching the Final of the English Cup. This was one of the best seasons Notts ever had in the League. In the following season they were eighth, but in 1892–3 they had fallen to fourteenth, and lost their position in the League, being beaten by Darwen in a test match.

But Notts faced their disheartening task nobly. They were in the Second Division for four years, and then in the season of 1896–7 they finished at the head of the Second League table, and so rejoined the First Division, and they have kept their place ever since.

Their first season in the Second League, indeed, was a great success, for they finished third, and accomplished the task which had always proved too much for their neighbours, the Forest—they won the English Cup ! The Oval was not available for football, and the Final between the County and Bolton Wanderers took place on the Everton ground on March 31, 1894. Thanks to the brilliant play of Logan, who went to them from Aston Villa, and whose dribbling and shooting on that day were magnificent, they defeated the Wanderers, who were pronounced favourites, by 4 goals to 1. It is only right that the names of the men who accomplished that feat should be given. They were : G. Toone (goal) ; T. Harper and J. Hendry (backs) ; C. Bramley, D. Calderhead, and A. Shelton (half-backs) ; A. Watson, A. Donnelly, J. Logan, D. Bruce, and H. B. Daft (forwards).

Notts rank as the only Second League club that have ever won the English Cup, and their triumph aroused great enthusiasm in Nottingham. It quite won back their lost following.

Notts have not done well in the League since they rejoined the Senior Division, except in the season 1900–1, when they totalled 40 points, and were third on the table to Liverpool and Sunderland. Once or twice they have had narrow escapes of again falling into the Second Division—notably in the season 1904-5, when they finished last on the League table with the meagre total of 18 points for 34 games, of which 5 only were won, 21 lost, and 8 drawn. The number of clubs in the League was, however, at the end of the season, extended from 18 to 20, and so the County retained their place ; it is to be hoped never to lose it again.

Howard Barrett, Southwell.]

FOOTBALL ON THE TRENT BRIDGE GROUND—NOTTS COUNTY *v.* MIDDLESBOROUGH.

Heading the ball.

NOTTS COUNTY FOOTBALL CLUB—FIRST LEAGUE TEAM, SEASON 1905-6.

Back Row: S. Robertson. E. Wright. F. P. Emberton. M. Reilly. J. Montgomery. T. E. Harris (Secretary).

Scott and Co., Manchester.]

Front Row: J. Dean. P. Humphreys. N. L. Mainman (Captain) R. Fountain. E. Gee. R. Craythorn.

Seaman and Sons, Chesterfield.]
THE RECREATION GROUND, SALTERGATE, THE HOME OF THE CHESTERFIELD TOWN FOOTBALL CLUB.
Note the famous crooked spire to the left of the grand stand.

CHESTERFIELD TOWN FOOTBALL CLUB.

By GEORGE ORAM.

The club founded in 1866—The rules that were drawn up in 1871-2—Chesterfield win their first cup—Further cup successes—Sheffield United defeated—The club joins the Midland League—A limited liability company formed—Chesterfield join the Second Division of the League—Six seasons' results in that competition—A bright future before the club.

Colours: Green and white striped shirts, dark-blue knickers. *Ground: Recreation Ground, Saltergate.*

THE Chesterfield Club, known chiefly away as the "Team of the Crooked Spire," and by many clubs as the "team of surprises," is undoubtedly one of the oldest clubs still in existence at the present day.

Founded as long ago as 1866, the original members played friendly matches; but in the season 1871-2 a meeting of those interested in football was called, and rules were drawn up, adopted, and printed. And through the kindness of Mr. T. H. Wardle, auctioneer, of Chesterfield, who is the proud possessor of a framed copy of the original rules, I am enabled to give a copy of the same for the edification of present-day football players and enthusiasts. They were as follows:

CHESTERFIELD FOOTBALL CLUB.

President:

J. CUTTS, ESQ.

Committee:

MR. MARRIOTT, MR. STANTON, MR. SYMES, MR. MUGLISTON, MR. NALL, MR. TOPLIS, MR. THOMPSON, MR. WHOMERSLEY.

Hon. Secretary and Treasurer: MR. C. W. ROLLINSON.

BYE-LAWS, RULES, AND REGULATIONS. SEASON 1871–2.

1. That this Club be called the Chesterfield Football Club.
2. That a Committee of Management be annually appointed, to consist of a President, Eight other Members, and a Secretary, who shall also act as Treasurer; both President and Secretary to be considered as ex-officio members of the Committee.
3. That an Election of Officers take place at the Annual Meeting of the Club, to be held the second week in September.
4. That the Committee shall meet at least once a month during the season, and that four form a quorum.
5. That the season commence in October, and end in March, and that practice days be Wednesday and Saturday.
6. That the subscription be Two Shillings each year, due at the commencement of each season, but the committee be empowered to make such further call as shall be necessary.
7. That the Secretary have the sole management of the matches and the selection of teams, subject to the approval of the Committee.
8. That prior to the commencement of each season the Secretary shall render an account of all moneys received and paid by him on behalf of the Club, which account shall be audited by two members of the Committee and verified by their signatures and then submitted to the Club.
9. That, if it should appear by the accounts that there is a balance in the hands of the Secretary, the amount shall be carried to the club funds of the ensuing year.
10. That any member, feeling himself aggrieved by any other member, or members, may bring his complaint before the Committee for their decision, and that the Committee have the power either to fine or expel such members complained of, and that such fine shall not exceed five shillings.

The majority of the promotors of the club in its early days are now dead, but Mr. John Marriott, a past mayor of the local borough, can often be seen sitting as a magistrate at the police-court, and also as a spectator at the "Town" football matches on Saturday.

Mr. John Marriott, Mr. John Cutts—at that time a well-known solicitor acting as Town Clerk, but now deceased—with Mr. C. W. Rollinson, who is still alive and who acted as secretary and treasurer, were the moving spirits in the enterprise.

Sheffield Wednesday, Nottingham Forest, Nottingham County, Sheffield Garrick, Sheffield Gentlemen, Rotherham, and other clubs were met in those days, and one match was won by the stupendous score of 22 goals to 1.

All the matches in this early period were friendlies, and no competition was entered into until the year 1891. In that year Chesterfield entered the Barnes competition, the winner holding a cup presented by the late Alfred Barnes, Esq., who was a large colliery proprietor in the district and member of Parliament for the Chesterfield division until defeated by the present sitting member, Thos. Bayley, Esq. The club succeeded in winning this competition, and became the holders of the cup. In 1892 Chesterfield managed to win the Sheffield Cup and the Derbyshire Minor Cup, and also won the Barnes Cup for the second time. During that season they created a tremendous surprise, beating Sheffield United by 3 clear goals, the losing team playing such well-known players as Ernest Needham, Bob Cain, Harry and Will Lilley, Scott, and Watson.

In 1896 Chesterfield joined the Midland League, and remained members of that body until they gained promotion to the Second Division of the English League in 1899. Amongst the honours they gained between 1891 and 1898 inclusive were the following: Barnes Cup, 1891-2-3; championship of the Sheffield and District League, 1892-3; Derbyshire Cup, 1892-3, 1898-9; championship of the Sheffield and Derbyshire League, 1896-7; championship of the Derbyshire Senior League, 1897-8.

In 1899 a meeting was called to consider the advisability of making application for admission to the Second Division of the English League, and it was decided to form the club into a limited liability company, with the late Mr. Edward Mitchell as president; Messrs. W. H. Eyre, W. H. Wagstaffe, and W. C. Brinson as vice-presidents, with nine directors; Mr. George Gillies (now secretary-manager of Leeds City F. C., Ltd.) as club secretary, and Mr. A. E. Mitchell as secretary of the company. The capital was £1,000, in £1 shares.

Mr. W. H. Eyre and Mr. G. Gillies attended the annual League meeting, and were successful in persuading the representatives present to accept the newly formed club as members of that body. The new company generously took over all the old club's liabilities and paid them, even though they had a severe struggle to keep financially sound.

Chesterfield finished their first season very creditably, winning 16 matches, scoring 65 goals, and gaining 38 points, with seventh position on the Second League table.

Meritorious victories have been secured at home, as numerous teams can testify, and the better the club pitted against Chesterfield the better their play, the team, with few exceptions, always rising to the occasion. Since joining the Second Division of the League, Chesterfield's performances in that competition have been of a fluctuating character, as will be seen by the following tabulated record of six seasons' work:

	Played	Won	Lost	Drn.	Goals For	Goals Agst.	Pts.	Psn.
1899-1900	34	16	12	6	65	60	38	7
1900-1901	34	9	15	10	46	58	28	14
1901-1902	34	11	17	6	47	68	28	16
1902-1903	34	14	11	9	67	40	37	6
1903-1904	34	11	15	8	37	45	30	11
1904-1905	34	14	9	11	44	35	39	5

It will be seen by the above that, after the season 1901-2, Chesterfield had to go, cap in hand, to seek re-election, but I am proud to be in a position to state that the whole of the thirty-three clubs voted for their return, showing their appreciation of the fact that the Chesterfield Club, in spite of not being a rich organisation, had always honourably kept to their engagements and arrangements with the other clubs with which they had come into contact.

Chesterfield, as a first-class football club on a limited liability basis, has never been blessed with a superabundance of wealth, but, through all its troubles and trials—and there have been many—it has had the unswerving support of loyal directors, and, what is rarer still, loyal players. Colonel Allen, of Wingerworth Hall, the club's president, has stuck to the club in many a crisis, and, with all working for one common end, there is no reason why the season of 1905-6 should not be the most prosperous in the club's history. The club has never received the support it quite deserved from the "Town of the Crooked Spire," but there are signs of public awakening, and in the future more extraordinary things than the regular visit of First League clubs to Chesterfield may occur. Who knows?

THE BOOK OF FOOTBALL *Copyright.*]

CHESTERFIELD TOWN FOOTBALL CLUB—PLAYERS AND OFFICIALS, SEASON 1905-6.

Back Row (left to right): GEORGE ORAM (Director). TYE. MARPLES. H. C. CLARKE (Director). COPE (Goalkeeper). T. H. FURNISS (Director). W. BANNER. G. E. CLARKE (Director). W. MACHENT (Committee). BAKER. J. T. HOSKIN (Secretary and Manager).

Bottom Row: NEEDHAM (Trainer). DYAL. HAIG. LUNN. TAYLOR. MUNDAY (Inside-left, the goal-getter). THACKER. BULL.

A BRIEF HISTORY OF THE RUGBY GAME IN WALES.

HOW THE CLUBS HELPED THE PRINCIPALITY.

By A. T. HABERSTRAW.

The origin of the Rugby game in Wales—To whom the honour should be given—Early games—A battle royal at Llanelly—The development of the game—The frigid attitude of England towards the Principality—The first International—The names of the Welsh fifteen—A gradual levelling up of form—Wales beat England for the first time in 1890—The four three-quarter game introduced by Cardiff—Famous Welsh clubs—Influence of Welsh play in the Northern Union games—Newport, Swansea, and Cardiff—Why Wales baffled New Zealand—Llanelly—Welsh Rugby football—Rugby football at its best.

IT is not within the recollection of everyone that there was a time, and that not so very far back either, when the Principality of Wales was nothing like the football centre it is now and its men no such players of subtlety and renown as all the world is now acclaiming. Time was when the Englishman gave Taffy fixtures more out of condescension than any desire for a sporting game, and when the Welshman saw the reverse side of the shield so frequently and disastrously that it is recorded in the secret annals of the game in Wales—annals few can gain access to—that it was proposed to abandon any attempt to place a representative Welsh team in the field, and to permit the individual club and player to "gang their ain gait" and take to the Association code should he or they so choose.

The actual origin of the Rugby game in Wales, or, to be more precise, in the southern portion of the Principality, is but vaguely known. A few isolated writers who have tackled the subject from time to time have had to contend with the claims of some half-a-dozen towns and communities who aver that there, and there only, was the first implant of the oval-shaped leather of any pretensions and permanency. Thus we have Newport, Swansea, Neath, Llandovery, Brecon, and even demure little Cowbridge, claiming to have been the birthplace of the Rugby code in the Principality. The claims most entitled to credence are those of Newport and Swansea, although the collegians of Llandovery and Brecon at one time contributed a goodly quota to the representative teams of the Principality, and undoubtedly played the game from early in the Seventies.

The personnel and composition of the Welsh fifteen against England at Richmond this year was indeed a striking contrast with the first few representative Welsh fifteens, in which the working-man element was conspicuous by its absence only, and indeed comprised of elements much like the Scottish and Irish teams of the present day. What old Welsh "sport" does not recall with sparkling eye the Hancocks, the Hills, the Goldsworthys, the Richardsons, and the Meagers; the old cup-tie (and earlier) days, going far back, when Neath trounced Swansea and Carmarthen accounted for Llanelly with quite natural ease. In those days the man who would have predicted that the time would come when "gates" of 30,000 at football matches would be common occurrences in the larger Welsh towns would have been looked on much as the man would to-day who might tell us we would all be made millionaires by Act of Parliament. In the early days of the Welsh game players clubbed together to pay the rent of their fields, and old Swansea footballers tell stories of how the Richardsons, of copper-ore trading fame, used to unwittingly open the early pages of the Welsh game by miniature Internationals on a field in the St. Helen's district of the town, now thickly built over with houses.

INTERNATIONAL RUGBY—ENGLAND v. WALES AT CARDIFF, 1905.
Wales get away.

The best-known families indeed of West and East Wales associated themselves with the handling code and its development, and to the Clarkes of Neath much of the present strength of football in the West is really due.

To-day, indeed, the Neath team can hold its own on its "ain midden" a deal more surely and confidently than it can on other fields.

People did not write descriptive articles to the Press in those early days every time a player twisted his ankle or perchance annexed the ball from underneath an opponent's nose with some newly studied subtlety. The writer recalls with gusto how in the streets of the grimy tinplate town, Llanelly, a string of wounded footballers, some limping, some being carried, were being escorted to their headquarters. "What sort of game was it, Dai?" shouted a tradesman from his door to a friend in the cortege. "Game!" echoed Dai beamingly. "Man, you missed something! Five 'urt on our side, and seven with the others!"

The game developed—almost unconsciously to the players. From one half-back and two full-backs down to the formation at the beginning of the 1905-6 season is a long step; but, like all other phases of devolution, the change came about quite naturally. In 1878 the South Wales Football Club exchanged the term "union" for "club," as the calibre and skill of the Welsh players was inspiring hopes in

Bowden Bros.]

INTERNATIONAL RUGBY—WALES v. SCOTLAND AT CARDIFF, 1902.

After a remarkable piece of play right on the line, Gabe gets over and scores the third try for Wales.

the breasts of its principal friends that there were other fields to conquer beyond the Principality. The early efforts to induce the footballers of haughty old England to meet the men of the Leek were, the present-day admirer of the conquerors of New Zealand will be interested to learn, met with a certain amount of frigidity, not unmixed with amusement. It was in 1881 that the first approach to anything like an International encounter took place at Blackheath. The memory of that day is still recalled with an admixture of mirth and gloom by the "old hands." The score was: England, 8 goals, 5 tries; Wales, nil. And the few newspaper critics of the day dismissed the Welshmen's pretensions in entering the inter-country arena with amused scorn.

The effect of this decidedly bad start was that no further Internationals were attempted by the Principality until 1882, and that was not strictly an inter-country fixture, being billed ".Wales v. North of England." The Welshmen only lost by a goal to a try, and this encouraged them to try their luck against their Blackheath victors once more, and the match took place at Swansea before an attendance that the present club fifteen there would consider a very small company indeed. Although there was no reversal of the previous result, the score was not so crushing, the verdict being: England, 2 goals, 4 tries; Wales, nil.

Succeeding matches up to 1887 showed that the Cymry were gradually getting the measure of their opponents until the eventful day in 1890, when, at Dewsbury, the Cardiff idol, "Buller" Stadden, got over with a wriggle worthy of a David James or an Owen, and scored the only try of the match, winning the first match of the International series to be won by Wales. The subsequent meetings between the two countries produced results of the fluctuating order, the most noteworthy being the swamping of Wales by the English forwards at Birkenhead in 1894, and the 1905 Saxon debacle at Cardiff. The first match played by Wales with Scotland was in 1883 at Edinburgh, the homesters being victorious by 3 goals to 1, and the first Ireland v. Wales fixture was an auspicious beginning for the men in red, who won at Dublin by the substantial margin of 2 goals, 2 tries to nil. The Hibernians were then in their embryo days, and the Gaelic style had up to then made the cult of Rugby difficult to establish in the Emerald Isle.

The four three-quarter game which was, so it is claimed, first tried by the Cardiff team under F. E. Hancock, was introduced into the Welsh match with Scotland in 1886, but as the men of the bagpipes vanquished the exponents of the innovation on their native soil by 2 goals and a try to love, not much enthusiasm or confidence was forthcoming. The Welsh clubs, however, continued to play it regularly—much as the present Cardiff, Swansea, and other fifteens play a wing-forward, as the fancy suits them—until 1890, when, truth to tell, popular jubilation over the unexpected victory of Wales at Dewsbury condoned the claim that the four three-quarter game—as played that day—was really responsible for Stadden's try. The opinion of those who saw the match, however, is just as favourable to Stadden's dash as to any preceding movement leading up to it. In any

A. and G. Taylor, Swansea.]

THE MAGNIFICENT FOOTBALL ENCLOSURE AT SWANSEA, THE HOME OF THE SWANSEA RUGBY FOOTBALL CLUB.

case, the other countries—who were really, England in particular, simply experiencing that period of transition from good to ill-luck which falls to all clubs sooner or later—thought a change would "do no harm," and they straightway adopted the four three-quarter game. Ireland alone appears to have mostly benefited by the change, and, truth to tell, the English teams have never really played the game as it was intended to move by the introduction of a fourth three-quarter. The fourth man was simply brought out to increase the scoring possibilities of a passing movement, and as English back play has never assumed an aspect of more than, at the most, clever individualism, it is not quite intelligible to the writer why England ever adopted the fourth man!

Coming to clubs, the names of Newport and Swansea stand out in the annals of Welsh football with singular boldness and brilliance. Their records are held up in every "Rugger" community as types and patterns to attain to, and Welshmen in Northern Union clubs have brought their wiles to Yorkshire and Lancashire and aided many an English side to victory. Partisans of both clubs claim that theirs is the better record of the two, but for consistent play the palm can hardly be withheld from the Swansea Club, or, as they are popularly known in Wales and the West, the "All Whites." It is, perhaps, appropriate that the only club team in the kingdom whose line the redoubtable "All Blacks" were unable to cross should be the "All Whites," and this at a period when, by general consent in the Principality—and what critics they are, to be sure!—the Swansea Club is not possessed of a side of anything like similar strength to that of two seasons back.

And at the risk of being accused of singling out the Swansea Club for special mention, let it be said that if the Cardiff Club—the famous "blue and blacks"—whose Hancocks, Biggses, Fitzgeralds, and Sweet-Escotts have ran with many a brilliant try—if this side made the four three-quarter system the game of machine-like precision it grew to, so did the Swansea Club develop every phase of the passing game until the mechanical aspect of it was confined to the accuracy of the transfers, and not to the certainty of their whereabouts. It is to Cardiff and Swansea primarily that Wales owes her present-day preeminence over any other exponents of the Rugby code in the world, which, as you know, includes the Antipodes. Newport developed the idea of the co-operation of the forwards with the three-quarters in the loose, and this, too, was a powerful factor; and it can never be forgotten that this club produced the most brilliant three-quarter of all time, the famous Arthur Gould, who, it is said, could score whenever he had really decided to do so! Newport, Cardiff, and Swansea can be safely regarded as the three top-sawyers in Rugby in the United Kingdom at the present day.

They may lose matches occasionally—invincible seasons are not for all time—but they are in skill and ensemble far above anything that can be produced in the other countries.

The excellence of the Welsh game cannot be wholly attributed to the play of the backs. Without the ball one cannot score tries. Therefore it is that every present-day effort of your "class" Welsh club is concentrated on "feeding the three-quarters."

The much-talked-of "secret formation" of the New Zealand forwards, who were said to be able to heel the ball out to their backs by some intricate and well-studied process, didn't "come off" at Cardiff, Swansea, or Newport, simply because these clubs are past-masters at the game themselves. To watch the forwards of a Welsh club working the ball out at their heels to their inside-half is quite a study in movement. And once it is out, your Welsh "up" does not regard his duty as finished or confined to leading dribbling rushes or indiscriminate kicks whenever possible. The Newport forwards in the days of Graham and Gould in 1890 and 1891 were as near like three-quarters in the open as anything the writer has ever seen.

A SECTION OF THE CROWD AT THE INTERNATIONAL RUGBY FOOTBALL MATCH—ENGLAND v. WALES AT CARDIFF, 1905.

Then we come to Llanelly, that strenuous little team of ups and downs. Once the terror of all the clubs—even now a "hot lot" on their own ground. The writer mentions the "Scarlet-runners"—as they are suitably dubbed—because of their indisputable contributions to the component parts of the Welsh system. Cardiff invented the "machinery," Swansea and Newport improved on it, and little Llanelly made it go faster! Whoever saw Badger, Davies, and Co. "on the travel" in the early Nineties saw very little of what transpired during the movements. The ball left the scrummage in some occult manner, and there was a flashing in and out of the opposing ranks of scarlet jerseys. Then someone would remark, "They're over!" Nobody saw precisely how it was done. Oftentimes the players themselves couldn't, but there it was.

It is, in short, the welding and blending together of all that is best and most effective of the club methods that has brought Welsh football to its present high pinnacle. The team representing the Principality in its inter-country matches may not be invincible always, but the name of Welsh football will continue to stand as a synonym for Rugby football at its best for many seasons to come, or until such time as those who control its official destinies choose to experiment too far and tread in unreliable paths to the detriment of a virile and picturesque system.

NEW ZEALAND'S CONQUERORS—THE FIFTEEN THAT REPRESENTED WALES AT CARDIFF December 16, 1905.

Ack. Llewellyn (Touch-judge).

Back Row: Tom Williamson (W. F. U.). J. F. Williams. George Travers. D. Jones. W. Joseph. R. T. Gabe. Sir J. T. D. Llewelyn, Bart. (President W. F. U.).

A. and G. Taylor, Cardiff.]

Middle Row: C. M. Pritchard. J. J. Hodges. W. M. Llewellyn. E. Gwyn Nicholls (Captain). H. B. Winfield. Cliff Pritchard. A. F. Harding.

Bottom Row: E. T. Morgan (who scored the winning try). R. M. Owen. P. F. Bush.

Howard Barrett.]
A LEAGUE MATCH ON THE CITY GROUND—NOTTINGHAM FOREST v. DERBY COUNTY.

NOTTINGHAM FOREST FOOTBALL CLUB.

Winners of the Football Association Cup, 1897-8.

How the club came into being—The "shinney v. football" rivalry—Nottingham Forest's first match—Forest beat the County by 1 goal to nil—Rapid progress of the club—The collapse of Notts Castle F. C. in 1878 adds to the Forest's power—English Cup games—The era of professionalism—Mr. H. S. Radford—The great Tinsley Lindley—Forest win the Cup—The team in the Final of 1897-8—The Forest's grounds.

Colours: Red shirts, white knickers. *Ground: City Ground, Nottingham.*

ALTHOUGH Notts Forest — or, rather, Nottingham Forest, to give the club its correct title—does not rank as one of the original League clubs, it has a history which is sufficient to make some of the more mushroom organisations of that combination blush for their aggressive newness. We have to go back to 1865 to reach the beginning of things in connection with the Notts Forest Club.

The Forest Club owed its existence to a number of active young fellows, many of whom are now well-known in the public life of Nottingham, who were accustomed to play the old-fashioned game of bandy on the Forest Recreation Ground. The game was known as shinney, and it was, of course, the pioneer of the now highly developed science known as hockey. The old racecourse was on the Forest, and there was a magnificent stretch of ground, some of the striking scenes on which have been graphically described by William Howitt, the possessor of a name well-known in Nottingham for generations. It was called the Forest because it had once been covered with the trees of Sherwood. The great feats of Richard Daft, and the other members of the Notts County team who disported themselves elsewhere, naturally fired the imagination of the young men who met on the Forest; and one Saturday afternoon quite a debate took place among them as to whether it would not be possible to play Association football as well as shinney, or, in the alternative, adopt Association football in place of shinney. But the advocates of shinney did not like to see the old game displaced by what they regarded as a fad, and finally it was decided to adjourn the impromptu meeting and call a definitely constituted one. Mr. J. S. Scrimshaw accordingly undertook to summon a meeting, and this was held at the Clifton Arms Hotel, not far from the ground. That meeting saw the definite formation of the Nottingham Forest Football Club. Among those who took part in the deliberations were several men who long remained active and loyal members of the Forest, including C. F. Daft, W. R. Lymbery, R. P. Hawksley, T. G. Howitt, W. Brown, J. H. Rastall, W. H. Revis, T. Gamble, J. E. Richardson, J. Tomlinson, J. S. Scrimshaw, and J. Milford. Mr. Milford was the first hon. secretary, and Mr. W. Brown had charge of the finances. Mr. Brown remained in office until comparatively recent times. He is now no more; but it was always one of his proud boasts that he remembered going to Mr. C. F. Daft's shop and buying a dozen red-flannel caps for the use of the players. They were the "Reds" then, and the "Reds" they have always remained.

The Forest played their first match in 1866, a year after the formation of the club, when they met their great local rivals—Notts County. This was the first of a great series of local fights, the like of which have rarely—if ever—been known in the history of the game. Both clubs survive; both have never ceased to be first class. The match took place on the old racecourse, in close proximity to the grand stand, and the most exciting, and, indeed, thrilling incident was when Hugh Browne, of the County, and W. H. Revis, of the Forest, had an exciting race after the ball. After crossing the palings near the grand stand, the Forester touched down, and so scored in a way which is honoured to this day under the Rugby code, but which seems strange in connection with the sister game. The ball was brought out in the legitimate Rugby way, and a place-kick was taken fifteen yards away at right angles to the goal-line. There was no crossbar; the ball merely had to go between the posts, at an infinite height it might be, and the kick being successful the Forest won by a goal to nil. Oh, yes; it was an Association match! Those were the normal happenings in those early days. You never knew where the Rugby method ended and the Association began; but it was good sport, I doubt not.

The club made splendid progress after this. The members were real enthusiasts, and they could not fail to succeed. They joined the Sheffield Association, and had many pleasant matches with the Sheffield and District clubs under Sheffield rules. In 1870 the historic Notts Forest athletic sports, destined to become the great meeting of the North of England, were originated, and were held on Trent Bridge, where they have so long been a recognised attraction. The expenses amounted to £60, but

THE NOTTINGHAM FOREST ELEVEN—1905-6.

Howard Barrett, Southwell.]

From left to right: NIBLO. HENDERSON. CRAGGS. WOLFE. DUDLEY. MORRIS. CRAIG. LINACRE. TIMMINS. SPOUNCER. WEST.

the attendance was so large that a handsome profit was realised, and the club have never failed to make the meeting a financial success.

The clubs met at this period were Notts County, Sheffield Norfolk, Newark, Notts Manufacturing Company, and some of the colleges in the neighbourhood of Nottingham and Derby. It was in the December of 1873 that the Forest had their first lesson in really scientific football. The famous Royal Engineers then made the first football tour on record. They met the Foresters and defeated them by 2 goals to 1. Such a result was regarded as creditable to the losers, because the Royal Engineers then shared with the Wanderers the credit of ranking as the first exponents of the game. Major Marindin, later destined to become the president of the Football Association, was the goalkeeper in that match. It occurred to S. W. Widdowson that combination was the key-note of the Engineers' success, and from that time forward the Forest made combination their watchword. Still, they did not lose their individual dribbling power, for Widdowson ranked as one of the greatest individual forwards that ever played the game. It was he who invented shin-guards, which he registered in 1874. The Forest also introduced the referee's whistle, this being used for the first time on the Forest ground in 1878 in a match with Sheffield Norfolk.

The Forest now went further afield for their games, and when in 1878 the Notts Castle Club collapsed, most of their members threw in their lot with the Forest, and the club became exceptionally powerful. They entered for the Association Football Cup competition in that season—1878-9—and have always been identified with the competition since. They were drawn with their neighbours—Notts County—and the teams met on a proper ground, where a "gate" could be taken, on November 16, 1878. The Forest won by 3 goals to 0, and beat the then well-known Sheffield club in the second round. They were then drawn against the Old Harrovians, and met the latter in London on January 27, 1879. This was the first appearance of a provincial club in a Cup-tie in the Metropolis. The Forest won by 2 to 0, and in the fourth round they beat Oxford University, then particularly strong, at the Oval by 2 to 1. They were now in the Semi-final stage, and they encountered the Old Etonians at the Oval. The absence of F. W. Earp, one of their most brilliant forwards, handicapped them considerably; but they were only defeated by 2 goals to 1. The Old Etonians were the final winners.

In 1879-80 the Forest made their headquarters at Trent Bridge, and again qualified for the Semi-final of the English Cup, only to be beaten by Oxford University by 1 goal to nil. Those were the palmy days of the Forest. They taught Birmingham people their football, and were the greatest missionaries the game had known. In 1885 the Forest, still under the leadership of genial Sam Widdowson, again reached the Semi-final of the Cup, and played a great match with Queen's Park at Derby. The game was drawn, but on being re-played at Merchiston, Edinburgh—the only English Semi-final ever played in Scotland—Queen's Park won.

Then came the era of professionalism, and the Forest would have none of it. But the club went down steadily, until its very existence was threatened. Notts County once more passed them in the race for position. Then, in 1889, Mr. H. S. Radford came into office as hon. secretary, and he saw that the policy of drift would not do. A modified system of professionalism was adopted, and at once the prospects of the club changed. Whereas in 1889 they were last but one in the Alliance table, in the following year they finished fifth, and applied for admission to the League, but only received one vote. Then they won the Alliance championship in 1891-2, and were elected to the First Division of the League in 1892-3. Thus in three years the Forest had completely regained their lost position. They have never lost their place. Among the notable players who assisted them at this period were Sandy Higgins, Adam Scott, and Ritchie. Scott was a magnificent footballer, and for his size was one of the grandest full-backs ever known. The assistance which the great Tinsley Lindley gave them at various times must never go unrecognised. He was one of the ablest centres that ever played football. He was in the Cambridge eleven for four years, and for ten years—namely, from 1881 to 1891—he rendered the Forest magnificent, if not regular, service. Then John McPherson, a wonderful captain, must not be forgotten. And Leonard Benbow, Arthur Capes, T. McInnes, P. McCracken, and R. Norris all did good service. Other names which occur in later days are: J. Iremonger, C. H. Richards, A. Spouncer, F. Spencer, and Frank and Fred Forman; while still more recently A. G. Morris, one of the ablest forwards ever known, Shearman, and their International goalkeeper, Linacre, have done much to keep the club famous.

The solitary victory of Notts Forest in the English Cup competition must not be forgotten. They reached the Semi-final in 1892, the year that Davie Russell was their leader, but were beaten in a sensational match in a snowstorm at Derby by West Bromwich Albion. However, in 1897-8 they appeared in the Final for the first time, and carried off the Cup. This was under Frank Forman's captaincy, and they beat Derby County by 3 goals to 1. Perhaps it might be interesting to give the team which won the Cup. It was: D. Allsop; A. Ritchie and A. Scott; Frank Forman, J. McPherson, and W. Wragg, T. McInnes, C. H. Richards, L. Benbow, Arthur Capes, and A. Spouncer.

Howard Barrett.]

THE RE-PLAYED SEMI-FINAL CUP-TIE AT THE CITY GROUND, 1905—ASTON VILLA (Cup Winners) v. EVERTON

(the Villa won by 2 goals to 1, after a draw, 1—1, at Stoke).

The Villa repel the Everton attack.

Moyse, Putney.]

THE TEAMS IN THE INTERNATIONAL TRIAL MATCH—AMATEURS *v.* PROFESSIONALS OF THE SOUTH.

Played at Craven Cottage, January 8, 1906, and won by the professionals by 1 goal to nil. Amateurs, white; professionals, stripes.

Back Row (from left to right): P. R. HARROWER (Referee). CAPTAIN E. G. CURTIS (Linesman). P. H. FARNFIELD. J. G. WITHERINGTON. C. D. MCIVER. H. A. NULTON. ASHCROFT. WALTON. CROSS. CHAMBERS. F. STYLES (Linesman).

Middle Row: S. H. DAY. V. J. WOODWARD. H. SMITH. S. S. HARRIS (Amateur Captain). BULL (Professional Captain). BLACKBURN. RILEY. THRELFALL.

Front Row: E. G. D. WRIGHT. T. S. ROWLANDSON. G. C. VASSALL. COLLINS. COLEMAN. HARRISON.

ENGLAND'S INTERNATIONAL TEAMS, AND HOW THEY ARE SELECTED.

By ALFRED DAVIS.

The first England v. Scotland match—Scotland's early sequence of victories—Disasters to Scotland checked in 1896 by the inclusion of players from English clubs—The personnel of the F. A. Selection Committee—How the teams are chosen—The arrangements made for International players—Scottish enthusiasm.

THE Football Association Council and the committees appointed by the Council have many and various duties to perform. The draw for the Football Association Cup rounds is, perhaps, the business that excites the greatest amount of interest and excitement for the general public, and, second only to the Cup draw, comes the selection of the teams to represent England in the International matches. This matter of selection is the medium for a vast amount of gratuitous advice and criticism of a more or less severe character, and I imagine that an International eleven has never yet been chosen that pleased everybody. Beyond the Border the interest in the choice of the Scottish teams outweighs even the Scottish Cup draw, and it is no uncommon event to find a big crowd awaiting the verdict of the selectors outside the hotel or offices in which the committee are deliberating.

The International contests, like the game of Association football itself, have made vast strides in popular favour in recent years. In the early days the spectators were numbered in hundreds instead of thousands, but I doubt not that the matches were fought out with just as much keenness as in the present day.

MR. ALFRED DAVIS,
Member of the International Selection Committee, and representative of the Berks and Bucks Association upon the F. A. Council.

The International rivalry between England and Scotland dates back to 1870-1, in which season two games were played on Kennington Oval. These matches are not recognised in the official records, owing to the fact that the Scottish teams were selected from Scots resident in England. November 19, 1870, was the date of the first encounter, and England scored the only goal of the match. The teams were made up of the following players:

England: C. W. Alcock (Old Harrovians), captain; A. J. Baker (Wanderers), T. N. Carter (Eton College captain), J. Cockerell (Brixton), W. P. Crake (Barnes), E. Lubbock (West Kent), T. C. Hooman (Wanderers), W. B. Paton (Harrow School captain), H. J. Preston (Eton College), R. W. S. Vidal (Westminster School), and R. S. F. Walker (Clapham Rovers). Scotland: J. Kirkpatrick (Civil Service), captain; A. F. Kinnaird (Old Etonians), R. E. W. Crawford (Harrow School), H. W. Primrose (Civil Service), C. E. Nepean

(University College, Oxford), Quintin Hogg (Wanderers), W. Lindsay (Old Wykehamists), W. A. B. Hamilton (Old Harrovians), G. F. Congreve (Old Rugbeians), R. Smith (Queen's Park, Glasgow), and G. G. Kennedy (Wanderers).

A return match, on February 25, 1871, ended in a draw (1—1). A few changes were made in the teams, the late W. H. Gladstone, M.P., being amongst the Scottish players.

Two seasons later (1872-3) the first officially recognised matches between England and Scotland were duly decided. The Scottish F. A. had not at that time been formed, and the selection of the teams to represent Scotland was undertaken by the Queen's Park F. C. The first game was played on the West of Scotland C. C. ground at Partick, and it resulted in a draw with no score. The match was witnessed by a large gathering, and it undoubtedly laid the foundation for the rapid growth of the game beyond the Border.

The teams which took the field were as follows :—

England : C. J. Ottaway, captain ; F. C. Maddison and A. Kirke Smith (Oxford University), J. Brockbank (Cambridge University), C. J. Chenery (Crystal Palace), J. C. Clegg (Sheffield), C. J. Morice (Barnes), R. C. Welch (Narrow Chequers), E. H. Greenhalgh (Notts), R. C. Barker (Herts Rangers), and W. J. Maynard (First Surrey Rifles). Scotland : R. W. Gardner, captain ; R. Leckie, W. McKinnon, A. Rhind, J. Weir, D. Wotherspoon, R. Smith, J. Smith, J. Taylor, W. Ker, and J. J. Thomson. All the home players were past or present members of the Queen's Park Club.

MR. WILLIAM PICKFORD,
Representative of the Hampshire Association upon the F. A. Council, and member of the International Selection Committee. There is no sounder authority on the game, and as a writer on football topics he has scarcely a superior.

In this match the formation of the English team was one goalkeeper, one back, one half-back, and eight forwards ; whilst the Scots played one goalkeeper, two backs, two half-backs, and six forwards. For the return match at the Oval on March 8, 1873, the Englishmen copied the Scottish formation, and with such success that a victory by 4 goals to 2 was recorded. In this match England only had two players that took part in the game at Glasgow, and the team all round was a much stronger one, with W. E. Clegg (Sheffield), Hubert Heron (Uxbridge), Captain Kenyon-Slaney (Household Brigade), and R. G. Von Donop (R. E.) included. Scotland made four changes — A. F. Kinnaird (Wanderers) and H. W. Renny-Tailyour (R. E.) being included, the first-named (now Lord Kinnaird) being the present popular President of the Football Association. Three thousand spectators witnessed the Oval match—a record crowd up to that period.

Pages might be written on the long series of determined struggles between the two nations which followed, but in this article no more than a brief review can be attempted. From 1873-4 only one fixture was played each season. Scotland gained the first of their many triumphs at Glasgow

Gunn, Ltd., Richmond.]

THE ENGLISH INTERNATIONAL ELEVEN AGAINST SCOTLAND AT RICHMOND, 1893.

Back Row: W. McGregor. R. C. Gosling J. J. Bentley. Holt. J. C. Clegg. Kinsey. Holmes. Goodall.
Middle Row: W. I. Bassett. Reynolds. G. H. Cotterill. L. H. Gay. A. H. Harrison.
At Bottom: Spikesley. Chadwick.

in 1874, and the fact that ten thousand spectators were present afforded a pretty substantial proof of the early growth of Scottish enthusiasm.

For some years Scotland proved almost invincible, and between 1873 and 1888 England only won one match, whilst Scotland was credited with victories by such substantial majorities as 7—2, 6—1, 5—1, and 5—0.

England's solitary victory during this period was at the Oval in 1879, when the match was postponed owing to snow until Boat Race day. The Scotsmen led by 4—1 at half-time, but the English forwards got going in the second half, E. C. Bambridge and "Billy" Mosforth giving a brilliant display on the left wing, and England finally won by 5 goals to 4.

Charles Campbell and W. McKinnon, of Queen's Park, were two of the heroes of these early matches. Campbell played ten times for Scotland against England between 1874 and 1886. This record has never been surpassed, although it was equalled by another Queen's Park player in Walter Arnott, who played behind Campbell in the latter's last three matches.

The Football Association legalised professionalism in 1885, and the strong objections made by the Scottish F. A. to professionals being played in International matches almost brought about the abandonment of the International fixture. However, both Wales and Ireland supported England in the matter, and Scotland eventually gave way. England, however, played only one professional in the 1886 match—J. Forrest, of the Blackburn Rovers.

MR. C. J. HUGHES,
Vice-President of the Football Association, and member of the International Selection Committee.

For some years the Scottish F. A. steadily refused to recognise professionalism, and a large number of Scottish players crossed the Border to join English clubs as professionals. In 1893 the Scottish F. A. accepted the inevitable and admitted professional clubs, but it was not until 1896 that the authorities consented to call in the help of the Scottish professionals engaged with English clubs. In the meantime, England had gained some striking successes. Between the match of 1886, when England first played a professional, and that of 1896, when Scotland first called upon men from English clubs, England won five matches, drew two, and lost two by the odd goal in five.

During this decade England placed some exceptionally fine teams in the field. The team of 1888, which gained the record victory of 5—0 at Hampden Park, was made up of W. R. Moon (Old Westminsters), goal; P. M. Walters (Old Carthusians) and R. Howarth (Preston North End), backs; Allen (Wolverhampton Wanderers), G. Howarth (Accrington), and Forrest (Blackburn Rovers), half-backs; Woodhall (West Bromwich Albion), Goodall (Preston North End), T. Lindley (Notts Forest), F. Dewhurst (Preston North End), and Hodgetts (Aston Villa), forwards. There were some veterans in this team, but they gave a brilliant display, and the Scots were hopelessly outplayed from start to finish.

Another great team was that of 1892, which gained a 4—1 victory at Glasgow. Some good judges regard the 1892 team as the best that ever represented the Rose. The team was composed of Toone (Notts), goal; Holmes (Preston North End) and A. T. B. Dunn (Old Etonians), backs; Reynolds (West Bromwich Albion), Holt (Everton), and Shelton (Notts), half-backs; Bassett (West Bromwich Albion), Goodall (Derby County), Southworth (Blackburn Rovers), Chadwick (Everton), and Hodgetts (West Bromwich Albion), forwards.

Another big victory fell to England in 1893, when the Scots were beaten at Richmond Athletic Ground by 5—2. In this match the brilliant wing tactics of Bassett and Spikesley brought disaster to the opposition, and the play of the English forwards in the second half will not soon be forgotten by those who witnessed the match. A portrait group of this fine eleven is given as one of the illustrations to this article.

The 1894 match witnessed the first appearance of Needham and G. O. Smith, who played seven times in all against Scotland. Bloomer appeared in 1895, and kicked the first of the numerous goals he has had the satisfaction of scoring against the Scots. Bloomer has played altogether in nine England v. Scotland matches —a record second only to that of N. C. Bailey, who played for ten consecutive years (1878—1887)—a magnificent record never likely to be equalled.

During the last decade (1896—1905) honours have been equally divided with four victories to each nation and two drawn games. The members of the Scottish Council who advocated the inclusion of players from English clubs were justified by results, for, after six barren years for Scotland, the Thistle once more won (2—1) in 1896, when five Anglo-Scots (as players from English clubs are called) were selected. Scotland won again (2—1) at the Crystal Palace in 1897, when a particularly strong English forward line was held by one of the best trio of halves that ever represented Scotland — Gibson (Glasgow Rangers), Cowan (Aston Villa), and Wilson (Sunderland). England then won two consecutive games, the 1899 match at the Aston Villa ground being memorable for the magnificent defence of Crabtree at a period when the Scots were pressing heavily. The happenings of the last few years need hardly be recalled—the accident to W. J. Oakley and 4 to 1 defeat of

Russell and Sons.]
ENGLAND v. SCOTLAND AT THE CRYSTAL PALACE, 1905.
A throw-in from touch for Scotland. Stephen Bloomer can be seen anxiously watching the flight of the ball.

England at Glasgow in 1900; Bloomer's thrilling equalising goal at the Palace in 1901; the disaster at Ibrox and re-play at Birmingham in 1902; and the narrow victories for England at Celtic Park and the Palace in 1904 and 1905.

The matches with Wales date back to 1879, and those with Ireland to 1882. Wales succeeded in winning two of the first four matches, but no further successes have been achieved by the Principality at the expense of England. In recent years, however, with the Welsh eleven almost entirely drawn from Welshmen who have perfected their football as professionals with English clubs, the matches have been more closely contested. In the last six years Wales drew three matches and lost two by a very narrow margin. The other match—played at Newcastle in 1901—was won by England (6—0), after some magnificent forward work by R. E. Foster and Bloomer.

MR. HENRY WALKER,
North Riding of York Association. Representative of the North-Eastern Division upon the F. A. Council, and member of the International Selection Committee.

Ireland has never beaten England, drawn games in 1894 at Belfast and 1905 at Middlesborough being the best efforts of the representatives of the Emerald Isle. Irish football, however, is improving, and the results of the last five years have been distinctly creditable. Up to the last decade England frequently played experimental teams against both Wales and Ireland, and many players, whose chances of appearing in the big match against Scotland were small, gained well deserved caps. In 1894 England played eleven professionals against Ireland, and eleven amateurs (all members of the Corinthian F. C.) against Wales. Experiments of this character are no longer possible with the recent levelling-up between the four nations.

The selection of the teams to represent England was originally carried out by the Council, but the increase in the number of members eventually made it necessary for a Selection Committee to be appointed, and, in 1888, a committee of seven members were duly elected. The new committee were warmly slated by the critics for their first attempt at team-building, for Scotland won (3—2) at the Oval, after being beaten by five clear goals at Glasgow the previous year. However, this was the only success the Scots gained for some time, and the Selection Committee has since been appointed annually, the number of members being increased from seven to nine in 1897. Since the number was increased, the Council have made it a practice to select six members from the North and Midlands and three from the South. The present members of the Selection Committee are Mr. J. C. Clegg, a vice-president and chairman of the Council, who played against Scotland in 1872, and who has been closely identified with Sheffield football throughout a busy life; Mr. Chas. Crump, the senior vice-president, and who is known as "the member for Birmingham"; Mr. C. J. Hughes, another vice-president, who has acted as hon. secretary of the Cheshire F. A. for twenty-five years; Mr. G. S. Sherrington, a vice-president and old Public School player; Mr. J. J. Bentley, the latest addition to the list of vice-presidents, who is president

R. P. Gregson, Lytham and Blackburn.]

ENGLAND'S INTERNATIONAL TEAM v. SCOTLAND, 1904 (England 1, Scotland 0).

Names (from left to right): BLOOMER. JONES (Reserve). WILKINSON. LEAKE. COMMON. BLACKBURN. RUTHERFORD. ALFRED DAVIS (Linesman). V. J. WOODWARD. BURGESS. WOLSTENHOLME. CROMPTON (Captain). S. S. HARRIS.

This photograph was taken outside St. Enoch's Hotel, Glasgow, after the match by Mr. R. P. Gregson. Snow was falling, the light was bad, it was six o'clock in the evening—a magnificent testimony to the skill of the photographer.

of the Football League, and one of the best-known men in modern football; Mr. W. Pickford, who has acted as hon. secretary of the Hants F. A. since its foundation; Mr. R. P. Gregson, a very old member of the Council, and hon. secretary of the Lancashire F. A.; Mr. Alfred Davis, the hon. secretary of the Berks and Bucks F. A.; and Mr. H. Walker, who is closely connected with the Cleveland district, and represents the far North-eastern corner of the country. All the selectors have rendered long service on the Council.

The members of the Selection Committee do not spare time or trouble in their efforts to get together the best side to represent England. Prior to the Internationals a trial match between North and South is usually played, and this has been of considerable value in weeding-out the candidates for the honour of a cap. Last year a Southern trial match between Amateurs and Professionals was played prior to the selection of the team to represent the South, and the experiment was so successful that it was repeated this season. The real work of the selectors begins about December, when candidates for the trial games are talked about; but the majority of the members live in football centres and see first-class matches the season through. From December onwards it is customary to find two or three members gathered together at some of the best matches played by such clubs as Aston Villa, Everton, Stoke, Tottenham Hotspur, and the Corinthians. After the Southern trial, the teams are selected for the North v. South game, with reserves for all positions.

The committee attend the trial match in full force, and the team for the first International (usually against Ireland) is selected immediately after the trial. If the form of the players engaged has come up to expectations, an eleven is built up mainly from the North and South teams. But disappointing form from men who have done splendid work in club football is by no means rare, and it frequently happens that other players are called upon for the International. The Irish match proves the possibilities of the eleven, and the committee then endeavour to strengthen any weak spots when choosing the team to tackle Wales, a task for which the very best side England can put in the field is required. By this time the form of nearly all the leading players has been under review, and if the team does well against Wales, the task of making the final choice for the great game against Scotland is an easy matter. But it is quite likely that one or two of the men will fail to come up to the standard required for the final encounter. Matters are discussed immediately after the Welsh match with a view to remedy any pronounced weakness, and if deemed desirable, the final choice is deferred to enable the committee to watch other players in their club games. The team against Scotland being selected, the duties of the committee are over for another season, and there remains the anxiety of watching the players on the field and receiving a due meed of congratulation or blame, according to the result of the match.

THE ENGLISH PLAYERS OUT FOR A STROLL ON THE MORNING OF THE MATCH AGAINST SCOTLAND AT THE CRYSTAL PALACE, 1905.

Every player appreciates very highly the honour of an International Cap, and thoroughly enjoys taking part in a match that affords a pleasant interlude from the routine of League and Cup-tie football. No distinction is made between amateurs and professionals in travelling and hotel arrangements, and for the matches in Ireland and Scotland the members of the committee travel with the players. Each player who represents England is presented with a white shirt on which the English arms are worked, and a cap on which the match and date are embroidered. The professionals also receive a fee in addition to travelling expenses, and I have no hesitation in saying that the majority of the men would rather forego the remuneration for their services than lose the highly-prized shirt and cap.

If the match is in Scotland or Ireland elaborate travelling arrangements are made. For the Scottish match, which is played in Glasgow every other year, the players and officials meet at a convenient railway centre, such as Hellifield (Midland) or Preston (L. & N.-W. Railway), and there board a specially reserved first-class dining-car, and on arriving at Glasgow they put up at one of the first-class hotels. For the Irish match the sea passage is taken on the Thursday before the match, which allows time for the ill-effects of the crossing to wear off. Many good footballers are poor sailors, but some excuse may be found in the fact that the Irish Sea is seldom in a peaceful mood during the month of February. Belfast is the venue for the matches in Ireland, and quarters are secured at a quiet watering-place within easy reach of that city.

MEMBERS OF THE INTERNATIONAL SELECTION COMMITTEE WATCHING A TRIAL GAME AT QUEEN'S CLUB.

In conclusion, I may add that I hope to see the English football public some day develop the whole-hearted enthusiasm for the International contests that permeates our friends over the Border. National pride with an Englishman should be as strong as with a Scotsman, but apparently a Cup Final, in which very few of us have any direct interest, is far more attractive than a match in which the football supremacy of our country is at stake. In Scotland the International is paramount, and on the day of the encounter Glasgow is invaded by thousands of enthusiasts from the Highlands and the Lowlands. In 1900 there were 62,000 spectators at Celtic Park, and the gate receipts amounted to nearly £4,400. We have never approached these figures in England.

THE UNIVERSITY FOOTBALL GROUND AT OXFORD.
A Rugby game in progress.

UNIVERSITY FOOTBALL (RUGBY).

By H. MAINPRICE.

Early Rugby at the Universities—The trial games—The football season—Principal opponents of the 'Varsities—College matches—The question of a League or Cup competition for the Rugby game at the 'Varsities—A difference in the forward game at Oxford and Cambridge of recent years—The Lent term—The modern open game a great strain on the player.

RUGBY football appears to have been played at the Universities as early as 1855, if not a little before that date. At Cambridge matches were played between 1855 and 1860, Rugby and Marlborough supplying the bulk of the players. But it was not until 1863 (Cambridge) and 1870 (Oxford) that the Rugby game became thoroughly established at the Universities; and we have to wait until the season 1873-4 before Oxford and Cambridge first met to play the Rugby game against each other. The first meeting under the present conditions—fifteen a side—took place two seasons later, up to which time twenty players a side had been the usual number. From this season, then, dates the formation of the University clubs.

At Cambridge the captain and secretary are supported by a committee of old Blues, usually three or four in number; while the president of the club is elected annually at a general meeting held at the beginning of each season. Cambridge have always been lucky in this respect, and for some years now the Rev. J. H. Gray, of Queen's College, has filled the office of both president and honorary treasurer, to whom the C.U.R.U.F.C. owes a deep debt of gratitude.

The one idea in view in the selection of a University side is, of course, the great match at Queen's Club, and all the other matches are regarded, rightly or wrongly, as trial games to help the captain and committee in their final selection.

The University season opens with a trial game between two sides of seniors chosen by the committee from the most promising members of the various college teams of the previous season. This is a comparatively easy task, as the form of each individual is pretty well known to the committee, who make a point of refereeing in and watching as many college matches as possible during the season.

To select two fifteens of Freshmen—the next trial game—is by no means such an easy matter, as the authorities have very little to guide them in their selection beyond the lists of prominent Freshmen sent in to them by the college secretaries. These lists are, of course, based principally on school reputations, which are apt to be misleading. Often it happens that players with big school reputations, for many obvious reasons, fail to produce anything like the form reported of them. These games, although serving their purpose to a certain extent, are practically of no great value as trial matches.

The University football season is naturally a short one, and latterly has also been a very heavy one; often as many as three hard matches a week are played in the latter half of the Christmas term. Far too many matches are crowded into the short term of eight weeks which immediately precedes the University match; and directly after it follows a week's tour of four matches in Scotland or Ireland. This means five hard matches in eight consecutive days, which is no small undertaking, and is, no doubt, to a very large extent the chief cause of the great number of accidents amongst members of the University sides of recent years.

Besides the leading London clubs—Blackheath, Richmond, London Scottish, Harlequins, Old Merchant Taylors, etc.—the principal Scottish and Irish clubs are met, and Scotland and Ireland are visited in alternate seasons.

In Scotland our chief opponents for some seasons now have been Edinburgh University, the Edinburgh Wanderers, the Academicals, and the West of Scotland. The first three matches are played in Edinburgh, and the fourth at Glasgow. While in Ireland, Dublin University, Monkstown, and the North of Ireland at Belfast, plus Irish hospitality, form an extremely powerful combination.

Tours of this description are always most enjoyable socially, but from a football point of view it has often been said that they are a farce. And certainly there is a great deal of truth in this assertion, as you can hardly expect a side to be at its best at the end of a heavy five weeks' continuous football, however strong the men may be.

It is a pity that nowadays none of the great Welsh sides find a place on either University's fixture list. Until quite recently both Oxford and Cambridge had matches with Newport and Cardiff, but owing to various reasons these matches have now been abandoned.

Matches with these two famous Welsh clubs were always popular at the Universities, and as trial games were certainly most instructive.

UNIVERSITY (RUGBY) FOOTBALL—OXFORD v. CAMBRIDGE AT QUEEN'S CLUB, 1901.
Collared!

chosen, together with one resident official, who is also elected by the players. This managing committee is very delightful and simple, and works extremely well. The captain is really all powerful, and on his shoulders naturally rests the chief responsibility. The secretary, who is usually captain the following season, has a very busy time and can hardly call a moment his own. The committee can be called at any time by the captain; but, as a rule, after the first fortnight of the season, the captain and secretary between them manage the whole business of the club. And it is usually found that this arrangement works very well.

Of late years the great strength of the Cambridge sides has lain in her forwards; in fact, so strong have the packs been that the outsides have suffered in consequence. This appears, on the surface, a somewhat illogical statement, but it is nevertheless a fact. And certainly one University match at Queen's Club was simply thrown away quite recently because the forwards were considered strong enough to win the game off their own bat, when the back division might have been used to more advantage.

Latterly especially a marked difference in the style of forward play has been noticeable at the two Universities. At Oxford the packs, as a rule, have been fast and rather on the light side, but extremely clever in their foot-work.

The Oxford forwards in the University match of the season 1903-4 were a wonderfully clever pack, and such an exhibition of clean, smart heeling and dribbling as they gave will long be remembered by all who were present. The Cambridge forwards, although considerably heavier and physically stronger than the Oxford pack, appeared quite unable to cope with their skill and dash. Cambridge, on the other hand—probably due to the Scottish element—have always favoured the strong, robust type of forward; individually, perhaps, not so clever as the Oxford forward, but amply making up for any lack of skill by more vigorous methods. J. R. C. Greenlees and D. R. Bedell-Sivright, both old Cambridge captains, are perhaps the best Scottish school forwards that have led the University forwards of recent years. Both were good scrummagers, fine dribblers,

College matches are played regularly throughout the Christmas and first half of the Lent term. Two, and often three, matches take place each week, and the competition for places in a college side is usually very keen. Unlike the matches under Association rules, there is no league or cup competition; and, judging from the keenness displayed in these matches, no artificial stimulus such as a cup competition or University league is needed. The non-existence of such a league has often been deplored by people, who were evidently not too well acquainted with the keenness and vigour of these inter-college games. It is stated, however, that the feeling in favour of a league competition at Oxford is growing stronger every season. As long ago as 1876 the Oxford Rugby Union decided to have a college championship, but the competition was abandoned two seasons later on account of the roughness of the games. The hospitals have their annual cup-ties, which are by no means exhibitions of scientific football, and are by common consent the roughest matches seen in London during the season. Surely the formation of such a competition would to a very great extent spoil the great charm of these college games, and a struggle for points would not only defeat its own object—to improve the standard of play amongst the colleges—but would be conducive to rough and dangerous play. We have only got to turn to the North of England to see what cup-ties have done for the Rugby game. The committee of the Yorkshire Union had to issue special rules to deal with rough play in these matches. It cannot, of course, be said with any truth that the standard of college football at the Universities is a very high one; but, still, the inter-college matches are so keen that no artificial stimulus is necessary—a stimulus, too, which is entirely foreign to the true spirit of the game.

At the Universities Rugby football is not troubled by any professional question, and therefore the game is played, as it ought to be, in the best spirit. Again, there are no complications caused by a committee of management who are non-players and have to provide for dividends and return on capital invested. Everything at the Universities is managed by the players themselves, from whom the officials for the year are

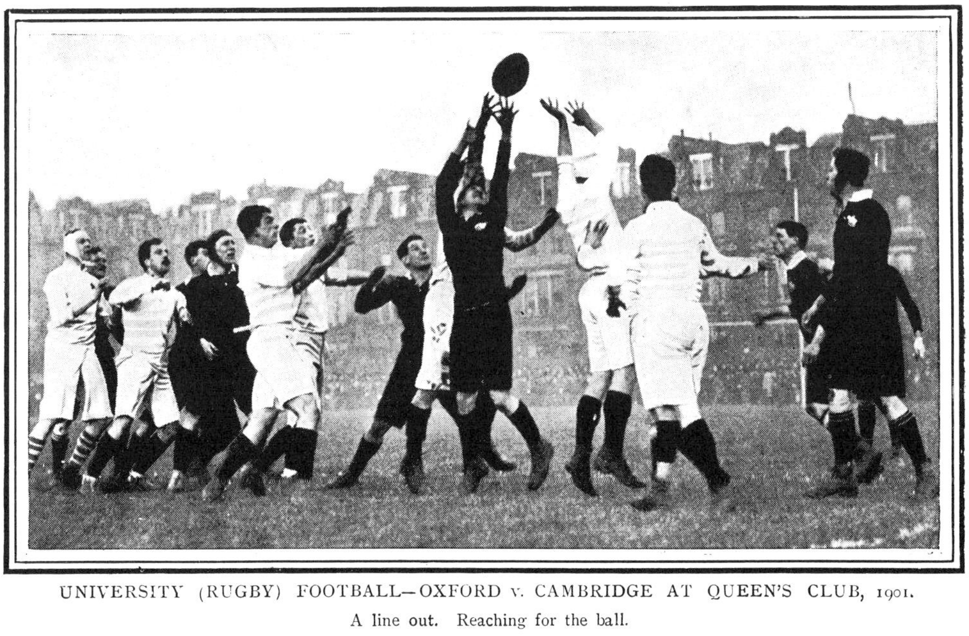

UNIVERSITY (RUGBY) FOOTBALL—OXFORD v. CAMBRIDGE AT QUEEN'S CLUB, 1901.
A line out. Reaching for the ball.

UNIVERSITY (RUGBY) FOOTBALL—OXFORD v. CAMBRIDGE AT QUEEN'S CLUB, 1901.

Rushing the ball through a scrum.

and magnificent tacklers. Amongst English scrummagers who have appeared in the Cambridge ranks during the last few seasons, undoubtedly the finest all-round player was J. Daniell, who, unfortunately, has been lost to English football since his unlucky accident in the match against Scotland two seasons ago. In fact, although Cambridge has supplied her full share of famous players outside the scrummage, perhaps the main feature of recent years has been the sound school of forwards turned out by the club. In this respect the University have always been very well served by the two great Scottish schools, Fettes and Loretto. And it is really quite phenomenal what a number of fine forwards these two famous Scottish schools have sent up to the Universities, and especially to Cambridge. And it is not only for forwards that we are indebted to the Scottish schools, for many of the most distinguished three-quarters, halves, and full-backs who have represented either University have hailed from across the Border. The secret of the success of the Scottish schoolboy at the Universities is undoubtedly due to the excellent way in which he is taught the game while at school; and in this respect he has a great pull over the boys at most of the English public schools. During the season the average boy at a Scottish school sees a good deal of first-class football in Edinburgh, so it is not surprising that he learns to play the game.

After the University match—that is to say, in the Lent term—Rugby football is not taken quite so seriously, but usually some six or eight matches are played. And, as a rule, the opportunity is taken to try fresh blood and to discover capable men to take the place of those who are going down. Some of the best and most enjoyable matches are those played in the second half of the short University season. Many well-known critics have described these matches as farces, pointing out that little interest is taken in the University matches after the match at Queen's Club, and that it would be better in every way that the inter-University match should be played at the end of the Lent term. However, the objections to the adoption of such a course are so obvious and so well known that there is no necessity to dwell on them here. Judging from the number of spectators present at the matches in the Lent term, perhaps there is less interest taken in the University sides than in the Christmas term. But certainly at Cambridge these matches are played in the same spirit, and are just as keen and vigorous as those in the earlier half of the season.

It will be interesting to see whether the New Zealand tour will influence the style of play at the Universities to any great extent in the near future. Our visitors have clearly demonstrated that seven forwards work better than eight under all conditions; and the formation of the back division—three three-quarters and two five-eighths—holds out great possibilities both in attack and defence. The Universities are proverbially conservative in such matters; nevertheless, it seems practically certain that a change is bound to take place at no very distant date. All modern changes in the game aim in one direction—namely, to make the play more open and consequently more interesting from the spectacular point of view. This tendency naturally puts a greater strain on the player, and demands a more thorough system of training than is at present observed. The result, as far as the Universities are concerned, must be a reduction in the number of matches played, unless football is to become a serious business and cease to be the game it is at present.

Bowden Bros.]

UNIVERSITY (RUGBY) FOOTBALL—OXFORD v. CAMBRIDGE AT QUEEN'S CLUB.

Breaking up a scrimmage.

THE FOOTBALL PARLIAMENT—THE COUNCIL OF THE FOOTBALL ASSOCIATION AT WORK.

Standing (from left to right): J. W. CARTER. JOHN LEWIS. W. H. HASKINS. F. STYLES. J. ALBERT. NAT WHITTAKER. KEMP. S. A. NOTCUTT. N. MALCOLMSON. W. J. WILSON.

Photo by kind permission of the Football Association.] [THE BOOK OF FOOTBALL Copyright.

Sitting (on left of table): R. P. GREGSON. MCKENNA. R. E. LYTHGOE. D. B. WOOLFALL. F. J. WALL. J. C. CLEGG. C. CRUMP. C. S. SHERRINGTON. C. J. HUGHES. J. J. BENTLEY.

Sitting (on right of table): W. H. BELLAMY. H. S. RADFORD. A. G. HINES. A. KINGSCOTT. M. T. ROBERTS. W. PICKFORD. ALFRED DAVIS. W. MCGREGOR. G. W. SIMMONS.

THE LEEDS CITY ASSOCIATION FOOTBALL CLUB.

By A. W. PULLIN, Vice-Chairman of Directors.

The club's first season—A menace to the Rugby game—The experimental teams of 1904-5—Formation of a limited liability company—The officials connected with the club—Reconstruction of the ground—Formation of the team—The players.

Colours : Blue and gold. *Ground : Elland Road, Leeds.*

THE Leeds City Association Football Club is the newest and most striking finger-post in Yorkshire football. It stands in the very centre of what for thirty years was a Rugby stronghold, and it points unerringly to the direction in which the future popular pastime is to be found. This is the club's first year as a Second League organisation, yet half way through the season the attendances have exceeded those seen at the headquarters of all the old-standing Rugby clubs within the city area combined.

The foundations of a first-class Association club in Leeds were really laid by the West Yorkshire Football Association. In a quiet and unobtrusive way this Association has for the past ten years been educating the new generation in the points and principles of the "Soccer" code. The split in the Northern forces of the Rugby Union, and, one is compelled to add, the lack of managerial capacity and foresight in the Northern Union, assisted the educational process, and thus when the Leeds City Club was formed it had an eager and willing constituency to its hand. The club's neighbourhood—Bradford, nine miles away—made a similar discovery two years ago. In each case, moreover, the Association club occupies a ground that was in turn the home of a successful Rugby and Northern Union organisation.

The Leeds City Club is really built out of the ashes of the old Hunslet Club, which kept the Association game quietly going at a time when the Leeds public had no eye or ear for anything but the handling code. Hunslet "went under," but, after the lapse of a season, some of its old members foregathered, and, being reinforced by many enthusiastic new-comers, the club was resurrected and given the representative name of "The Leeds City Association Football Club." At first the enterprise was nebulous and visionary, but the outlook cleared when the Holbeck Northern Union Club became defunct and placed its ground in the market. Leeds City became the tenants, and afterwards contracted to purchase the enclosure, and to-day, so rapid has been the club's stride into popularity, the directors are faced with the necessity of having to considerably increase the 22,000 spectators' accommodation which the Elland Road Ground provides.

In the season 1904-5 Leeds City ran experimental teams, with the view of feeling the public pulse. The results were so satisfactory that not the least doubt was left as to the future success of the club in the event of admission to the Second League being secured. Preparatory to this a limited company was formed, with a nominal capital of £10,000, though there was no intention of asking anything like that sum of money from the public. As a matter of fact, up to the time of writing, only about £2,000 in shares has been issued, but it is known that this amount can be increased at any time the club may require it. By accepting the chairmanship of the board of directors, and contracting to purchase the ground for the club if necessary, Mr. Norris R. Hepworth, one of the oldest and best-known sportsmen in Leeds, enabled the whole scheme to take practical shape. But for his timely assistance it is doubtful if the club would have been in a position to apply for admission to the Second League in May last. As it was, Mr. Hepworth, on behalf of the club, was able to put so good a case before the League delegates that Leeds City secured election to the Second Division by a clear majority of votes over all applicants.

The directors were fortunate in securing the services as secretary-manager of Mr. Gilbert Gillies, who was formerly the manager of the Chesterfield Club. Prior to his appointment much hard work had been cheerfully performed by Mr. Frank Jarvis in the capacity of honorary secretary, by Mr. M. Mycroft (now of Derby) as honorary treasurer, and a committee of whom Mr. John Furness, one of the most hard-working of the present directors, was chairman. Mr. Gillies brought to bear upon the fortunes of the club all the loyal and enthusiastic services of which he is capable, and his football experience, like that of Mr. R. M. Dow (late honorary treasurer of Woolwich Arsenal), Mr. John Oliver (formerly of Tottenham Hotspur), Mr. F. G. Dimery, and Mr. Oliver Tordoff, who with the vice-chairman form the management committee of the club, has proved invaluable in enabling Leeds City to thus early reach a high standard among Second League clubs.

Since last August the ground has been almost entirely reconstructed, and a fine covered stand, capable of accommodating 5,000 spectators, erected. How the public of the city and district appreciate the improvements, as well as the football fare provided, is forcibly shown in the fact that the gate receipts at the end of December—that is, after only four months' operations as a Second League club—amounted to over £3,500. On the occasion of the match with Bristol City £430 was taken, while when Bradford City appeared at Elland Road, on the last Saturday in December, over 20,000 persons were present, and the receipts amounted to £487.

In building up their League team, the management committee of the club were careful to secure players who would, in every sense of the word, do credit to professional football. As captain, an excellent appointment was made in Richard Ray, full-back, who has had experience with Manchester City, Stockport, and Chesterfield. The responsibility of steering a new team seemed to occasionally sit heavily upon him, to the detriment of his play, but latterly he has thrown off this and proved himself alike a skilful leader and a full-back of courage and class. His fellow full-back, John Macdonald, formerly of Ayr and Blackburn Rovers, was the first player to be engaged for the League eleven, and he, too, has given full satisfaction. Latterly, D. B. Murray, who came from a Scottish junior club to England and has played with Everton and Liverpool, was secured from the Liverpool Club, and as partner to either Ray or Macdonald he has played exceptionally well.

Prior to joining Leeds City, H. Bromage did most of his goal-keeping for Derby County and Burton. He has done splendid work with his new club; indeed, there are few, if any, better custodians in the League than the Leeds City representative. His understudy is Dixon, formerly of Aston Villa. The halves are Charles Morgan (Liverpool and Tottenham), H. Stringfellow (Everton and Portsmouth), and James Henderson (Bradford City), with F. Walker, late captain of Barrow, reserve. The forward rank is composed of G. Parnell (Derby County), R. Watson (Woolwich Arsenal), J. T. Hargraves (Burton United and Aston Villa), R. Morris (Liverpool and Welsh International), H. Singleton (Queen's Park Rangers), T. Drain (Bradford), and D. Wilson (Hull City), the last named having been added to the club's strength late in December. The team are under the care of George Swift, who has proved himself to be in every way well qualified for the office of trainer. The average weight of the team is 11st. 4lb.

LEEDS CITY FOOTBALL CLUB—THE PLAYERS AND OFFICIALS, SEASON 1905-6.

Back Row: R. YOUNGER (Director). R. S. KIRK (Director). MORGAN D. WHITAKER (Director). DOOLEY. MACDONALD. AUSTIN. WALKER. SINGLETON. R. M. DOW (Director). G. SWIFT (Trainer).

R. Scott and Co., Manchester.]

Middle Row: G. GILLIES (Secretary and Manager). PARNELL. WATSON. HARGRAVES. RAY. MORRIS. CLAY. O. TORDOFF (Director).

Bottom Row: "THE CITY DOG." STRINGFELLOW. DRAIN. HENDERSON

PROUD PRESTON NORTH END.

Winners of the Football Association Cup, 1838-9; Finalists, 1887-8. Champions of the League, 1838-9, 1839-90; Runners-up in 1890-1, 1891-2, 1892-3.

Pioneers of professionalism—The early history of the club—"Soccer" introduced—William Sudell—The Scottish invasion—The beginning of Preston North End's greatness—A ready admission hastens the legalisation of professionalism—Magnificent playing records—The English Cup and the League championship won in 1889—The secret of the club's phenomenal success—A fall from grace—In the Second Division—Back to higher realms—Players and officials—The old Deepdale Ground.

Colours: White shirts, dark-blue knickers. *Ground: Deepdale Road, Preston.*

PRESTON NORTH END form a connecting link between the golden age of amateurism and latter-day professionalism. Pioneers in the introduction of the paid player, they rose to greatness through his prowess, and in the Eighties built up a reputation which has no counterpart in the history of English football. There were great teams, no doubt, in the old days when the famous Wanderers achieved their five triumphs in the Football Association Cup competition, three of them in consecutive seasons, and since then we have seen Blackburn Rovers win the trophy the same number of times, three of them also in succession, so that the record of the Wanderers has been repeated. The exploits of Sunderland's splendid side, "the team of all the talents," as they were called, are well within our memories, and Aston Villa, with their wealth of Cup and League successes, rank above all their rivals for consistent excellence over a really long period. And yet it is doubtful if any of these great teams, brilliant as they undoubtedly were, attained to quite the same standard as Preston North End in the glorious days twenty years or so ago.

Founded as a cricket club in 1862, North End did not take their famous name for several years, and it was fourteen or fifteen years after the formation of the organisation that a football section was tacked on with the object of making the club pay its way. Even then it was not Association football they played, but Rugby, the adoption of the handling code being due, in all probability, to the enthusiasm aroused in the town by the doughty deeds of the then famous Preston Grasshoppers, whose ranks included many brilliant players, of whom Mr. A. N. Hornby, the Lancashire cricketer, was one of the most notable. Rugby, however, did not prove a great success with North End, and after a very short time the "oval" was forsaken for the "circular" ball, the popularity which the Association game had already gained in East Lancashire having very likely suggested the change. This happy departure was made in 1880-1, and, though the new exponents of "Soccer" soon sustained a 16—0 thrashing at the hands of Blackburn Rovers, they gradually attained a measure of proficiency, and the season 1883-4 introduced the era of success which, for half a dozen years, was the leading feature in the football world.

The guiding spirit in the North End Club at this time was William Sudell, one of the old cricket and Rugby players who had joined in 1867. A keen observer and a smart business man, as well as an enthusiastic footballer, he had noticed that certain Scotsmen had come to England, not so much to obtain work, as was commonly reported, as to play football. Moreover, he could see the worth of these players, and his appreciation of Scottish talent was all the greater because an old Glasgow centre-forward, named Belger, working at Preston, had given North End valuable assistance in 1882-3. These were days when professionalism was illegal, but Mr. Sudell, nevertheless, conceived the idea of doing, on a large scale, what a few other clubs had done in a far more modest manner, and he set himself to get the pick of Scottish footballers so far as that was possible. He chose his players with excellent judgment, and by-and-bye a number of brilliant players from the land o' cakes were located in the proud town on the banks of the Ribble. "Nick" Ross, captain of the Heart of Midlothian, was one of the first to be brought down—as a slater—and, in due course, Geordie Drummond, Sandy Robertson, David Russell, Johnny Graham, Sam Thomson, Jimmy Ross, and Jack Gordon, were all in the team. In the meantime the local players had made great strides, and some of them, notably Fred Dewhurst, Bob Howarth, W. Joy, and Bethel Robinson, were footballers of a high type. With more than half the team composed of Scotsmen anyone could read between the lines, and when North End drew with Upton Park in the Cup competition in 1884, the latter protested on the ground that the Preston club paid their players.

The charge was not denied, and there can be no doubt that North End's action in candidly admitting payment hastened the legalisation of professionalism, which took place in the following season. North End were now a power in the land. In 1883-4 they had won 30 matches and only lost 4, and in this and the five succeeding seasons they won 294 games and lost only 35, while their goals numbered 1,502 to 385. One season furnished 59 victories and 2 defeats, the team going as far as Easter Monday before sustaining their first reverse—surely a remarkable record! Each season brought fresh talent to the team, but in Cup-ties West Bromwich Albion proved North End's bete noire, beating them in the Semi-final in 1887, and in the Final in 1888; but a year later the Preston men ousted the Albion in the Semi-final, and defeated the "Wolves" in the Final at Kennington Oval, thus winning the elusive trophy for the first and only time in their career. The players who accomplished this performance at the Oval were: Dr. Mills-Roberts, goal; R. Howarth and R. Holmes, backs; G. Drummond, D. Russell, and J. Graham, half-backs; J. Gordon, J. Ross, J. Goodall, F. Dewhurst, and S. Thomson, forwards. One of the eleven, Mills-Roberts, was a Welshman; three of them, Howarth, Holmes, and Dewhurst, were locals; Drummond, Russell, Graham, Gordon, Ross, and Thomson were Scotsmen; and Goodall was a Londoner, who had learned his football at Kilmarnock. "Nick" Ross was then having a short spell of service with Everton.

This was the season in which North End brought off a dual achievement which is never likely to be equalled, for they won the League—then in its first season—without a defeat, and they secured the Cup without a goal being scored against them in any of the ties.

Aston Villa have obtained the League championship and the Cup in one season, but not with such remarkable records, and Bury have won the Cup without having a goal put up against them in the competition, but the Preston club's double record in all its wonderful detail stands supreme. In the early years of the League, North End were strikingly successful, securing the championship in the first and second seasons and being second in the following three, while altogether they obtained 174 points in those five seasons, or 30 more than any other club, Everton being next with 144. Enough has been said to indicate the super-excellence of North End, but we should be neglecting a cardinal feature of the play which compassed these many fine results if we omitted to state that the club owed their success, not merely to the introduction of talented Scotsmen and to the cultivation of the best local talent, but to the style of play adopted. North End carried combination to a perfection never previously known; as a team they were the greatest masters of the passing game that football has produced; and the combination extended to all departments, forwards and halves working in wonderful harmony, and even the backs and goalkeeper having the same delightful understanding with each other and with the players in front. Many of the great players who built up the Club's reputation are no more than names to most of the present generation, but to old football followers they were familiar figures. It is not easy to compress into limited space all that might be said about these fine players. In goal alone they had W. Joy (now a director), W. C. Rose, Dr. Mills-Roberts, and Trainer, the last-named of whom was accorded the title of "Prince of Goalkeepers." At full-back there was "Nick" Ross, in the opinion of many the best back ever seen, a fearless and magnificent defender, with two locals in R. Howarth and R. Holmes, both of whom have often played for England. Robertson, Russell, and Graham rank with the best half-back lines the game has produced, and forward there were such stars as Gordon, Jimmy Ross, Thomson, John Goodall, Dewhurst, and Drummond, all players of the highest type. The wonderful doings of these brilliants will stand for all time, and Preston can never forget the great place the Club has filled in the football world.

With all its historic treasures, however, the past cannot be allowed to crowd out the present, and the North End Club, as it has been in more recent years and is to-day, claims considerable attention. As often happens, great success was followed by days and even years of disappointment, and the company, which took over the club in 1893, have had to fight an uphill battle. It took the Preston public a long time to realise that the changed conditions made it utterly impossible to get the cream of football talent as the club had done in the Eighties, and even in more recent years, when this fact has been recognised, the directors have had a task of no little difficulty, for the "gates" on which, of course, they rely are not nearly so big as those of the majority of the leading League clubs. Consequently, it has often been hard work competing against the more wealthy organisations. At the end of the season 1900-1 the club, which was one of the original members of the League, had to fall into the Second Division, and only those who have been through the mill can realise how difficult it is to get back into the higher circle. For two years North End tried in vain to regain their place, but, happily, the third season's attempt was more successful. They and Woolwich Arsenal ran a splendid race together, each striving first and foremost for promotion, and, incidentally, for the championship, with Manchester United coming along strongly in the later stages and pressing close upon them. Almost to the finish the championship was in doubt, but finally the Arsenal unexpectedly dropped a point at home, and this allowed North End to secure first place by defeating Blackpool in their last match. This was a memorable season for the Prestonians. In their 34 League matches they secured 50 points and scored 62 goals to 24. Only once was more than a single goal put up against them at home, and in 17 of their 34 games, 9 at home and 8 away, the opposing side failed to score at all. Such a record merited promotion. Among the players who helped towards this happy issue were Peter McBride, who fully sustains the traditions of Trainer as a goalkeeper of the most polished type; Derbyshire, a rising full-back, who plays a conspicuously fair game; Orrell, a defender of the dashing order; McLean, Hunter, and Tod, halves of the lion-hearted kind, fearless in tackling, and determined to achieve their purposes; and excellent forwards in Bond, Smith, Bell, etc. Without a doubt, one of the best strokes of business North End have done in recent years was the engagement of Bell, for though he is no longer young as footballers go, he has been invaluable, his sound judgment and his skill in pulling the team together having been

PRESTON NORTH END—THE FAMOUS TEAM THAT WON THE ENGLISH CUP AND THE LEAGUE CHAMPIONSHIP, SEASON 1888-9.

Back Row: Right Hon. R. W. Hanbury. Sir W. E. M. Tomlinson. Mr. Sudell.
Middle Row: G. Drummond. R. Howarth. D. Russell. R. Holmes. J. Graham. Dr. Mills-Roberts.
Front Row: J. Gordon. James Ross. J. Goodall. F. Dewhurst. S. Thomson.

(The championship of the League was won without a defeat, and the Cup without a goal being scored against the eleven—a unique record in the annals of the Association game.)

worthy of the highest praise. Having returned to the highest rank, North End have proved themselves worthy foemen of the best. Their team includes most of those mentioned as figuring prominently in the extrication from Division II., and others to be mentioned are Rodway, a talented full-back of the steadiest sort; Lyon, a keen and pertinacious half; and Wilson, Maher, and Lockett, forwards, with others well able to give a hand when required. Bond, who was capped twice for England last season, has never played so brilliantly as during the present campaign, 1905-6, and his wonderful success for an outside winger may be gauged from the fact that he scored 11 out of the team's first 23 goals in League matches.

Other players of note who have been associated with North End at different times have been Dunn, a burly full-back from Scotland; Sandy Tait, who has since passed a good many seasons with Tottenham Hotspur; R. Kelso; Moses Sanders, who made his opponents laugh until they couldn't play; W. Orr, now of Glasgow Celtic; Frank Becton, an English International; Tom Smith, who played with the "'Spurs" when they won the Cup; John Cowan; and Adam Henderson. Not to the players alone must be given all the credit for steering the North End barque through the troublesome storms encountered in the Nineties and through the treacherous waters of the Second Division. The directors have worked steadily and loyally, and, though it is impossible to mention all who have served with success in this capacity, reference must certainly be made to Mr. W. E. Ord, the chairman, Mr. W. Pomfret, the vice-chairman, and Mr. Tom Houghton, all of whom joined the directorate when the company was formed in 1893, and to Mr. R. Turner, who came on only a year later, and all of whom are still sticking to their guns.

Mr. Ord is a sportsman through and through, and is undoubtedly the most popular leader the club could possibly have. Mr. Pomfret, whose connection with the club goes right back to its cricketing and Rugby days, is a man of that dogged, resolute type so valuable in fighting an uphill battle as North End have had to do. Mr. Houghton has travelled many thousands of miles further with, and on behalf of, North End than any other person, searching for players when necessary, and, otherwise, accompanying the team on every possible occasion. Year after year he scarcely misses a match, and his North End journeyings probably total little short of forty thousand miles. Mr. Turner, the other old hand, takes a keen interest in the financial side of the club's life, and the colleagues of these four gentlemen work with just the same desire for the continued prosperity of the old club. At present they have a sound, business-like team, specially strong in defence, and if the close of the season finds the funds in a sufficiently healthy state to justify extensive improvements at Deepdale, the management will be supremely happy.

It is now more than thirty years since Deepdale became the headquarters of North End, then only a cricket club, and no one would ever wish to remove from a ground which is easy of access and which is so wonderfully rich in historic associations.

Dewhurst, Preston.]

PRESTON NORTH END—THE TEAM AND OFFICIALS, SEASON 1905-6.

Back Row: G. Tod. J. Derbyshire. P. McBride. T. Rodway. J. Turnbull.
Middle Row: Mr. T. Houghton (Director). G. Drummond (Trainer). J. McLean. J. Hunter. W. J. Lyon. Mr. H. Worthington (Secretary). D. Maher.
Bottom Row: R. Bond. J. Wilson. P J. Smith. J. Bell (Captain). A. Lockett.

INTERNATIONAL RUGBY FOOTBALL—ENGLAND v. SCOTLAND AT RICHMOND, 1903

A line out.

THE RUGBY GAME IN SCOTLAND.

By W. S. DOUGLAS.

The introduction of the Rugby game into Scotland—An International day in Edinburgh—A dive into history—Scottish Rugby a product of the schools—Loretto and Merchiston foster the game—Great school players—The Club Championship—A bit of International history.

FOOTBALL dates a long way back in Scotland. Centuries ago there were statutes passed in Edinburgh prohibiting the people from playing it, in order that archery for the national defence might be fostered. Sir Walter Scott saw the game played at Carterhaugh and elsewhere. Long before him, Sempill, of Beltrees, had written of a rural celebrity who had this trait among others that "at the football full fierce he ran."

The queer, old "handba'" games annually played in several country towns are a survival of such football. Their very name might be held to show a predilection for "the carrying code." But the Rugby Union game is, of course, an importation. It might be considered a "swop" for golf; and some even think that England sent us a better article than she got from Scotland. But they do not venture to say so on the links.

It is well-nigh half a century since they made a start with the game North of the Tweed, in a small way. Much water has flowed under the bridges since those days, and now Rugby is one of the most popular games of the country, from Aberdeen to the Borders. In the Highlands it does not count, any more than cricket. Lord Lovat once decried all football (at a shinty meeting) as alien and anti-Gaelic. But in Edinburgh, Rugby may fairly be said to be well-nigh as popular as Association—partly because Glasgow rules the roost so decidedly in the latter game. And the Scottish Football Union holds sway over Border factory operatives and "tony" West-Enders of Glasgow and the capital alike, and justly claims to have the best-equipped ground—its own property—in the three kingdoms; and we cock our bonnets because we have beaten England at the game more often than England has beaten us. "Set us up!" as we say in the North. We shall never do the same at cricket, so we are entitled to some rejoicing over that per contra item.

The Internationals and the club championship are the great affairs of each season. The jolly intercourse that the former brings about between Scots and their brother sportsmen of England and Ireland and Wales ought not to be left out of account. Princes Street of a fine Saturday forenoon in early spring, when the wearers of the Rose or the Shamrock or the Leek have been let loose upon it, is a memorable sight. It is one of the occasions on which Edinburgh unbends, as she does for the Carnival at Christmas.

Luckily, the Gould testimonial dispute is a half-forgotten affair; and the present generation hardly recalls the knock-on rumpus at Blackheath, in 1884, and the subsequent rupture of relations for two successive years, with the attendant throes and pangs that heralded the birth of the International Board. All goes smoothly, under its ægis, between the Unions now. Those of Scotland and Ireland, alone among the four, have never had a row with each other; and a match with the "bhoys" from over the water is reckoned the height of good sportsmanship in the North.

One feels inclined to dive into history. The old stager who can recall over two score Scottish International matches that he has witnessed has superabundance of material to draw upon. He might propose to himself a survey of well-nigh thirty years' modernised International encounters since twenty a-side was given up and Malcolm Cross dropped the winning goal in the first fifteen a-side match in 1877; and still relegate to limbo the older game, along with the two umpires who used to be in charge, more or less, of a match, with the scoring system under which a goal beat any number of tries, with the two half-back arrangement (we used, till quite lately, to have quarter-backs in Scotland, where three-quarters then were half-backs), and with the tasselled and piratical cowls which all the players were accustomed at one time to wear.

Any such survey, in anything like detail, cannot, of course, be attempted here. Yet merely to pass over the earliest days of Scottish Rugby with a word or two costs one a pang. It should, at least, be mentioned that, before most of to-day's celebrities in the game were born, men like "Bulldog" Irvine, "Tom" Chalmers, J. H. S. Graham, Ninian Finlay, Stuart Carrick, and Leslie Balfour — whose name, with

E. D. SIMSON
(Merchistonian).
Scottish half-back, 1902-3-4-5-6. In the opinion of many good judges he is the finest half-back of the day.

the Melville now added, is kept green in Edinburgh by an annual tax-paper, and recalled to a wider public by the batting exploits of which he is still, happily, capable—had won renown for themselves in it.

But the mere setting-down of the names of those giants of the past recalls to mind the fact that Scottish Rugby is peculiarly and distinctively the product of its schools. Each man of those on the list just given was either an Edinburgh Academical or a Glasgow Academical—a member, that is to say, of the clubs formed by the former pupils of the Edinburgh and Glasgow Academies. Those schools, and Merchiston Castle—which, by the way, was Malcolm Cross's school—were the birthplaces of the game amongst us. There were associated with their representatives, in the first challenge to England for the opening match of the long series in 1871, the St. Andrew's University and West of Scotland Clubs. But the old grey city hardly claims the same pre-eminence (by the way, one of its backs who played in that match was one of the Rosses, the "Kings" of the out-of-the-way Cocos-Keeling islands) in the game of football as in that of golf. And the West of Scotland then, as now, largely consisted of public school men vying in this sport with the day-school which has had Sir Archibald Hunter as one of its most famous pupils.

To such headmasters as the late Dr. Hely Almond, of Loretto, and the late Dr. Rogerson, of Merchiston, may be ascribed in great measure the hold which the Rugby game has secured in Scotland. Very many who know little else about that, too, are well aware of the renown of the Fettesian-Lorettonians who annually tour in England in the last week of the year. But it is not only at Pinkie, Merchiston, and Fettes that fine players are trained up for Scotland. In days gone by, Blairlodge combined with its cramming the production of International men; and Craigmount gave Mason Scott to England and "Tom" Scott, of Langholm, to Scotland. Dollar Institution still is a good school for budding Rugby men, and so, in a less degree, are Stanley House and Glenalmond.

The still older tradition of the day-schools in this respect is, however, worthily maintained. Edinburgh Academy and George Watson's College meet all the public schools of Scotland on level terms. In the west, Kelvinside Academy has entered into keen rivalry with Glasgow Academy at Rugby — its F. P. team, in the days of G. W. Lamond, the still-renowned Bristol three-quarter, J. T. Tulloch, and the Wingates, was one of the cleverest in Scotland—and Glasgow High School, proud of its very renowned International forward, J. M. Dykes, holds somewhat the same position in its City as do Stewart's and Heriot's in the east.

There remain to be named at least two other schools of great fame in Scottish Rugby—the Royal High School, of Edinburgh, whose former pupils have never held the club championship, but claim that they have in only very few years been without a representative in an English International (their most famous ones have been J. P. Veitch, Dr. J. W. Simpson, and Mark Morrison), and the Edinburgh Institution, which has not had a man in a Scottish fifteen for an exceedingly long time, but turned out one of the most renowned former pupil teams that ever played together a quarter of a century ago.

H. J. STEVENSON
(Edinburgh Academicals).
He played for Scotland 1888-1893. He was one of the best centres in the three three-quarter days, but was relegated to full-back in favour of Gregor McGregor.

The "'Stution," indeed, formed in those days such a side as the older Rugbyites of the North look back upon to this day with even more fond recollections than they have of those early Fettesian-Lorettonians whom the success of the great Vassall team at Oxford, and the contemporary exploits of the matchless A. R. Don Wauchope at Cambridge, brought together as a conjoint team.

Naturally, considering the possibilities of the bigger schools Fettes and Loretto have turned out very many more famous players since those days than the Institution. There have been no successors to the International half-back pair of the latter school, nor to such forwards as the Ainslies and Dr. Brewis, and their International comrades "Garry" Maitland and Dr. Philp. To enumerate all the Fettesian - Lorettonians who who have played for Scotland in the last twenty years, on the other hand, would be a large order indeed. To the Oxonians, J. G. and A. Walker, who were contemporaries of Wauchope and Asher, there succeeded such great scrummagers as J. D. Boswell, H. F. Menzies, W. J. Thomson, and D. R. Bedell-Sivright; and behind the scrum there has been a series of noted backs, from the late G. C. Lindsay and D. J. Macfarlane, P. R. Clauss, and G. T. Campbell, to W. Wotherspoon, C. J. N. Fleming, the Rev. H. T. S. Gedge, and W. P. Donaldson, and so on to A. R. Smith, the late Lieutenant D. B. Monypenny,

THE SCOTTISH SIDE AGAINST ENGLAND, 1905.
Back Row: A. Ross. H. G. Monteith. W. T. Ritchie. R. S. Stronach. W. Kyle. D. G. Schulze. G. A. W. Lamond.
Middle Row: W. P. Scott. A. B. Timms. A. G. Cairns. L. West.
Front Row: J. C. M'Callum. T. Elliott. E. D. Simson. P. Munro.

and the Cantabs, L. M. and K. G. McLeod. With these names there should be coupled famous Merchistonians past and present—the Malcolm Cross and Allan Arthur, the J. A. Campbell and T. Begbie, of the past; the R. G. McMillan, of the middle period; and, to come to quite recent years, F. H. Fasson, W. H. Welsh, A. W. Duncan, and E. D. Simson. But that list is incomplete indeed without mention of the Neilsons, the famous Merchistonian family which holds the record for having had one brother or the other in Scottish fifteens for well-nigh ten years continuously through the Nineties and on to the beginning of this century—first, George and William (the present President of the S.F.U.), forward and three-quarter; and then Gordon and Robin, forward and three-quarter again. With these, moreover, should be bracketed such renowned Edinburgh Academicals of more recent times as W. E. Maclagan, who just about tied with Mark Morrison in the number of International caps—some twenty-five—that he has worn; Dr. Charles Reid; H. J. Stevenson, prince of centre three-quarters; the brothers McEwan; J. M. Reid and Phipps Turnbull; J. I. Gillespie; and J. E. Crabbie. Nor should renowned Glasgow Academicals be forgotten, though their number has been few—R. C. Greig almost the sole one, indeed—until the happy revival of the club of late years—G. R. Fleming, J. E. Junor, J. H. Smith, J. B. Brown, W. A. Walls, H. Ker, and J. French, whose successors in a Scottish pack have been R. S. Stronach, the "timber-topper," and W. M. Milne, with R. S. McCowat behind them.

If it were possible in the space at one's disposal to tell the history of the club championship, it should duly be set forth how some of these men encountered others in notable struggles of the past. But only a summary can be attempted. It must be set down as, at first, the tale of how the Institution were the first to break in upon the charmed circle of Edinburgh and Glasgow Academicals twenty-five years ago; how they, in turn, were ousted from the championship by the West of Scotland, captained by D. Y. Cassells, and including the Oxonian Walkers; what tussles J. B. Brown's Glasgow Academicals then had with the "West" (some even say that the former were clearly champions in 1883), but how the Edinburgh Academicals, instead, wrested the honour away, with a team which, under Dr. Charles Reid, comprised also his fellow International forwards, M. C. McEwan, A. T. Clay, T. W. Irvine, and T. B. Whyte.

Then followed the decline of the Raeburn Place team, and the revival of the West of Scotland. The "West," under great Boswell, were the team of the beginning of the Nineties, and they fairly claimed the championship honour.

New rivals had been creeping up, however. The Watsonians, under M. M. Roddick and H. T. O. Leggatt, had cultivated such a forward game as the Gurdons taught England. They ruled the roost from 1893 to 1895, till Hawick obtained the championship by beating them.

An unsatisfactory division of the honours between Jed Forest, the Watsonians, and the Clydesdale was the outcome of season 1896-7; but after that the Edinburgh Academicals asserted themselves irresistibly, and from 1898 to 1901 they were champions, under the younger McEwan and J. I. Gillespie. The turn of Edinburgh University followed. They had a claim to divided honours with the Raeburn Place team in 1899-1900. Now they made sure of it, and in 1901-2 were the only undefeated side in Scotland. Next year they had to share the honour with the Watsonians, and in the following year with the Glasgow Academicals. Last season the latter defeated them decisively in a postponed match played at Craiglockhart on Boxing Day; and for the first time for at least twenty years the honour returned to Anniesland.

As to International history, one can only say that 1893 was a turning-point, not only because of Wales forcing the adoption of four three-quarters upon us, but because it was the eve of the Northern Union secession, since which event a fully representative English team has never taken the field. But it is only partly in consequence of that fact (since the prowess of some of the Edinburgh men last-named helps to explain it) that Scotland has had such a series of victories recently. Between 1877 and 1893 she only won two matches to England's five; since 1893 she has won eight out of the twelve. Per contra, Wales ominously broke, last year, the alternation of wins at home and losses in Wales to which we had got accustomed; and Ireland, never victorious in Scotland till 1899, has since that year won as many matches as she has lost to us.

W. S. D.

GLASGOW ACADEMICALS, RUGBY CLUB CHAMPIONS OF SCOTLAND, 1904-5.

Back Row: D. Russell. R. D. Waddell. D. N. Sloan. J. Knox (President). W. M. Milne. J. A. Brown. R. S. Stronach.
Middle Row: W. Church. J. Hally. W. Russell. L. L. Greig (Captain). A. C. Frame. J. McGill. B. Dunn.
At Bottom: William Macfarlane. R. H. McCowat.

MANCHESTER UNITED FOOTBALL CLUB

(Late Newton Heath).

The early days of Newton Heath—A poor playing field—Steady advance of the club—The Manchester Cup won—Some famous Newton Heath players—The "Heathens" join the Alliance—In the Second League—Beaten in the test matches—A desperate struggle for existence—Mr. J. H. Davies to the rescue—A new ground and new prospects—Overwhelming success of the old club under the title Manchester United.

Colours: Red shirts, white knickers.

Ground: Bank Street, Clayton, Manchester.

SOMEWHERE about 1878 there were Association football clubs in a small way in the Manchester district, and one of the best known of these was undoubtedly Newton Heath. Originally the title was Newton Heath L. and Y. R. Cricket and Football Club, but later the title was considerably abbreviated, and for many years it was known as simply Newton Heath. Their earliest matches were with Manchester Arcadians, Naughton Dale, Oughtringham Park, Hurst Brook Rovers, Dalton Hall, and Blackburn Olympic Second. The visit of the latter was naturally looked upon as a great attraction, for they were, relatively speaking, giants. But the Newton Heath Club did not have very inviting playing headquarters, for even in the early Eighties the field was little better than a clay-pit, and all round the ground was a perfect quagmire. There was no dressing tent on the ground. Bless you, the arrangements were far too primitive for that! The team changed at the Three Crowns public-house, Oldham Road, and then had a sharp run to the playing-field. After you had played in a hard match you had a sharp run back, a wash and a rub down, and you felt as fit as a fiddle.

By March, 1886, the club had advanced to such an extent that Sam Black, one of the most enthusiastic players they ever had, E. Moran, J. Blears, and Fulton were selected to do duty for Manchester and District v. Liverpool and District. The following season, Association football came to the front more generally in Manchester, and Newton Heath became known as a great goal-scoring team. They were designated the "Coach-builders"—the why and wherefore of the title is self-evident—and that year they won the Manchester Cup, defeating Manchester before a crowd of 8,000 strong.

In the latter part of 1886 the team came into much greater prominence, for it secured men of national reputation. With a team which included Beckett in goal, Powell at back, J. Davies and Burke at half, and R. Doughty in the centre, Manchester were beaten in hollow style by 8—1. In 1887 we hear of Pat McDonnell being acquired. McDonnell was not doing well at the time, and he walked all the way from Glasgow to find employment at Newton Heath. McDonnell came in August, and in September of the same year Newton Heath's great goalkeeper, Tom Hay, arrived from Staveley. "Gates" were beginning to be numerous, and Newton Heath extended their stand accommodation. The Manchester Cup was again won, Denton being defeated by 7—1. The club made a draw with Preston North End on May 5, 1888, and then came a magnificent series of results, the following clubs being beaten in succession: Bolton Wanderers, 1—0; Blackburn Rovers, 2—1; Walsall Town Swifts, 2—1; Darwen, 4—3; Gainsborough Trinity, 5—1; and Leek, 5—1.

In the season of 1889-90 the Alliance came into being, and Newton Heath formed one of the new combination, but the record of the club in the Alliance was not satisfactory, for they only finished third from the bottom of the table.

In the season of 1892-3, however, the club made rapid headway, and the great ambition of the management was realised. They finished second to Notts Forest in the Alliance table, winning 12 matches, losing only 3, and drawing 7, out of a total of 22. They scored 69 goals, and lost 33. How well old supporters of the club remember September 10, 1892; it was indeed a red-letter day in the history of Manchester football, for on it the first League match ever seen in Manchester was played. Burnley furnished the opposition, and the result was a draw, 1—1.

They were now in the Second League, and they finished third in the season of 1894-5. When the club became a company, Mr. A. H. Albutt, a well-known Aston Villa director, became the first secretary, and he did splendid work on behalf of the club. In 1896-7 Newton Heath finished second in the League, but were unsuccessful in the test matches. Cassidy was doing excellent service for the team now. They won the Lancashire Cup in 1898, beating Blackburn Rovers by 2—1 at Everton. But they had some very poor seasons in the Second League, and, finding themselves heavily in debt in 1901, they had a bazaar, and made a substantial sum of money.

But the Newton Heath Club was always floundering. They could not get higher than tenth in the Second League in the season 1900-1, and the public naturally did not manifest much enthusiasm in their games. There was nothing wrong with their home performances, however; it was away that they failed. They drifted from bad to worse, and in the following season they were fifteenth on the list. Still, there were three clubs below them. Finally they drifted into bankruptcy, and it seemed all over with the organisation. But when there were no funds, and very few players, Harry Stafford, the famous back, who had ably captained the side, and Mr. West, the secretary, who left Lincoln City when Mr. Albutt retired, made a gallant effort to keep the concern afloat. The Football Association were indulgent, as indeed they ought to have been under the peculiar circumstances, and the men played the games in their Second League programme, and shared what money they took.

Messrs. West and Stafford carried on the club in this way until a good friend turned up in the person of Mr. J. H. Davies. He was a wealthy man, and he was induced to take an optimistic view of the future of an organisation in the district. He thought the matter over, and at last decided to act. But he was shrewd enough to see that the project could only be a success if it were worked on really enterprising lines, so he spared nothing in the way of capital. A good side was got together, and the club, under the name of Manchester United, went straight ahead, and continued Newton Heath's programme in the season of 1902-3. The ground which Mr. Davies laid out was a model for the whole country. There was a separate dressing-room and bath for each player, and the stands and general appointments were magnificent. Mr. J. J. Bentley threw in his lot with the club, and at present (1905-6) acts as chairman of committee. There was some inquiry on the part of the Football Association as to the position of Mr. Davies, and the Association insisted that the club should have a proper constitution.

The new team met with much success. They drew enormous "gates," and they finished fifth in the Second League. There was tremendous enthusiasm everywhere. In the following season the team made a splendid effort to gain First League honours, but they had a heavy programme at a critical time, and were beaten by Woolwich Arsenal for second place by a single point. Last season they again had a disappointment, for they finished 3 points behind the second club—Bolton Wanderers. This season they are sanguine of achieving the object for which they have fought so ably and so strenuously. They hold second position, and are likely to retain it. If they succeed, they will have richly deserved their success.

Should the United get into the First League, they will speedily become one of the richest and most powerful clubs in the competition. They have the population to draw from; other clubs have not.

MANCHESTER UNITED FOOTBALL CLUB—THE TEAM, SEASON 1905-6.

Back Row: ALEC DOWNIE. H. MOGER (Goalkeeper). R. BONTHRON

E. J. Care, Manchester.]

Middle Row: J. MANGNALL (Secretary). J. PICKEN. C. SAGAR. T. BLACKSTOCK. J. PEDDIE. FRED BACON (Trainer).

Bottom Row: J. BEDDOW C. ROBERTS. ALEC BELL. T. ARKESDEN.

THE COLLEGE GAME IN THE STATES.
A desperate scrimmage in mid-field.

FOOTBALL IN AMERICA.

By EDWARD B. MOSS.

Early football in the United States—Yale introduce an annual contest in 1840—Mr. E. S. Shaff, from Rugby, helps to systematise the sport in 1873—A meeting of college delegates in New York—Inter-collegiate football—The Association game—Rugby in Canada—Evolution of the laws of the Rugby game in the States—The Rules Committee for 1905—The field of play—How the teams line up—How the game is played—The "interference"—The worst feature of the game—Leading teams in the United States—The great inter-college games—Attendances at big games—The stadium at Harvard University—Dangers of the game.

FOOTBALL in the United States, like many other branches of American sport, traces its ancestry back to England, and claims Rugby as its progenitor. Yet the present-day football could hardly be recognised by its forebears, so radical are the changes made in the Rugby Union code during the past thirty years to meet the New World ideas. To trace the origin of football in the United States to its beginning is almost as difficult as to discover the fundamentals of the game in Great Britain. Undoubtedly the Pilgrim Fathers brought the essentials of the old English game with them from the fatherland, and it is a well-established fact that a crude game of kicking football was played in New England as far back as 1750. There are records of town matches played on Thanksgiving Day between unlimited sides as far back as a century ago, in which a pig's bladder, inflated, was kicked back and forth by men and boys. Later, the New England colleges took up the sport, and played a rough sort of dribbling and kicking game, modelled after the play then in vogue in England.

About 1840 Yale University—which it may be stated has always been a leader in American football—adopted an annual contest between the Freshmen and Sophomore classes. As was the case in all the play at that time, the game was an extremely crude affair, and eye-witnesses have described it as a sort of open riot, in which an unlimited number of players took part, and participated in what resembles a modern class rush, in which more attention was paid to the opposing side than to the ball. These conflicts—for such they must be termed—continued until 1861, after which they appeared to have lapsed. In 1870 there was a revival of the sport, but on more clearly defined lines. A Mr. E. S. Shaff, who entered the class of 1873 from Rugby School, England, did much to systematise the sport, and records show that games were played between the various classes. Other colleges followed suit, and in October, 1873, the first meeting of delegates from educational institutions interested in the game was held in New York City. There were present at this gathering, Yale, Columbia, Princeton, and Rutger's College delegates, and rules were adopted, paving the way for the first inter-collegiate football matches in the United States.

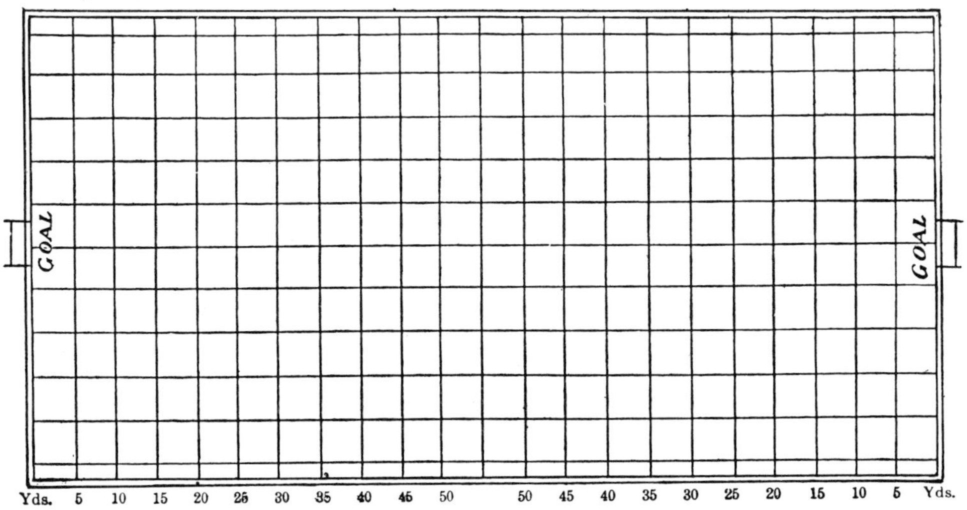

DIAGRAM OF THE FIELD OF PLAY IN THE AMERICAN GAME.

This marked the second epoch in American football and the beginning of the evolution of the game now known as inter-collegiate football. It is pertinent to state here that, so far as the United States is concerned, football is distinctly a scholastic and collegiate sport. All the important games are played between teams of schools, colleges, and universities. Attempts to professionalise the sport have failed utterly, and while here and there athletic clubs and towns foster teams, they are purely local affairs, never heard of outside their own limited boundaries.

QUARTER-BACK RECEIVING THE BALL FROM CENTRE TO PUT INTO PLAY.

Association football is played to some extent in the larger cities by independent teams, and Gaelic football by Irish and Irish-Americans. Within the past two years the Association game has been taken up by students of some of the larger colleges who do not care to go in for the more strenuous inter-collegiate game, and, aided by the enthusiasm created by the visit of the Pilgrims' team from England in the fall of 1905, the Association game is rapidly increasing in popularity.

PLAYER HOLDING THE BALL PREPARATORY TO A TRY AT GOAL FOLLOWING A TOUCH-DOWN, WITH KICKER ABOUT TO KICK SAME.

In Canada, Rugby, played under the English Rugby Union rules, prevails in Halifax, Winnipeg, and the Victoria sections; while in Ontario, Quebec, and other quarters Canadian teams play under what are known as Canadian Rugby rules.

The delegates to the meeting of the Eastern colleges interested in football in 1873, in their attempt to secure a general system under which to play the game, naturally turned to England and the Rugby regulations. As a result, the present game of inter-collegiate football may be said to have been derived from the game as played by the Rugby Football Union teams from 1871 to 1875.

The first games on record were those played between the teams of Yale and Princeton and Yale and Harvard Universities in 1876. During the same year Princeton and Pennsylvania University teams also played. The Rugby rules were not thoroughly understood by the college students during those days, despite the fact that Canadians, who were more familiar with the game, in some cases gave a helping hand in untangling and making clear the obscure points. The play was extremely crude, and the teams consisted of from fifteen to twenty players. The scoring system was the same as that in vogue in England at that time. Almost immediately came a demand for changes, and thus the inception of the American or inter-collegiate football was at hand. A convention to consider new rules was called in the fall of 1876, and one of the first moves was the altering of the form of scrummage, or, as it is termed in the United States, "scrimmage."

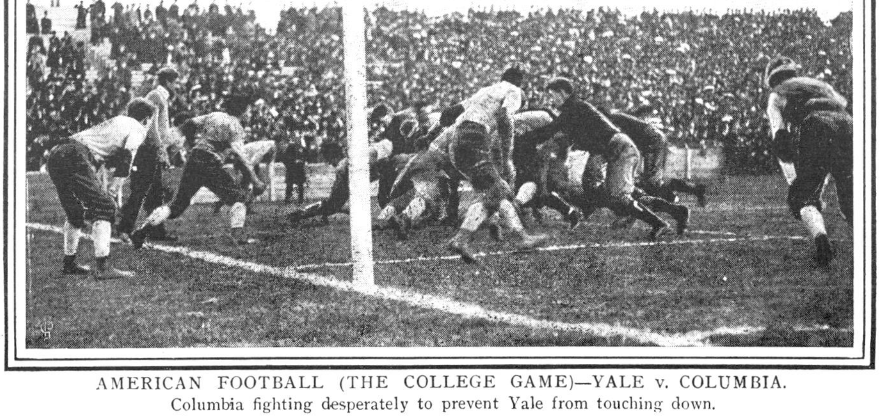

AMERICAN FOOTBALL (THE COLLEGE GAME)—YALE v. COLUMBIA.
Columbia fighting desperately to prevent Yale from touching down.

The first rules changed were known as Rugby Union Rules Nos. 8 and 9. In place of the general kicking in scrimmage, a regular heel-out was adopted, which was soon followed by a regular line-up in place of the English "scrum" or circle. Other changes followed rapidly, notable among them being one which necessitated the side in possession of the ball gaining five yards in three "tries" or scrimmages, or else forfeit possession to their opponents.

At first the games continued for one and a half hours, and were divided into three periods of play. Later, the playing time was reduced to two 45-minute halves, which, in turn, were shortened to 35-minute halves, the present playing time. At first only goals counted in the scoring. Next, in case of a tie, "tries" or touch-downs, as they were called, counted. Later it was ruled that, in case of a tie, a goal kicked from a touch-down took precedence over a field-goal. Then safeties were allowed to count, and where no goals or touch-downs were scored, the side that made four or more safeties less than their opponents were decided the winners. A still more radical move was the giving of values to the various forms of scoring. This was done shortly after 1880, and under the new ruling a touch-down counted 4, a touch-down and goal 6, a field-goal 5, and a safety 2.

These rules, during the existence of the Inter-collegiate Association, were made by an advisory committee of college graduates. In 1896, after the demise of that organisation, the present rules committee system was adopted, and this season—1905-6—consists of seven members, as follows: Paul J. Dashiel, U.S. Naval Academy; John C. Bell, University of Pennsylvania; L. M. Dennis, Cornell University; Robert D. Wrenn, Harvard University; J. B. Fine, Princeton University; A. A. Stagg, Chicago University; and Walter Camp, Yale University.

This committee formulates the rules, making changes or additions as its members think wise each spring for the following season of play, which consists of practically three months—from September 1 to December 1. Throughout the entire country these rules are accepted as the code for the year, and every college, university, and school team governs its play in accordance with them.

The game is played upon a rectangular field 330 feet long by 160 feet wide, marked with lines 5 yards apart running both lengthwise and crosswise of the field, which has caused the same to be nicknamed a "checker-board." On page 244 is a diagram of the field marked for play. The goals are placed in the middle of each goal-line, and consist of two upright posts, not more than 20 feet in height, placed 18 feet 6 inches apart and with a crossbar 10 feet above the ground. Teams consist of eleven players on a side, and the ball is a prolate spheroid of leather enclosing an inflated rubber bladder. The contending teams line up as a general rule as follows, although there are a number of variations used, according to the attack and defence planned by the rival elevens:

Left end.	Left tackle.	Left guard.	Centre.	Right guard.	Right tackle.	Right end.
*	*	*	*	*	*	*

quarter * back.

Left * half-back. Right * half-back.

Full * back.

There are two methods of advancing the ball—kicking and running. After the opening kick-off, which is the same as in Rugby, the team in possession of the ball, when the runner is tackled and his progress stopped, line up, as shown in the above plan, and the centre passes the ball to the quarter-back who, in turn, passes it to the runner elected to try for the advance. The latter may be one of the half-backs, the full-back, or even one of the line players, but in no case must the pass be a forward one. In case the quarter-back is chosen to make the try, he must run at least five yards to the right or left of his position when receiving the ball before turning down the field towards his opponent's goal-line. This rule, however, applies only to the quarter-back. The team holding the ball is required to advance the same at least five yards in three tries for downs, and in case they fail to make the distance the ball goes to the opposing team, where the last try is held. As a rule, however, when a team fails to gain the requisite distance in the first rushes, it elects to punt or kick on the final try in order that the ball may fall into the possession of its opponents as far from its own goal as possible. The runner carrying the ball has the right to use his open hands to ward off tackles, and the opposing team players can tackle, hold, or throw him to the ground, providing they tackle him between the shoulders and knees.

MEMBERS OF THE U.S. CARLISLE INDIAN SCHOOL TEAM AT PLAY.

Clean tackle of a runner carrying the ball by a member of the opposing team.

The greatest difference between American football and Rugby is in the interference. In the inter-collegiate game the runner may be protected, covered, or guarded by as many of his team-mates as can gather round him in his rush, either in front or behind him, but they cannot use their hands or arms to ward off the tacklers endeavouring to reach the man carrying the ball. Shouldering and body blocking is the means adopted to protect the runner from these tacklers. Under the present ruling, a touch-down is made when the player carrying the ball places it behind his opponent's goal-line, and this counts 5 points for his team. A free try at goal, in which the ball is first either brought or punted out from the goal-line to a point in front of the goal proper, is allowed after a touch-down. In case the ball is kicked over the cross-bar and between the uprights in such a free try, an additional point is scored. A field-goal, which can only be made by dropping the ball to the ground and kicking it on the rebound, or following a fair catch, in which the catcher signifies his intention of trying for a goal from placement, scores 5 points. A safety is made when the ball in the possession of a player guarding his own goal is declared dead by the referee behind such player's goal-line, the impetus which caused it to pass from outside the goal to behind the goal-line being given by the side defending the goal, and such safety counts 2 points for the opposing team. These, roughly, are the cardinal points in the inter-collegiate game.

The play has reached a most scientific point, the attack being directed in turn by the quarter-back at various points along the whole of the opposing line, from tackle to tackle, or outside the ends when a long run is attempted. The worst feature of the play is the using of heavy and powerful linesmen to lead the attack. They are drawn back to lead tandem drives at the opposing tackles or guards, or rushes around the end, and it frequently happens that the runner and his interference is thrown at a single individual player, who, in his attempt to break through such interference and reach the man with the ball, is obliged to face three or four men under full headway. When the attack is directed at the line positions from tackle to tackle, the forwards on the side possessing the ball try to make an opening for the runner and his interference by throwing the opposing line players out of the way, using their shoulders and bodies for the purpose. As the players of the team not in possession of the ball are allowed to use their hands, this is a difficult task, and frequently results in the attack being smothered as soon as it reaches the line of scrimmage, piling up the players of both teams in a promiscuous heap. When these tactics are repeated over and over again, as is frequently the case, the game becomes decidedly slow and uninteresting to spectators. This has given rise to a demand for a more open and spectacular style of play, with less pushing, piling, and hauling, and more long runs around the ends, and quick dashes through a wide, open line.

The play this year has been more in this direction, and in another year it is expected that the rules will be further changed to encourage this form of advancing the ball. The present system cannot be laid entirely to the playing rules formulated by the rules committee, for its members have done much to encourage more open play. The fault lies rather with the coaches in charge of the various college elevens—for the players are trained by graduates of their colleges, or professionals—who, until very recently, had directed their attention to developing play along the line on the driving and rushing system rather than toward open playing. The advent of several Canadian Rugby teams playing in the United States this season has done much to demonstrate the possibilities of the open Rugby game with its double and triple passes, and it is not unlikely that something upon these lines will be incorporated into inter-collegiate football within the next twelve months.

As stated before, there are no independent clubs of importance playing football in the United States. Every school, college, and university of any size, however, is represented by a team, and the rivalry between the elevens of the various institutions is intense. This is true throughout every section of the country. In the eastern part of the United States the Yale-Princeton, Harvard-Yale, Pennsylvania-Harvard, Cornell-Princeton, and

AMERICAN FOOTBALL—A FINE SNAPSHOT TAKEN ON THE FIELD OF PLAY.

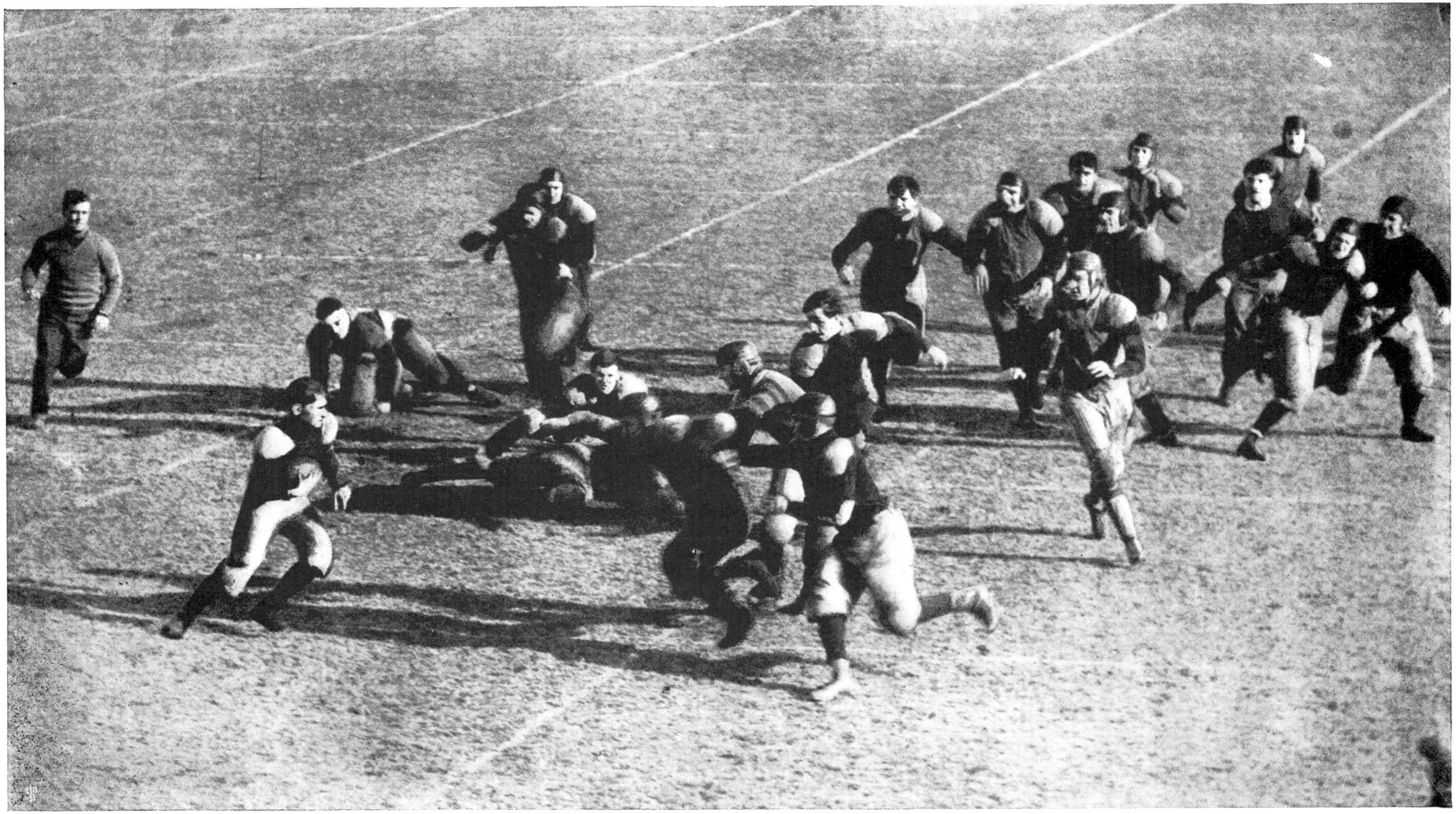

The photograph shows a runner opposing the encircling team's end, after having first made a run across the field. Note how his team-mates have upset several of the opposing players who have tried to tackle him, and the opposition running up to bar his further progress with the ball.

Columbia-Yale games draw thousands of spectators. In the middle west the Michigan-Chicago, Wisconsin - Minnesota, and Michigan-Wisconsin contests are the big games of the year; while the Pacific coast has its California-Leland Stanford game, and the South its Georgetown-Virginia match. In every case the contesting elevens are composed of students pursuing courses in the competing universities. The annual match between the teams of the United States naval and military academies is a national affair, and the leading army and navy officials, foreign diplomats, and, not infrequently, the President of the United States, attend this game. Some of the colleges have been meeting in annual football games each year since 1876, notably Yale and Princeton; while others have continued with an occasional break of a season or two from the same date.

So far as the popularity of the game is concerned, it shows no signs of diminishing, despite the recent attacks made upon American football. Games between rival school teams of the same city draw crowds of from 5,000 to 7,000 spectators, while those in which the contesting elevens represent schools of different large cities, such as New York and Chicago, the attendance reaches at times as many as 12,000. In the big games of the year between the larger university teams the attendance is limited only by the capacity of the stands surrounding the field of play. This is true of both the games played in the East and West.

In the annual struggle between Yale and Princeton Universities 30,000 spectators are all that can be accommodated, in round numbers, at either the athletic fields of the colleges. These games are played in almost every case on the private grounds of the respective university athletic associations. The undergraduates and alumni of these universities have first call on the tickets, and, as a rule, four are as many as one person can make application for.

In cases where there is a surplus after these favoured classes are satisfied, the residue of tickets are placed upon public sale. The charge is the same in every case. Seats in every part of the stand bring 2 dols. each. It frequently happens that when the teams appear to be evenly matched, judging from their early season games against smaller college elevens, there is such a demand on the part of both alumni and students, their families and friends, that the general public is unable either to secure seats or admission to the grounds. Thousands travel from New York, Boston, Philadelphia, and other cities to the small college towns to witness the play.

Harvard University, situated at Cambridge, Mass., two years ago erected an immense stone stadium at a cost of close upon a quarter of a million dollars, the seating capacity of which is approximately 40,000. At the Yale-Harvard games played there in 1903 and 1905, many thousands of prospective spectators were unable to gain admittance. The few seats that fell into the hands of speculators brought from 10 dols. to 25 dols. each, according to their location in the stands. The same conditions prevail in the middle west in the games between teams of the Universities of Chicago, Michigan, and Wisconsin, and are equally true of the California-Leland Stanford contest on the Pacific coast.

The proceeds of the sale of tickets, which, in the case of the Yale-Harvard game is close upon 80,000 dols., is divided, after the various expenses are paid, between the athletic associations of the contesting colleges. The average attendance at the larger college games throughout the country is approximately 20,000, but, as stated before, it is in almost every case governed by the capacity of the stands. Including the cost of tickets, railway fare, and hotel expenses, it can be conservatively stated that the average cost of witnessing a big college contest is from 10 to 15 dols., and in cases where the spectator travels more than the usual distance the expenses will amount to as many as 30 dols., or even more.

It has been said, and with much truth, that American football is not a game for weaklings. To indulge in the sport, with the danger of bodily injury reduced to a minimum, requires that the player be in the full possession of the strength and agility which comes with early maturity. As the game is played at present, it is not a sport for either schoolboys or those whose scholastic duties or business pursuits prevent them from training in the arduous manner which is necessary to fit a contestant for inter-collegiate football. This is borne out by the number of serious injuries and even deaths which occur to those who indulge in the play without first having prepared themselves physically to withstand the buffeting and bodily contact which is the portion of every player in a hard contest.

A careful analysis of the tabulated list of casualties each season shows, almost without exception, that the players seriously injured are those who, as members of high school and public school elevens, were, owing to their youth, not capable of withstanding the bodily strain imposed upon them in the game. The other class are players who compete in athletic club or town teams, and whose means of livelihood are such as to make careful training and preparation for the play entirely out of the question. From these two classes come practically all the serious cases of injury and death charged against American football. It is seldom that members of the big college elevens, guarded as they frequently are with leather helmets, nose and shin guards, and heavily padded suits, are more than temporarily injured in the play.

AMERICAN FOOTBALL. (THE COLLEGE GAME.)

Protective formation showing the ball being passed back to full-back for a kick, with opponents trying to break through line to prevent the same. Note how well the line is holding, with the secondary defence in backs ready to stop any players of the opposing team who may succeed in breaking through the line

THE ART OF CAPTAINCY.

By JOHN DEVEY

Professionalism and captaincy—The qualities that go to make a good captain—The ideal position the captain should occupy on the field—Archie Hunter—The value of tact—Defensive tactics—Dennis Hodgetts and Allen—The English Cup Semi-final of 1894-5—The Villa v. Corinthians, and Mr. C. B. Fry's comment on the match—Signalling—Players and temperament.

THE question of captaincy receives far too little attention in modern football. Very often, I fear, the management of a team give the matter a minimum of consideration; they seem to think that all a captain has to do is to spin a coin at the beginning of the game, make his choice of ends, and then his afternoon's work is done. But those of us who recall some of the grand leaders of old know that those two points were regarded by them as among the most insignificant duties they were called upon to perform. Some of the old leaders had a lofty conception of their duties, and when one recalls the influence they exerted upon the teams they led, it seems inexplicable that the high office should have come to be so lightly regarded. But the work of the football captain may mean much or it may mean little—that depends upon the man who fills the office. Speaking broadly, however, one is forced to express regret that professional clubs, who are prepared to spend unlimited sums in the acquiring of men, should be so indifferent to the circumstances which go so far to ensure loyalty and enthusiastic co-operation amongst the players on the field.

Singularly enough, this short-coming is general. The impression prevails—of course, there are notable exceptions—that almost any member of the team is good enough for a leader, provided that he possesses a reasonable experience. No greater fallacy was ever propounded. In the early days the choice of captain was due to seniority, ability, or geniality. Often the selection was due to all three, and no happier combination could be imagined. The advent of professionalism altered all this, and the result is that, instead of the average football captain being a real factor in the control of the team, he is largely a player with an official title and nothing more. The majority of professional footballers would endorse this, and probably regret it at the same time, because it is not calculated to produce that enthusiasm which, when fully roused, goes far to carry an eleven on to victory. There will be a reaction some day, but it cannot be denied that the present-day captain is not playing the part that his official capacity should entitle him to play.

The captain should be the mouthpiece of the team; it is necessary for the welfare of the players and of the club generally that he should be their mouthpiece, for, after all, the interests of players and committee are identical. The captain should be proud of his men; and the men should be proud of their captain. They should look up to him. It is not necessary that the captain should be chosen merely because he is a hard worker, and yet that is in the case of many clubs the basis of selection. It is important that the captain should be able to set an example to his men in this respect, but it may happen that he is not physically fitted to outshine all his rivals in respect of hard work. A man may be a great captain and yet lack the power to rank as the greatest worker. You play a captain for the manifestation of his brain power; it is conceivable that a man may be invaluable as a captain when he is no longer the most sprightly member of the eleven.

You want the office of captain to be invested with a certain sense of dignity. The captain should be the brainiest man in the eleven; he should be looked up to by both management and players alike.

There are two excellent positions for the captain to occupy—centre-half and centre-forward—but the ideal position for the leader of a team is centre-half. He is there in close touch both with attack and defence, and he can control the game perfectly, because he sees everything that is happening. But it was remarkable how Archie Hunter, a centre-forward, used to get into touch with his defence. You could often see him giving them a helping hand, and not only helping them but inspiring the defence. He seemed to get back by instinct when anything was likely to go wrong. I have never seen any man—and I have seen all the great League captains—exercise the same influence on a side that Archie Hunter did. Of course, he was favoured by condition and environment.

Archie Hunter came from Scotland when the game in the Midlands was in its infancy, and he was a hero in everyone's eyes. The players looked up to him as they never looked up to any man who came later. But he was a grand leader, and his captaincy won almost as many games as his executive skill. I daresay present-day players who do not recognise the conditions as we who knew them are able to do may feel inclined to think that too much adulation is heaped upon some of the heroes of the past, but, to-day, captaincy is practically a lost art if you compare it as it was in the days of Archie Hunter. But while a captain is better placed at centre-half or centre-forward, a good captain at outside-left, or in goal, would be infinitely preferable to a moderate captain in the most favoured position.

One great difficulty a captain has to deal with is the attitude of a man who has made a high-class reputation. If he has to perform in a big match, say the English Cup Final, or an International encounter, or any special game, his attitude is all that a captain need desire. But in an ordinary game, one in which there is nothing special at stake, he is apt to put on airs and to flout the authority of the captain. The "skipper" then has to try to induce such a one to drop such conduct by appealing to his temperament. If that appeal should fail, then sterner measures have to be adopted. I have more than once advocated the claims of a player of less ability in preference to a player of distinction on account of the impossibility of getting good results with such a man in the team. There is no necessity for any man to play to the gallery merely because the match in which he is engaged is not an English Cup Final or a game of special importance. It seems to me all the more contemptible that a player who must know better should be guilty of conduct which amounts to insubordination and is provocative of insubordination in others. I have had experience of this. The last four years of my captaincy of Aston Villa was the most trying period of my life. There comes a time when you cannot yourself do quite so much as you were once able to accomplish, and that is the time that the yearning for your old maximum power comes to you. You want a little help yourself then, and you do not always get it. That is a trying time indeed for a captain.

A captain should never be dictatorial; he should strive to obtain a community of interest among the players under his charge. It is not a bad thing for a captain to go to a man and say, "Now, you use me as your tool. We should all be tools to one another; all should be tools in turn. Every time you have the ball and cannot get away with it, I am there to help you out of a difficulty; use me as your tool. If I have the ball, you be my tool."

An indifferent captain is better than several captains on the field. Nothing is more disastrous than a conflict of authority. The captain should be in sole control; and no one should venture to usurp his prerogative. I believe in a captain consulting his players. You may agree with their conclusions or not, but I believe in soliciting their opinions. If your ideas are strengthened as the result of an interchange of opinion, well and good; if the result is in the opposite direction, then no

Howard Barrett.]

THE FOOTBALL ASSOCIATION CUP—SEMI-FINAL, 1904-5.

Aston Villa v. Everton in the re-played tie on the Notts Forest Ground. Fine forward play by the Villa. Bache running with the ball. Aston Villa won the match by 2 goals to 1.

harm has been done. It may be that things have been presented to you in quite a different light to that in which you had previously viewed them. At the same time, it is gratifying to all the men to know that their opinion has been asked. It is a nice feeling for the youngest man in the team to think "He appreciates my opinion, although I am the youngest player on the side." He feels flattered, and will play better football if he thinks his skipper is interested in him than he would if he held the idea that he was regarded as a mere cypher in the team.

We want to look deep down into football; there is too much surface watching done. If we look right into the science of football—and it is a more wonderful science than most people think—we can detect deep schemes. The spectators may not see them—nay, they cannot see them. The captain has to watch the game most critically. He sees, perhaps, at a certain time that his opponents have the run of the ball. He has to bring every ounce of intelligence to bear upon the process of staving off the daring and impetuous attacks which are being made upon his position. He has to counteract those attacks, and it often happens that if he does so diplomatically he converts his side from one which is being overrun into a winning team. Just when the tide is flowing against his side, he grasps the situation, and then we see an example of defensive combination. The inside-forwards silently fall back and help the halves, but the two outside men and the centre are ever ready to dash off and, maybe, find a weak place in the opposing defence. They do not waste their energies; they conserve them, but they keep the other defenders playing all the time while the hostile forwards are working at twice the pace that a vanguard normally does. But the defence is so systematic that the whirlwind attack gradually dies away, and then the side which has been content to remain on the defensive gradually raises the siege, and it becomes their turn to attack. The game is won, but few of the crowd can do full justice to the tactics which made victory probable.

I can recall many occasions in the seasons when Aston Villa won the League championship when diplomacy won us games in which our opponents were excessively dangerous. We would be occupied in resisting impetuous attacks when suddenly one of our men would get off; in would come a flying centre, the ball would come to John Campbell, he would send in one of his brilliant shots, and the whole position would be changed. We seldom received the credit for this to which we were entitled; it was not realised that we were following a carefully thought-out plan of campaign; sometimes we were told that we had scored "a lucky goal." There is more method in some of these lucky goals than some of the critics realise. You have all watched games in which one side has manifested infinitely more devil for a given period than they have shown in any other portion of the match. It is the captain's duty to watch the play of his opponents during that period, and if he can cope with it he will have broken the backbone of that team. Indifferent captaincy at such a time would probably mean a lost game; and yet the position of captain is one which many would treat lightly!

Here is an anecdote showing the veneration, almost the awe, in which the greatest captain I have ever known was held. When I was captain of St. George's, I was playing in a match, Birmingham v. Cheshire, at Crewe, in which I was inside-right, with Archie Hunter in the centre, and Dennis Hodgetts and A. Allen on the left. Allen, a beautiful dribbler, came sailing through the defence and went for goal. Suddenly Archie called for a pass, but Allen, seeing what a great chance he had, went through and scored. As we were walking up to the centre, I heard Hodgetts say, "Well played, Al., but didn't you hear the captain ask for the ball? You ought to have done what he said, you know." Such absolute confidence had Hodgetts in the judgment of his skipper that, although a goal had been scored, he could not get it out of his head that nine times out of ten Archie would have been right. Archie, of course, was quite content; he would be the last man in the world to desire his players to be automata. I give the incident, not to prove that Allen was wrong, but just to illustrate the hold which Archie had on the men under him. Do you think such a thing would happen in regard to any First League captain of the present day? I trow not. Ah, what a delightful thing it would be for a captain—and for the team—if the prevailing sentiment among the men was "Well, he is our captain; if we can help him we will." A good captain can settle a team from a confused side into a well-balanced set of players. The captain should work largely by force of will. He has to give instructions, but the good captain never shouts and bawls at his men. Sometimes he has to be more emphatic than at other times. I remember a case in which one of our backs would persist in kicking straight up the field. We had fleet wing-men; but he was giving them no chance. Usually he kicked straight to the other backs, and, of course, the ball was returned, and we never had an opening made for us. At last I had to get very emphatic. "Kick obliquely," I kept telling him, and at last he did so. Our fleet wingers got going; and we did well.

Even in a great game a little diplomacy may work wonders.

The finest match I ever took part in was the Semi-final for the English Cup at Blackburn in 1894-5, when Aston Villa beat Sunderland. Geordie Russell, left half-back, had a very awkward wing to face in Miller and Gillespie. Russell played well, but in the second half he realised that he had more than he could do, and he kept appealing to his inside-forward to fall back and assist him. Now I fancy that the man appealed to had quite as much as he could manage, and these continual cries from the half-back seemed to worry him considerably. Still the appeals came, and at last Hodgetts got rather out of temper and told the half-back to stop worrying him. I, therefore, exhorted them, "Now, lads, don't play into the hands of our opponents like this. You must not take one another's remarks so seriously. I will help you," I said to Russell, and, turning to Hodgetts, who was just off with the ball, I remarked, "Now, Dennis, get on and show them how to play football." I could see Hodgetts literally jump again. He put fresh spirit into his play, and that game was won.

I daresay I have said some hard things without meaning them. I often used to try to get Spencer fully roused, because he never plays so magnificently as when he is on his mettle. I always used to like to see opponents ruffle Howard just a little. It takes a great deal to even ruffle him slightly, but when ruffled just a little he used to play his greatest game.

Here is a good story illustrating the value of advice. I call it a good story because it is rather against me, in a sense. I was the captain, and we were playing against the Corinthians. It was towards the close of my career, and I felt the strain of the hard game. James Cowan suddenly said to me, "Why don't you go on the wing and let Athersmith come inside?" I thought it a good suggestion, and took it, and almost immediately gave Athersmith a nice opening. He raced through at a speed which I could not then have shown, and scored. Mr. C. B. Fry, in commenting on the match, spoke of the masterly judgment of John Devey in bringing Athersmith inside, whereas it was solely Cowan's idea. Certainly I made the opportunity for Athersmith, but it would never have come about had not Cowan made the suggestion he did.

By the exercise of discretion the captain may train his men to promptly interpret the word he may utter, or any action he may go through in the form of signalling. When danger threatens, a motion of the arm may send back both inside-forwards to strengthen the half-back line, and the casual onlooker marvels at the manœuvre. It is the science of the game, and a captain who has studied football from all its offensive and defensive bearings is able to take advantage which the moment may suggest. But first-class players do what is required naturally; it is part of their football education to watch how the game is going.

It is not essential that all the instruction should come from the captain; indeed, it is far better that the men, following the advice of their skipper, should institute a system whereby exchange of thought can be readily understood. Secret signalling in this sense is invaluable, and it has seldom been carried into effect with more striking result than in the case of the famous Preston North End eleven which carried the country by storm in consequence of the unison with which they worked.

Another important function which devolves upon the captain is the correction of any misapprehension which may exist as the outcome of injudicious criticism from the crowd. The tendency of spectators is to judge a player by exactly what catches the eye. A captain who knows what's what should lay himself out to correct disparagement from the onlookers by offering personal encouragement to the player concerned.

A captain should make a point of encouraging the players on every possible occasion. He should try, too, to study the individual temperaments of all the men under his care. It is here that the complexity of a captain's work lies. He has ten players to deal with, and there may be ten altogether different temperaments among them. There is the hot-headed player; he is an easy man to manage, because you get at the bottom of him at once. Then you have the sulky player; he is a very different individual to deal with; you never get at the bottom of him. Still, an encouraging word is not often wasted, even on the sulkiest of players. Football brings out a man's characteristics very pronouncedly. If you see a man sticking closely to the ball and never giving his colleagues a chance, you may rely upon it that that man is a selfish man off the field. If, on the other hand, you come across a player who is ready to do anything for you, and delights in making openings for you, you may depend upon it that he is good-tempered and unselfish.

But whatever a man is, you have to so shape your conduct as to get the best out of him. After all, we are ruled by our temperaments. Sometimes a man can master his temperament, but oftentimes it is too strong for him.

Having captained Aston Villa for eight of the most prosperous years the club has known, my observations upon the captain's art may not be uninteresting. I am convinced that the relations between club and captain on the lines I have outlined would prove an inestimable boon to all concerned.

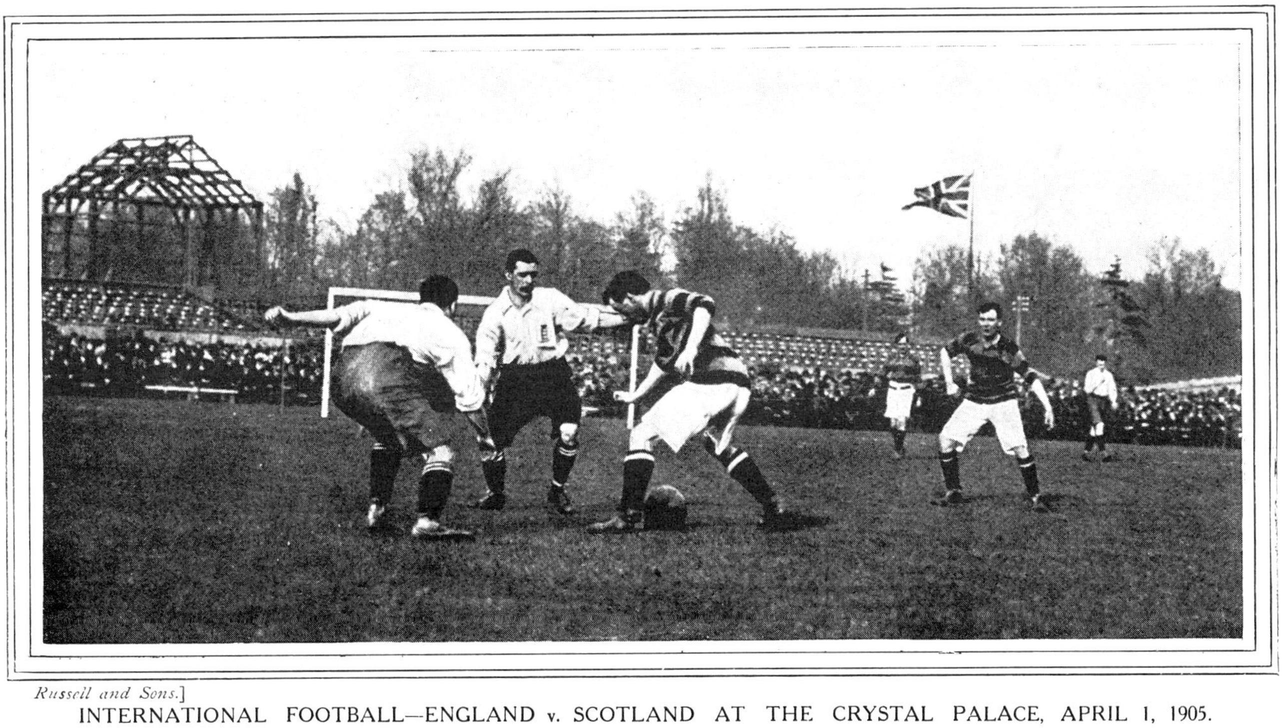

Russell and Sons.]

INTERNATIONAL FOOTBALL—ENGLAND v. SCOTLAND AT THE CRYSTAL PALACE, APRIL 1, 1905.

England, 1; Scotland, 0. (Bache scored for England.) A tussle for the ball in mid-field.

J. H. Wilson, Leicester.]

THE LEICESTER FOSSE FOOTBALL GROUND, FILBERT STREET, LEICESTER.

LEICESTER FOSSE FOOTBALL CLUB.

Early football in Leicester—Formation of the Fosse Football Club—Derivation of the name—The first cup won—Fosse enter for the English Cup and join the Midland League—Elected to the Second Division of the Football League—Fluctuating fortunes—Officials of the club.

Colours : Dark-blue shirts, white knickers. *Ground : Filbert Street, Leicester.*

IT seems quite a long time ago since the Leicester Fosse Football Club was first started upon its more or less eventful career. Looking backward for a period of twenty-two years—1883-4—it is not difficult to call to mind the entire absence of local public interest in "Soccer" football in Leicester. At this time there were few Association clubs in the town, the Leicester Town, Wyggeston School, and Mill Hill House being the most prominent. This was when two to three thousand people would "spectate" free round the ropes on the Victoria Park to witness the performances of the premier Rugby club, whilst the number of spectators interested in Association matches played at the same end of the Park, and within a few yards of the Rugby games, would be represented by the few officials only.

The Fosse Club was really formed in the following season—1884-5. A combination of youths, mostly Old Wyggestonians, subscribed the sum of ninepence each for the purchase of a ball, and with the aid of a carpenter they turned out a set of roughly-finished goalposts, etc. A further call of ninepence each raised the total to one-and-sixpence as the club membership fee for the first season. These ardent spirits, residing principally in the West End of the town, and in the neighbourhood of the old Roman Fosse, decided upon a club name possessing local significance, and were led to adopt the name of "Fosse" at the suggestion of one of the officials, who argued that as "The Fosse" was known throughout the length and breadth of the land, so should the new football club be known in the future. The ancient and historical neighbourhood was thus responsible for the name of the club.

The first season terminated with a balance of one shilling and tenpence in hand, but the club began to create such interest that two seasons later the membership had increased to such an extent as to necessitate a reserve team being organised.

The season of 1887-8 saw the membership augmented still further, and to meet the wishes of the playing members it was deemed necessary to run three teams. The first team took on a more ambitious programme than previously, and entered into engagements with such clubs as Burton Swifts, Notts County, Rovers, Kettering, and Loughborough Town. These clubs proved too strong, however, and the season's results were consequently not of a very satisfactory nature.

Still plodding along, the club had to face a serious difficulty in the season 1888-9, the Leicester Rugby club outbidding its Association rival for the use of the Belgrave Road Ground. No alternative remained but to resort to the Victoria Park again. The following season, however, saw the opening of a new ground, and it was at this particular juncture that the club entered into really serious business. Two cup competitions were entered—Kettering and Leicestershire—and although the club early received its quietus in the Kettering competition, no mistake was made with regard to the local trophy, which was won by the following players: Goal, C. Walker; backs, S. Rowson and W. Davis; half-backs, J. Johnson, J. Murdock, and A. Vickers; forwards, C. Bentley, F. Gardner, E. Johnson, A. West, and E. Thompson.

Great things were accomplished in the subsequent season. For the first time the club entered the English Cup competition, and the outcome of really excellent work on the field was the election of the Fosse to the Midland League in May, 1891. This, of course, meant a much more serious class of football than the club had previously engaged in; but the change was warmly welcomed by those whose only aim was to see Association football thrive in Leicester. And it did thrive, too, so much so that the third season in the Midland League saw the Fosse finish second to Burton Wanderers. This was a state of affairs which was well calculated to satisfy the appetite of the most exacting of the club's supporters, and when, on May 21, 1894, the club secured election to the Second Division of the Football League, the enthusiasm of the ever-increasing army of "Fossites" knew no bounds.

The season 1894-5 thus saw the club embark upon its campaign in the Second Division, and such an excellent show was made that at the close of the season the club was only debarred from participating in the test matches owing to an inferior goal average. The following three seasons were not nearly as successful, however, and the result of moderate play on the part of the team was that the club was placed in very grave difficulties financially. This was the state of affairs when the season 1898-9 was entered upon, and the prospects of the club did not appear to be any too bright at this juncture. Suddenly an electrifying change took place, the outcome of two or three smart performances on the part of the team being that a really determined effort was commenced to gain First Division honours. Up to the close of this season the team made a keen bid for premier honours, but Glossop—after appearing to be out of it—managed to secure the second position to Manchester City, and the Fosse had to be satisfied with third place.

Having raised the interest of the club's supporters to such

LEICESTER FOSSE FOOTBALL CLUB—THE PLAYERS, SEASON 1905-6.

Back Row: MORGAN. GOULD BLESSINGTON. SMITH. MOODY. TRUEMAN. POLLOCK. THOMPSON (Trainer).

J. Herbert Wilson, Leicester.]

Front Row: MR. GEORGE JOHNSON (Secretary). BRADSHAW. HUBBARD. BANNISTER (Captain). OAKES. ASHBY. HODGKINSON.

DURRANT.

a pitch, it was imperative almost that this self-same interest should be sustained if the club was to succeed. For the second time—1899-1900—a bold bid was made for First Division honours, and when the first three months went by without the team meeting with defeat, there were justifiable hopes that the coveted goal would be reached. Disappointment was, however, once again in store for the Fosse, and Sheffield Wednesday and Bolton Wanderers were successful in getting back to the First Division fold.

The most disastrous season in the club's career was next experienced. Determined, if possible, to get a "star" team together, money was spent by the directors rather lavishly. The team, however, did badly, and interest consequently waned. With a heavy wage-bill to meet each week this was bound to prove disastrous, and altogether the sum of £600 was lost as the result of this particular season's work. From this stage—1900-1—up to the close of last season nothing seemed to move in the right direction for the club. Matches were lost with irritating frequency, and the culminating point was reached in May, 1904, when the club had to apply for re-election to the Second Division. The position at this time was a humiliating one, both for officials and supporters, and although there was never any doubt that the club would be again elected to the League, it was felt that the ordeal ought never to be faced again. This season matters have turned out much more favourable, as at the time of writing the club occupies a very creditable position on the Second Division chart.

A few remarks concerning past and present officials of the club will not be out of place. It only seems the other day that the late Mr. Frank Ashwell was taking an active part in controlling the club's affairs, and those ardent supporters who were acquainted with Mr. Ashwell will always remember with deep gratitude the great efforts he made to advance the club's interests. Another good old official was Mr. Thomas Seddon, who even now gets to the matches as often as he can, and continues to take an interest in the club's welfare. Other names that suggest themselves to one's mind are those of Messrs. W. G. Jones, H. Chitham, J. J. Curtis, A. W. Staines. Councillor S. Hudson, and Ernest Marson. The latter acted as hon. secretary of the club for a number of years, previous to which Mr. Frank Gardner also wielded the secretarial pen

Alluding now to the present directors—for the club has been a limited liability concern for nearly ten years—it can truly be said that each and everyone of them has done all that is possible to further the interests of the club. Mr. A. H. Vass, the present chairman of directors, has devoted both time and money to the club, and this gentleman and his colleagues on the board have, during their eight years' service, experienced to the full what a perilous time a football club is sometimes called upon to face.

The most remarkable feature of the club's career is the bad luck which has been experienced with regard to the English Cup competition. It seems impossible to get a good match at home, and one has to go as far back as 1893-4 to recall a Cup-tie at Filbert Street in the competition proper. This was the memorable drawn game with Derby County. Each time since that the Fosse has reached the competition proper a strong club has had to be met away from home, and it is questionable if any other club in the country can produce as disappointing a record in this respect. Of the players who have in the past assisted the club, one is deserving of particular mention. This is the redoubtable "Billy" Darrell, who, no doubt, was greatly instrumental—in the club's earliest stages—in arousing the enthusiasm of supporters. Another old warrior was Jack Lord; whilst, coming to more recent times, Arthur Collins is deserving of reference. The latter was taught his football in Leicester, and he has earned golden opinions at Fulham this season, so much so that he was chosen to represent the South against the North at Leeds.

Langfier, Glasgow.]

A SAD AND UNIQUE FOOTBALL PHOTOGRAPH—THE IBROX PARK DISASTER.

The wreck of the stand after the International match between England and Scotland, April, 1902.

THE PRINCIPAL AMATEUR CLUBS OF THE PAST.

By C. W. ALCOCK, Vice-President of the Football Association.

"Let others hail the rising sun,
I bow to that whose course is run."

The survivors of 1863—The Sheffield Club—Decline of the old Forest Club and rise of the Wanderers—Esprit de corps—The Wanderers win the Football Association Cup outright—Travelling to Glasgow in the good old days—The Royal Engineers—Lord Hawke as a footballer—The Shropshire Wanderers—The dawn of the professional era and rise of the Blackburn Rovers

WHERE are the stars of yestere'en ? In other words, where are the clubs which made history by bringing the Football Association into being ? How many of these are still alive, even in name ? As a mere matter of football record, the question is not without its importance. Fortunately the answer is easily given. Of the eleven clubs represented at the meeting at the Freemasons' Tavern on October 26, 1863, when the Football Association became a living body, only three are still going concerns, and one of them a recent renaissance after a long interregnum of inactivity. Of the "only and original" clubs forming the Football Association, one alone has throughout the ages been an active and faithful member of the Association without a break up to the present time.

As a matter of fact, the Barnes Club has never had bare justice done to it for the splendid work it did for the Football Association in its early days. The earliest code of rules was formulated by Mr. E. C. Morley, the first hon. secretary, a gentleman learned in the law, who subsequently secured well-deserved promotion to the presidency of the Football Association, and is still—the gods be praised!—going strong, a fitting illustration of the benefits of the physical cult. The fact that the Barnes Club also supplied his two successors in the post of hon. secretary—R. W. Willis and R. G. Graham to wit—will of itself show the important part it played in safeguarding and consolidating the Association in its infancy. *Floret, Floruit, Floreat!*

This tribute to the Barnes Club must, however, not be understood to mean that it was the first to carry on football in any organised form. There were brave men before Agamemnon. Other clubs playing the dribbling game in one shape or another were undoubtedly in evidence before the Football Association was formed. I can well remember, in the middle of the Fifties, reading occasionally of the doings of a metropolitan team which fretted its brief hour on the football stage under the name of Dingley Dell. The Crusaders, a combination on much the same lines, and composed mostly, if my memory serves me rightly, of old public school men, made rare appearances on the scene about the same time.

In both cases the football was of a fitful character, which it was bound to be, considering that the only opponents to be found at this period in London or even Greater London were Westminster and Charterhouse Schools—the old Charterhouse, that is, then in the heart of the City in Charterhouse Square.

Yorkshire, always to the fore where sport is concerned, had, it is certain, taken up football in the latter half of the Fifties. The Sheffield Club was formed in 1855, its neighbour the Hallam Club two years later. The Sheffield Club has a unique record in Association football, and one of which it has good reason to be proud. Its antiquity is beyond dispute—all credit and honour to it. Whether it was the first to organise seriously with a view to a regular programme of football is, however, a little open to doubt.

The first club to work on a definite basis with the distinct object of circulating and popularising the game, I am inclined to think, was a club known as the Forest Club. Founded in 1859 by a few old Harrovians, it had an uninterrupted career of success, playing its home fixtures on a part of Epping Forest in the immediate vicinity of the Merchant Seaman's Orphan Asylum at Snaresbrook. The first captain was J. F. Alcock, and among the original members of the team were J. Pardoe, who subsequently contributed largely to the development of Association football in Hitchin and Hertfordshire, C. W. Alcock, A. and W. J. Thompson, and C. A. Absolom.

Fired by the zeal and energy of the Foresters, other clubs soon saw the light, with the result that the Forest F. C. had in a short time quite an imposing programme to fulfil. Matches with Mincing Lane, Richmond, then a scratch team but soon to emerge from the chrysalis stage into the brilliant butterfly as one of the bright particular exponents of the Rugby Union game, and others supplied the chief items in the Forest programme during the four years of a flourishing career.

A variety of causes led to the decision of the old Forest Club, after four years of unbroken triumph, to seek a wider scope of football utility. The chief was the fact that the local element in the team had become fine by degrees and beautifully less. Whatever the reason, the conversion of the old Forest Club into the Wanderers in 1863 marked a new era in the history of the Association game.

What an important part the Wanderers played in the development of Association football, not only at the moment but for all time, the record of its extraordinary success from 1864 into the Eighties will fully testify. Originally composed exclusively of University, public school, and military men, a place in the Wanderers team represented the highest ambition of the best players. The esprit de corps which characterised the Wanderers in those early days was truly remarkable. I can vividly recall the details of a visit I made to Gresham Street one Friday afternoon to get a goalkeeper to play against Queen's Park at Glasgow the following day.

"Can you play to-morrow, G—— ?" was my salutation.

THE OFF-SIDE RULE EXPLAINED.

DIAGRAM NO. 6.—OFF-SIDE.

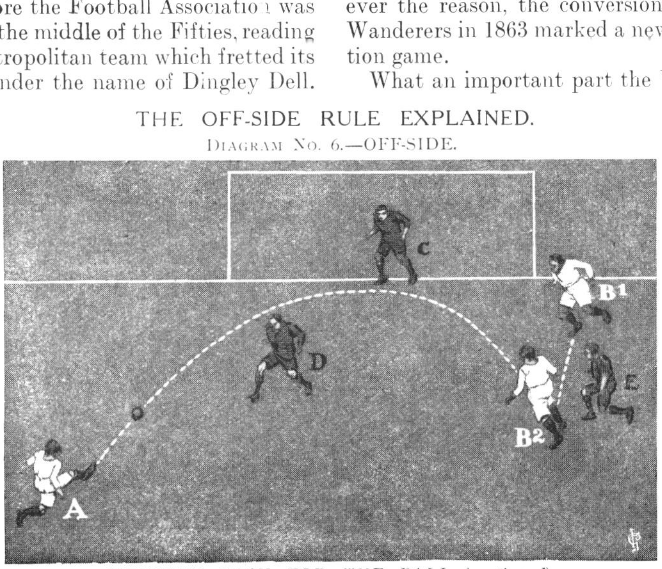

RUNNING BACK FOR THE BALL (*continued*).

A makes a high shot at goal, and the wind and screw carry the ball back. **B** runs from position 1 to position 2, and scores. **B** is off-side, because he had not three opponents between him and the goal-line at the moment the ball was last played by **A**.

"Yes," was the reply; "where?"

When I responded "At Glasgow," he said cheerily:

"All right! When do we go?" It was then late in the afternoon.

"From Euston at eight."

"I shall be there," he returned with a smile.

And he was there. Very much there in fact, in a more than usually stubborn contest. No wonder that the club made history as it did with such splendid material.

It is hardly necessary, indeed, to recall the remarkable achievements of the Wanderers in the early days of the F. A. Cup. They were Cup fighters before anything, as the Old Etonians, the Blackburn Rovers, and West Bromwich Albion showed themselves to be subsequently, and they had the happy knack of rising to the occasion, which is always characteristic of special excellence or particular keenness. Five times in the first seven years of its institution was the F. A. Cup in the possession of the Wanderers. They won it, too, outright in 1878, after three successive wins, but returned it to the F. A. on the condition, which was accepted, that it should never again become the property of any club.

The formation of the Old Boys' clubs weakened the foundations of the Wanderers to such an extent that it gradually subsided, and though it lingered on as a name for some time afterwards, its career as a fighting body was over when the Eighties had begun.

They were glorious days in the way of enjoyment, those of the late Sixties and throughout the Seventies. Then it was at least the game pure and unadulterated. No "gates" to speak of—down our way, at least. It was real sport, *sans* exes., *sans* records, *sans* everything of the modern up-to-date order, in any case. Those were the days primeval, long before the turnstiles had begun to sing their merry song to the tune of the club manager, years prior to the era of luxurious travelling, of saloon carriages and sleeping berths, and every possible comfort. To go to Glasgow—a railway journey of over 800 miles there and back—in the good old days for an hour and a half's football and at one's own expense was not in a way grateful and comforting. How we did it is not so easy to say. But it was done, and plenty of fun it brought with it, if one had to travel through the night in draughty carriages with hard seats—in fact, in a severely economical style, to which the new footballer—good luck to him!—is happily a stranger.

But this is not the place for sentiment, and I am getting off the line. Times are changed, and footballers naturally changed with them. To return to the old clubs. How quaintly some of the methods in those days read now! I have before me as I write a card of the match between the Wanderers and Queen's Park, Glasgow, played on Hampden Park, Mount Florida, Glasgow, on October 9, 1875, which is well worthy of reproduction in facsimile. Though each side wore its own jerseys of uniform colours, the various players had caps or stockings of distinctive colours, duly recorded on the card, so that everyone could be easily identified. The positions of the Scottish team stand out strangely. Harry McNeil was "left-front," his brother, Moses McNeil, was "left back-up," W. Mackinnon was "centre-front," J. B. Weir "right-front," with C. Herriot and T. Lawrie respectively "centre back-up" and "right back-up." At the bottom of the card is a plaintive appeal in bold type: "Please do not strain the ropes"!

FOOTBALL MATCH,

WANDERERS, London, v. QUEEN'S PARK,

Played on Hampden Park, Mount Florida, Glasgow, on Saturday, 9th October, 1875

H. W. CHAMBERS,
Goal Keeper.

A. H. STRATFORD,
Back.

A. F. KINNAIRD, *Right X Half-back* Blue and white cap — **W. S. RAWSON** *Left X Half-back.* Blue cap

J. TURNER, *Left X Wing.* — **W. D. GREIG,** *Right X Wing* Blue stockings.

R. L. GEAVES, *Centre X* Red and white cap — **C. W. ALCOCK,** *Captain X and Centre.* Cap—blue and white chequers. — **H. S. OTTER,** *Centre. X* Pink cap.

HUBERT HERON, *Left X Wing.* Grey stockings, and orange, violet, and black cap. — **J. KENRICK,** *Right X Wing.* Cerise and French-grey cap

UMPIRE—ROBERT GARDINER, CLYDESDALE CLUB.
REFEREE—THOMAS HASWELL, 3RD L.R.V. CLUB
UMPIRE—W. C. MITCHELL, QUEEN'S PARK CLUB.

HENRY M'NEILL, *Left X Front* Orange and black stockings. — **W. MACKINNON,** *Centre X Front* Red stockings. — **JAMES B. WEIR,** *Right X Front.* Red and white stockings.

M. M'NEIL, *Left X Back-up* Blue and white stockings. — **C. HERRIOT,** *Centre X Back-up* Black and white cap—no stocking. — **THOMAS LAWRIE,** *Right X Back-up.* White stockings.

JAS. PHILIPS *Left X Half-back* Red and black stockings. — **CHAS. CAMPBELL,** *Right X Half-back* Red, white, and black stockings.

R. W. NEIL, *Left X Back* Heather mixture stockings — **JOSEPH TAYLOR,** *Captain and X Right Back.* Black and white stockings.

JOHN DICKSON,
Goal Keeper.

Colours: Wanderers, White Jersey — Queen's Park, Black and White Stripe.
Play will begin at 3.30 p.m. and end at 5 p.m.

PLEASE DO NOT STRAIN THE ROPES.

This match-card is a full-sized facsimile of the original printed for the match between the Wanderers (five times winners of the Football Association Cup) and Queen's Park, Glasgow, played on Saturday, October 9, 1875.

Queen's Park, Glasgow, looms so largely among the amateur clubs with a brilliant past that a glance at its history cannot fail to provide interesting reading. But there are plenty of other clubs which deserve an enduring record. The Sheffield F. C. has already had mention, and, taken all in all, the Sheffield Club has perhaps the best record, considering the conspicuously active part it has played throughout the last forty years of the Association's history.

The whirligig of time has brought with it no greater revenge than the practical disappearance of the Royal Engineers from the area of Association football. Memories of Marindin and Merriman, of Renny Tailyour and Von Donop, of Rawson and Hedley, of Wood and Goodwyn crowd into one's mind as one goes back to the palmy days of the R.E. Who can forget the picturesque appearance they presented in their red-and-black jerseys, with their long brewer caps of the same colours? For twenty years and more they were a dominant factor in Association football. N. L. Jackson, in his excellent history of the game, claims for them that they were the first club to go on tour, referring to their visit to the North in 1873. As a football chronicler, "N. L." took infinite pains, and no doubt in this case he is right. Still, I "hae me doots," remembering as I do vividly the effects of a week's visit to Cambridge in the early days of the Wanderers, and the painful experiences of six days of successive football.

Contemporary with the Royal Engineers at their zenith were the Clapham Rovers, who are still to the fore—a strictly amateur club; the Old Etonians, the champions of many a hard-fought Cup-tie; the Old Carthusians, prominent among them J. F. Prinsep and E. G. Wynyard, W. N. Cobbold and J. Vintcent, with many others of equal fame. The Swifts, like the Wanderers, have long gone under. They were the creation of the Bambridge family, and a fine quartette of players "the Bams" were, with W. S., G. F. E. H., E. C., and A. L. in order of seniority. The Remnants, if I remember rightly, were in some respects of Eton growth; and it is not without interest to recall that Lord Hawke, the great cricketer who has made Yorkshire what it is, was one of the Remnants who opposed Darwen in one of the later Cup-ties at the Oval in the early Eighties.

Another old team which played a prominent part in the

THE OFF-SIDE RULE EXPLAINED.

DIAGRAM NO. 7.—OFF-SIDE.

SHOT AT GOAL RETURNED BY GOALKEEPER.

A shoots at goal. The ball is played out by **C**, and **B** obtains possession, but slips, and passes the ball to **F**, who scores. **F** is off-side, because he is in front of **B**, and when the ball was passed by **B** he had not three opponents between him and the goal-line.

DIAGRAM NO. 8.—NOT OFF-SIDE.

SHOT AT GOAL RETURNED BY GOALKEEPER (*continued*).

A shoots at goal. The ball is played out by **C**, but **B** obtains possession and scores. **B** has not three opponents between him and the goal-line when the ball is played by **A**, but, provided he is not obstructing an opponent, he is not off-side, because the ball has been last played by an opponent, **C**.

F. A. Cup for many years about the same time was the Shropshire Wanderers. The moving spirit was J. Hawley Edwards, an old Salopian, a sturdy forward of the type which prevailed in the days when a good honest charge, shoulder to shoulder, was a part of the game, and taken in the best of spirit. This was in the halcyon time, before the referee had come into vogue, and a game was played without the need of a controlling official or officials hampered by repressive powers of increasing severity.

About the same time the Pilgrims had made a name in the east of London. C. E. Hart, who came in time to be treasurer of the F. A., one of the best-hearted fellows Association football has ever known, came out, if I remember rightly, as a player, first as goalkeeper, for the Pilgrims. H. A. Swepstone, the English goalkeeper of 1882-3, was a Pilgrim, too, and a fine specimen of the pocket-Hercules he was. An offshoot, in a sense, of the Pilgrims was the Ramblers; but the club was not destined to flourish very long. A more enduring relic of East London football is the Upton Park Club, which has had an uninterrupted career.

The Hertfordshire Rangers had for a number of years a fairly strong combination, as combinations went then. One of their leading spirits was R. C. Barker, who represented England in the first International match in 1872, and was also one of the stalwarts of the Wanderers in that club's best day.

Memories crowd on me as I write of other giants of the ante-professional period, of the sturdy players of the Midlands, of the stout-hearted lads of Lancashire, of the hardy and good-tempered sons of Yorkshire, full of grit, who never knew when they were beaten. Many of the clubs to which they gave bold advertisement remain, though the necessities of the times have prevented them retaining their old amateur status. Lincoln, one of the earliest to enrol itself under the banner of the Football Association; Nottingham, now Notts County; Notts Forest, Blackburn Rovers, Sheffield Wednesday, Everton, Darwen, Stoke, Bolton Wanderers, and Aston Villa, with a little later the Wolverhampton Wanderers and Preston North End—all these contributed largely at different periods to the teams which represented England in the Seventies and early Eighties.

But even the triumphs of Sheffield and Nottingham pale before the brilliant doings of some of the East Lancashire teams. One has only to take the Blackburn Rovers for an illustration. Three times in succession winners of the Football Association Cup and five times its holders in eight years, their record stands out as the most remarkable achievement in a competition that has produced unlimited sensations. What a galaxy of talent they had, too, those same Blackburn Rovers pretty well throughout the Eighties! Who can forget H. Arthur, one of the very best goalkeepers England has ever produced; Jimmy Brown, speediest of forwards; "Dock" Greenwood; Jimmy Forrest, a prince of half-backs; the brothers Hargreaves, F. W. and J.; with J. Lofthouse, to mention the chief of the players who carried the flag of the Rovers triumphantly to the highest pinnacle f ofame?

But enough. The past is said to be the interpreter of the future, and one can hardly express a better wish than that the best traditions of the good old days will never cease to influence the play of the generation that are to come.

DIAGRAM NO. 9.—OFF-SIDE.

BALL REBOUNDING FROM GOAL-POSTS OR GOAL-BAR.

A shoots for goal, and the ball rebounds from the goal-post into play. **B** secures the ball, and scores. **B** is off-side, because the ball is last played by **A**, a player of his own side, and when **A** played it **B** had not three opponents between him and the goal-line and was in front of **A**.

DIAGRAM NO. 10.—OFF-SIDE.

BALL REBOUNDING FROM GOAL-POSTS OR GOAL-BAR (*continued*).

A shoots for goal, and the ball rebounds from the cross-bar into play. **A** follows up from position 1 to position 2, and then passes to **B**, who has run up on the other side. **B** is off-side, because the ball is last played by **A**, a player of his own side, and when **A** played it **B** had not three opponents between him and the goal-line, and was in front of **A**. If **A** had scored himself at the second attempt, instead of passing to **B**, it would have been a goal.

HISTORY OF THE BURY FOOTBALL CLUB.

English Cup-holders, 1899-1900 and 1902-3; four times Lancashire Senior Cup-holders, and six times Manchester Senior Cup-holders.

How the Bury F. C. introduced the Association game in a Rugby centre—The first officials of the club—The Gigg Lane Ground—A match in June—Poor financial support in the opening season—The Lancashire League formed—Origin of the club's nick-name, "The Shakers" Bury's grand record in the Football Association Cup competition—A limited liability company formed—Some facts about the Gigg Lane Ground.

Colours: White shirts, Navy-blue knickers. *Ground: Gigg Lane, Bury.*

MR. H. S. HAMER.

Mr. H. S. Hamer is probably one of the best known club secretaries in the North of England. He took a leading part in the agitation which culminated in fixing the wages limit for professionals. At home he is universally esteemed as a man thoroughly conversant with his business, and with the best interests of the club at heart.

FEW clubs can boast of a more interesting career than the Bury Football Club. Right from the inception of the organisation in the early months of 1885 their career has been marked by a series of triumphs which has won the club distinction even among the high-class company in which they now figure. Starting from the very humblest level, the highest sphere has been attained only by the exercise of much self-denial by real enthusiasts and unremitting attention to the well-being of the organisation by its committee and directors. In the course of their career Bury have won every cup and trophy for which they have entered, with the sole exception of the League (First Division) championship and the Sheriff of London Shield.

It was in 1885 that a number of gentlemen assembled at the Waggon and Horses Hotel, Bury, and started the movement which culminated in a further meeting at the Old White Horse Hotel, Fleet Street, Bury, on April 24, 1885, at which the club was definitely given life. Bury was then a hotbed of the Rugby code, but when the dribbling system was introduced Rugby soon succumbed to the pangs of starvation.

GEORGE ROSS.

George Ross, the veteran captain of the Bury F. C., first played with the Bury Wesleyans, and joined the Bury Club in 1887. He is a Scot by birth, but came to Bury when only a few months old. He has risen with the club from its infancy to the giddy heights of fame, and probably no player in the country possesses a more varied or valuable collection of gold medals which he has won during the nineteen years he has played for the club

At the aforementioned meeting Mr. J. Hall was elected president, Mr. W. Barritt hon. treasurer, Mr. J. D. Turner secretary, and Messrs. J. Veitch, J. Harrison, W. Bentley, G. Holgate, C. Hartley, J. Taylor, R. Weir, G. Black, G. Bolton, Tom Hargreaves, J. Hoyle, and F. Hill the committee.

At first some difficulty arose in procuring a playing-pitch, but eventually the site of the present ground was obtained on one of Lord Derby's farms at Gigg Lane, and it is now everywhere regarded as one of the best playing surfaces in England, being well drained and covered with a thick carpet of grass even at the end of the season.

In 1885 there was no close season. The committee, therefore, early got to work, Accrington and Church playing the first match on the ground on June 6, 1885, when the visitors won by 4—2. At the end of two months the secretary resigned, and Mr. Tom Hargreaves undertook the duties, and to him the club owe a great debt of gratitude.

The first season was opened with a match at Little Lever against the club of that name, the Bury team being as follows: Wolstenholme, goal; L. Rostron and McAllister, backs; Lonsdale, J. Ross, and Clark, half-backs; Pollock, Douglas, Holgate, Rostron, and Barlow, forwards. Wigan were the first team entertained and beaten (4—3), the receipts at the seat of custom amounting only to £1 16s. 7d. Bad as this was it was princely when compared with the 4s. 6d. realised by the visit of Colne, in a Lancashire Junior Cup-tie, on September 26.

Undeterred by this lack of financial support, the committee persevered, and gathered to themselves some promising local talent and a number of experts from other districts, Pollock and Douglas acting as coaches. At the end of the first season Bury had played 32 matches, won 12, lost 11, drawn 9, and scored 88 goals against 71. A second team was also run, their record being a brilliant one, winning 17 out of 20 engagements, losing 2, and drawing 1, while they scored no fewer than 107 goals to 26. The match receipts for the season amounted to £140 9s. 2d., of which £105 11s. 8½d. was paid to the players, the adverse balance on the year amounting to £8 0s. 1d.

Gradually the playing strength was improved, and ambition began to soar high. The notion was conceived in 1889 of forming a Lancashire League, and Bury issued circulars with that object in view. The league was formed, 13 clubs taking part. Higher Walton just headed Bury off as first holders of the championship by one point; but the latter won it the next season, and also held it on one other occasion, but were never lower than the third stave. Bury also won the Lancashire Junior Cup at this time.

Bury now stepped into

MR. ALBERT DUCKWORTH.

Mr. Albert Duckworth, vice-chairman of the Bury F. C., is a native of Bury and a sportsman to the core. He joined the committee in 1889-90, and has continuously served upon it up to date. For three years he was chairman of the club, but resigned at the end of that time, preferring to take his present subordinate position, and Mr. Alfred Wardle (the present chairman) took his place He is regarded as a valued friend by all the local cricket and football leagues in the town and district.

the Lancashire Senior Cup competition, and from this time ranked as a senior club. They won the cup at the first time of asking by as brilliant a performance as lies within the annals of the club. They beat Newton Heath on the latter's ground by 3—2; Accrington (then members of the First Division of the League) were trounced by 4—0 at home; Everton were decapitated in the semi-final at Deepdale by 2—0; and in the final round Bury beat Blackburn Rovers by 2—0. The reception given the team on their return home exceeded in its wild enthusiasm that which marked their two later triumphs in the English Cup tourney.

It was this series of performances which gave rise to the club's sobriquet of "The Shakers." The then chairman of the club (Mr. J. T. Ingham) exclaimed: "We'll give them a shaking up; in fact, we are 'The Shakers'!" The phrase was an expressive one, was instantly seized upon by the club's supporters, and soon became widely used. The team which won the cup on this memorable occasion was: J. Lowe, goal; T. Cooper and A. Warburton, backs; L. Pemberton, R. Jobson, and G. Ross, half-backs; A. Wilkinson, A. Spence, R. Conway, G. Bourne, and J. Plant, forwards. That was in 1891-2, and Ross and Plant are still in the service of the club!

The only occasion upon which the ground has ever been encroached upon by the crowd was when Bolton Wanderers were entertained in the Lancashire Senior Cup, which was then regarded as one of the most attractive trophies in the football world—at any rate, in Lancashire. The gate receipts amounted to £455, and, the ground accommodation proving inadequate, the crowd burst on to the playing-pitch and stopped the game 35 minutes from the finish, with the Wanderers leading by 3—0. The Wanderers won (1—0) in the re-play at Bolton.

In 1893-4 the County Palatine League was formed, and lasted only one season, in which Bury ran out the champions, although all the First Division clubs in Lancashire were in membership.

Only one year have Bury spent in the Second Division—1894-5. They won the championship with 48 points, or 9 more than their nearest rivals, and in the test matches defeated Liverpool by 1—0. In 1895-6—exactly ten years from the inception of the club—they became members of the First Division, in which they have remained ever since.

Bury have scored two signal triumphs in the National Cup competition. In winning the Cup for the first time in 1900, they beat Southampton by 4—0, this being the most pronounced victory in the history of the Cup, except that of the Blackburn Rovers against Sheffield Wednesday (6—1) in 1889-90—ten years previously. But Bury eclipsed this record in 1902-3 by going right through the competition without having a goal scored against them, and winning all their ties at the first attempt—Wolverhampton Wanderers, at Gigg Lane, 1—0; Sheffield United (the Cup-holders), at Bramall Lane, 1—0; Notts County, at Gigg Lane, 1—0; Aston Villa (Semi-final), at Goodison Park, 3—0; and Derby County (Final), at the Crystal Palace, 6—0. Bury, therefore, accomplished a finer record than that established by Preston North End in the early days of the game.

Bury twice won the English Cup; have already won this season the Lancashire Senior Cup, this making the fourth time they have held it; they have four times held the Manchester Senior Cup, and twice have held the same cup jointly with Manchester City, after several indecisive attempts to settle the question of sole ownership.

Since the Eighties there have been few changes in the personnel of officials or directors. The present secretary, Mr. H. S. Hamer, has been in office since 1887, with the exception of one year (1890) when he was elected a director. The chairmanship has been in the hands of only three gentlemen since the Eighties—the late Mr. J. T. Ingham, Mr. Albert Duckworth, and Mr. Alfred Wardle, who still occupies the post. The secretary has for the last eight or nine years been helped, as an assistant-secretary, by his brother, Mr. Frank Hamer.

Nearly ten years ago the club was formed into a limited liability company, and Mr. Wardle has been chairman ever since.

The accommodation of the ground is now estimated at 30,000, and the largest gate has been between 28,000 and 29,000—on the occasion of the visit of Southampton in the third round of the English Cup, two or three years ago, when £1,096 was taken at the turnstiles.

Howard Barrett, Southwell.]

THE BURY FOOTBALL CLUB TEAM, SEASON 1905-6.

JOHNSTON. RICHARDS. PLANT. MULLINEUX. THORPE. WOLSTENHOLME. HODGKINSON. SIMPSON. ROSS. LINDSAY. DOW.

A SECTION OF THE CROWD AT CARDIFF ARMS PARK ON THE OCCASION OF THE RUGBY INTERNATIONAL, WALES v. SCOTLAND, FEBRUARY 3, 1906.

THE RUGBY GAME.

PART III.—HALF-BACK PLAY.

By the REV. R. H. CATTELL, B.A. (Oxford University, Blackheath, and English International).

The qualifications necessary for a Rugby half-back—Alterations in the style of half-back play—The New Zealand formation adds to the half-back's difficulties—The half-back as scapegoat to the team—The importance of combination—The half-back's duties in attack—How to pass the ball—Defensive play—The need for courage in a crisis—Never push the ball back into the scrum—The throw-in from touch—Practice makes perfect.

"NASCITUR non fit" is a generally accepted fact with regard to a first-class cricketer, and it may be applied with scarcely less truth to a half-back in Rugby football. Of course, by constant practice and careful coaching, you may produce a player of machine-like excellence who will pass for the real thing as long as circumstances are favourable, but, like all machinery, he is liable to be thrown out of gear by some unforeseen circumstances. What I mean is this—you may train a man to pick up and pass out with the greatest accuracy, to stop a forward rush with the greatest skill, but you cannot teach him *when* to pass and *when* to "cut in," or *when* to kick instead of doing either. That is a matter for his own judgment, and requires an innate capacity for seeing in an instant what is the right thing to do, the thing least expected by his opponents, and therefore sometimes quite unorthodox.

Is it useless, then, to lay down rules as to half-back play, or is all literature on the subject superfluous? By no means! The young player has to conform to certain written rules and regulations; he can pick up many hints which will prove useful to him in trying to improve his game, but all the rules and regulations and advice in the world will never in themselves produce a first-class half-back. The innate capacity must be there. Of what, then, does this consist? Well, there are many qualifications necessary for a half-back. First, and foremost, perhaps, is the ability to see in an instant an opportunity and to make the most of it; a sort of intuition which cannot be acquired by reading or any kind of instruction. For this reason a young player should be given plenty of scope for developing this, and not be bound down too strictly to hard-and-fast rules. Many promising half-backs are spoiled at school by their coach—possibly a three-quarter or forward—insisting that they shall conform to certain regulations laid down by himself. Of these at the present time the principal one is that he must pass the ball out under any circumstances. It is some people's idea of the Welsh game, and may possibly be one explanation of the deterioration in the last few years of half-back play in this country. How far removed it is from the Welsh theory and practice, anyone who watches a first-class Welsh game will see at once.

It will perhaps be interesting here to notice the wonderful alteration that has taken place in the style of half-back play. When Rugby football became a recognised game in the Sixties, and for some fifteen or twenty years afterwards, the half-back was practically the only scoring medium. He was by far the most important player behind the scrum; he did nearly all the running, and most of the tackling. He was never expected to pass unless he possessed the unenviable reputation of funking. Then when the number of forwards was diminished, and that of the three-quarters increased, he had to change his methods. But it was not until about 1881 that the system of passing out to the three-quarters was adopted.

The late Alan Rotherham was the first to show this method to advantage; in fact, he may be said to have completely altered the game. He showed that a half-back's real duty was to feed the three-quarters, to make openings for them to score, as well as to run and score himself when he had an opportunity. Both halves then passed out direct from the scrum to a three-quarter without much idea of combination between the two. The introduction of a fourth three-quarter and the reduction in the number of forwards to eight brought about another change, one which tended to make the game still faster. The three-quarters claimed a far greater share of the game, and the half-back's lot became not quite such a happy one. He had not only to do the hard work of stopping forward rushes and tackling, but he had to keep up with the ball when it was in the hands of the three-quarters. Then it was the custom for the half-backs to work the scrum in turn, and while one was getting the ball the other fell back as a sort of fifth three-quarter.

Now the custom generally adopted is for one half-back to devote himself entirely to working the scrum and to passing the ball out at once. This, to many lovers of the forward game, seemed to be the outside limit to which anyone could go in trying to open out the game without abolishing the scrum altogether. Then suddenly all our preconceived ideas on the subject were ruthlessly upset by the overwhelming victories of the New Zealanders. They not only introduced a new arrangement of the players by reducing the number of forwards to seven, but compelled their opponents to adopt their system in self-defence. It was thought at first that with only seven forwards against eight the backs would be literally starved, but here it was proved conclusively that the scrum formation of seven was vastly superior and more effective than that of eight. Here, too, the difficulties of the half-back are increased. He has not only his opposing half-backs to contend with, but an extra man to worry him and obstruct him in his attempts to get the ball. Though, as a matter of fact, this is not an original conception on the part of the New Zealanders, for as far back as 1893-4 A. H. Colvile was included among the Oxford forwards for the express purpose of spoiling the play of the Cambridge halves. How successful he was in his attempt is a matter of history.

But to return to the qualities required of a first-class player. They are much the same as they ever were. He must be strong, active, fearless, and clever with his hands and feet. Given these qualities, let us see how he can bring them into practice with the greatest advantage to his side. I must, however, preface these remarks with the confession of fallibility. People's ideas on the subject are so varied that, though mine are the results of many years of practice and study, they will probably meet with much adverse criticism, but no one will deny that the difficulties or the importance of the half-back are supreme. The scoring power of a team depends very much upon him. Yet he very rarely gets any credit. The forwards blame him when they heel badly, and the three-quarters do the same when they drop his passes. Yet, to a real lover of the game, who is fond of plenty of hard work, there is no position on the field which appeals so strongly.

INTERNATIONAL RUGBY—ENGLAND v. IRELAND AT LEICESTER, FEBRUARY 10, 1906.
(Ireland, 16 points; England, 6 points.) A line-out.

Strength, but not necessarily bulk, is essential to a half-back. He has to give and take a good deal of hard tackling, and with a beaten pack of forwards in front of him, a weak or very light half-back is quite useless. The best halves that come to mind were all on the heavy side. A. Rotherham, Don Wauchope, C. M. Wells, W. P. Donaldson, Selwyn Biggs, J. W. Simpson, and W. Marshall could all hold their own in a trial of strength. But no matter how brilliant a man may be as an individual, he loses most of his effectiveness unless he works well with his partner. Combination, important as it is in all departments of the game, is all important between the half-backs. I don't believe that the two most brilliant men in existence coming together for the first time would be equal to two inferior players who thoroughly understand each other's game. Half-backs, then, should come to a thorough understanding with each other before every game begins, and possibly one of them, the more experienced, should be in command, so to speak.

We will now consider the half-back's duties in attack, as being quite the most important branch of the game. That attack is the best method of defence is a truism which they ought to realise, though many half-backs overlook it. They have more opportunities of turning the tables on their opponents than anyone else; for an attack set up in your own "25," when your three-quarters are unmarked, is far more likely to be effective than when the opposing three-quarters are lining up as near to them as they can get. The Welshmen and New Zealanders quite frequently score tries from the neighbourhood of their own goal-line. In contrast to this, it was maddening to see one of the English halves in the England v. New Zealand match pushing the ball back into the scrum with his foot as if he didn't know in the least what to do with it in that part of the field. And this in spite of the fact that the opposing three-quarters and half-backs were standing well back from the scrum! In any case he could have saved his forwards a lot of unnecessary work by a kick into touch, and could probably have gone right through himself, or made a grand opening for his three-quarters.

Although these chances occur frequently—and are almost as frequently overlooked—yet the most usual thing is to attack from inside your opponent's territory. Here your forwards make special efforts to heel the ball out straight and cleanly. It is then the duty of one of the halves to get the ball. To do this he should not stand too near (about a yard back), so that he gets a good view of the ball, and avoids the danger of having it heeled too swiftly past him, or of being interfered with by the opposing half. He has then to transfer it in the shortest possible time to his partner standing seven or eight yards back. The transfer should be made in one movement, the ball being swept off the ground and passed hard and low about the level of his partner's hips. A fraction of a second gained or lost in effecting this pass often means the gain or loss of a try. So there must be no fumbling, no turning round to run after it or to see where the other half is standing. He must, as a rule, pass at once. But even to this rule there are exceptions.

There are times when a dash for the line is the best policy, and as to that a player must use his own judgment, and if he sees an opening he must try for it with every ounce he has got. The half-back who is standing back from the scrum should try to get into his stride before the ball reaches him; then, if he is not marked, he will go straight through; if he is marked, he will draw his man and then transfer the ball to the nearest three-quarter. He must remember always to go *straight*, never across the field. It may be wise sometimes to attack on the side of the scrum nearest to the touch-line—the blind side as it is called. This intention he must convey to his partner by some pre-arranged signal unperceived by his opponents. Both halves should be accurate in their passing, for a wild or a bad pass is most likely to reach an adversary's hands. It should be passed well in front of the taker, so that he doesn't have to stop or

AN INTERESTING RUGBY PHOTOGRAPH.

The New Zealand Fifteen singing their Maori War Cry prior to the opening of their first International match against Scotland, at Inverleith, November 18, 1905 (New Zealand, 12 points—4 tries; Scotland, 7—1 dropped goal, 1 try).

slacken his pace in order to take it. A pass taken standing still is generally quite useless, and very often disastrous to the man taking it. It is impossible to tell a man when to feint to pass; he must be guided by the character of the man opposed to him; but it is often successful if the tackler shows any hesitation as to which man to go for.

The next important feature of the half-back's play is defensive work. It consists in stopping the rushes of the opposing forwards by falling on the ball and tackling, and in preventing the opposing halves from passing out or running in when their forwards have got possession of the ball. Stopping a forward rush appears to be a most difficult and dangerous performance, and it is certainly an unpleasant one, but to the half-back who doesn't funk, but knows how to fall, it is quite easy and comparatively free from danger. At any rate, a man who cannot do his share of this kind of work is never likely to become a really first-class half-back. He should never fall with his face or the front of his body towards his opponents, but throwing himself on the ball he should at once turn the broad of his back to the attackers and bend his head over into his chest. In that way he will protect his most vital parts and his head from any chance of a kick or other injury. Never let a half-back attempt to stop a rush with his feet, or take a flying kick at the ball. He is very likely to miss it, and in any case will be simply hustled out of the way.

Again, he must not make half-hearted grabs at the ball, but throw himself at it bodily. Funk is responsible for most of the accidents in football, just as it is in hunting. "He who hesitates is lost" is a very sound maxim here. Next comes the question of how to spoil the opposing halves when their forwards are heeling, and how to prevent them passing out. Of course, as only one is taking the scrum and the other has fallen back clear of it, it seems unnecessary for both to keep watch over the same opponent. But, as a matter of fact, if one of the defenders leaves the scrum to mark his vis-a-vis, he opens up a clear run through for the half with the ball that he would at once take advantage of. No, both must follow the ball as closely as possible without being off-side, and as soon as it emerges from the back of the scrum make a dash for it, and if possible spoil the pass or even get possession of the ball. If too late for either, they must both rush immediately to the assistance of their three-quarters. They should always let their forwards know where the ball is and when it has left the scrum. In the event of their own forwards getting possession and letting it out in home territory, a punt into touch is often advisable. It gives the forwards a rest, and tends to dishearten the enemy.

A half-back must never punt into the middle of the field in his own "25," as a dropped goal or a try to the other side may result. But as to whether he should kick into touch or run himself, a man must use his own judgment. Many a try has been scored by an unexpected attack of this sort. But never, oh, never, let him push the ball back into the scrum! It is so unenterprising and shows such a want of originality.

There is just one more branch of a half-back's work that is worth consideration. It is the throw-in from touch. This is very important, and can only be done by practice. A half-back should be able to see at a glance if one of his side is unmarked at the line-out, and without any fuss send the ball to that player. If he is a forward close in, it is quite easy; but if he is a three-quarter in the middle of the field, it requires some skill to throw it quite straight so that it falls at the desired spot. But as I have said before, it can be done with practice, and as a final word of advice to a young player who wishes to become an expert half-back, I say *practice, practice, practice!*

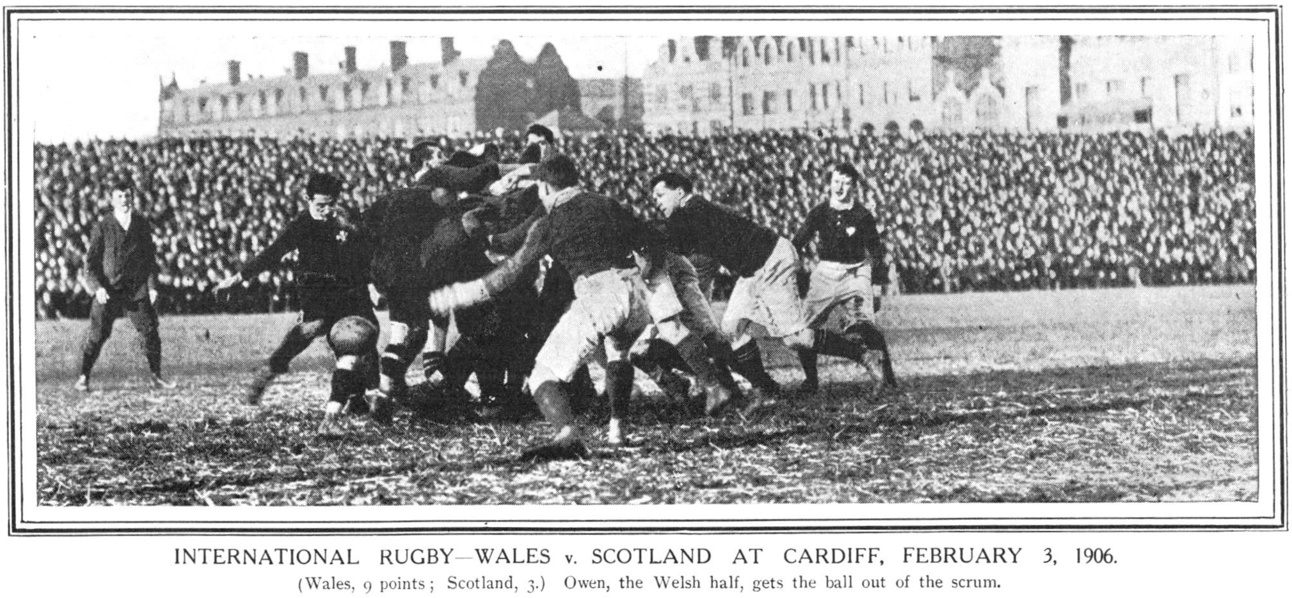

INTERNATIONAL RUGBY—WALES v. SCOTLAND AT CARDIFF, FEBRUARY 3, 1906.

(Wales, 9 points; Scotland, 3.) Owen, the Welsh half, gets the ball out of the scrum.

THE MUCH-ABUSED REFEREE.

By JOHN LEWIS.

The football referee—His relation to the Football Association—Spectators and their criticism—The referee has the last word—The necessity for tact on the field—"Spoil sports"—The eternal whistle—The off-side law—What the crowd does not see—The referee as time-keeper—Refereeing a pleasure as a hobby, a poor thing as a profession.

THE referee in Association football has always been a much abused official, and to-day we hear more of his misdeeds than ever before. The reasons are not far to seek. Twenty years ago the leading matches were all of the "friendly" kind—in name at least—and if the spectators had a crow to pluck with the referee they did it there and then. The Football Association extended little or no protection to its representative, and if he were mobbed or stoned as he left the field it was "all in the day's work," and there was no redress. Since the pre-professional days, however, the conditions under which a referee works have been altered very considerably. He now officiates as the direct representative of the game's rulers, and any insult to or assault upon him, no matter whether his task has been well or ill-performed, is treated as an outrage upon the Football Association. The severe penalties which have been found necessary in order to enforce respect for the referee and ensure the proper conduct of the game have had the effect of practically putting an end to disorder upon our leading grounds; but nothing has sufficed to muzzle the angry spectator or to prevent vocal or printed criticism from making itself felt.

This, of course, is as it should be. Half the enjoyment of the game lies in the subsequent criticism of the players and the referee, and so long as the criticism is intelligent no sensible referee will object to it. For myself, I would take no objection to hooting or groaning by the spectators at decisions with which they disagree. The referee should remember that football is a game that warms the blood of player and looker-on alike, and that unless they can give free vent to their delight or anger, as the case may be, the great crowds we now witness will dwindle rapidly away. It is always a consolation to an official who is being badly baited to bear in mind that, after all, he has the last word, and that his opinion prevails.

There are times—although, as I have said, they are fortunately very infrequent—when a crowd's hostility to a referee gets beyond mere hooting, and when it is necessary for him to stop the game and announce that offensive conduct will have to be reported to the F. A. Such an intimation is usually effective, for the prospect of a ground closed to football for weeks on end would appal the stoutest partisan. There are, however, many referees who hardly realise the responsibility they undertake in this matter of preserving order on the field. They do not, in so many words, make any promise to the Football Association, but in asking for registration they tacitly pledge themselves to do their best to see that the game is played in accordance with the laws, that players behave themselves as sportsmen and gentlemen, and that spectators do nothing to bring the game into disrepute. It is, therefore, no light task they undertake, and before submitting their actions to the eager scrutiny of ten thousand pairs of eyes they should convince themselves that, besides that passionate love of the game without which no referee can be imagined, they also possess a thorough grasp of the laws, and a physique which will carry them through a long period of bodily as well as mental exertion.

Another possession which is not so common as folks imagine, and which has much to do with the behaviour of crowds towards the referee, is a comprehension of the spirit of the game as opposed to the mere letter of the law. It is just as impossible to erect football laws which shall convey the full meaning of their proposers as it is to draw an Act of Parliament through which a quibbling lawyer may not drive a coach and four. Thus we have referees who are temperamentally unable to disregard the printed word, and we have others, all too few, who read between the lines and recognise that the first object should be to ensure the game being played honestly, fairly, and in a truly sporting spirit—that, in short, everybody concerned should behave in a "gentlemanly" manner, as the laws put it. When these laws were framed, of course the paid player had not been born, and although we had plenty of good, forcible charging, there was little or none of that skilful foul play or shady work just within the four corners of the law which developed in the Nineties, but which happily is becoming less noticeable owing to altered laws and an improved public sentiment. Many of these cleverly conceived and skilfully executed offences altogether fail in their object, and the F. A. has wisely decreed that in such cases the referee may ignore them, because to do otherwise would really penalise the side already wronged. The literalists, however, cannot, or will not, understand this instruction, and thus we have referees of great experience who blow their whistle for every offence, or attempted offence, they notice. These are the "whistling referees," who more than anybody else rob the game of its charm as a spectacle by continually stopping play to

Howard Barrett.]

MR. FRED. KIRKHAM REFEREEING IN A LEAGUE MATCH, STOKE v. NOTTS COUNTY.

The game is stopped owing to the temporary disablement of a Notts County player.

award free kicks. It is curious how the referee who "sees everything" is hailed by many crowds as great in his class, whereas, if the people only knew it, he is a real spoil-sport, acting not only contrary to the spirit of the game, but in direct opposition to the express instructions of its legislators. Referees should aim at allowing play to proceed without stoppage just as far as it is possible to do so without incurring the risk of disorder. All, or nearly all, the alterations made in the laws of recent years have been for the purpose of impressing this upon officials, and this year it has even been laid down that when a penalty kick has been scored it shall not be disallowed even though, during the taking of the kick, the defending side have committed a further offence. Referees should realise that the punishments prescribed in the laws are for offenders against the laws, and that any rigid adherence to them which is calculated to put the offending side in a better position than it would have occupied had it played fairly is not only illegal, but stupid. I do not wish to blame all the referees responsible for such decisions as are alluded to, because I know that, unless men are born with certain qualities—good judgment, power to discriminate, and quick decision—all the practice in the world will not enable them to acquire them.

Some referees evidently believe that they are compelled to whistle for all free kicks, penalty kicks, corner kicks, and goal kicks to be taken. This is not so, and those officials who make themselves so frequently heard may become less conspicuous by using other signals to intimate that they are ready for such kicks to be taken. For many years it was my own practice to abstain from whistling for corners and goal kicks, because I considered it unnecessary; and for penalty kicks, because I believe a quiet intimation to the men concerned when they are ready is far preferable to a signal which sets every man instinctively on the run, and leads to frequent breaches of the law. Another reason for not using the whistle for goal kicks and corner kicks is that it seems desirable for everybody to know, when the whistle sounds near the goal or the goal-line, that it is for some offence against the laws of the game, and not for a merely automatic move in the play.

The most frequent cause of complaint against referees is the way they administer the off-side law. I have always held that, puzzling as many people seem to find it, this law is a very easy thing to understand once you grasp the main idea. The fact remains that spectators and referees continually differ as to its application, and it must be admitted that the spectators at the side of the ground are frequently in a much better position to judge of the facts than the referee in the middle of the field. Just as often, however, the referee has the advantage in this respect, and spectators would make his task the more pleasant if they would remember this and give him credit, even when they think he is wrong, for acting to the best of his ability. It is a difficult—nay, impossible—feat for any referee to keep in line with the ball throughout a game, and in many cases he is compelled to give decisions about which he may have a doubt. He has, of course, two linesmen to assist him, but it would never do to stop the play every time he felt uncertain about the facts.

If a referee is up to his work he will, in spite of his position in the middle of the field, know more about the run of the game than the spectator on the ropes. While the latter concentrates his attention on the ball and the man immediately in possession, the official is always on the look-out for eventualities. The crowd, as a rule, pay little attention to the position a player occupies "at the moment the ball was last played," and persists in judging him by the place at which he plays the ball, which, of course, has nothing whatever to do with the question of his violation, or otherwise, of the off-side law. The referee should remember, when the people howl at him for what they regard as a mistaken decision, that he is probably right and they are probably wrong, because he has taken in the relative positions of all the men concerned and they have not. I remember, a few years ago, four men, all thoroughly conversant with the laws of the game, standing shoulder to shoulder at a match on the Aston Villa ground, and while three of them completely disagreed with an off-side decision, the fourth was convinced I was right. It turned out that the fourth man was the only one who could remember the position the player occupied when the ball was last played, and, what was still more curious, the other three all held different opinions about the last player's position. It is really remarkable how different men looking on at the same incident gather totally different impressions, and the fact explains much of the apparent discontent of spectators, which, at the time, seems inexplicable to the referee. It is a frequent occurrence for two friends to dispute, say, whether a player handled the ball or the ball struck the man's hand, and however the referee may decide in such a case one of his critics will be displeased.

Russell and Sons.]

MR. A. J. BARKER REFEREEING IN THE CUP FINAL OF 1903-4 AT THE CRYSTAL PALACE. (City 1, Bolton 0.)

Manchester City make a hot attack on the Bolton Wanderers' goal.

A little point which deserves attention from referees anxious to avoid misunderstandings is the necessity of "clocking" the game accurately. In the history of the Cup and the League there have been many occasions on which faulty timekeeping has been alleged, and with truth; and the bitterness of feeling which may be aroused among the supporters of a side deprived of a minute or two within which it might have saved the game needs no description. The consequences attending failure in the League and Cup competitions are so extremely serious that no referee ought to go on the field without a good, reliable stop-watch, which he should be able to start and stop easily, so that at most he will only be a few seconds wrong when he blows for time.

Notwithstanding the abuse and the fault-finding to which he must inevitably subject himself, a man with a real enthusiasm for football may find much pleasure in refereeing—as a hobby. As a profession, as some unkind people choose to speak of it, refereeing is a very poor affair indeed. I do not, as many do, believe that an official with such great responsibility should be paid at least as much as the worst-paid professional among the teams under his control, but, all the same, I cannot regard the guinea or so which is given for Cup-ties and League games as adequate "pay" for the work. There are many referees of my acquaintance whose enthusiasm for football must have involved them in the loss of hundreds of pounds through the neglect of their ordinary business. The clubs have, in most cases, done a great deal for the comfort of the referee by providing properly-equipped dressing-rooms and so forth, and it only remains to raise the scale of fees to something like an adequate recognition of earnest, strenuous, and often thankless work.

SOME FAMOUS REFEREES

MR. A. KINGSCOTT (*Derby*).

MR. P. R. HARROWER (*London*).

MR. A. J. BARKER (*Hanley*).

MR. JOHN ADAMS (*Birmingham*).

MR. T. KIRKHAM (*Burslem*).

MR. JOHN LEWIS (*Blackburn*).

THE SCOTTISH FOOTBALL LEAGUE AND ITS HISTORY.

By R. M. CONNELL.

The historical meeting at Holton's Hotel, Glasgow, March 20, 1890, and formation of the Scottish Football League—The League tolls the death-knell of the amateur constitution of the Scottish Football Association—The legalisation of professionalism in Scotland—Queen's Park elected to the League in 1900-1—Growth of the League—The pioneers of the Scottish League movement resign—Scottish League officials—The clubs that have won the championship—The Second Division of the League—The League International and its record—Inter-League games with Ireland—The Scottish League and charity—The Scottish League and the Scottish Football Association.

WHETHER it be that the colder temperature of the North is responsible for the conservatism of the Scot in clinging to traditional methods, the fact remains that the national characteristic is exemplified in football as in the ordinary affairs of his life. Sandy is slow to move. He likes to "bide a wee" to see how the thing works out ere following a lead. Scotland followed England's lead in organising football, and a study of all important legislation and development in the game reveals that Scotland has always played the part of following the leader.

On March 20, 1890, the writer attended a meeting held in Holton's Hotel, Glasgow, convened at the instigation of the Renton Football Club to discuss a proposal fraught with momentous issues to the game in Scotland.

The Football League had been in existence one year, and many of the leading clubs in Scotland were groaning under the existing cup-tie arrangements, the frequent derangement of the fixture-card, and the inferior class of matches they were often compelled to play.

To this gathering were invited the following fourteen clubs: Queen's Park, Rangers, Celtic, Third Lanark, Heart of Midlothian, Cowlairs, Clyde, St. Mirren, Abercorn, Renton, Dumbarton, Vale of Leven, St. Bernards, and Cambuslang. All the clubs save Queen's Park and Clyde responded to the invitation, each being represented by two delegates. Queen's Park was a more powerful club then than it is now. As holders of the Scottish Cup, its officials were staunch pillars of the Scottish Football Association, and, as the extension of the league system to Scotland was suspected in high places to be a covert move against the Association and amateurism, Hampden Park did not countenance the movement.

To disarm the spirit of distrust abroad, the majority of the speakers at that conference promoted by Renton when the Scottish Football League came into existence emphasised their allegiance to the Scottish Football Association and the principles of amateurism.

Mr. Alex. Lawrence, of Dumbarton Football Club, who gained fame with the rifle by winning the Queen's Prize on Wimbledon Common, was a bitter antagonist to the professional spirit that had crept into Scottish football. From the chair he took pains to make clear that the agitation for a league was but the germination of a scheme propounded five or six years previously by the representative of the Dumbarton Club for the exemption of a proportionate number of clubs from the preliminary rounds of the Scottish Cup competition. Others who championed the proposed league on the lines indicated included the late Mr. John Mellish (Rangers), afterwards Dominican Consul in Glasgow and president of the Clydesdale Harriers, Messrs. J. H. McLaughlin (Celtic), Tom Lamb (St. Bernards), R. Smith (Heart of Midlothian), Peter Campbell (Renton), D. R. Montgomery (Third Lanark), and A. Towns (St. Mirren). Mr. McLaughlin moved the resolution that a league be formed, and that proposal was carried without a dissentient.

MR. ALEXANDER LAWRENCE
(Dumbarton),
First President of the Scottish Football League.
He is a crack shot, and has had the honour of winning the Queen's Prize, to say nothing of numerous other trophies. His name is indelibly associated with the history of the Scottish Football Association and the Scottish Football League.

A league was not absolutely necessary for amateurism. It was necessary, perhaps vital, for professionalism. Club expenses were on the increase in those amateur days. Crowds used to watch Groves, Madden, Dunbar, Coleman, Neil McCallum, Kelly, and other Celts in their practice games.

The Hibernian Club, too, it should not be overlooked, had "tholed the assize" on a charge of professionalism three years previously at the instance of the Vale of Leven Club. But professionalism was bound to come.

Six years before the Scottish Football League was formed, it was legalised in England, and although the League clubs in Scotland professedly vowed to support the Scottish Football Association in its pathetic attempts to ignore the existence of the paid player, it was the powerful clubs of the League that tolled the death-knell of the amateur constitution of the Scottish Football Association.

The dawn of the League in Scotland hastened the professional era just as the birth of the Celtic Club quickened the League. "You might as well attempt to stop the flow of Niagara with a kitchen chair as to endeavour to stem the tide of professionalism," was the historic utterance of Mr. J. H. McLaughlin, when his proposal for its legalisation was first rejected at the annual meeting of the Scottish Football Association. It was singular that his fiercest opponent on that occasion should be his League colleague, Mr. Lawrence; the one persuasive and logical, pleading for "common honesty in club dealings," and the other strenuously and passionately urging the "voice of the country" to maintain its traditions.

Professionalism was legalised in Scotland in 1893, and two years before that as much as £2,000 was paid in one season to players in Glasgow professedly amateur. A few years later we find the League clubs mutually congratulating each other on the prosperity that had followed in its wake, and the annual report testifying that "Professionalism has been a boon to us all."

Originally, the Scottish Football League comprised eleven clubs, and the opening matches took place on August 16, 1890, when the fixtures were: Celtic v. Renton, Rangers v. Heart of Midlothian, Dumbarton v. Cowlairs, and Cambuslang v. Vale of Leven. The other three clubs completing the federation were Third Lanark, St. Mirren, and Abercorn. At that time the Airdrieonians, Greenock Morton, Partick Thistle, Port Glasgow Athletic, and Kilmarnock were members of the Scottish Football Alliance, for there was no Second Division of the League until the season of 1894-5. Old clubs long since defunct connected with the Alliance included Thistle, Northern, and Linthouse, all in the Glasgow district.

The second year of the League saw it increased to twelve clubs. Cowlairs dropped out, and Clyde and Leith Athletic secured admission. A year later—1892-3—the membership was reduced to ten clubs, and at this total it remained till the season of 1900-1, when Queen's Park was elected without having to qualify as a Second Division club. Next year Partick Thistle dropped out, and the complement was ten once more. An agitation to extend the League's sphere of influence by the addition of two clubs resulted in the election to the First Division in 1902-3 of Port Glasgow Athletic and the return of Partick Thistle. The broadening influence continued the following year, and another two clubs—Motherwell and Airdrieonians—were incorporated in the First Division, both clubs being keen Lanarkshire rivals.

The current season—1905-6—witnessed the advent of another two—Aberdeen and Falkirk—raising the membership to sixteen, at which total it is likely to remain for some time.

The League has always been happy in its choice of officers. Mr. Alex. Lawrence continued to act as chairman till the Dumbarton Club lost its place in the First Division in 1896, and throughout this period Mr. J. H. McLaughlin acted as secretary. The Celtic chairman, who succeeded the ex-Queen's prizeman, a year later expressed the regret of the League that the Dumbarton Club should have dropped out of the League altogether. By a fatal freak of fortune, the Renton Club did not long survive the old Boyhead champions, and resigned because it could not pay its way. What a sorry fate for the pioneers of the movement in

Maclure, MacDonald.]
MR. ARTHUR GEAKE,
President of the Scottish Football League.

Scotland, and a one-time dreaded opponent of the old Preston North End combination in the days when Scottish clubs fought for the English Cup! Had the rule whereby the clubs "pool" the "gates" in League matches been in operation in the early days, it is reasonable to assume that those once powerful clubs — Dumbarton, Renton, and Vale of Leven—all located within a few miles of each other, would have been among the prosperous clubs in Scottish football to-day, and managed to retain the bulk of their players. But up till 1905 the drawings in League matches in Scotland were allocated in the proportion of two-thirds to the ground club, and a third to the visiting club, with the result that the Dumbartonshire clubs, with practically village populations, could not maintain their position or keep their best players from joining the wealthier organisations in England and nearer home.

After the Celtic chairman, who resigned office in 1899, when he had the honour to be elected president of the Scottish Football Association, the subsequent presidents were Messrs. J. McFarlane (St. Bernards), D. R. Montgomery (Third Lanark), J. K. Horsburgh (St. Mirren), and Arthur Geake (Queen's Park). Another official who rendered much good service was Mr. W. Wilton (Rangers) in the capacity of secretary from 1896 till 1899, when he resigned office, as the result of a resolution carried by the casting vote of the chairman whereby the secretary should not be a member of, or connected with, any club in the League. Mr. W. McAndrew, solicitor, Glasgow, was appointed in his stead, and the League is thus fortunate in having the benefit of expert legal advice at its ordinary meetings.

Only six clubs have won the championship: Celtic (five times), Rangers (five times), Heart of Midlothian (twice), Dumbarton (twice), Hibernian (once), and Third Lanark (once). In the first year of the competition, Dumbarton and Rangers, after tieing, decided to hold the championship jointly after a rubber match. Goal average is ignored in Scotland, so that a deciding

Maclure, MacDonald and Co.]
HEART OF MIDLOTHIAN FOOTBALL CLUB, SEASON 1905-6.
Back Row: G. GOODFELLOW (Asst.-Trainer). G. PHILIP. D. BAIN. F. M'LAREN. H. M'NAUGHT. WM. LINDSAY-WAUGH (Secretary). J. CHAPMAN (Trainer).
Front Row: D. LINDSAY. R. WALKER. A. MENZIES. C. THOMSON (Captain). J. DICKSON. D. WILSON. G. WILSON.

Maclure, MacDonald and Co., Glasgow.]

RANGERS' FOOTBALL CLUB, SEASON 1905-6.

Back Row: A. FRASER. T. SINCLAIR. A. CRAIG. F. SPEEDIE. J. STARK. J. MAY. J. WILSON (Trainer).

Front Row: R. DALRYMPLE. J. GRAY. R. S. M'COLL. R. C. HAMILTON. A. KYLE. A. SMITH.

match is necessary. The Rangers also tied in 1904-5 with the Celtic, and a rubber game at Hampden Park gave the "Celts" premier place, as they won by 2 goals to 1. The Rangers enjoy the coveted distinction of winning the championship four years in succession—1898-9 on till 1901-2—a record that is without parallel in first-class League football anywhere. In 1898-9 the club went right through the competition without losing a single point, and with a goal record of 79 against 18.

So far as Edinburgh is concerned, the Heart of Midlothian has alone retained an unbroken connection with the League, although in 1901 the club had to seek re-election. Leith Athletic was four years in the First Division, St. Bernards seven, whilst the Hibernians boast of a ten years' affiliation.

The Second Division of the League was created in 1894-5, with Mr. Peter Campbell (Renton)—one of the original founders of the First Division—as its chairman. It was an independent body, and remained such until the annual meeting in 1899. At the annual meeting of the First Division in 1895 the Hibernians, champions of the Second Division, were elected to the First Division, on the understanding that the size of the playing pitch would be increased. And it is worthy of note that the Hibernian is the only promoted Second League club to win the First Division championship. The Clyde, Partick Thistle (twice), and Abercorn are the only clubs that regained their place in the First Division after being dropped. And but for the tacit understanding among the clubs, whereby Glasgow should not have more than five clubs in the First Division, the Clyde, as winners of the Second League championship last year, would to-day be figuring in a higher class. There is no automatic system of promotion in Scotland whereby the two top clubs in the Second Division take the places of the two at the bottom of the First.

The Football League benefited by the inception of the League in Scotland, and the annual match between its representatives, designated by the Press the "League International," ranks second in importance to the major event between the two countries. As the Football League takes one-half of the drawings—and as much as £1,457 18s. 5d. has been taken in Glasgow, where the match secures its greatest patronage—no inconsiderable portion of its revenue accrues from this convenient fixture.

Over the series of fourteen League games England claims eight victories and Scotland three, while three were drawn. I saw the first match on the old ground of the Bolton Wanderers, at Pike's Lane, played on a Monday evening—April 12, 1892. A faster or more brilliantly-contested struggle I have never seen, and a fitting termination to a memorable game was the result —2 goals each. W. Groves, H. Gardiner, Donald R. Gow, and T. McInnes, all noted Anglo-Scots, were of the England team; but ever since the sides have comprised purely national players. The result of the match afforded some little consolation to the Scottish public for the overthrow of the Scots in the national match played at Ibrox Park that year, when Bassett and Southworth gave such a brilliant and impressive display.

Inter-League games were established with Ireland in 1893, but the fixture lapsed in 1905, the Scottish officials being dissatisfied with the financial returns when the game was played in Belfast. Altogether twelve games were played between Scotland and Ireland, the Scots winning nine times and Ireland thrice.

The bond between the officials of the Leagues of England and Scotland became closer as the years rolled on. In 1897 the consummation of a long desired agreement was realised, whereby the respective Leagues decided upon a mutual recognition of players' registrations. This important resolution was discussed at a joint conference held in Douglas, Isle of Man, in the July of that year, and ratified by the Scottish Football League five months later. Slight concessions were made on either side. Scottish players, who had played in England previously but were in Scottish teams at the date of the agreement, were held by the League club for which they were registered in England as well as by the Scottish club to which they were attached, and no other club in England could treat for their transfer without the consent of the interested parties in Scotland.

Another important point was the cancelment of the registrations of Scottish players who had never played for the English clubs holding their registration with the Football League. All amateur League players in Scotland had to be registered thenceforth.

The logical outcome of this International agreement was the institution of the International League Board for the adjustment of transfer disputes, and the first Scottish representatives on this Board—whose labours have been exceedingly light—were Messrs. J. H. McLaughlin (Celtic), N. Burke (Hibernian), A. Grant (Leith Athletic), and W. Wilton (Rangers).

Maclure, MacDonald.]
MR. W. McANDREW.
Secretary of the Scottish Football League.

If self-protection is at the root of the League system, the League has not existed entirely to serve its own ends. As much as £200 has been voted in one year from its funds in aid of the charities of Glasgow, Edinburgh, Leith, Renton, Dumbarton, and Paisley. One recalls, too, how in 1891, when the Scottish Football Association Charity Cup committee refused an official and reasonable request by the League to alter its dates to permit of the expedition of the League competition, that the League clubs interested—Celtic, Rangers, and Third Lanark—withdrew from the Scottish Football Association Charity ties, which fell flat in consequence, but along with Dumbarton organised a supplementary charity competition under League auspices, with such influential citizens as Bailie Simons (chairman), Sir John Ure Primrose, Bart. (treasurer), and Councillor Angus Campbell, independent voluntary assistants. Mr. T. E. Maley, the present Manchester City manager, acted as secretary, and the League raised £943 15s. 3d., and was in a position to disburse £840 among the public institutions.

Again, in 1902, Sunderland and Everton—the top clubs in the English League—journeyed north to assist the Ibrox Park Disaster Fund, and competed against the two top clubs in the Scottish League—Rangers and Celtic—for the Glasgow Exhibition Cup (won by the Celtic) put up by the Rangers to help the sufferers. By this means £840 5s. 2d. was raised.

The actions of the League have often been misjudged, largely because of its relations between club and player and in matters affecting club agreements requiring Scottish Football Association adjustment. But as one who has maintained personal touch with the officials from the start of the League, I have ever found them ready to co-operate with the parent Association in all that tended to better the game, and as loyal adherents of the Association, subordinating League interests where there was the semblance of conflict.

Of the benefit to the game which fixity of fixture gave, there can be no two opinions, and nowhere has this been more in evidence than in Glasgow. As showing the remarkable equality between the two crack League clubs in Scotland—Celtic and Rangers—in twenty-one consecutive League games, beginning 1895 and ending 1905, there is only one goal of difference, the Celtic getting forty-three and the Rangers forty-two; while each club gained twenty-one points. No club match excites the same interest, and the record League attendance of 65,000 on the Rangers' ground on January 2, 1905, was the occasion of their League match. That same day the Corinthians and Queen's Park, at Hampden Park, attracted about 30,000 spectators, so that Glasgow may be justly regarded as the City of Football.

Maclure, MacDonald and Co.]

PARTICK THISTLE FOOTBALL CLUB, SEASON 1905-6.

Back Row: JOHN NUTT (Trainer). ANDREW SWAN. DAVID MELVILLE. CARRICK HAMILTON. WM. HOWDEN. GEORGE GILCHRIST.
Front Row: JAMES SOMMEN. HARRY WILSON. SAM KENNEDY. THOMAS HARVEY. DAVID WALKER. ROBERT GRAY.

F. B. Bedford, Barnsley.]

BARNSLEY FOOTBALL CLUB—THE OFFICIALS, SEASON 1905-6.

A. FAIRCLOUGH (Gen. Sec.). T. PLEASANT. J. HAWKE. T. H. FISHER (Chairman). J. MURTON. F. B. BEDFORD. G. HAIGH. J. CHARLESWORTH.
T. KENWORTHY. J. PEMBERTON. H. FOUNDHERE (Fin. Sec.). T. BOTT.

BARNSLEY FOOTBALL CLUB.

By F. LODGE.

The introduction of "Soccer" in the Barnsley district—Its rise to popularity—Progress of Barnsley Football Club—Some talented Barnsley players—The club's officials—Future prospects.

Colours: Red shirts, blue knickers. *Ground: Oakwell, Pontefract Road, Barnsley.*

THOUGH the Barnsley Club, in a comparative sense, cannot boast of ancient lineage, it is approaching the twentieth year of its existence. Curious though it may seem, still it is a fact that in the early Eighties, whilst so popular in the Sheffield district—but fourteen miles away—little was seen of the "Soccer" code in the Barnsley locality. Then the Rugby game was in full swing, while now it is little followed; whilst quite a network of clubs playing with the round ball are full of life and vigour.

In narrating the history of the Barnsley Club reference has at first to be made to the doings of a band of "old schoolboys" who, under the title of Barnsley Wanderers, were the pioneers of the game in the district. These devotees of the game troubled nothing about "gates," and were glad to see spectators at the games; but there were but few, though the team produced football which made them worthy rivals to the amateur combinations of Sheffield and other provincial towns.

The legalising of the professional, however, brought into being the Barnsley Club and gave the game a much wider popularity, though progress was scarcely instantaneous. The tale of the inception of the present club, in 1887, must be a repetition of the circumstances attending the birth of so many other clubs—its first connection being with a place of worship. This was St. Peter's Church, situated in a purely working-class part of the town, and the leading spirit in its promotion was the Rev. T. T. Preedy (now in London), whose persistent work in launching the club will not readily be forgotten.

The Rugby game, as stated, was then a strong force, and in other parts of the town came Association clubs following the appearance of the "Saints," as they were then fondly termed. That the club had behind it a band of earnest workers is shown by the fact that it soon became the chief club in the district, and not long afterwards, in the struggle with the Rugby element, won the favour of local enthusiasts, and became, if not in name, the town's organisation, adopting the title of Barnsley Football Club on the death of the Rugby combination.

Association clubs sprung up on every side, and there quickly followed in 1888 the formation of the Barnsley Association Football Union, with the inevitable challenge cup competition. The local club, in the second year of its existence, had found admittance to the Sheffield and Hallanshire Cup competition, but did not meet with any great success, the calibre of competitors being then much stronger than at the present day. Then—in the first year of the local cup competition—Ecclesfield was too good for Barnsley; but in subsequent years the trophy was secured by the Barnsley Club, and, eventually becoming too strong a force for the district class, the club withdrew, rather than bespoil the general interest in the fight for the local trophy.

Incidentally, as showing the early popularity of the game, it may be recorded that in 1889, on the occasion of the final for the local cup, when the club conquered Mexbro' Town at the second attempt, the gate receipts were respectively £156 and £111, both figures being well ahead of Barnsley's average receipts for Second League games at the present time. The club quickly made progress, and in 1891 was considered strong enough for the Sheffield and District League.

It was in 1894 that the name of Barnsley Football Club became more widely known. The team had won their way through the qualifying stages of the Football Association Cup competition, and found themselves drawn against Liverpool in the first round of the competition proper. The First Leaguers made an objection to the Barnsley ground, which was then certainly not all that could be desired, but their objection was overruled by the Football Association, and Liverpool had to journey to Oakwell where, to the astonishment of the whole football world, the locals made a draw of the game. At the second meeting of the clubs at Liverpool Barnsley were well beaten, but their plucky play had won for the club a wide renown.

The year 1895 saw the club promoted to the Midland League, while they again fought their way into the first round of the English Cup, only to be beaten by Derby County. In 1898 Barnsley entered the Second Division of the League, and have retained their position in that select circle up to now, though they had on one occasion to seek re-election.

During Barnsley's football history the club has produced many young and talented players, and of these Harry Davis, the Sheffield Wednesday right-winger, who was transferred from his native town club to the First Leaguers, has gained International honours; whilst it is reputed the club received £1,000 in one season for the transfer of "Benny" Green, another local youth, to the new-styled Birmingham Club, and of Alf. West, the smart right-back of the Liverpool Club. Last season Birmingham renewed their love for Barnsley talent, Frank Cornan, Aaron Jones, and Anderson (who was with Barnsley for a brief period) having been transferred to the Midland organisation, which has been further strengthened by securing the services of Will Norman, who, for a couple of seasons, was Barnsley's clever trainer.

The club has always had a useful set of men guiding its destinies. Mention has already been made of the founder, the Rev. T. T. Preedy. Another early worker was Mr. J. Raley, now chairman of the local Association Football Union; and Mr. F. G. Senior, the genial president, and Mr. T. H. Fisher, the present chairman, have also lent their valuable assistance to the club. In the earliest period of the club's history Mr. S. Ruston was a hard worker in the capacity of secretary; whilst, coming to recent times, Mr. J. McCartney—now in charge of the destinies of Paisley St. Mirren—first in the capacity of player and captain and then as secretary and manager, was a stout-hearted worker. Mr. Arthur Fairclough, a former secretary, is now discharging the secretarial duties, and his long experience of the game and connection with the club is of much value to the organisation.

The management of the club is now in the hands of the following: President, Mr. F. G. Senior; directors, Messrs. T. H. Fisher (chairman), J. Charlesworth (vice-chairman), F. B. Bedford, T. Bott, E. W. Buswell, G. Haigh, J. Hawke, T. Kenworthy, F. Lodge, J. Pemberton, T. Pleasant, H. Morton, W. Wood, and Dr. J. P. Shine; financial secretary, H. Foundhere; and general secretary, A. Fairclough.

The Oakwell Ground is the original club enclosure, and whilst its situation and equipment are not ideal, still it will bear favourable comparison with that of many of the League clubs. The playing pitch may be considered as almost perfect, for the ground was thoroughly overhauled and levelled at great expense: while ample stand and covered accommodation has been erected for the comfort of the spectators. Last season the sum of £600 was expended in the construction of a grand stand alone. The ground will hold 10,000 people with comfort, and it is to be hoped that "gates" of this magnitude will soon regularly attend the home matches.

Barnsley, within a near radius, has a population of 100,000. For years those in charge of the club's affairs have yearned for the development of the game in Yorkshire, and now the long-hoped-for growth of Yorkshire rivalry is an accomplished fact. Bradford, Hull, and Leeds are now in the Second League, and whilst this increased competition of neighbouring towns should arouse added interest, does it not give birth to heavier responsibilities? Can Barnsley hold its own against the new forces? Can the club give the desired response?

F. B. Bedford, Barnsley.]

BARNSLEY FOOTBALL CLUB—LEAGUE TEAM AND PLAYERS' COMMITTEE, SEASON 1905-6.

Back Row: A. Fairclough (Secretary). T. H. Fisher (Chairman). J. Hay. F. B. Bedford (Director). E. Rounds. H. Stacey. T. Pleasant (Director). T. Bott (Director). F. Lodge (Director). J. Marston (Trainer).
Middle Row: H. Silto. J. Wilkinson. S. Robertson.
Bottom Row: H. Ryalls. J. Beech (Capt.). A. Hellewell. J. Bell. G. Wall.

A BRIEF HISTORY OF WATFORD FOOTBALL CLUB.

By ALBERT MILLS.

Forerunners of the Watford Football Club proper—Amateurism v. professionalism—Amalgamation—Early Southern League experiences—Back to the Second Division—Again in the First Division—A successful season—The club's patron—Further disappointments—The future—Players and members—The club ground.

Colours: Red. green, and yellow stripes. *Ground: West Herts Club Ground, Watford.*

THE town of Watford has ever boasted the possession of the premier football team in the County of Herts. One has to go back to the early Seventies to note that—in 1872, to be exact—the Hertfordshire Rangers, who played in a meadow off the Langley Road, furnished R. C. Barker as goalkeeper for England against Scotland at Glasgow, the result of which game was a goalless draw. The exit of the Rangers made way for the Watford Rovers, in their day a powerful team, who won the County Cup in the seasons 1888–9 and 1890–1.

In 1891 came the formation of the West Herts Club and Ground, and the Rovers joining this body, played four seasons as West Herts, winning the County Cup in the seasons 1891–2, 1895–6, and performing generally with remarkable success. Eventually, the various league competitions had the usual effect of making the "friendlies" less and less attractive, the ultimate result being that admission was sought and obtained to the Southern League (Second Division) in the season 1896–7. The growth of professionalism in the South at this period had the effect of strengthening most of the teams met, and the end of the season found West Herts ninth on the list.

There had meanwhile sprung into existence a local club, St. Mary's, which received a considerable amount of gate money, and the competition between the "Saints" and West Herts is a memory that still sets the tongues of all old Watford enthusiasts wagging.

In 1897–8 West Herts pluckily adopted professionalism; and the "Saints'" secretary urged his committee to do likewise, notwithstanding the fact that during the season the amateurs had defeated a West Herts team containing three professionals—Vernon, Wilcox, and Marsh. It was, of course, apparent that the town could not support two professional organisations, and amalgamation of the two clubs under the present name resulted. So, in 1898–9, Watford turned out a strong side, finished second in the Metropolitan section of the Southern League, and carried off the championship of the Bucks and Contiguous Counties League.

The following season witnessed the longed-for possession of the championship of the Second Division; the test match with Sheppey United was won by 2 clear goals, and entrance to the First Division secured. Football enthusiasm was at fever heat when the season 1900–1 was entered upon, but the club and supporters had by experience to learn that the First and Second Divisions of our Premier Football Leagues spell "difference," and the end of the tourney found Watford last but one on the chart. The farcical test match with Gray's United produced no goals, and the Essex club being anything but anxious for First Division strife, we again entered the fray in September, 1901, hoping for better results, and realising hopes to the extent that we finished with three clubs below us and 22 points for 30 games.

The season 1902–3 was most disastrous, Watford being in the last two and set to play Brighton and Hove a test match at the Memorial Grounds, Canning Town. This proved to be an extraordinary affair, concerning which many ugly rumours got about, and we were trounced by 5—2.

With finances in a parlous state, a season in the Second Division could not have been entertained but for the generosity of Mr. R. A. Thorpe, chairman of the Watford Urban District Council, who came forward and said, in effect, "Get a good team and manager, win back the club's prestige, and I will see to the financial side of the business." Not without a struggle did we renounce our right to a place in the extended "Upper House," and we vied with Fulham and Plymouth Argyle in setting forth our claims, and to such effect that at the annual Southern League meeting on the Friday night we were re-elected, but ignominiously thrown out at a subsequent meeting on the Saturday afternoon, between which assemblies various forces were brought to bear, but over which I will draw a veil in the same manner as did the Fulham secretary in an earlier part of this book.

With the famous John Goodall engaged as player-manager, and a splendid body of players—several of whom are still with us—we simply "fooled" through the Second Division, and we were subsequently received back amongst the elite of Southern professional football. John Goodall remained, Mr. Thorpe stood by with the money, and several "class" players were secured, including our present goalkeeper, William Biggar, who came from the unthankful task of understudying Fryer at Fulham; Main, the old Arsenal favourite; and Peter Turner, the latter crossing from Luton to join his old Arsenal-Middlesborough left-wing partner, James Tennant.

Thus, back in the First Division, Watford commenced to make history. The team performed most creditably, and the close of April, 1905, found them ninth from the top. The exact reading was: Played, 34; won, 15; drawn, 3; lost, 16; goals for, 44; against, 44; 33 points.

This present campaign opened with the introduction to Watford people of C. Aston, a full-back from Burton United, and formerly with the Villa and Queen's Park Rangers at Kensal Rise. He has proved a great acquisition. The halves have a clever understudy in Fyfe, who played last year for the Hibernians. Forward, the ex-Notts County inside-right, J. Reid, came to fill the manager's position when required, and "Johnny" was successful in securing Foster, the most prolific scorer in the Midland League. Kelly came down from Chesterfield to fill the position so long occupied by Jamie Tennant, and things promised well. Remarkable to relate, the so little altered team has performed but very poorly.

The club progressed further in the Cup tourney than ever before, but at the time of writing the position is most precarious, and the debt to the more than generous chairman, Mr. Thorpe, stands at a big figure. This is most undesirable—and for more than ordinary reasons. The Cassio Road Ground is as near perfection as could be desired. Larger than Lords' Cricket Ground, just as level, beautifully drained and kept, the football portion is well-provided with a substantial club-house and stands. Watford is but thirty minutes from Euston by London and North-Western main line, and the fine route taps a populous district, while the town itself boasts, with its neighbouring district of Bushey, well over 40,000 inhabitants. Within hail are the towns of St. Alban's, Rickmansworth, and Hemel Hempsted, all of which send big bands of enthusiasts to the West Herts enclosure. Above all, the supporters have ever been worthy of the name, attending the matches, for the most part, in goodly numbers; and with such support, despite the troubles that seem to loom ahead, we feel sure that first-class football is anything but a dead letter in Watford.

WATFORD FOOTBALL CLUB—THE PLAYERS, SEASON 1905-6.

Standing: Brooks. Aston. McCartney. John Goodall (Manager). Upton (Trainer). Biggar (Goalkeeper).

Sitting: Badenoch. Reid. Main. Foster. Fyfe. Eaton.

Turner. Kelly.

THE HISTORY OF THE NORTHERN UNION.

By J. H. SMITH, President.

The causes of its establishment—The working-man player—The advent of professionalism—The "Works Clause" and subsequent developments—The formation of the Northern League and its result—The Northern Union style of play—Stability of the Union—The men in charge.

FOUNDED in 1895, the Northern Union has had a somewhat eventful career, and therefore, in attempting to trace its history in the space allotted to me, the initial difficulty is to determine the main points calling for consideration. It will, however, be imperative to explain the causes of its inception, and briefly these are as follows: For many years previous to 1895 the Rugby world was full of rumours as to alleged professionalism. The increased popularity of the game among the working-class population of the North, and the consequent increase in "gates," enabled clubs to offer inducements too great to be resisted, and the migration of skilful players became so pronounced as to admit of no doubt that professionalism existed. The English Union strengthened their rules with the avowed object of preventing anything but pure amateurism, but, in Lancashire and Yorkshire particularly, it was recognised that where large sums were taken in gate money, payment for time lost, at least, was inevitable. Consequently, an organised attempt to legalise the payment of bona-fide broken time was made; but at what was I believe the best attended meeting on record, the Southern element proved too strong, and we were defeated. However, although actual steps were not immediately taken, the breaking away of a section of the North only became a question of time, and it was not long before events took definite shape. In the summer of 1895 the leading clubs of Lancashire and Yorkshire held a large number of meetings, and although some of those who engaged in the undertaking hesitated and withdrew before matters reached a climax, the ultimate result was that, at a meeting held at Huddersfield on August 29 of that year, the resignations of twenty-two clubs were sent to the English Union, and the new organisation was then and there inaugurated. The founders were Bradford, Brighouse Rangers, Batley, Broughton Rangers, Halifax, Hunslet, Hull, Huddersfield, Liversedge, Leeds, Leigh, Manningham, Oldham, Rochdale Hornets, Runcorn, St. Helens, Stockport, Tyldesley, Wakefield Trinity, Warrington, Wigan, and Widnes. Of these, Tyldesley, Liversedge, Manningham, and Stockport have since disbanded.

MR. JOHN H. SMITH,
The president of the Northern Union, is justly renowned and respected in the North of England, where he has taken a leading part in football as player, official, and referee for more than twenty-five years. He has been officially connected with the Northern Union from its inception; has been twice president of the Union, twice president for Lancashire County, president of the Lancashire Senior Competition, and ten years president of the Lancashire Referees' Society.

For the first season the clubs were all included in one huge league, which involved the playing of forty-two matches by each club. Fortunately the winter proved an open one, and the big programme was successfully completed. At the end of the season, as expected, a large number of Rugby Union clubs came over to the new organisation. Amongst these were Salford, Swinton, Morecambe, Castleford, Bramley, Heckmondwike, Holbeck, and Leeds Parish Church. It therefore became necessary to reconstruct the League, and separate Senior competitions were established in Yorkshire and Lancashire, supplementary leagues for junior clubs also being provided.

In this year the Challenge Cup competition was inaugurated, and at once caught the popular taste, success being assured from the outset. The following particulars show the progress of this competition:

Year.	Winners.	Where Played.	Attendance.	Gate Receipts. £	s.	d.
1897	Batley	Leeds	13,492	624	17	7
1898	Batley	Leeds	27,491	1,506	3	0
1899	Oldham	Manchester	15,763	946	16	1
1900	Swinton	Manchester	17,864	1,110	1	0
1901	Batley	Leeds	29,563	1,644	16	6
1902	Broughton R.	Rochdale	15,006	846	11	0
1903	Halifax	Leeds	32,507	1,834	8	6
1904	Halifax	Salford	17,041	936	5	6
1905	Warrington	Leeds	19,468	1,261	3	0

When the new Union was floated, it was freely stated by its opponents that the lost-time question was a mere expedient and only a means to an end, which had for its object professionalism pure and simple; but that this was not the case was fully demonstrated by the determined efforts made by the authorities to keep payments within the limits laid down, and some of the wealthy clubs found this out to their cost. The majority of those who risked their existence at the time of the split were certainly sincere in their desire to confine payments to bona-fide time lost in pursuit of the game, and subsequent expansion was due to force of circumstances, which I shall now proceed to explain. The great fillip given to the Rugby game by the establishment of the Northern Union, and the increased desire to win matches which the league principle had created, rendered competition for skilful players keener than ever; and after three years working of the original scheme, the powers that be found the difficulty of preventing surreptitious payments to players beyond their control, and consequently decided to legalise unrestricted professionalism. That is, unrestricted so far as disbursements in actual cash were concerned. They were, however, reluctant to go the whole hog, and although the new scheme permitted unlimited remuneration, a clause was inserted in the rules which provided that if a player did not work at some additional occupation he should not play football. The wisdom of this clause was from the first made the subject of controversy, but, in spite of strenuous opposition from within and ridicule from without, for seven long years the Northern Union strove to carry out their ideal. It is unnecessary to enter into any lengthy description of the reasons which prompted the adoption of the much-abused "works clause"—suffice it to say that its subsequent abolition was not due to any inherent defects in the clause itself, or the conviction on the part of its adherents that their original ideas were based upon false premises, but rather to questions of expediency brought about by the unpopularity of the measure in the minds of the average supporter, who, as the man who finds the funds to carry on the game, has, of course, a claim for consideration. The knowledge that this feeling existed, and the conviction that the spirit of unrest which had permeated the Union ever since its inception was not calculated to further the interests of the game, perhaps did more than anything else to turn the scale in favour of out-and-out professionalism.

It will be seen that the history of the Northern Union and the history of professionalism are synonymous terms, and the evolution from pure amateurism to the present state provides a very interesting study. First, the payment for time lost, followed by the legalisation of compensation in the form of wages, but restricted by a stipulation of a supplementary occupation; and now an extreme system practically unrestricted.

After the adoption of professionalism in 1898, the Northern Union acquired a constant accession of strength from outside, and between that date and 1901 a steady influx of new clubs necessitated a corresponding increase in the number of leagues and cup competitions. In 1901 we reach a period in the history of the Union when the first discordant note was sounded, and an event occurred which was fated to have far-reaching consequences. I refer to the formation of the Northern League. enclosure in the very heart of Bradford at a moment's notice. It is certain that had it not been for the chagrin of the Manningham officials at being left out in the cold, and their determination not to continue in second-class company after their brilliant achievements of the immediately preceding seasons, they would not have resigned their membership of the Northern Union, and the Bradford City club would have been compelled to seek a home elsewhere. In such manner do great events from little causes spring.

However, the new League became an accomplished fact. The first season it consisted of fourteen clubs only, but in 1902-3 this number was increased to eighteen, and a Second Division, also consisting of eighteen clubs, was added. The latter competition, having regard to the class of clubs of which it was composed, proved unwieldy, chiefly owing to the wide area covered and the consequent heavy item incurred in the cost of long journeys, and after three seasons' trial it became apparent that

OLDHAM FOOTBALL TEAM—WINNERS OF THE NORTHERN LEAGUE CHAMPIONSHIP, SEASON 1904-5.

Back Row: H. Topham. D. Thomas. A. Jardine. H. Ellis. A. Lees (Captain). J. Vowles. G. Frater. J. Wright. A. Glossop (Trainer).
Middle Row: T. White. J. Wilkinson. T. Sellars. G. F. Tyson. C. Civil. S. Lees. J. Owens. R. Carpenter.
Bottom Row: R. L. Thomas. F. Spottiswoode. T. Cash. D. J. Lewis. T. McLean. J. R. Lawton.

THE LEAGUE CUP.

Up to this time one of the predominant factors in building up the edifice of the professional Union was the unanimity with which the authorities worked to render the interests of the richer clubs identical with those less fortunately placed. In all my experience I have never been associated with a committee where the spirit of mutual dependence was so fully recognised, or where concession and conciliation were so pronounced. The establishment of the Northern League, however, altered all this, and we have certainly never been the same happy family since. The provision of opportunity for the leading clubs to meet in League matches irrespective of their geographical position was only the natural and logical development of the League principle, and some scheme which would group these clubs together was sooner or later bound to be demanded, but, unfortunately, the establishment of the new League, or, to be exact, the manner of its formation, was keenly resented by those left out of the select circle, and was the direct cause of our losing one or two prominent clubs. But for the friction caused, the promoters of Association football in West Yorkshire would not have been able to secure a ready-made and fully-equipped the weak financial condition of the Second Division was such as to render continuance of this section an absolute impossibility, and, therefore, unless the premier clubs were content to stand alone and allow a number of old-standing organisations to lapse, reconstruction became a *sine qua non*. It was consequently proposed to combine both divisions into one league, open to an unlimited number of clubs, who would not be required to play the whole of their competitors. Any club which could mutually arrange fixtures with ten others would be included, and the position in the table determined by the percentage of points gained in the matches actually played.

As was only to be expected, this proposal met with strong opposition from many members of the First Division, because the premier League had, from the first, been a pronounced success, and, naturally, its members hesitated to give their support to a scheme primarily adapted for the amelioration of less important organisations unless their own interests could be adequately safeguarded. In the end, however, wiser counsels prevailed, the opposition was withdrawn, and reconstruction accepted on the lines laid down.

That the disintegration of the original League is, in a sense, a retrograde step goes without saying, but it has been rendered imperative by the peculiar circumstances of the situation.

It must be said, however, that while the new competition cannot claim all the advantages of an exclusive league, it has its compensations. For example, the scheme is calculated to raise the standard of play, as owing to there being no compulsion in regard to the arrangement of fixtures, any team which cultivates an unattractive style of play or systematically indulges in shady tactics will probably find their fixtures with the leading clubs seriously curtailed. Those who are fully cognisant with the desire to win at any cost, so frequently practised under the league system, will appreciate the importance of this point. Another advantage is the opportunity afforded for expansion. The Northern Union has for several years been handicapped by the limited scope of its operations. The ultra development of the league principle had established a close corporation which practically precluded the acquirement of new clubs of good standing, and, as a matter of fact, no new members of importance have been admitted since the formation of the Northern League in 1901. The adoption of the present scheme has again opened the door for the accession of strength from outside, and the sequel will be awaited with interest.

C. F. Shaw, Batley.]
THE NORTHERN UNION GAME—HALF-TIME, BATLEY v. WARRINGTON.
The Warrington forwards discuss the state of affairs.

Before leaving the subject of competitions, the County championship calls for brief notice. By reason of the superiority of the individual players, this tournament ought to be regarded as of premier importance, and that such is not the case is due partly to the limited character of the contest, but principally because the very nature of the league system causes club interest to dominate all other interests. The annual meeting of Lancashire and Yorkshire, however, has an importance of its own quite apart from any question of championship, and this match alone is sufficient justification for the continuance of county football. Lancashire have won the championship on six occasions, Yorkshire have been champions three times, and Cheshire once.

Passing on to the style of play practised; when the Northern Union was formed the existing rules of Rugby football were adopted just as they stood. Subsequently, in the endeavour to produce a more attractive exposition, slight changes have from time to time been made. Of these, the point which has commanded the greatest attention has been in respect to the method of bringing the ball into play from touch. The line-out, although theoretically an ideal system of restarting the game from the side boundaries of the field, was anything but satisfactory in practice owing to the frequency with which it resulted in a scrummage, and, in 1897, in the hope of minimising the time lost from this cause, a punt-out from touch was substituted. After an extended trial, however, the method developed objections on its own account in the shape of increasing opportunity for foul charging, &c., and in 1902 it was abolished in favour of the present method of forming a scrummage ten yards from the line, opposite the point where the ball entered touch. The only point of difference between the English and Northern Union with respect to this feature of the game is, that in the former there is the option of either the line-out or a scrummage, while in the latter the scrummage is proceeded with forthwith.

The statement has often been made that the Northern Union introduced such drastic alterations in the laws that the game as now played under their auspices is unrecognisable from that of the parent body, but this is totally inaccurate. In addition to the method of touch play, there have only been two changes of any importance. The first of these is that during the time a scrummage is in progress all the backs are compelled to keep behind the last row of forwards—i.e., behind the scrummage altogether, and not simply behind the ball, as in the amateur code. The second item has reference to the compulsory playing of the ball after a player has been tackled and the ball fairly held. This has been abolished, and, under the circumstances named, a scrummage has to be formed before play can proceed. Other differences are merely matters of detail which more immediately concern referees, and do not call for explanation.

NORTHERN UNION FOOTBALL—FINAL TIE, HALIFAX v. SALFORD, AT HEADINGLEY. APRIL 25, 1903.
Rigg (Halifax) and Lomas (Salford) tossing for choice of ends. The referee and touch-judge are evidently enjoying a joke.

The Northern Union is sometimes referred to as a moribund organisation, and there are those who express the belief that its extinction is only a matter of a few more seasons. Probably this is, in some instances, a case of pious wish rather than an expression of honest conviction, but, as no success of the English Union or development of the Association game is ever allowed to pass without the fact being advanced as indicating Northern Union decay, it may, perhaps, prove interesting to quote a few facts in support of the contention that professional Rugby football is anything but a spent force.

The success of any organisation embracing professionalism is, of course, largely determined by questions of £ s. d., and is, therefore, reflected in the income derived from the general public.

In this connection, the figures quoted in the early part of this article show the great interest evinced in cup-ties, but support is by no means confined to representative matches of this character. Ordinary League games regularly attract large crowds, and as much as £710 has been taken at the gate of one of these encounters.

While it would be idle to deny that some few clubs are not in a prosperous condition, others are in a very sound position indeed. For example, the Bradford club own their own grounds, which are valued at £25,000, upon which they have a mortgage of only £7,000. Since 1892 the football section, after paying full proportion of rates, taxes, and all other charges, have made a clear profit of £3,700 from Rugby football. Hull have spent £12,000 upon their grounds, and now owe less than £2,500; the difference having been paid off out of profits derived from football. Oldham have spent about £8,000 upon their enclosure, all paid for, and have £1,500 invested in loan as well as a satisfactory working balance, while the grounds of Huddersfield, Leeds, Salford, etc., are among the best in the kingdom.

MR. JOSEPH PLATT
(Oldham),
Hon. Secretary of the Northern Rugby Union.

As regards numerical strength, the number of clubs in membership, direct and through the County Unions, is 129. The various district leagues include about 130. Intermediate competitions—that is, competitions for youths who have left school—74, and schoolboys 87, making a total of 420 clubs.

As the junior of to-day is, of course, the senior of to-morrow, the strength of junior football is particularly encouraging, and while the Northern Union will be pleased to admit into their ranks any outside club which believes in professionalism, the above facts show that even without accession of strength from outside the Union is still capable of being maintained in a state of efficiency.

This history would not be complete without brief reference to the gentlemen who have engineered the Northern Union. According to the official guide for 1895, the first committee was composed of Messrs. H. H. Waller (president), J. E. Warren (vice-president), J. Platt (hon. secretary), D. F. Burnley (hon. treasurer), A. H. Briggs, J. Clifford, T. Wright, H. Hutchinson, J. Hampshire, J. Nicholl, C. A. Brewer, H. Sewell, A. Fattorini, W. Carrol, E. Gresty, J. Underwood, E. Rothwell, H. Rowson, F. J. Dennet, J. M. Mills, O. S. Quigley, and J. H. Smith.

As showing the rapid changes which take place, only Messrs. Platt, Nicholl, and myself now remain in office. Mr. Platt has been secretary from the commencement, and if anyone may be singled out for commendation, Mr. Platt is that one. His grasp of detail and faculty for organisation has been of incalculable service to the cause of Rugby professionalism, and his strong personality and sound commonsense have often enabled the management to solve the most difficult complex problems. Mr. Nicholl has been treasurer since 1897, while the writer was president in 1899-1900, and has again been elected to the position this year.

The names of other gentlemen who have occupied the presidential chair are Messrs. J. E. Warren, D. F. Burnley, H. Hutchinson, J. H. Houghton, J. Clifford, R. Collinge, and F. Lister.

The present board of management is composed of the three already mentioned and Messrs. J. B. Cooke (vice-president), H. Ashton, J. Goodall, J. H. Houghton, J. W. Wood, H. Taylor, J. E. Kirkham, J. W. T. Aldred, G. Taylor, H. Speight, W. D. Lyon, C. Pownall, R. Collinge, W. Fillan, F. Lister, and J. W. Ingham.

J. H. Cartwright, Warrington.]

WARRINGTON FOOTBALL TEAM—WINNERS OF THE NORTHERN UNION CUP, SEASON 1904-5.

Back Row: I. HACKETT (Trainer). T. HARMER. F. SHUGARS. J. PRESTON. A. S. BOARDMAN. J. BELTON. G. JOLLEY. F. HEESOM (Trainer).

Middle Row: W. SWIFT. T. KENYON. G. DICKENSON. J. HALLAM (Captain). D. ISHERWOOD. J. FISH. T. COOK.

Bottom Row: G. THOMAS. DIA DAVIES. **THE CUP.** E. BROOKS. A. NAYLOR.

THE BRENTFORD FOOTBALL CLUB.

Foundation of the Brentford Football Club — Early cup triumphs — Brentford win the London Cup — Professionalism adopted — Brentford Champions of the Second Division of the Southern League—In the Southern League Premier Division.

Colours : Blue and gold stripes. *Ground : Griffin Park, Brentford.*

THE Brentford Football Club was founded in the year 1888, having a membership of about a score of persons, and started playing in a field owned by Mr. Underwood, at the back of the Wesleyan chapel adjoining the present ground, under the captaincy of Mr. J. J. K. Curtis, and with Mr. Archer Green attending to the secretarial duties. He, however, died shortly afterwards, the position being taken up by Mr. R. Beaver, who was subsequently followed by Mr. A. E. Harris. In the year 1896 Mr. W. G. Brown was secretary; but the following year he was succeeded by Mr. J. Hinton Bailey, who held the position for three years.

The club made very little progress until 1893, when they won their first cup, becoming champions of the West London Alliance. The following year the West Middlesex Junior Cup was won, and in the next season the West Middlesex Senior Cup was captured.

In 1896-7 they could not lay claim to any of the honours, their best performance being in the London Senior Cup, in which they were defeated by the Old Carthusians in the semi-final at Leyton. The same season they played their first match against a professional club—viz., a friendly with Edinburgh St. Bernard's, the result of which ended in a goalless draw. In 1897-8 the club reached its proudest position as an amateur organisation by winning the London and also the Middlesex Senior Cups, and finishing second in the London League. The same year the Reserves won the Kingston League Challenge Cup. At this time the club were playing on Shotter's Field in Windmill Road.

The London Cup was practically won by defeating the Casuals at Leyton in the semi-final round by 4 goals to 3, for Ilford were beaten by the fine score of 5 goals to 1 in the final. The teams in the game with the Casuals were as under:

Brentford—C. W. Gillett, goal; P. G. Swann and A. W. Lugg, backs; A. H. Charlton, H. G. Edney, and W. A. Smith, half-backs; R. H. Dailley, D. Lloyd, E. Booth, C. Field, and T. H. Knapman, forwards.

Casuals—H. R. Blaker, goal; W. G. Adams and S. L. King, backs; J. E. Lea, C. O. Hatton, and H. I. Pickering, half-backs; R. Hilleary, H. R. Barrett, G. P. Wilson, S. S. Taylor, and C. F. Drake, forwards.

Amongst the players who composed the Brentford team that year were such fine players as Pennington (goalkeeper), now of Notts County; Field (inside-left), now of Birmingham; and A. Charlton (half-back), who for a time played with Notts Forest. All these left before the succeeding season commenced; but, despite this, the committee got a good side together. Affairs, however, were not well managed, and the players did much as they pleased. They were unsuccessful in winning matches, failed in the cup competitions, the supporters of the club dwindled away as the result of this, and there was a big deficit at the end of the season. The prospects for 1899–1900 were very poor. Only a moderate team turned out to do duty for the club, and, consequently, they were not very successful. It should be mentioned that in 1898-9 the club had to find a new ground, and a most unsuitable pitch was obtained in the Cross Roads. This, together with the distance from the town, affected the "gates" very considerably.

Nearly half the season of 1899-1900 was over when the club was hauled up before the Football Association for certain alleged misdeeds. The club was suspended for one month and fined £10; in addition to this, many officials of the club were suspended. On resuming after their enforced rest, the club embraced professionalism.

The next year Brentford won the championship of the Second Division of the Southern League without losing a match and only having 11 goals scored against them.

Having won the championship of the Second Division of the Southern League, after a great tussle with Gray's United, the management of the club rightly considered its position, and came to the conclusion that they must go forward. They only made a draw in the test match with Swindon, and had they won they would have been saved much of the trouble that followed. As it was, they had to make application to the Southern League for admission to Division I.; but their strong claims were passed over in favour of the two Midland clubs Wellingborough and Northampton, much to the disappointment of Brentonians, who felt that they had not been fairly treated. The same policy still seems to obtain in the Southern League to-day in respect to rising London clubs. The club, however, were admitted to the Southern League during the summer of 1901, owing to the collapse of Gravesend who withdrew.

They had considerable trouble to get a team together, then, to compete in first-class company, but they succeeded, and amongst those engaged were Roddy McLeod, W. Regan (of Millwall), and "Bob" Storment (of the "'Spurs"), who captained the side. They opened the season with a draw at Swindon, but it was not until November that they notched their first victory. On the whole, they did fairly well, winning 7 games, losing 17, and drawing 6, which gave them 20 points. They had, however, to play a test match with Gray's United, who did not want promotion, and this ended in a draw. The following season was the worst the club had ever experienced in Division I., for though they had the assistance of players like Warren (of Derby County), Shanks, Maher (now of Preston North End), Pickering, Regan, Spicer, and Green (now of Burnley), they won only two League matches, and finished last in the League table with only 5 points.

Of course, the season was also a bad one from a financial point of view. They had to play Fulham in a test match, and, though the Craven Cottagers scored first, the "Bees" won by 7 goals to 2. Then Mr. Dick Molyneux was appointed secretary-manager, superseding that genial sportsman Will Lewis. He was a man eminently suitable for the position on account of his great experience with the Everton Club. From the time he arrived the fortunes of the club, which had been transformed into a limited liability company a season or so previously, improved. He got a good side together for 1903-4, the players including Frail, Parsonage, Underwood, Howarth, Watson, Davidson, Jay, and Bell. They won 9 games, drew 9, and lost 16, gaining 27 points, which gave them fourteenth position in the table.

The following season their fine new enclosure Griffin Park was opened. Amongst the players engaged for 1904–5 were Whittaker, Shanks (who returned after a season and a half with the Arsenal, whom he had rendered splendid service), Hobson, and Tomlinson.

They improved on the previous season's record, making 29 points, but dropped a place or two in the table. The present season—1905-6—is the best the club ever had. They opened with a win over Southampton at the Dell. In some of the following matches they were inconsistent, but since October their record will compare favourably with any team in the country. For the first time in their history, they reached the Competition Proper of the Football Association Cup. In this they beat Bristol City, Lincoln City, and then had to play Liverpool at Anfield Road, when they were defeated by 2 goals to 0. They have a grand defence, which was strengthened by Riley, a fine young back from Blackburn, and Parsonage, who is one of the greatest captures made by Mr. Molyneux —and that is saying something.

Amongst the great supporters of the club are Messrs. Devey, Harvey, Buck, Stephenson, Knight, W. G. Brown, N. Jason, and Saunders.

BRENTFORD FOOTBALL CLUB—THE PLAYERS, SEASON 1905-6.

Back Row: Watson. Whittaker (Goalkeeper). Riley.

Second Row: R. Molyneux (Manager). Cross. Howarth. Greaves. Dewhurst. R. Crone (Trainer).

Third Row: Gates. Jay. Parsonage (Captain). Shanks. Tomlinson.

Front Row: Corbett. Hartley. Underwood. Cookson.

[*Wakefield, Brentford.*]

THE RUGBY GAME—NEW ZEALAND v. BLACKHEATH AT THE RECTORY FIELD, BLACKHEATH, NOVEMBER 4, 1905—A GRAND RUSH.

This was the fifteenth match of the New Zealand tour, and the New Zealanders won by 32 points (5 goals—1 penalty—and 3 tries) to nil.

THE RUGBY GAME.

PART IV.—FULL-BACK PLAY.

By J. F. BYRNE, ex-Captain of the English Rugby Fifteen.

The full-back as individualist—Qualifications for the position—How to catch the ball—Kicking into touch—The use of both feet in punting—Dropping at goal—Stopping a forward rush—Good tackling indispensable—Safety before brilliance should be the full-back's maxim.

The changes which have taken place of later years in the game of Rugby Union football have affected the position of full-back less than any other position in the field.

The full-back to-day stands out, as he always has done, the solitary figure whose play is absolutely individual; he may not partake in attack in combination with the other players of his side, and seldom gets material assistance when the opposing attack has successfully penetrated to his position; he is there to combat the attack of the opposition when it has overcome the defence of his comrades, and also, let it not be forgotten, to rectify the errors of players on his own side, which very often are the outcome of too wild and reckless attempts at attack.

In present-day football, where the chief factors of success are pace, quick following-up, combination, novelty in methods of attack such as the kick across and other innovations, the work of a full-back is much more onerous than in the old days of slow, heavy forwards, tight scrummages, and individual effort.

The full-back to-day should be strong, fast, quick in his movements, and, like all other players, should be possessed of plenty of pluck; if he can add to these advantages the other necessary qualifications, he should be all that is desirable for the position.

Of all the qualifications which a full-back should possess, I should place first accurate fielding of the ball and accurate kicking into touch.

How often a full-back who fumbles the ball lets his side down, and if his mistakes do not lead to immediate disaster, they give the other players of his side a feeling of uneasiness, and destroy the confidence which they should have in him, with the result that his three-quarters are continually feeling the necessity for backing him up in order to cover his possible mistakes, and consequently are often deprived of chances for attack which perhaps might fall to them if they were able to keep in their proper positions. But possibly the worst evil is that he is needlessly tiring the already hard-worked forwards, whose strength and lasting power are the basis of success, in continually running them about in order to get back to scrummage where his mistake has occurred. On the other hand, the accurate fielder and kicker is of immense value in tiring the other side, and saving his own. He will field the ball cleanly and quickly, and while making his opponents follow up, will give them no chance of tackling him, but will kick the ball back over the heads of his own forwards into touch, to where all opponents who have followed up must run back.

The matter of accurate fielding is greatly assisted by the position which a full-back takes up. There can be no set rule in regard to this; it is to be determined by the conditions of wind and weather, and, in some degree, by the methods employed by the opposing side. In this very important matter of position, the man who has what may be termed the football instinct will generally be able to intelligently anticipate the movements of the other side, and will naturally take up the best position to frustrate those movements. Hence when an opposing player is in possession of the ball and is going to kick, a back so gifted will frequently gauge to within a few yards where the ball is going, and will already have taken steps to get into the best position for securing it.

In fielding, it should never be forgotten that whenever it is possible the ball should be caught before it touches the ground, not only because there is an immense saving in time, but because it is safer. When once a Rugby ball hops it is impossible to tell which way it may bounce, or whether it will bounce high out of reach, or short, and run end over end. In any event, if the ball is allowed to bounce, there is a great risk that the kicker will have time to follow up and place his fellow players on-side, in which case the full-back is always in a tight corner.

In kicking, the full-back must remember that he should almost invariably kick into touch, and that it is much better to kick not quite so far and find touch than attempt a kick which may be a little longer but which drops the ball just short of the touch-line. It is on very few occasions that it is desirable for a full-back to kick into the field of play. Perhaps with a strong wind behind him, and particularly if the ball is wet and greasy, he may break what may be almost termed the golden rule, and kick high in the chance that the players on the other side may miss the ball or fumble it.

A full-back should be able to punt with either foot, not only because, when close to the touch-line, it is easier to get a longer kick, and more surely find touch with the foot furthest away from the line, but because, when hard pressed, there is not always time to get into position to kick if he can only use one foot. The full-back should also be able to drop well, for at times he has opportunities for dropping at goal, and it is highly useful if for once in a way he can turn defence into attack and score four points for his side.

Probably the part of a full-back's work which requires the most courage is that of saving from the feet of dribbling forwards. There are times when it is impossible to pick the ball up, and it becomes an absolute necessity for the back to throw himself upon it, and intervene his body between the ball and the feet of the opposing forwards.

Good tackling is indispensable to a good full-back. In the old days, when there was very little, if any, combination, a back could concentrate all his attention on the man with the ball, and put forth all his efforts to bring him down; and although it remains to-day the golden rule to tackle the man with the ball, it is equally necessary, when an opponent gets away, for the back to quickly take note of other opponents who are in positions to act in combination with the player in possession, and also of players of his own side who may be following up, and are in positions to help in frustrating the attack. He must then adapt himself to the circumstances, and, while being ready to tackle the man with the ball, must also be on the alert to guard against possible disaster in the quarter most unprotected, and where the ball is likely to be passed.

H. D. THOMPSON,
Of the New Zealand Rugby Team, 1905-6, making his mark.

Nowadays the combination which a full-back is most generally called upon to contend with is that by three-quarter backs, and when this combination is successful, it is usually a centre three-quarter with his wing man in attendance who gets to the back. In this case the full-back should endeavour to get into a position so that when going to tackle the man with the ball he will be between the centre and his wing man; this position will make the intended pass from the centre man to the wing extremely difficult, because in its execution the ball will have to be thrown past or over the full-back. And further, if the back should miss his man, he has upset the preconceived plan of attack, and has probably compelled the centre man to cut in, which gives a possible chance for tackling him to any of the defending side who may have followed up. On the other hand, if the full-back simply follows the ball across, and goes for his man on the near side, a centre three-quarter may, with advantage, as soon as he has passed the ball, allow himself to be tackled, or even throw himself into the arms of the full-back, and so protect his wing man, who then has a clear run in.

When there is only one man to deal with, the full-back, as a rule, should account for him, but the player with a good, quick swerve is always difficult to tackle, and if such a one gets clear up the centre of the field, it should be odds on him scoring, because when he gets to the full-back he has got up his top pace, and has the knowledge of what he intends to do, whereas the back is without that knowledge, and cannot get on pace until his opponent has disclosed his intention. Under these circumstances, the full-back, without stirring sufficiently to get out of touch with his opponent, should move a little, and get into a line just on one side of him, and so endeavour to rob him of the opportunity of going either side—in fact, compel him to go one way. In conclusion, it should not be forgotten that a full-back, above all things else, must be safe. He is the last line of defence, and when once the ball or the man are past him, it generally spells disaster to his side.

Baker and Dixon.]

THE RUGBY GAME—NEW ZEALAND v. LEICESTER AT LEICESTER, OCTOBER 1, 1905—A STRUGGLE ON THE LINE.

This was the fifth match of the New Zealand tour, and the New Zealanders won decisively by 28 points (5 goals and 1 try) to nil.

NORTHAMPTON TOWN FOOTBALL CLUB.

By HOWARD SLEIGH.

The rise of the "dribbling" code in Northampton—Formation of the Town Club—Its early football history—Championship of the Northants League won—In the Southern League—English Cup reminiscences—Agents steal Northampton's best players—Increasing success of the club and popularity of the "Soccer" game in Northampton.

Colours : Claret and white striped jerseys, black knickers.

Ground : County Cricket Ground, Northampton.

ACCORDING to tradition, and the private opinions of the folks known for brevity's sake as the "Rugby people," Northampton ought not to be a centre of Association football. It should be devoted entirely, so far as football is concerned, to the Rugby code. Until a few years ago this practically was the case, for against one of the strongest clubs in the Rugby Union and hosts of minor Rugby combinations "Soccer" followers could only point to a few small Association clubs, with, for some little time, a town amateur team. The real invasion of Northampton by the "dribbling" code was in considerable measure the outcome of good football played by two Second League teams. The acting president of the Northampton Town F. C. made a journey to Leicester with an Association team of Northampton boys, who were to meet a Leicester side. The match was played off immediately prior to a Second League match between Leicester Fosse and Notts County.

Remaining to witness this, Mr. Darnell experienced for the first time the real fascination of the Association game, and returned to Northampton fired with enthusiasm. In the spring of 1897 a number of assistant schoolmasters—then the ruling body of the Northampton and District Elementary Schools' Athletic Association—met and discussed the formation of a professional "Soccer" club in the town. Mr. A. J. Darnell, the hon. secretary of the Northants County Cricket Club, president of the Schools' Association, and a great figure in local sport, was called in. His advice and enthusiasm clinched the matter. A public meeting was called, and at the present headquarters, the Princess Royal, it was decided, in face of the Rugbyites' upraised eyebrows and innumerable cheerful prophecies of an early doom, to form an Association club on professional lines.

The presidential chair was accepted by Mr. Pickering Phipps, of the well-known brewing firm, whose influence has been of the greatest assistance to the organisation ever since. Mr. Darnell became acting president, Mr. C. Gyde was appointed hon. treasurer, and Mr. Arthur Jones secretary. The same men occupy these positions to-day. The first committee numbered twelve. The following composed it : Messrs. W. J. Westmorland, H. Davis, F. Heritage, G. Clarke, T. Johnson, T. James, A. Stockwin, F. Harris, D. Elson, F. Fry, H. W. Smith, and T. Haynes. Shortly afterwards it was decided to increase the number to thirteen. Far be it from me, however, to hand down to posterity the name of that added member—unhappy man !—who brought the total up to the unlucky figure. The club has had more than its share of misfortune from the beginning, and superstitious people might be inclined to blame No. 13.

However, the club made a capital start in the season 1897-8. Admission was obtained to the Northamptonshire League, and the present ground—a portion of the magnificent County Cricket Club Ground—was obtained as a field.

The Town, or the "Cobblers" as the crowd loves to call them, began well by winning their first match, a friendly encounter with the 48th Regiment, whose depot is at Northampton, and on its first essay the club reached fourth position in the Northamptonshire League—not bad for a start against clubs which took their football as seriously as did the Northants Leaguers of that day. The old Northampton players, for instance, retain vivid memories of having once to run for their lives from the Raunds field, pursued by a howling crowd. The "Cobblers" had won, and Raunds did not like it.

Financially, this first season was not successful, for with "gates" worth but £3 or £4 each, as a rule, the club lost £65.

Northampton took a step forward in 1898-9. They entered the English Cup competition. That season they possessed a capital team, which included Brawn, the famous Villa right-winger, locally known as "Gansey." He was picked up from Wellingborough at the price Northampton have always paid for their players—namely, nothing. It is a curious fact that Northampton Town have never yet paid a penny in transfer fees, though last year alone they made over £300 by the sale of players.

In the season under review Northampton pulled off the championship of the Northants League, and did well in the Cup-ties. After beating Hinckley, at Hinckley—where they had the misfortune to lose their centre-forward Scriven, whose leg was broken—they met their near and dear neighbours Wellingborough, at Wellingborough, and set the Nene on fire by triumphing over the senior club. Unfortunately, a technical irregularity necessitated a re-play, and Wellingborough restored the river to its normal condition by winning the tie. The "Cobblers" had some revenge, however, by knocking the Wellingborough men out of the Wellingborough Cup, and depriving them of the opportunity of winning the trophy outright.

Moving onward still, Northampton in the following season joined that splendid school, the Midland League, their reserve team taking their place in the Northants League. The "Cobblers" found themselves among old acquaintances—Wellingborough, Kettering, and Rushden all being members of the Midland League. "Gates," of course, had grown by this time, and the County Cricket Club Company erected a grand stand on the ground, opposite the distant cricket pavilion—a stand capable of sheltering 900 people. The Northamptonshire clubs had some rare tussles, and eventually the Town finished behind Kettering and Wellingborough, third from the top of the League chart.

Early in 1900 Northampton transferred Brawn to Sheffield United for £125 and a match, but, luckily, soon picked up another brilliant right-winger in James Frost, who is still sporting the claret-and-white jersey. At the end of the season 1900-1 Northampton were again third from the top of the Midland League.

The following season found the "Cobblers" tossing on the stormy waters of Southern League football, their application to join that exalted company having been successful. Once more they fell among friends, for Kettering had been admitted the year before, and Wellingborough joined alongside the "Cobblers." Here is Northampton's first Southern League team : Cook (now with Portsmouth) ; Bennett (Blackburn Rovers, Leicester Fosse, and Luton) and T. Turner ; Pell, Murrell, and Howe ; Frost, Chapman, Farrell (Stoke, Southampton, and New Brighton Tower), Coleman, and Lawrence. This season, though finishing eleventh among sixteen clubs in the Southern League, Northampton had a fine time in the Cup competition. Drawn away for the first three ties, they beat Gresley Rovers, Burton United (in a re-play caused by fog), and Kettering ; while they overcame Darwen at Northampton in the old intermediate round. The long string of successes brought its reward, for Sheffield United were eventually drawn to visit "Bootdom." The attendance broke all previous records. Four hundred pounds all but a few shillings was the sum taken at the receipt of custom, and about 15,000 people watched the "grate fite," though all did not pay, the gate being rushed. Northampton were beaten by 2 goals to 0.

The "Cobblers'" team that year proved highly attractive to other clubs, and at the end of the season Northampton was regularly invaded by agents looking for players. At ten minutes past the midnight hour which concluded the season, Woolwich Arsenal snapped up Coleman and Lawrence; West Ham got Farrell; Chapman was pounced upon by Sheffield United; Glossop signed Pell; and a few hours later Turner was induced to sign for Portsmouth. The whole business was like a clearance sale, with the notable exception that the poor sellers never saw a farthing for their goods.

With the courage and determination which have always characterised them, the club authorities buckled to the task of building up another side. For a start they got that splendid centre-half Herbert Dainty, of Kettering, Leicester Fosse, New Brighton Tower, and, later, Notts County. Other captures were Peter Durber, from Glossop, Len Benbow (Stoke and Notts Forest), and Crump (Glossop).

Notwithstanding the disruption of the team, Northampton at the end of the season under review figured in the top half of the League table. But they collided with their old Staffordshire opponents, Burton, in the Association Cup contest, and were beaten.

In the season 1903-4 Cook and Brown, both locals (the latter is now in the Southampton forward line), were transferred to West Bromwich Albion; while Perkins was obtained from Liverpool, and Clarke (like Brown, with the "Saints") from Sheffield United. Bert Neal, Ralph Howe, McIntyre (Notts County), and Murray were conspicuous members of the side. This season saw a change in the fortunes of the club. Previously the "Cobblers" had never won a trophy; but in the season 1903-4 the club lifted the Northamptonshire Senior Cup, the Northamptonshire League championship trophy, the Wellingborough Charity Cup, and the Northamptonshire Junior Cup; but the club's position in the Southern League went so low as fifteenth. Wellingborough defeated the Town at Wellingborough in the Cup-tie, and the "Cobblers" are sore over that beating to this day.

Murray was the biggest loss at the end of the season. Northampton could not afford to keep him in face of Tottenham Hotspur's offer to him. Still, the club picked up some good men. They obtained that popular player, Arthur Chadwick, the old International, still one of the best halves in the South; Chapman returned from Sheffield, Marriott joined from Bristol, and Wallace Smith was picked up from Kettering. The club lost Howard by an accident at Portsmouth, and—the biggest loss it has ever sustained, perhaps—Benbow disappeared as a fighting force, the result of a kick received at Reading. The Cup produced four games—with Burton, Kettering, and Leicester (two). At the end of the season the club was in the thirteenth position on the League table. For the first time a profit (about £100) was shown on the year's working. This, however, was due greatly to the transfer fees received for Clarke, Smith (Bradford City), and Chapman (Tottenham).

The chief new players this season are Drennan (Aston Villa), Tirrell, a promising local, Platt (Portsmouth), Gooing (Woolwich), Turner (New Brompton), A. H. Vann (a local amateur), and Dilks (a former player, who has also seen service with Leicester Fosse and Reading); while Harold Springthorpe, the amateur inside-left, has developed so wonderfully that in one sense he also may be called a "new man."

The chairmanship of the club committee has been held by Mr. W. J. Westmorland, Mr. J. R. Blunt (two years), Mr. H. T. Bradley (four years), and Councillor D. Staton, the present popular occupier (two years). Len Benbow, who is a chartered accountant and Conservative agent, took up the duties of financial hon. secretary when Mr. R. W. Dykes left the town.

"A good heart breaks bad luck," said Sancho Panza. The Northampton Town F. C. has had a lot of bad luck since its inception, but there are men with good hearts and plenty of grit at its back, and some day they will succeed in breaking the club's bad luck. One inspiring fact, at all events, they can show. Apart from the club's success in popularising the Association code among the rising generation of Northantonians, its own displays have risen steadily in the town's favour, and the gate receipts have gone up every year.

Greenway, Northampton.]

NORTHAMPTON TOWN FOOTBALL CLUB—THE TEAM, SEASON 1905-6

Back Row: LOAKES (Trainer). B. NEAL. T. DRENNAN. W. PERKINS (Captain). P. DURBER. R. HOWE. A. CHADWICK.
Front Row: J. FROST. J. PLATT. W. GOOING. J. COLE. J. TURNER.

THE SOUTHERN LEAGUE.

ITS RISE AND PROGRESS.

By ALFRED DAVIS (Football Association).

The inaugural meeting in 1894—A curious chapter of football history—The old public school clubs hold aloof—Millwall's early successes—Southampton's great record in 1896-7—Tottenham Hotspur's popular triumph—Constitutional changes for the season 1903-4—Southampton's sixth championship—The future of the League.

THE Football League had been in existence for six seasons before the South woke up to the possibilities of the new form of competition; and a reason for this may be found in the fact that professionalism—first legalised by the Football Association in 1885—was practically unknown in the South of England at a period when it had been adopted by nearly all the leading clubs in the North and Midlands. The actual *raison d'etre* for the formation of the Southern League forms an interesting chapter in football history. During the early Nineties the leading clubs in the South relied upon friendly guarantee matches at home with First League clubs for their most attractive fixtures. Millwall, with a view to strengthening their team, and having followed the lead set by Royal Arsenal in 1891 in adopting professionalism, persuaded two Scottish players named Mackenzie and Robertson to come to the Metropolis. A little later the Millwall executive had an unwelcome surprise in the shape of a demand from Everton for £100, on the ground that that club held the League signatures of the two players, who had never before crossed the Border. Millwall flatly refused to admit any liability, and properly so. But the League clubs promptly applied a boycott by scratching the guarantee matches arranged to be played at Millwall, and leaving the London club with a sadly decimated fixture list. The matter was eventually settled by a payment of £25 to Everton, but it convinced Millwall and other clubs that the time had arrived for the South to be up and doing, and the inauguration of the Southern League was the result.

Although it was the Millwall Club that actually took the lead in founding the Southern League, the first circular on the subject came from the Royal Arsenal Football Club. This was issued during the season 1892–3, and the circular stated that the Arsenal directors were of opinion "that the time has arrived when some effort should be made to improve the game in the South by the strongest clubs forming themselves into a combination or league." Invitations to attend a meeting were issued to the Casuals, Chatham, Clapton, Crusaders, Millwall, London Caledonians, Old Carthusians, Old Etonians, and Old Westminsters. Two meetings were held, and as the old public school clubs were averse to the idea, other clubs were invited, but nothing definite was done. Before the next season the Royal Arsenal had sought and obtained admission to the Second Division of the Football League, and, for good or ill, they have remained members of that League ever since.

The meeting which resulted in the Southern League being formed was convened by the Millwall Club and held on January 12, 1894. The delegates present on that notable occasion were Messrs. Henderson and Dickinson (Millwall), Clark and Hayward (Clapton), Dowsett and Davies (Ilford), Arnold and Austin (Luton), Harman and McLeod (Chatham), Rogers (Reading), and Murray (2nd Scots Guards). The minutes of the proceedings record the fact that Mr. W. Henderson proposed, and Mr. W. Rogers seconded, "That this meeting is of opinion that it is in the interests of football that a Southern League should be formed, and pledges itself to do all in its power to form a league." This resolution was carried unanimously, and it was decided to invite the Casuals, Crusaders, Crouch End, Old Carthusians, Old Westminsters, Royal Ordnance, and Swindon Town to join the clubs represented at the meeting in forming the League.

MR. NAT WHITTAKER,
Hon. Secretary of the Southern League.

Mr. Whittaker was elected secretary of the Southern League before the first playing season commenced, and has held the position ever since. He has also had the honour of representing the Southampton Division upon the Football Association for eight years. Mr. Whittaker is also well known as a referee, and this season is one of the three Southern referees on the Football League list. He was born at Oswaldtwistle (Accrington), Lancashire.

The meeting was adjourned for a week for the purpose of receiving replies, and it was then decided that the League should include the nine clubs that had accepted the invitation—viz., Chatham, Clapton, Ilford, Luton Town, Millwall, Reading, Royal Ordnance, Swindon, and 2nd Scots Guards. Mr. R. H. Clark (Clapton) was elected chairman of the League, Mr. Colin Gordon (Millwall) hon. treasurer, and Mr. W. Henderson (Millwall) hon. secretary. In view of later developments, it is interesting to note that at a meeting in February applications for membership from Southampton St. Mary's and Tottenham Hotspur were declined, although two months later the resignation of the 2nd Scots enabled Southampton to obtain admission. Mr. John Oliver, an enthusiastic and liberal supporter of the game in London, kindly came forward with an offer to present a shield for the championship trophy, and this offer was accepted.

In May it was decided to form a Second Division, and Bromley, Chesham, Maidenhead, New Brompton, Old St. Stephen's, Sheppey United, and Uxbridge joined the lower division for the first season. The representatives chosen to form, with the officers, the management committee for the first year, were Messrs. J. Dowsett (Ilford), T. P. Moore (Royal Ordnance), J. G. Stone (Chesham), and W. J. Wadham (Old St. Stephen's). Before the season opened—in July to be exact—Mr. Henderson resigned the position of hon. secretary, and Mr. N. Whittaker was elected as his successor. Both Mr. Whittaker and the treasurer—Mr. Colin Gordon—have retained their offices ever since.

The League competition therefore started in the 1894–5 season with nine clubs, five of whom —Millwall, Luton, Southampton St. Mary's, Chatham, and Swindon—included professionals in their teams. Millwall went through the campaign without defeat, and had the honour of being the first club to hold the championship trophy.

At the first annual meeting in April, 1895, the balance-sheet for the year showed receipts £70 7s., and expenses £36 9s. 1d., leaving a balance in hand of £33 17s. 11d. It was decided to increase the number of clubs to ten. New Brompton, who had won the championship of the lower division, were promoted, and Swindon, whose position at the bottom of the table necessitated their coming up for election, were given the tenth place in preference to Tottenham Hotspur and Sheppey United. Millwall retained the shield for the season 1895–6 with 33 points out of the possible 36, followed by the same two clubs as the previous season—Luton (27 points) and Southampton St. Mary's (24 points).

At this time test matches were played between the two bottom clubs in Division I. and the two top clubs in Division II., and at the end of the season Wolverton and Sheppey United deposed Royal Ordnance and Ilford through the medium of the "tests."

At the annual meeting of 1896 it was decided to increase the clubs to fourteen, and Tottenham Hotspur, Gravesend United, Northfleet, and Royal Ordnance were elected, the latter in spite of their failure in the test match. But the numbers were reduced to twelve by Clapton and Luton resigning their membership. Luton joined the Second Division of the Football League, but, after an absence of four seasons, the Bedfordshire club came back to the fold.

Only eleven clubs actually took part in the League in the season 1896–7, for Royal Ordnance came to grief early in the season. Southampton St. Mary's finished at the top of the table, and so gained the first of a long series of championship honours. Moreover, they followed the example of Millwall in the first season by going right through the competition without defeat—a record that has not been equalled since.

For the season 1897–8 Dr. Russell Bencraft, the famous Hampshire cricketer and a rare good sportsman to boot, was elected president of the League, and he has held the office ever since. The constitution of the League remained unaltered, with the addition of Bristol City, who altered their title from Bristol South End on coming into the League. A change was made in the method of playing the test games by the arrangement of home-and-home fixtures between the clubs concerned, instead of a single match on neutral ground. Southampton—who had dropped "St. Mary's" from their title—finished at the top of the table with 37 points out of 44, after a most exciting struggle with Bristol City, whose record of 33 points was a fine performance for a club new to the competition.

For the season 1898–9 the rules were altered to admit eighteen clubs to membership, but only fourteen actually took part, and one (Warmley) collapsed during the playing season. Northfleet and Wolverton disappeared from the upper division, and Bedminster and Brighton United were elected with the Royal Artillery and Warmley, who came up from Division II., which was divided into two sections for 1898–9. Southampton for the third time won the shield (35 points out of 48) after another prolonged struggle for supremacy with Bristol City (33).

The season 1899–1900 witnessed some important alterations in the rules. The League was becoming an important body, and the entry fee was increased to £21, and the subscription to £5 5s. Neutral linesmen were appointed for the matches, and the management committee was increased to ten members. The Fletcher system of arranging fixtures was also adopted for the first time. The Royal Artillery resigned membership, but the list was increased to sixteen clubs by the election of Portsmouth, Bristol Rovers, Queen's Park Rangers, and Thames Ironworks. The latter, now known as West Ham, came up from Division II. Unfortunately, Brighton United collapsed towards the close of the campaign, and the final record was made up with fifteen clubs. Tottenham Hotspur won the championship with 44 points, and their success gave immense satisfaction in North London, where the popular "'Spurs" had secured a large and loyal following.

The next season witnessed the return of Luton to the fold, and Kettering were elected at the same time. Chatham started the season in the League, but eventually collapsed, and their records were expunged from the table. Bedminster had also been absorbed by Bristol City, so that fifteen clubs again took part in the competition, which proved to be the keenest in the history of the League up to this period, 5 points covering the first five clubs. Southampton eventually topped the table once more with 41 points out of 56.

The annual general meeting of 1901 was marked by the

Globe Photographic Co., Southampton.]

SOUTHAMPTON ST. MARY'S FULL LEAGUE FOOTBALL TEAM—WINNERS OF THE SOUTHERN LEAGUE CHAMPIONSHIP, SEASON 1896-7.

Back Row: Meston. Clawley. McKie.
Middle Row: Shenton. McMillan. Littlehales. Hodgkinson. Haynes. Dawson (Trainer).
Bottom Row: Naughton. Buchanan. Farrell (Captain). Keay. Turner.

retirement of Mr. R. H. Clark from the office of chairman, and Mr. W. H. Lawson, of Swindon, was elected as his successor. Bristol City resigned membership to join the Second Division of the Football League, and Northampton and Wellingborough were elected. Sheppey United and Gravesend also resigned before the season opened, and Brentford were given one of the vacancies, bringing the membership to sixteen clubs. Portsmouth played most consistently throughout the season, and finished up with only three defeats and a total of 47 points out of the possible 60. Tottenham Hotspur and Southampton came next with 42 points.

For the season 1902–3 the constitution of the League remained unchanged, and Southampton deprived their local rivals of the honour of holding the shield with an aggregate of 48 points. Reading were a good second (45), and Portsmouth (41) third.

The following season (1903–4) was marked by some important constitutional changes. At the annual meeting the membership was increased to eighteen clubs, an amendment in favour of twenty being lost; the test matches were abolished; the subscription was increased to £10 10s., with a levy of £5 5s. for delegates' expenses; the management committee was altered to one representative from each club; and reserve teams of First Division clubs were made eligible for membership of the lower division. Fulham made their entry into the upper circle this season, after winning the championship of Division II. in the two previous seasons, and Brighton and Hove Albion also came up from the lower division. Watford failed to secure re-election, preference being given to a new club in the far west formed under the title of Plymouth Argyle. Southampton won the trophy for the sixth time, and for the second consecutive year, with 50 out of 68 points.

The happenings of last season, when Watford took the place of Kettering, are too recent to call for detailed reference. Bristol Rovers gained a thoroughly well-earned triumph with 48 points. Reading and Southampton coming next with 43 points each. For the present season Wellingboro did not seek re-election, but Luton survived the ordeal of applying for a place, and the other vacancy was given to Norwich City in preference to Crystal Palace, Clapton Orient, Leyton, and Grays United.

From a small beginning the League has developed into the second most important organisation of its kind in the country, and its influence in developing and consolidating professional football in the South cannot be over-estimated. The individual and collective strength of its clubs will probably continue to grow, for football has yet to reach its high-water mark in London and the South; and if the executive shape their policy with due regard to the best interests of the game, the League should attain still greater heights of prosperity and influence.

R. W. Thomas. Cheapside.]

MILLWALL ATHLETIC FOOTBALL TEAM—WINNERS OF THE SOUTHERN LEAGUE CHAMPIONSHIP AND SHIELD, SEASON 1894-5.

Back Row: W. Lindsay (Trainer). C. Gordon (Chairman). A. Law. J. Dewar. E. R. Stopher (Treasurer).
Second Row: T. B. Kidd. G. King. J. Matthew. J. Graham. W. Davis. H. Matthews. J. Higson.
Third Row: W. Jones. M. Whelan. A. Geddes (Captain). D. McInroy. G. A. Saunders.
Bottom Row: E. Clark. J. Rhodes. THE SHIELD. C. Leatherbarrow. J. Beveridge (Secretary).

SOME FAMOUS GOALKEEPERS

Reeves.] KITCHEN (*West Ham*).

Wakefield.] WHITTAKER (*Brentford*).

EGGETT (*Tottenham*).

Taylor.] WILLIAMSON (*Middlesborough*).

Moyse.] FRYER (*Fulham*).

Burgess.] CLAWLEY (*Southampton*).

Stuart and Winfield.] LAWRENCE (*Newcastle*).

Elbourne.] ASHCROFT (*Woolwich*)

Wilkes.] BADDELEY (*Wolverhampton*).

A GENERAL VIEW OF THE NEW BROMPTON FOOTBALL CLUB'S GROUND, PRIESTFIELD ROAD, GILLINGHAM, KENT.

THE NEW BROMPTON FOOTBALL CLUB.

By W. I. GROOMBRIDGE.

How the military element introduced the Association game into New Brompton—Some famous local players—New Brompton Excelsior win the Kent Junior Cup—Formation of the New Brompton Football Club Company, Ltd.—Professionalism adopted—The Second Division of the Southern League Championship won—In the Southern League—Football Association Cup-tie performances—The five games with Woolwich Arsenal in 1899-1900—The present season.

Colours: Black and white stripes. *Ground: Priestfield Road, Gillingham, Kent.*

THERE can be no doubt that the military element have by example and precept taught the youth of New Brompton (now Gillingham) how to appreciate field sports, manly pastimes, and athletic exercises generally. Little wonder, then, that Association football has for some thirty-five years had a great fascination for Gillingham. The Royal Engineers, stationed in Gillingham Municipal District, four times fought their way to the Final of the Football Association Cup, better known as the English Cup, and on one occasion succeeded in winning the trophy.

In the old days the events of the season were the matches between the R. E. and Old Carthusians, R. E. and Old Etonians, R. E. and Old Westminsters, and R. E. and Swifts, and the players taking part no doubt included the cream of the country. There were Von Donop, Sealy, Vidal, Wingfield Stratford, Renny Tailyour, and Rawson among the "Sappers," while Cunningham, Hunter, Weston, A. E. Turner, F. G. Guggisberg, Symons, &c., will be remembered by many present-day followers of the game.

The players in the small local clubs of those days, who also played on the "Great Lines," were to be found trying pluckily to adopt the tactics of the famous men above-named. Such clubs as the Victoria, St. Mark's, and Excelsior were in the front of local football and played several hard games to win the local cup before the introduction of the league principle, and while the R. E.'s and their star visitors had their followers, the local clubs were not wanting for their supporters.

Of the Brompton players the best remembered are Stedman, Roberts, Scott, West, Mattock, McLeod, Hore, Evans, Morley, Shepherd, and the brothers Mark and Walter Branfield. A little later we come to George Ekins, who, like his brother Harry, made for himself a big name as a player. He was the first to leave the district and join one of the professional clubs in the Midlands; later Joe Dickenson went to Bolton Wanderers. C. Hibbard, J. Hibbard, and W. Leitch are others who have helped to keep up the Brompton district reputation for turning out some of the best football players.

HIS WORSHIP THE MAYOR OF GILLINGHAM, LIEUT.-COLONEL J. B. RIDOUT, J.P., President of the New Brompton Football Club.

In April, 1893, New Brompton Excelsior won the Kent Junior Cup and the Chatham and District League, in which competition they did not lose a single match. This success prompted a number of enthusiastic supporters to come to the decision that it was quite time to foster and cultivate talent in New Brompton. A number of preliminary meetings were held, the attendance including some of the directors of the present day, viz., the chairman, Mr. Alderman J. Barnes, Messrs. W. Checkerfield, A. W. Parker, J. Evans, Alderman J. R. Featherby (then High Constable), Messrs. F. Bloor, W. C. Snow, A. W. Partridge, W. I. Groombridge, H. G. Croneen, W. Croneen, Dr. Warren, R. J. Passby, and others, resulting, in June, 1893, in the formation of a limited liability company, the purchase of land for athletic purposes, and the establishing of a club under the name of the New Brompton Football Club Company, Limited, the land being situate in Priestfield Road, Gillingham, four minutes from the railway-station.

Previously the Excelsior team had played on the "Great Lines" between New Brompton and Chatham. The share capital was fixed at £1,500 in £1 shares, all of which were very soon taken up.

On January 12, 1894, the Southern League was formed, and New Brompton, who adopted professionalism in the July of that year, together with Sheppey, Old St. Stephen's, Uxbridge, Bromley, Chesham, and Maidenhead were included

OFFICIALS OF THE NEW BROMPTON FOOTBALL CLUB.

COUNCILLOR G. C. SWAIN (Hon. Treasurer).

F. CRADDOCK (Trainer).

ALDERMAN J. BARNES (Chairman).

W. F. PATON, Esq. (Hon. Doctor).

W. I. GROOMBRIDGE (Secretary).

in the Second Division. New Brompton playing practically the same team as in the previous year, with the addition of Dan Pellatt (the Chatham captain), J. Dickenson (the ex-Bolton Wanderer, who was born and learnt his football at New Brompton), A. Russell (late of Dartford), and Arthur Rule (of Sheppey United). The other members of the team were A. Ashdown, A. Jenner, Albert James, Fred Manning, Harry Buckland, and David Hutchinson.

This was an excellent team, as is proved by the splendid record they had in the Second Division of the Southern League at the end of the season. They played twelve matches, won eleven, drew none, lost one, and scored 57 goals to their opponents' 10, thus gaining twenty-two points out of a possible twenty-four. Then came the test match, in which the black-and-whites defeated Swindon by 5 goals to 1. This gained them a well-deserved place in the First Division, where they have remained ever since. The positions held each year in the Southern League are as follows: 1895-6, sixth; 1896-7, eighth; 1897-8, sixth; 1898-9, sixth; 1899-1900, tenth; 1900-1, eleventh; 1901-2, tenth; 1902-3, sixth; 1903-4, sixteenth; 1904-5, ninth. The League consisted of eighteen clubs during the last two seasons.

The team won the Chatham and District Charity Cup in 1893-4 and 1895-6, and they were finalists in 1898-9 and 1899-1900. They have also won the Thames and Medway Combination Championship Cup and Flag on two occasions. In 1898 and 1899 the team got as far as the first round of the competition proper of the Football Association Cup, and were then defeated by Southampton by 1 goal to nil. In the season 1899-1900 they were drawn against Woolwich Arsenal at Woolwich in the third qualifying round of the Football Association Cup, the match resulting in a drawn game of 1 goal each. The re-play at New Brompton also ended in a draw, so that a third meeting was necessary. This was played at Millwall, both teams scoring twice, and a fourth game was played, this time at Tottenham, the match ending in a draw of 1—1. In fact, it was not until the fifth match that a definite result was arrived at, and then, at Gravesend, New Brompton were victorious by 1 goal to nil. In the fourth round New Brompton were drawn against Thames Ironworks (now West Ham) at New Brompton, the match ending in a draw. In the re-play at Canning Town the Ironworks won by 2 goals to nil. The following season, 1900-1, West Ham succeeded in ousting New Brompton from the intermediate round at West Ham after a drawn game at New Brompton.

In 1901-2 the club survived in the great national competition until the intermediate round, when they were beaten by Walsall at Walsall. In 1902-3 Glossop defeated them in the intermediate round by a lucky goal scored in the last minute. In 1903-4 New Brompton, exempt until the intermediate round, drew with Bristol City at New Brompton, but were beaten in the re-play; and in 1904-5 Brighton defeated them in the Cup by the odd goal in a strenuously fought match.

This (1905-6) season the club did not take part in the F. A. Cup until the first round competition proper, and by a decided win over Northampton (2—1) qualified to meet the well-respected Cup-fighters Southampton; and it was not until the re-play at Southampton that the match was won by the "Saints" in the last half-minute, one goal only being scored in the two matches.

The directors have each year had a hard uphill fight, but population, support, and enthusiasm grow each season, and before many years New Brompton should rank as one of the strongest clubs in the Southern League.

NEW BROMPTON FOOTBALL CLUB—SOME PROMINENT PLAYERS.

P. BARNFATHER (Outside-right).

He has made quite a reputation in the Southern League.

J. MARTIN (Goalkeeper).

John Martin came to New Brompton as a centre-half from Sheffield, but his ability as a goalkeeper was discovered at practice, and he has performed consistently well in that position.

F. GRIFFITHS (Goalkeeper and Captain).

He has seen two years' service with his present club, and has played for Wales against both England and Scotland.

J. ELLIOTT (Junior International, 1898).

He has seen four years' service with New Brompton, is a very consistent player, and rarely misses a match. His position in the field is left half-back.

J. WALTON (Back).

He is only twenty-three years of age, but already gives evidence of developing into one of the best backs playing Southern League football. He has been with New Brompton two years.

RECORDS OF THE DERBY COUNTY FOOTBALL CLUB.

Football Association Cup Finalists 1897-8, 1898-9, 1902-3; Semi-finalists 1895-6, 1896-7, 1901-2.

Formation of the club in 1884—Aston Villa beaten in 1885-6—Derby County absorbs the Derby Midland Club—The arrival of Stephen Bloomer—Fluctuating fortunes—A limited liability company formed—Magnificent performances in the Football Association Cup competition—The Final and Semi-final reached thrice in eight years—Derby County's League points since the Football League was formed in 1888—The club's officials.

Colours: White shirts, black knickers. *Ground: Baseball Ground, Shaftesbury Crescent, Derby.*

THE Derby County Football Club came into existence during the spring of 1884, its inception being entirely due to the energetic action of Mr. William Morley, of Derby. The first match played, history tells us, was against the Great Lever Club, and in this memorable opening game, in which Derby were defeated by 5 goals to 0, John Goodall played for the first time for an English club.

Derby County quickly showed that they were no mediocre side, and in the season 1885-6 they beat Aston Villa, the match, played on the County Ground, being an English Cup-tie, which the Villa lost by 2 goals to 0

With varying fortunes the club progressed until the season 1891-2, when its playing strength was increased by the absorption of the Derby Midland Club, from whom Derby County obtained such sterling players as Hickinbottom and Staley, and two dangerous forwards in Mills and W. Storer. John and Archie Goodall joined the team in the season 1889-90.

The season 1892-3 is notable for the fact that an important recruit was secured in the person of Stephen Bloomer, whose name has since become a household word.

In 1893-4 a brilliant series of victories towards the latter end of the season carried the club to the third position on the League table. They played, in all, 53 matches—won 32, lost 13, 8 were drawn, and they scored in the aggregate 141 goals against 88.

As if Fate intended to balance matters, the season 1894-5 proved to be one of the most disastrous in the club's history. They sank to the last place but one on the League table, and in the test match against Notts County only escaped relegation to the Second Division by a goal scored in the last few minutes of the game.

The following season (1895-6) the Derby County team, by consistent and really brilliant play, proved itself to be about the best in the country. The League championship and the English Cup were both nearly won, and the County had the best goal average of any club in the League. Aston Villa beat Derby County for the League championship by 4 points only.

Before the next season opened the club was turned into a Limited Liability Company, but although they reached the Semi-final of the English Cup competition and finished third on the League table, a loss on the year's working of £323 was incurred. The end of the season 1897-8 found Derby County in the Final of the English Cup. In this competition Aston Villa, Wolverhampton Wanderers, Liverpool, and Everton were successively beaten but in the Final Notts Forest triumphed by 3 goals to 1. Financially the season was about the best on record, a profit of something like £1,066 being returned.

In 1898-9 Derby County, as the result of magnificent play, again went right through the great Cup competition, but only to be beaten in the Final, this time by Sheffield United, who scored 4 goals to 1. Their position in the League was but moderate. In 1899-1900 the club was knocked out of the English Cup in the first round, and a financial loss was the result.

In 1900-1 Derby County were again defeated in the first round of the national competition, and finished last but two on the League list. The following season the Semi-final of the Cup was again reached, and Derby County took £2,000 as their share of the Cup-ties.

1902-3 saw Derby County again in the Final. They, however, were beaten by Bury at the Crystal Palace by 6 goals to 0, and the loss of 7 League points out of a possible 10 in the month of April robbed them of their position at the head of the League list. It was hard lines upon a club whose team had played so brilliantly for two seasons.

1903-4 was a disastrous season both on the field and financially. For the second time they had to figure in the test matches in order to retain their position in the Premier Division of the League, but they scraped through in the last minute of the game against Notts County at Leicester.

Last season (1904-5) Derby County finished eleventh on the League list with 32 points to their credit, but they were defeated in the first round of the English Cup, and the balance-sheet at the end of the season showed a deficit of £1,467.

Derby County share with Aston Villa, Wolverhampton Wanderers, Everton, and Blackburn Rovers the distinction of being one of the survivors of the twelve clubs which first formed the Football League in 1888, and their total of League points scored from the season of 1888-9 to the end of 1904-5 reaches the round total of 497.

The club's officials are: Sir Clement Bowring, president; Messrs. W. T. Morley and A. Wilson, J.P., vice-presidents; Messrs. F. Bennett, Edward H. Cox, Bendle W. Moore, T. Clifford Newbould, G. D. Moon, J. Ryley, W. H. Sargent, Dr. C. H. Taylor, and Morgan T. Roberts, directors; with Mr. H. J. Newbould secretary and manager.

[*Winter, Derby.*]

STEPHEN BLOOMER,

England's famous inside-right, was born at Cradley Heath in 1874, removing to Derby when he was very young. Prior to joining Derby County in the season 1892-3 he played for Derby Swifts. He is a great example of the brainy player, and a deadly shot. He is the proud possessor of twenty-one International caps—nine against Scotland, six against Wales, and six against Ireland. He stands 5ft. 7½in., and weighs 11st. 3lb.

DERBY COUNTY FOOTBALL CLUB—THE FIRST LEAGUE TEAM, SEASON 1905-6.

Dereske, Derby.]

1. H. J. NEWBOULD (Manager). 2. J. W. DAVIES. 3. S. BLOOMER (Captain). 4. B. WARREN. 5. J. METHUEN. 6. H. MASKERY. 7. C. MORRIS. 8. MR. SERGEANT (Asst. Sec.). 9. T. H. PATON. 10. B. HALL. 11. G. W. RICHARDS. 12. F. MIDDLETON. 13. A. WOOD.

MANCHESTER CITY FOOTBALL CLUB.

CONCILIO ET LABORE

Winners of the Football Association Cup 1903-4.

The birth of the West Gorton Football Club—A change of ground and change of title—The title Ardwick Football Club adopted—From the Alliance to the Football League Second Division—Promotion secured—Mr. Edward Hulton, Jun., becomes chairman of directors—The arrival of Mr. T. E. Maley—The Football Association Cup won—Fine League performances—The need of a larger ground.

Colours : Blue shirts, white knickers. *Ground : Hyde Road, Manchester.*

LIKE many famous organisations, Manchester City began in a small way. 'It came into existence in the year 1880, and the father of the club was Mr. W. Chew. It was originally called the West Gorton Association Football Club. The first field procured was situated just off Clowes Street—the site is now covered by Messrs. Brooks & Doxey's works. In the following season the club migrated to the present Kirkmanshulme Cricket Ground, but owing to the damage wrought to the cricket-pitch the followers of the summer game were very irate, and West Gorton's sojourn there was a short one.

When the club lost the use of the Kirkmanshulme Cricket Ground, they were temporarily without a home, and virtually the club was disbanded, but an effort was made to revive it, and in 1884 the club started again as the Gorton Association Football Club. The need of an enclosed ground, where a "gate" could be taken, was now severely felt, and eventually a Mr. Fortune secured the tenancy of the present ground in Hyde Road. The club migrated there in the year 1889, and for the third time there was a change of name, the title of the Ardwick Football Club being adopted.

Ardwick started under more pretentious auspices than the two former clubs had done. The change of name arose out of a meeting convened by Mr. W. Chew and Mr. L. Furniss at the Hyde Road Hotel in August, 1887. The club became members of the Manchester Association, and Mr. Furniss, who had been captain of the Gorton Club, became secretary. It was at this point that the late Alderman Chesters Thompson and Mr. J. Allison became identified with the club. Thanks to the generosity of Mr. Allison and Mr. Chapman, it was decided in 1889 to advertise for players, but J. Hodgetts, the inside-right, was for some time the sole professional, and he only received five shillings per week.

It was in 1890 that the forward policy really began, and in 1891 they defeated Bury in a Lancashire Junior Cup-tie, and got into the final, but were beaten by Blackpool. The first trophy was won on April 18, 1891, when they secured the Manchester Cup, beating Newton Heath by 1—0.

This brought them fame, and in the season of 1891-2 they were elected members of the Alliance. They finished seventh in the Alliance table, and in the following year they were fifth in the Second Division of the League. Then came the last season of Ardwick, when they were thirteenth in the competition. The club was in a bad way financially, bad management being largely responsible for this, and the Ardwick Club became extinct, only to be restarted under the title of Manchester City Football Club as a limited liability concern in the year 1894.

Mr. J. E. Chapman was the leading spirit of the new venture, and the first secretary was Mr. Joshua Parlby. It was his influence and persuasive tongue that secured the club a position in the Second League before they had played any practical football whatever. Their first League match was with Bury, and they lost. But recruits were speedily obtained ; Walker and Robson, two capable full-backs, were added, McBride appeared, and on October 27, 1894, against Newcastle United, W. Meredith, of Chirk, made his first appearance for Manchester City.

The team gave a fine show in 1895-6, only missing the championship through an inferior goal average ; Liverpool were successful, the City securing the same number of points (46). In the season of 1897-8, Burnley won the championship with 48 points ; Newcastle were second with 45, and the City were third with 39. The season of 1898-9 was eventful ; James Ross, the famous old North End player, came into the team, and the following eleven won admission to the First League : C. Williams ; Read and Di Jones ; Moffatt, B. Smith, and W. Holmes ; Meredith, Ross, Gillespie, F. Williams, and Dougal. Ross, a consummate master of football, made Meredith a magnificent partner. Gold medals were presented to the team to mark their promotion to First League football.

But Manchester City found, as many other clubs had found before them, that there was a vast difference between the class of First League and Second League football. It is true that they did fairly well in the first season, when they and Glossop North End displaced Bolton Wanderers and Sheffield Wednesday. They were seventh on the table, and had 34 points to their credit. But in the following season they could only finish eleventh with 32 points, and the next season they were last on the list, scoring only 28 points, and they had perforce to again enter the ranks of the Second League. The City were now sorely in need of a good friend, and they found not only a friend with money, but, what was almost as essential, a friend with first-class business ability. Mr. Edward Hulton, Jun., became chairman of the directors, and provided the funds for obtaining new players. The value of good business ability was evident from the appointment of secretary, for the redoubtable Tom E. Maley, of the Celtic, was induced to take the office.

With a fine team at their disposal, the City had no difficulty in carrying off the championship of the Second Division. They had the following record : Played 34, won 25, lost 5, drawn 4 ; 49 goals for, 29 against; 54 points. They were once more members of the First League, and their next season—1903-4—was a most brilliant one. They finished second to Sheffield Wednesday in the League, being only 3 points (44—47) behind the champions; and they won the English Cup. They met Bolton Wanderers at the Crystal Palace, and won by a goal (scored by William Meredith) to nil.

The club's greatest loss since then has been, of course, William Meredith, who was suspended for attempting to bribe an Aston Villa player on the occasion of a notable match at the end of last season. He was, without doubt, the finest wing-forward in football. The City again made a bold bid to carry off the championship last season, but they had to be content with third place. Still, they had another exceptionally good season. Naturally, with such an enormous population to draw upon, Manchester City get exceptionally big "gates," and they would get larger did they possess a better constructed and more commodious ground. That is their chief want, but some selfish people have stood in the way of what everyone with common-sense must regard as a legitimate advancement. Before leaving the club, mention must be made of the secretarial work of Mr. Joshua Parlby and Mr. Sam Ormrod, and of the good service of Broad, who has trained the team from the starting of the club.

THE END.

INDEX